P9-DFI-317

THE DEATH PENALTY

AN HISTORICAL AND THEOLOGICAL SURVEY

by
James J. Megivern

Paulist Press
New York/Mahwah, N.J.

The Publisher gratefully acknowledges use of the following materials: Selected quotations from "*Killing ex officio:* The Teachings of 12th and 13th Century Canon Lawyers on the Right to Kill," by Sally Anne Scully; Cambridge, Mass.: Harvard University Unpublished Dissertation in History, 1975. Selections from *The Frederick Douglass Papers,* Vol 3 (1979), edited by John W. Blassingame, copyright © 1979, Yale University Press, New Haven, Conn. Excerpts from *Voices Against Death: American Opposition to Capital Punishment 1787–1975,* edited by Philip E. Mackey, copyright © 1976, Burt Franklin & Company, New York. Excerpts from *Heresies of the High Middle Ages,* edited by Walter J. Wakefield and Austin P. Evans, copyright © 1974.

Book design by Theresa M. Sparacio.

Library of Congress Cataloging-in-Publication Data

Megivern, James J.
    The death penalty : an historical and theological survey / by James J. Megivern.
        p. cm.
    Includes bibliographical references and index.
    ISBN 0-8091-0487-3 (cloth : alk. paper)
    1. Capital punishment—History. 2. Capital punishment—Religious aspects.
3. Capital punishment—Moral and ethical aspects. I. Title.
K5104.M44   1997
364.66—dc21   97–4216
                                                                            CIP

Published by Paulist Press
997 Macarthur Boulevard
Mahwah, New Jersey 07430

Printed and bound in the
United States of America

CONTENTS

iii

94/15

Gratefully dedicated
to the memory of

JOSEPH CARDINAL BERNARDIN
(1928–1996)

A Wise and Gentle Teacher who
courageously led the way back
to the broader Gospel vision of a
Consistent Ethic-of-Life
...all Life...every Life.

PREFACE

The origins of this work date back to a call which I received from a North Carolina public defender in the summer of 1979. She wanted someone to explain to the jury in the sentencing phase of a murder case that the Bible does not require that all killers necessarily and always be executed. I had not previously had occasion to give the issue much thought, but the many anomalies surrounding it gradually absorbed my attention. The lack of English-language histories that explained how capital punishment came to be the common practice throughout centuries in Christian Europe I found puzzling. How had it come about that churchmen in the High Middle Ages had adopted a position of staunch support of this singular practice of deliberately destroying human life? There simply had to be more of a story behind this intriguing phenomenon, but, whatever it was, the standard literature did not seem to include it. The widely used church histories, especially, were strangely silent, seeming to take it for granted that there was nothing incongruous in such endorsement.

Little by little, the search for "the missing story" became both my hobby and my chief research project, even though I was only able to work on it at times when my other academic and administrative duties allowed. So many people assisted me in so many ways over so many years that it is impossible to name them all, but some mention must be made here of at least a few.

• The staff of UNCW's Randall Library must be acknowledged first. They never gave up on my many requests for out-of-the-way works in odd languages from obscure places with uncertain dates and convoluted titles. Without their gracious cooperation, the project could simply not have been kept alive.

• A visit to the University of Bonn in the summer of 1982, after an exchange of letters with Professor Franz Böckle, opened the first promising avenues for deeper exploration. It was he who kindly introduced me to the special *Todesstrafe* collection in the moral theology section there and gave me access to its many resources, which have still only been partially tapped.

• A summer 1984 UNCW faculty research and development grant made it possible for me to spend time at the library of St.

Louis University, where I got a good start in organizing some of the medieval materials.

· A summer 1987 trip to Rome provided me with the opportunity to track down missing pieces of the story in the Vatican Library.

· Another UNCW summer grant in 1992 enabled me to use the resources of the Institute for the Study of American Religion at the University of California, Santa Barbara. The director, Dr. J. Gordon Melton, provided valuable suggestions and encouragement for which I am grateful.

· Multiple visits to Washington, D.C., throughout this entire time allowed me to pursue materials at the Library of Congress, the Catholic University of America, and the libraries of Georgetown University, in all of which I received gracious assistance. These visits were always greatly facilitated by the ready hospitality of my sister Kathleen and her husband, Jim, in Alexandria.

There were, of course, many other kinds of personal assistance over the years. I am grateful to department colleagues Maurice Stanley and Jim McGowan for reading various parts and different versions of the manuscript; and to Chairman Walt Conser and Dean Carolyn Simmons who did what they could to remove obstacles and provide encouragement.

I also benefited from the kindness of many who answered my request for help in piecing together some of the American Catholic story. These included: Monsignors Joseph Gremillion, Salvatore Adamo and Charles Rowland; Fathers Robert Drinan, S.J., Bryan Hehir and Charles Curran; and Messrs. Frank Butler, Germain Grisez and Richard Rufo, to name but three trios.

Fathers Kevin Lynch and Larry Boadt of the Paulist Press offered patient encouragement for more years than I had any right to hope. Without them the finished project would surely not have materialized.

One special source of information and encouragement throughout these years was the National Coalition to Abolish the Death Penalty. Their annual convention became a regular item on my summer calendar, and the inspiration derived especially from conversations with the exceptional people who were involved, especially Henry Schwarzschild, Hugo Adam Bedau, Gil

Wanger, Bob Domer and Father Jim Sunderland, S.J., gave me renewed determination to see it through.

In the last couple of years, Dr. Robert C. Schultz of Seattle proved to be more than a friend in the time and care which he willingly devoted to the manuscript. He regularly offered quality recommendations at several levels, all of which I appreciated, even those that were not finally incorporated. His vision always included further valuable pathways down which the search should continue if the tangled story is to be fleshed out more fully, as it certainly should be.

Among the many others who have assisted and wished me well in "the project," special thanks must first go to my wife Marjorie for her unflagging encouragement and support of what often seemed an impossible dream.

I would also like to thank belatedly certain teachers of a bygone era—Vincentians in the U.S., Dominicans in Switzerland and Jesuits in Rome—who valued, imparted and encouraged the use of tools for retrieving the past, so as to perceive its strengths as well as its flaws, and re-vision the story. When that story touches on something so basic and important as the value and dignity of human life—all human life—it is certainly worth the effort to tell it as well and as truly as possible, no matter the years required nor the cost expended.

James J. Megivern

FOREWORD

The sheer magnitude of James Megivern's historical and theological survey of the death penalty, quite apart from the book's more important merits, warrants the greatest admiration. Here, for the first time, we have a comprehensive collection of views on punishment by death in western civilization as seen through the eyes of Christian thinkers across two thousand years. Thanks to hundreds of quotations from as many different writers, the reader can savor the flavor and texture of unfamiliar voices from the past.

To tell this story with anything like the detail it deserves requires prodigious scholarship, endless patience and unerring judgment—a combination of talents rare in any case and infrequently evident in work on the death penalty. Thanks to Megivern's labors, we now have under one set of covers a broad survey of the entire field that lays the basis for futher work.

Megivern's book is not, however, dry-as-dust tombstone polishing; he does not pull back the curtains of neglect that conceal the past, only to leave it at that. On the contrary, *The Death Penalty: An Historical and Theological Survey* is history with an attitude, scholarship in the service of an angument. Our author never lets the reader lose sight of the rhetorical interrogative which the entire book is designed to answer: How does it come to pass that the religion founded in the legacy of Jesus of Nazareth would for centuries—indeed, until a decade or so ago—not merely tolerate but actively defend death deliberately and intentionally inflicted as punishment as a right of the state and as a desirable and necessary institution? Nor are we ever in doubt as to the author's own unequivocal rejection of the death penalty on empirical, political, moral and—above all—religious grounds.

Under Megivern's guidance, we see the story unfold during the two millenia of Christian culture in the west. Central to the story he tells is the Christian church's long struggle against heresy; as he explains, had it not been for the church's belief from the earliest decades that only death could stamp out heresy, a very different legacy might have unfolded. As it is, the history Megivern relates—to put it as briefly and bluntly as possible—is the struggle within the church between two opposed value systems: belief in the *right* of the state to kill as punishment and the *necessity* of exercising that right, versus belief in the *sanctity* of human life, the *right* to life, and the equal *dignity* of all persons. In our time, as the evidence he assembles shows, the latter trio at last dominates.

But not without a struggle. We learn of the early and solitary voices raised against the church's endorsement of the death penalty, voices drowned out by centuries of clerical manuals arguing for death, epitomized in St. Thomas of Aquinas's grim (and unfortunate) metaphor of the criminal—whether heretic, witch, traitor or murderer—as a "diseased member" necessarily amputated if the otherwise healthy body politic is to survive. We read also of the all but insurmountable difficulties the church faced in accommodating the Enlightenment protest against the death penalty without embracing Enlightenment principles hostile to the church itself.

Megivern writes as an American for an American audience; as he says, his "chief interest is to trace the remarkable change in attitude toward the death penalty among the contemporary leaders of the American Catholic Church." Roughly the latter half of the volume is devoted to this part of the story—a mere two centuries out of the twenty spanned by the book as a whole. Here the author is especially concerned about placing each step of the church's self-transformation on this issue in the context of objective events in American legal, constitutional and political practice as they affect the death penalty in this country. As he makes plain, while American Catholics (and, he could add, American Christians generally) give nominal support for the current death penalty, American Catholic clergy are increasingly united in outspoken and unequivocal condemnation of capital punishment. As Megivern says more than once, this gap dividing the laity from the clergy presents a formidable challenge to the church's teaching mission.

Within the past few years, students of the history of capital punishment have been fortunate to have several magnificent volumes published: Peter Linebaugh's and V.A.C. Gatrell's works on the death penalty in England, Richard Evans's study of the death penalty in Germany and William Schabas's account of the developing international law against capital punishment. To these monuments of scholarship we can now add another—this volume by James Megivern.

Hugo Adam Bedau

INTRODUCTION

When the encyclical letter *Evangelium Vitae* was released by Pope John Paul II in late March 1995, its statements on capital punishment were singled out in the media as surprisingly newsworthy. Throughout the previous quarter-century national groups of Catholic bishops had regularly and repeatedly made forthright statements of opposition to capital punishment, but there always seemed to be enough room left for those who so desired to contend that this opposition was somehow not really the "official" position of the Catholic Church. After all, that church had for long centuries been identified not only as a staunch public defender of the state's right to execute but also as a quiet observer of the lavish use that was made of that "right." All the moral theology manuals provided cautious justifications from scripture and tradition. Such a tradition of support, it seemed, must surely have a solid enough basis that it could not simply be jettisoned overnight. It was not uncommon for some to suggest that the right of the state to execute wrongdoers was close to being a Catholic dogma, due to the prestige of its defenders in earlier ages.

Cardinal Joseph Ratzinger told a March 30, 1995, news conference that the new encyclical's teaching, which restricted the use of the death penalty to "very rare, practically nonexistent" cases, represented "important doctrinal progress" that would require some "reformulation" of what had been written in the *Catholic Catechism* published only a short time earlier.[1] The multiple confusions surrounding the issue could be seen less than a month later when, in the emotional aftermath of the terrorist bombing of a federal building in Oklahoma City, a journalist for the Religion News Service declared in a national news release that "the Oklahoma blast poses a tough and practical question to bishops, theologians, ethicists and lay Catholics: Does the crime fit John Paul's 'rare' circumstance meriting death?"[2]

This was neither the first nor by any means will it be the last instance of absolutely astonishing incomprehension of the position expressed by the pope in the encyclical. The principle he was articulating was so simple and solid that the agitated reporter missed it completely. But the instance stands as a good

1

example of the confusion that surrounds the issue of capital punishment today, due in part to the strange history of Christian
involvement with this practice over the centuries. It is so sensitive
a topic that normally there is far more emotion than sober
reflection expended on it. It is one of those "gut issues" surrounded by long-standing mythologies that elicit such commitment from their adherents that most would prefer to repeat
rather than reexamine the past.

It is the purpose of the present work to call attention to
some elements of Western Christian history that may provide
some insight into why there has been such confusion and to suggest that the awareness of some of these historical developments
may help to make some sense of what has happened. One might
think that, given the past two millennia, during most of which
the death penalty was routinely imposed hundreds of thousands
of times as standard penal practice throughout the many realms
and ages of Christendom, there would be little need to discuss or
defend either principles or practice. The long tradition of outright support would seem to require little justification, having as
it did the endorsement of many of the best Christian minds and
hearts in the centuries since its origins.

The situation is admittedly unusual and delicate. It is the
kind of anomaly that readily invites simplistic reactions of one
extreme or the other. One might simply underline the undenia-
bility of the traditional acceptance of capital punishment in so
much of Christian history and go no further, maintaining that
what was the acceptable tradition throughout so many centuries
cannot reasonably be discarded or called into serious question
today. On the other hand, given the kind of cumulative case that
has been built against capital punishment internationally in our
own day, one might be tempted to see the history of the gallows
in Christendom simply as proof of a basic deficiency in Christian
ethics and opt, without further ado, for some superior "post-
Christian" ethic that puts a higher value on human life. Either
way, any closer examination of the record is thereby rendered
superfluous; either because one sees the use of the death
penalty as "a sacred tradition" in no further need of defense, or
because one views it as "an anachronous barbarism" that is an
unthinkable mode of conduct in a civilized, enlightened age.

For those who are uncomfortable with either of these extremes, however, the record is obviously a matter of interest, if only to try to account for some of the surprising twists and turns that could never have been anticipated or predicted in the growth of a tradition that took its start from the gospel story. The full history remains to be written, but it seems that several developments can safely be singled out as factors that contributed to the institutional complications that led to the extraordinary historical entanglement of Christian churchmen with the death penalty. Some of these developments have only recently been subjected to critical scrutiny by modern historians, and this has created the current opportunity of trying to make a fresh start in our day. By reassessing some of the troublesome departures of the past, it is possible to bring different priorities and to retrieve overshadowed principles that can now be applied anew.

The case to be made here is, in a nutshell, that there were particular periods in the first eighteen centuries of Western Christian history in which escalating developments occurred, each resulting in an ever greater entanglement of churchmen in the use (and then the justification of the use) of the death penalty. Those periods were roughly as follows:

1. **The fourth and fifth centuries,** when all the challenges of the Constantinian revolution had to be dealt with, determining how the new status of Christianity as the "established" religion of the Roman Empire should affect its teaching on the ethics of the use of lethal force, especially in war and capital punishment. The challenge was daunting, to say the least.

2. **The eighth and ninth centuries,** when the Western church allied itself with the newly ascendant Frankish powers, whose militant lifestyle raised further challenges concerning the use of lethal force that thus had to be confronted. The level of violence was admittedly beyond comprehension, let alone control.

3. **The eleventh to thirteenth centuries,** when the emergence of the "papal monarchy," faced with the sudden proliferation of popular heretical movements, had to make further choices. Theological and canonical reflection on the agonizing

problem of further direct church involvement with lethal force modified both Christian theory and practice.

4. **The fifteenth to seventeenth centuries,** when the complex heritage of inquisitorial use of lethal force formed in the earlier eras led to such dire social consequences that protest and reform were inevitable. The complications, difficulties, and failures that had to be endured before change or recovery of a more defensible Christian position on the use of lethal force occurred is the story of what happened, beginning with a few lonely voices (Lollard, Anabaptist, Quaker, etc.) that were hardly heard until a broader protest movement arose.

5. **The eighteenth to twentieth centuries,** starting with the critiques of the Enlightenment. Thereafter the combination of secular and religious forces labored haltingly but tirelessly to undo the official immersion in violence and achieve abolition of the aberration of capital punishment throughout Europe by the late-twentieth century.

As is evident, the problem being addressed extends far beyond the issue of capital punishment as such, since this practice is symptomatic and only one piece of the much larger puzzle, the puzzle of accounting for the oxymoronic phenomenon of "Christian violence" in its many forms. Other kinds of study in our own day, such as those inspired by the work of René Girard,[3] are grappling with the problem of the radical disorder of violence at the deepest level of human society. All that can be attempted here is a brief survey of some of the relevant historical material relating to the practice of the death penalty in Western Christendom, with the hope of providing some light on past departure from ('perversio'), as well as contemporary return to ('conversio') a more consciously gospel-based perspective on the dilemmas associated with the use of lethal force in the conduct of human societies.

After a brief look at the earlier developments, attention is turned to the contemporary struggle to free the world from the death penalty, and how that movement has emerged from the confluence of two other movements: 1) the movement to reinvigorate the church by redirecting its members toward retrieved gospel values, as articulated by Pope John XXIII and Vatican II, and 2) the worldwide movement to awaken nations to a greater appreciation of universal human rights, especially the basic inviolable right to life itself, on which all others are necessarily founded. The post-World-War II formulation of international laws and covenants to protect these rights is one of the success stories that provides hope for a world that may ultimately be made up of free nations that do not engage as a matter of policy in routine killings. From the mood of modern America, that seems highly unlikely, but, as everyone knows, moods can change as dramatically and quickly as the weather. More important is the retrieval of higher values when presented with the information and opportunity for doing so.

CHAPTER 1

————⊰✳⊱————

The Death Penalty and
Early Christianity

I. Prologue—On Interpreting the Bible
   A. Genesis 9
   B. Romans 13

II. Pre-Constantinian Christian Writers (A.D. 175–325)
   A. Athenagoras of Athens
   B. Minucius Felix
   C. Tertullian of Carthage
   D. Clement of Alexandria
   E. Origen
   F. Cyprian of Carthage
   G. Lactantius
   H. Hippolytus of Rome

III. The New Religion of the Roman Empire (313–450)
   A. Julius Firmicus Maternus
   B. Pope Damasus I
   C. The Execution of Priscillian
   D. St. Ambrose of Milan
   E. Pope Innocent I
   F. St. Jerome
   G. St. John Chrysostom

IV. The Ambivalent Legacy of St. Augustine (354–430)
   A. His Many Writings
   B. Seventeenth-Century Contentions
   C. Twentieth-Century Corrections

V. The Theodosian Code and Its Legacy (438–866)
   A. Pope St. Gregory I
   B. Pope Nicholas I

VI. A Postscript on the Greek Orthodox Experience
   A. Emperor Justinian I and His Code
   B. Afterword

I. PROLOGUE—ON INTERPRETING THE BIBLE

The history of the use of the death penalty is a story of extraordinary human conduct replete with all manner of anomalies. It involves religion at almost every step of the way and touches on virtually all aspects of a culture. Our interest is largely limited to the place of capital punishment in Western Christendom. The deep involvement of Christian church leaders over the centuries in this practice of sanctioning the deliberate destruction of human life brought about an entire complex of beliefs and practices that constituted a kind of tradition. What follows is only a partial overview of selected events in Christian history. Justice cannot be done to the story here, but we hope at least to provide a glimpse of the twisting road that led to capital punishment being enshrined in a privileged position and the painful retreat from that position in modern times.

In looking at this history many different starting points could be justified. But some treatment of the Bible would inevitably have to be included, since its central role in the formation of outlooks in Western Christendom is beyond question. There is, however, a very real problem in making it a starting point due to the rise of historical-critical consciousness. The biblical literalism that dominated the past has given way to methods that demand greater sophistication in using the Bible. This important change and its impact will be increasingly obvious as we proceed. There is nothing so fruitless as wrangling over the meaning of the Bible when the real object of debate should be the presuppositions brought to its interpretation. For now, only a few points will be touched on to give some idea of the changes required in approaching these ancient texts.

An obvious problem right at the start makes the issue of capital punishment very different from many others. The single most influential factor accounting for the early and widespread Christian acceptance of the death penalty was undoubtedly the Bible. If death had not been so strikingly represented as a divinely ordained penalty for dozens of human misdeeds in the Hebrew Bible, the practice of executing wayward fellow human beings would never have gained the kind of central position that it did in Christian history.[1] The ancient Hebrew law codes, as they were often invoked and applied in past ages, raise hard questions for Jewish and Christian believers. Controversy has swirled around "the great paradox" for centuries. [2]

The kind of proof-texting that has characterized the conversation, where the law codes of the ancient Israelite theocracy are taken literally as divinely given directives assumed to have perennial relevance for all later societies, even for modern secular states, is acknowledged by some Christians as valid, but by many others as simply wrongheaded in our day. A postcritical treatment and analysis of all the texts on capital punishment in the legal codes of the Hebrew Bible certainly constitute an important and worthwhile project yet to be fully accomplished, but promising efforts have been begun in recent years, even though the jury is still out on how successful they have been.[3] For our purposes, however, it will be enough to give some idea of how the biblical "problem" has been viewed in the past and how it is handled today in traditions where historical-critical methods have been accepted as valid and valuable parts of the contemporary search for fuller understanding and appreciation of the Bible.

First, a brief overview of the capital crimes found in the law codes of the Hebrew Bible is given, if only to help recall how large the problem is. By one Jewish scholar's count, thirty-six capital offenses are found in the Mosaic Law (eighteen calling for death by stoning, ten by burning, two by decapitation, and six by strangulation), and these in turn fall into variations of thirteen classes of misdeeds[4]:

> (a) adultery (2); (b) bestiality (2); (c) blasphemy (1); (d) idolatry (7); (e) incest (12); (f) kidnapping (1); (g) maladministration (1); (h) murder (1); (i) pederasty (1); (j) rape (1); (k) violations of filial duty (3); (l) violation of the Sabbath (1); (m) witchcraft (3).

Mendelsohn further notes that of these thirteen classes, four (c,d,l,m—which add up to twelve offenses) are crimes more immediately offending God, whereas the other nine categories (which add up to twenty-four offenses) are more immediately repugnant to human society.

This is not the place to delve into what actually went on in ancient Israelite society, but one cannot simply assume that these law codes literally reflect the general practice or that they served as more than symbolic reminders of the demands implicit in living according to the Covenant.[5] That is a rather academic question more for historians of ancient Israel than for contemporary Christian ethicists. But it is clear that at least by the time of the Talmud there was strong Jewish sentiment against the death penalty. "The most important passage in Rabbinical literature on the topic of capital punishment" records a conversation in which a rabbi said that a Sanhedrin which executes once in seven years is known as destructive. Whereupon "Rabbi Eleazar ben Azariah says, 'once in seventy years,' Rabbi Tarfon and Rabbi Akiba say 'if we were in Sanhedrin, no man would ever have been executed.' Rabbi Shimeon ben Gamliel says 'they (Rabbi Tarfon and Rabbi Akiba) would cause the proliferation of blood-shedders in Israel.'"[6]

This discussion, although dating from well over a century after the destruction of Jerusalem by the Romans, is nonetheless revealing.

> These Rabbis are advocating the abolition of the death penalty despite the Bible sanctioning such punishment in a number of instances. They evidently believed that biblical law was intended as a solemn warning to the extreme seriousness of crime but that the courts were justified in circumventing the law so that it becomes a dead letter. The statement...which concludes the passage is the stock argument of the antiabolitionists even today.[7]

The fact that laws might be read in different ways seldom received much attention in many of the Christian controversies over the role of the Bible. Language has many uses. Law codes are not automatically to be understood literally as simple mirrors of practice. One function of the juridical death threat was to get people's attention, to lay down a solemn warning, to alert all to the extreme seriousness of certain misdeeds. This pedagogical function of the law is accomplished by the texts themselves. They articulate what the society's top values are and what is beyond the range of acceptable behavior in the ideal order. If they were ever implemented literally, however, the streets of the community would run red with blood, the populace would be slaughtered by its own courts. There is little evidence that ancient Israel was ever such a sanguinary society.[8] While the expressive language of the law codes forcefully taught the essentials of proper conduct, the procedural protections largely circumvented their literal implementation, in that sense making these codes a relatively "dead letter." There is thus a striking irony in the way that these Hebrew law codes took on unprecedented new life outside of Israel in later Christian history.

Once they became part of the Old Testament of the Christian Bible, the capital mandates in these codes were seriously pondered over the centuries and subjected to a variety of interpretations. One infrequent way of handling them was to say quite simply that these harsh stipulations of the Old Law, however they may have been used in Israel, were totally and absolutely abolished by the New Law of Christ. So, at the end of the nineteenth century, John McMaster wrote that his chief aim was "to show upon the authority of the Bible 1) that the necessity for capital punishment was swept away by the atonement of our Lord and Savior Jesus Christ; 2) that the continuance of the death penalty is not merely inconsistent with, but antagonistic to, the express teaching of Christ and His Apostles; 3) that Christ by act and word repealed it; 4) that in the anti-Christian *(sic)* period of Jewish history, capital punishment...was necessary to reveal God's character and purposes, and to foreshadow the atoning death of our Savior."[9]

This particular kind of solution had no problem reading the law codes literally as a standard part of the old, pre-Christian order, but then held them inapplicable because they were relics of a time that was completely done away with by the advent of a new order initiated by Christ. This supersessionist theology reduced the Hebrew Scriptures to little more than quaint reminders of how bad things were before Christ and how ethically advanced the New Covenant was over the Old. It has, needless to say, not only been challenged but largely left aside today as an indefensible kind of Christian triumphalism.

At the other end of the spectrum, however, and much more common, are numerous varieties of Protestant evangelicalism that take the Pentateuchal texts as eternal and immutable mandates of God, just as much in force for obedient Christians of modern secular society as they are presumed to have been for ancient Israelites and all the ages in between. One group arguing in this fashion is the Theonomist or Christian Reconstructionist school, represented in the United States in recent years by Rousas J. Rushdoony, Gary North, and Greg Bahnsen.[10] Rushdoony, for example, insists that "murder requires the death penalty whether the offender is an animal, an 'insane' man, a child, or a feeble-minded person."[11] In less rigid form the basic position is also supported by Carl Henry, although he puts some qualifications on it:

> The Old Testament does not teach that capital punishment is always mandatory even when intentional killing is involved. Discretion is necessary in applying the mandate that the murderer is to be punished by a sentence of death; the deliberate murderer need not under all circumstances be put to death.[12]

But even in this less extreme form any advocacy of abolition of capital punishment is dismissed as stemming from "a non-Christian view of man, a secular theory of criminal law, and a low estimate of the value of human life."[13] It is somewhat surprising to encounter this kind of denigration of all opponents as "non-Christian" in a work explicitly intended to show that there are prominent Protestant evangelicals on both sides of the issue. In the very same pages of *The Genesis Debate* evangelical Malcolm Reed argues "for the strong counter-thesis that Genesis 9 is irrelevant to the issue of capital punishment," and that anyone who tries to use it for that purpose "faces textual, contextual, hermeneutical, and moral difficulties that, taken together, are insuperable."[14] But he does not excoriate fellow Christians who happen to hold the opposite position, which he personally repudiates as untenable.

This contemporary intra-Protestant dispute is mentioned simply to point out that capital punishment necessarily presents problems in Christian circles where precritical assumptions filter the reading of the Old Testament law codes. It is in many ways a modern American Protestant replication of outlooks found in earlier European Christianity, both Catholic and Protestant. Only when biblical literalism has been modified by modern critical methods does a different reading result, one that can bring new insights and understanding. The creation of an atmosphere in which alternative positions can be adjudicated and serious critical questions can be raised publicly must be counted as one of the significant beneficial "signs of the times."[15]

The recent change of stance in Catholic evaluation of the death penalty may reasonably be seen as merely one of the many benefits stemming from the advent and acceptance of modern historical-critical studies. The sea change that has occurred since Pope Pius XII's 1943 encyclical, *Divino Afflante Spiritu,* promoting the adoption of such studies, has undoubtedly brought problems with it, but it has enabled Catholic interpreters to escape the fundamentalism that invariably plagues ahistorical approaches to the Bible. It may thus be worth looking briefly at a couple of the biblical texts that were always at the center of the earlier debates about capital punishment, if only to see why the proof-text method of old has been definitively left behind. One example from each Testament is all that will be attempted here by way of illustration.

A. *Genesis 9*

> v. 3. Every creature that is alive shall be yours to eat. I give them all to you as I did the green plants. 4. Only flesh with its lifeblood still in it you shall not eat. 5. For your own lifeblood, too, I will demand an accounting. From every animal I will demand it, and from man in regard to his fellow man I will demand an accounting for human life. 6. If anyone sheds the blood of man, by man shall his blood be shed; for in the image of God has man been made. (*NAB* translation)

In the history of Christian theological legitimation of the death penalty, Genesis 9:6 has probably been cited more frequently than any other text as basic proof of the propriety of humans executing fellow human malefactors. For centuries it was taken as a divine command, promulgated in the Covenant with Noah, imposing the death penalty on murderers; the conclusion was drawn in literalist interpretation that the Bible here places upon the state the solemn duty to execute all persons duly convicted of murder and that the failure to do so would be an abominable act of disobedience. Such a reading was always faced with manifold difficulties, including the problem of explaining why, five chapters earlier, the primeval murderer did not have his blood shed, but rather "the Lord put a mark on Cain, lest anyone who came upon him should kill him" (Gn 4:15). But there were various ways to get around that objection, such as by contending that, while murder was always wrong, God did not impose the death penalty until after the Flood.[16]

Another objection provoked by a critical reading of this verse is the fact that "no distinction is made between accidental, negligent, and willful homicide; and within willful homicide no distinction is made between crimes of passion and those which are planned with scheming malice."[17] Those who appeal to it as their authority for blanket approval of the death penalty invariably narrow its application without further ado to the single case of first-degree murder. This kind of arbitrary restriction, devoid of any textual basis, is a good example of why such proof-texting has been thoroughly discredited.

Modern scholars have pointed out that the text actually has a chiastic structure, typical of Hebrew wisdom literature. Recent translations, including the *NAB*, indicate that the verse is thus poetic in form, yet biblical laws were never written in poetic form.

> This is a very convincing argument why Genesis 9:6 must not be understood as an imperative, commanding any state to administer capital punishment. We seem to be dealing here, accordingly, not with a piece of legislation but with something like a proverb. Expressions falling into this literary genre are familiar to all, and are not foreign to the Bible. We are told, e.g., that "he who lives by the sword shall perish

by the sword"; or again, "what a man sows that shall he
reap." There is a profound truth in these utterances...but
they are ill-used when given legal application. Proverbs are
not juridical in nature, and are not to be taken as legal prescriptions. By this same token, neither is Genesis 9:6a.[18]

Thus the "traditional" use of Genesis 9:6 to bolster the infliction of capital punishment has been judged unwarranted,
because such a reading fails to take into account the literary
genre of the passage. *The New Interpreter's Bible* incorporates
such an understanding:

> The chiastic formulation of v. 6 provides a shorthand
> expression, probably proverbial, of the repercussions that
> fall upon a murderer....The chiasm formally expresses the
> point; in such cases, justice will involve the principle of mea-
> sure for measure....This text does not advocate or authorize
> or justify capital punishment; rather it recognizes the way in
> which human beings would participate in the moral order as
> executors of the divine judgment....This saying expresses
> God's point of view, regarding the high value of human
> life.[19]

There are other anomalies and anachronisms in employing
this verse to support modern state executions. There was no
established state involved when the text came into being. What it
was originally sanctioning was the tribal practice of blood-
vengeance, whereby the nearest relative of the victim had the
duty to avenge the slaying of his kinsman. In that sense, the verse
has nothing to do with authorizing a state to kill. To be consistent, if one treats the verse as a divine law, the modern application would be, not the authorization of state-regulated
executions, but the legitimation of blood-feuds, whereby a victim's relatives are invited to take their revenge on the killer.[20]
    Arguments over such points, however, are seldom fruitful,
precisely because of the uncertainties that come with the plurality of possible interpretations. A dogmatic stance, insisting that
one's own interpretation is the only possible one, leads to the
demonizing of opponents.

B. Romans 13

> v. 1. Everyone must submit himself to the governing authori-
> ties, for there is no authority except that which God has
> established. The authorities that exist have been established
> by God. 2. Consequently, he who rebels against the author-
> ity is rebelling against what God has instituted, and those
> who do so will bring judgment on themselves. 3. For rulers
> hold no terror for those who do right, but for those who do
> wrong. Do you want to be free from fear of the one in
> authority? Then do what is right and he will commend you.
> 4. For he is God's servant to do you good. But if you do
> wrong, be afraid, for he does not bear the sword for noth-
> ing. He is God's servant, an agent of wrath to bring punish-
> ment on the wrongdoer. 5. Therefore, it is necessary to
> submit to the authorities, not only because of possible pun-
> ishment but also because of conscience. 6. This is also why
> you pay taxes, for the authorities are God's servants, who
> give their full time to governing. 7. Give everyone what you
> owe him: If you owe taxes, pay taxes; if revenue, then rev-
> enue; if respect, then respect; if honor, then honor. *(New
> International Version)*

This New Testament passage vies with Genesis 9:6 as the
most popular and frequent proof-text invoked to justify the practice of state executions over the centuries. It has traditionally
been loaded down with multiple assumptions. Some have found
in it not only grounds for permitting but for actually requiring
that the state execute all criminals. The passage, however, merely
acknowledges the validity and propriety, even the necessity, of
the punitive function of the state. It does not address questions
about the actual form or extent of punishment. As a symbol of
authority, the sword, like a policeman's handgun in our time, is a
kind of last-resort warning. In and of itself, it may suggest that in
certain circumstances its possessor may be authorized to use it to
wound or kill a law breaker. In that sense, one could say that the
state's penal power may extend as far as capital punishment. But
having "the power of the sword" is a symbolic way of expressing
the legitimacy of the state's general penal authority, not a suggestion that in practice it ought to engage in bloodshed. In fact,
as is well known, violence is the hallmark of failure, the open

admission that all other efforts and solutions have proved fruitless. The success of one who has the power of the sword is ideally
measured in terms of never having to use it. In light of the rest of
Paul's teaching about God's love manifest in Christ, it can certainly be argued that "scriptural principles and Christian compassion point in the direction of judicial restraint toward the
minimal use of the sword, toward the bracketing of capital punishment as a rarely used weapon of last resort."[21] As Voltaire
observed centuries later, it is the sheathed, not the unsheathed,
sword that is the best symbol of legitimate power.

But, just as in the case of the Genesis passage, turning
Romans 13:4 into a proof-text for capital punishment is even less
persuasive when its context is more fully taken into account.
Judging from verse 2, what Paul had in mind was not individual
malfeasance but "rebellion" such as that which had led Emperor
Claudius to expel the Jews from Rome a short time before.[22]

> The mention of the sword is, in our opinion, more probably
> to be understood as a reference to the authority's possession
> of military power than to the power of capital punishment—
> a reminder that it is in a position to quell resistance.[23]

These two examples are meant simply to give some indication of why it is not satisfactory in our day to repeat precritical
positions. There is widespread recognition that texts, biblical or
otherwise, must be approached in a broader way than ahistorical
proof-texting. Understanding must precede exposition, and
exposition must precede application.

> The order cannot be reversed. We cannot apply a text until
> we have expounded it, i.e., stated its meaning, and we can-
> not state its meaning until we have understood it. Conse-
> quently it is incorrect to try to apply a biblical text until we
> have discovered its meaning by paying attention to its origi-
> nal context. It is equally incorrect to think that we can dis-
> cover its context without first grasping the type of text it is.[24]

Such critical procedure in itself is not the whole answer, but it is
certainly part of the corrective action that has invalidated earlier

simplistic usage of the Bible to sanction the familiar. None of this is meant to suggest that the necessary transition is easily made.

> These biblical texts, thanks to an uncritical and naive exegesis, inspired and sustained across the centuries the legislation of the death penalty in our traditional civilization. This pseudo-biblical foundation must be demythologized. If the Bible has something fundamental to say to us, it is on a different level; it cannot be on the level of juridical and temporal institutions, but on that of human destiny, of relationship with God, of the meaning of life and death, of sin and pardon, of the primacy of contributing absolutely to human values and realities in the realm of brotherly love.[25]

It is precisely this kind of shift in the use of the Bible that is illustrated in the best contemporary church statements against capital punishment.

Much more needs to be said, especially about the bearing of the teaching of Jesus on this practice of deliberate killing, but it seems best to postpone that until after surveying the historical record. Since the story of the capital execution of Jesus is central to the message of the Christian gospel, it is worth asking whether his early followers had anything special to say about this practice of destroying human life.

II. PRE-CONSTANTINIAN CHRISTIAN WRITERS
(A.D. 175–325)

In trying to determine what early generations of Christians may have thought about the death penalty, there is not a large body of surviving literature to be consulted. Remarks in passing give an occasional glimpse of how the capital practices of pagan Rome were viewed, but it must be remembered that the Christians of the time, as members of an illegal religion, were among the likeliest targets of capital punishment. This is a fact of considerable significance for later events. Roman Law in its pre-Constantinian formulation had gradually come to include an extremely harsh penal code.[26] One might have thought that, since it was under this code that Jesus himself was cruelly and unjustly executed, his followers could have had special reason to be critical of the practice. Undoubtedly it would be fascinating to know if this were actually the case to any great extent, but there is unfortunately not very much to go by. Struggling minorities in any age are not often in a position to have their story well preserved for transmission to later generations, and the early Christians were no exception.

In the 1950s historian Bernhard Schöpf set out to examine the pre-Constantinian literature for observations touching on the ethics of terminating human life, whether by murder, suicide, euthanasia, self-defense, gladiatorial games, abortion, capital punishment, tyrannicide, or war. Although his findings tell us much about early Christian perspectives on the ethics of killing, only a handful of passages in the surviving works touch on capital punishment as used in their day, and none of these is very enlightening.[27]

A. Athenagoras of Athens

The earliest was philosopher Athenagoras of Athens in his eloquent *Plea for Christians*, addressed to Emperor Marcus Aurelius and his son Commodus soon after the latter had been given the imperial title in A.D. 176. Toward the end of the plea, when dealing with the wild allegation that Christians ate human flesh in their assemblies, Athenagoras asks: "What man of sound mind will affirm...that we are murderers? For we cannot eat human flesh till we have killed someone." Furthermore,

> When they know that we cannot endure even to see a man put to death, though justly, who of them can accuse us of murder or cannibalism? Who does not reckon among the things of greatest interest the contests of gladiators and wild beasts, especially those which are given by you? But we, deeming that to see a man put to death is much the same as killing him, have abjured such spectacles. How, then, when we do not even look on, lest we should contract guilt and pollution, can we put people to death?[28]

It is only a remark made in passing, hardly a basis for building any broad theory about early Christian ethical beliefs, but it is nonetheless an intriguing comment, reflecting as it does the sensitivity of a second-century member of a Christian community that would have nothing to do with human bloodshed. It can hardly be read as having more than an indirect bearing on the evaluation of capital punishment as such, but it does seem to take for granted that the death penalty could be imposed "justly" by the pagan Roman courts. At the same time, however, it judges the practice totally incompatible with Christian sensibilities.

This stance of "Christian separatism" was understandable and perfectly defensible as long as Christians were a persecuted, relatively powerless minority in the Empire. Their challenge then was one of survival in a hostile world. Only later would they have to concern themselves with the problem of the ethical use of public power. It is interesting to note that in virtually the same breath Athenagoras notes the silliness of accusing Christians of cannibalism and murder when it is common knowledge that they are so strongly opposed to killing that they reject abortion and infanticide. Hence, in this early Christian philosopher's brief remarks a "consistent ethic of life" appears that leads him to demand that those accusing Christians of cannibalism explain "on what principle would we commit murder?" With the confidence of a traditional Greek philosopher in the power of simple logic, Athenagoras rests his case: killing is killing, and Christians are well known to be opposed to it in all its forms, so stop the silly allegations that are in open contradiction with that principle!

B. Minucius Felix

The chronology is not entirely clear, but the *Octavius* dialogue of Minucius Felix, from the same general period, has a similar passage, rebutting the allegation that "Christians worshipped monsters, devoured infants, and mingled in incestuous banquets." Their known opposition to abortion was likewise appealed to as counter-evidence, as was the fact that "for us it is not permissible either to see or to hear of human slaughter; we have such a shrinking from human blood that at our meals we avoid the blood of animals used for food."[29] Once more, the general renunciation of any kind of bloodshed would presumably rule out any Christian involvement with the death penalty (other than as its victims, as in the case of Jesus) but tells us nothing more about how it may have been evaluated. The focus of these writings is intra-Christian, concerning the survival of a religious minority in a hostile environment, so they could hardly be expected to engage in more theoretical considerations.

C. Tertullian of Carthage

Tertullian had different things to say about the death penalty at different times in his writings. In his *Apology* (A.D. 197) he criticized Roman law for being excessively severe and would have welcomed a milder replacement. In *On Idolatry* and *On the Crown* (c. A.D. 211) he voiced two objections to Christian participation in the Roman army: first, soldiers were required to take part in pagan sacrifices; and second, they were required to carry out capital punishments. Once again, the brief passages are hardly adequate for drawing general conclusions. It is tempting to read them as indicating total opposition to any kind of killing as such, and much of the later Christian pacifist literature has interpreted them in this way. But such a reading may go beyond what is warranted by the texts, especially since in his treatise *On the Soul* and elsewhere, Tertullian, invoking Romans 13, acknowledges that rulers have the power of the sword.[30] Schöpf ends up uncertain of exactly how to interpret Tertullian on this issue, but notes that "people in general—not only Christian thinkers—often approve of the death penalty, but at the same time, detest the one who carries it out."[31] Such has been the lot of the hangman in many cultures.

D. Clement of Alexandria

In his famous *Miscellanies* (written after A.D. 202) Clement (c. A.D. 150–211) was, as far as Schöpf could determine, the first Christian writer to provide theoretical grounds for the justification of capital punishment. In this he was not especially original, but rather, like Seneca a century and a half earlier, appealed to a rather questionable medical analogy rather than to anything of specifically Christian inspiration. Punishment, Clement suggests, should work like a diet or an enema ordered by the physician to restore health. "When a punishment is just, it can lead a soul back to the right path." But if someone "falls into incurable evil—when taken possession of, for example, by wrong or covetousness—it will be for his good if he is put to death."[32] This seminal remark, extending the medical analogy to the bizarre extreme of treating the patient with the "final solution," will be encountered in later contexts, but it never makes any more sense then than it does here. It is a highly misleading if not fallacious analogy, because it parallels removal of a physical part to save a person's life with removal of a person's life to save a society. It begs the question about the ethics of capital punishment, which is supposedly the subject under discussion. Schöpf points out that it could just as easily be used to justify euthanasia (which Clement certainly does not do) and concludes by citing the logical rule: "He who proves too much proves nothing."[33] But it is hard to base very much on this brief remark, if only because of its casual nature.

E. Origen

Origen (A.D. 185–254) clearly takes for granted the state's right to impose death on malefactors and also defends the prominence of capital punishment in the Old Testament against critics who made accusations of its being terribly cruel for divine conduct.[34] His only real concern, just as in the case of war, was to prohibit Christians from taking part in such killing. His ecclesiology envisioned Christians as "spiritual warriors" who keep their own hands unbloodied while praying for the success of the others (pagans) who must do battle and engage in politics for the good of the Roman Empire.[35] This kind of separatism had its own charm but could not be seriously maintained once church membership represented more than a small minority. "When Origen wrote, the problem of defining a Christian group identity in pagan society was only just arising....[Later] Christians had to guard against the threat to their identity by becoming too assimilated."[36] But in Origen's day the separatist model was still an operational possibility, so direct ethical problems of involvement with the penal system and its administration of capital punishment were yet to arise.[37] It is quite unfair to expect Origen to have foreseen and formulated the kind of theology that would be required for the unimaginable circumstances of a century later.[38]

F. Cyprian of Carthage

In the passages cited by Schöpf, Cyprian (d. A.D. 257) does not deal directly with the death penalty. In one of them he merely sets up a rhetorical dilemma: "Either being a Christian is a capital crime or it is not. If it is, why not execute those who profess to be Christians? If it is not, why persecute the innocent?" Does Cyprian thereby imply that he regards the death penalty as a legitimate practice of the Roman government? Probably so, but that is certainly not the focus of his argument, which is an exercise in rhetoric with a very different point. Such a text cannot be used in any general argument about the ethics of capital punishment, since the focus is obviously elsewhere.

Another passage of Cyprian's, found in his letter to Donatus, may be an allusion to the way the death penalty was being used, but on the other hand, it may simply be a barb thrown at the corrupt society of his day:

> Consider the roads blocked up by robbers, the seas beset with pirates, wars scattered all over the earth with the bloody horror of camps. The whole world is wet with mutual blood; and murder, which in the case of an individual is admitted to be a crime, is called a virtue when it is committed wholesale.[39]

Of a more challenging nature is his letter to Cornelius, describing the persecution in which the "soldiers of Christ" prevailed by making their persecutors aware that

> they cannot be conquered, but that they can die; and that by this very fact they are invincible, that they do not fear death; that they do not in turn assail their assailants, for it is not lawful for the innocent to kill even the guilty; but that they readily deliver up both their lives and their blood; that since such malice and cruelty rages in the world, they may the more quickly withdraw from the evil and the cruel. What a glorious spectacle was that under the eyes of God![40]

The higher standard for Christians was taken for granted; it was not lawful for them to kill. If confronted with the choice of killing or being killed, there was no ambiguity about what their faith required, as far as Cyprian was concerned.

G. Lactantius

Lactantius (d.c. A.D. 320) lived through the turbulent transition from violent persecution of Christians under Emperor Diocletian to the total reversal of fortunes under Emperor Constantine I. The significance of this change is obviously fundamental for all subsequent Christian history. In the decades before Constantine, Christians were more likely to be concerned about the death penalty only from the victim's viewpoint. Thousands of them paid for their faith with their lives in persecutions launched by Roman imperial forces, the worst bearing the names of Decius (A.D. 249–251) and Diocletian (A.D. 303–311).[41] Then suddenly the roles were reversed. It is difficult to miss the enormous irony, for example, in Constantine's order of 324, not only commanding the destruction of all copies of Porphyry's work *Against the Christians,* but, in the process, prescribing the death penalty for any and all who might secretly retain it.

The writings of Lactantius are of interest more for their style than for their intellectual content, although some of his formulations of Christian moral positions are notable enough. In *Epitome,* for example, he says that "the first duty of justice is to acknowledge God as a parent, to fear him as a master, and to love him as a father," and that God thus has "the authority to correct us and the power of life and death....The second duty of justice is to acknowledge man as a brother...and he who does not acknowledge this is unjust." Such ruminations are entirely relevant to the project of Christians groping for proper ways to use their newly acquired political power and responsibility, but such theological ideas were not actually destined to make much impact on imperial policy for the next century.

As for the death penalty, however, Lactantius has with good reason been cited by both advocates and opponents. In his *Divine Institutes* one of the most celebrated passages of early pacifism occurs. Christians, he says, are not allowed to engage in any kind of bloodshed:

> When God forbids killing, he is not only ordering us to avoid armed robbery, which is contrary even to public law, but he is forbidding what men regard as ethical. Thus, it is not right for a just man to serve in the army since justice itself is his form of service. Nor is it right for a just man to charge someone with a capital crime. It does not matter whether you kill a man with the sword or with a word, since it is killing itself that is prohibited. And so there is no exception to this command of God. Killing a human being, whom God willed to be inviolable, is always wrong.[42]

This absolutist interpretation of the fifth commandment, understood as prohibiting any kind of killing whatsoever, no matter when, where, why, or by whom, remained a minority interpretation that was to recur in the Middle Ages and again in more recent Christian history. But it seems safe to say that Lactantius went on to modify his views after the Constantinian victories, and that he came to share some of the providentialist views of Eusebius, regarding Constantine as "God's divinely appointed agent to restore justice and exact divine vengeance on the wicked." So, overall, at least consecutively, he seems to "embody both traditions that we have seen in the early church.... Lactantius's *volte-face* anticipates the position that will become the majority view from this point onward."[43]

Before moving to the next period, it is worth mentioning another fairly well-known text that Schöpf did not include, presumably because of the multiple uncertainties surrounding it. We place it here with the awareness of those continuing questions (who wrote it? who is speaking? when? and so on).

H. Hippolytus of Rome

Hippolytus (c. A.D. 170–236) may have been the author of the original part of the much revised and transformed *Apostolic Tradition*. Article 17 reads:

> A soldier who is in authority must be told not to execute
> men; if he should be ordered to do it, he shall not do it. He
> must be told not to take the military oath. If he will not
> agree, let him be rejected.

To what is this referring? The statement is so general it is
ambiguous. It could be alluding to "the killing of criminals in
connection with the gladiatorial games, persecution, or simply
capital punishment. It seems clear that the train of thought
before and after rules out the taking of life in combat as its meaning."[44] In any event, it cannot be invoked as contributing very
much, precisely because of its ambiguity.

III. THE NEW RELIGION OF THE ROMAN EMPIRE
(A.D. 313–450)

The new religion of the Empire did not start off with any
greater tolerance or any less use of capital punishment; there was
only a switch as to who the chief victims were.[45] This is only one
example of the legislation and policies that led Imbert to conclude that "Christianity had absolutely no real influence on the
repressive system of the Roman Empire."[46] While that may be
somewhat of an overstatement, it seems closer to the mark than
the occasional claims in the opposite direction by some earlier
church historians.[47] Personalities and power politics combined to
keep in place most of the harsh imperial penal policies of the past.

The century and a quarter from Constantine I to Theodosius
II, when Christianity was adapting itself to its new role as the
established religion of the Roman Empire, was a crucially formative time. The complex intertwining of Christian creed and
Roman law definitively marked "Imperial Christianity" in manifold ways destined to last for centuries to come.[48] This is the initial
context for understanding the history of the use of capital punishment in Christendom. Ironically, the lethal combination of the
Bible and Roman law provided surprisingly cruel penal codes,
invariably viewed as directly willed by God. The entire repressive
system of Roman Law was brought to bear actively on the project
of "Christianizing" the Empire when it was under challenge
from external "barbarian" forces. During this period successive

emperors passed at least sixty-six decrees against Christian
heretics, and another twenty-five laws "against paganism in all its
forms."[49] The violence of the age was extraordinary, and Christians were becoming more and more deeply involved in it, confronted with major decisions about how to respond appropriately
when the instruments of power were placed in their hands. To
underline the troublesome developments of this transitional time,
it is worth noting a few problematic incidents that need to be more
carefully evaluated in any overall assessment of the age.

A. Julius Firmicus Maternus

In 346, Julius Firmicus Maternus, a recent convert, addressed
to the sons of Constantine an inflammatory booklet, *On the Error
of Pagan Religions,* issuing thereby "the earliest-known instance of
an appeal by a Christian to 'the secular arm' to enforce Christianity and destroy other religions without mercy."[50] This vigorous call
for eradicating paganism by ferocious use of state power strikes an
unfortunate new note in Christian literature. "The express conviction of such humane thinkers as Tertullian and Lactantius had
been that enforced conversion is unreal and ineffective for salvation."[51] Ten years earlier, while still a pagan, Maternus himself had
compiled a lengthy book on astrology, revealing that he had a
thorough familiarity with the common beliefs about the gods of
paganism. In his later profoundly ironic call for violently uprooting paganism in favor of Christianity, he explicitly stated that the
reason for engaging in such horrendous bloodshed was because
the grossly immoral conduct of the pagan gods gives their followers "seminal ideas for almost all the types of crime, and allows
their doomed souls to commit misdeeds with impunity, (and) they
defend themselves with greater authority by the foregoing examples of wrongdoing."[52] His lengthy list of the sins that the followers
of the Roman gods might imitate is impressive, but at the same
time he seems totally oblivious of the immorality of what his own
violent appeal advocated: "Be not afraid to strip the temples of
their ornaments. May these gods melt in the fire for the minting of
your coins, and in the flames of your lead-mines. Confiscate for
your own benefit all their gifts; make it all your own property!"
With high rhetoric he urged the "Most Holy Emperors...to casti-

gate and punish this evil!" In a classical formulation of the legitimation of unlimited violence, he insisted that "the Law of the
Supreme Deity enjoins on you that your severity should be visited
in every way on the crime of idolatry." After citing Deuteronomy
13 as proof, he went on to insist that God "bids you spare neither
son nor brother, and thrusts the avenging sword through the body
of a beloved wife. A friend too He persecutes with lofty severity,
and the whole populace takes up arms to rend the bodies of sacrilegious men. Even for whole cities, if they are caught in this crime,
destruction is decreed." In the next breath, after urging the Christian emperors to an ethic of total violence, he called upon them to
act

> with a pure heart, a devout conscience, and an incorrupt
> mind....Let your clemency ever fix its gaze upon heaven,
> ever look for help from God....So will all things come to you
> in happy success: victories, riches, peace, plenty, health, and
> triumphs, so that borne forward by the power of God, you
> may govern the world in fortunate sovereignty.[53]

With counsel such as this there was little chance that Christian Rome would be any less violent than pagan Rome had been.
In fact, in light of the increased heavenly rewards promised for it,
an increase in repressive violence might reasonably be expected.
But if this call for killing outsiders so as to make the whole world
Christian illustrates one major dimension of the problem of violence, the same century records yet other foreboding developments marked by extraordinary bloodshed.

B. Pope Damasus I

In 366 one of the most scandalous papal elections in history
occurred. The talented Pope Damasus I (366–384) (who later
commissioned St. Jerome to produce the Latin Vulgate translation of the Bible) was ultimately the successful candidate, but not
before his partisans had stormed the Basilica of Liberius (now
Santa Maria Maggiore), in which the supporters of his rival, Ursi-
nus, had barricaded themselves. By the time they were dis-
lodged, 137 corpses littered the church pavement.[54] If the
nonviolent ideals of the Prince of Peace were to be advanced in

the church of the future, some very definite changes obviously would have to occur in the conducting of Roman church politics. But no sooner was Damasus dead than an even more ominous event occurred, one that was to cast a long shadow down the corridors of Christian history.

C. The Execution of Priscillian

In 385/386 Priscillian of Avila and his companions were executed in what was most likely the first instance of Christians killing fellow Christians because of doctrinal differences.[55] The victims were treacherously put to death in Trier by the usurper Maximus.[56] This scandalous action was severely denounced by Martin, bishop of Tours, by Ambrose, bishop of Milan, and by Siricius, bishop of Rome. All three condemned Ithacius, the bishop of Ossonuba, who had manipulated Maximus into ordering the execution, and all three refused communion to any bishops who associated with Ithacius.[57]

But this "healthy protest against something which closely resembled the later handing-over of heretics for execution by the secular arm"[58] was not effective. Of much greater impact for the future was the fact of the execution itself, which set a tragic precedent. Even though the pope during whose pontificate it happened (Siricius) registered his strong disapproval, less than two generations later a different and much more influential pope, Leo I (440–461), looked back and expressed his full approval of the execution of Priscillian on the grounds that his killers "saw...that both divine and human law would be subverted, if ever it should have been licit for such men to live with such doctrine."[59] This was to be the single most intractable problem for Christian churchmen for the next fourteen centuries: how were they to deal effectively with heretics? This dilemma bewildered and entangled churchmen more and more inextricably, involving them in all the incongruities and cruelties of a policy of thoroughgoing, routine capital punishment.[60] If it had not been for this agonizing dilemma, there is good reason to believe that Christian church leaders would never have allowed themselves to become so supportive and accepting of the policy of sanctioning the deliberate destruction of life with the death penalty.

D. St. Ambrose of Milan

The reaction of St. Ambrose, bishop of Milan, to the Priscillianist affair has already been mentioned. But a few years later a far more horrendous case of bloodshed by a Christian emperor occurred, to which Ambrose had to respond.

> In the summer of 390 the troops stationed in the Balkan city of Thessalonica were unleashed upon the civilian population: "for three hours the city was given over to the sword, and very many innocent were slain." The massacre was evidently a mistake and it dealt a potentially catastrophic blow to the reputation for competence and clemency that (Emperor) Theodosius had cultivated.[61]

Although there is still much controversy over exactly what happened and why, it was a gross instance of mass imperial capital punishment carried out by the military. The ultimate surprise, however, was the masterful way in which Ambrose "turned the catastrophe into a public relations triumph for the emperor. To the admiration of his Christian subjects Theodosius was seen to humble himself before the discipline of the church; he took his place...among the sinners who gathered at the basilica to demonstrate their repentance to God, and tearfully solicited the prayers of the faithful."[62] Of course, what the emperor was repenting of, and what the bishop was requiring him to do penance for, was not the use of the death penalty as such, but the overhasty and irresponsibly excessive use of it on one occasion in Thessalonica. In the long run, the fact that the entire incident ended up establishing a much closer "partnership... between bishop and emperor"[63] ironically may have helped reinforce the model of church and state as two coordinated arms, the religious and the secular, with the former arm able to rely on and use the latter arm to do the dirty work, handing over condemned heretics to this "secular arm" for execution, while maintaining an appearance thereby that all church responsibility for the bloodshed was avoided.[64]

On the other hand, the emphasis that Ambrose himself placed on God's readiness to forgive, especially in his refutation of hard-line Novatianism, was certainly an important source deeply influencing Augustine, who would soon make it central to his own Christian pastoral lifestyle. A truly forgiving spirit cannot help but look disapprovingly on the very idea of the death penalty, which is in effect an act of total despair in the potential of the individual to repent, to be rehabilitated, and/or to make meaningful reparations.[65]

Perhaps the most famous text of Ambrose that merits pondering here is the one expressing the high ethical standard of his description of the duties of the clergy. Referring to a question asked by his beloved Cicero, the answer of Ambrose was different:

> Some ask whether a wise man ought in case of a shipwreck to take away a plank from an ignorant sailor (in order to survive). Although it seems better for the common good that a wise man rather than a fool should escape from shipwreck, yet I do not think that a Christian, a just and a wise man, ought to save his own life by the death of another; just as when he meets with an armed robber he cannot return his blows, lest in defending his life he should stain his love toward his neighbor. The verdict on this is plain and clear in the books of the Gospel. "Put up thy sword, for everyone that taketh the sword shall perish with the sword." What robber is more hateful than the persecutor who came to kill Christ? But Christ would not be defended from the wounds of the persecutor, for He willed to heal all by His wounds.[66]

This kind of insistence that the hard teachings of Jesus were relevant and ought to be taken seriously in ordinary Christian ethics says much about Ambrose. The only problem is that this nonviolent gospel is apparently directed as obligatory only on the Christian clergy. This "split-level" Christianity leaves the way open for accommodating violence on the lower-level (laity), and from there even to find its way back into the upper-level (clergy). But blame for such later anomalies can hardly be laid at Ambrose's door. This eloquent passage, calling for the clergy to be peacemakers, became part of the textual fund that was passed on to enrich medieval university students with solid ideals for their grounding in moral theology.

E. Pope Innocent I

The deeply traumatic sack of Rome by Alaric and his marauding Goths in 410 was symbolic of the end of an age and provoked Augustine to write his famous *City of God.* But a different kind of transition was also reflected in a letter that Innocent, the bishop of Rome at the time of the sack, wrote. He gives us a rare look at how some Christians thought about the death penalty in this chaotic time of barbarian invasions. Earlier (382), when Damasus was pope, one of the canons of the Roman Synod directed to the bishops of Gaul set forth the clear policy that state officials who "have handed down death penalties, given unjust judgments and administered legal torture cannot be regarded as free from sin."[67] Now, a generation later, Innocent was explicitly asked: "How should one regard those who, after having received the sacrament of baptism, have assumed public office and administered torture or pronounced capital sentences?" The pope's explicit reply was: "On this point nothing has been handed down to us."[68]

Compagnoni, in pondering this strange exchange, theorizes that it was part of the church's pragmatic adaptation policy as the number of Christian officials in the Empire increased after A.D. 400. "The shift had taken place in the problem...not only in the solution...in spite of all the reservations of an Augustine."[69] While that may be so, it is also possible in retrospect to ask whether such an adaptation policy entailed, willy-nilly, the abandonment of a higher ideal and the tacit acceptance of a lesser one, with unfortunate long-range consequences.

F. St. Jerome

The reason for including Jerome (d. 420) at this point is the fact that a couple of passages from his biblical commentaries later came to be applied to the death penalty by medieval authors. There is no doubt that they were being invoked out of context to support positions that had not even been formulated in Jerome's day. But, if they are to be included at all, perhaps this is the proper place:

In the first, Jerome was commenting on one of the fiery oracles of Jeremiah (22:3): "Thus says the Lord: Do what is just and right. Rescue the victim from the hand of his oppressor. Do not wrong or oppress the resident alien, the orphan, or the widow, and do not shed innocent blood in this place." This last command (not to shed innocent blood) led Jerome to comment that the prohibition did not apply to "murderers, blasphemers, and poisoners," because they were not innocent and thus punishing lawbreakers "is not the shedding of blood but the administration of laws."[70] This was little more than a rhetorical flourish, a bit of hyperbole meant to emphasize the difference between two acts of bloodletting, one authorized, the other unauthorized, but the statement lent itself to something more. It would come in handy when the medieval search was on for greater legitimation of the death penalty.

In the second passage, Jerome was once again commenting on a major prophet, this time examining the angry words of God in the vision of Ezekiel (9:1) when God "cried in my ears with a loud voice, saying, 'Draw near, you executioners of the city, each with his destroying weapon in his hand,'" and they were then commissioned to slaughter the inhabitants wholesale, causing Ezekiel to fall on his face and plead (9:8): "O Lord God, will you destroy all that remains of Israel in the outpouring of your wrath upon Jerusalem?" Once more, Jerome's choice of words is the point. He first corrects the Septuagint translation, noting that the verb should be in the present, not the past. Then he goes on to remark that "he who strikes the evil (idolators) insofar as they are evil, and has the 'destroying weapon' for executing the worst (of them), is a minister of the Lord."[71] As is evident, it would be a long stretch to say that Jerome was here remarking in any way on the legitimacy of the state's use of capital punishment. He was dealing with the far more vexing problem of the God of the Israelites, as Ezekiel saw him, using the enemies of Israel to slaughter Israelites and destroy the Temple of Solomon in punishment for their infidelity to the covenant. But the language of Jerome, once again, was ideal for being taken over in a later medieval context that elevated allowable killing as a kind of ministry or divine service.

G. St. John Chrysostom

Before turning to the complex case of St. Augustine to close out this part of our survey, it is worth recalling a homily of his great contemporary in the East, John Chrysostom (d. 407), on the parable of the wheat and the weeds (Matthew 13), which was to play a curious role and receive a surprising variety of interpretations in the capital-punishment debate of later centuries. When the servants asked the master if he wanted them to pull up the weeds immediately upon finding them, the master said "No, lest you root up the wheat with them." Chrysostom commented that this was said "to hinder wars from arising, and blood and slaughter. For it is not right to put a heretic to death, since an implacable war would be brought into the world....He does not forbid our checking heretics, and stopping their mouths, and taking away their freedom of speech, and breaking up their assemblies and confederacies, but [he does forbid] our killing and slaying them."[72] This drawing of the line just short of the death penalty in repressing religious dissent was to prove extremely problematic in practice. Once the use of violence is authorized, as the history of war all too well illustrates, it is virtually impossible to draw such idealistic lines. Violence follows its own laws, which do not realistically accommodate any significant measure of restraint, no matter who advises it.

IV. THE AMBIVALENT LEGACY OF ST. AUGUSTINE
(A.D. 354–430)

A. His Many Writings

Shortly after the execution of Priscillian, Augustine was baptized by Ambrose and was soon thrown into bitter battles with the Donatists back home in North Africa. Despite all the frustrations he had to face, the early Augustine flatly rejected Maternus's idea of using force to make heretics renounce their errors.

> It is not my desire that anyone should against his will be
> coerced into the Catholic communion, but that to all who
> are in error the truth may be openly declared, and being by
> God's help clearly exhibited through my ministry, may so
> commend itself as to make them embrace and follow it.[73]

This was Augustine writing in 396. But after another decade of
brutal terrorist killings, bloody quarrels, and incredible social
chaos, he found himself moving to a different position. As he
acknowledged in a famous letter of 408:

> I was formerly of the opinion that no one should be forced
> to the unity of Christ, that we should agitate with the word,
> fight with disputation, conquer by reason, lest we substitute
> feigned Catholics for avowed heretics. This opinion of mine
> was changed, not by the words of critics, but by the logic of
> events. My own town rose up to convict me. It had been
> entirely devoted to the Donatist party, but now was brought
> to Catholic unity by fear of the imperial laws.[74]

In retrospect, one can both sympathize with his battle-weari-
ness and understand his relief when some semblance of social
order was restored by force of Roman arms. But at the same time
one cannot help but wonder whether he really thought that "fear
of the imperial laws" was a likely foundation for any lasting, worthwhile kind of "Catholic unity."[75] In any event, there are few positions of Augustine that have been more criticized than this
countenancing of the use of state coercion in support of religion.[76]
     That said, however, it is immediately necessary to add that
Augustine all too often has been criticized for positions he never
held and blamed for many excesses that others committed later,
after passing through the door of coercion that he unfortunately
left ajar. Even though he has been referred to as the "father of the
Inquisition" because of this unfortunate change of mind on the
use of force, he can hardly be blamed for the unthinkable horrors
that later came to be associated with some forms of that institution.[77] This is especially the case in regard to the death penalty.
     Twentieth-century clarifications wrought by more careful
study of Augustine's letters are of special interest here because—
strange as it may seem—his stance on the death penalty was

obscured for centuries due to later misrepresentations. His reputation in our day has consequently been undergoing appropriate
rehabilitation in this area in the name of simple justice.[78]

To explain why this is so will require a brief review of a controversy which occurred in European theological circles as of the
seventeenth century. Defenders of the Spanish Inquisition
claimed legitimacy for the operations of that institution on the
basis of the writings of Augustine. Because he had dealt with the
subject so many times from various angles, and had been
involved in so many cases in his own pastoral experience, some
of them very complex, Augustine had written things to which
both protagonists and antagonists could appeal, depending on
what passages were selected and how they were interpreted.

B. Seventeenth-Century Contentions

The interpretations of Augustine over the centuries are too
numerous to catalogue. Our immediate interest is to see the particular interpretation of his position on the death penalty, which
was to become the center of controversy in our own century. For
purposes of brevity, the starting point is Salamancan theologian
Hurtado de Mendoza, who in 1631 published the results of his
examination of Augustine's statements about the ethics of condemning heretics to death.[79] His conclusions were obviously
amenable to the Spanish authorities and were regularly repeated
for the next three centuries. Hurtado had come to the conviction that Augustine thought "the extermination of heretics by
the civil authorities was not only legitimate, but also pious and
laudable."[80] As proof he appealed to four different series of texts,
drawn chiefly from the letters of Augustine.

C. Twentieth-Century Corrections

1. In 1910 German Catholic theologian Otto Schilling published a work on Augustine's social thought challenging Hurtado's
interpretation and conclusions; Schilling suggested that the misunderstandings surrounding Augustine on the death penalty
could be cleared up by more carefully reading all his texts in context, taking into account the circumstances in which each was written. Of all the different categories of statements, Schilling

concluded that it was only (a) when pagans (not heretics) were involved, and (b) when the cause of the church as such was not involved, that Augustine recognized in principle the state's right to execute for the sake of the common good and state security[81]; in principle, he insists, but not in practice, because even here Augustine was personally and pastorally opposed to the state actually exercising this right. As Schilling saw it, Augustine's true Christian humanism was operative here. In maintaining the supremacy of the mandate of forgiveness, capital penalties, even if theoretically justifiable, should never actually be carried out. His episcopal intercession for the pardon of the condemned was not arbitrary but rather a special mission inherent in the very nature of the Christian priestly ministry, as Augustine understood it. In one of his famous sermons, he declared:

> "Man" and "sinner" are two different things. God made man; man made himself sinner. So, destroy what man made but save what God made. Thus, do not go so far as to kill the criminal, for in wishing to punish the sin, you are destroying the man. Do not take away his life; leave him the possibility of repentance. Do not kill so that he can correct himself.[82]

2. In 1913 N. Noguer, unpersuaded by Schilling's delegitimizing of Hurtado's interpretation of Augustine, attempted a refutation.[83] In doing so, however, he found little on which to base his dissent. All he could manage was the simple repetition of Hurtado's claims, praising him for his "notable wisdom" but not pointing to any kind of weaknesses in Schilling's arguments against Hurtado.

3. That same year N. Merlín joined the conversation, pointing out the inadequacies of Noguer's apologetic for Hurtado and calling for greater attention to be given to the "most valuable study" of Schilling and for a fairer and more accurate understanding of the socio-political doctrine of Augustine. It was time to "rehabilitate" the reputation of the great African bishop if it was indeed true that he never approved of executing heretics.[84] Such a realization would undoubtedly have given many an inquisitor pause, since the tradition had regularly assured them that in performing their somber tasks they were simply being

true to the spirit and letter of what the great Augustine had taught as required in the real world.

4. In 1958 an American writing his doctoral dissertation in Rome, Fr. Geoffrey Keating, touched on the question in the final chapter of his treatment of a broader problem in Augustine's moral theology.[85] He, too, like Schilling a half-century earlier, found it necessary to sort the Augustinian material more carefully. The distinction he found necessary was between ecclesial and secular causes as they occurred in Augustine's writings, the former being those in which the church and its spiritual role in the world were specifically implicated. Keating concluded that Augustine denied the legitimacy of the death penalty in any and all ecclesial causes due to lack of proportion between the penalty and the crime. At the same time, it seemed clear to him that Augustine never doubted the legitimacy as such of the proper civil authority imposing the death penalty when done in accord with the law in cases of extreme gravity. The decisive reason for this legitimacy was the common good of the whole society, reinforced by reasons of a psychological order, for example, deterrence. But this did not prevent Augustine from interceding on behalf of the condemned; such intercession could by no means be interpreted as denying the civil authorities' right to punish in general or to execute in particular in the name of the common good, as far as Keating's reading of Augustine was concerned.

5. With these preliminaries, Blázquez then reviewed the claims made, did his own study of the clusters of texts, and drew his own conclusions. They do indeed present a different assessment of Augustine regarding the death penalty than had prevailed at least since Hurtado's day. Blázquez's major conclusions can be briefly summarized thus[86]:

a. Augustine never did a theoretical, academic study of the death penalty as such, the way he did with so many other topics like the Trinity, original sin, and so forth. His treatments of capital punishment were always "occasional," that is, dealing with particular cases pending in the courts at the time he was writing about them.

b. Augustine's episcopal career coincided with the worst possible combination of social circumstances; the Christian emperors were issuing ever more hostile edicts against pagans

and proscribing the very existence of Donatists, some of whom
were turning to terrorist activities as they lost their battle against
their hated Catholic opponents. This context cannot and must
not be ignored.

   c. Every text of Augustine on the death penalty was written
in this atmosphere of grave public conflict; his statements need
to be classified into two quite different categories, if he is to be
understood properly.

   Rather than secular and ecclesial, Keating's categories,
Blázquez distinguishes between what he calls the "deprecativos"
and the "polemicos-interpretativos" texts. The first series (deprecativos) is a group of serene, meditative texts flowing from the
pen of a Christian bishop authoritatively engaged in exercising
his pastoral ministry. Directed for the most part to Christian
magistrates, they unconditionally oppose the execution of any
prisoner whatsoever. There is no ambiguity, no evolution of position, no exceptions in this whole set of texts; the wrongdoer
should be judged and punished proportionately, but always with
humanity. He should never be executed, not in the name of anything or anybody.

   The second series (polemicos-interpretativos) of texts is
much more difficult to interpret. In these Augustine is not dealing with cases of executions about to take place that might still be
prevented. These texts have to do rather with executions that
were carried out in the past and thus are irretrievably over and
done with, such as incidents narrated in the Bible. Augustine's
intention in these passages is very different. The last thing he
would want to do as a Christian peacemaker would be to inflame
emotions in the volatile atmosphere of his day by any kind of
easy justification of bloodshed; on the other hand, neither would
he ever engage in interpreting biblical texts or incidents in other
than a most respectful way.[87] This is what creates the ambiguity in
this second set of texts. He views these past events from a "providentialist perspective," always allowing for the likely good will
and rectitude of the executors but not making a value judgment
on the morality of their actions. In this way he can always draw a
"spiritual lesson" from the incidents, seeing that "from the
inscrutable designs of Providence, God can draw good even
from the greatest evils."

d. Augustine always defended the right of the state to punish wrongdoers in the name of justice and in defense of the common good. Theoretically there can be no doubt about this. He expressed it clearly in the very first book of *The City of God:*

> The same divine law which forbids the killing of a human being allows certain exceptions, as when God authorizes killing by a general law or when he gives an explicit commission to an individual for a limited time. Since the agent of authority is but a sword in the hand, and is not responsible for the killing, it is in no way contrary to the commandment, "Thou shalt not kill," to wage war at God's bidding, or for the representatives of the State's authority to put criminals to death, according to law or the rule of rational justice.

He gives as examples Abraham, Jephthah, and Samson in the Bible, and he ends up insisting that "apart from such men excepted by the command of a just law in general or of God, the very Source of justice, in a special case, anyone who kills a human being, himself or another, is guilty of murder."[88]

This was the basic theory, and, in practice, as we have seen, his thought evolved from a milder to a more severe position on the use of force, especially in dealing with the complicated question of heresies, opening a new chapter in the pedagogy of fear. Man's radical freedom as the work of God must be respected; but wrongdoing as the work of man had to be restrained. Where to draw the line? How to strike the balance? What to make the limits? These were the practical questions that inevitably had to be faced.

"One thing is clear," insists Blázquez. For Augustine himself the limit in coercing heretics "NEVER extended to the death penalty or to those tortures that in practice usually result more in the expression of naked revenge...than justice."[89]

e. So, how is the following basic question to be answered: Would Augustine defend the moral legitimacy of the death penalty as a just punishment when inflicted by legitimate authorities on particular wrongdoers convicted according to all of the precisely observed formalities of the prevailing law? Or would he not?

It is Blázquez's contention that this question cannot be answered with certainty simply because it was never actually addressed by Augustine in any of his surviving writings. Commentators who presume to answer it for him invariably do so by reading their own bias into his texts, trying to enlist his support for their own opinion when he is actually addressing other points or questions. A valid diachronic reading of any text forbids such ignoring of its internal and external context.

f. But this one uncertainty should not be allowed to blur what was learned from the study of the first series of Augustinian texts (deprecativos). His unmitigated opposition in practice to every particular case involving the death penalty reflects his profound conviction that, from the perspective of Christian faith, death is invariably and always an inappropriate punishment that a Christian minister regularly ought to urge magistrates to commute, reminding them of the mercy and love of God as shown in the example of Christ.[90]

The significance of this Augustinian stance for the rest of our story can hardly be exaggerated. In assessing the doleful experience of Augustine in the bloody conflicts that plagued his time, Peter Brown remarks that "he was no Ambrose; he lacked the streak of obstinacy and confidence that he could control events that is so marked in the great ecclesiastical politicians of his age."[91] But on this issue, even if he could not actually save the lives of the condemned, he had the courage of his convictions and left an ethical heritage to which Christian churchmen can return with gratitude after long centuries of mistaken and uncritical legitimation of bloodshed. One may endlessly defend the right of the state to execute wrongdoers when absolutely necessary, but in the last analysis, the Augustinian position was that that right, no matter how valid or well founded, ideally should never actually be exercised. Rather than simply going along with the system, Augustine saw the Christian churchman's role as requiring that he do everything in his power to prevent all avoidable bloodshed every time a case arose. Augustine is thus a model of immense relevance for today.[92]

Many unprecedented problems confronted church leaders in this strange new state-church relationship. The situation had been further complicated by Emperor Constantine's moving of the imperial capital to the East, resulting in the bishop of Rome gradually assuming a multiplicity of new functions. The emperors touted their Christianity, but it seldom had any visible impact on their policies. To take one relevant example, in 391 Emperors Valentinian, Theodosius I, and Arcadius issued an edict (incorporated into the Theodosian Code forty-seven years later) granting the following right to citizens:

> We grant to all men the unrestricted right of resistance if any soldiers or private citizens should enter their fields as nocturnal ravagers or should beset frequented roads by attacks from ambush. This right is granted to everyone in order that whoever so deserves shall be subjected immediately to punishment, shall receive the death which he threatened, and shall incur that danger which he intended for another. For it is better for a man to fight back at the proper time than for him to be avenged after his death. Therefore, We entrust the right of vengeance to you, and what it is too late to punish by trial We repress by edict. Let no man spare a soldier who should be resisted with a weapon as a brigand.[93]

The edict is untouched by Christian teaching. The reigning Christian emperors, in literally laying down the law, make no reference whatsoever to the fact that Jesus taught his followers something quite specific about not taking revenge, just as he gave quite clear instructions on the ideal manner of relating to enemies. Such an edict, issued in the very year of Augustine's ordination to the priesthood, guaranteed to Christian citizens a legal "right of vengeance," providing imperial authorization to ignore the hard sayings of the gospel and to have no qualms about engaging in the time-honored cycle of violence and revenge. It is tempting to see this edict as a signal of the troubles ahead. The vicious cycle of violence and counterviolence was hereby given a comfortable public place in Christian ethics for the future, sanctioned by the full force of imperial law.

Augustine certainly knew of this edict, but he never allowed it to cancel the teaching of Jesus against revenge. Just because it was offered by the highest Roman authorities did not establish any Christian "right to revenge" as ethically valid. Consider, for example, the striking contrast between the spirit of this edict and that of Augustine the pastor in dealing with a particularly vicious case of lethal violence. Donatist clerics had been arrested and convicted of murdering one Catholic priest (Restitutus) and of brutally mutilating another (Innocentius). Augustine wrote two of his more famous letters on this occasion in 412.

Letter #134 was written to the Christian magistrate Apringius. Augustine, knowing that the execution of the culprits was virtually certain, nonetheless urgently pleaded that they not be killed lest

> the sufferings of the servants of God...be sullied with the blood of their enemies...If there were no other punishment...extreme necessity might require that such men be put to death, although, as far as we are concerned, if no lesser punishment were possible...we would prefer to let them go free, rather than avenge the martyrdom of our brothers by shedding their blood. But, now that there is another possible punishment by which the mildness of the Church can be made evident, and the violent excess of savage men be restrained, why do you not commute your sentence to a more prudent and more lenient one?[94]

Letter #133 is the third of five surviving letters written to Marcellinus, the brother of Apringius, on the same occasion. Hearing that the Donatist attackers had gouged out an eye and cut off a finger of Innocentius, Augustine acknowledged that "this news has plunged me into the deepest anxiety, lest perchance your Excellency should judge them worthy, according to the laws, of punishment not less severe than suffering in their own persons the same injuries as they have inflicted on others." Here was a classical instance where the literal application of the *lex talionis* was simple and extremely tempting: an eye for an eye, a finger for a finger, then a life for a life. But Augustine had a high opinion of Marcellinus, "Wherefore I write this letter to implore you by your faith in Christ, and by the mercy of Christ the Lord himself, by no means to do this or permit it to be done." In one of the finest pages of his truly pastoral theology, he tried to motivate Marcellinus to tame the urge to revenge:

Fulfill, Christian judge, the duty of an affectionate father; let your indignation against their crimes be tempered by considerations of humanity; do not be provoked by the atrocity of their sinful deeds to gratify the passion of revenge; but rather be moved by the wounds which these deeds have inflicted on their own souls to exercise a desire to heal them....If you do not hearken to me asking this favor as a friend, hearken to me offering this counsel as a bishop....Let not the sufferings of Catholic servants of God be sullied by the retaliation of injuries on those who did them wrong, but rather, tempering the rigor of justice, let it be your care as sons of the Church to commend both your own faith and your Mother's clemency.[95]

This is the often forgotten Augustine, the compassionate pastor who knew the gospel and desperately tried to communicate its ethical imperative to others by both his words and deeds, despite the fact that Roman law and Roman emperors fostered and favored the taking of revenge. But circumstances converged to obscure this particular Augustinian heritage so that for centuries, despite his towering prestige and the influence of so many of his ideas, this vital dimension of his teaching fell into oblivion.[96]

V. THE THEODOSIAN CODE (438) AND ITS LEGACY
(A.D. 438–866)

The Theodosian Code is a work of central importance to Western jurisprudence. Done in the decade after the death of Augustine, it has within it no fewer than 120 laws that assign death as the proper penalty; they are the accumulation of all the earlier laws of the pagan empire plus the even stricter ones enacted over the previous century for the express purpose of "Christianizing" the empire.[97] The full history of the use of the death penalty among Christians in Europe from the fifth to the eleventh century is yet to be written, but it seems safe to say that some of the "barbarian" law codes were originally more humane before coming into contact with "Christianized" Roman law, at least in some regards. In the first version of the Salic Law, for instance, as issued by Clovis in the early sixth century, there was no death penalty for homicide; the punishment was financial compensation (*wergeld*).[98] Precise monetary values were assigned for long lists of crimes, and their relative gravity was indicated by setting the price higher or lower. In later revisions of the law, under the influence of Roman law, the use of the death penalty grew, but initially only for three crimes.[99] Savey-Casard noted some of the unpredictable variations in barbarian legislation:

> The death penalty is more frequent in the Edict of Theodoric....It is much less so in the Salic Law....It is called for rather rarely in Visigothic law...being replaced in several instances by corporal punishment, or exile, or financial compensation....Bavarian law, dating from the end of the seventh century, deserves mention as making the maximum use of financial compensation and doing away with the death penalty the most often. It says, regarding the right of asylum: "No crime is so grave that life cannot be accorded to the culprit for the fear of God and the respect of the saints. For the Lord has said: 'The one who forgives will be forgiven' (Title I,7)."[100]

Such sentiments will be sought in vain in the Theodosian Code.

A note of caution is necessary, however, since the law codes tell only part of the story. Other sources detail executions, torture, and a high level of violence at least in parts of this period. In practice, the envisioned financial compensations were undoubtedly often beyond the ability of poor folks to pay, so these presumably had to pay with their lives. As in most cases in cultures where capital punishment has been used, it was predominantly imposed on the poor. And yet, as in other ages, there were instances when no amount of money could offset the passionate popular urge for revenge. In such cases, even if offered, the *wergeld* could be refused and the culprit summarily executed to satisfy the tribal bloodlust.

Certain capitularies also occasionally reflect harsher practices than the law codes might suggest. Savey-Casard cites one of Childebert from 511, stipulating death as the penalty for theft with violence, and another from 596, forbidding financial compensation because "the one who knows how to kill must know how to die."[101] A third capitulary, from Paderborn in 785, aimed at the Saxons, prescribed death as the penalty for three specific offenses: 1) eating meat during the Lenten season; 2) burning a cadaver in pagan style instead of burying it in a Christian cemetery; and 3) going into hiding rather than presenting oneself for baptism.[102] Seeing such surprisingly harsh penalties on the books again raises questions about what actually was practiced in the societies concerned. As in the case of the biblical codes, the gravity of the penalties is certainly a forceful way of communicating to a populace the seriousness with which certain offenses are to be viewed. Edicts assigning death as the fate of anyone who should dare to teach a "barbarian" how to build a ship or how to forge counterfeit money may be examples of this kind of pedagogical function, but their enforcement undoubtedly varied according to how great and imminent a danger they were perceived to represent at the particular time of arrest.[103]

A. Pope St. Gregory I (590–604)

A rumor had circulated after the death of a bishop Malchus in prison in Rome that he had been killed for money. Gregory wrote to Sabinianus to set the record straight. The story is too complex to go into here, but in telling it, Gregory made a comment that speaks volumes and has been used as a summary of his pastoral stance regarding bloodshed: "Since I fear God, I shrink from having anything whatsoever to do with the death of anyone."[104] This great papal ideal, however, was to be forgotten all too often in later centuries.

B. Pope Nicholas I (858–867)

Another gem in the papal archives is an extraordinary letter written to the newly converted Bulgars in 866 that actually recommends doing away with the death penalty. Nicholas I challenges the new Christians to adopt the high New Testament ideal:

> You must act like the apostle Paul, who, having been a persecutor, was converted....You must give up your former habits and not merely avoid every occasion of taking life, but also, without hesitation and in every possible circumstance, save

the life of body and of soul of each individual. You should save from death not only the innocent but also criminals, because Christ has saved you from the death of the soul.[105]

For a moment the Christian pastoral example of Augustine over three centuries earlier was the explicit advice being advanced by the bishop of Rome. The call to break the cycle of violence and not to embrace the legacy of avenging bloodshed by bloodshed was issued as the Christian ideal, no matter what might be found in Roman law. The pope's counsel was a breath of fresh air, the call to a gospel ideal. It would be a very long time, however, before such advice could be heard again, largely because of a bewildering outbreak of heresy in the eleventh century in the west, which began to complicate matters.

VI. A POSTSCRIPT ON THE
GREEK ORTHODOX EXPERIENCE

A. *Emperor Justinian I and His Code*

In closing out this overview of developments in the use of the death penalty in early Christianity, it is obvious that it is selective and restricted largely to the experience of the Western church after Constantine moved the imperial capital from Rome to the East (A.D. 330). A complete history would have to follow the developments of both the Western Latin and the Eastern Greek traditions as they more and more went their separate ways. The present work is intentionally limited to the former, but a word about the latter is not out of place, if only to point out that neither church was able to find a viable solution to the intractable problem of dealing with heretics.

The Greek church had to face the issue of heresy on a broader scale at an earlier time than the Latin church did. The Council of Chalcedon (451) resulted in a bitter feud between the Monophysites and the "Chalcedonians." Emperor Justinian I (527-565) undertook a lengthy campaign attempting to achieve unity and, in the process, issued a series of edicts that included liberal use of the death penalty. After early efforts of persuasion in the 530s, he "turned to persecution, and...Monophysites were imprisoned, tortured, and executed."[106] Justinian undoubtedly accomplished much for the advancement of Byzantine Christianity,[107] but there is also no doubt that he carried the harshness of the Theodosian Code yet further, especially in the notorious "Libri Terribiles" (Books 47 and 48) of his *Digest* and Book IX of his *Code*.[108] The 51 Titles of the latter enshrine all the sanguinary legislation of the earlier centuries of Roman law, while giving them greater legitimation in the name of Christianity than they ever had before.[109]

The next two centuries of Eastern Orthodox Christian history saw the problem worsen in some quarters.

> Suddenly, with the coming of the eighth century, a heresy with a new name appears (the Paulicians) and concentrates upon itself the attention of right-thinking Christians.... Emperor Leo V instituted the bloodthirsty methods that drove the Paulicians to seek Moslem protection....[A century later] officers of the Empress...with a ferocious thoroughness, fell upon the heretic [Paulician] churches, till, according to the chroniclers, 100,000 victims perished.[110]

These Eastern Christian disasters, stemming from much the same problem—how to deal with theological differences perceived as heresies—occurred earlier than the series of comparable bloodbaths that plagued the medieval Christian West, and it is intriguing to note the role that the Crusades—bringing the West to the East—played in immersing Christians yet more deeply in interminable bloodshed.[111]

B. Afterword

With all these complications, it is safe to conclude that the experience of the early Christian church left it with a terribly ambiguous legacy regarding capital punishment, both in the East and in the West. On the one hand, it embraced as fundamental to Christian ethics the fifth "word" of the Decalogue: "Thou shalt not kill." This straightforward prohibition in its simplicity of expression set the standard for ideal conduct. Human life was to be seen as sacred, the gift of God. Its dignity and value could be conferred and withdrawn only by the authority of its

Creator. The function of Christian churchmen to practice, proclaim, and protect this ideal was beyond dispute.

On the other hand, the reality of human sin complicated the maintenance of this ideal from the very start. Side by side with the ideal of not killing stood specific exceptions in the scriptures, sometimes ordering the killing of certain malefactors in the community. No one in early Christianity struggled with this dilemma more consistently and under more difficult circumstances than St. Augustine. While his late concession to the use of state coercion against dissenters tarnished his name, his persistent example as a Christian churchman opposing all recourse to the death penalty in practice, advocating clemency in every case, was often forgotten. It was principally the problem of what to do about heretics that clouded the picture. A simple reading of the biblical law codes, reinforced by the harshness of "Christian" Roman law and unrelieved by the gospel, created an explosive situation, and even the solid pastoral efforts of an Augustine could not prevent the bloodshed. Once Christianity had become the state religion, the imperial values articulated in Roman law tended to overwhelm gospel values. "Citizenship and membership in the state religion were inseparable. The emperor deemed it his duty as the repository of religious authority to regulate the church, and this seemed entirely natural to contemporaries."[112] As a result, the legacy of Constantinian-Theodosian Christianity to subsequent ages was highly ambiguous on the ethics of killing, whether in the case of war or capital punishment. Less and less attention was paid to that most troublesome of the teachings of Christ: the prohibition of the taking of revenge.

CHAPTER 2

―◈―

Movement in the Medieval Church

I. Aspects of Departure from Earlier Christian Ideals
    A. The Rise and Repression of Heresies
    B. The Romanticization of Fighting
    C. The Invention of the Crusade
        1. Pope Urban II (1095)
        2. St. Bernard of Clairvaux (1140s)
    D. The Legitimization of Revenge

II. An Aside on the Benefit-of-Clergy Exemption

III. Conflicting Evaluations of Christian Violence
    A. Otto of Vercelli (c.940)
    B. Peter Damian (d.1072)
    C. Guibert of Nogent (1108)

IV. Early Scholastic Theologians and Homicide
    A. Peter Abelard's *Sic et Non* (c.1123)
    B. Hugh of St. Victor (c.1140)
    C. Peter Lombard's *Sentences* (c.1155)
    D. Peter of Poitiers' *Sentences* (c.1170–1180)
    E. Peter the Chanter (c.1177–1197)

V. Early Canonists and the Authority to Kill
    A. Anselm of Lucca (c.1085)
    B. Bonizo of Sutri (c.1086)
    C. Ivo of Chartres (c.1093)
    D. Gratian's *Decretum* (c.1140)
    E. Huguccio's *Summa* (c.1188)
    F. Johannes Teutonicus' *Glossa* (c.1215)

The imposition of death as a penalty for a broad array of human misdeeds was a fact of life in the Roman Empire both long before and long after Emperor Constantine I made Christianity the preferred state religion. It seems, in fact, that the practice of executing malefactors not only continued but became even more deeply entrenched under Christian auspices, due to the biblical warrant being added to the Roman law authorization. The justification for capital punishment as it was worked out in Christian thought followed much the same path as its justification of war. The two were initially seen as similarly problematic because of their frontal collision with another biblical element, the mandate "Thou shalt not kill." The Creator-God was the only Lord over life. Even more, the sayings and deeds of Jesus as narrated in the New Testament surely ran counter to any human conduct that would deliberately engage in the shedding of human blood, especially the distinctive teachings on nonretaliation, forgiveness, love of neighbor, and his hard saying about loving even those designated as enemies.

The names of Ambrose and Augustine are forever intertwined with the early struggle of conscience over how engagement in lethal violence might sometimes be deemed compatible with these Christian values. While they found a way to justify some restricted, controlled, limited, carefully conditioned use of force, even lethal force, they were never comfortable with that compromise. Augustine's reasoning on Christian involvement in war has been accurately described as "agonized participation," allowed only under strictly limited conditions. Killing fellow human beings was so patently contrary to the Great Commandment that, as far as Augustine was concerned,

> a private Christian could not (even) kill an attacker in self-defense, for that would entail hatred and loss of love....Only rulers and officials acting in the line of duty were able to kill without giving vent to hatred and other sinful passions.[1]

This severely restricted Augustinian sanctioning of the exceptional use of violence by Christians loomed large in the tradition as it was passed on from the fifth century. Even in the few cases where bloodshed was justifiable, churchmen themselves were required to abstain from it. They were to keep their own hands clean and do what they could to be peacemakers, resolving conflicts by pointing to the example of Christ rather than merely condoning the use of violence. The stark ambivalence of this Augustinian position left room for abuses, undoubtedly, but the general perspective prohibiting most Christians from involvement in most bloodshed most of the time prevailed into the early Middle Ages. Developments then took place, however, that were to have a radical impact on the way in which some forms of killing, including the death penalty, came to be evaluated. Modern medievalists have thrown light on these complex developments; what follows is simply an attempt to gather some of their pertinent insights.

I. ASPECTS OF DEPARTURE FROM EARLIER CHRISTIAN IDEALS

With the final breakup of the Roman Empire, the emergence of the Papal State, and the ascendency of the Franks under Pepin and Charlemagne, Western Christendom underwent dramatic changes.[2] "The church had to absorb and assimilate vast numbers of new Celtic, Germanic, and Slavic Christians, who brought with them doctrinal and liturgical peculiarities and magical and cultic practices from their pagan past."[3] Until the turn of the millennium, the unsettled situation was marked by broad diversity. The death penalty was being used as an inherited "Christian" institution, enshrined in the Bible and in Roman law, but it did not receive much attention because of the greater problems that had to be confronted. The unusual violence that marred the papacy itself in the ninth and tenth centuries is evidence enough that it was not a time when the pursuit and development of more peaceful policies were very likely.[4]

> Even if we eliminate the gross scandals which are on record,
> it must be admitted that the personal character of almost all

of the Popes of those days was very far removed indeed from the apostolic ideal.[5]

Some departure from earlier ideals had already occurred, but a particularly troublesome challenge began to emerge at the turn of the millennium, the response to which was to constitute the greatest single complication in the entire history of Christian involvement with capital punishment. The intractable problem of what to do about heretics gradually led churchmen into the quicksand of lethal repression. The basic period was the eleventh through the twelfth into the thirteenth century, when the pattern of action and a concomitant rationale were put firmly in place and retained for four or five centuries, before the tradition itself was able to undertake the retrieval of the ideal. Four intertwined developments need to be looked at for their cumulative consequences.

A. *The Rise and Repression of Heresies*

A curious rash of early eleventh-century outbreaks of heresy in southern France and northern Italy signaled that special troubles were brewing, ones that would have far-reaching consequences. "The Church was singularly ill-equipped to deal with heresy when it first became a serious problem in the west. Half a millennium had passed since the collapse of the Roman Empire and during that time western society had become barbarized."[6] A series of incidents on record set the tone.

Around A.D. 1000, Leuthard, a peasant of Vertu in Champagne (according to chronicler Rudolphus Glaber) began claiming that his teaching was inspired by God and given to him while he was at work in the fields. He attracted a sizable following and taught them, among other things, that it was foolish to give tithes. When Gebuin, in whose diocese he lived, quizzed him about his beliefs, the wise bishop easily got the better of him and declared that "the lunatic (Leuthard) had become a heretic." His followers were called back from insanity and reinstated, but the humiliated Leuthard "threw himself to his death in a well."[7] The story depicts an early outbreak of popular heresy, but differs from most which follow in that the bishop acted quickly and effectively and the heretic destroyed himself before anyone else was tempted to do so.

A.D. 1022 in Orléans—The first known case of a heresy actually being treated as a capital offense in the medieval West was that of an unusual French group claiming direct enlightenment by the Holy Spirit. One of their number defied his ecclesiastical interrogators by testifying:

> "You...may believe the fictions of carnal men scribbled on animal skins....To us, however, who have the law written upon the heart by the Holy Spirit,...you spin out superfluities and things inconsistent with the divinity in vain."[8]

This case caused a major scandal, because the people involved this time were not unlettered peasants but respected members of the clergy, including the former confessor to the queen and confidant of King Robert the Pious, who himself presided over the trial, a dozen accounts of which survive. Two archbishops and three bishops rendered the verdict.

The execution of the thirteen defendants was the first instance of the burning of heretics in the medieval West, and a recent study concluded that

> the charges made against the Orléans heretics were to a large extent literary clichés....There is no way of being certain how many of these accusations had a basis in reality, but they do show that in the period 1000–1150 A.D. heresy and witchcraft were increasingly identified with each other and both of them associated with diabolism.[9]

Tragic as this development was for Western Christian history, it was only the smallest of beginnings; the worst consequences would not come to climax until the great witch-craze four to five centuries later. But the tragic trail of blood and tears tied to the repression of heretics in medieval Western Christendom was hereby entered upon.

A.D. 1025 in Arras—A certain Gundolfo drew crowds to his sermons rejecting the sacraments of baptism and the Eucharist when performed by morally unworthy clergy. This was "the first instance of medieval Donatism...and foreshadowed the widespread growth of antisacerdotal heresy in the next century."[10] This incident had a happy outcome when Gundolfo was persuaded to abjure his position, but the discontent with aspects of the church and its clerical leaders reflected here was clearly on the upswing. Criticism of clerical shortcomings gave rise to alternate beliefs that bypassed the clergy. Frustration over the maddening problem of what to do about this kind of dissent from "official" beliefs and practices was to plague church leaders for centuries to come and played an obvious role in ever-deeper church entanglement in the use of the death penalty.

A.D. 1028 in Milan—Bishop Aribert was informed of the presence of a group of heretics in the castle of Monforte. They denied the authority of the Roman pontiff in favor of that of their leader, Gerard, who, among many other things, insisted that they hold all goods in common. Once arrested, they were subjected to long and heavy preaching by the local clergy in a desperate effort to get them to conform. But when they would not convert, the crowd "took matters into their own hands and, despite the bishop's protests, burnt those heretics who refused to recant."[11] The glimpses of these groups that emerge from the records suggest that other issues were also at play, including class status, as competing ideologies and mores arose. With the increase of urban populations, older tradition and privilege carried less weight. The new world of town merchants and artisans was very different from the ecclesiastical world, and the collision of the two was virtually inevitable. But whatever the combination of causes, there was no easy remedy on hand, and the lynch-mob's solution to the new and unfamiliar has appealed to many ages and societies besides this one.

A.D. 1043–48 in Châlons-sur-Marne—According to a remarkable account, the bishop of Châlons, upon learning that groups of "Manichaeans" had appeared in his diocese, consulted with Bishop Wazo of Liège for advice on how to deal with the situation. Among their errors the heretics "abhorred marriage and not only avoided the eating of meat but also considered it wicked to kill any animal at all, assuming as justification for their error the command of God against killing in the Old Law." The bishop wanted Wazo's advice on "whether or not the sword of earthly authority should be directed against them." In his extraordinary response Wazo acknowledged that the heretics do indeed "go out of their way to entangle themselves with numerous incongruities, misinterpreting the commandment...'Thou shalt not kill'...wherein only homicide was forbidden." But he goes on to apply with eloquence the parable of the wheat and the weeds in the same vein as St. John Chrysostom had done over six centuries earlier. "What does the Lord reveal by these words but His patience, which He wishes His preachers to display to their erring fellow men, particularly since it may be possible for those who today are weeds, tomorrow to be converted and become wheat." Nor does he stop with this basic advice. He commends his fellow bishop for "the fervor of spiritual zeal burning in your breast for souls deceived by devilish fraud." But this must not be allowed to lead one to act impatiently.

> Lest you do this hastily, lest it be done before its time, the holy text is rather to be obeyed so that, although we think we are practicing righteousness by punishing transgressors, whose impiety is veiled under semblance of strict life, we do no disservice to Him who desires not the death of sinners nor rejoices in the damnation of the dying, but rather knows how to bring sinners back to repentance through His patience and long-suffering....Let us not seek to remove from this life by the sword of secular authority those whom God himself, Creator and Redeemer, wishes to spare....It is possible for an omnipotent God to make those whom we now consider to be enemies of the way of the Lord superior even to us in that heavenly home.

To illustrate his point, Wazo appealed to the New Testament case of Saul, who assisted at the stoning of Stephen, but whom Stephen now "rejoices to recognize as a superior apostle." But Wazo was not simply counseling inaction; his real concern was that the wrong thing not be done.

> We who are called bishops do not receive at ordination the sword which belongs to the secular power, and for that reason we are enjoined by God our Father not to do unto death but rather to quicken unto life. There is, however, another point about the aforesaid schismatics which should be carefully heeded, one of which you are not at all unmindful. They and those associating with them should be deprived of Catholic communion.[12]

This was Wazo's final word on dealing with obstinate heretics: excommunication, yes; execution, no. Like Chrysostom and Augustine before him, he was a conscientious Christian bishop inspired to hold the line against capital punishment for heretics in spite of the prescriptions of Roman law and the great aggravation the dissenters were causing. He had no doubt about what the Christian ministry required of a "good shepherd" in such a situation, and he raised his voice to repudiate the death penalty as an inappropriate substitute for a solution.

A.D. 1051 in Goslar—According to the same record, only three years after the death of Bishop Wazo his wise counsel was totally ignored and the troubling trend of the future was demonstrated:

> A comparable sect was seized at Goslar. After much discussion...and a proper excommunication for obstinacy in error, they were sentenced to be hanged. When we carefully investigated the course of this examination, we could learn no other reason for their condemnation than that they refused to obey one of the bishops when he ordered them to kill a chicken....I can truly say, and I will not keep silent, that if it had happened in his time, our Wazo would not at all have agreed with this verdict, after the example of Blessed Martin, who, in order to intercede for Priscillianists condemned by edict of the depraved Emperor Maximin, on advice of the priests who basely flattered him, preferred to incur a slur on his most excellent virtue than to be unsolicitous even for heretics who were soon to die. We say these things not because we seek to defend the error of heretics, but to show that we do not approve of that which is nowhere sanctioned in the Sacred Laws.

The whole issue of heresy thus continued to provoke the entanglement of churchmen ever more deeply in the use of the death penalty. The wise pastoral protests of John Chrysostom, Martin of Tours, Ambrose of Milan, Siricius of Rome, and Augustine of Hippo were still echoing in the sound advice of Bishop Wazo, all of them rejecting the use of the death penalty against heretics, considering it a policy in conflict with the teaching of Jesus. But these voices were being drowned out by those

calling for the simplest solution to the vexing problem—the elimination of the dissenters by capital execution. Things presumably
could have gone otherwise, if an Augustine or a Wazo had
emerged in a major leadership position at the time. Had the long
tradition of opposing the execution of heretics prevailed, a very
different history of the use of the death penalty in the Christian
West might well have resulted, because those entrusted with the
preaching of a proper ethic would not have found themselves so
compromised.

Identifiable patterns of discontent were becoming more
and more prevalent: unhappiness with aspects of clerical
lifestyle; an urgent new "search for the apostolic life,"[13] with its
invitation to higher morals and stricter discipline, including
detachment from material goods; refusal to kill or eat animals,
and so on.[14] Even the occasional "academic" heretic (like Beren-
gar of Tours, who was twice tried and condemned in the 1050s
for heretical teaching about the Eucharist) can be seen as falling
within this pattern. If one were basically unhappy with a non-
apostolic clergy, a belief or teaching that diminished or omitted
the central role of the Eucharist had its obvious attractions.[15]

Some frustrated ecclesiastics rejected Bishop Wazo's idealistic call for patience and preferred to take direct action against
nonconformists, convicting them of obstinate heresy, excommu-
nicating them, and executing them directly, thus doing away with
the "diseased members" of the church body but also thereby
casting aside the ancient tradition of Christian clerics abstaining
from the shedding of human blood. The persistence of this tradition testifies to the deep ambivalence toward bloodshed that
marked Christian history and was still clearly reflected in canon
984 of the 1917 Code of Canon Law.[16] It is remarkable that this
tradition was always kept on the books, even though on occasion
it was effectively bypassed in times of elevated violence.[17]

But the indirect strategy was more commonly adopted:
church courts would judge the culpability of those accused of
heresy, then the lay power ("secular arm") was called upon to
carry out the sentences on the guilty. If the lay power failed to
take over and dispose of the heretics, their subjects could be
released from the bonds of obedience and all their other feudal
obligations.[18] Given the advantage of hindsight, it is easy enough

to see the drift away from Christian ideals which this whole development involved, resulting in the enshrinement of the death penalty at the very heart of church policy for dealing with heretics. This anomaly facilitated a second, closely-related area of departure from the earlier Christian ideal.

B. The Romanticization of Fighting

This second problem area is more difficult to isolate precisely because it became so all-pervasive. It may thus help to identify some of its overlapping dimensions or manifestations. Its roots certainly go back at least to the early Frankish period. If part of the problem of the Constantinian-Theodosian era (fourth to fifth centuries) was the fact that the newly Christian Roman emperors ignored Christian values in their legislation and politics, that problem was only magnified and aggravated in the Merovingian-Carolingian-Ottonian periods (seventh to tenth centuries), especially because of the almost uninterrupted waging of war. For instance, "the pattern of annual campaigns... established in the first decade of Charlemagne's reign continued throughout the whole of his long life—more than 50 important campaigns in 47 years, some 30 led by the king himself"; his tactics became "ever more severe, from forced baptism to the execution of thousands of prisoners and the deportation of thousands more."[19] Despite the considerable achievements of a handful of scholar-monks in the Carolingian renaissance, it was a time of appalling ignorance and immorality among the clergy, who were thus unable to communicate much of the gospel to the masses. This is part of the reason for the appeal of the antisacerdotalist heresies. Without a body of minimally competent preachers and/or catechists, the church was in no position to do much more than tolerate the belligerence and bloodlust fostered by the violence of the warriors of these chaotic times.

Nor was that violence only a problem on the periphery. The papacy itself, caught in the middle of extremely "violent clashes between two (Roman) families,"[20] took on a corresponding image. Pope John VIII (872–882) personally took charge of military operations, "building a defensive wall around St. Paul's basilica, and commanding a small papal fleet which he founded" for fighting against both Christian and Muslim enemies.[21] This first occurrence of a strange new model—a warrior-pope—is a striking example of departure from the earlier ideal; once demonstrated, it was a model that would surprisingly recur numerous times over the next six centuries. Whatever justification one may attempt, the central point is beyond reasonable dispute: the message conveyed by such a model of the papacy was counterproductive, to say the least. Christian leadership, inextricably tied up with military violence as its most visible interest, occupation, and mode of operation, was a gross liability in dire need of reform. Its bearing on the question of capital punishment is evident. Once the use of violence is so domesticated at the center, there is no need to justify it elsewhere. The destruction of human life becomes a relatively easy routine, an integral part of any totally militarized lifestyle.[22]

This leadership problem remained even when clerical reform groups developed and made surprising advances against other problems. For instance, a new chapter in the history of the papacy opened, after some of its most dismal days, with the election of Pope Leo IX (1049–1054), at the very time that these new heresies were arising.

> Leo accomplished the first significant breakthroughs on behalf of the early reform in Rome. By the time of his pontificate, renewal of religious life had become a matter of the deepest concern for many monks and for members of the clergy and the laity. With the ascent of Leo IX, the pope became the leader of the eleventh-century reform movement.[23]

But the bad news was that this reform spirit, despite its many positive features, entailed a cluster of other changes, some representing further engagement in violent conduct as the norm. Leo IX not only raised his own Roman militia to defend church lands from the threat of Norman invasion, but in 1053 he actually chose to lead these troops into battle himself. This "battlefield-warrior-pope" is a model of Christian ministry that St. Augustine would have found bewildering, but, once developed, it was destined to find its place periodically for the next five centuries before being definitively renounced.

The reform party led by Hildebrand, first as papal advisor, then as Pope Gregory VII (1073–1085), fostered the romanticizing of violence in yet another way: the transformation of traditional figurative speech into a very literal usage.[24] This Hildebrandine shift appropriated the military language that had long been part of Christian vocabulary (St. Paul, for example, depicted Christian life as a spiritual combat, a war against sin and the forces of evil, in which one had to arm oneself and fight like a good soldier to overcome temptation, conquer evil, destroy vice, and so on).[25] But now it was transferred and applied in a blatantly literal sense, elevating military life to a positive new status. The dream of a totally Christian world, united under the pope, could not be realized without doing real battle against real political enemies, as the warrior-popes had already illustrated in their actions.

> Gregory took the critical step of proclaiming that earthly warfare could, after all, be an authentic part of the *Militia Christi*. During his struggle with Henry IV of Germany, he called, in an altogether novel way, upon the knights of all lands to dedicate their swords to the service of Christ and of Saint Peter, and to realize their Christian vocation by doing so.[26]

Gregory's reign thus opened the way to promoting a new kind of soldier-saint for general emulation. Earlier Christian soldier-saints, like St. Maurice, St. Sebastian, St. George, and St. Martin, were revered because they led saintly lives *despite* being soldiers. But Gregory began honoring contemporaries as saintly precisely *because* they were soldiers, men who used their military skills to do battle literally. He assured them that by fighting the church's wars, they were performing positive service to God in a most necessary and praiseworthy way.

The mystique of the medieval Christian knight, dedicated to doing the work of God with his military weaponry, was significantly advanced by this change.[27] Earlier church misgivings about authorizing warriors had been grappled with as recently as at the Council of Narbonne in 1054. It had given knights of the time a surprisingly graphic warning: "Let no Christian kill another Christian, for there is no doubt that he who kills a Christian spills the blood of Christ."[28] But such efforts to put limits on military conduct were being offset by the needs of the church for warriors. Knowing how to fight and kill when necessary, whenever and wherever called upon, was now needed to complete God's work. Earlier misgivings were left behind as "the Cluniac Pope Gregory VII invited the laymen of Europe to form a militia which he called the Knights of St. Peter, bound to the Pope as its head and dedicated to the defense of the Church."[29] Thus violent fighting was thoroughly domesticated, naturally encouraging other military characteristics as well, for example, the expectation of blind obedience from all in its ranks.[30] The whole complex of militaristic attitudes provided an atmosphere in which the death penalty was viewed as just one more violent measure authorized by God for the success of the church. The sword lifted to execute heretics and other criminals was totally parallel to the sword lifted against enemies in the midst of territorial warfare.[31] But there were other important factors at play as well.[32]

C. The Invention of the Crusade

The romanticizing of military violence was fairly complete by the end of Gregory's reign, except for one final step that was to come ten years after his death. The drift away from earlier Christian ambivalence and restraint came to a significant turning point with the launching of the First Crusade.[33]

1. POPE URBAN II

Pope Urban II, Gregory VII's able protegé, took this definitive step at the Synod of Clermont in November 1095, calling for a holy war, something quite new that dramatically changed the face of Western Christianity in a variety of ways, some of which also had an important bearing on the future of capital punishment.

Urban could not have realized it at the time, but he sparked a conflagration that quickly escaped his control. Speaking on that historic occasion as a Frenchman to Frenchmen, his eloquence was no doubt irresistible....But he had not reckoned on the speed with which his popularity and the enthusiasm generated at the synod would spread....It is hard to believe that his persuasive power alone inspired at least 100,000 men to quit their homes and suddenly set out for the unknown east....The economic and social reasons for seeking an outlet from con-temporary miseries—overpopulation, poverty, lack of cul-tivable land, subjection to oppressive lords and the general drabness of life—were probably as potent as religious ideal-ism, but it was the Pope's visionary exhortation that first pointed the way of escape and the opportunity of adven-ture.[34]

His address revealed how far official attitudes toward war and the use of violence had really drifted by this time.

Hitherto you have waged unjustifiable warfare....Now we set before you wars which have in themselves the glorious reward of martyrdom, and the halo of present and everlast-ing fame.[35]

But the new theology that built into crusading the promise of pardon for all sins and the prospect of a martyr's crown for those who fell in battle appealed strongly to the common Christian lay-man of the time.

Only thirty years before Urban's speech at Clermont, Nor-man troops had fought at Hastings (1066) under a papal banner in what was judged to be a just war. Even though they had won the battle, traditional Christian ambivalence toward bloodshed was still strong enough that the soldiers were summoned before the bishops to receive the customary penalties for whatever vio-lence they had inflicted during battle: "for killing a man, a year's penance; for wounding one, forty days, and so forth."[36] The long-standing negative assessment of any engagement in bloodshed, even "justifiable" bloodshed, still made this ritual meaningful and therapeutic and necessary. But no such reservations or sense of guilt would be called for or even considered appropriate on the part of Christian troops soon to be fighting in the newly created holy war. The agonized deliberation over whether one's cause was just and whether all the other necessary conditions were adequately fulfilled, which was the very heart of Augustine's doctrine, was not needed here. The cause was guaranteed to be just, the explicit will of God, and thus fighting in this war was actually sanctifying, an activity that in itself conferred spiritual merit that enabled one to escape hellfire, that admitted one to the heavenly legions. The ideas were all there in Gregory VII, but it was Urban II who put them together in a concrete call, specifying when, where, and how these eternal blessings were to be achieved.[37]

To appreciate more of the impact of this innovation, it is helpful to look ahead for a moment to the Second Crusade in order to get a sense of how great a change the invention of the Christian holy war really represented.

2. St. Bernard of Clairvaux

St. Bernard of Clairvaux (1090–1153), was a towering church figure in his day who made many valuable and lasting contributions. On the dilemma of Christian violence, however, he was a product of his time, and his time was that of preparing for the Second Crusade, which he enthusiastically preached. Carrying forward the Hildebrandine use of "metaphors of war," he was called upon to write the rules for the fledgling Knights of the Temple, and in his *De Laude Novae Militiae* he weaves together the military and monastic lifestyles "despite the existence of a profound anomaly in their position. They were a contradiction in terms, a confusion of spiritual and secular estates."[38] Bernard himself seems to have been caught in the middle. His general stance was that of the long tradition against churchmen being directly involved in bloodshed. He minced no words in affirming that "it is a disgrace to the kingdom that a cleric should command soldiers, just as it is a disgrace to his orders that a cleric should take money from the King in payment for fighting for him."[39] But no such restrictions held when it came to the Knights Templar. They were "a new kind of soldier," pledged to combine spiritual and temporal warfare, whose weapons only resulted in, not homicide, but "malicide."

Frederick Russell remarks that "the glorification of Christian militarism" was never "more intoxicatingly expressed" than by St. Bernard. It was the novelty of the very idea of the Crusade—a near contradiction in terms—that "enabled Bernard to achieve a mystical amalgam in which pacifism and religious bellicosity, clergy and laity, lost their separate forces and identities."[40] He saw the hand of Providence clearly manifested in the fact that the most violent elements of European society were conveniently removed and sent off to be installed as God's faithful monk-warriors, defending the Holy Land. Darkness had somehow been turned into light, even though there was confusion as to how this transformation had been accomplished (and even more, how the failure of the Second Crusade and especially how the successful recapture of Jerusalem by the "infidels" in 1187 could be made to fit into this divinely providential picture).

The only thing more astonishing than the development of this amalgam of incompatible ideals was the uncritical acceptance that it enjoyed for so long in Christian history. It is not surprising that it is at the root of additional deviations from earlier ideals, the most striking of which is undoubtedly the legitimization of revenge.

D. The Legitimization of Revenge

The invention of the Crusade with all its promises of spiritual benefits suddenly made unprecedented armed forces available to the church. The crusading ideology touched laymen where they lived. Their world was one of violence and brutality, in which death was no stranger and often came at the hands of others. The feudal system of contractual relationships, in which men were bound to one another by ties of protection, tenancy, and service, fostered an atmosphere in which *vendetta* was a natural outgrowth of the group feeling. The blood-feud held a prominent place in this system. Kinsmen were expected to defend the members of their group and to take revenge on manslayers.[41]

This pre-Christian cultural residue resisted evangelization (just as it does today in mafia-like clans), even in areas where proper Christian preaching had long taken place. The notion of the Crusade drew upon this subculture by calling for volunteers to join with a broader, like-minded group devoted to a higher

cause under divine auspices. Even before Urban II's inspired volunteers could form into proper armies, many of them went on a
rampage in 1096, slaughtering Jews all along the Rhine.[42] It was
soon possible to see the Crusade as a kind of church-sanctioned
vendetta that, instead of bringing earthly infamy upon its perpe-
trators, would lavish on them all the purported gifts of heaven.
They were not just recovering land, they were repaying earlier
anti-Christian violence in kind. No sooner was it born than this
strange notion of warring for Christ by destroying his "enemies"
took Christians deeply into the wasteland of endless violence.

        This disturbing development was dramatically articulated
in the *chansons de geste,* which accurately mirrored the popular
outlooks of their day. The ignorance of Christian ethical values
that these songs reveal is no surprise, given the level of learning
in church and society, but the new "twist" is the opening given
for the infiltration of views that are blatantly antithetical to the
gospel. The appalling anti-Semitism and the disgraceful
pogroms have already been mentioned.[43] Just as the Crusades
fostered a manifest desire for revenge upon the Jews for the crucifixion of Jesus, they also prompted a thirst for revenge upon
the Muslims for holding the Holy Sepulchre and reportedly mis-
treating Christian pilgrims visiting Jerusalem. Western Christendom found itself afflicted in the twelfth century with an ailment
from which it has never entirely recovered.

        The most extraordinary example of subversion of the
gospel is dramatically illustrated in the *Chanson d'Antioche,* the
greatest of the vernacular epics of the First Crusade. As he hangs
dying on the cross, Christ is portrayed as reassuring the good
thief thus: "Know for certain that from over the seas will come a
new race which will *take revenge* on the death of its father." The
fundamental justification for the Crusade herein has taken on a
life of its own and reached its most forceful and vindictive
expression. It was the call of the dying Christ himself for revenge
that provided the basic motive, a call accompanied by a confident prediction that the Crusaders would come centuries later
and fully vindicate his execution, finally settling accounts with
the godless Jews and Muslims.

        This astonishing mythology gave extraordinary prestige to
the Crusaders' calling, since it assured them that they were not

only directly obeying the Lord but actually avenging his death as they set forth to slaughter infidels and Jews long centuries after the fact.[44] The irony of such an offensive mythology is beyond measure. It was forged only at the cost of a total reversal of the actual teaching of Jesus, repudiating the sentiments attributed to him on the cross, especially in Luke's gospel, and thus turning the meaning of the whole scene upside down. Far from loving or forgiving his enemies, the suffering Jesus is presented in quasi-blasphemous terms as seething with sentiments of hateful revenge. He predicts in the most "unChristian" fashion imaginable that his followers will nurse a vindictive grudge against the Jews for over a thousand years, and then will finally explode, unleashing the bloodbath not only upon the Jews but on all of God's enemies by means of the glorious Crusade. This theological absurdity, worlds apart from anything ever consciously intended by Pope Urban, is what the Crusade amounted to when it came to be viewed through the popular prism of the blood-feud. Christian knights on Crusade were the holy executioners, justly authorized to impose the death penalty on the descendents of those who had imposed it on Christ.

The bearing of this kind of apocalyptic vendetta mentality on any honest reappraisal of capital punishment is obvious. It was a twelfth-century parallel to the fourth-century distortion when "Christian" Roman emperors, totally oblivious of what Jesus taught about the matter, assured Christians, and legislated accordingly, that they had an imperial right to take revenge on their enemies. Just as the legend told of Constantine having the cross of Christ put on the shields of his soldiers before the battle of the Milvian Bridge (312), so the legend tells of the crowd listening to Pope Urban II nearly eight centuries later and pulling out "as though from nowhere...strips of cloth cut in the shape of a cross, and everybody busily sewing them on," thereby creating the well-known Crusader's badge.[45] In both cases the symbolism of the cross was not just distorted but totally and ironically reversed. Instead of the dying Savior's call from the cross for divine forgiveness of his executioners and enemies, the call from this revised version of the story was rather for naked revenge, a very different "gospel" indeed, and one that can still be heard in some discussions of capital punishment today. This ready accommodation of revenge may be the most disturbing heritage of the Crusades, the most blatant departure from Christian ideals. It puts Christian leaders in an extremely embarrassing position. To preach Jesus' message of forgiveness of enemies and rejection of revenge would mean to call for nothing less than "conversion" from the attitudes fostered by the Crusader blood-feud mentality.

Many eleventh and twelfth century forces were at work transforming Western Christendom in this direction, entailing often unintended degrees of departure from earlier ideals. The whole complex of notions touching on violence, war, bloodshed, killing, and revenge was in significant transition. As in any such evolution, there were many interacting factors, which cannot be easily or neatly separated by hindsight. The need for adjustment to new experiences, as always, played a central role, and the unanticipated rise of popular heresies, the low level of education, the barbarity of social customs, and the invention of the Crusade all played their parts. Conflicting voices understandably could be heard during this volatile period, some cautioning against, some cheerleading for, the changes. Before sampling them, however, it is worth taking note of a curious development that had a major impact not only on the practice of capital punishment but on Western law more generally for subsequent centuries.

II. AN ASIDE ON THE BENEFIT-OF-CLERGY EXEMPTION

There are fascinating studies of this strange custom, which can only be alluded to here.[46] But behind it is the troublesome distinction fostered by monasticism that has plagued Christendom from early times. The gospel was interpreted as teaching that there were two different levels of response to Jesus. All Christians were to follow his call, but some at a higher level than others. The commandments were to be observed by all, but the "counsels of perfection" were not meant for all. These were a higher standard meant for clergy and religious, who were thus called to be Christians of a higher order and thus were naturally to be judged by different criteria. Since "the church abhors bloodshed," church courts could never impose the death penalty, so one "benefit of clergy" was automatic exemption from the death penalty, no matter how serious the ecclesiastical offense. Clergy who became heretics initially posed a serious dilemma for church authorities in this regard until the convenience of "handing over to the secular arm" was worked out. This legal fiction worked to the advantage of those in power and the disadvantage of accused heretics, to say the least.

But the cognate legal fiction of benefit-of-clergy worked in a surprisingly generous way for laity. Any person on trial for a capital crime could claim to be "clergy" if the person knew how to read. The very structure of the legal trial in England came to reflect this practice. The allocution before sentencing included

> an inquiry whether the accused has anything to say why sentence should not be pronounced. This is the point at which an appeal for mercy is usually made. In origin the function of the allocution is to afford an opportunity for the convicted felon to inform the expectant court that he is a minister of the gospel; prove it by reading the neck verse; and escape the gallows.[47]

Thus, this legal fiction benefited large numbers of lay prisoners, protecting them from the death penalty.[48] Of course, none of this addressed the basic problem of the two different standards of Christian ethical conduct. In fact, it left open the even greater development of second-class status for laypeople. They were not prohibited from engaging in bloodshed, revenge, war, and other forms of public violence, which were prohibited for clergy. The very presence of the benefit-of-clergy exemption thus reinforced the two-class model of Christianity, but it provided a touch of clemency by way of a convenient fiction, and thereby occasionally softened the rigors of the capital code for those who were fortunate enough to know how to exploit it.

III. CONFLICTING EVALUATIONS
OF CHRISTIAN VIOLENCE

Was the nonviolent gospel message preached by Pope Nicholas I to the Bulgars in the ninth century still alive in the following century? There are at least a few occasional writings suggesting that it was, even though its future was in danger. One of the figures in this vanishing minority was a distinguished bishop in Italy.

A. *Otto (or Atto) of Vercelli*

Otto (c.940) wrote a work in which he put together an extraordinary pastiche of peace-advocating texts preserved in the Latin tradition, weaving together verses from the gospels with others from Acts, St. Paul, and texts of Ambrose, Augustine, and Gregory. He emphasized with the assistance of this gallery of authorities how inappropriate it would be for clerics to engage in bloodshed or violence.

> Since David was commanded not to build the visible temple because he was a man of war who frequently shed blood, how could priests go to war or battle even for justice, since they must build the temple, i.e., teach the Church of God?[49]

It was a *tour de force* in making the case for a nonviolent clergy, but in so doing it was witnessing to a fading ideal in danger of being overwhelmed by a tidal wave of forces. Circumstances favored the advocates of a more aggressive church policy unapologetic about the use of lethal force in pursuit of heavenly goals. But witnesses to a nonviolent message were still there.

B. *Peter Damian*

A prestigious cardinal of the following century, Peter Damian (d.1072) was an early and important figure in Hildebrand's reform efforts. He died the year before Hildebrand became Pope Gregory VII. Peter Damian was still able to assert confidently his conviction that

> in no circumstances is it licit to take up arms in defense of the faith of the universal church; still less should men rage in battle for its earthly and transitory goods.[50]

Peter's old-fashioned ecclesiology was on the wane, and his straightforward criticism of the militaristic spirit, which he saw escalating around him, is a valuable reminder that there were

churchmen who recognized and resisted the drift toward violence that was soon to prevail.

C. Guibert of Nogent

Guibert (c.1108) represents the very antithesis of Peter
Damian. He may be best described as a Christian intoxicated with
postwar euphoria. The unbelievable had happened. The First
Crusade had actually been victorious! The Holy City of Jerusalem
had been taken back from the infidels by the rampaging soldiers
of Christ. Guibert saw this in nothing less than cosmic terms: it
was the providential moment when God in his eternal plan lifted
the former ban on Christians embracing military life and practice. The earlier reservations about the use of violence, which
seemed to be what Jesus taught, were no longer in force. The
weapons of war were now transformed into the blessed means of
Christian sanctification by a God who wanted a militant people to
honor him by warring mightily against his enemies.

> In our time God has instituted holy warfare so that the
> knightly order and unsettled populace, who used to be
> engaged like the pagans of old in slaughtering one another,
> should find a new way of deserving salvation. No longer are
> they obliged to leave the world and choose a monastic way
> of life, as used to be the case...but...by performing their own
> office, they may in some measure achieve the grace of
> God.[51]

Rather than finding any fault with the new Crusader theology,
Guibert enthusiastically endorsed it, but he did not provide
much insight or theoretical foundation for this reversal. The
thrill of the conquest of Jerusalem apparently swept away all misgivings. Victory was the manifest proof, the revelation of God's
will (as the Crusaders' slogan had confidently proclaimed). Who
had the audacity to quarrel with such military success achieved
under the very banner of the cross? God could not have manifested himself more plainly.

For our purposes, it is worth noting that similar reasoning
applied to the role of the hangman as well. The early Christian
abhorrence for shedding blood made both roles—soldier and

executioner—problematic for the same reason. Now it was possible with this new theology to give both of these states a much more positive standing. As men who were officially commissioned in the name of God to kill the enemies of God, their function took on a virtuous hue it had never borne before. The trend toward a fully positive evaluation of Christian engagement in bloodshed met with Guibert's full approval, but some theoretical justification had yet to be worked out. It was a challenge calling for the attention and talent of gifted interpreters if the transition to the new understanding was to be facilitated.

IV. EARLY SCHOLASTIC THEOLOGIANS AND HOMICIDE

One might have expected that the emerging theologians of the age would have been the ones in the best position to take up the challenge and address this difficult question. At issue were basic concepts affecting all of Christian life and society. But this was not the case, for reasons that will become clear.

A. *Peter Abelard's* Sic et Non *(c.1123)*

Peter Abelard dramatically influenced the direction of twelfth century theology, especially by his adept use of dialectics on some of the problems in the tradition. One difficulty with his work, however, was the fact that he often "simply left his readers with the conflicting statements, yes and no, without providing a resolution."[52] His personal troubles with church authorities may have played a role in this, but the result was that, while he often brought fuller attention to problems, he did not necessarily help in solving them. That was the case with his treatment of "the Christian-killing dilemma." Of his 158 "yes and no" topics gathered together with appropriately conflicting texts found in the tradition, numbers 156 and 157 dealt with the delicate ethical question of Christian participation in bloodshed.

Number 156, in rounding up conflicting statements found in the tradition, summed up the situation thus: "It is never licit for Christians to kill anyone for any reason...and the contrary."

One can readily see both why the method got quick attention and why it was considered radical, even dangerous. In using it one could momentarily endorse all manner of wild positions, then turn around and embrace their opposites a moment later, leaving many a reader totally befuddled as to what to believe. In this case all six of the passages he cites were well-known excerpts from Augustine, reflecting his notorious ambivalence. The sixth one, for example, asks why it was said that "he who takes up the sword perishes by the sword," unless because no one but a judge is allowed to kill anyone with the sword.[53] The passage as formulated fairly begs for clarification, completion, or at least some further illuminating comment, but it receives none of these at the hands of Abelard.

Number 157 has a sharper edge and includes over twice as many passages to illustrate the conflicting positions: "It is licit to kill a man, and (it is) not." Three texts are taken from St. Jerome, one from pseudo-Cyprian; the remaining nine are once again culled from the writings of St. Augustine. The use of the dialectic here reinforces the Augustinian insistence on the primacy of the inner disposition:

> When a soldier in the line of duty kills a man, he is not guilty of homicide under any state law; rather, if he fails to do so, he is guilty of imperial desertion and contempt. If he did it on his own authority, he would be guilty of the crime of shedding human blood. Hence, as he is punished for acting (killing) when not ordered to do so, likewise he will be punished for not acting (not killing) when ordered to do so.[54]

The strange ambiguity in killing fellow humans could hardly be put more starkly, and the problem formulated in this manner was guaranteed to receive continued attention from posterity. The nub of the entire issue, however, is hereby narrowed to one factor and one factor only: that of proper authority. The action of killing by one who has the authority to kill is seen as something entirely different from—in fact, totally opposite to—the very same action performed by anyone who kills without authority. It is not surprising that it was from the canon lawyers rather than the theologians that a more comprehensive exploration of the

question was going to have to evolve. The legal question pre-
empted the ethical question.

It should not be forgotten that there had regularly been
some very practical efforts on the part of churchmen to restrain
violence. For example, the Peace of God and the Truce of God
were worthy ecclesiastical efforts to limit military activities by
restricting them to certain times, places, and persons,[55] but in the
long run these were relatively ineffective counter-measures,
which could not offset the more general turn to violence as
acceptable policy.

> Violence was a double-edged instrument in knightly hands.
> Its acceptable basis lay in custom permitting vengeance,
> redress, and self-defense in noble society....More equivocal
> was the frequency of feuds, homicides, duels, and other acts
> of violence...for they contradicted the solidarity and reliabil-
> ity of loyal service...and undermined justice.[56]

The policy of fostering elite bands of knights, specially trained
and devoted to the most effective use of violence in the political
causes of the church, resulted in a less demanding ethic in the
evaluation and protection of human life.

B. Hugh of St. Victor

The reason for including Hugh (c.1140) is an intriguing
remark that he made about the impropriety of executing thieves,
which had become regular legal practice in his day. As far as he
was concerned, "this is by no means the justice of the Gospel,
that a man be killed for (stealing) a horse or an ox, nor is such a
precept to be found anywhere in the entire gospel. Nor does the
church do it, but only permits it."[57] One senses that Hugh realized that something had gone awry, that use of the death penalty
had gotten out of hand in executing petty thieves. It was being
used as a routine instrument of the rich to protect their property
and material goods from the poor.[58] This was a recurring problem that would receive further cynical comment from other
medieval Christian observers, but an astute churchman like
Hugh here seemed to be acknowledging the unfortunate fact,
while at the same time being resigned to his inability to do much

about it. Perhaps it would not be too far off the mark to see it as a kind of trade-off: because the death penalty was being used for the church's benefit in repressing heretics, its use could not easily be denied to wealthy laymen for the benefit of protecting their goods.[59]

If so, it was another case where church theory "had lagged far behind practice, and it remained to be seen (among other things) what distinguished crusades against infidels and heretics from ordinary just wars waged on ecclesiastical authority."[60] And, as always, the positions adopted in theorizing about war would invariably have a bearing on the understanding of capital punishment as well. Dealing with heretics set the scene for the general legitimation of the death penalty that would hold sway for the next six or more centuries in Western Christian church life.[61] If the death penalty had not been routinized as the official sanction for dealing with heretics, it is unlikely that it would ever have gained the kind of universal endorsement that it did for all kinds of other crimes, religious and secular, grave and petty, in subsequent Western society. If church officials were to function as ready collaborators, even outright advocates, in the execution of heretics, there was little room for them to register any kind of credible objection to the way that secular authorities were imposing the same penalty for crimes of any and all kinds in their jurisdiction.

C. *Peter Lombard's* Sentences *(1152–1158)*

There is no need to dwell on the key role played by Peter Lombard in the development of medieval scholastic theology. All the giants of the thirteenth century stood on his shoulders, answered his questions, started from his collection of opinions. His distinguished teaching career in Paris ended in 1159 when he was elected bishop of the city, but he died only a year later in that office. His reputation is basically tied to his most celebrated work, the four books of *Sentences,* because of their subsequent impact on conceptions of Christian doctrine.[62]

Although Peter's four books set the framework for those of later theologians, his successors seldom followed him exactly because his plan had some serious drawbacks. Briefly put, his four books arranged the content of the Christian faith thus:

Book I—Trinity; Book II—Creation and Fall; Book III—Incarnation, Redemption, and Virtues; Book IV—Sacraments and Eschatology. "The genius of this work lies in its organization and in its brevity." It became "a standard textbook in the theology curriculum into the 17th century."[63] But a closer look reveals at least one reason why some who followed him experimented with alternatives. If, for example, one wanted to find what Peter had to say about Christians using lethal force, whether by engaging in warfare, imposing the death penalty, or shedding blood in other ways, where might one find his opinions? From the above headings, Book III would be the likeliest candidate, and, in fact, it is organized into forty distinctions with a total of 143 chapters. Twenty-nine of those distinctions deal with traditional questions of Christology (Incarnation and Redemption), leaving eleven for discussion of the Virtues. Six of these eleven are taken up with the theological and the cardinal virtues and the seven gifts of the Holy Spirit, which leaves only four distinctions (37 to 40) for the handling of the Ten Commandments, a limitation that is not especially promising from the start.

Then distinction 37 sets out to explain how Jesus reduced the Ten Commandments to only two commandments—love God, love your neighbor—pointing out that this was actually the way they were originally presented to Moses, on two different tablets. A few words follow about each tablet, the first containing the three commands regarding duties to God. When Peter gets to the second commandment on the second tablet, regarding duties to one's neighbor ("thou shalt not kill"), this is what he has to say:

> The act of homicide is prohibited according to the letter, but, according to the spirit, so is the desire (*voluntas*) to kill [which is forbidden]. Hence, to this commandment according to the letter a superaddition is made in the Gospel, because the letter of the Gospel expresses what the letter of the Law did not.[64]

Granted that it is only an overview, one nonetheless gets the distinct impression that there were no special problems surrounding this commandment, that it was clearly understood and ordinarily obeyed, and that its demands were perceived as calling for no special treatment. That perception was wrong, of course, but it underlines the fact that in this crucial time, when a monumental change was taking place in so delicate an area, the division of labor was such that the theologians were content to leave this thorny issue to the canonists, as we see in one of Lombard's more famous students.

D. Peter of Poitiers' Sentences (1170–1180)

Peter taught theology in Paris from 1167 until his appointment as chancellor in 1193, a post he held till his death in 1205. He drew heavily from Lombard's work but added freely, more than doubling the number of questions addressed, and he reorganized the contents from four books into five books: I–Trinity; II–Creation; III–Grace and Virtues; IV–Christology; and V–Sacraments and Eschatology. This gave him more leeway to include and do greater justice to pressing questions of his day, but "he also avoids scrupulously questions belonging to the canonists rather than to the theologians."[65] Nonetheless, the issue of "Christian killing," which had already made its brief appearance at the end of Peter Abelard's work, could not be left entirely to the canonists. This is how Peter of Poitiers dealt with it:

In Book Four he has six treatises on [six of] the Ten Commandments (On False Gods; On Killing; On Theft; On Adultery; On Lying; and On Perjury), and in dealing with them he regularly asks whether it is ever lawful to act contrary to any of these commands. When he comes to "thou shalt not kill" and asks if it is ever licit to kill, his answer is that "it seems as though it is," and he points to the incident in First Maccabees when a thousand Jews were slaughtered after refusing to defend themselves, and the decision was made by the Jewish leaders that "if anyone attacks us on the Sabbath...we will resist him; we must not all be killed as our brothers were" (1 Mc 2:41). Peter notes that this decision was reached under "the instruction of the Holy Spirit." He also invokes the classical dictum we will see in the canonists, that "it is lawful to repel force with force," but then he adds a fascinating new thesis, an argument from victory (or, nothing succeeds like success): "If the Church had not permitted and approved, our soldiers overseas would not have killed the pagans"[66]; that is, they would never have won the First Crusade! Needless to say, it was a dangerous, double-edged argument, available for use only for a very short time; obviously it had to be dropped once the Christians started losing all the subsequent Crusades.

Against the presumed legitimacy of the death penalty, in good scholastic fashion he builds the best case he can, citing the gospel passage of offering the other cheek and not resisting evil (Mt 5:38f., Lk 6:29). He grants that the death penalty does not seem to be in accord with the spirit of the Beatitudes. In the same sense he cites Paul's recommendation that we not take justice into our own hands, but leave it to God (Rom 12:19). Also he notes that Jesus reproached Peter for striking the servant of the high priest, and that this was equivalent to a negative moral judgment being declared on Peter's aggressive conduct.

Peter of Poitiers then gives his response to these objections in the following manner: It is not licit to kill when it is done with animus and hatred, but killing is licit when motivated by zeal, by justice, in defense of truth, and to protect the faith. To sustain his thesis he uses the "traditional" text from Jerome that we have already seen.

Peter goes on to adopt a position that is at once understandable and shocking. He says in so many words that the teaching of the New Testament had only a temporary and circumstantial validity:

> The divine Spirit, carefully considering everything, foresaw that in the time of the primitive Church, when it was small, it was useful for it to bear its sufferings and maintain itself with patience. But when its numbers grew, it found that (to be) licit which previously was not licit.[67]

Applying this principle to the death penalty explains why such punishment was not allowed in the early days of the church, but later, because of its growth and expansion and victories, the evangelical and apostolic objections to bloodshed had been set aside and no longer applied. It is a fascinating passage that makes this metamorphosis sound like a normal growth process without any moral implications, a kind of "winner take all" philosophy. The idea is faintly reminiscent of Paul's words "When I was a child...I acted as a child; when I became an adult, I put an end to childish ways" (1 Cor 13:11), but to use it here would be cynical in the extreme. It would be to suggest that early Christian nonviolence was itself merely a ploy, a pragmatic policy decision that was to be casually discarded once Christians had acquired enough strength to overpower their enemies. It is a kind of anticipation of Machiavelli. But there was yet another Peter in Paris at the same time who had something more impressive to say about the death penalty.

E. Peter the Chanter

Peter the Chanter (d.1197) taught theology in Paris from 1173 to his death in 1197, so he was centrally positioned to note the events and anomalies in this crucial period of change.[68] His criticism of some of the more obvious abuses of capital punishment was trenchant. For instance, in France, England, and elsewhere the royal forests had become the sacred hunting grounds for the rich, and summary hanging had become the routine punishment for poachers. Something was clearly amiss, and the incongruity cried out for attention. As we saw earlier, the subject was a sore point a generation earlier in the time of Hugh of St. Victor. Now Peter ventured to ask: "Why is it that in the Old Testament, adultery was punished by death but theft was not, while today we hang a petty thief but not an adulterer?" It was not the kind of question likely to make him popular at the royal courts or in high society. He nonetheless wasted no time drawing the conclusion that, however adultery might best be punished in a society, no one had any right to kill a person who had committed simple theft. He challenged anyone to point to any biblical legitimation for such an inhumane policy, noting rather that the Hebrew prophets could be cited at length against such tyrannical unjust treatment of the poor by the rich.

But Peter also had his own position on the more delicate question about heresy. Should churchmen approve and advocate executing heretics? The precedent for endorsing such deliberate infliction of death on the part of those who claimed to represent the Lord of life, seen as early as the fourth century case of Priscillian, had indeed been given formal standing in the Roman law codes. But these provisions had nonetheless not been much used in the West for more than five hundred years. The issue was revived only in the century before Peter in the infamous Orléans case. That there was still a great deal of ambivalence, despite the increasing instances of heretics being executed, is not surprising. As with many other controversial topics, it was still an open question that could be freely debated by responsible Christian theologians with conflicting viewpoints.

Some canonists advocated using the death penalty outright as a necessary means for protecting orthodox faith from the contagion of heresy, while others were not so sure about its propriety. But pressure from the escalating outbreaks of heresy increasingly tended to settle the debate for the foreseeable future in favor of execution as the appropriate way to deal with obstinate heretics.[69]

During the height of Peter's teaching career in Paris, the Council of Verona, under Pope Lucius III, issued the ominous decretal *Ad Abolendam* (1184), which has been called "the founding charter of the Inquisition."[70] It changed the climate by setting an official attitude toward heresy, naming indiscriminately a whole list of groups as heretical, including the Waldenses. It provided for specific procedures according to which any who were judged by ecclesiastical courts to be incurably heretical were henceforth to be handed over in the last resort to the secular prince to receive their "due punishment" (*animadversione debita*). By leaving the nature of that punishment open, the pope allowed recourse to the death penalty as an obvious possibility for those who chose to use it.[71] Peter was a disapproving witness of the hard-line shift that was taking place in church policy toward heretics. He was neither willing nor able to agree with those who justified killing heretics but rather aligned himself in the tradition with the pastoral position of St. Augustine and Bishop Wazo. In opposing those who preferred to kill heretics, Peter marshalled familiar passages from the Bible and the Fathers, and cited the Council of Reims of 1148, where Pope Eugenius III had chosen not to have the convicted Breton heretic Eudo de Stella executed but consigned him rather to a life sentence in the archbishop's prison.[72]

Peter's common sense and Christian compassion also led him to raise his voice in criticism of the superstitious practice of ordeals. He pointed out that they were in violation of the scriptural injunction "thou shalt not tempt the Lord thy God," and he lamented the many cases of innocent people being condemned to death after failing in a trial by ordeal. There is good reason to think that Peter the Chanter's critique was one of the major factors that finally led to the banning of all ordeals in the canons of the Fourth Lateran Council in 1215.[73] But Peter's dissenting voice had hardly been stilled by death (1197) when a new pope was elected (1198). The new pope would soon be pushed not only to permit but also to legislate lethal punishment as standard policy against heretics.[74]

V. EARLY CANONISTS AND THE AUTHORITY TO KILL

While several theologians had a variety of things to say about the death penalty, it was especially in the realm of canon law that the question had to be faced more broadly. For the canonists it was not just a theoretical question but a very practical one: When (if ever) could capital punishment be justified? Who (if anyone) could be killed? By whom (if anyone) was such authority held? Why (if for any cause) should it ever be imposed? These were hard questions over which there were long debates and canonical struggles. Only a few of the steps can be summarized here, but it is this canonical development that would seem to be at the heart of the entire history of the use of capital punishment in Western Christianity. The events and ideas that prevailed in twelfth-century canon law established the theory and practice of almost the entire time since, both European and, by extension, American. All too little exploration of the relevant materials has as yet been done, but it is clear that there is much to be learned here. It will thus be necessary to double back to pick up the canonical trail running parallel to the theological developments we have just been exploring.

A. *Anselm of Lucca*

Anselm had produced a collection of canons around the time of Pope Gregory VII's death (1085) to support the growing trend arguing the right of the church and churchmen to use the sword and armed force against any and all heretics and infidels. It was an arsenal meant to enable one to counter the objections of a Peter Damian or anyone else of that period who tried to hold the nonviolent line. It has been said of Anselm of Lucca that he was "the first canonist to give extensive consideration to the problem of ecclesiastical coercion and war" and his work "in all essentials...forms the basis for the later scholastic theory of war."[75] Gregory VII's bitter feud with King Henry IV had awakened a militaristic mentality among his supporters that was to be the wave of the future. The fact that there are three surviving biographies of Anselm has made it possible to trace a distinctive type of hagiography, which Golinelli calls "a hagiography of battle."[76] Anselm is celebrated as a holy bishop, but because he was caught up in the battle over lay investiture, his approving biographers highlight his aggressive militancy for the church as that which especially made him a saint and thus a model to be emulated by others. Anselm himself was still "too subtle a thinker to sanction reckless assaults; he rejects revenge, joy over the defeat of the enemy, and enrichment from enemy property," but his reservations about bishops using force were personal. He was too familiar with the tradition not to realize that the restraints on violence are binding on Christian leaders, when they are serious in following the teaching and example of Christ. But the new militancy that marked the eve of the Crusades made it extremely difficult to draw the line short of violence.

B. *Bonizo of Sutri*

A more feisty colleague of Anselm's, Bonizo produced a comprehensive book of canons. He was an uncompromising advocate of reform whom Gregory VII knew he could trust and whom he also employed as a legate. "In the course of the investiture struggle he was captured by Emperor Henry IV (1082), escaped, and took refuge with Matilda of Tuscany, where he wrote his most famous work, *Liber ad amicum*...designed to rally all reformers after Gregory's death in 1085."[77] In this work he set out to answer two questions: (1) Why is the church now in such sad straits? And (2) Are Christians permitted to take up arms to fight for the faith? The latter question soon became the one he waxed most eloquent upon, while engaging in a fascinating bit of revisionist church history. The warrior-pope of a generation earlier (Leo IX) was, according to Bonizo, not a deviation or departure from the Christian norm but the actual culmination of a long line of Christian fighters who had taken up the sword and died for justice, and, if anyone had doubts, "miracles proved their elevation into the ranks of the saints, thereby giving living hope to all future fighters for righteousness."[78]

"Bonizo coarsens Anselm's work by almost entirely bypassing the Augustinian teaching that an attitude of love should be taken toward the enemy; he even goes so far as to attribute to Augustine the statement that those men are holy who *practice* persecution for the sake of righteousness." He also creates other militaristic texts that he puts in the mouth of Jerome. This is classical propaganda, produced in the heat of real conflict, geared to influence the wavering. Bonizo raises the pitch to another level in his conclusion, with an attempt at an *a fortiori* argument, designating the crisis of his time as the preeminent moment in church history:

> If a Christian has ever been allowed to use weapons for any cause, then he is *NOW* allowed to wage war in any way at all against the Wibertines.

In some ways Bonizo was too much too soon. He certainly represented the path that was beckoning, but the nonviolent message of Christ could not be completely swept aside quite so quickly and easily as Bonizo had done. His effort to portray all of Christian history, even the pre-Constantinian church, as the story of a glorious march of the *"milites Dei"* battling for truth and righteousness is overdrawn, to say the least, as is his episcopal prayer that "all heresy may perish in fire."[79] But, while other canonists would have to struggle in a more sophisticated process of accommodation, it is Bonizo who stands as the most striking exemplar of the marked militarism that was to dominate all too much of Christendom's immediate future.

C. Ivo of Chartres

Ivo of Chartres (d.1116), a man of great ability and influence, was "the most famous canonist of the eleventh century....It was mostly through his efforts that Roman law became known North of the Alps."[80] He was present at Clermont in 1095 for Pope Urban II's historic call for the First Crusade, and at that time had probably only recently completed his massive (seventeen volumes) *Decretum* (between 1093 and 1095). Part Ten is a long collection of texts (188 chapters) reflecting hundreds of bizarre cases that had confronted churchmen with all kinds of questions about bloodshed over the centuries. The introductory rubric summarizes its contents as being about "homicides, spontaneous and non-spontaneous; parricides and fratricides; and the killing of legitimate wives, and elders, and clerics; and that not every one who kills a man is a homicide; and about penances of the above."[81] Ivo is of great interest because he explicitly had to confront not just the question of "Christian war" but also the question of the death penalty as such.

Ivo's timid but clear defense of the death penalty, based on appeals to 2 Peter, Jerome, Augustine, and Gregory, has to do with cases of homicide and theft. He cites the handy text of Jerome seen earlier, that one who punishes evil persons for their malice and bestows death to the worst of them conducts himself as a true "minister of God." He goes on to cite 1 Peter 2:14, where obedience to authorities for the love of God is recommended. Governors are commissioned as delegates of God to chastise the evil and praise the good. Without any comment on the quotation, Ivo turns anew to Jerome's commentary on Jeremiah to cite a text that was to have a long history. Chastising those who commit murder, sacrilege, and poisonings with the penalty of death does not constitute a deed guilty of blood but a legal act of ministry of the law. An irrelevant allusion to Augustine is also brought in, evoking Exodus 22:17, where there is talk of the legal death of sorcerers. In his judgment Elijah caused the just death of many by divine inspiration. A quotation attributed to Gregory remains difficult to authenticate. Then he ends his appeal to authorities by citing the incident of Ananias and Sapphira in Acts 5 as an example to persuade all that capital vindictiveness is not extraneous to the New Testament. The text says that "when Ananias heard these words (of Peter), he fell down and died" (v. 8), and that a moment later Sapphira likewise "immediately fell down at his feet and died" (v. 10), punished by God on the spot for their fraud. This is indeed an unusual instance of a "death penalty," but, contrary to Ivo's insinuation, it is hardly a case of Peter doing the executing, although it could obviously serve as a great proof-text, if it were not for all those other canons about clerics being required to abstain from bloodshed.

Ivo does not use the expression "death penalty" or "capital punishment." In speaking (elsewhere) of lay obligations, he says that thieves and malefactors "duly convicted according to the law" should also "die according to the law."[82] It is precisely here that the greatest questions should be raised about what was happening in the canonical realm. Ivo simply transposed from the Old Testament to the New Testament the same penal prescriptions, among them the death penalty. This recourse to the authority of the Old Testament as if it automatically justified capital punishment in the New Testament is problematic in the extreme. For instance, his chapter 72 simply refers to Deuteronomy 13:6-11 as if it were self-evident that a Christian of his day still belonged to a society like the ancient Israelite community:

> If anyone secretly entices you...even if it is your brother...your own son or daughter...or the wife you embrace, or your most intimate friend, saying "Let us go worship other gods,"...show them no pity...kill them; your own hand shall be the first...to execute them....Stone them to death....Then all Israel shall hear and be afraid, and never again do any such wickedness.

Putting aside for the moment all the other questions that such a passage raises, consider the strain it puts on everybody, including the poor canonist. Using the unchallenged principle that "the church does not shed blood," there was only one conclusion at hand. Laymen, in their second-class capacity as the secular arm, were the ones called to do the blood-letting for the first-class (clerical) Christians. Needless to say, something had to give; the situation cried out for resolution; something simply had to be done to alleviate the canonical strain of leaving things at this perplexing level.[83] It was time for some kind of creative new thinking.

D. *Gratian's* Decretum

Gratian's work (c.1140) did in fact open a new era in the history of canon law, not only replacing earlier poorly organized collections like Ivo's, but also providing a systematic, logical ordering of the documents. "It quickly established itself as the basic text for the study of law in the schools," and held that position for at least the century following its appearance.[84] The work was meant to highlight, in order to lessen or resolve, the contradictions and incongruities that littered the canonical landscape. Gratian had "examined fearlessly the discrepancies between his grouped extracts, and then sought, by means of distinctions, to reconcile them."[85] Compared to Abelard's work, Gratian's cast a far wider net and made fuller use of the dialectical method. He gathered sources from scripture, church Fathers, decrees of councils and synods, papal letters of all kinds, and Roman law. How to reconcile conflicting texts was the challenge, and he freely added his own opinions (*dicta*) in working to settle disagreements.

Of the three parts of the *Decretum,* the first is taken up with questions of ecclesiastical governance, whereas Part Two (the longest of the three) is a series of "Causae" treating the problems of Christian laypeople. The section from Causa 23 through Causa 27 is known as the *Causae Haereticorum,* and the first one of these (Causa 23), an unusually long collection of texts, has been described both as "the first serious discussion on problems of war in medieval Europe"[86] and "the first development of an international code or law of toleration."[87] Thus, Causa 23, on the one hand, tries to justify war, and, on the other hand, tries to control its violence through moral injunctions.[88] In this ambivalence it is thoroughly Augustinian in spirit.[89]

Causa 23 obviously has a great bearing on the history of Christian thought about capital punishment as well as about war, because the sanctioning of both has the same basis. The timing is also noteworthy. Not only was the *Decretum* composed as Gratian was struggling with the old problem of the use of coercion in a Christian society plagued by heresy, but he did this between the end of the First Crusade and the call for the Second Crusade. Among later commentators, his Causa 23 was to serve as the classical locus for bringing up all aspects of the thorny subject of deliberate killing within the Christian ethical tradition, and in that context there was no way to ignore the numerous texts recalling the teaching of Jesus on love of enemies and nonretaliation.

Drawing from the earlier collections of Ivo of Chartres and Burchard of Worms, Gratian organized the material into eight basic questions, the very asking of which tells us much about how the dilemma of "Christian killing" had come to be developed in church thought and legislation throughout the first ten Christian centuries: (1) Is it a sin to wage war? (2) What is a just war? (3) Should a wrong done to an ally be repelled with arms? (4) Ought one to take revenge? (5) Is a judge permitted to condemn criminals to death? (6) Can one restrain wrongdoers? (7) Can one deprive heretics of their goods? and (8) Are bishops or clerics permitted to take up arms on their own, without the command of the emperor?[90]

A fascinating feature of Causa 23 is the intensity of its dialectic. Gratian makes no effort to soften the stark tension between the teaching of Jesus in the Sermon on the Mount and the sanctioned killing that had come to be permitted and practiced in Christian society in the aftermath of the Ambrosian-Augustinian just-war teaching. Christ's counsel to "turn the other cheek" (Mt 5:38) is cited six different times in Causa 23; the commandment "thou shalt not kill" is repeated three times. Christ's command to Peter to put up his sword and the warning that those who live by the sword will die by the sword (Mt 26:52) are also cited half a dozen different times. The only Old Testament passage occurs early and is from Deuteronomy 32:35, God's insistence that "vengeance is mine," not man's. Gratian was not only not dodging the oxymoronic problem of "Christian violence," but actually confronting it in its strongest terms. Moreover, he did not merely present this fundamental conflict between scripture and current practice *pro forma* in the first question, but rather returned to it at the beginning of each of the subsequent questions as well. The problem for him was not an easy one that could be permanently set aside, as Bishop Bonizo had managed to do. It was rather a troublesome, problematic, paradoxical, continuing difficulty for Gratian, and he grappled with it manfully. Christ's precepts were repeated and seriously acknowledged but then by-passed, as it were, due to the Augustinian assurance that they only applied to the internal disposition of the warrior/punisher, not to his external acts. So the answer to the first question, despite the seeming clarity of the teaching of Jesus to the contrary, was that "it is not a sin to wage war...[Christ's] precepts of patience must be observed in the preparation of the heart, not the conduct of the body."[91]

This Augustinian move, making the hard sayings of Jesus apply, but only in the order of intention not in the order of action, was the uneasy path that had circuitously led to the conclusion that all deliberate killing of fellow humans was not necessarily sinful. As long as the intention was one of "justice," a Christian could morally engage in a war, as long as several other important conditions were also satisfactorily met. So, in question two, Gratian proceeds to objectify this subjective attitude by identifying the legal conditions for a war to be just, since this was obviously the only kind of war that a Christian could even consider engaging in without abandoning the noblest teachings of the Lord. Thus, in question three, Gratian follows St. Augustine into the thicket of Old Testament wars in search of insight into this disturbing dilemma. He emerges with two (and only two) examples of "just wars": First, a war is just when it is explicitly commanded by God (*ex edicto*), and second, a war is just when it is waged to avenge injuries, as in the case of Joshua destroying Ai (Joshua 8). Ominously, as Scully notes,

> no New Testament examples of war can be found; the Old Testament is relied upon to establish even the existence of a just war. Nor are New Testament texts used to establish an opposite pole...against which these texts can be dialectically opposed and then resolutely resolved by the master.[92]

Gratian just "passes quickly" to the next question.

The most obviously embarrassing aspect of Gratian's treatment is its failure to grapple with the teaching of Jesus on nonretaliation, despite all the earlier citations. Avenging injustice is offered as a "just cause" of war merely by appeal to the one case in Joshua. This was no great problem for the ancient Israelite theocracy, since divine vengeance was by definition something very different from human revenge. The problem with the example holds just as much for capital punishment as for vindictive war in ancient Israel. Who can reliably claim to have the power of God to do the will of God by inflicting lethal violence on other human beings? And when, why, and how is this to be confidently determined? The number of problems confronting the honest inquirer was bewildering.

Gratian's failure to find any New Testament support left the dilemma completely unresolved. He accepted and propagated the Augustinian attempt at a solution, but his many readers, past and present, could sense how embarrassingly uncomfortable he was with it. The canonists who followed him turned elsewhere in search of an alternative solution to the problem of Christian killing rather than live with the tension of the "apparent conflict between the law of scripture and the reality of society's use of violence and force. The necessity of justifying, theologically and morally, such seemingly unchristian behavior absorbed much of the space and attention Gratian gave the questions raised by Causa 23."[93] But his successors were to turn in a very different direction, one that was more in tune with the *Zeitgeist*.

It is impossible to do justice here to Scully's extensive analysis of the canonists. She traces the growth of the two main branches, the Bolognese school and the French school, pinpointing how each succeeding commentator accepts, rejects, modifies, or passes on what is found in Gratian. In admittedly oversimplified fashion, we select from her study the two canonists whose work represents a two-stage departure from Gratian in answering the delicate question of the right to kill.

E. Huguccio of Pisa's Summa Decretorum *(c.1188)*

The most brilliant of the Bolognese canonists, Huguccio was also "the last great Decretist" and, not to be overlooked, the

teacher of the canonist who was shortly to become Pope Innocent III (Lothario of Segni).[94] One of Huguccio's strong opinions
is of special interest: he was convinced that clerics were forbidden from fighting, no matter how just the cause. "It is always a
sin for them to be soldiers."[95] In the process, however, he thus
"seems almost to define a layman in terms of his military capabil-
ity, as one for whom fighting is licit." There is no narrowing
down to any particular sub-group empowered by authority to act
in defense of the whole, that is, those with the office of soldiers
or executioners. "As yet, presumably, all laymen may kill in a just
cause." His focus is on the traditional internal dispositions, the
need to keep mind and heart free from hatred of the enemy
even, or especially, as one carries out his duty involving the shedding of blood. In this he continues to stay close to both Augustine and Gratian, heightening the agonizing tension between
loving and killing.

But he also takes another step. "For the first time in the context of a discussion of Causa 23," a Bolognese canonist intro-
duces a principle which Gratian had used elsewhere, claiming
that

> natural law is common to all nations, so that everywhere by
> an instinct of nature, not by some constitution, force is
> repelled by force.

Here was a way of going beyond the New Testament's moral
demands and justifying not only self-defense but necessity as
grounds for using violence. This is probably reflective of the
"growing dissatisfaction with the patristic rationalizations of violence"; but the fact that he chose not to make it the "foundation
of his discussion of Causa 23 shows that he did not understand
the legal use of violence to be its basic issue."[96] But the stage was
set for an important move soon to be taken by the other branch
of canonists.

F. Johannes Teutonicus's Glossa Ordinaria (c. 1215)

Johannes provided the capstone of the French school and is
of special interest for our purposes because "he arrives at his
position by a way which had not occurred to Gratian and which

was external to the problems considered within the Causa (23)."[97] It was his work that set the stage, altered the tone, and determined the direction of Christian thought about killing and war for the centuries to come.[98] The major change that Johannes and the other members of the French school of canonists introduced into discussions of Causa 23 was to make central the single principle of Roman law—*vim vi repelleret*—that force can be used to repel force. Gratian knew the principle, citing it elsewhere, but never used it in Causa 23 as a way of by-passing the nonretaliatory teaching of Jesus. Huguccio, as we have seen, introduced it into Causa 23 but did not make it basic. It was Johannes who now made it the cornerstone, constructing a whole new theological position around it.

Once the "vim-vi" principle is invoked, it puts killing in an entirely different, much more positive light. It is simply a reasonable part of the natural order of the everyday world. Like "turnabout is fair play," "tit for tat," "what goes around comes around," and "kill or be killed," it changes the context of the conversation from theological-ethical considerations to a straightforward legal-pragmatic category, expressed in so-called common-sense slogans rather than hard sayings, like the directive of Jesus to "turn the other cheek."[99]

This shift signified a fundamental change in understanding. By its introduction killing came to be treated, not in the negative (Augustinian) way as something to agonize over and do penance for, but as a positive aspect of the natural order, part of "the way things are," a fact of life in the real world, thus implicitly seen as accepted, intended, and approved by the God of nature. The remaining task of the canonists was to fix the limits placed on this positive right to kill. There was no further need to focus on the negative, justifying the very thought of Christians engaged in killing. The moral dilemma was "solved" by the introduction of the natural-law principle. Using force to offset force needed no further apology, so attention was diverted from the ethical to the legal question of proper control of this killing sanctioned by natural law; that is, who has the right to do such killing *ex officio*? It is a fascinating move taking one down a respectable path of philosophical ethics, pondering the degrees of counterviolence that can be legitimately brought to bear against the violence of an unjust aggressor, without running into awkward prohibitions attributed to Jesus.

In closing, it is interesting to note a fascinating parallel in the case recently made by two contemporary Christian authors who contend that

> to maintain a consistent belief in Christianity is antithetical to supporting vengeful punishment and capital executions. These two positions cannot conceivably be joined together, except by a reinterpretation of the positions to rectify the cognitively dissonant conflict.[100]

This sounds for all the world like a description of what Johannes Teutonicus and others ended up doing in the century after Gratian. The introduction of the "vim-vi" principle, notes Scully, settled the authorization question because it was "seen as an aspect of natural law, and killing is thus seen as an aspect of the natural order....Moral questions, such as intention, become secondary to legal questions, such as the details of damages incurred by an official." Office, particularly the judiciary,

> was focused upon to an unprecedented degree as the single licit vehicle for retaliation....All the resources of both schools are pooled (by Teutonicus) to sharply delineate the judicial office as the sole jurisdiction empowered and entrusted with the positive right to kill licitly.[101]

Teutonicus used the "vim-vi" principle as justification for by-passing the troublesome texts of the New Testament. As a result, the thirteenth-century canon lawyer saw "nature and natural law as a surer criterion of the divine law."[102] This novelty, strangely enough, occurred on the very eve of the most important formative period in the history of Catholic theology. The focus on the legalities of *ex officio* killing distracted from the agonizing over bloodshed that was characteristic in the earlier tradition. A case can be made that it was precisely this fixation upon the question of the basic legality of the death penalty (the state's "right" to execute) that sidetracked consideration of more important questions (such as the necessary fulfillment of stringent conditions) in the intervening centuries.

It is difficult to decide how to proceed at this point because so much was happening within basically the same time frame. In one sense, the rise of the Waldensian movement is not all that important, given that we do not even know for sure what Peter Waldès himself believed about the death penalty. On the other hand, it was in the context of this movement that a unique papal intervention occurred, for whatever reasons, that guaranteed for the future that whenever the death penalty was discussed in Roman Catholic circles, the text of that intervention had to be considered. So, it seems feasible at this point to sketch the rise of the Waldenses and then take a look at the first theologian to attempt a major response to this issue.

CHAPTER 3

The Waldensian No and the Thomistic Yes

I. Peter Waldès and Followers (1170s–c.1205)

II. Alan of Lille's *Against Heretics* (c.1200)

III. A Crucial Half-Century of Papal Policies
    A. Innocent III (1198–1216)
    B. Gregory IX (1227–1241)
    C. Innocent IV (1243–1254)

IV. St. Thomas Aquinas (1225–1274)
    A. The Purposes of Punishment
    B. Capital Punishment
    C. Recent Critiques

V. John Duns Scotus (1266–1308)

VI. Reaping the Consequences
    A. Executions of the Apostolici (1296–1306)
    B. The Knights-Templar Disaster (1307–1312)
    C. Inquisitorial Excesses (1335–1401)
    D. The Execution of John Huss (1415)
    E. The Execution of Joan of Arc (1431)

The Waldensian connection with capital punishment in the medieval West is something of an oddity. Opposition to the death penalty was only one small item on a long list of objections and disagreements that the group assembled in the late twelfth and early thirteenth centuries, and its place on that list was not destined to survive very long. It thus had an impact on subsequent Catholic treatment of capital punishment out of proportion to any initial significance.[1] The reason for this is that some forty years after the group's origins a statement renouncing the rejection of capital punishment was inserted into the profession of faith that a group of returning Waldenses was required to affirm upon reconciliation with the church. This papal addition was one of the few "official" Catholic affirmations about the death penalty before modern times. It thus held its place at the center of virtually every subsequent Catholic discussion of capital punishment. And yet, lacking Waldensian records, there are numerous uncertainties as to what actually occurred, why and when it became a problem, and who were its originators. To put things in more of a context will require a brief overview of earlier events.

I. PETER WALDÈS AND FOLLOWERS (1170s–c.1205)

Waldensian history is not a simple story to unravel.[2] This is true especially regarding the alleged objections to capital punishment. Exactly what those objections were and when they may first have been raised can only be surmised from other sources. There are no surviving accounts from the Waldensian side that can provide definite answers.[3]

In the mid-1170s a prosperous merchant of Lyons named Waldès gave up his family and fortune to undertake a life of penance and poverty, and set about preparing himself for preaching to the uneducated poor.

By 1177 he was traveling around Lyons as an itinerant street-preacher. In 1178 the archbishop of Lyons forbade this activity, but Waldès decided to fight for his right to preach. He and some companions went to Rome at the time of the Third Lateran Council (1179) to present their case. Pope Alexander III is said to have embraced Waldès and approved his poverty and piety, but he forbade him to preach unless invited to do so by local clergy. Englishman Walter Map was appointed to interrogate Waldès and his followers, and his mocking account of their ignorance is of interest, but nowhere in it is any mention made of any kind of Waldensian problem with the death penalty.[4] On his return to Lyons Waldès seems to have observed the prohibition against preaching for a time, but before long started again.

In 1180/1181 a grand diocesan council summoned Waldès to make a full profession of Catholic faith. He agreed. The document used on this occasion was a lengthy expansion of earlier professions used with recanting heretics and was "orthodox in every way."[5] It made no mention whatsoever of the death penalty. Waldès and his followers, in this early phase at least, were not heretics so much as "conscientious objectors" to clerical corruption, convinced that they were called by God to preach renewal by teaching the Bible to the people.[6]

In 1184 at the Council of Verona Pope Lucius III officially included the "Poor of Lyons" on a list of heretics condemned for preaching without permission, and this made them technically subject to repression and persecution, along with the Cathars and others whom they, ironically, strongly opposed. The surviving documents of this occasion contain no mention of any problem with the death penalty.

Two decades later, in 1205, there were conflicts occurring within the prospering Waldensian movement. Waldès himself was opposed to certain proposed organizational changes, and this led the "Poor of Lombardy" to split away from the original Poor of Lyons group. Waldès died, probably in this same year, so, strangely enough, we have no record from his lifetime about his personal stand on the death penalty. In other words, it is uncertain whether the Waldensian challenge to the legitimacy of the death penalty came from Waldès or from one or more of his followers.

In 1207 Durand of Osca, the only confidant of Waldès whose name and activities are known to us, took part in a three-way public debate at Pamiers among Waldensians, Catholics, and

Cathars. He found himself vehemently disagreeing with the Cathars and defending the right of the Catholic clergy to their office even when they were guilty of leading sinful lives. He also opposed some of the newer ideas of his own fellow preachers. So, according to the chronicler William of Puylaurens, he and associates "approached the Apostolic See and received penance. I have heard that they were given permission to live under a rule." As a new religious community, accepted as such by Pope Innocent III (three years before Francis of Assisi made a similar request), these "Catholic Paupers" (or Poor Catholics), prospered for a time and spread to parts of Italy, France, and Spain.[7]

In December 1208, when Durand and associates made their submission to the church, "Pope Innocent III accepted from them a profession of faith derived directly from the one made by Waldès in Lyons [twenty-four years earlier], now amended so that it...repudiated the errors commonly charged against the Waldenses."[8] Once again, there was no mention of the death penalty in this document.

In 1210, however,

> under the leadership of one Bernard Prim, some former Poor Lombards were also received into the Church, as the Poor Catholics had been, and took as their new name "the Reconciled Poor"....A new profession of faith was drafted....It included specific disavowal of the charges that were being made against the Poor Catholics: that they, like the Waldenses, denied the right of secular justice to impose the death penalty and that they did not show proper deference to the Catholic clergy.[9]

It was the statement about the death penalty, which was added to this profession of faith (that is, the 1210 version) and required of this second group of returning Waldenses, that was later incorporated into collections of official Catholic teachings. As it stands today in Denzinger's Handbook, it is the affirmation that

> the secular power can, without mortal sin, exercise judgment of blood, provided that it punishes with justice, not out of hatred, with prudence, not precipitation.[10]

The statement is obviously minimal and temperate, worth pondering as much for what it does not say as for what it does say. As Msgr. Charles Journet noted years ago, "Innocent did no more than defend a biblical and traditional truth."[11]

Thus it seems that in the Waldensian encounter, perhaps for the first time ever in the post-Constantinian church, the ethical validity of capital punishment was called into question.[12] Along with many other "unorthodox" assertions was apparently a contention that homicide (killing humans) was absolutely forbidden by the fifth commandment. God's law, it was claimed, is above human law, which must bow to God's supreme will. Judging from the content of Catholic responses, the Waldensian objectors used an arsenal of texts from the Bible and the Fathers, including a maxim of Pope Gregory I, who extended sanctuary "to those who had shed blood"; they also noted the irony of the fact that "Christian laws," which they felt should show mercy and kindness, were far more implacable and bloody than those of Moses. He, they pointed out, had limited revenge to "an eye for an eye," but Christian laws exacted a life for an eye or a tooth, or even for the theft of a piece of petty property. How was such action to be reconciled with the command of Christ to "love your enemies and do good to those who hate you"? The objectors seem to have granted that the state had the right to defend itself against wrongdoers but insisted that this right did not include or justify letting a state defile itself with a new crime by shedding the blood of criminals. They faulted a society that would kill heretics rather than bring them back to the way of justice and help them repent of their misdeeds. To execute people without such efforts would be to strike at their souls as well as their bodies, possibly condemning them to eternal perdition.[13] Such was apparently the Waldensian stance, at least as far as it can be reconstructed from the surviving works of their opponents.

The revolutionary challenge to the justifiability of the death penalty had an impact that still reverberates. It seized the high moral ground and pointed out the worst features of using the death penalty. It thus put the defenders of the system in an extremely awkward position, having to argue primarily for the legitimacy of an exception to the high Christian ideal of loving, preserving, and valuing all human beings, even one's worst enemies. It forced the "orthodox," ironically, to take up the defense of a very questionable practice.

The Waldensian challenge provoked a reaction that resulted in yet deeper church involvement with the death penalty. The real problem was more the practice rather than the general principle, as in the case of war. But this critique assailed the revered Roman legal system at its very heart, contending that it was in basic conflict with the teaching of Christ, and it did so in an unparalleled way. It would be a very long time indeed before Catholic thinkers would feel free enough to start reevaluating capital punishment. Before anything else could be said or done, the Waldensian critique would have to be rehearsed and put to rest. It forced proponents of the "traditional" use of the death penalty onto the defensive from the start.

Such a radical critique of the very institution of capital punishment in a Christian context was unparalleled. It was an affront to the basic belief system of the period. Churchmen found themselves in the curious position of having to leave other questions aside in any conversation about capital punishment and devote themselves first and foremost to defending the state's right to kill malefactors. It is thereby one of the oddest legacies in Western church history, resulting in a strangely skewed discussion that made preachers of the "good news" diligently elaborate arguments for the state's right to kill wayward members. If it had not been for the path taken after 1184, accepting burning at the stake as the proper way to deal with obstinate heretics, despite all the earlier objections, it does not seem likely that full ecclesiastical support would ever have been given to execution as a normal part of the legal systems of Christendom. Meantime, a man remembered more for his literary contributions in other areas seems to have been the first to attempt a more or less systematic response to the embarrassing Waldensian challenge.

II. ALAN OF LILLE'S *AGAINST HERETICS* (c.1200)

The "Universal Doctor," Alan of Lille, was an original thinker who taught at Paris from c.1157 to 1170, then spent the following fifteen years in the Midi, during which period he wrote

Against Heretics, rather cavalierly refuting all the theses of various "Waldenses, Albigenses, Jews, and Saracens." His defense of the basic legitimacy of the death penalty, countering the Waldensians' arguments against it, affords him the place of being in all likelihood the first direct apologist for capital punishment in the medieval church. By the same token, his polemic also seems to be the first and thus the oldest account of the Waldensian position itself, as viewed from the outside.[14]

Was the Waldensian objection to the death penalty just one more item stemming from the prevailing biblical literalism of the day? Was it picked up from the Cathars? Why was it conspicuously absent from Waldensian sources after 1400? These are questions in need of further attention, and Peter Biller has offered interesting and debatable hypotheses on all of them. In any event, Alan began his refutation of the purported Waldensian claims by agreeing completely with Peter the Chanter that death is indeed not the proper punishment for heresy as such. But then he immediately gave the argument a peculiar twist:

> Heretics ought not to be killed for their heresy, but should, on account of the Christian character they bear, be brought back to the bosom of the Church. But if they labor under any of those sins for which temporal death is assigned, they can be punished by a secular judge, provided he does so justly, not out of anger or rancor of spirit.[15]

In other words, heretics are not to be killed for their heresy, but if they can be convicted on any of the other capital charges in Roman law, it is quite all right to kill them, as long as your motives are pure. As in the case of the just-war theory, the potential for self-deception, manipulation, and abuse is obvious.

The passage reflects escalating tensions, and Alan's was a relatively moderate voice. The rising tide of heresy seemed to many to threaten the entire social order, so heretics had to be contained and punished. But Alan was aware of the patient pastoral stance of Augustine, which many of his contemporaries were putting behind them. Difficulties in establishing a uniform and effective policy stemmed in part from the disarray caused by conflicts between pope and emperor, but in 1177 Pope Alexander III and

Emperor Frederick Barbarossa made peace (the Treaty of Venice) and thereupon were able to unite imperial and ecclesiastical forces for an all-out war on heretics as simultaneously the greatest enemies of both church and state. The next eight decades were to be crucial as ecclesiastical and secular leaders joined in adopting full repression of all dissent as the official policy. Many factors contributed to this, and the accuracy of Henry Lea's overall analysis is beyond dispute.[16]

Alan of Lille was, incidentally, also in agreement with Hugh of St. Victor and Peter the Chanter that "ordinarily, death should not be the punishment for theft, but rather a thief should be made to pay restitution and be corrected by flogging." But after these minor concessions, Alan went on to repudiate what he saw as the basic Waldensian errors by countering their citations of authorities with a set of quotes of his own, presented as self-evidently restoring the truth. He insisted that his opponents had missed the original sense of the maxim of Pope Gregory I on sanctuary; it was, he said, simply meant to put ecclesiastical judges on guard against the temptation to pronounce the capital sentences themselves. As Imbert noted, the simplistic nature of the arguments on both sides is depressing. The texts, whether biblical or patristic, were read ahistorically, out of context; they were made to mean what the writer was already convinced they must mean to support his own presumptions. The exchange illustrates the perennial problem of proof-texting, a popular mode of argument used especially when the participants never have to confront one another in person. They speak out of worlds that seldom converge and never converse.[17]

It was only after Alan's death (1202) that the papal response to the Waldensians' objection to the death penalty took place, so it is worth asking again: What was the Waldensian objection really all about? It appears so seldom and so peripherally, and in such different formulations, that it is difficult from the documents alone to make absolute statements. A catalogue drawn up after 1250, attempting to summarize heretical tenets, has four variations on what the heretics' error or errors about capital punishment may have been:

1. "It is not permissible for anyone to kill." This is the most

straightforward version and would presumably be the expression of a belief derived from a simple reading of the fifth commandment taken literally, much as Lactantius had in the fourth century. It is a denial of any legitimate exceptions to the commandment against killing fellow humans, a stance of total pacifism.

2. "Punishments ought not to be inflicted." This could be quite a different and much broader objection, rejecting not just capital punishment but any humanly imposed punishment. It could conceivably be derived from a belief that only God has the authority to punish, and that humans claiming such authority are abusing their role and "playing God." It could thus be a kind of anti-authoritarianism that fits rather easily with the anti-sacerdotalism and anti-ecclesiasticism that were in the air and which characterized many of the dissenters of the day, especially the Cathars. As is obvious, it is a far greater threat than mere opposition to capital punishment, since it would be an attack upon the whole penitential system of the church as well as on all secular penal systems of any kind. It seems in effect to be a radical claim that no one in this life has the right to punish anyone else for anything at all.

3. "Justice ought not to be rendered by man." This in some ways parallels the previous objection, rejecting far more than capital punishment alone, but the key word here suggests a more specific objection. It is not punishment so much as judgment that is repudiated, recalling the admonition of Christ: "Judge not, and you will not be judged!" This was, after all, an explicit Christian teaching, one of the challenges that loyal evangelical followers had to try to take seriously and put into practice. Only God can know the heart of man, so how can the elaborate "judicial" systems of either church or state be justified? Thus, it is one more expression of the tension between canonical and evangelical outlooks.

4. "Justice should be deferred for the purpose of conversion."[18] This is yet another kind of objection to the death penalty, one which has a certain perennial relevance, especially for churchmen. Deliberately terminating a malefactor's life before he has made, or at least had a fair chance to make, his peace with God is reprehensible from virtually any pastoral perspective. But, as is quickly recognized, this is not at all as radical or comprehen-

sive an objection as the others, since it would seem to be concerned chiefly with the timing of an execution rather than with the execution itself. As long as the criminal were given all possible support for full repentance of his crimes, the point of this objection would seem to be basically met and the execution presumably sanctioned. This kind of thinking will account for some of the later forms of special gallows ministries within the church.[19]

All in all, many historical uncertainties remain about the precise nature and prevalence of objections to the death penalty in circulation at the end of the twelfth century. One certainty, however, is that none of them was effective enough to interfere with the trend that had cleared the way for ever deeper commitment to its use in the struggle to curtail the spread of heresy. The real irony was that the thirteenth century produced some of the ablest men ever chosen to occupy the papal chair, but they had to expend an extraordinary amount of their unusual talent on the bewildering and intractable problem of dealing with heresy. Understandably, they looked back to Augustine and the legacy of Roman law for solutions and were not only lured into using coercion, as Augustine and many others had, but also into using the final repression, the death penalty, which Augustine and many others had resisted.

III. A CRUCIAL HALF-CENTURY OF PAPAL POLICIES

A. *Pope Innocent III (1198–1216)*

The 1201 execution of Evrard of Chateauneuf as an incorrigible heretic included a revealing exchange. When he was handed over to the secular prince by the ecclesiastics who had found him guilty, the prince was willing to do one of two things: either execute him forthwith or set him free. The third option, which he rejected in the negotiations, was Peter the Chanter's preferred solution—life imprisonment. The prince's reasons for refusing were very practical, especially in view of the sudden upsurge of heresy: his prisons were simply too small and too costly to be used in such a way.

This exchange must be kept in mind when the role of Pope Innocent III is examined. In his famous decretal *Vergentis in Senium* (1199), announcing that "heretics were traitors to God, exactly comparable to traitors to Caesar in Roman Law,"[20] the penalty nonetheless was at that point only confiscation of property. In later letters he also proposed the use of legal infamy or exile as penalties. But when it came time for an official strategy to be put in place by the Fourth Lateran Council (1215), Innocent included the consignment of heretics to the secular authority for "due punishment." It is true that he did not mention or openly advocate the death penalty, but

> of equal significance, nowhere did he forbid it....By leaving
> the penalty to the prince's discretion, the Lateran Council
> of 1215 set the pattern for the thirteenth century, in which
> the *autodafé* became a standard fixture. The protests of Peter
> the Chanter and others...were relegated to oblivion for the
> remainder of the Middle Ages.[21]

Innocent III was undoubtedly one of the great popes in history and was faced with extraordinarily difficult decisions. Jerusalem's fall (1187), Emperor Henry VI's death (1197), the wildly powerful prophesying of Joachim of Fiore (d. 1202), and the upsurge of uncontrollable Catharism all contributed to the apocalyptic fear that gripped much of Europe when Innocent was elected pope at the age of 37. With unparalleled energy he undertook a broad array of activities to deal with the escalating problems.[22] Two of his strategies are of special interest in connection with capital punishment.

First, in trying to find worthy preachers to offset the errors of the Cathars, Innocent hit upon a new strategy: he decided in 1204 to invite the Cistercians to take a kind of emergency leave from their cloisters and enter the lists as popular preachers to provide solid instruction in Christian doctrine for the people. It was a good idea in theory, but the monks proved unsuited to the task. In eventually approving the founding of two new orders better suited to undertake that specific task, the Dominicans and the Franciscans came into being. They dramatically changed the face of the Christian church in myriad ways for the rest of the

Middle Ages and beyond. Part of their story is the use to which they were soon put, not only as preachers but also as inquisitors, in the escalating war against heresy.[23]

Second, during this time another damaging incident occurred. In January 1208 Innocent III was outraged when the Cathars murdered his faithful legate, the Cistercian Peter of Castelnau. The frustrated pope thereupon turned to the military model and launched the Albigensian Crusade (the first Crusade ever directed at internal Christian enemies). He offered this new kind of Crusader the same incentives and indulgences as those attached to the campaigns against the "infidels" in the Holy Land.[24] At Béziers, in one of the many bloodbaths that followed, some "7,000 people were massacred and the cathedral was destroyed...but what was intended as a forty-day punitive expedition dragged on for twenty years, and set the seal of approval on later violence."[25] The law of unintended consequences prevailed and what started out on the pretext of eradicating heresy turned into an all-out war of conquest between rival political parties enlisted to "save the faith."

Despite his energy, talents, and good intentions in trying to cure the church of the "sickness" of heresy, Innocent III found himself pushed to adopt yet harsher measures in the Lateran Council of 1215. Canon 3 made it official policy henceforth that heretics found guilty were to be handed over to the secular power for punishment; feudal lords were expected to expel them; bishops were to force the laity to denounce any known to them, and the accused were to be called before a special episcopal tribunal, where all the sanctions of canon law were to be applied. Any bishops who did not actively implement this process were subject to removal from office for neglect of duty.

This was already more than a rough sketch on the way to a fully elaborated Inquisition.[26] There is a parallel here between Innocent and Augustine: in their earlier days patience and persuasion were the chosen responses, but, disheartened by the obstinacy of some, their later frustration and loss of patience led them to accept the use of coercion in dealing with persistent heretics.[27]

B. Pope Gregory IX (1227–1241)

The actual foundation of the Inquisition came as a result of several developments in the first six years of the pontificate of Innocent's nephew, Pope Gregory IX. The decisive step was his constitution *Excommunicamus* of February 1231. Its most ominous feature was its incorporation into canon law of the harsh 1224 constitution of Emperor Frederick II, explicitly permitting the burning of heretics at the stake. This meant in effect that the previous ambiguity of *animadversio debita* was removed, and for the future the unambiguous meaning of the phrase for convicted heretics was that death was the standard punishment and burning at the stake was its specific form.[28]

A rash of executions quickly resulted from the zeal of the early inquisitors. In Germany, Conrad of Marburg waged such a campaign of terror in Mainz that he was assassinated in June 1233. In France, a Dominican, himself a former heretic, Robert le Bougre, staged notorious theatrical spectacles, burning ten heretics at once in the town square of Douai in March 1236 and managing a veritable holocaust in the presence of the King of Navarre, burning 183 Cathars in Champagne in May 1239. In 1244 over 200 Cathars were burned at the stake after the bloody siege of Montségur, provoked by the assassination of the inquisitor of Toulouse, William Arnaud.[29] In Italy, inquisitor Peter of Verona "turned the fight against heresy into a bloody political battle with what Hamilton has called 'Catholic gangs' (quasi-military lay confraternities) roaming the streets of Florence with the blessing of the Church."[30] Peter was bludgeoned to death by a group of Cathars in April 1252.

C. Pope Innocent IV (1243–1254)

Peter's assassination provoked Innocent IV to issue "the most terrible of all Bulls in the history of the Inquisition on May 15, 1252, *Ad Extirpanda.*"[31] The ablest in the line of extremely active lawyer-popes, Innocent with this bull "sought to render the civil power completely subservient to the Inquisition, and prescribed the extirpation of heresy as the chief duty of the State."[32] Something had obviously gone terribly awry in the initially legitimate search for a proper policy for dealing with heresy, and with this bull the policy went even further awry. The use of torture was officially introduced into the inquisitorial procedure as one more tool for ferreting out secret heretics. In effect, all the elements of a police state were assembled. The trend was further intensified by the 1256 decretal *Ut Negotium* of Pope Alexander IV, permitting inquisitors to absolve one another of any canonical irregularities incurred in their work. Torture thereupon had "a secure place in ecclesiastical inquisitorial procedure."[33]

Medieval European Christendom produced many marvelous results, of which its heirs can be justifiably proud, but one dark side of its evolution was this turn of events in standard penal practice. The high ideal of giving primacy to the other-worldly purpose of Christian faith, as conceived at the time, had unwittingly led to an inhumane this-worldly social order. By mid-century even the best of Christian theorists were hard-pressed to justify the situation on gospel ideals, and one effect was the ever deeper entanglement of churchmen in the unlimited sanctioning of violence.[34] It is impossible to know what the medieval Christian ethical assessment of the death penalty might otherwise have been if this intractable heresy dilemma had not overridden all other concerns.

IV. ST. THOMAS AQUINAS (1225–1274)

This was the ominous social setting in which Thomas Aquinas had to do his theorizing about the death penalty, and that fact cannot safely be set aside in reading him. Circumstances in his day were vastly different than they had been for Peter the Chanter and Alan of Lille some three-quarters of a century earlier, when it was still possible to take a public position maintaining that burning heretics was wrong. By mid-century a sea change had occurred, and the use of capital punishment for heresy was no longer a subject open to academic debate. Hundreds of people had been executed in the interim, and there was no sign of a slowdown in Thomas's lifetime. Because his limpid Latin style is so calm and unemotional, he makes it easy for his reader to forget the chaotic repressive social world in which he lived and wrote. But use of the death penalty is such a culturally conditioned question that it is essential to recall its historical context whenever it is being evaluated. So, especially in light of the tremendous influence Aquinas had on subsequent Catholic thinkers, his thoughts on the subject fully merit unusual attention, although he would have been the last to expect his work to be taken over wholesale without any critical questions being raised. The tradition he had inherited, combined with the context in which he lived, made for an especially problematic enterprise.

Thomas was only a teen-ager when the extraordinarily bitter feud between Pope Gregory IX and Emperor Frederick II reached a boiling point in 1239. "This was the signal for the outbreak of an ideological war which in fierceness, ferocity and depth of passion and disregard of all the accepted norms of warfare, has few, if any, parallels in medieval history."[35] And the family of Aquinas apparently was not on the sidelines. Rinaldo Aquino, thought to have been Thomas's older brother, served in the emperor's military forces up until 1245 when another pope, Innocent IV, formally deposed Frederick at the Council of Lyons. At that point "Rinaldo changed allegiance and fought with the armies of the Pope against Frederick."[36] The following year Rinaldo was arrested and executed with others for involvement in an alleged conspiracy to assassinate Frederick. It was clearly a terrible time for anyone to have to speculate about proper papal (and/or imperial) policies on capital punishment.[37] The lines were already too sharply drawn, the power-politics too belligerent, the atmosphere too volatile.

A. *The Purposes of Punishment*

Aquinas gave much thought to the topic of punishment in general in his published works.[38] This part of his teaching is so clear, so logical, and so sensible that some specific remarks made about capital punishment are all the more surprising when they are first encountered. One clearly needs to proceed carefully.

Thomas treats the role of punishment in his first major organic composition, *Commentary on the Sentences of Peter Lombard,* written in Paris in the mid-1250s. The question that raises the issue is "whether one sin could be punishment for another sin," and in his reply his first observation is that punishment functions as "medicine," sometimes to cure the wrongdoer, and at other times to deter others from imitating his misdeeds.[39] This dual remedial purpose for inflicting punishment recurs regularly in his later writings, but he also makes it clear that this is not the whole story. Citing Aristotle a few pages later, he notes that, even though it is justified, punishment is not always effective as medicine, "but it restores something lacking in the state of the universe...on account of the order of justice."[40] And he writes, "Punishment is satisfactory in two ways: as payment of a debt, and as medicine for preventing sin."[41] Drawing these texts together we see that he already has the major ingredients of what would become his mature formulation of the triple purpose of punishment. In modern terms, these purposes are usually given as *retribution* (repayment of the debt that is due), *rehabilitation* (medicine curing the individual wrongdoer), and *deterrence* (social "medicine" discouraging others from following the wrongdoer's example).

These texts do not reflect any special originality on the part of Aquinas, nor should they be expected to. By definition, what he was doing was commenting on traditional data found in Peter Lombard's collection of earlier opinions. He found the metaphors (both the fiscal and the medicinal) already prevalent in the standard sources of Christian thought, and he affirmed them as appropriate to his own understanding as well.

A few years later Aquinas started a second organic composition, his *Summa Contra Gentiles* (1258–1264?). In Book III he repeated his earlier position, explaining that "punishments are imposed by human law for the correction of vices; hence they are a kind of medicine," whereas divine punishments are imposed, not for their own sake, but "to maintain that order in which the good of the universe consists."[42] The same images recur, but with the interesting distinction that the medicinal goal is associated with human punishment and the retributive goal with divine punishment.

Aquinas's fully formulated thought on the purposes of punishment is found in Quaestio 87 in the Pars I–II of his *Summa Theologiae,* entirely given over to discussion of "the debt of punishment." He starts with the basic observation that punishment makes sense only in terms of its restoring some kind of violated order. Thus, one can be punished with a threefold punishment, corresponding to the three orders to which the human will is subject. First, a man's nature is subjected to the order of his own reason; secondly, it is subjected to the order of another human being who governs him in either spiritual or temporal matters, ... and thirdly, it is subjected to the universal order of divine government. Now, each of these orders is disturbed by sin, for the sinner acts against his reason, and against human and divine law. Wherefore he incurs a threefold punishment: one inflicted by himself, viz. the remorse of conscience; another inflicted by man; and a third inflicted by God.[43]

This concise passage, integrating into a harmonious whole all that has gone before, is characteristic of Aquinas at his best. At the same time, it serves as an excellent reminder that it is impossible to dig out of his writings a social or political philosophy that is not dependent on his theology.[44] Any distinction between sin and crime is "telescoped," since the human agent is subject to all three of these orders. Thus, one and the same deed disrupts the divine order, the human order, and the self order. The triple debt thus incurred calls for triple punishment to restore the triple order to which the human will should conform.[45]

If God provides the punishments that pay the debt incurred by violation of the divine order, and remorse of conscience is the punishment exacted by the self order, the only area that is left open is that of the violation of human law. The entire problem is how to determine appropriate punishments to enable the wrongdoer to pay his debt for disrupting society, civil or ecclesiastical. This is the perspective to be kept in mind when we move to Pars II–II, where, in Quaestio 68, he states that "in this life there is no punishment for punishment's sake. The time of last judgment has not yet come. The value of human punishment is medicinal, contributing either to the sinner's correction or to the good of the republic, the tranquility of which is secured by the punishment of sinners."[46]

At a later point he contends that "punishment may be considered in two ways:...under the aspect of punishment as such...whereby the equality of justice is restored...or under the aspect of medicine, not only healing the past sin but also preserving from future sin." (And, significantly,) "the punishments of this life are more of a medicinal character."[47]

B. Capital Punishment

Aquinas's general, balanced, humane theory about the purposes of punishment should be kept in mind when we come to the troublesome passages about the death penalty. Capital punishment, as we have seen, had entrenched itself deeply in church policy right before and during his time, especially because of the intractable problem of heresy. He had to make the best of a very bad situation, which continued to worsen throughout his own brief lifetime. He was not writing or thinking in a vacuum but rather was surrounded by the same extraordinary social turbulence in which the papacy and empire of his day were enmeshed.

There are two "celebrated" treatments of capital punishment in his writings. The first occurs in the *Summa Contra Gentiles* while he is arguing in defense of the general thesis that it is lawful for judges to inflict punishment. The Waldensian denial had set the parameters for this discussion. The first three paragraphs are straightforward, making standard logical points in general penal theory with which most reasonable persons would be likely to agree: 1) "It is just for the wicked to be punished, since by punishment the fault is restored to order." 2) "Men who are in authority over others do no wrong when they reward the good and punish the evil." 3) "What is needed to preserve the good cannot be evil in itself."

But then, after opening a fourth paragraph with the axiom that "the common good is better than the particular good of one person," the argument suddenly turns to the death penalty, using this principle as its justification:

> But the life of certain pestiferous men is an impediment to the common good, which is the concord of human society. Therefore, certain men must be removed by death from human society. Furthermore, just as a physician looks to health as the end of his work, and health consists in the orderly concord of humors, so too the ruler of the state intends peace in his work, and peace consists in "the ordered concord of citizens." Now, the physician quite properly and

beneficially amputates a diseased organ if it threatens the corruption of the body. Therefore, the ruler of a state executes pestiferous men justly and sinlessly, in order that the peace of the state may not be disturbed.[48]

The final sentence is undoubtedly another allusion to Pope Innocent III's addition to the ex-Waldensians' profession of faith a half-century earlier. But there is something deeply disturbing about the whole "gangrene analogy," and Aquinas himself seems to be aware of this.[49] He first (para. 6) invokes as would-be support for his position questionably relevant passages from 1 Corinthians 5, Romans 13, and 1 Peter 2, before taking up (para. 7) the texts used by his opponents from Exodus 20 and Matthew 5 ("thou shalt not kill") and Matthew 13 (the parable of the wheat and the weeds). After noting that they draw from this parable the lesson that "the wicked are not to be removed from among the good by killing them," and that they join to this (para. 8) the argument that "so long as a man is existing in this world he can be changed for the better,...and so he should not be removed from the world by execution, but kept for punishment," he dismisses all these out of hand (para. 9) as "frivolous arguments."

This is a rather bewildering assessment, coming from Aquinas. What he thereby tosses aside as not even worth considering happens to be the time-honored pastoral position adopted by St. Augustine, St. John Chrysostom, Bishop Wazo, and others, in applying the parable of Jesus in Matthew 13. This is certainly a very uncharacteristic move for Aquinas, since he is usually so respectful of his saintly predecessors' ideas, even when he ends up disagreeing with them. One thus gets the impression that something has spoiled the conversation here. Aquinas does not look any further than the latest source of these arguments, the condemned heretics of the previous generation, taking little note of the otherwise significant fact that highly respected Christian forebears found the very same arguments entirely persuasive rather than "frivolous." The real problem was that in the changed atmosphere and context of his day, these objections could no longer be safely entertained.

And yet, even after this curt dismissal, he ends up acknowledging that under certain circumstances "the execution of the wicked" could indeed be forbidden. It would have been most helpful for his later students and admirers had he at this point spelled out what he thought those special circumstances might be, but his cryptic remark is left without elaboration.

Some ten years later, when writing the *Summa Theologiae*, Aquinas showed that he was indeed aware of the very text in Chrysostom's homilies, as well as others, teaching that the meaning of the parable in Matthew 13 is that "the weeds signify heretics,...and therefore (it teaches that) heretics should be tolerated." But he circumvents this conclusion by, in effect, arguing that the parable cannot be applied here: "If heretics be altogether uprooted by death, this is not contrary to our Lord's command, which is to be understood of a case when the weeds could not be pulled up without uprooting the wheat."[50] In other words, if the weeds (heretics) are clearly identifiable targets that can be carefully isolated from the rest of the community, it is not only possible but appropriate to eradicate them, for then the conditions are sufficiently different that the parable does not apply.

Later in this section Aquinas has occasion once more to argue that capital punishment is not a violation of the divine commandment not to kill, and once more he does so with his "social security" argument.[51]

> Men may kill brute animals insofar as they are naturally ordained for man's own use, on the principle that the imperfect is for the sake of the perfect. But every part is related to the whole precisely as imperfect to perfect....If, therefore, the well-being of the whole body demands the amputation of a limb, say in the case where one limb is gangrenous and threatens to infect the others, the treatment to be commended is amputation. Now every individual person is, as it were, a part of the whole. Therefore, if any man is dangerous to the community and is subverting it by some sin, the treatment to be commended is his execution in order to preserve the common good.[52]

Thomistic commentators have been notoriously uncomfortable with this passage and the one that comes right after it, describing the sinner as "worse than a beast" and thus properly subject to execution.[53] Crowe remarks, "It is difficult not to see it as an argument that proves too much. A carrier of infection or a maniac may be as upsetting to the peace of society as any murderer; but one cannot accept that such should be executed."[54] Furthermore, it says nothing at all about limits, about proportion, about last resort, about the dangers of abuse or arbitrary application.[55]

Capital punishment was by this time so firmly entrenched, especially for dealing with obstinate heretics, that it was shielded from serious criticism, even from one as astute as Aquinas. This may be understandable, given the atmosphere of the time and the pressures on church leadership. Hindsight can criticize such policies long after the fact, but those immersed in them and unable to see any way out were obviously in a much more regrettable situation. It is thus all the more unfortunate that these passages, which are an embarrassment today,[56] and are so far from reflecting Aquinas at his best, were nonetheless destined to be repeated with confidence, even complacency, for some six or seven centuries, as virtually the last word on capital punishment by many Catholic moralists.[57]

C. Recent Critiques

At this point it is worth recalling those earlier passages of Aquinas on punishment in general. A case can certainly be made that, if it had not been for the fact that capital punishment had recently and regrettably become the final "authoritative" solution in the battle against heresy, his position on it might well have been otherwise. To speak of the purposes of punishment as being retribution, rehabilitation, and deterrence (individual and social), and to acknowledge that the first is more appropriately left to divine punishment, and that the aim of human punishment is more appropriately medicinal, quickly leads away from capital punishment as any kind of acceptable or defensible solution.

1. NICETO BLÁZQUEZ, O.P. (1985)

Recently commentators have been taking a more critical look than ever at the problematic passages of Aquinas on the death penalty. Niceto Blázquez, whose work in rehabilitating Augustine from earlier misconceptions has already been seen, turned his attention a decade later to Aquinas on the same subject.[58] Only a few of his major points can be summarized here.

a. The deep ambivalence over Christians having anything to do with the deliberate shedding of human blood is reflected by the canonical prohibition that made killing of any kind an impediment to ordination. Bloodshed was viewed as totally incompatible with the priestly ministry of the New Law, a position with which Thomas not only fully agreed but elaborated on.[59] "The act of homicide, even if inculpable, entails an irregularity. So a judge who justly condemns someone to death, or a cleric who kills someone in self-defense, incurs the irregularity, even if there was no intention of killing." Blázquez makes the point that this prohibition is rightly based on the "spirit and ethic of the Gospel," but that there is absolutely no biblical basis for restricting it to the clergy. It is this distinction that is at the root of the medieval problem: (a) the demands of the New Law are limited to the clerical caste, leaving the laity to live by a lower standard, which includes engaging in necessary bloodshed; (b) the clergy, however, while obligated to keep their own hands clean, were to appeal to the "secular arm" to do the necessary bloodshed for them in battling heretics.[60]

b. Blázquez has a number of criticisms of the passages on the death penalty in the *Summa*. In general, Thomas proceeds here more as an Aristotelian philosopher, drawing cold rationalist conclusions from a notion of natural law, than as a Christian theologian, dealing directly with the pastoral goals of the gospel.[61] Especially in his medical analogy, justifying the killing of malefactors as gangrenous members that threaten the welfare of the whole body, the argument bristles with difficulties of equivocation. *Whole* and *part* do not mean the same thing in a social body as in a physical body. "A person is not related to a society as to his ultimate end as an arm is to the body. So it is not reasonable to deduce that a person can be killed in function of the society to which he belongs, since the specific goal of every human person transcends the community."[62] Otherwise, the analogy is open to absolutizing the social order, submerging the human person to inferior status, thereby giving excessive authority to Aristotle and not taking sufficient account of the New Law.

c. Blázquez concludes by saying that "the thesis sustained by Saint Thomas is wrong." Even on the level of strict human reason it is deficient, because it tries to apply the physical principle of the whole and its parts to the field of human justice. But it is a characteristic of Aquinas's genius that among the principles and criteria he teaches are those needed to correct his own occasional slips, as in this case of capital punishment.

2. BRIAN CALVERT (1992)

Another recent critic of Aquinas's position is Brian Calvert, who has suggested that "there is more than an even chance that if Aquinas were alive today he might well turn out to be an abolitionist."[63] He bases this conjecture on two straightforward points, using Aquinas's own logic. First, the traditional principle of the ethics of self-defense, as expressed in the *Summa* (II–II, q.64, a.7): "It is legitimate to answer force with force, provided it goes no further than due defense requires." Second, "if he (Aquinas) were persuaded that such a level of force (as the death penalty) was not necessary and the same results could be achieved without it, then...he would be committed to the use of less severe penalties." The logic of this argument is so transparent that it has become a standard point in modern Catholic discussions of capital punishment.[64] Nor is this the only argument pointing in the direction of Calvert's conjecture. The death penalty, as used in modern Western society, has great difficulty fulfilling any of Aquinas's own stated purposes of punishment. In the open climate of our day, it is by no means fanciful to suggest that Thomas himself would be the first to admit this and to cast his vote for the sanctity of life over death.

There is thus good reason for contending that, if Aquinas had not been burdened with all the cultural baggage of the imperial state religion, struggling with the maddening problem of how to deal with heretics, and crippled by the earlier acceptance of execution as specifically the due punishment of obstinate offenders, higher gospel values could have come back into play.[65] But the complications of history are not so easily disentangled. The first serious questions about the legitimacy of the death penalty had come from sources that were branded as heretical, and that set the framework in which all subsequent discussion would have to take place. Doubts of any kind about the propriety of the death penalty were thus likely to put one under suspicion of heresy, ironically qualifying one as a prime candidate in inquisitorial eyes for becoming a victim of that very punishment. The ecclesiastical dilemma thereby created was destined to remain without solution for another five centuries, and even thereafter was only slowly, partially, and imperfectly addressed.

As one final reflection of what had happened in Western Christendom by Aquinas's day, there is a unique work that appeared less than ten years after his death. Philippe de Beaumanoir's *The Books of the Customs and Usages of Beauvaisians* (1283) has as its longest chapter the one devoted to crimes, detailing which were capital and how death was to be administered. The major capital crimes were "murder, treason, violent homicide, rape, arson, robbery, heresy, counterfeiting, escape from prison, poisoning, and attempted suicide." The normal method for imposing death was by "dragging and hanging," except that "heretics were burned to death and counterfeiters were boiled before being hanged."[66] The penal system of Christian Europe had become a veritable nightmare and was destined to get a lot worse in its prodigious use of the death penalty after the thirteenth century before there was enough serious thought, effort, and agitation for doing anything positive to change it.[67]

V. JOHN DUNS SCOTUS (1266–1308)

The particular nuance for which the "Subtle Doctor" is remembered in discussing capital punishment came in his best-known work, *Commentary on the Sentences of Peter Lombard*. There he initially interpreted the fifth commandment in an absolute sense, much as Lactantius had in the fourth century. The prohibition of the killing of humans by humans in any deliberate way must be understood "ut jacet," that is, literally and absolutely, equally valid whether concerning innocent or guilty parties. "Thou shalt not kill." Period.

With the general principle thus established, the implication is that if any killing is ever to be considered licit, it could only be by way of some explicit exception made by God himself. To override the absolute nature of the prohibition, it would thus be necessary to show the exception as clearly stated in the revealed word of God, the Bible. Some such exceptions are present in the Old Testament: adultery, blasphemy, and other offenses that have death assigned to them as the divinely mandated penalty.

The novelty of this Scotist position was that at least it set limits to the lawfulness of capital punishment in two ways: (1) there was no justification for making something a capital crime if it was not already so characterized in the Bible. An obviously relevant example was theft. No one was authorized anywhere in the Bible to take the life of someone who had stolen material goods. Hence, the death penalty was improper, not being a divinely authorized punishment for theft. The same lack of authorization also made suicide wrong.

There were, moreover, cases where the New Testament had canceled the penalties of the Old. For example, the woman taken in adultery whom Jesus refused to condemn (John 8). He had, in Scotus's opinion, thereby explicitly annulled death as the assigned penalty for the female in cases of adultery.[68]

It was an interesting position that at least put some limits to the kinds of crimes for which the vaunted "right of the state to execute" could be used, but it was not an argument that was likely to convince anyone who was not already committed to a "voluntarist" theory of law.

VI. REAPING THE CONSEQUENCES

The practice of capital punishment and the theory sanctioning it, as worked out in classical form by Aquinas, remained firmly in place without significant modification for the following centuries. The repressive program to try to curtail and control the "disease" of heresy by lethal violence was the order of the day. It is worth pondering some of the later history that might have unfolded in different ways and had different consequences, had it not been for this development and the fondness for the "final solution" of capital punishment of dissenters that went with it. Examples could readily be multiplied.

A. Executions of the Apostolici (1296–1306)

The history of the group known as the Apostolici illustrates the tragic dimensions of the problem. Gerard Segarelli had founded this group in Parma in 1260 to pursue the ideal of poverty. The suspicion of heresy automatically descended on such groups, and they often came into conflict with the local clergy, especially in their practice of begging. Four of Segarelli's followers were burned at the stake in 1296. He was imprisoned until 1300, when he too was executed. This use of the death penalty did not deter Friar Dolcino from taking over as leader and enjoying great success in winning over hundreds of peasants by his preaching. So the incumbent warrior-bishop of Vercelli and his inquisitors raised their own army and laid siege to the camp of the Apostolici, killing about 400 of them and taking 140, including Dolcino, captive. The elimination of the "cancer of heresy" in a small part of rural Italy was undoubtedly achieved quite effectively by torturing and burning to death all the survivors, including Dolcino, in 1306.[69] But the peace achieved was the peace of the graveyard and brought little more than sadness to church, state, or posterity.

The death penalty had become a major instrument for maintaining religious uniformity; it had been officially embraced as appropriate and integrated into both theory and practice of church life. Voices of disapproval had fallen silent, and the scaffold and the stake became more and more entrenched as unquestionably appropriate, standard features of a "Christian culture," a normal part of the status quo. It is sobering to realize how unnecessary some of the most unfortunate episodes and incidents of Western church history were, tragedies that would not have happened if this ready accommodation and approval of sanctioned bloodletting had not so centrally established itself at the heart of Christendom. An especially painful instance was the following, which was due more to the greed of a French king than to any kind of justice.

B. The Knights-Templar Disaster (1307–1312)

The use of the death penalty to exterminate groups that held identifiably heretical views was bad enough. But, once allowed, it provided a gruesome tool for more nefarious uses as well. This danger was nowhere better illustrated than in the tragic history of the destruction of the Knights Templar by King Philip IV of France. "The trial of the Templars was a scandal of injustice which hardly has its equal in history."[70] And Pope Clement V not only went along with the sordid executions of hundreds of innocent Templars but issued the bull *Pastoralis Praeeminentiae* ordering "the kings of all Christian lands to follow Philip's example and arrest the Templars in their countries...in the name of the papacy."[71] Even though the Council of Vienne found almost unanimously that the order was not guilty of the heresy of which it was accused, Clement, with King Philip seated at his side in solemn conciliar assembly, abolished the Order of the Temple "by an irrevocable and perpetually valid decree," *Vox in Excelso,* of April 3, 1312, at the expense of both his own reputation and integrity and that of the office he held. His sorry address on that occasion, with its "farcical explanation" to cover up what was really going on, remains one of the lowest points in all papal history. Both Clement and Philip died the following year, and Dante, in his *Divine Comedy,* saw fit to put both of them firmly in hell.[72]

The bewildering episode fairly bristled with ironies. (Such an order would never have come into being in the first place without the invention of the Crusade; the creation of such unlikely "monk-knights" would have been virtually inconceivable without the total romanticization of soldiering; the imposition of repeated torture and the final burning of the victims would have been impossible without the anti-heresy inquisition apparatus put in place during the previous century, etc., etc.) But once more, the worst part of it could not have happened if the abusive availability of capital punishment to get rid of human obstacles to royal ambition had not enjoyed the church's full seal of approval.

The tragedy of the Templars unfolded at the start of the "Babylonian Captivity" of the papacy in Avignon (1305–1403), where Clement had decided to settle. This prolonged absence from Rome in turn provided "an alternative papal capital and administration" that helped to provoke and prolong the Great Western Schism (1378–1415) with its scandalous proliferation of popes, anti-popes, and anti-anti-popes. By developing a greater papal bureaucracy and upper-class lifestyle, Avignon also contributed to the atmosphere that allowed many of the aberrations of the "Renaissance Papacy" to develop, all of which contributed greatly to the dissipation and virtual collapse of papal prestige and authority. The drift from ideals and some of the lamentable consequences were more accentuated and scandalous than in the previous ages.[73]

C. Inquisitorial Excesses (1335–1401)

If the Albigensian Crusade in Languedoc stands out as a tragic turning point for engaging in intramural Christian bloodshed, the place that came to be called "the fourteenth-century Languedoc" because of the purging that took place in "purifying the faith" was Bohemia. (Archbishop Jan IV of Prague [1301–1343] had to stay in the Curia in Avignon for eighteen years to free himself and his diocese of the suspicion of heresy.) The impact was unparalleled for the future of central Europe. Inquisitor Havel of Hradec, for instance, according to the surviving records, tried over 4,400 people between 1335 and 1355, condemning about 5 percent of them to execution at the stake.[74]

The controversies over the meaning and requirements of evangelical poverty plagued the Franciscan movement throughout the thirteenth and fourteenth centuries, and church policy stiffened first toward the "Spiritual Franciscans," then turned violent toward their successors, the Fraticelli. One of the surviving narratives depicting an ugly slice of medieval life describes "how Friar Michael was burned." It is an anticlerical account of the execution of Friar Michael da Calci, burned at the stake in Florence in 1389, by the bishop's wicked "college of Pharisees" (Inquisition), who lie, cheat, and torture Michael as he patiently accepts his suffering like Christ, falling to his knees dead when his ropes burn through, and deeply impressing the bystanders by his pious courage.

> While folk went homeward, the greater part thought it an ill deed, and they could not say enough evil of the clergy. One said, "he is a martyr," and another, "he is a saint," and

another the contrary. And thus there was greater noise of
this deed in Florence than there ever had been.[75]

Inquisitor Petrus Zwicker found there were enough Waldensians flourishing in the fourteenth century to keep a full-time
inquisitor busy. Prior of a Celestine monastery, he took his
assignment seriously and began hearings in 1391 in Erfurt
(where Luther was to become a student a century later). He then
went to the Brandenburg March and Pomerania, where he discovered a hitherto unknown Waldensian center, and in two years
there (1392 to 1394) "he tried some 500 Waldenses....In 1401 he
condemned Waldenses in Hungary, and also made trips back to
Austria and Slovakia. In the space of ten years, more than 1,000
people stood before him, and the numbers of those who feared
and hated him must have been much vaster." It is understandable
that the earlier Waldensian rejection of violence (including the
death penalty) disappeared from their tenets as "the constant
pressure of the Inquisitions also radicalized Waldensian teachings."[76] One of their most popular preachers and leaders, Frederick Reiser, linked the Waldensians with the Hussites, stimulating
the exchange of religious ideas between the two groups. He was
captured by the Inquisition and executed in Strasbourg in 1458.
In the Alpine Valley the conflict continued, and a Crusade was
actually organized against the Waldenses there as late as 1488.

D. The Execution of John Huss (1415)

In England John Wycliffe and his followers came into conflict with the authorities, and the result was that eventually the
first national anti-heresy law was enacted, the parliamentary
statute of 1401, *De Haeretico Comburendo*. It spelled out the way in
which the full apparatus of state authority was to be brought to
bear on those accused of preaching and teaching "new doctrines
and heretical opinions," and if offenders did not abjure, they
were to be "burnt before the people in a conspicuous place, that
such punishment may strike fear into the minds of others, so that
no such wicked doctrines...or their supporters...may be in any way
tolerated."[77] Lollard William Sawtrey was the first victim to be
burned, and, once the rebellion of Sir John Oldcastle was put

down in 1414, his burning followed in 1417. It must be admitted that, especially when their numbers were small, the extermination of heretics was often effective in stemming the tide of heresy. But it is highly questionable whether instilling the fear of being arrested and subjected to capital prosecution for personal religious views is a commendable way to motivate any kind of sincere Christian belief or conduct. A thousand years of the Constantinian-Theodosian policy of using state force to maintain religious uniformity had passed, and its lure was as attractive as ever.

Religious dissent, of course, does not cease just because more mechanisms of control have been developed and selected individuals and groups of dissenters have been wiped out. When the fathers of the Council of Constance condemned and burned John Huss in 1415 and his colleague Jerome of Prague in 1416, their presumed intentions backfired badly. King Richard II's marriage to Anne of Bohemia was one factor not taken into account, since it brought with it opportunities for Wycliffite and Hussite ideas and outlooks to intertwine, proliferate, and anticipate some of the yet greater dissent of the next century.[78] Had there been a St. Augustine, Bishop Wazo, Peter the Chanter, or Alan of Lille among the Council Fathers at Constance to protest the idea of burning the Hussite leaders, on the basis of early Christian abhorrence of bloodshed, how much of the subsequent carnage might have been avoided?[79]

But such was not to be. As soon as word of Huss's execution reached Bohemia, the Czechs rioted in Prague, "the nobility united in a Hussite brotherhood, quite openly supported by the queen...and obedience was practically withdrawn from the bishop."[80] A papal interdict on the city only made things worse. City councillors who opposed Huss were thrown from the windows of city hall, and before long all Bohemia was in revolt, declaring itself for Huss and against the official church in council in Constance. The tangled history of the next two centuries illustrates all too well the potential for catastrophe when the chosen route is violence. The emergence of the ultra-militaristic Taborites, convinced that they were called to annihilate the enemies of God by the sword, was not that far removed in ideology from the Crusader myths. Much of the killing may have occurred anyway, but it is certainly worth pondering the fact that it was sparked by well-meaning churchmen at Constance, acting in open violation of the emperor's promised safe-conduct to Huss. Their decision to use the death penalty as the instrument of choice for dealing with John Huss marks one of the bleakest, blindest moments of Western Christian history. Historian J. W. Thompson was of the opinion that "the Reformation of the sixteenth century might have been prevented if the Wycliffite and Hussite movements had been given a hearing at Constance."[81] At least, such a hearing would have been far more in line with the ethical principles to which the churchmen at Constance were supposed to be committed but which were obscured by the illusion of an "easier" way of dealing with differences, that is, by executing the persons who held them.

E. The Execution of Joan of Arc (1431)

The burning of Joan of Arc a few years later was another graphic illustration that something was very wrong with the system. Once the compromise was accepted, and the ecclesiastical system immersed in the power politics of the time, with no principled objection to the use of lethal force against heresy, it was open to manipulation in untold ways. Even though Joan's rehabilitation trial of 1456 was "a better example of inquisitorial procedure at work,"[82] the pathos is all the greater, since even the fairest of trials could not undo the principal consequence of the first trial; because of the ready availability of capital punishment, Joan was twenty-five years dead before her name was cleared.

Admittedly, Joan of Arc will forever be an enigma when it comes to Christian principles and bloodshed. If the very notion of a Christian warrior is in itself paradoxical and ambiguous, it becomes agonizingly so in Joan. "She felt called by God, she thought her battles just and her actions correct...[but] despite her armor, her sword, and her willingness to lead troops into the thick of battle," she carried a white banner with the fleur-de-lys on it, so that she would not have to draw her sword, and later she proudly insisted that she had never killed.[83] The greater shame was that her executioners could not say the same.

The upshot of four centuries of justifying ever more strongly the use of the death penalty as a necessity for defending orthodoxy and preserving society was that the stage was set for even worse immersion in Christian bloodshed. The nagging questions had long since been put aside and with full theological warrant a culture of death flourished at the center of Western Christendom as well as throughout its many provinces. It would not be long before other than Waldensian voices began to be heard expressing their disapproval.

CHAPTER 4

Renaissance and Reformation Dilemmas

I. Six Renaissance Popes and the Spiral of Violence
   A. Nicholas V (1447–1455)
   B. Pius II (1458–1464)
   C. Sixtus IV (1471–1484)
   D. Alexander VI (1492–1503)
   E. Julius II (1503–1513)
   F. Leo X (1513–1521)

II. Three Reformation Era Writers
   A. Thomas More's *Utopia* (1516)
   B. Martin Luther's Augustinianism (1520)
   C. Francisco de Vitoria's Thomism (1530s)

III. Popes of the Tridentine Reform and the Death Penalty
   A. Paul III (1534–1549)
   B. Julius III (1550–1555)
   C. Paul IV (1555–1559)
   D. Pius IV (1559–1565)
   E. Pius V (1566–1572)

IV. Roman Executions After the Council of Trent
   A. Gregory XIII (1572–1585)
   B. Sixtus V (1585–1590)
   C. Clement VIII and Giordano Bruno (1592–1605)
   D. The Dilemma of Gallows-Pietism

V. Sixteenth-Century Catholic Catechesis
  on Capital Punishment
   A. The Catechisms of Peter Canisius (1554–1557)
   B. The *Roman Catechism* (1566)
     1. Its Composition
     2. Its Teaching About the Death Penalty

After the developments of the eleventh century, which involved departures from earlier ideals, it is tempting to ask whether these changes may help to account for some of the later church problems. The notorious deficiencies of the Renaissance popes need not be rehearsed here other than to note that

> a new era began with the election of Nicholas V in 1447, and ended during the pontificate of Clement VII with the sack of Rome in 1527. Through the whole of this period the Popes acted more as monarchs than as pontiffs, and the secularisation of the See of Rome was carried to its utmost limits.[1]

Some of their less than ideal conduct during these eighty years was in the troublesome areas of violence, killing, warfare, and revenge. The particular anomaly of interest here is their ready use of capital punishment without any qualms. Although they were clearly acting in conformity with the expectations and standards of their time, proper valuing of human life was an area as much in need of reform as simony, concubinage, and materialism. A half-dozen examples may serve as potent reminders of how papal conduct in this strange period had strayed far from gospel ideals.

I. SIX RENAISSANCE POPES AND THE SPIRAL OF VIOLENCE

Why was the Renaissance plagued with such an extraordinary escalation of violence and vengeance? The question has often been asked, though attempted answers have not always won consensus. Well over a half-century ago Gabriel Maugain pointedly raised the issue of how to account for the "shocking antithesis" of Renaissance Italy, with its extraordinarily high cultural achievements side by side with its unsurpassed indulgence in vicious, inhumane violence.[2] Maugain catalogues the unbelievable bloodshed—by individual serial-killers, by bandits, by

133

mobs, by clerics, by the nobility, by the courts, and so on. The way in which lethal violence was condoned and used even at the highest church levels during this period was, it seems, part of the legacy derived from the earlier lapses already spoken of. Basic Christian values were being totally ignored. The following are by way of example.

A. Pope Nicholas V (Tommaso Parentucelli) (1447–1455)

The first of the Renaissance popes, Nicholas V was a learned man with broad cultural interests, a bibliophile who was the real founder of the Vatican Library. He did many useful things for the Rome of his day, such as taking measures to eliminate its mercenary troops. Two memorable events during his reign tell much about the time. In 1452 he presided over the crowning of Emperor Frederick III in St. Peter's Basilica, the last such imperial coronation to take place in Rome. The old order was indeed passing away in Latin Christendom. But the very next year, 1453, brought the shocking news that Constantinople—the city of Constantine—the second Rome—the center of Eastern Christendom for over a thousand years—had fallen to the Turks. Nicholas belatedly tried to organize a Crusade to resist the disaster, but to no avail. The Mediterranean world had changed dramatically and was soon to be transformed yet further.[3]

Another incident earlier in 1453, however, well illustrates the point being singled out here. A plot was discovered, the brainstorm of Stefano Porcaro, a republican dreamer who wanted to take over Rome and deliver it from "priestcraft." Nicholas had dealt with him leniently in several earlier encounters. This time, however, when it became clear that Porcaro was fully armed and ready to assassinate Nicholas and his entourage, if necessary, there was no thought of mercy. Nicholas had Porcaro and his fellow conspirators promptly executed.[4] In the power politics of the day this was taken for granted as the only appropriate reaction, but it raises troublesome questions as to what had happened at the core of Western Christendom. What would have been done in such a situation if the age-old teaching and example of Jesus had been consulted instead of the norms of the violent culture of the day?

B. Pope Pius II (Aeneo Silvio Piccolomini) (1458–1464)

Perhaps the most fascinating of the popes of the high Renaissance, Pius II so converted and reformed his own lifestyle upon election to the papacy that he made many enemies in high places and became the object of at least one conspiracy, which was easily foiled. But his conception of what an ideal pope ought to be was surprisingly narrow. Still shaken by the loss of Constantinople ten years earlier, he called a secret consistory in 1463 to lay before the College of Cardinals his master plan. He began with a sober confession, acknowledging humbly that

> the luxury and pomp at our Court is too great, and this is why we are so detested by the people that they will not listen to us, even when what we say is just and reasonable. What do you think is to be done in such a shameful state of things?

With that pointed question forcefully asked, it was a promising moment of potential reform, but the only answer he could come up with for changing things was the old military model:

> We have determined to proceed in person against the Turks, and by word and deed to stir up our Christian princes to follow our example. It may be that, seeing their Teacher and Father, the Bishop of Rome, the Vicar of Christ, a weak and sickly old man, going to war, they will be ashamed to stay home. Should this effort also fail, we know of *no other means* to try. We are well aware that at our age we are going to meet an almost certain death. But let us leave all to God, his holy will be done! Nevertheless, we are too weak to fight sword in hand, and this is not the priest's office. But we will imitate Moses, who prayed upon a height while the people of Israel were doing battle with the Amalekites. On the prow of a ship or on the summit of a mountain, we will beseech our Lord...to grant us deliverance and victory.[5]

Pius continued his dream by challenging the cardinals and the Curia to join him after selling all superfluous chalices and ornaments, so as to outfit a major fleet that could sail off to win the world for Christ by holy war. On June 18, 1464, in failing health, he took the Crusader's cross in St. Peter's and led the papal procession to Ancona to set sail, but they found no fleet ready for them upon arrival. Finally, on August 12, a mere twelve galleys showed up in the harbor and the heart-broken pope died two days later. The fiasco stands as a sad commentary on faded ideals. Leading Christians into holy war, armed to the teeth and determined to kill all enemies, had somehow become the violent vision of where and how Christian leadership ought to lead.

C. Pope Sixtus IV (Francesco della Rovere) (1471–1484)

The name of this gifted Franciscan is forever associated with the magnificent Sistine Chapel. He also founded the Sistine Choir, the Vatican Archives, and was the "second founder" of the Vatican Library. With his manifold building projects and boundless energy he "transformed Rome from a medieval into a Renaissance city."[6]

Sixtus, however, was also more than marginally associated with the unseemly domestication of violence. Besides proclaiming two different Crusades against the Turks, neither of which received much response, he immersed the papacy in the petty politics of the Italian peninsula to an unprecedented degree. He actually launched a full-scale war against Florence, incited the Venetians against Ferrara, then changed sides, imposing ecclesiastical penalties on Venice with no apparent qualms about such flagrant abuse of his papal power.

Two other events, both in 1478, also contributed to the trend of Christians wantonly shedding the blood of other Christians: (1) Sixtus authorized Ferdinand and Isabella to establish a Spanish Inquisition under virtually unlimited government control, a development that was eventually to result in one of the most disastrous chapters in Western church history; and (2) his proximity to the Pazzi conspiracy against the Medicis was nothing less than scandalous. (1478 was actually the year of the birth of the illegitimate son of Giuliano de' Medici, Giulio de' Medici, who later became Pope Clement VII.) The Pazzi conspirators fell upon Giuliano de' Medici and assassinated him during High Mass in the Cathedral of Florence. The very setting seemed to cry out for the Christian world to awaken from this sacrilegious nightmare. Giuliano's brother Lorenzo was injured in the same plot, but escaped from the cathedral alive. Francesco de' Pazzi, Girolamo Riario (a nephew of the pope), and Francesco Salviati, the archbishop of Pisa, were the chief conspirators, and vengeance against them was swift and bloody.

> The slaughter of the guilty at once began. Salviati, his brother, and his nephew, with de' Pazzi, were all hung up together from the window-bars of the Signorial Palace. Then the ropes were cut, so that the bodies fell amidst the crowd, where they were torn to pieces, and the severed heads and limbs borne in triumph through the streets. All who were supposed to be enemies of the Medici, whether guilty or innocent, were butchered. The two assassins who had fallen upon Lorenzo had their noses and ears cut off before they were killed.[7]

Even though Sixtus apparently was not directly responsible, his well-known hatred for the Medici clan and his fear of their power politics played a crucial role. Ludwig Pastor expressed his personal opinion that "open warfare (against the Medici) would certainly have been more worthy of a Pontiff than participation in a political plot, even had it involved no bloodshed." Whether or not waging "open warfare" could ever be a "worthy" project for a pope, it is abundantly clear that Sixtus's policies left the gospel entirely out of the equation. The long-accepted cycle of violence had been more than domesticated. In a dramatic reverse of the practice of sanctuary, here it was the house of God that was intentionally selected as the scene for perpetrating the bloodshed. The virus of violence was out of control with no sign of any effective antidote.[8]

D. Pope Alexander VI (Rodrigo Borgia) (1492–1503)

Alexander's misconduct in manifold ways is legendary, so it may be superfluous to single out his shortcomings involving violence, since so many other Christian standards were being violated. Even though the degree of his direct involvement in the worst skulduggery of his son, Cesare Borgia, is debatable, there were yet instances where there is no doubt of his participation, such as the case of the execution of four leaders at Senigallia in 1502.[9]

However, the most notorious instance of his recourse to capital punishment was the execution of the fiery Dominican friar Girolamo Savonarola and his companions in Florence in 1498. The surviving letters between Alexander and Savonarola as the conflict intensified stand as a permanent record testifying to the extreme difficulties and bitterness in which both were immersed before the "final solution" was carried out. The totally different worlds they lived in could hardly have been painted more graphically as each traded thunderbolts, seriously pronouncing one another excommunicated and eternally lost. But the pope's religio-political use of the death penalty to exterminate the bothersome preacher was an action that should have been unthinkable rather than taken for granted and was "the blackest mark of all on the disgraceful reign of Alexander VI."[10] It seemed perfectly logical at the time only because lethal violence had long since been adopted as the normal way of settling differences in that cultural context. Ironically, part of Savonarola's "heresy" was his daring (Augustinian) belief that the death penalty was wrong, that "no one ought to be put to death."[11]

E. Pope Julius II (Giuliano della Rovere) (1503–1513)

With the collapse of the Borgia faction, a rival force came into power. This time it was not a pope's son who wielded the sword (as Cesare Borgia had for Alexander VI), but the pope himself who took it in hand. Julius II, the endlessly warring soldier-pope, insisted on leading his own troops on the battlefield in a long series of convoluted combinations and conspiracies in petty Italian politics. The people called him "il Terribile" as he carried the military model to its logical conclusion, actually a *reductio ad absurdum*.

> His efforts...caused infinite bloodshed and distress....He exhausted and demoralized Italy by his wars....He betrayed his spiritual trust by his extreme concentration on secular affairs.[12]

This bizarre chapter in church history demonstrated that once the earlier tendencies were allowed to prevail, the trend toward diminished regard for human life led to the acceptance of violence and bloodshed as ordinary conduct, the way things are in the "real" world, even at the heart of the church. Capital punishment as a link in this chain, readily justified and regularly applied as part of God's work, was one more weapon by which to extend political goals. When Michelangelo made a three-times life-size bronze statue of Julius, it was Julius who, quite fittingly, instructed him to place a sword rather than a book in his upraised hand. This symbolism was all too lucid. The gospel had been put aside for the weapons of war. But the irony could hardly have been missed when, in 1511, a disenchanted crowd pulled down the statue of the warrior-pope while he was still alive and broke it into a thousand pieces. The message was clear.

F. Pope Leo X (Giovanni de' Medici) (1513–1521)

Our final example takes us to the start of the Protestant Reformation. Leo X became a cardinal at 17 and pope at 37. This second son of Lorenzo the Magnificent happened to be on the papal throne at the time of Martin Luther's initial protest against Roman abuses (1517). Leo X was a man of considerable talent but nonetheless became known as "a devious and double-tongued politician and an inveterate nepotist"[13] who was constantly involved with war. Before he became pope he marched at the head of the papal army and, in 1511, in a battle at Ravenna, was taken prisoner but managed to escape. The next year he regained political control of Florence and was its temporal ruler when he was elected pope. His total immersion in Italian peninsular politics led him to wage a disastrous war in 1516, trying to install one of his nephews as duke of Urbino. Then, in 1517, the year that Martin Luther posted his ninety-five theses in Wittenberg, Leo made a preemptive political strike, invoking the death penalty against Cardinal Alfonso Petrucci, the leader of a group of disaffected cardinals whose plot to poison him had been discovered and thwarted.

It would be difficult to imagine a more deplorable departure from nonviolent ideals than this series of events. Besides avenging himself on the captured conspirators, Leo waited three years to lure back to Rome the one conspirator who had escaped, Gianpaolo Baglioni. By subterfuge he had him seized and beheaded in the Castel Sant'Angelo in 1520, the year in which he also issued his bull of excommunication against Martin Luther.[14] Such was the use of the death penalty by some of the Renaissance popes, and few, if any, objections or criticisms were raised against it.

II. THREE REFORMATION ERA WRITERS

A. *Thomas More's* Utopia *(1516)*

In 1516 Sir Thomas More published a highly original Latin work, called by the freshly minted Greek name *Utopia* ("No place"). It was "perhaps the greatest of the Humanists' many reform tracts."[15] The reason for mentioning it here is due to a much-noted passage in Book Two, chapter 7, dealing with the Utopian penal system:

> Usually the most serious crimes are punished by slavery. For they think that this is just as unpleasant for the criminals and more profitable for the state than if they hurried to execute the guilty and do away with them immediately. For their work brings more profit than their death, and by their example they can deter others from similar offenses for a longer time. But if in this treatment they rebel and fight against authority, then they are slaughtered like wild beasts that no prison or chain can confine. Yet if they are patient, not absolutely all hope is taken away. If after being subdued by long misfortune they clearly show enough repentance to demonstrate that their sin is more displeasing to them than their punishment, then sometimes by the President's prerogative, sometimes by the vote of the people, their slavery is mitigated or altogether remitted.[16]

This is by no means a call for abolition of the death penalty, but, given the time and place of its appearance, it is a remarkably novel passage, suggesting dissatisfaction with the status quo nearly two centuries before similar criticism would begin to be heard in the Enlightenment. More himself would later be responsible as King Henry VIII's lord chancellor for imposing the death penalty on several people convicted of heresy, and still later would himself be the victim of capital punishment for opposing the king's divorce. These subsequent developments make it all the more intriguing to realize that he once had envisioned an ideal society with a very different kind of spirit and penal practice.[17]

B. Martin Luther's Augustinianism (1520)

While the major Protestant Reformers called for change in many other things, they had no objection to the death penalty as such. The first time it became any kind of issue was in Leo X's bull *Exsurge Domine*, condemning Luther. Among the forty-one excerpts from his writings which the bull judged erroneous, proposition #33 was Luther's statement "It is against the will of the Spirit to burn heretics."[18] This is one of the very few references to capital punishment found in papal documents, so it has received considerable attention. It was undoubtedly an allusion to the 1210 addition of Innocent III to the profession of faith administered in the reconciliation of ex-Waldensians, affirming that the secular power can "exercise a judgment of blood" without committing a mortal sin, as long as it is not done out of revenge or hatred.[19] There is more than a little irony in this, for Luther was no Waldensian by any stretch of the imagination and was very far from denying the state's right to execute. On the contrary, he developed an understanding of the respective roles of church and state that included strong support for the state's use of the death penalty, a characteristic of much Lutheran theology right down to recent times.[20] But in drawing the line by objecting to the use of capital punishment against heretics, he was merely joining hands with St. Augustine and other prominent earlier theologians, like Peter the Chanter and Alan of Lille, all of whom agreed in practice that execution was entirely inappropriate as an instrument against heretics.

It is true that Luther used language that was so graphic he could easily be caricatured in the course of bitter controversy. Because the state was viewed as God's instrument holding back chaos, he could insist that

> severity must be used, and people must be kept from sin by
> force. If a thief will not quit his stealing, let him be hanged
> on the public gallows. If a malicious scoundrel wants to
> harm everybody as he pleases...let justice be meted out to
> him at the place of public execution. Then he will no longer
> disturb anyone's peace; he will no longer beat or stab any-
> body. The executioner will nicely keep him from doing
> that.[21]

The language may be harsh, but the practice advocated was
exactly what had been going on in much of Christendom for centuries. By Luther's time the reigning mythology included the
axiom that the death penalty was essential to the social order. It
was a given that few doubted, a veritable cornerstone of the prevailing system. In 1524 Luther expressed this clearly in another
passage:

> Let no one imagine that the world can be governed without
> the shedding of blood. The temporal sword should and
> must be red and bloodstained, for the world is wicked and is
> bound to be so. Therefore the sword is God's rod and
> vengeance for it.[22]

From all of this, two things might safely be said about Luther's
impact on Christian thought about the death penalty:

1. On the one hand, because of his sharp distinction
between the two kingdoms, maintaining that each has its appropriate sphere and that the temporal sword is given by God to the
state alone, the state's practice of capital punishment has full
religious sanction. It is a God-given instrument for punishing
evildoers. This emphasis goes far in explaining the subsequent
Lutheran "tradition" of endorsing the political status quo and
often viewing abolitionism as merely part of the secular Enlightenment attack on the entire body of Christian theology.
2. On the other hand, because the church holds only the
spiritual sword and is forbidden to shed blood, "it is against the
will of the Spirit to burn heretics." This restriction obviously creates significant ambivalence. It is not capital punishment as such
that Luther targeted as wrong; on the contrary, properly used it

is part of the providential order. But, in his opinion, it is improper to use it as a weapon in the war against heretics, since by definition they are fellow Christians. It is wrong for Catholics to kill Lutherans and Calvinists, and, presumably, for Lutherans and Calvinists to kill Catholics; as for infidels, atheists, and others who threaten the social order, that is a different question.

From a contemporary perspective one is inclined to say "a pox on both your houses," and dismiss the disagreement as irrelevant since neither side is engaging the real issue. But in all fairness it must be acknowledged that Luther's drawing of the line short of death in the case of heretics has its value. It harks back to an earlier day when there was still a consciousness among many that the imposition of capital punishment did have limits and using it to silence heretics was beyond justification. That may not seem like much until one looks more closely at what was being said simultaneously by the best of Catholic thinkers.

C. Francisco de Vitoria's Thomism (1530s)

Vitoria, the brilliant Spanish Dominican theologian who put the *Summa* of Thomas Aquinas at the center of theological study at the University of Salamanca, was an exact contemporary of Luther. He brought exciting new challenges and progressive ideas to his teaching, especially in the area of international law and social justice. He criticized the clergy for indifference toward the poor and raised embarrassing questions about the morality of Spain's conquest of the New World and whether the subjugation of native peoples could be justified. He put stricter limits on the ethics of war and defended the individual's right to object in conscience to specific wars.[23] What did such an unusually sensitive and creative thinker have to say about capital punishment as it was being used in the rapidly changing world of his day?

Spanish Dominican Niceto Blázquez recently set out to examine this question, just as he had done with the writings of St. Augustine and St. Thomas. He found that Vitoria had pondered all the traditional citations drawn from all the works of Aquinas and commented on their strengths and their logic. While encountering and acknowledging many valuable insights in Vitoria's works, Blázquez found major weaknesses, especially his misreading of some of the Augustinian and biblical texts (Acts 5, Galatians 5, Romans 13). After reviewing these in detail, Blázquez comes to this conclusion:

> Vitoria brings nothing new to the arguments of St. Thomas. Rather than a study of Thomistic thought, he offers an apologia, taking for granted that Thomas' reasons are beyond question. I have at least shown that the Thomistic thesis is more debatable than Vitoria supposed. His position regarding heretics and schismatics is understandable from an historical and psychological standpoint, as is that of Aquinas. But I think nonetheless that when seen in the light of more rigorously applied Christian principles, it is unacceptable. Vitoria had the merit of having solemnly affirmed the fundamental character of the human *right to life,* as did Aquinas. But he did not draw all the practical consequences from this principle. He was conditioned by his excessive fidelity to the authority of St. Thomas, by the religious and social circumstances of his time, and by a lack of historical perspective....Vitoria is on this question an example of a Thomistic commentator unconditionally faithful to the letter of the master....On other questions he comments with geniality and originality, but when it comes to the concrete reality of the death penalty, he makes no effort to bring anything new to what he has literally encountered in Aquinas.[24]

This incisive criticism makes an extremely important point. If the difficulties and complexities of the next four centuries associated with the death penalty are to be understood, the experiential dimension must be brought in to complete the picture. The practice of capital punishment had found a virtually impregnable position to occupy in the social order of Western Christendom and was surrounded by protective theory by the best theological minds. Add to this combination the polemics that became the order of the day once Reformation quarrels began, and it is clear that there would be no real opportunity to challenge the status of the scaffold from within the church for a very long time to come. Meantime, the presence of the institution of capital punishment at the heart of Christendom continued to compromise otherwise commendable efforts to reform.

III. POPES OF THE TRIDENTINE REFORM
AND THE DEATH PENALTY

The recorded use of the death penalty in the Papal States by the Tridentine Reform popes has seldom been dwelt upon in standard histories, but it cannot reasonably be omitted.[25] Execution was, at this time, a standard mode of social control throughout Europe for both religious or secular crimes. The 1532 Code of Emperor Charles V ranks among the harshest in all of Western history.[26] It is evident that the practice of these popes was no better or worse than that of contemporary temporal rulers. As leaders of the Tridentine Reform, they clearly had the power—but apparently not the will—to extend their reforms to the legal system's use of death as punishment. There were, after all, good grounds within the Christian heritage for rejecting the death penalty. But rather than returning to a more merciful approach, they chose in the atmosphere of the time to maintain the rigors of Roman imperial law, and apparently some of them administered it with enthusiasm.

What follows is only a sampler from the scattered surviving records of the use of capital punishment in the pontificates of these Tridentine popes. This is part of the experiential component that must inform any serious discussion of what happened and what should be expected in a Christian context where the dignity of the human person is given precedence.

A. Pope Paul III (Alessandro Farnese) (1534–1549)

Paul III began his career in an enormously different world than the one in which he found himself when he was elected pope at the age of 67. By force of circumstances he had to change his lifestyle radically. It was he who finally excommunicated Henry VIII of England (1538); it was he who finally opened the Council of Trent (1545). But in between it was also he who deeply affected the church's involvement with the use of the death penalty by agreeing to reconstitute the Roman Inquisition. His bull *Licet ab Initio* of July 1542 provided for the appointment of six cardinals as inquisitors-general.

> Cardinal Carafa, the chief originator of the new institution, proceeded to put it into working order with fiery enthusiasm....The punishments to be meted out were specified: imprisonment, execution, and confiscation of goods in the case of those condemned to death.[27]

It had been tragic enough that this route of institutionalized violence was chosen in the thirteenth century to counter the bewildering new heretics of that time. But this renewal of the extermination approach in the controversies arising over three hundred years later was an even greater tragedy, given the differences of the time. There was ample blame on all sides, undoubtedly, but it is intriguing once more to ponder what the outcome might have been if the dignity of the human person and the sacredness of human life had been convictions sufficiently imbedded in the culture of the age so as not to permit even dreaming of having recourse to executing people.

B. Pope Julius III (Antonio del Monte) (1550–1555)

Julius was the first of the "new breed" of popes sincerely dedicated from the start to the internal reform of the church; he was responsible for reconvening the Council of Trent for its second period. As a young man, during the traumatic 1527 sack of Rome by the mercenaries of Emperor Charles V, he had been one of the hostages whom Pope Clement VII had been forced to provide as security. When the pope could not raise the full amount of ransom demanded, the hostages were led in chains to a gallows in the Campo di Fiori to be hanged. This happened to him twice within five months, and this personal experience of "death row" probably contributed to his later policy. Even as a cardinal, he tried diligently to persuade convicted heretics to recant rather than handing them over to death. Nonetheless, the gallows had been chosen as the preferred way of settling Protestant-Catholic differences. The only question was which side had the power to impose its will.

Even though relatively few, the executions on Julius III's watch were seized upon and graphically described in Germany in bitter anti-Roman pamphlets that bore such titles as *True Report of Three Martyrs Killed by the Pope* (1551); *A History of How Anti-Christ in Rome Again Murdered Two Christians* (1553); *True Story of Montalcino, Who Was Martyred in Rome for His Confession of Faith* (1554); and *True Story of Fanino of Favencia and Dominico of Basana, Killed by Pope Julius III on Account of the Scriptures* (1554). Entries in a diary quoted by Pastor mention proceedings against "Lutherans," including notice of the September 4, 1553, execution of the preacher Montealcino and ten others.[28]

Ironically, it was this very same year that the broadest Protestant endorsement of the death penalty was dramatically illustrated by the execution of Michael Servetus in Geneva (October 27, 1553) under John Calvin. The controversy that surrounded that incident was notable for how broad the consensus in Protestant circles was that this was the right thing to do.[29] Almost a year later (October 14, 1554) Melanchthon in a letter to Calvin wrote: "The Church...owes you gratitude for the present as for the future. I entirely concur with your judgment. I maintain that your magistrates have acted rightly by condemning a blasphemer to death after a proper trial."[30]

Granted, there were dissenting voices. Note must especially be taken of "the first methodical investigation of this topic," the originally anonymous work of Sebastian Castellio, *De Haereticis, an sint Persequendi* (published in March 1554), soon followed by a French version, *Traité des Hérétiques*. Lecler sums it up thus: "The death penalty, which is retained for rebellion and crimes of common law, is utterly rejected in the case of religious error, according to the spirit of the early Church."[31] This stance, basically a return to the position of Augustine, however, was not popular. Sixteenth-century European Christian leaders on all sides (with a handful of exceptions to be seen shortly) were more than ever convinced of the necessity of using the death penalty to eliminate those whose ideas were "unorthodox."[32]

When Marcello Cervini was elected to succeed Julius as Pope Marcellus II (1555), there was great enthusiasm in reform circles. "Few elections have aroused such eager hopes....Able and experienced, upright and zealous for reform, he seemed the chief-pastor for whom the crisis-ridden church was crying out."[33] But he died after only twenty-two days in office, not only dashing hopes, but leaving the way open for a very different kind of successor with truly tragic shortcomings.

C. Pope Paul IV (Gianpietro Carafa) (1555–1559)

If the Renaissance popes (especially Alexander VI and Leo X) had given great scandal by their sensuous lifestyles, by mid-century that problem was effectively remedied. Asceticism had become the trademark of the Reform popes, including Paul IV. But another kind of scandal came with the politicized extremism exemplified by Paul. A man of many gifts, he let his absolutist "fixed ideas" blind him to many things, including the worthlessness of his nephew Carlo, whom he elevated to cardinal and whom his successor felt obliged to put to death for his part in the scandalous "Carafa War" with Spain, which blighted Paul's entire pontificate.

Becoming pope at the age of 79, Paul IV had a will of steel, which could have assured good progress in the church reform to which he was committed. But he wasted much of the first half of his brief pontificate on the Spanish political fiasco, until the humiliating defeat of papal forces at the hands of the Duke of Alva and the signing of the Peace of Cave (September 12, 1557).[34] But this proved to be only part of his problem. Although dedicated to reform, he was entirely opposed to reconvening the Council of Trent and devoted his full authority rather to the Roman Inquisition as the most reliable instrument of church reform. He faithfully attended its Thursday sessions week after week and arranged for the Commission of the Inquisition to take precedence over all other bodies in Rome.[35] He let his fierce anti-Protestant passion override considerations of justice and humanity, and his paranoid suspicion of Jews as secret promoters of Protestantism led him to force them ignominiously into ghettos in the Papal States and to insist that henceforth they wear distinctive yellow headgear.[36]

It is an irony of the history of the Inquisition that the records of this ruthless period were largely destroyed at the time of Paul's death.

> The fury of the (Roman) populace broke out and vented
> itself principally on the buildings of the Inquisition....Not
> even the number of cases tried, or even of the executions
> which took place partly in the Piazza Navona, and partly in
> the Campo di Fiore and the Piazza Giudea, can now be
> stated with accuracy.[37]

The full record has thus been lost, but the names of some of the
victims executed under Paul IV are known from other sources:
On June 15, 1555, Gisberto di Milanuccio was killed. On June 15,
1556, Ambrogio de Cavoli was strangled and burned. On August
19, 1556, on the square before the Ponte Sant'Angelo, Pomponio
de Algerio di Nola "suffered a horrible death in a caldron of boiling oil, for persisting in his denial of papal authority, purgatory,
and the sacraments as taught by Rome; he was not entitled to the
more merciful death by the sword before being burned."[38]

It was also during the pontificate of Paul IV that the Spanish Inquisition crested with the notorious auto-da-fé of October
8, 1559, attended by King Philip II himself, the royal family and
some 200,000 spectators, curious to see how the twenty-six
Protestants and a handful of other dissenters paraded before
them would fare.[39] Something was terribly amiss in a system that
allowed such institutionalizing of violence in making the destruction of human life part of the church's liturgy in the elaborate
ceremonies of the auto-da-fé.

D. Pope Pius IV (Giovanni Angelo Medici) (1559–1565)

Pius IV provided a greatly needed breath of fresh air after
the Carafa disaster. Pius finally reconvened the Council of Trent
and successfully shepherded it to conclusion despite formidable
obstacles. He furthered the compilation of the *Roman Catechism*
but did not live to see it completed. And yet, full use of the death
penalty took place under him as well. The following death sentences are among those on record: On August 13, 1560, Luigi
Pasquali, Waldensian preacher in Calabria, and two companions
were executed for heresy. There were at least two other executions held in this first year of Pius's pontificate (on September 15
and 25, 1560).[40]

Even as he was arranging for the final session of the Council, Pius IV had his predecessor's two corrupt nephews, Cardinal Carlo Carafa and his brother Giovanni, duke of Paliano, executed for treason (March 5, 1561).[41] Then, on June 13, 1562, Macarius of Macedonia, an "obstinate monk and a Greek bishop," was executed. Like so many of the ones that follow, he too was a "stranger" in Rome (a common characteristic of the prime victims in any scapegoating scheme). Other executed strangers included: on January 23, 1563, a heretic from Holland; on September 4, 1564, a heretic from Cyprus and on December 16, 1564, Thomas de Fabianis and Giovanni Micro of Naples, executed "pro fisco."

On January 27, 1565, three conspirators (who had planned to assassinate the pope but froze once in his presence) were arrested, condemned, tortured, and "barbarously put to death as guilty of high treason."[42] The fanatical leader of this bizarre plot was apocalypticist Benedetto Accolti, and his co-conspirators were Taddeo Manfredi and Antonio di Canossa.

At least four more "strangers" were executed in Rome in the final year of Pius IV's pontificate: on February 28, 1565, Johannes Baptista Saxum of Caserta; on April 12, 1565, J. Paganum of Caserta; on September 16, 1565, Marco Bergamesco of St. Germano; and on October 4, 1565, Aurelius della Vista di Santo Angelo.[43]

It is true that there were many instances of other kinds of much greater bloodshed among Christian groups in this chaotic period.[44] These records of executions ordered in papal Rome, however, show how heavily even the most reform-minded church leaders relied on the death penalty as a matter of course. This was part of the social reality of the very time when the *Roman Catechism* with its particular treatment of the ethics of capital punishment was being composed. It was very far from being an abstract issue.

E. Pope Pius V (Michele Ghislieri) (1566–1572)

Pius V was responsible for the vigorous implementation of the reforms of the Council of Trent, including the completion and promotion of the *Roman Catechism*. He also oversaw in his reforming zeal "more executions...in a single month than in four years under Pius IV."[45] He had been pope only a few months when the beheading of Pompeo de' Monti, a Neapolitan nobleman and relative of Cardinal Colonna, was ordered and carried out (July 4, 1566). Right from the start, Pius launched a vigorous campaign against all forms of misconduct. A papal bull of July 13, 1566, threatened the death penalty for all who dared to give shelter to murderers or outlaws and assigned exile as the fate of all their relatives. On September 21, 1567, Pietro Carnesecchi, once the private secretary of Pope Clement VII, was beheaded and his body burned.[46]

On December 6, 1568, three of fourteen suspects who had been sent from Faenza were condemned for heresy by the Roman Inquisition and decapitated, then burned. On February 28, 1569, an "obstinate Lutheran" was hanged. On May 22, 1569, Bartolomeo Bartoccio, persisting in his voicing of objections, was burned at the stake. On July 3, 1570, Antonio della Paglia, better known as Paleario, a professor of belles-lettres in Siena, Lucca, and Milan (and later revered as a Protestant saint) was strangled and his body burned.[47]

On June 7, 1571, Alessandro Pallantieri, appointed in 1567 as governor of the March of Ancona, was accused of bribery, deception, and possible heresy. His tangled case was argued in the presence of Pope Pius himself for some three hours, and the outcome was his conviction and prompt execution.

On August 18, 1571, the governor of Anagni was beheaded for immorality. On February 9, 1572, five persons, four of them women accused of witchcraft, were burned at the stake. It is also recorded that Niccolo Franco was "hanged by order of Pope Pius V for publishing the *Priapeia*" (a pornographic book).[48]

Pius V's ambitious efforts to eliminate immorality from the Holy City, no matter how high the cost, led him to abolish the longstanding right of sanctuary, "since justice must be able to lay its hands upon the guilty everywhere, even in the Apostolic Palace."[49] And for several years a plan to legislate death as the standard punishment for adultery was high on his agenda.[50] It was extraordinary how dramatically things had changed in Rome in the half-century since Luther's initial protest.[51] But the continued use of violence to achieve good ends left grave questions about the overall quality of the achievement.

IV. ROMAN EXECUTIONS AFTER THE
COUNCIL OF TRENT

The Council of Trent corrected, or at least lessened, much of what had gone wrong in the Roman church. But, as in any reform, there were areas that escaped detection and correction. The papal use of the deeply entrenched death penalty was not given any attention. Many other things would have to change before it could be addressed. The Tridentine reforms brought no relief in this regard, as is evident from the records of two highly talented men who were chosen as popes in this period. Many other noteworthy reforms were implemented, but capital punishment was utilized virtually without restraint.

A. *Pope Gregory XIII (Ugo Boncompagni) (1572–1585)*

Gregory is remembered as one who "gave the Counter-Reformation a more militant slant."[52] He had made useful contributions at Trent and was subsequently made cardinal-legate in Spain, where he gained the good graces of King Philip II. But "he was almost exclusively preoccupied with the fight against Protestantism and the mobilization of all the Church's resources...for that purpose."[53] In his first year as pope the infamous St. Bartholomew's Day massacres took place in France, the basis of the most enduring "myth" in the history of Protestant-Catholic conflict. Kingdon's recent analysis of the rise of this mythology concludes on the hopeful note that a valuable lesson may yet be learned:

> Violence in the name of religion continues to plague society....It continues to feed on the mutual incomprehension we saw in the sixteenth century. French Protestants then simply could not and would not understand why Catholics valued objects...that to them were symbols of blasphemous sacrilege. French Catholics simply could not and would not understand why Protestants wantonly destroyed objects that to them were cherished reminders of the most holy. Perhaps this book's account of the appalling violence that can result from such incomprehension will encourage modern readers to seek understanding of beliefs other than their own...and

lead us all to hope that good may yet come from other periods of fanatical conflict.[54]

Even though his policies, on the whole, may have been somewhat milder than those of his predecessor, Gregory's pontificate saw Protestant-Catholic hostilities reach unparalleled ferocity, not only in France and Germany, but also in England. Cuthbert Maine was the first Catholic priest executed by Queen Elizabeth I in 1577, and 124 more priests as well as 61 laymen suffered the death penalty before her reign was over.[55] Simultaneously, however, Pope Gregory XIII was using the same "remedy," presiding over such cases as the following in Rome: On May 24, 1573, "eleven men and two women had made their abjuration; one of these was condemned to death, four to imprisonment, and the others to the galleys."[56] On November 30, 1574, an obstinate heretic ended his days at the stake. On August 13, 1578, seven Portuguese Marani were put to death at the Porta Latina.[57] On June 13, 1579, two relapsed Lutherans were executed. In fact, 1579 saw a Roman auto-da-fé in which more than twenty unfortunates were handed over to the executioner.[58]

The year 1581 was one of the ugliest times in the exchange of Protestant-Catholic atrocities. On August 2 an Anabaptist Englishman, Richard Atkins, had his right hand cut off, then was burned alive, and his ashes scattered to the winds in Rome.[59] Shortly after, Jesuit Edmund Campion was hanged, drawn, and quartered at Tyburn under Elizabeth I. Divided Christendom was producing a torrent of blood as virtually all parties to the controversies invoked the death penalty as their God-given instrument for eliminating those who held other convictions.

On January 20, 1582, a Castilian who had snatched the chalice from a priest at Mass in Rome was executed in secret "in order to avoid scandal," but ten months later a crazed Frenchman who claimed to be pope also attacked a priest at Mass, and was burned alive in a Roman public square.[60] On February 13, 1583, another Portuguese Marrano was executed at an auto-da-fé held at the Minerva. And on March 22, 1585, Giacomo Massilara, a Dominican brother also known as Teodoro Paleologo, was beheaded and his body burned. He had several times been condemned for heresy but saved himself once by flight from Rome and once by the intervention of St. Philip Neri, but after two years he was again arrested and this time done away with.[61]

But besides these executions on religious grounds, there was another group that caused particularly troublesome problems in Gregory's day. The Roman countryside, for a variety of reasons, had become more and more infested with brigands, who caused so much robbery and bloodshed that the pope had to gather additional Swiss troops even to protect his own palace. As this chaotic situation grew worse, he was "unable to master the plague of brigandage" despite having executed one notorious ringleader, Giovan Battista Pace, on June 4, 1583. Two months later "four bandits of Frascati were beheaded, together with a brigand chief who with his own hand had committed 65 murders."[62] Dealing with this bandit crisis was the first order of business for the next pope, who took extraordinary means in addressing it.

2. Pope Sixtus V (Felice Peretti) (1585–1590)

Sixtus V was, with good reason, dubbed "The Iron Pope."[63] He launched a ferocious anti-crime campaign during his first month in office. He "set himself to remove the bandits from Rome and from the whole of the States of the Church by measures of the greatest severity."[64] His blistering bull Hoc Nostri of July 1, 1585, made it clear that he meant business.[65] His desperate decision was to have recourse to the death penalty in a far greater way than any other pope in history. Over seven thousand bandits were executed in his initial campaign, and a report from Rome, dated September 18, 1585, noted that the severed heads of bandits exposed on the Ponte Sant' Angelo outnumbered the melons brought to market that season.[66] That this kind of carnage alleviated the immediate problem, making travel in the countryside safer, and was thus appreciated by the local populace, is undeniable. But as a papal program it underlined the regrettable gap that had developed between religious ideals and temporal reality. Other necessary reforms were undoubtedly put in place, but this bewildering reliance on massive lethal violence to eliminate wrongdoers had yet to be confronted.[67]

On August 5, 1587, a major auto-da-fé was held at Santa

Maria sopra Minerva and included four executions: "two were burned for offenses against the Church, the other two for their libertine views, which in the case of one—the priest Pomponio Rustico—had clear materialist tendencies."[68] The record notes that one, Gasparo Ranchi, remained impenitent to the end, while the other three, Rustico, Antonio Nuntio, and Giovanni Bellinello, died "with good sentiments."[69]

This brief reminder of the deep involvement with and recourse to the death penalty on the part of the Reform popes emphasizes the magnitude of the problem of honest reassessment. It was in some ways the worst of times for composing a catechism that had to include treatment of the issue. While the thirteenth century accounted for how the burning of heretics became the standard practice, despite all earlier objections to killing, the sixteenth century created the intolerable situation in which there was less and less restraint on its use.

Yet, even this is not the complete picture of the extremes to which the embracing of capital punishment had led. As a practice it always fosters corruption in a social system, although those directly involved in its use are the last to recognize this. Administrators of the Papal States devised methods of execution that competed with and in some instances surpassed those of other regimes for cruelty. One example was the *mazzatello:*

> Mazzatello—a decidedly brutal method of execution developed by the Italians in the papal states, the States of the Church in central Italy ruled by the popes until 1870. The mazza or mazzatello, named after the mallet or pole-ax used in the killing, began with the prisoner, accompanied by a priest, being led to a scaffold erected in a public square. On the platform lay a coffin. Above it the executioner, masked and dressed in black, raised the mallet, swung it round in the air to gain momentum, and brought it down on the head of the prisoner, much like the mallet-swingers in a stockyard on the heads of cattle. Finally the executioner would cut the throat of the fallen man to make sure the job was done. Not until the coming of the Italian patriot and master of guerilla warfare, Giuseppe Garibaldi, and the formation of a United Italy in 1861 was the practice abolished.[70]

This is part of the concrete reality being blessed and defended, legitimated and camouflaged, by respectable abstractions such as "capital punishment" and "death-penalty."

D. The Dilemma of Gallows-Pietism

There was another way in which the church by this time found itself even more deeply immersed in the business of capital punishment. When Pope Innocent VIII had established the Archconfraternity of St. John the Beheaded in 1488, he assigned to it the functions of comforting the dying and burying the dead, but especially of concerning themselves with those condemned to death. Their charge was to be with the condemned all during their final hours, doing whatever they could to get them to repent of their misdeeds and make their peace with God and the church. It was an unusual kind of ministry, to say the least, and Firpo makes a pertinent remark about it after examining the records:

> The only point that seemed to concern the "confratelli" was that the condemned ascend the scaffold "with good dispositions," i.e., reconciled to the church, contrite and repentant, to the edification of all, without ever a word about the enormity of the crimes or the atrocity of the punishments.... Obstinacy and final impenitence were seen as inhuman monstrosities, or manifestations of insanity, without ever provoking the slightest doubt about the evangelical compatibility of repression, or any sense of respect for people of inflexible conscience.[71]

For nearly four centuries (1490–1870) the members of the Archconfraternity performed these services in Rome. Their archives became a center of attention toward the end of the nineteenth century, when scholars found in them a previously unknown account of the early part of Giordano Bruno's trial, including descriptions of the tortures he endured.[72] Confusion and controversy followed when it was realized that, for whatever reasons, much of the four-century record of Roman executions was missing. On the other hand, the third or so that survived included information about executions not recorded elsewhere.

There are two lists of executions held during the Tridentine period we have been discussing. The first records twenty-two of the executions prompted by the Roman Inquisition between the years 1567 and 1657, eight of which are not documented elsewhere. Ludwig Pastor knew of this list and used it in his work. The second list, however, which records eighty executions for other offenses between 1569 and 1671, seems to have escaped Pastor's attention. Neither of these lists is a complete record of all the Roman executions held during these years. But to get an impression of the Archconfraternity's work, the first half of the second list is summarized below, indicating the ruling pontiffs of the period.

Under Pius V:
1. May 1, 1569—Filippo Borghese, decapitated and burned.
2. July 24, 1570—Paris, son of Girolamo della Genga, decapitated.

Under Gregory XIII:
3. July 8, 1574—Giovanni Aldobrandini, decapitated and burned.
4. October 25, 1574–Giovan Bernardino Ghisilerio, strangled after being reconciled in prison.
5. December 8, 1581—Cesare de Totis, decapitated.
6. March 11, 1582—Fulvio di Tiberio Alberini, decapitated.
7. June 13, 1583—Captain Giovan Battista Pace, decapitated.
8. July 8, 1583—Alfonso Ceccarello, physician, decapitated.
9. April 10, 1584—Captain Fabio Nini d'Ascoli, blindfolded, *mazzatelloed,* then drawn and quartered.
10. April 2, 1584—Giovanni d'Agostino da Bertinoro, hanged on the Ponte Sant'Angelo.

Under Sixtus V:
(There is no mention of the seven thousand brigands executed in his first year; these were presumably not committed to the Archconfraternity's care.)

11. May 30, 1586—Count Vittorio Monte Mellino, decapitated.
12. July 28, 1586—Captain Nicolò Azzolini, decapitated.

13. February 19, 1587—Virgilio di Montaco, decapitated.
14. August 13, 1587—Ramberto Malatesta, decapitated.
15. May 11, 1588—Spaniard Martino de Suria, hanged in the Piazza of St. Peter's.
16. March 4, 1589—Druso Delfino d'Amelia, decapitated.
17. April 28, 1589—Antimo Capizucchi, decapitated.
18. May 23, 1589—Lelio de' Massimi, decapitated.
19. October 12, 1589—Camillo Voltri, decapitated.
20. May 25, 1590—Mutio Treppet of Vienna, hanged on the Ponte.

Under Clement VIII:
("He sharpened the severity of the Inquisition, which in his reign sent more than thirty heretics...to the stake."[73] But besides these unfortunates, whose crime was heresy, there were other culprits committed to the "program" of the Archconfraternity in preparation for paying with their lives for other crimes.)

21. April 17, 1592—Baron Troilo Savelli, decapitated in Castel Sant'Angelo, along with nine others.
22. June 26, 1592—Rafaello d'Accursio Tarugi, for murdering during Mass in St. John Lateran, decapitated.
23. June 28, 1592—Three men (Captain Ceccone di Sebastiano da Monte Santo, Polifemo de Utozzi di Servigliano, and Giacomo di Michelangelo Grifoni da Righello) were tortured, their right hands cut off, then they were beaten, drawn, and quartered.
24. September 11, 1592—Cornelio Clementini, decapitated.
25. June 15, 1593—Captain Nofrio Tartaro da Montefalco, hanged along with five others, and one who was *mazzatelloed.*
26. August 20, 1593—Giovanni Stuniga da Seranzar and Marco de Tussi, brother, along with five others, hanged.
27. October 1, 1593—Fr. Alessandro Cioschi da Supino, hanged.
28. October 22, 1593—Antonio Benozzi, hanged and quartered.
29. December 12, 1593—Prospero Grifoni, decapitated.
30. April 22, 1594—Spaniard Luis Perez de Roa, hanged.
31. May 12, 1595—Mercurio Grillo da Cervetri, hanged.
32. September 20, 1596—Francesco Pichio, hanged.

33. August 6, 1596—Sebastiano d'Andrea Ancarini and his brother Gesualdo, decapitated.
34. August 17, 1596—Oratio di Federico Conti and Oliverio Saracinello, decapitated and heads exposed on Pontc.
35. May 9, 1597—Francesco Barberini, hanged on Ponte.
36. April 15, 1598—Captain Giovanni Calcalara, hanged on Ponte.
37. June 16, 1599—Marcantonio Massimi, decapitated and quartered.
38. September 10, 1599—Giacomo Cenci, hanged and quartered; Lucrezia and Beatrice Cenci, decapitated.
39. January 18, 1602—Prospero Gaetano, decapitated.
40. January 31, 1603—Marcantonio Albrizi, hanged on Ponte.
41. January 30, 1604—Baron Onofrio Santacroce, decapitated.

The most notorious of the executions under Clement VIII, however, was that of ex-Dominican Giordano Bruno. He had been detained in prison for more than seven years and still refused to retract his unusual and unorthodox ideas.

> Pope Clement VIII ordered that he should be sentenced as an impenitent and pertinacious heretic. On February 8, 1600, when the death sentence was formally read to him, he addressed his judges, saying: "Perhaps your fear in passing judgment on me is greater than mine in receiving it." On February 17 he was brought to the Campo di Fiori, his tongue in a gag, and burned alive.[74]

Understandably, as Aquilecchia continues, Bruno became a "symbol of freedom of thought...[and] inspired the European liberal movements of the 19th century, particularly the Italian Risorgimento."

From all of this it becomes clear that it was in the century after Trent that "Gallows-Pietism" reached its climax. The social-security argument, which was the chief buttress legitimating the death penalty in Scholastic theology, was admittedly a cold-hearted calculus. The gangrenous member of society had to be amputated for the good of the whole body politic. The prescription for the health of the society was the excision of the cancerous

organ, and that was simply part of the harsh reality of sixteenth-
and seventeenth-century European life.

But this could not be the final word for one with any Christian sensitivity, since, as St. Augustine had demonstrated so
graphically, the condemned person cannot simply be abandoned
to cruel fate like an animal marked for slaughter. No matter how
much the culprit may have "forfeited" by his crime, there is still a
human soul involved and some hope for "good news," at least in
the next life.

Hence, a second theme became increasingly prominent in
the Reform era, which might be labeled the "celestial-security"
concern. It served to alleviate the hard-heartedness of the social-
security argument. To define the criminal as human garbage, fit
only to be discarded and burned, may answer to a primal instinct
but could make no claim to reflect the compassionate teaching
of Jesus. So, offsetting the stark reality of the grim natural-law
condemnation was a more spiritual element, a divine-law dimension that offered some relief.

Cardinal Robert Bellarmine was a principal contributor to
the growth of this trend, as seen in his influential book *The Art of
Dying Well*. His eloquence, in fact, impressed a modern historian
to describe Bellarmine's approach in these terms:

> The condemned man was actually rehabilitated by his suf-
> fering and repentance. His piety transformed his execution
> into an expiation, and his death became a good death, better
> than many others. "When they have begun to depart from
> mortal life," Bellarmine wrote almost admiringly of con-
> demned criminals, "they begin to live in immortal bliss."[75]

The stress on bringing greater piety to the gallows was one way
of rising somewhat above the gruesome realities of torture and
bloodshed. Capital punishment as it was being practiced was so
horrendous that one simply had to try to see it through different
eyes. Just as one had to see the shedding of the blood of Jesus as
having deeper meaning than could be discerned on the surface,
so the torrent of blood deliberately shed by state executioners
had to be given a more exalted sense than met the eye. The celestial-security (or atonement or expiation) arguments provided a

religious veil that diminished the stark brutality of what was taking place on the scaffold.

The seventeenth-century French and Italian schools of Catholic spirituality had, for various reasons, an unusual preoccupation with death, and one anomalous consequence was that the condemned criminal could thus become an object of special admiration, his death a kind of blessing in disguise. One condemned to undergo capital punishment was provided with an opportunity to snatch eternal victory from the jaws of temporal defeat, to become ideally the envy of all true Christians. Here was a person for whom the customary human uncertainties surrounding death (its time, place, and manner) were providentially removed. The precise moment and mode of departure from this life were clearly assigned well beforehand. This "privilege" meant that death row could become a veritable model setting with ideal conditions for a "mors bona Christiana."[76] All other distractions were removed. The prisoner had only to turn his thoughts to God, repent of his sins, confess them humbly, and accept the suffering imposed on him as expiation for his guilt and preparation for possibly immediate entry into heaven.

This celestial-security emphasis combined with the social-security argument became standard in many Catholic works. It can be found eloquently expressed as recently as 1945 in a classic work of Heinrich A. Rommen:

> Capital punishment is atonement on the part of him who suffers the extreme penalty for the grave injustice he has committed against the unity of order, against the common good. As long as we believe in immortality this idea of atonement, apart from the idea of determent, justifies the death penalty. The evil-doer atones, and thus he can be received into paradise. That the priest accompanies the condemned person to the portal of eternity, is what makes such death penalty bearable. The socio-political order that has been gravely disturbed is restored by the sacrifice of life, so that in his death the condemned person helps to restore that order.[77]

The passage, by implication, suggests much about the misgivings inseparable from the social-security defense by itself, even when backed with the authority of Aquinas and the major moral theologians. Here the gruesome reality of deliberately destroying criminals is veiled and attention diverted from the harsh, distasteful system with its direct intentional killing. So construed, the death penalty became even more deeply entrenched and taken for granted as totally sanctioned by God and natural law, so that questioning its propriety was virtually impious. Woven into the social fabric, a natural ingredient of the long-established legal-political-religious system, capital punishment was applied relentlessly and without remorse even by the most upright rulers. Regarded as an unpleasant duty, yet authorized by God, it was a burden that simply had to be shouldered bravely and carried out solemnly for the common good (social security).

This theological emphasis, placing execution squarely in the "model-Christian-death" category, attracted a broad array of pastoral workers. Full-scale chaplaincy on "death row" was encouraged, much the same as on the battlefields of war. It was a prestigious form of Christian ministry, and prison chaplains were challenged to develop new skills as "technicians of guilt." Their exalted task was to persuade the condemned to accept their plight, confess their guilt, and cooperate completely with their executioners, so that they would become "role models" in facing death and thereby greatly edify the vulgar mob crowded around the scaffold. When it worked, it was obvious to all that the gallows was a special work of God, a providential occasion where proper dispositions for a good Christian death were ideally enacted in a grand public liturgy from which all could learn important lessons in both living and dying as good Christians.

But as attitudes toward the scaffold changed, so did the role of the prison chaplain in a transformation that complicated this "compensatory piety." It is easy to see how the celestial-security emphasis, as long as it held, directly augmented Christian legitimation of the scaffold. The presence of the chaplain helped make even the most brutal execution "the awesome act of a Christian community fulfilling the will of God; its chaplains lent a religious aura to the whole solemnity."[78] But this meant that churchmen were seen as co-opted, performing what was obviously a very worthwhile ministry to the lowly but, at the same time, giving the death penalty a special legitimacy as a pedagogical tool for the good of the entire society. This kind of intimate intertwining of

Christian ministry in the state's machinery of death augmented the burden by increasing the likelihood that the larger questions about such a system would remain both unasked and unanswered as long as no significant protest arose. Religious orders to focus on the condemned proliferated, such as the *Hermandad de la Paz y Caridad* in Spain and the *Confrerie de la Miséricorde* in France, modeled to match the Italian original, the Archconfraternity of John the Beheaded (*San Giovanni Decollato*). Sueiro describes their modus operandi in minute detail, observing that "the scaffold was turned into the new means of apostolate," but at the cost of losing balance. A religion centered entirely and solely on how to die, without any focus on how to live and forgive, does less than justice to Jesus.[79]

All of this was part of the social reality, not just background but central to the entire prevailing world view. Who would have the wisdom, the insight, the ingenuity, the gall to challenge this providential plan? The scaffold was part of the "sacred" order of the era, and the era was the time when the *Roman Catechism* was composed, to be distributed and taught all across Europe.

V. SIXTEENTH-CENTURY CATHOLIC CATECHESIS ON CAPITAL PUNISHMENT

What were the people actually being told, and how was the instruction being given by the churchmen of the day? One striking pedagogical development was the rise of the *catechism* as a special instrument in the effort to improve and revitalize Christian education and more effectively communicate Christian teachings on the popular level. Even though the first use of the word *catechism* seems to have been in the title of a 1357 work in England, and the first use of the basic form was developed by Jean Gerson in the early 1400s, it was Martin Luther who brought the genre to center stage in 1529 with the publication of his two catechisms, which were soon being widely distributed and effectively used.[80] In eight days of November, 1541, John Calvin wrote his counterpart, called *Formulaire d'instruire les enfants en la Chrétienté*, and it too began to exercise broad influence.

It was thus no surprise that, at the very beginning of the Council of Trent in 1545, many Council Fathers expressed their desire to have a comparable Catholic catechism produced. But it was more easily asked for than achieved. After being twice suspended, the second time for nearly ten years, the Council had still not progressed very far with the arrangements when the final session closed on December 4, 1563. On that day the Council Fathers left the catechism as one of four major projects for the pope to carry to completion.

A. *The Catechisms of Peter Canisius (1554–1557)*

As the work of the Council of Trent dragged on, King Frederick of Austria tried persistently to get the University of Vienna to prepare a Catholic catechism for the proper education of his subjects. The University Senate finally entrusted the task to a Jesuit theologian, Claude Lejay, who in turn asked a colleague, Peter Canisius, to help him with it. When Lejay died in 1552, Canisius continued the task alone. He produced three different works: (1) in 1554 a *Summa doctrinae christianae, per quaestiones tradita*...also known as the *Catechismus major,* with 213 questions and answers; (2) in 1556 a *Catechismus minimus,* with 59 questions and answers; and (3) in 1557 a *Catechismus minor,* with 124 questions and answers. The three, translated into German, rapidly took their place as the Catholic standard and were soon translated and circulated in all the major languages of the rest of Western Europe.[81]

It is worth taking a brief look at these works of Canisius because of their enormous impact both in the decade before and in the long years after the *Roman Catechism* finally appeared in 1566. In its Ante-Tridentine version it touched on the question of killing in three different places: (a) the simple statement of the fifth commandment—"Thou shalt not kill"; (b) the follow-up question: "What does the fifth commandment include?" with the answer:

> It prohibits not only external murder and all violence which injures the body and life of a neighbor, but it also excludes anger, hatred, rancor, indignation, and any other internal dispositions inclined toward harming one's neighbor. It also requires meekness of spirit, humanity, clemency, fellowship, and beneficence, so as to forget injuries easily, not to

demand revenge, but to forgive one another's offenses just as God has done for us in Christ.

(c) A later section dealing with the types of sins includes questions about the four "sins that cry to heaven," the first of which is voluntary homicide. One of the questions is: "How does Scripture teach that voluntary homicide is to be vindicated?" The answer begins with the words of God to Cain (Genesis 4:10) "What have you done?...The voice of your brother's blood is crying to me from the earth. Now therefore you will be cursed from the earth." Then comes Genesis 9:6 "Whoever sheds the blood of man, by man his blood will be shed. For God made man in his own image." And then follows Psalm 54:24 "Men of blood shall not live out half their days."

However much one may want to read into these biblical texts, there is nothing explicitly taught about when, how, or by whom the bloodletting is to be done. It is thus interesting to note that in the Post-Tridentine revision of Canisius, two sentences were added to introduce another factor:

> It [homicide] is a very great crime and anyone who takes a life *without legitimate authority* does the most atrocious injury to his neighbor. Hence the saying of Christ: "All who take the sword will perish by the sword."

Provision is thus quietly made for legitimately authorized exceptions, such as war and capital punishment, as had been done by the canonists after Gratian, but no such exceptions were actually spelled out in the catechism. The accent was kept very definitely on the positive requirements of the commandment, instilling appreciation for the inviolability of human life. It is a good example of Peter Canisius at his best, capturing the sense of the gospel and expressing clearly the teaching of Jesus that the full meaning of "thou shalt not kill" included the responsibility of renouncing revenge. No matter what might have been happening elsewhere, those who learned their Christian ethics from the catechism of Peter Canisius were still basically instructed in the nonviolent message of Christ.

B. The Roman Catechism *(1566)*

1. ITS COMPOSITION

The catechism called for by the Council of Trent was finally promulgated by Pius V in the first year of his pontificate, 1566, twenty-one years after the opening and three years after the closing of the Council.[82] It was initially composed in Italian by three Dominicans: Archbishop Leonardo Marini of Lanciano, Bishop Egidio Foscarari of Modena, and Francisco Fureiro (a Portuguese priest who was a close friend of Cardinal Carlo Borromeo), who had "distinguished himself at the Council." Pastor appropriately remarks that "the principal credit for the Roman Catechism must be ascribed" to the Dominican Order.[83] The text was printed by Paulus Manutius, who had been summoned to Rome in 1561 to start a printing business to publish "editions of the Fathers of the Church."[84]

2. ITS TEACHING ABOUT THE DEATH PENALTY

This manual, intended chiefly for parish priests, has four major sections: Part One—the Creed; Part Two—the Sacraments; Part Three—the Decalogue; and Part Four—the Lord's Prayer. Its chapter in Part Three on the fifth commandment is the focus of our interest. It is carefully constructed and more elaborate than its counterpart in Canisius and can be outlined as follows:

I. Introduction—The Importance of Instructing on This Commandment

II. The Two Parts of This Commandment
    A. The Negative (Prohibitory) Part
        i. the exceptions (kinds of killing not prohibited):
          a. the killing of animals
          b. the execution of criminals
          c. killing in a just war
          d. killing by accident
          e. killing in self-defense
        ii. the prohibitions:
          a. murder

          b. suicide
          c. sinful anger
   B. The Positive (Mandatory) Part
      i. love of neighbor inculcated
      ii. charity toward all commanded
      iii. patience, beneficence, and mildness
         commanded
      iv. forgiveness of injuries commanded

III. Special Advice on How to Persuade Men to
    Forgive Injuries
     A. all we have to endure comes from God
     B. advantages of forgiveness
     C. disadvantages of revenge
     D. remedies against hatred

One may indeed marvel at the neatness of the arrangement, a logical orderliness worthy of the best Scholastic tradition. Several influences of Canisius are quite evident. And yet, there is something disturbing about the prominence given to the exceptions, which are spelled out in great detail even before the substance of the commandment itself is set forth. This may have been a pedagogical ploy, so that the negatives could be dealt with first and then closed out allowing full attention to be given to the positive part of the teaching. On the other hand, it may also be read as reflecting a psychological defensiveness on the part of the authors as they anticipated the multiple objections that would be thundering through the minds of readers in view of the astonishing amount of violent bloodshed accepted as part of Christian life since the twelfth century. Embarrassing questions as to what the fifth commandment really should require, and what churchmen ought to be teaching about it might thus be best treated "up front." In any event, a closer look at the individual segments of the chapter may yield further useful insights.

The three-paragraph Introduction opens on a promising note, immediately connecting the commandment with the Sermon on the Mount, reminding pastors to stress the duty of Christians to be peacemakers and thus automatically reinforcing the prohibition against the killing of fellow humans:

> The great happiness proposed to the peacemakers, of being
> called "the children of God," should prove a powerful incen-
> tive to the pastor to explain to the faithful with care and
> accuracy the obligations imposed by this Commandment.
> No means more efficacious can be adopted to promote
> peace among mankind than the proper explanation of this
> Commandment and its holy and due observance by all.
> Then might we hope that men, united in the strictest bonds
> of union, would live in perfect peace and concord.[85]

This extremely idealistic start confirms what has often been
noted about the catechism in general, that is, that it is remarkably free from the usual polemics that marred so much of the
theological writing of the sixteenth century, both Catholic and
Protestant.[86] Care clearly had been taken to keep the instruction
on as high a plane as possible.

The second paragraph of the Introduction turns to a central text of the Old Testament to note that, after the flood in
Noah's time, "this was the first prohibition made by God to man.
'I will require the blood of your lives,' He said, 'at the hand of
every beast and at the hand of man' (Genesis 9:5)."

Interestingly enough, the quote stops short of verse 6, which
Canisius had used by itself and which is still the most frequently
quoted Old Testament verse in any kind of proof-texting defense
of capital punishment: "Whoever sheds the blood of man, by
man shall his blood be shed; for God made man in his own
image." Whatever the explanation, it is not used here in the place
where it might have been most expected. Verse 5 has its own difficulties; the reader is confronted squarely at the very start with
the core paradox about capital punishment that has plagued
Bible-believers from time immemorial:

(A) You shall not shed another's blood, but
(B) If you do, I (God) will require (someone to shed) your
      blood.

Simplistic approaches that refuse to recognize the problem are
not very helpful. Merely to let *A* be obliterated by a hasty assumption that *B* has authorized someone to shed blood without any
other considerations is naive, to say the least.

The third introductory paragraph goes on to insist that the

purpose of the commandment is "to protect the life of each one,...emphatically forbidding homicide; and it should be heard by all with the same pleasure as if God, expressly naming each individual, were to prohibit injury to be offered him under a threat of the divine anger and the heaviest chastisement." An admirable statement indeed, it personalizes the commandment, challenging the Christian to maintain priorities: first and foremost, the protection of human life.

Thereupon the move is made to divide the content of the commandment into two parts, (A) the negative, and (B) the positive.

The prohibitory part (A) advises that "it should first be taught what kinds of killing are not forbidden by this Commandment," and the first such exception is:

1. The killing of animals, "for if God permits man to eat them, it is also lawful to kill them." This non-biblical quote, the first such in the chapter, is from Augustine's *City of God.* The very brevity and casualness of its use suggests that this was a common position on which little disagreement was expected, and thus there was no need for further elaboration. Whether it was meant to justify not only killing animals for food but also the practice of executing them when they harmed humans is not clear. The chronology at least suggests the possibility that there may have been a connection between the proliferation of such proceedings and the witch-craze.[87]

Without further ado the text then moves on to the second exception.

2. "The execution of criminals." This is the key passage, and is in fact the only one in the entire catechism that directly addresses the question of the morality of capital punishment. It is interesting to note its position: it is the very first instance of allowable killing of fellow human beings, standing as it does ahead of the brief treatment of the problem of war. Again, the casualness of the treatment would lead one to believe that the penal practice of the day (examples of which we have seen above) was generally accepted without reserve, if not actually endorsed as inevitable.

The single paragraph devoted to the justification of the death penalty is carefully crafted, but there is a touch of defensiveness indicating that the authors were indeed aware of some kind of controversy in the background, but nothing that had to be taken very seriously. It was only isolated outsiders/heretics, like the Waldenses some four centuries earlier, who saw fit to suggest there was something wrong with this everyday practice of state-authorized killing of lawbreakers. Such objections could be dismissed safely as the utterances of critics like Castellio, who had already shown themselves to be "unorthodox" Christians. Opposition to the death penalty was just one more of their many errors.

One can certainly wonder why there were not more protests, given the inhumanity of the methods used, but sensitivities in Christendom, it seems, had toughened. The widespread, ordinary use of sword and gallows, axe and wheel, seen as God's regular way of maintaining the social order through his princely proxy and supported by church teaching and practice, were part of everyday life. The Bible was read as providing full legitimacy for execution as the providential way to deal with social problems, and the powerful voice of Christian tradition was there to reassure, should anyone begin to waver on the propriety of the practice.

It is in this context, then, that the key passage of the *Roman Catechism* on the death penalty must be read. It is made up of five sentences, each of which is worth close scrutiny:

> 1. Another kind of lawful slaying belongs to the civil authorities, to whom is entrusted power of life and death, by the legal and judicious exercise of which they punish the guilty and protect the innocent.

> 2. The just use of this power, far from involving the crime of murder, is an act of paramount obedience to this Commandment which prohibits murder.

> 3. The end of the Commandment is the preservation and security of human life.

> 4. Now the punishments inflicted by the civil authority, which is the legitimate avenger of crime, naturally tend to

this end, since they give security to life by repressing outrage and violence.

5. Hence these words of David: "In the morning I put to death all the wicked of the land, that I might cut off all the workers of iniquity from the city of the Lord (Psalm 100:8)."

(1) The first sentence is a triple affirmation: (a) that civil authorities have power over life and death; b) that they must exercise it in a legal (according to the law) and judicious (according to good judgment) way; and (c) when they do so, they punish the guilty and protect the innocent.

This is a fairly concise summary of traditional teaching about the general legitimacy of the political order, reflecting the Constantinian conjunction of church and state. Paul's teaching in Romans 13, as traditionally understood, is in the wings, although it is not actually cited.

The only restriction mentioned is that the authorities have the responsibility to use their awesome power over life in a "legal and judicious" way, and it is here that questions arise. Two traditional justifications are given: "to punish the guilty (retribution), and to protect the innocent (social security)." No attention is given to the problem of the uniqueness of death as a punishment that does not punish in any ordinary sense of the word, but rather exterminates the subject.[88] Nor is there any attention given as to whether it makes any difference if the protection of the innocent can be achieved by other means. The confident tone of the statement, given as if it were an obvious matter of fact beyond all dispute, reflects a precritical outlook. There was not yet any inclination to grapple with the very real questions arising from blanket approval of state-imposed executions, as if they were all clearly mandated by God himself.

(2) The second sentence is likewise problematic. Its defensive quality is more evident than in the first sentence. The authors are looking over their shoulders, very much aware of someone making the claim that killing criminals is murder. Without identifying their opponents, they dismiss this opinion out of hand as not worthy of further attention. But in doing so, they

endorse an *a fortiori* argument that leaves them open to ready caricature. They argue, in effect, the opaque proposition that killing killers is somehow the very best way to obey the commandment not to kill. It is a bit of empty word-play that would escape challenge only so long as it could be taken for granted that no orthodox Christian would be likely to suggest that capital punishment might itself be a violation of the commandment. As long as one could dismiss such allegations as coming only from fringe groups, there was no challenge to develop more serious arguments to justify the routine of frequent executions.

Here, just as in the case of war, there seemed to be no evidence of the least suspicion that something might be wrong with the time-honored institution of capital punishment. The acid remarks of Voltaire two centuries later, describing Western history as one massive scaffold on which thousands upon thousands of people were regularly slaughtered by the authorities, civil and ecclesiastical, were gross exaggerations. But this statement is also an exaggeration in the other direction, providing no awareness of the very possibility of abuses. Violence perceived as divinely sanctioned without reservation or restriction is before long carried out relentlessly and without qualm.

(3) "The end of the Commandment is the preservation and security of human life." This beautiful statement has unfortunately been drained of sense by being placed back to back with the previous one. If it were allowed to stand on its own, it would obviously lead in the opposite direction. But "the preservation and security of human life" have already been greatly diminished by the way in which exceptions were multiplied so as to offer adequate cover for all Crusaders, inquisitors, and "just" warriors without any identifiable limits.

(4) "The punishments inflicted by the civil authority...naturally tend to this end, since they give security to life by repressing outrage and violence." The key word here is the adverb *naturally*. It is a statement of bald idealism that romanticizes penal practice in detached isolation from reality. No distinction is made regarding the different kinds of punishments, capital or corporal, humane or inhumane, but only the affirmation of blind faith in

the natural goodness of any and all policies adopted or authorized by a legitimate civil authority, because this meant that at
base they were delegated by God. Such ivory-towerism collapses
into total disrepute with the reality checks introduced by the
social sciences. The statement as it stands cannot take the empirical realities of abuse seriously into account. The myth of social
security as an automatic consequence resulting from ritual
bloodshed was uncritically accepted and dogmatically affirmed
without adequate warrant. And the suggestion that executing
people "represses violence" underscores how little the reality of
capital punishment had yet been understood or investigated.
The myth of deterrence enjoyed unconditional acceptance without ever being called to account for itself.

(5) Even if one were not disturbed by anything else in the
paragraph, the use made of verse eight of Psalm 100 (101) as the
final flourish is unfortunate, to say the least. It speaks volumes
about what was wrong with the whole system. It suggests that in
the ideal biblical order the civil authorities would schedule multiple executions every morning before breakfast. Deprived of any
rational context and used in such a setting, the text becomes an
entirely unwarranted endorsement of routine violence, a good
example of how the Bible should not be invoked.[89] It suggests
that virtually any officeholder of any petty state of any era, no
matter how godless, can be presumed to hold the total power of a
King David in his role as God's anointed.

The text itself is not necessarily that violent. It may hold an
allusion to the death penalty, but it also may not. The New International Version, for example, renders it: "Every morning I will
put to silence all the wicked in the land; I will cut off every evil-
doer from the city of the LORD." And it should certainly count
for something that the psalm begins with the promising excla-
mation: "I will sing of mercy and judgment....I will behave
myself wisely in a perfect way."[90] But even if the more violent
sense of the psalm is conceded, its application here is regrettable. That the daily use of capital punishment should come to
mind as a social ideal suggested by the text says more about the
state of the culture of sixteenth-century Rome than it does about
the psalm.

Granted, the catechism was written before the Thirty Years War, before the French Revolution, before World Wars I and II, and so on. Nonetheless, it helps to show what was wrong with the unquestioned view of the death penalty as God's will. There is, of course, no way of gauging how much influence the catechism itself may actually have had in promoting or sustaining this mentality. Gerard Sloyan concluded his overview of the Roman catechism's influence with the remark that "the lip service paid to it and the little use (more accurately the highly selective use) made of it by catechism authors since 1566 is perhaps the most notable feature about it."[91] This particular passage was among those well worth not selecting.

CHAPTER 5

Post-Tridentine Troubles and Tribulations

I. Internal Liabilities—the Burdens of Bloodshed
   A. The Wars of Religion—Military and Theological
      1. Cardinal Robert Bellarmine (1542–1621)
      2. Lutheran Theologian Johann Gerhard
         (1582–1637)
   B. The Spanish Inquisition
      1. Recent Studies
      2. Francisco Suárez, S.J. (1548–1617)
   C. The Witch Craze

II. External Liabilities—the Voices of Dissent
   A. Fourteenth-Fifteenth Centuries:
      Wycliffite-Hussite Voices
      1. John Wyclif (1330–1384)
      2. John Coryngham (1384)
      3. Nicholas Hereford (1391)
      4. Peter Chĕlcický (1421)
   B. Sixteenth and Seventeenth Centuries:
      Anabaptist Voices
      1. Conrad Grebel (1498–1526)
      2. Michael Sattler (1490–1527)
      3. Jakob Hutter (d.1536)
      4. Menno Simons (1496–1561)
      5. Marcin Czechowic (1575)
      6. Fausto Socino (1539–1604)
      7. Valentinus Smalcius (1572–1624)
   C. Seventeenth Century: Quaker Voices
      1. George Fox (1624–1691)
      2. John Bellers (1654–1725)

There is undoubtedly great irony in the unfolding story of Christian accommodation to the routine use of capital punishment. Three transitions have been identified as milestones on that journey, and all three were complicated by exceptional, unrelated, more or less simultaneous events or conditions.

First, in the fourth century, when the new religion was embraced by the Roman emperor, its "official" adoption might have introduced a higher ethic for a broader public, especially given the new religion's message promoting a way of life based on love of neighbor and devoid of revenge and violence. But the legacy of Roman law, reinforced by biblical literalism and other complications, led in the other direction. The ways of Firmicus Maternus and the Theodosian Code outweighed gospel priorities, for example, on the vendetta question.

Second, in the thirteenth century, when so much of the best of the earlier Christian heritage flowered in the intellectual spring of Scholastic theology, once more there was a series of severe practical problems, especially connected with controlling heresy and conducting crusades, that led both theologians and canonists to justify positions which had already been embraced, some of them in unanticipated directions. When Aquinas pondered the death penalty, he had to do so not in a vacuum but in an explosive age of violence between pope and emperor that is hardly conceivable.

And third, in the sixteenth century, when a catechism was prepared to guide teachers through the whole spectrum of Christian faith and practice, the context was a society already profoundly addicted to the use of capital punishment as its chief "problem-solver." Capital punishment was daily becoming more deeply entrenched in its use with increasingly enthusiastic approval by churchmen, both Protestant and Catholic, more so than in any other age in Christian history. The authors of that catechism were obviously working, not in a vacuum, but in a boiling cauldron of religious conflict where the absence of the gallows was unthinkable.

But that is not the whole story. The thesis of this chapter is that there were additionally some extremely important developments concerning the use of the death penalty during the first two centuries after Trent. More problems aggravated the situation, making it ever more difficult and unlikely for any serious critique to emerge from within. These complicating factors were both internal and external to the Catholic community's immediate experience.

I. INTERNAL LIABILITIES— THE BURDENS OF BLOODSHED

It is a well-known phenomenon that institutionalized capital punishment has always and everywhere carried very unpleasant consequences for all involved in the system, not just its direct victims. Administrations that engage in the business of planning, performing, and cleaning up after the systematic killing of people naturally have many things to do that other administrations do not. Although we have already seen much evidence of this, the two centuries after Trent are also illustrative.

A. The Wars of Religion–Military and Theological

The immediate aftermath of the Reformation saw days of uncommon destruction of life. For nearly a century, especially from 1559 to 1648, the conflict was exceptionally "passionate and highly disruptive....The battles fought between Protestants and Catholics...were tumultuous and anarchic because they characteristically took the form of civil war and rebellion."[1] They provided a special atmosphere for looking more longingly beyond this bloodied and war-torn "vale of tears" to a more peaceful and harmonious life after death.[2]

Recent historiographers, making greater use of the social sciences, have opened wider perspectives on the role that capital punishment played in the Tridentine era. Seventeenth-century Europe was, with good reason, a time and place marked by the widespread prevalence of profound fear. For many adults the world of their youth seemed to be disintegrating before their very eyes, and religion with its bitter divisions had become an unusually large part of the problem. The brutality of the Thirty Years War; the deep uncertainties reflected, for example, in Descartes' method of "universal doubt"; and other developments that challenged the traditional world view left many people confused and without moorings, open to growing cynicism, pessimism, and despair.

> Why was there, on both sides of the confessional abyss, that hyperacute awareness of sin, that obsession with hell, that emphatic and almost morbid delight in the original fault? Why was man so disparaged? Why was there that atmosphere of fear? A society which is afraid needs reassurance....The multiplicity of condemnations and warnings, anathemas and repudiations...give some measure of the enormous fear of Satan in the mentality of the west at that time.[3]

In such an age the prolific use of capital punishment as an integral part of the social-security program served as desperate consolation. Delumeau notes that in the catechism of Peter Canisius "the name of Satan is quoted 67 times, and the name of Jesus only 63."[4] The death penalty played a vital, necessary part in this cosmic clash with Satan. It was considered by the fearful populace to be a crucial instrument for eliminating the satanic agents proliferating throughout the society. In a world where war over clashing religious beliefs was virtually continuous, summary execution of enemies and traitors and other diabolical forces was an inevitable part of the endless campaigns, practiced systematically by all the churches. Part of the dogmatism on all sides of the theological controversies was inevitable, a kind of bravado in the face of uncertainty. It is fascinating to see the kind of extensive theological exchange over capital punishment that occurred at the time and has been grandly ignored (with good reason) in subsequent Christian history.

In classical Catholic-Lutheran *Controverstheologie* of the time, the exchanges often bore such extreme bitterness and hatred that they are embarrassments for later generations of both sides. The intensity of the religious wars of words paralleled the military and judicial assaults on opponents' lives. There were exceptions, however, and two of the most talented, erudite, and urbane participants deserve mention, even if their contributions are not of great significance today precisely because of the rigid ideologies they reflect.

1. CARDINAL ROBERT BELLARMINE (1542–1621)

The use of the death penalty had increased in dramatic fashion in this violent age. In the German diocese of Trier, for example, "in a mere seven years, from 1587 to 1593, 368 people from twenty-seven villages...were burned alive for sorcery."[5] It is understandable that theologians of the day found themselves having to devote more and more attention to such a tragic and troubling social trend. Even though their works, as noted, are largely historical curiosities today, due to their being so time-bound and ideological, it is worth taking a brief look at them.

Bellarmine was one of the great churchmen of the time, and the quality of his many contributions has been acknowledged by friend and foe alike. He wrote massive commentaries on most of the Catholic-Protestant theological controversies that raged during his lifetime. In Book III of his magnum opus he included two lengthy chapters summarizing the church's stance on capital punishment over the centuries, as he saw it.[6] The first of these, chapter 21, starts with the forthright fashion: "Can heretics, when they are condemned by the church to temporal punishments, also be punished with death?" Huss, Luther, and the Donatists of Augustine's time are introduced by Bellarmine as people who had made the mistake of denying this power in the past, whereas "all Catholics and even some heretics, including Calvin, teach the contrary." Then comes a barrage of biblical quotes meant to prove his contention beyond all doubt.

Of special interest is his remark on Acts 5, where he actually says "Peter killed Ananias and Sapphira." Such a reading of the New Testament text could go far toward justification not only of state use but also of papal use of the death penalty. In speaking of Theodosius, Valentinian, and the other emperors who were responsible for enacting the capital statutes against heresy in Roman law, Bellarmine has no hesitation in describing them as "most religious." Some of the liabilities of the comfortable union of church and state are readily discernible just beneath the surface.

For patristic support Bellarmine then lines up quotations from Cyprian, Jerome, Augustine, Leo, Gregory, and Bernard, thus interpreting a millennium's worth of authorities as approving and defending the policy of killing heretics. Then, with all this biblical, imperial, and patristic evidence on his side, he turns finally to a fivefold "proof from natural reason" to cap it off. Pointing to the fact that the law of God and the law of the land provide death as the penalty for "lesser" crimes, such as murder and adultery, so it stands to reason that heretics—guilty of a far greater crime—ought to be executed. Some of his assessments paint a grim picture of the age; for example, he apparently agrees with a certain Galeno that "often it is useful to kill [heretics] because otherwise they would only get worse, and it is improbable anyway that they could ever be restored to mental health."

Chapter 22 is devoted to answering objections. In considering the famous restriction of Luther, Bellarmine runs short on patience:

> The church, says Luther, from its beginnings down to the present, has never ordered the execution of a heretic, so it does not seem to be her will to burn them. I answer that this argument perfectly proves, not the opinion, but the ignorance or impudence of Luther. As a matter of fact, that great numbers have been burned or otherwise killed either Luther does not know [the truth], and thus is incompetent, or he knows it, and is impudently lying. In fact, that heretics have often been burned by the church can be demonstrated by recalling a few from among many examples.

This is the level of discourse henceforth to prevail on both sides in much of the Protestant-Catholic polemics. Bellarmine unabashedly admits that the church has been killing heretics for centuries and does not suggest that there was anything wrong with this; on the contrary, he cites a list of executions, beginning with Priscillian's in the fourth century, and seems to be boasting rather than expressing any regret or embarrassment. He proceeds to formulate no less than eighteen different arguments to refute Luther, some of them extremely thin and hardly worthy of someone of his stature.

In argument #18, for example, he concedes that "the Apostles did not invoke the secular arm against heretics," but immediately goes on to explain that this was simply "because there was no Christian prince [at that time]....Later, in the time of Constantine, the church suddenly had available the help of the secular power." This political gratuity is seen as an unmixed blessing with no note of caution or criticism. The mere fact that something happened in church history enabling churchmen to prevail in the physical realm seemed to be reason enough to confer legitimacy and make it a practice worthy of perennial imitation. To the political victors belong the spiritual spoils.

2. LUTHERAN THEOLOGIAN JOHANN GERHARD (1582–1637)

Gerhard's magisterial *Loci Theologici*, published in nine volumes over a span of a dozen years (1610–1622), included a treatment of capital punishment even lengthier than Bellarmine's.[7] He expended great energy in defending Luther and refuting Bellarmine by all available means. The most striking aspect, however, is his long list of theological propositions drawn from Christian history, which he held in common with Bellarmine, both of them staunchly defending the validity of capital punishment in most cases. Both appealed to the Bible in literal fashion to show not only that the death penalty was legitimate but that it was divinely sanctioned, that it was unquestionably necessary for an orderly state, that executioners perform a virtuous act when they carry out their important office, that such killings do not violate the law of love but are rather an actual fulfillment of it, and that pardon of prisoners should certainly not be given in every case, even though mercy was occasionally an appropriate Christian response.

The one place where the battle lines were most clearly drawn was at the troublesome thesis #33, condemned by Pope Leo X, regarding Luther's contention that the execution of *heretics* was contrary to the will of the Holy Spirit. On this issue Catholics and Calvinists were dead wrong, as far as Gerhard was concerned. Matching opponents in the numbers game, he piled up figures on mass killings and told horror stories of the cruelties of the Spanish Inquisition. He discoursed for pages on the lessons of the parable of the wheat and the weeds, seeing it as his most powerful weapon against both Bellarmine and Calvin.[8] Jesus had taught that the heretical weeds must be allowed to coexist until the harvest, as Chrysostom and Wazo and so many others had also taught before the thirteenth-century papal crackdown made it an unacceptable position for Catholic theologians.

But this was virtually their only area of real disagreement. Gerhard found nothing wrong with the death penalty as such; on the contrary, it was basic to the divine plan. The state possessed the temporal sword given by God and could hardly do without it. The only thing wrong and "against the Holy Spirit" was extending the circle of its victims to include heretics. Yet, as the case of Servetus had demonstrated over a half-century earlier, this was a fragile restriction indeed and did little to curtail the increasing "legal" bloodbaths in seventeenth-century Europe.

> Little distinction was made in practice between moral and religious offences, including blasphemy and heresy, and secular offences such as murder or theft; all were seen in the first instance as violations of the godly order which the secular authorities were divinely appointed to enforce....An offense against the law was thus an offense against God. Secular authority wielded the sword of justice by divine ordinance....Punishment...was couched in the language of religious ritual...a Christian ceremony that signified the unity of the godly and the secular order.[9]

Gerhard and Bellarmine shared much of this world view, even as they employed often tendentious arguments against one another. All around them the Protestant-Catholic controversies escalated. An example is found in a surviving booklet printed in 1621.[10] It shows how the harsh reality of the religious clashes led to bloodshed with inexorable logic. Catholic Gaspar Schoppius[11] is reported by Lutheran Justus Meier as having set forth to the authorities this impeccable syllogism:

> [Major] All heretics and schismatics are banned by Roman Imperial Law and should be subject to the supreme punishment, and (thus) rightly ought to be killed immediately.

> [Minor] All Protestants are heretics and schismatics.

> [Conclusion] Therefore, all Protestants are banned by
> Roman Imperial Law and should be subject to the supreme
> punishment, and (thus) all ought to be killed immediately.

Here the death penalty in Christianity was driven to its all-time logical climax as a God-given instrument for authorizing the wholesale extermination of one another. All who professed other than totally orthodox Christian faith were by definition subject without exception to execution. Who was to do the judging, and how, were questions left to be answered by whoever had the greater political power at any moment. The point had been reached where all previous debate was irrelevant. The death penalty had been incorporated as a constitutive part of the church. Wherever heresy appeared, the scaffold had to be set up or the eternal plan of God would be gravely violated. It is easy to see how theologians got trapped in this logical calamity; and it is considerably less easy to see how to get out of it without a revolution in thinking. We shall see later a more recent instance where this very dispute was replayed in a bitter English-Irish controversy.

Reflection on this impasse can give one a new appreciation for what was attempted in the Treaty of Westphalia (1648), which desperately tried to separate Catholics and Protestants geographically to curtail the bloodshed. It also highlights the wisdom of Augustine, who, even though he had granted potential legitimacy for the death penalty, concluded that the ideal in Christian practice was that it ought never in any circumstances actually be used.

B. The Spanish Inquisition

1. RECENT STUDIES

The Spanish Inquisition was at its zenith in this same period, and it too may be viewed as due at least in part to institutional departure from higher ideals. Due to lingering Protestant-Catholic biases it is still difficult to be fair in any assessment of it in its extreme complexity, as Edward Peters has shown in recent years. Easily overlooked is the fact that medieval Spain had far more experience than other Christian societies in living peacefully with large numbers of people of different beliefs (Jews and

Muslims) in its midst. It was only from the mid-fourteenth century that an extremely ominous change began to occur:

> A series of economic and natural catastrophes...from the Black Death (1348–1349) on increased widespread resentment against the tax collectors, and at the same time a more intense and widespread anti-Semitism began to circulate throughout the kingdom....The older kinds of tolerance and cosmopolitanism began to give way before the increasing power, wealth, and world-view of the higher aristocracy, which perceived itself chiefly as a Christian military nobility superior to Muslims and Jews.[12]

Christian militarism escalated throughout the next century, with Moors and Jews being forcibly expelled, and "religious anti-Semitism changed into ethnic anti-Semitism" as the descendants of the old Christian Visigoths grounded their superiority in the racist myth of "purity of blood." This doctrine became the new ideology that "shaped the history and society of early modern Spain."

The Inquisition is admittedly the saddest chapter of Spanish Christianity, and the November 1, 1478, bull of Pope Sixtus IV, permitting Ferdinand and Isabella to choose their own inquisitors, paved the way for this aberration.

> When an alleged *converso* plot to take arms against the inquisitors was uncovered in Seville in 1481, the first large-scale condemnation of Judaizing *conversos* was held, along with the first public burning of condemned heretics. The public sentencing of convicted heretics in solemn paraliturgical ceremonies came to be known as the *auto-da-fé*, the "act of faith."[13]

Peters sets the record straight on certain aspects of the Spanish Inquisition. For instance, on the question of how many persons were actually executed, he writes:

> The Spanish Inquisition, in spite of wildly inflated estimates of the numbers of its victims, acted with considerable restraint in inflicting the death penalty, far more restraint than was demonstrated in secular tribunals elsewhere in

Europe that dealt with the same kinds of offenses. The best estimate is that around 3,000 death sentences were carried out in Spain by Inquisitorial verdict between 1550 and 1800, a far smaller number than that in comparable secular courts.[14]

Henry Kamen has pointed out the factors that made Spain unique in terms of the Protestant Reformation: (1) "Medieval Christianity in Spain was too busy to produce dissent of its own....One has to go back to the sixth century to find a heresy (Arianism)....This astonishing freedom from heresy was matched by an absence of repressive institutions."[15] (2) Rome gave almost total control over the church to the Spanish crown, which from 1508 had the "Patronato"—the right to make all church appointments in America, and from 1523, the same right for Spain itself. This meant that the crown had extensive control not only over church personnel but revenues as well. Thus, unlike the situation in northern Europe, the king of Spain was "the last monarch in Europe to want to use the Reformation for political advantage....Quite simply, he did not need it." (3) The history of the Reformation in Spain is thus extremely brief.

> It was not until the events of 1558-62 that a real heresy crisis erupted....The *autos-da-fé* at Valladolid in May 1559 and at Seville in September began the bloody repression, which continued with a series of further *autos* up to 1592. With these executions, Protestantism in Spain was almost totally extinguished.[16]

But, after full provision is made for correcting distortions and exaggerations due to the bitter animosities of the past, the central question still remains. If the legitimacy of deliberately killing people for having different beliefs had not become a Christian cultural given, how different might Western history have been? The exporting of the death penalty to the colonies of the New World, for example, was nowhere more tragic than in the case of Mexico. When the massive human sacrifices practiced by the Aztecs were discovered, Cortès and his conquistadores could think of no better response than to execute them. Thus, Aztecs who were caught offering human sacrifices were condemned to become human sacrifices in order to show that human sacrifice was wrong![17] It was only one of the more irrational instances of using capital punishment as a would-be solution to a troublesome problem.

The timing of these events was, to say the least, unfortunate for the native peoples of the New World. The European colonizing period happened to coincide with the precise era when Christian addiction to the death penalty was most firmly in place among both Protestants and Catholics. As one of the worst features of European Christianity it thus aggravated the colonizing impulse. The Mexican Inquisition staged an auto-da-fé as early as October 17, 1528, in which two Jews were burned for heresy. Eighty years of inquisitorial activity in New Spain was observed with an auto-da-fé on March 25, 1601, during which "143 heretics [were] paraded and 4 of them burned at the stake." Soon afterward, the English brought to Massachusetts Bay and to Virginia, and the French brought to Canada, the full seventeenth-century European legal codes with all their heritage of lethal violence confidently imposed in the name of God.[18]

During Vatican Council II Karl Rahner, S.J. reminded his fellow Catholics that basic changes of mind and heart in evaluating these aberrations would have to be made if the incipient renewal were to be ultimately effective:

> Certainly, the history of the persecution of heretics, of the Inquisition, and of the internal Christian "wars of religion," is a terrible chapter in the history of Christianity, full of horrible events which must not be defended, least of all in the name of Christianity.[19]

But "not defending" them requires at least identifying them as tragic departures from gospel ideals. Not only the practices but the ideologies that accounted for their development and survival needed to be replaced. Otherwise, the cycle of violence could never be broken, and Christians would be free to go on supporting the death penalty as if it were merely an incidental part of the woodwork rather than the hallmark of a culture of death.

2. Francisco Suárez, S.J. (1548-1617)

In the case of Suárez we have an example similar to what we have already seen in Aquinas, Vitoria, and Bellarmine. Like them, Suárez was an original and highly gifted thinker, recognized as one of the great Catholic theologians of that or any other age. His positive contributions in many areas were monumental. So effective was his refutation of the divine right of kings theory, for example, that King James I had a copy of his work burned on the steps of St. Paul's Cathedral in London (1613). He was well ahead of his time in his view of the state as the result of a social contract involving the consent of the people. His arguments for the natural rights of the human individual to life, liberty, and property, as well as his repudiation of the Aristotelian notion of slavery as the natural condition of some kinds of people, also put him on the cutting edge of progressive social thought.[20]

It is thus all the more unfortunate to see Suárez burdened with the task of trying to justify the execution of heretics, as was called for in his time, the heyday of the Inquisition. Less than two decades separate his major work from that of Bellarmine, but Suárez had incorporated his treatment of the death penalty into the core of his massive tract *De Fide Theologica* which runs to some six hundred pages in the nineteenth-century printing and is divided into twenty-four disputations.[21] The treatment of heresy as a part of the theology of faith begins with definitions and descriptions in Disputatio #19; in #20 he delves into the thorny problem that had been bedeviling the Western church for some thirteen hundred years: how to respond to heretics and heresy. Is it right for the church to prohibit and censure them? Can they be coerced to recant? Is everyone bound to denounce them to the authorities?

The questions reveal much about the existential context in which they were being discussed. Disputatio #21 then turns to the spiritual punishment of heretics, from censure to excommunication, while #22 takes up temporal punishment, especially the extent and severity allowed in the confiscation of goods and property. But it is #23 that goes on to deal with corporal punishments, enumerating four particular types to be treated: imprisonment, exile, flagellation, and death.

> The material of this disputation [#23] pertains more to the external than to the internal forum, and so we will dispatch it more briefly...only touching on what has to do with dogmas of faith or the forum of conscience in some way. The various corporal punishments can be reduced to four....We do not count *torture* because that is used not as a punishment but only to discover the truth...and we will dwell chiefly on the *death penalty,* because, if that can be justified, *a fortiori* all the rest can also be.

It is sobering to realize the kinds of changes that had taken place in the century since the Reformation began. Here we see the theologian who is often considered second only to Thomas Aquinas in Catholic history forced to spend an inordinate amount of the time available for discussing the mysteries of Christian faith on the intricacies of using the death penalty against heretics. Times had changed indeed. Aquinas at least only had to explore basic moral aspects of executions and the need for rational arguments to support them. But Suárez was unfortunately confronted with the need to take into account the entire "system" that had been constructed for the use of the royal Inquisition. He was held responsible for defending much that neither earlier nor later Catholic theologians would even dream of attempting in a treatise on theological faith. Such was his misfortune.

Suárez's Disputatio #23 has two sections, the first of which begins by asking the question: "Can the church justly punish heretics with the death penalty?" His answer, divided into nine parts, begins by pointing out the bad company one would be keeping by denying such power to the church: "That the church cannot impose the death penalty on heretics nor invoke the help of the secular arm to do so was an ancient heresy...that of the Donatists." After a half-dozen references to places in Augustine to support this, he goes on to note that "Wyclif, according to the Council of Constance, made the same mistake," and then Luther took it up and "was condemned for it by Pope Leo X." But then he summarizes the case made by those who oppose killing heretics. Augustine admittedly had his doubts "not whether it was lawful but whether it was expedient." The ancient church did prefer to exile rather than to kill heretics, but "this custom was

based on the church's mildness," making it view the death
penalty as "repugnant." And yes, it is also true that the church
does not kill some infidels and "even tolerates Jews; therefore, it
ought not and indeed cannot use this penalty against heretics."
So some would contend.

"Nevertheless, it is a Catholic assertion that the Church can
justly punish heretics with the death penalty. This truth is widely
defended against the heretics [who deny it]." He refers to Eck,
Bellarmine, Castro, Valentia, Osius, and a half-dozen others, and
then notes that it will not take long to prove this assertion
because

> for a penalty to be justly imposed, only two things are neces-
> sary: 1) it must be proportionate to the gravity of the crime;
> and 2) it must be imposed by one who has the power and
> jurisdiction to do so.

As might be predicted, his next step is to appeal to the Old
Testament, pointing out with all the appropriate references that
God ordered false prophets to be killed as well as those Israelites
who refused to obey the judgment of the priests. Then comes a
reference-filled appeal to church custom and the Fathers, and
finally a call to reason. It is interesting to see the medical analogy
surface at this point, with the note that putrid limbs must be
amputated for the good of the whole body.

This is only the first half of the first section. The crucial
question of power is then taken up in similar manner, with
lengthy elaboration on Christ having given the keys to Peter.
The parable of the wheat and the weeds is then discussed in
great detail with a basic distinction being introduced to defuse
it:

> Christ prohibited killing heretics when they cannot be
> known or identified by Catholics. But when they are suffi-
> ciently discerned and their crime is known and proved, then
> *the parable does not apply,* because, even though the weeds are
> being uprooted, there is no danger of thereby uprooting the
> wheat, i.e., Catholics, at the same time, which is what Christ
> taught should be avoided.

The second section of Disputatio #23 is even longer than the first, having no fewer than seventeen parts. The general question it addresses is the reach of the law: "Are *all* heretics subject to the death penalty according to the law of the church?" It does not get better. The greatest practical value of this section is the way in which it illustrates how institutionalized capital punishment invariably poisons the system that is burdened with it. Imagine if Suárez had had the luxury of living in a context where there was no capital punishment. He had already shown what great insights his extraordinary intelligence could achieve when he was free to focus on higher things. But this was just one more loss stemming from the burdensome inquisitorial system of legalized bloodshed that he was expected to defend.

C. The Witch Craze

The great witch craze overlaps the other burdens of bloodshed, but it needs to be recognized for what it was, one of the most bizarre cases of Western religion gone mad. Classifying witchcraft as a heresy under Roman law became a tremendous liability for the churches (Catholic and Protestant) during this episode. The real number of victims executed will never be known, but from combined sources the estimated totals have ranged from 200,000 to 500,000, and upward.[22]

The study of this aberration in recent years has produced much light where myths and biases previously ruled. Some of the discoveries have also made important corrections to the record; for example, Cohn's demonstration that three forgeries of the fifteenth, sixteenth, and nineteenth centuries were responsible for creating stories of atrocities that never really happened. He thereby eliminated as fictional a tale of mass trials in Toulouse from 1335 to 1350 in which four hundred witches were supposed to have been executed.[23]

But such revisions, resulting in the discarding of some legends, are more than offset by the closer study of what actually did happen, not in the fourteenth century but in the seventeenth century, the scandalous climax of the European witch craze, when, for example, the prince-bishop of Catholic Würzburg burned some 900 persons at the stake (between 1623 and 1631), while in much the same period 358 persons were burned at the stake in Protestant Scotland. In 1634 in France the Carmelite nuns of Loudun were executed as possessed by the devil. The year 1645 saw the Essex outbreak, the largest such collective execution in England, when 19 women were hanged. In 1649 another epidemic of over 300 executions took place again in Scotland. In 1669 Sweden had its attack with the Mora witch panic that left 85 persons executed, many of them children. In 1692 the craze infected the New World with the witch trials of Salem, Massachusetts, and in 1697 another 20 persons were executed at Paisley in Scotland. The worst was over, as the "cosmological infrastructure of the witchhunt was overtaken by enlightenment rationalism," although the last "legal" execution of a witch in Switzerland was in Glarus in 1782 and in Poland in 1793, five years after the death penalty had supposedly been abolished there.[24]

It is easy enough to dismiss these executions as aberrations of an age of sick religion that simply cannot be accounted for, but the seeds of such carnage are identifiable, even if the fruit of violence is seldom foreseen in its seeds. How different might the story of Western Christianity have been if churchmen had adopted the Augustinian response and said no instead of yes to the use of capital punishment as a privileged means of social control?

II. EXTERNAL LIABILITIES—THE VOICES OF DISSENT

The Christian ideal of nonviolent conduct has always had a strong biblical warrant but has regularly been circumvented in practice in a variety of ways. The accommodations made in the early Middle Ages, allowing capital punishment to gain its unusually privileged position in Western Christendom, were largely unintentional aberrations. Other issues held center stage. As internal disagreements and conflicts multiplied, however, it was not long before some Christians had misgivings about the acceptance of legalized bloodshed. Some of the Waldensians were apparently the earliest, within the century after the First Crusade. Even though they later left the nonviolent ideal aside, there

were others who took it up in the following centuries. Their role
in the eventual overthrow of the death penalty in Europe often
has been minimized or overlooked. Catholic historians, on the
one hand, have tended to dismiss them as minor heretical sectar-
ians without much importance. Secular historians, on the other
hand, have often ignored them as mere religious curiosities from
an earlier age.

The argument here is that these voices of protest ought to
be recognized for keeping the nonviolent heritage alive until it
was eventually more generally retrieved. This contradicts the
popular idea that initial efforts to get rid of capital punishment
came as a relatively unexplained bolt from the blue at the time of
the Enlightenment. Such can be maintained only by ignoring the
individuals and groups recalled here, people motivated by their
understanding of the gospel to criticize the death penalty as an
ungodly abomination long before the abolitionist movements
began. John Howard Yoder has spoken of "a constant undercur-
rent in earlier Christian history" opposing capital punishment.[25]
Six centuries before the Enlightenment, as we have seen in the
case of the Waldenses, there were Christian critics objecting to
Christian use of the death penalty. Their objections designated it
a violation of both the fifth commandment and the "hard sayings" of Christ, which gave priority to love and forgiveness and
rejected all revenge-taking among his followers.

Some of these groups quickly died out or were suppressed,
interrupted or transmuted. Their witness was nonetheless an
important factor in preparing for the time when, after several
centuries, less overtly religious protests would initiate a long and
arduous drive to rid European culture of the anomaly of capital
punishment. Although these contributors cannot be discussed in
detail, at least some acknowledgment of their important role is
called for. This requires us to double back chronologically to
pick up the trail of protest that coincided with the general acceptance of the death penalty, which we have already traced.

Reform movements desirous of translating and distributing
the Bible to the common people were invariably the wellsprings
from which disapproval of Christian bloodshed surfaced. There
was no way to escape the impact of the Sermon on the Mount,
for example, especially when stated in the familiar terms of

everyday speech. Even if the broader reform movements did not reject all violence, the appearance of individuals within them who did was common. Because their nonviolent witness was usually imbedded in a complex of other beliefs that were not only controversial but often declared heretical by the "mainstream" Christian churches, it was likely to be discarded as one more theological error. But their witnessing to the sacredness of the gift of life, sometimes at the price of life, provided an articulate challenge to the wider community.

A. Fourteenth-Fifteenth Centuries: Wycliffite-Hussite Voices

1. JOHN WYCLIF (1330–1384)

Often known as the "Morning Star of the Reformation," Wyclif played an important role in the history of "Englishing" the Bible. He was an innovative thinker whose radical theological ideas were taken home by Bohemian students at Oxford University. It was only in his latter days, however, that "something happened to change his attitude to war-making."[26] Wyclif had previously written about the conditions for a justified war, but the disastrous 1383 "Crusade" of pope against anti-pope led him to denounce warfare vehemently. In one of his last sermons he repudiated all war. He organized his objections as "Sixteen different ways that warfare violates charity." This was his major contribution to a more peace-minded Christianity, but some of his followers carried this strain of emerging pacifism into the explicit analysis of capital punishment as well as war.

2. JOHN CORYNGHAM

Coryngham was a country vicar who came under Wyclif's influence while at Oxford. Little is known of him except that he was accused in 1384 of teaching that "it is wrong for a Christian to take human life under any circumstances."[27] This fourteenth-century Christian pastor apparently reached the same conclusion as Lactantius had in the fourth century and some Waldensians had in the twelfth century: all killing is forbidden to Christians. Fuller information on exactly how he proceeded to arrive at this position is simply not available.

3. Nicholas Hereford

This Carthusian monk joined Wyclif's circle at Oxford and was one of the translators responsible for the Lollard Bible. He was condemned for preaching a sermon in defense of Wyclif and went to Rome to appeal his case. He was imprisoned there, but the pope saved him from execution. After escaping from prison, he went back to England but was rearrested there. This time he recanted and was given a position at the Hereford cathedral.

Before this final stage of his turbulent life, however, Hereford had espoused Christian nonviolence and spoken out against war. He was probably the author of the English tract *On the Seven Deadly Sins*, which includes the following passage:

> We should love our enemies....Men should not now [i.e., under the new law of love] fight. And therefore Jesus Christ, duke of our battle, taught us the law of patience, and not to fight bodily....It seems no charity to ride against thine enemy well armed with sharp spear upon a strong courser....What honor falls to a knight because he kills many men,...[acting] only as a "butcher of his brethren"?

Such scathing disapproval of knightly violence represents a disenchantment that was not much in evidence since the rise of the Crusader three centuries earlier. An episcopal courtbook of the bishop of Norwich for the years 1428 to 1431 reveals much about Lollard beliefs at that time and place, explicitly including "the rejection of war under all circumstances as well as of the death penalty."[28] One defendant, a miller named John Skilly, is on record as believing and saying publicly that "it is not lawful for a man to fight or do battle for a realm...or to go to law for any right or wrong." Killing human beings was condemned as contradicting a Christian's obligation to show love toward all his fellows. One witness says quite explicitly that "every man should remit all vengeance...to the sentence of God."

Voices like these, even though readily ignored, forgotten, or suppressed, were pesky reminders that the Christian compromise with killing, even though "canonized" for two or three centuries, still made some Christians very uneasy, especially those inclined to take the gospel literally.

D. PETER Chělcický

Chělcický holds an intriguing place in Czech history. The execution of John Huss and Jerome of Prague at the Council of Constance, and the bloodshed that followed in Bohemia, have already been noted. In the sordid aftermath of that tragedy an unusual person, acting out of Christian motives, embraced radical pacifism in that incredibly violent time. His first book was a running commentary on Ephesians 6:10–20 and can be seen as reversing the eleventh-century Gregorian tendency to use military language for religious ends.[29] Peter's whole point was to insist that the text urging Christians to "put on the whole armor of God" and fight manfully also makes it clear that the language is figurative, since "our wrestling is not against flesh and blood," but against "principalities and powers" in the spiritual order. His conclusion is that "all killing, including such as is incidental to war, is sin."[30]

Peter's classic work, however, was "The Net of Faith," written early in the 1440s, setting forth his attack on "the union of church and state,...and Christians serving as soldiers."[31] For him the problems began in the fourth century when "Constantine injected a poison into the body of Christ" and the secular order gained supremacy over the law of love. As the title indicates, the book is a kind of commentary on Luke 5:4–11, the miraculous draught of fishes. In his imaginative adaptation, Peter sees the net as a symbol of the church torn apart by the emperor and the pope. "When these two monstrous whales began to turn about in the net, they tore it to such an extent that very little of it has remained whole."[32]

Peter's anti-papal vitriol anticipated the trenchant language of Luther in the following century. It reflected the depth of dissatisfaction, anger, and frustration felt by many Christians of the day. One need not accept Peter's analysis of church history, his view of the papacy, his basic ecclesiology, or anything else to see that he was touching on an extremely important and sensitive issue, that is, how a Christian ought to respond to violence. His was an early voice, groping diligently for a solution to this agonizing problem. The need for church reform at the time was colossal. The only remedy for the "poison" of worldliness injected into the church by Constantine, as Peter saw it, was a radical separation of church and state. He came close to returning to the third-century position of Origen, admitting that Christians must submit to the state (as to a necessary evil) but must not participate in its practices of killing in war or capital punishment.

By the time of his death around 1460 a community had formed to try to live according to Peter's teachings. Spinka calls this "the beginning of the organization of that finest product of the Czech Reformation, i.e., the Unity of Brethren."[33] Such minority voices could not and did not stop the savagery of religious wars, but their witness to peace and against the slaughter of fellow human beings had long-range impact, even though they paid a high price in the short term.[34]

B. Sixteenth and Seventeenth Centuries: Anabaptist Voices

The Radical, or Left-Wing, Protestant Reformation was a notoriously complex series of developments, extremely difficult to analyze fairly, not only because of the speed with which it splintered but also because it "crystalized almost simultaneously in several [different] geographical areas."[35] It was made up of a variety of groups, some of them very different from others, some revolutionary, others pacifist. All we can do is mention a half-dozen members of Anabaptist sub-groups that had (and in some cases still have) an obvious bearing on our topic. The impact of their opposition to capital punishment was admittedly reduced by the way they objected, not just to the death penalty, but to the whole notion of humans functioning as magistrates, or at least to Christians serving in such a capacity. Nonetheless, they were part of the cumulative dissent to sanctioned violence, voices in the wilderness crying out against vindictive human judgment.

In our day it has been said that "the Anabaptists were neither Catholic nor Protestant, but stressed pacifism, the separation of church and state,...and the conviction that ethics are a part of the good news of Jesus Christ. [They] wanted to restore the New Testament church in both essence and form."[36] Their name ("Rebaptizers") was used pejoratively by both their Protestant and Catholic opponents, linking them with the fourth century Donatists, who were explicitly condemned as heretics in both civil and ecclesiastical Roman law. They were thus defined as subject to the death penalty according to the Justinian Code, making it all the easier to exterminate them.

Their opposition to the practice of capital punishment clearly derived from their interest in restoring a Christian ethic that more fully represented the teaching of Jesus as they understood it from the New Testament. The readiness with which such protest groups identified the death penalty as an aberration to be repudiated must give one pause. No matter how "heretical" many of their other positions seemed, their opposition to violence and bloodshed struck close to home and troubled other Christians who had compromised with war and capital punishment. Attacks upon the Anabaptist "disturbers" usually centered on other areas of disagreement, such as aspects of their views on the Trinity, Christology, ecclesiology, eschatology, and so forth. The union of church and state required the larger, established Christian communions, whether Catholic or Protestant, to defend the "traditional" acceptance of the legitimacy of bloodshed, since both were so inextricably involved in its everyday use. The thirteenth-century agreement of pope and emperor to make all-out war against heretics proved a heavy liability, since it obscured Christian witness to the sanctity of life in chaotically violent circumstances.

This fact also goes far in explaining why Catholics did not participate in the abolitionist debate for centuries. Since prophetic groups that raised objections to capital punishment also rejected important parts of Catholic teaching on other points, there was an understandable tendency to be leery of all their claims. For those convinced they were wrong in other novel beliefs, it was safer to believe they had recovered nothing at all valid in their reforming effort. The apologetic instinct to defend all past positions by pointing to the shortcomings of would-be reformers cut short the possibility of dialogue. At the end of the twentieth century, however, we may put aside those perceptions and try to acknowledge the positive achievements of the various parties.[37]

1. CONRAD GREBEL

Grebel was the early leader of the Anabaptist Swiss Brethren. A young scholar who had studied in Basel, Vienna, and Paris, Grebel was associated with Zwingli until they quarreled and parted ways over their differing visions of the church. He and his friends thought they might find kindred spirits in Thomas Müntzer's group, so in 1524 they wrote to explore that prospect, openly addressing some areas of concern that required caution. One of the issues was the Christian use of violence, and Grebel made his position clear:

> The gospel and its adherents are not to be protected by the sword, nor are they thus to protect themselves....True Christian believers are sheep among wolves, sheep for the slaughter; they must be baptized in anguish and affliction, tribulation, persecution, suffering, and death; they must be tried with fire, and must reach the fatherland of eternal rest, not by killing their bodily, but by mortifying their spiritual, enemies. Neither do they use worldly sword or war, since all killing has ceased with them—unless, indeed, we would still be of the old law. And even there, so far as we recall, war was a misfortune after they had once conquered the Promised Land. No more of this.[38]

The letter never reached Müntzer, and Grebel's leadership was cut short by his death in the plague of 1526 at age 28.[39]

2. MICHAEL SATTLER

Sattler took up Grebel's mantle and was the leading figure at the first synod held at Schleitheim near Zurich in 1527. He was the chief author of the "Brotherly Union" adopted there, an important document for Anabaptist groups. Sattler had been a Benedictine prior and was burned at the stake four months after the Schleitheim gathering.[40] One characteristic of the theology expressed by Sattler was its stark dualism:

> There is nothing else in the world and all creation [other] than good and evil...Christ and Belial, and none will have part with the other....Thereby shall also fall away from us the diabolical weapons of violence—such as sword, armor and the like, and all of their use to protect friends or against enemies—by virtue of the word of Christ, "You shall not resist evil."

In its sixth article, dealing with the state's use of violence, the document declared that "the Christian should not use the sword

against the wicked for the protection and defense of the good."
The signers of this confession thus concluded that "Christians
should not become magistrates or become involved in government
affairs. Government rested on coercion, and Christians could not
use force."[41] Whatever one might think of their conclusions, it was
clearly their earnest reading of the New Testament that ultimately
accounted for these convictions. "Thou shalt not kill" applied
across the board. Lethal violence was simply not Christian.

3. JAKOB HUTTER

Hutter reorganized a group of Swiss Anabaptists after they
had fled to Moravia because of persecution. He ended up being
burned at the stake in 1536, but his followers carried on both his
teaching and lifestyle of nonviolence and rejection of bloodshed
as part of their Christian heritage. These Hutterites migrated
further east to the Ukraine in 1756, then, when treated poorly by
the czarist regime, came in considerable numbers to the United
States and Canada in the 1870s. Their commitment to nonviolence cannot be overlooked as one of the continuing factors
keeping the ideal alive on this continent.[42]

4. MENNO SIMONS

Simons was a Dutch priest whose spirited writings provided
a community framework for his followers. They adopted his name
(Mennonites) to distinguish themselves from the fiercely militant
group of revolutionary Anabaptists (Münsterites), whose excesses
in Münster in 1534 were often used by Catholics and Protestants
"to discredit all Anabaptists as revolutionaries and terrorists."[43]
Simons is the only early Anabaptist whose careful explanation of his opposition to the death penalty has survived. He
began it by observing that

> it would hardly become a true Christian ruler to shed blood.
> If the transgressor should truly repent before his God and be
> reborn of Him, he would then also be a chosen saint and
> child of God, a fellow partaker of grace, a spiritual member
> of the Lord's body, sprinkled with his precious blood and
> anointed with his Holy Spirit, a living grain of the Bread of
> Christ and an heir to eternal life; and for such a one to be

hanged on the gallows, put on the wheel, placed on the stake, or in any manner be hurt in body or goods by another Christian, who is of one heart, spirit, and soul with him, would look somewhat strange and unbecoming in the light of the compassionate, merciful, kind nature, disposition, spirit, and example of Christ, the meek Lamb, which example he has commanded all his chosen children to follow.

Simons covers the best-case scenario of a repentant criminal, painting a faith-picture of how inappropriate the execution of such a person would be. Then he takes up the worst-case scenario of an impenitent criminal. What then? He declared that executing a person in such a condition

would unmercifully rob him of the time of repentance of which, in case his life were spared, he might yet avail himself. It would be unmerciful to tyrannically offer his poor soul, which was purchased with such precious treasure, to the devil of hell under the unbearable judgment, punishment, and wrath of God, so that he would forever have to suffer and bear the tortures of unquenchable burning, the consuming fire, eternal pain, woe, and death. Never observing that the Son of man says: "Learn of me, I have given you an example. Follow me; I am not come to destroy souls but to save them."[44]

It is a simple argument of individual Christian piety based on a rather traditional New Testament reading. For that very fact it could not be dismissed out of hand, even though its adherents were members of very small Christian groups. As has always been the case, it does not take much leaven to affect the mass, and this witness against killing influenced even those who found it objectionable. It inspired honest people to strive for a higher ideal by rejecting the violence of the death penalty some two centuries before the Enlightenment, a reminder that the privileged status of the gallows was never without its critics. Many of these dissenting Christians, ironically, suffered the death penalty in the very process of testifying to its anti-Christian inspiration. When that happened, the parallel between their experience and that of Jesus was unmistakable.

Opponents identified grave problems in Mennonite ecclesiology. Although the two men never met personally, John Calvin wrote a work against Menno *(Contra Mennonem)* in 1558 at the request of a friend who had debated the latter a number of times. Calvin conceded that the Anabaptists would be right in their pacifism "were we angels in this world...but the children of God are found mixed together with cruel monsters and with wolves and rapacious men....The rise of the sword will therefore continue to the end of the world." His deepest disagreement with the Anabaptists was what he saw as their confusion between the *regimen politicum* and the *regimen spirituale.*[45] They believed the sinful world needed a strong government to deal firmly with evildoers, said Calvin, but then they maintained that the New Testament called Christians away from the use of violence and to a life of patience and nonresistance. Israel used the death penalty, but Christians could use only the sword of the spirit to punish. "The sword of the Mosaic theocracy was transferred to the civil government,...not to the church."[46]

We have seen this problem before and will see it again. Nevertheless, this witnessing against Christian violence, while fraught with ecclesiological problems, was still a sobering counterpoint to its widespread acceptance.

5. MARCIN CZECHOWIC

Czechowic was a minister in the Minor Church. In 1575 he published his *Christian Dialogues,* showing that the Polish Antitrinitarian Anabaptists

> at the beginning at any rate, accepted nonresistance, too, as part of their religion. They rejected war and the magistracy as unchristian functions, just as the Swiss Brethren, and the German and Dutch Mennonites did. Their witness in this area, however, is still little known to students of Anabaptist and Mennonite history....This is the more regrettable in view of the fact that [they] produced the most interesting writings on nonresistance that have come down to us from the 16th century.

Two passages from Czechowic tell us much about his approach and what he had to say about appealing to the Bible:

> In the Old Testament many things were allowed which the New Covenant has forbidden the faithful to do. Whoever today would like to justify wars through examples in the Old Testament, as well as revenge and killing, must also justify and practice circumcision and polygamy and divorce as well as many other things which do not square with the Gospel of Christ.[47]

The question of how to use the Bible in the debate over capital punishment has continued in the four intervening centuries, but Marcin's words are as relevant today as they were when he wrote them.

The second passage, however, raised the recurring separatist problem seen as early as Origen:

> It is God's decision and his universal commandment that the wicked should be punished and the blood be shed of him who also sheds the blood of another (Genesis 9:6). It is right, I say, to do so for him into whose hand God himself gives the sword....The rulers of this world must willy-nilly punish the wicked and shed their blood, but not the disciples of Christ, who must be willing rather that their own blood be poured out for righteousness' sake than that they should shed the blood of any.[48]

Here once more is the theology of martyrdom as encountered in Michael Sattler a half-century earlier, but it poses serious problems for the broader question. It repudiates bloodshed by Christians on distinctively Christian grounds but retains capital punishment as a divinely mandated practice to be carried out by non-Christian statesmen. It is a separatist, not an abolitionist, position.

6. Fausto Socino

Socino was another fascinating character with a complicated history. He left Italy for Poland where he became an important leader among the Anabaptists but refused to be rebaptized himself. In 1581 he defended the nonresistant position in a lengthy Latin tract, but by 1601 he had profoundly modified his views. He moderated his pacifism so that church members were allowed to hold public office, but he still "sternly forbade them to cooperate with the state in imposing the death penalty,"[49] to which he remained staunchly opposed. Socino believed that executions were simply and blatantly incompatible with the teaching of Jesus, since 'thou shalt not kill' was a command addressed to magistrates as well as to all others.

7. VALENTINUS SMALCIUS

Smalcius was a close collaborator of Socino and, like him, moderated the earlier position. His arguments in 1614 focused on German Lutheran criticism of his church's position. He explained it this way:

> We believe it is lawful for a Christian to collaborate with the judiciary...with this one proviso, that nothing be done contrary to the laws of Christ, and above all, against the royal law of love, or anything smacking of revenge. For certain punishments under the New Convenant, which is a time of grace, are less severe than they once were under the Old Convenant which was a time of fear.

He condemned the death penalty without reservation, saying that "human laws must be brought into conformity with the gospel of Christ," and under no circumstances whatsoever was it permissible "for a Christian magistrate to shed human blood."

There were a few later voices maintaining the nonresistant message to one degree or another, especially Brenius and Wolzogen. But, as Brock indicates, they were dying out due to a number of adverse factors. In 1625 the Dutch jurist Hugo Grotius published his immensely influential *De Jure Belli ac Pacis,* which "argued cogently in favor of the just war and self-defense and against the nonresistant position; a Christian, he stated bluntly, might undertake both with a good conscience. Many of the Polish Brethren, who still hesitated, were won over by reading Grotius." In addition, the Russo-Polish war of 1632–1634 saw many a change of heart, as patriotism drew the younger generation into the military ranks. Then, in 1658 the Polish Brethren was declared an illegal organization and, in 1660–1661, forced into exile. But by this time most had abandoned their nonresistant stance, and "clergy as well as laity now believed in a Christian magistracy that wielded not the sword in vain."[50]

From this sketchy overview it is easy to see that the important century-and-a-quarter of the original Anabaptist movement offered prophetic opposition to the legitimacy of the death penalty in a society of Christians. That they were all classed as heretics and persecuted, and that they were only a small minority with very limited influence, are both true. But that cannot take away from the fact that they witnessed to a faded ideal, testifying that there was something amiss and unchristian in the way that the gallows had come to be used in standard conflicts between groups claiming to be followers of Christ.

C. Seventeenth Century: Quaker Voices

Waldenses, Wycliffites, Hussites, and various kinds of Anabaptists kept the ideal alive to one degree or another over some five centuries. Next it was the English Quakers who were to take up the cause and bring a different kind of attention to the death penalty as well as to the whole prison system that grew up with the Industrial Revolution.

1. GEORGE FOX

George Fox (1624–1691) saw the absurdities of the seventeenth-century British prison system firsthand and tried to do something about it. With over one-hundred-fifty capital crimes on the books, "the most serious matter was the lack of proper proportion between the punishment and the gravity of the offense....The existing law...which struck down the thief who had filched only a small amount as well as the murderer, inevitably destroyed all sense of justice in the popular mind."[51]

Fox was in jail in Derby in 1650 when he leveled this criticism against English judges:

> [They] put men to death for [stealing] cattle and money and small matters. I laid it before the judges what a hurtful thing it was that the prisoners lie so long in jail...showing how they learned badness one of another.[52]

Parliament appointed a commission in 1652, and the next year
the death penalty was in effect abolished for all but murderers
"through the pardon of all criminals convicted of other
crimes."[53] But this was only a very temporary respite for the brief
period when the Puritans gained power. The time for serious
penal reform in England, however, was not yet at hand.

Fox came to the position of total rejection of violence only
gradually. In his earlier days he had approved of the use of force
to put down irreligion and popery.[54] Soon after the restoration of
the Stuart monarchy and the reestablishment of the Church of
England in 1660, the Quakers felt the full force of government
intolerance and repression. Fully fifteen thousand of them were
jailed and nearly five hundred died as a result of imprisonment
by the time of the passage of the Act of Toleration in 1689.[55] Fox
and other Quaker leaders distanced themselves from associates
who wanted to counter violence with violence. He declared that
henceforth he would witness "against all violence and against all
the works of darkness, and to turn people from the darkness to
the light and from the occasion of the magistrate's sword....With
the carnal weapon I do not fight."[56]

Fox told of an instance when his appeal for clemency for a
condemned person had a happy outcome:

> While I was here in prison, there was a young woman in the
> jail for robbing her master of some money. When she was
> about to be tried for her life, I wrote to the judge and to the
> jury about her, showing them how it was contrary to the law
> of God in old time to put people to death for stealing, and
> moving them to show mercy.

The woman was condemned nonetheless. When she was led off
to be hanged, Fox wrote again. This time his statement was to be
read for the benefit of the crowd at the gallows. At the last
moment, "they did not put her to death, but brought her back
again to prison. And in the prison, she afterwards came to be
convinced of God's everlasting truth."[57]

One commentator makes the following general statement:

> Throughout their 300-year history Quakers have been opposed to the death penalty. One cannot believe in reformation while destroying the potential reformee. To be in favor of the abolition of capital punishment is a natural extension of the Quaker testimony that violence is the wrong way to achieve any goals.[58]

That may well be true in the abstract, but people are not always consistent in the concrete. The Quaker who is remembered for having publicly made that logical step and actually having become an outspoken advocate for the total abolition of the death penalty seems to have been not George Fox, but another English Quaker later in the century, John Bellers.

2. JOHN BELLERS

John Bellers (1654–1725) is often said to have been the first English abolitionist.[59] Fox, because he maintained the continuing validity of the biblical precepts, had trouble putting aside the death penalty as a just atonement for the crime of murder. Bellers took the decisive further step, initiating what subsequently became the standard Quaker goal: "utter abolition of the death penalty" without exception. Jorns says in an aside that "it thus appears that credit for priority in agitating the abolition of capital punishment, which is usually given to the Italian jurist Cesare Bonesano de Beccaria...belongs in reality to Bellers."[60] And Bellers' grounds for abolition were obviously religious. It was the teaching of Jesus that was at issue. By the time of Beccaria over a half-century later, a different kind of protest, largely couched in secular terms, burst on the scene, opening a brand new chapter in thinking about the death penalty.

CHAPTER 6

Enlightenment: Religious and Secular

I. A Major Complication: Conflicting Views of Death

II. Various Contributors to the Conversation
  A. Cesare Beccaria (1738–1794)
  B. Voltaire (1694–1778)
  C. Maximilien Robespierre (1758–1794)
  D. Immanuel Kant (1724–1804)
  E. The Works of St. Alphonsus Liguori (1696–1787)

III. A Sampler of Voices in a Chorus of Concern
  A. England:
      1. William Blackstone (1723–1780)
      2. Jeremy Bentham (1745–1832)
      3. Samuel Romilly (1757–1818)
      4. Daniel O'Connell (1832)
      5. William Ewart (1840/1850)
      6. John Jessop (1864)
  B. France:
      1. Joseph de Maistre (1753–1821)
      2. Alphonse de Lamartine (1790–1869)
      3. Charles Lucas (1803–1889)
      4. Victor Hugo (1802–1885)
  C. Belgium:
      1. Jean-Joseph Thonissen (1816–1891)
  D. Italy:
      1. Giuseppe Compagnoni (1754–1833)
      2. Pietro Ellero (1833–1933)
      3. Msgr. Giuseppe C. Zanghy (1829–1878)
  E. Spain:
      1. Manuel Pérez de Molina (1854/1878)
  F. Germany:
      1. Friedrich Schleiermacher (1768–1834)
      2. Karl J. A. Mittermaier (1787–1867)
      3. Ernst Wilhelm Hermann Hetzel (1820–1906)
      4. Fr. Franz X. Linsenmann (1835–1898)

I. A MAJOR COMPLICATION:
CONFLICTING VIEWS OF DEATH

Competing interpretations of the Enlightenment still abound, but it is generally agreed that it was a time of popular dissatisfaction with much of institutionalized religion.[1] Authority and tradition did not hold the same secure place they once had, thus allowing reexamination of previously unquestioned cultural features. In this context the death penalty began to lose its formerly privileged status. Eighteenth-century Europe abounded with chaotic contradictions and classical conflicts, symbolized for some by the contrast between Louis XIV, still strutting pompously before the mirrors of Versailles at the beginning of the century, and Louis XVI, losing his head to the guillotine at the end of the century. Massive changes were occurring, climaxing in the eruption of the French Revolution, and like many other things, perspectives on capital punishment were far different at the end of the century than they were at its beginning.

As the century began, the elaborate Catholic liturgy of capital punishment was still a broadly flourishing enterprise where the gallows-pietism of the Counter-Reformation found full expression. A society without the ready reminders of mortality provided by death-penalty rites was virtually unimaginable. The rituals portrayed the social reality in microcosm. A special Christian drama began as the death sentence was solemnly pronounced and the divinely deputized judge concluded: "May God have mercy on your soul!" (a sentiment not extended to the body).

Members of pious confraternities then went into action, systematically carrying out the duties of the deathwatch, urging the repentance and full cooperation of the malefactor in the ceremonies of his own execution. In France, Spain, Italy, and parts of Germany these brotherhoods directed religious processions, with altar boys at the front ringing bells as they wound their way through the town, alternating chanted litanies until they reached the place of execution.[2] Much of the liturgy had initially been

211

developed to dramatize the fate of heretics in the auto-da-fé. But it was only fitting that it was adapted for use with other victims of the hangman also, since the ceremonies served the desirable purpose of keeping the focus on helping the prisoner to die with good dispositions rather than on the brutality of the act of killing. Even so, it was hard to control such public displays when part of their central theme was the wrath of God on sinful humanity. Andrieux noted some of the mischievous rituals that had made their way into Roman executions:

> The Pope himself said a long prayer for [the victims] in his private oratory....The star criminals of the year would be reserved for carnival-time, when they were despatched in the Piazza del Popolo by executioners dressed as *pulcinelli* and derisive jesting was traditionally the last earthly sound they heard.[3]

Turning these otherwise somber occasions into carnivals was one way of dealing with their agonizing ambiguity. All around Europe the ubiquitous scaffold stood starkly at attention, grimly reminding passersby of the local rule of law. Church processions to these locales served to reflect the proper priorities of a "godly society." But this strange symbiosis of sacred and secular in the use of the gallows undoubtedly contributed to its gradual undoing in the Enlightenment.

The death penalty with its rituals had been more and more thoroughly grounded in religion over the previous five centuries. Its justification, even glorification, in theological and canonical treatises left even the best-informed observer with the understanding that it was an integral part of God's eternal plan. If tempted to waver on this, one needed only to consult the bedrock authorities from Aquinas to Suárez. Questioning it could seem an act of arrogant temerity. If one did not believe in the death penalty, what other parts of the Christian faith might one also be daring or arrogant enough to doubt or deny?

But the age of serene accommodation began to be disturbed from another quarter. It borders on the obvious to say that the meaning of "death penalty" depends upon the meaning of "death" and the meaning of "penalty," and changes in the understanding of both would invariably produce disagreement and confusion. Gallows-pietism rested on the conviction that the soul of the one whose bodily life was destroyed on the scaffold not only departed to a life beyond the grave, but that the nature and quality of that other life could be dramatically and eternally affected by the manner in which bodily death on the scaffold was endured. It took as a matter of faith that the state could do no more than affect this transition peripherally. Let human judges and courts of law think and act as they wished; the real judgment, the eternal judgment, was in the hands of God, not men.

Such religious faith is essentially subversive. It relativizes the significance and consequences of all earthly sufferings and failures. It allows society's losers to turn the tables so that it is the judges and executioners whose work might in fact be of little duration and importance, while the victims who are dispatched to the next life may not only be their equals but their superiors for all eternity. The awareness of such possibilities of reversed fortunes in a believers' universe has always given death a special fascination. The curious crowds flocked to the scaffold to see if some sign of the "real meaning" of this person's death was forthcoming.

But it was precisely this belief in an afterlife that underwent serious erosion in the process of Enlightenment secularization. Once the lenses of faith were removed, everything on the scaffold looked very, very different.

> It was the growing belief that death was final which prompted Enlightened and above all liberal thinkers to feel that capital punishment was indeed irreparable....The Christian Churches, Catholic and Protestant...were the most consistent supporters of capital punishment during this period, and the groups most hostile to them...were the most consistent advocates of abolition....Underlying changing attitudes to capital punishment were changing attitudes to death: from the death of the body and release of the soul into eternity, to the final death of the individual, to death as the elimination of a link in the chain of heredity.[4]

This was a tremendously complicating factor. For the next two centuries, even as evidence continued to mount that the institution of capital punishment was an aberration that should never have been allowed to establish itself within Christendom (the *religious* Enlightenment), a new danger was attached to the idea of abolishing it. Believers who would normally have joined in such efforts found themselves in danger of being misunderstood and misinterpreted as being on the other side of the great ideological divide.[5] Advocating retention of the death penalty was, oddly, one way of showing retention of belief in life after death, despite the attacks of the *philosophes*. Advocating abolition of the death penalty, on the other hand, could easily be understood as implying that one had abandoned that belief, which was part of the basic "crisis of the European mind" pinpointed by Paul Hazard as occurring between the years 1680 and 1715:

> In this era, so turbid, so crowded with events that it seems at first sight a mere welter of confusion, there took their rise two great streams which were to flow on through the whole century: one is the river of rationalism; the other...the river of feeling, of sentiment....The principle of equality and individual freedom...the rights of the individual as man and citizen...all these things were ancient history by 1760. For three quarters of a century and more they had been freely and openly discussed...in order to bring out anew the verities which govern and condition the life of man.[6]

The timing was ironic. Belief or disbelief in life after death did not in itself imply approval or disapproval of the death penalty, but there was literally a world of difference between the two positions. Thus divergent outlooks about the consequences of execution caused further complications for the capital-punishment question at the very time that the work of Beccaria appeared.

II. VARIOUS CONTRIBUTORS TO THE CONVERSATION

There is no way to do justice here to the large number of works on the death penalty produced by a host of Enlightenment thinkers. Bettina Strub devoted her doctoral dissertation to an examination of *the influence of the Enlightenment on the death penalty,* and her findings identified the particular nuances and directions opened up by some two dozen major contributors.[7] Needless to say, she found little Catholic participation to speak of, and it is not difficult to understand why. We will look at Beccaria and Voltaire as chief representatives of the thinking in this group.

A. *Cesare Beccaria (1738–1794)*

Even though many of his ideas were borrowed from Hutcheson and Montesquieu, it was Beccaria's work of 1764, *On Crimes and Punishments,* which caught the attention and imagination of the age.[8] Voltaire's enthusiastic embrace probably helped to guarantee its swift, revolutionary impact. Initial Catholic reactions were understandably negative. The book was quickly placed on the Roman Index of Prohibited Books, not because of anything it says about the death penalty but because of the philosophical presuppositions and rejections.

Beccaria's work has been undergoing some reassessment recently. Piers Beirne argues that "Beccaria's treatise must be placed in a trajectory radically different from the 'classical' one conventionally accorded it."[9] He insists that as a "text of the Enlightenment," neither the structure nor the content should be taken at face value, since authors in that context invariably "employed ubiquitous trickery to defeat the censor and the police and, in Beccaria's Lombardy, to avoid the prying eyes of the Inquisitorial Council of Ten. Beccaria was painfully aware of the fates of Machiavelli, Galileo, and the historian Giannone."[10]

The fact that the work was first published anonymously lends support to Beirne's thesis. This in turn emphasizes the monumental changes that were taking place in Christian Europe. The death penalty simply could not continue to maintain its privileged existence unchallenged. It would continue in use, to be sure, but the second half of the eighteenth century saw not only a decline but a total metamorphosis of the status of capital punishment. It would never again be a penal institution simply taken for granted the way it had been for some five centuries. The challenges to its propriety would come from ethicists and lawyers, historians and criminologists, Protestants and Catholics, and would come from every country in Europe. Churchmen who simply dug in their heels and held the line against any reassessment actually contributed to the decline of Christianity. The role of custodian of higher values had to be taken up by other forces speaking in support of a more humane ethic.[11]

If, from the viewpoint of Catholic theology, it can reasonably be said that "Beccaria rejected the death penalty for the wrong reasons,"[12] this obviously complicated the call for abolition. Many who were inclined to support the eminently sensible goals of limiting or eliminating the death penalty on humanitarian and/or utilitarian grounds were put off by some of Beccaria's novel arguments.

The first problem to be encountered is the text itself. Beccaria's famous work has an astonishingly complex compositional history, to say the least. *On Crimes and Punishments,* it has been pointedly summed up, contains "a mass of ideas from the French rationalists...hastily scribbled by Beccaria, transcribed and reordered by Verri, drastically revised by subsequent editors and translators, especially by Morellet, whose paragraphing and reordered sequence Beccaria willingly adopted as an improvement over the original."[13] Some of its eventual "chapters" are no more than single paragraphs. The two longest are the ones on the subjects of torture (sixteen paragraphs) and the death penalty (twenty-one paragraphs).[14]

The latter is, of course, our special interest and demonstrates how great a change had already taken place in some Western thinking about capital punishment by this time. Beccaria reflects the dramatic decline of the theological and the rise of a pragmatic philosophical approach to the subject. His very first sentence sets the tone by its contrasting usage of the two words "useless" and "useful."

> The useless profusion of punishments, which has never made men better, induces me to inquire: whether the punishment of *death* be really just or useful in a well governed state?

The next most striking feature here is the juxtaposition of "just" and "useful." The moral and the utilitarian dimensions are united to the point of virtual identity, so that the next sentence immediately demands: "What *right,* I ask, have men to cut the throats of their fellow-creatures?" Here, in a very different form, is the basic challenge raised in the twelfth century by some Waldensians. Who can claim to be sure of having such awesome authority to kill human beings deliberately? But this time the issue has not been raised based on anyone's reading of the Bible. On the contrary, the basis for objecting to executing human beings is

> certainly not that on which the sovereignty and laws are founded. The laws...are only the sum of the smallest portions of the private liberty of each individual, and represent the general will, which is the aggregate of that of each individual. Did anyone ever give to others the right of taking away his life? If it were so, how shall it be reconciled to the maxim which tells us that a man has no right to kill himself? Which he certainly must have, if he could give it away to another.

Whatever one may think of the argument, it is obviously a very different kind of objection than those that have gone before. It represents the dawning of an era when, for the first time, a basic secular objection is articulated against the death penalty. Characteristically, Beccaria is more interested in (and influenced by) the philosophical construct of the social contract than by anything in the Bible. He moves quickly in the second paragraph to conclude categorically that

> the punishment of death is not authorized by any right; for I have demonstrated that no such right exists. It is therefore a war of a whole nation against a citizen, whose destruction they consider as necessary or useful to the general good. But if I can further demonstrate that it is neither *necessary* nor *useful,* I shall have gained the cause of humanity.

This extremely interesting move not only binds war and the death penalty together but classifies the death penalty as a kind of sub-species of war. As a result, it is perfectly reasonable to apply traditional just-war criteria to the question of whether the death penalty ought to be used. His next statement is, in fact, a simple variation of the "last resort" condition:

> The death of a citizen cannot be *necessary* except in one case. When, though deprived of his liberty, he has such power and connections as may endanger the security of the nation; when his existence may produce a dangerous revolution in the established form of government. But even in this case, it can only be necessary when a nation is on the verge of recovering or losing its liberty; or in times of absolute anarchy, when the disorders themselves hold the place of laws. But in peace-time, in a form of government approved by the united wishes of the nation; in a state well fortified from enemies without and supported by strength within...there can be *no necessity* for taking away the life of a subject.

Once formulated in these terms, the abolition of capital punishment became the obvious ethical ideal. It is, ironically, the same practical position voiced over two centuries later by Pope John Paul II in his 1995 encyclical.[15] But the novelty of Beccaria was that this position was arrived at without any religious argument at all. Hence the ambiguities of the next two centuries. This ignoring of the Bible and attempted reliance on a rational argument alone allowed defenders of the tradition to dismiss the entire position. For the next two and a half centuries the secular proponents of a more humane society were, ironically, to be the chief defenders of the dignity of human life over against those who continued to invoke the Bible to justify the gallows, even as they were used against churchmen themselves.[16] The secular call for a higher ethic thus fell on deaf ears in church circles because it was perceived as (and in many instances was indeed) accompanied by a hostile rejection of biblical faith.

Other arguments of importance for the future were also made in Beccaria's famous chapter on the death penalty. One of them still has a rather contemporary sound to it, because it has been a prominent part in the anti–capital punishment arsenal ever since its introduction:

> The punishment of death is pernicious to society from the example of *barbarity* it affords. If the passions, or the necessity of war, have taught men to shed the blood of their fellow creatures, the laws, which are intended to moderate the ferocity of mankind, should not increase it by examples of

barbarity, the more horrible as the punishment is usually attended with formal pageantry. Is it not absurd that the laws, which detest and punish homicide, should, in order to prevent murder, publicly commit murder themselves?

It is easy to see why some of Beccaria's arguments had significant impact. He seized the high moral ground and asked embarrassing questions, questions that had lain dormant because of the deep entrenchment of the death penalty in Western Christian culture after the twelfth century. Now, with all religious arguments put safely aside, Beccaria forced citizens to confront the common-sense question: How does the state's killing of killers show in any rational way that killing is wrong?

B. Voltaire (1694-1778)

Beccaria acknowledged from the start that his ideas for penal reform were largely drawn from the new thinking coming out of France, and the French quickly recognized and welcomed home their intellectual offspring in Beccaria's work. Voltaire wrote a significant commentary that was published together with the 1766 edition of the French translation of Beccaria, and it gave added punch to the original by placing it solidly in a heightened historical context. As has long been recognized, the strongest occasions for protesting against the death penalty are the times when notorious instances of blatant abuse come to public attention. Much of the latter part of Voltaire's life was significantly affected by his personal involvement in three infamous capital cases. On the other hand, no other single factor was more responsible for bringing the death penalty into disfavor than the biting sarcasm and stinging wit of Voltaire. Like Clarence Darrow in a later context, an articulate lawyer can leave a devastating mark on an open target.

The most notorious case was the execution of Huguenot Jean Calas in Toulouse in 1762. Voltaire led such a strident press campaign that public outrage had to be confronted. Not only was a fifty-judge royal panel appointed to review the case, but the judges' verdict was a reversal of Calas's conviction three years after his execution. All that could be done practically was the indemnification of the family, but it was the system using capital punishment that was the great loser in the longer run. The coincidental appearance of Beccaria's pamphlet at precisely this time in French history accounts for some of the special enthusiasm with which it was received. The need for penal reform was urgent in any event. Using his most indignant rhetoric, Voltaire assailed the death record of Western Europe in unforgettable terms that became a standard part of later abolitionist campaigns:

> Christian tribunals have condemned to death more than 100,000 so-called witches. If you add to these juridical massacres the infinitely higher number of immolated heretics, this part of the world will be seen as nothing other than a vast scaffold crowded with executioners and their victims, surrounded by judges and spectators.[17]

Voltaire attempted to shame his contemporaries even further, claiming that France was trailing far behind England and Russia in contemporary efforts to correct its barbaric penal system. He reminded Frenchmen of their proud heritage with its roots in Roman law:

> A Roman citizen could be condemned to death only for crimes that threatened the security of the state. Our masters, our first legislators, respected the blood of their compatriots, while we lavishly waste that of ours!

Little did he realize the eerie accuracy his words would take on as a description of what was to happen in France in its revolution only a quarter-century later.

The same year in which the Calas verdict was posthumously overturned, Voltaire took up the case of the Sirven family. This time he had the satisfaction (in 1771) of seeing them declared innocent before rather than after execution. But meantime he had been unable to prevent the execution of La Barre in 1766. In all of this turmoil, it was evident that something very basic was changing. Across much of Europe the long-privileged position of the death penalty as the cornerstone of the penal system of Western Christendom was under unprecedented attack. And because many of the attackers were also antagonistic toward institutional Christianity, the reaction of many churchmen was to "circle the wagons" and defend everything of the past in an indiscriminate way.

One other ironic incident in Voltaire's dealings with the death penalty throws light on this changing scene. In 1759 the Jesuits were expelled from Portugal, where they had been under fierce attack. One of them, Gabriel Malagrida, had been a missionary in Brazil and returned with a reputation among the people for being a living saint. At an elaborate auto-da-fé orchestrated by the Portuguese Inquisition in Lisbon in 1761, Malagrida was strangled and burned at the stake. Even those who had no use for the Jesuits joined in the public outcry throughout Europe over this atrocity. It triggered a host of critical writings and events, including the production of a three-act tragedy in Paris in 1763. Voltaire himself wrote "The Sermon of Rabbi Akiba," and thus put on the lips of a Jew the strongest denunciation of the Jesuit's execution, including this prayer:

> "O Adonai, you who have created all of us and wish no unhappiness for your creatures! O God, our common Father, God of mercy, make it possible that on our little globe...there be neither fanatics nor persecutors."[18]

Voltaire did not call for abolition of capital punishment as such. It was "fanatics and persecutors" that raised his ire. He strongly supported the reformist utilitarian idea of forced labor in most cases, putting criminals to work to repay their debt to society. This made much more sense to him than killing them. But there was one case, "the only case," where he would continue to favor the death penalty: "when there is no other means of saving the lives of the greater number," that is, in the traditional limit situation ("last resort"). The image he invoked for comparison was that of a rabid dog that simply had to be killed if it continued to constitute an imminent danger to the entire community.[19]

But this exception did not soften his critique of the general practice. He mocked the infamous M. de Machaut, a French magistrate earlier in the century, who had condemned an average of five hundred criminals a year during his forty years on the bench. In thus sending some twenty thousand people to the gallows, de Machaut earned the gruesome nickname of "judge coupe-tête."[20]

Outraged over this wanton destruction of human life in a supposedly Christian culture, Voltaire preached the new Enlightenment ideal: "The sword of justice is in our hands; but we must blunt it more often than sharpen it. It is worn in its scabbard before kings to remind us to draw it rarely."[21] Unfortunately for France, Machaut rather than Voltaire was the model followed once the cataclysm began. One of the weirdest episodes in the history of the death penalty unfolded during the French Revolution.

But before turning to that history, we note in passing that this is the chronological point at which the earliest Catholic dissenter is usually recalled. A certain Cesare Malanima in 1786 published a work rejecting the death penalty.[22] He is quoted as saying that if the Old Testament capital precepts were still in force in the New Testament, so would the rest of it be, and Christians would have to observe the Old Law entirely and renounce the New Law. It is difficult to tell from this whether Malanima went on to adopt an abolitionist position or not, but the title of his work is reminiscent of Beccaria's, and he is treated by Skoda as his first Catholic "adversary," that is, the first Catholic writer to become a "defector" from the grand tradition of supporting the death penalty. Needless to say, Malanima had virtually no impact at the time or subsequently.

C. Maximilien Robespierre (1758–1794)

As for the French Revolution, it was the "incorruptible" Maximilien Robespierre who took up the "enlightened" position and made the most devastating rhetorical attack on the death penalty in the Constituent Assembly of May 1791. He had obviously absorbed the published work of Pierre Pastoret, summarizing the conversation begun by Beccaria and advancing it considerably.[23] Robespierre assured his colleagues that in reforming the penal code they were solemnly engaged in nothing less than "interpreting the eternal laws that were divinely dictated to men," and therefore they had an obligation to abolish from it completely all capital punishment. There was no longer any place for the laws of blood which sanction judicial murder, laws which are repugnant to the Frenchman's new way of life and to their new Constitution. I wish to prove: first, that the death penalty is fundamentally unjust; and secondly, that it is not the most effective of penalties and that, far from preventing crimes, it increases them.

He went on to maintain that the state, when it spills human blood, deadens moral sentiment among its people, brutalizes and degrades their spirit, and wears out the springs of government.

> Listen to the voice of reason and justice!...The laws must always afford peoples the purest model....If they shed human blood that they have the power to prevent and that they have no right to shed at all, ...then they pervert in the citizens' minds all idea of what is just and unjust....Human dignity is rated of lesser worth when public authority sets little store on life. The idea of murder inspires far less terror when the law itself sets the example of it for all to see. Horror of crime diminishes when its only punishment is by another crime....I conclude that the death penalty must be *repealed*.

Not only did his eloquence not prevail, but that same assembly adopted the guillotine and put dozens of them in place all over the country. Robespierre himself, eighteen months after his fierce attack on capital punishment, stood before the assembly again, this time arguing for the absolute necessity of beheading the king without even the formality of a trial. "To propose a trial for Louis XVI...is a counterrevolutionary idea, since it puts the Revolution itself on trial." He did what he could to justify his change of heart, assuring all that

> I abhor the death penalty....I have neither love nor hatred for the king; it is only crime that I hate. I demanded the abolition of the death penalty; it is not my fault that the Assembly thought this *heresy*....Now you ask for an exception to the death penalty for the one man in whose case it would be justified. Yes, the death penalty in general is a crime....It can be justified only in cases where it is necessary for the security of the state....Louis must die in order that our country may live![24]

Louis did die, guillotined five weeks after this address. Eighteen months later it was Robespierre's turn to be beheaded after a bizarre suicide attempt. But these were only two of the thousands of French heads that rolled as mechanical decapitation raised capital punishment to new heights of celerity and efficiency.[25] These are relatively small numbers when compared to the hordes of Frenchmen whose corpses would soon be littering Napoleon's battlefields, but they were nonetheless large enough to raise profound questions about the right of a state to execute its citizens. Respect for human life, so central to the teachings of the gospel and the Enlightenment, had been abandoned on such a broad scale that its continuation in any valid form was at stake.[26]

D. Immanuel Kant (1724–1804)

With Beccaria's work placed on the Index of Forbidden Books, Catholic participation in the death-penalty debate was not exactly encouraged. The staunchest defense for the gallows thus came from Protestant quarters, especially from those influenced by the staunch retributivism of philosophers Immanuel Kant and Georg W. F. Hegel. We cannot do justice to them here, but the role of Kant in the aftermath of Beccaria can hardly be passed over if the nineteenth-century controversies are to be understood. What follows is only the barest sketch of what happened, but it may give some idea of how distinctive the debate had become.

Beccaria's work had been circulating throughout Europe to great acclaim for three decades when he died in 1794. Three years later the eminent Königsberg philosopher Immanuel Kant caustically dismissed the work of "the Marquis of Beccaria," describing him as "moved by sympathetic sentimentality and an affectation of humanitarianism" in his argument that "all capital punishment is illegitimate."[27] (As we have seen, this is not an accurate reflection of what Beccaria said.)

Thus the second phase of the philosophical clash over the death penalty began. Kant had no use for utilitarianism. Only the law of retribution (lex talionis) could determine the kind and degree of punishment required of every crime if the moral order of the universe were to be kept in balance. He thus found Beccaria's arguments horrific as well as ridiculously sophomoric. The

two outlooks on the basis of punishment—utility or retribution—
were so far apart, as conceived, that the dilemma they present
remains unresolved.[28] As far as Kant was concerned,

> if a man has committed a murder, he must die....There is no
> substitute that will satisfy the requirements of legal jus-
> tice....There is no equality between the crime and the retri-
> bution unless the criminal is judicially condemned and put
> to death.

To underline how literally Kant meant this, we can point to his
famous example of a civil society on a desert island that decides
to cancel its social contract and disband, but there happens to be
one murderer left in prison as they are about to disband. What is
to be done with him? For Kant the answer was self-evident: they
had no choice but to execute him, for if they failed to do so, they
would be in open violation of legal justice. He accused Beccaria
of blatant sophistry in using Rousseau as a disguise for his own
soft-headedness about the social contract.

The reasoning of Kant's position exerted a vast influence
on nineteenth-century Protestant theologians who accepted this
reinforcement of their traditional biblical understanding as providential.[29] But this was by no means the whole story. While Kant
was deeply convinced that the utilitarian approach was wrongheaded and immoral, he was aware there were many lingering
problems with his own retributivism, and at least on occasion
touched on some of these.

There are also modern admirers of Kant who have made
the case that full fidelity to his own best principles would have
led Kant to oppose rather than endorse the death penalty. His
desert-island scenario, according to one critic, is "simply inconsistent with what he says in other places."[30]

There is a strange fascination about this philosophical
clash, which reverberated throughout the nineteenth century.
Kant and Beccaria left the Bible aside, even though both were
obviously familiar with it. They attempted to make their respective cases for and against the death penalty by invoking "enlightened" reason. The intensity of the ensuing debate, however,

often reached an emotional pitch indistinguishable from that of the religious debates.

Chief among the "other places" in Kant referred to by Scheid is a central teaching about the categorical imperative, especially in its second formulation ("Never use a human being merely as a means").[31] In 1985 philosopher Steven Schwarzschild revived the explicit position that had been formulated by the Marburg Neo-Kantian Hermann Cohen seventy-five years earlier, contending that "the logic of Kant's fundamental ethical principles should have made him a radical opponent of capital punishment." Cohen and Schwarzschild both attempted to call Kant before his own tribunal of consistency, "to understand Kant better than he understood himself, as Kant favored understanding Plato better than Plato understood himself." The clinching argument for Cohen was that "no legal action may aim at the annihilation of the moral person. The moral person is bound to physical life. Legal penalties must, therefore, stop short of human life."[32]

So the anomalous situation recurs. Just as there are loyal Thomists today who are convinced by their appreciation of Thomas Aquinas at his best that he would be an abolitionist in the current context, so there are loyal Kantians who take the bedrock principle of Kant and, reflecting upon its implications, conclude that today Kant would undoubtedly end up opposing capital punishment on the basis of simple consistency.[33]

Schwarzschild went on to make another strong argument in light of Kant's position on the "impenetrable privacy of personal morality," which should have made him "an inveterate opponent of the death penalty....It is exactly the unattainability by any second party (other than God) of this level of moral decision...that makes it logically impossible for the judiciary to deal with it."[34] It is inconsistent to admit that there is always a high degree of ignorance and uncertainty any time humans try to judge the inmost hearts and minds of other humans, and then apply the ultimate punishment of death as an appropriate penalty based on such judgments. To do so is at least anachronous. A judicial tribunal that knows better nonetheless decides to act as if it were in possession of privileged divine insight, something which a modern secular state has no reasonable basis whatsoever to claim.[35]

In the final analysis, Kant has probably been used more enthusiastically by both abolitionists and retentionists than any other single figure in the entire debate about capital punishment. For the retentionist, Kant's thoroughgoing retributivism says it all: an eye for an eye, the murderer must die. For the abolitionist, the second form of the categorical imperative creeps more and more into contemporary arguments. It rejects capital punishment as an inherent violation of human dignity, treating a person as a means instead of an end, despite all protests to the contrary.[36]

By the end of the process reviewed, the basic arguments against the death penalty had multiplied significantly. It is possible to group them as three different kinds: (1) the biblical-theological; (2) the humanitarian; and (3) the pragmatic or operational. After examining each of them, Michael Endres concluded that the "absolute theological and humanitarian arguments against the death penalty were...equivocal and inconclusive," but that once the third (pragmatic, operational) framework was brought in, the case against the death penalty became much clearer: "It has always been *unjustly applied* and, given the realities of human society, it can hardly be otherwise."[37] But it was another two centuries before the consequences of this realization would be fully felt in Catholic ethics.

E. The Works of St. Alphonsus Liguori (1696–1787)

The noted Catholic moralist Alphonsus Liguori was a contemporary of Beccaria and wrote extensively on moral issues of the time. He was a man of boundless energy and great achievements in many important areas. On the capital punishment issue, however, he too was basically hampered by what he had received and aimed to defend. This is not surprising, given the increasing complexity of the situation and the circumstances of his own career. He was made a bishop two years before Beccaria's work appeared and in his most productive years

> Alphonsus' interest was turned towards the apologetic defense of the faith against what he considered to be the clouds of threatening rationalism and deism. Instinctively, he was right, but the books themselves are defensive.[38]

The reference here is especially to his 1772 work, a massive review called *The History of Heresies and Their Refutation* or *The Triumph of the Church.*[39] As seen earlier in the cases of the other great theologians Vitoria, Bellarmine, and Suárez, their pre-critical apologias on this issue are best left aside as products of their troubled times. They were so ideological that they could be of help only to those inside the barricades, totally devoted to bolstering as well as they could the inherited positions under attack. Bitter controversy is never a good context for fruitful rethinking of anything, let alone so complex an issue as capital punishment had become. It would take much more than a single great thinker to address so intractable a problem.

III. A SAMPLER OF VOICES IN A CHORUS OF CONCERN

What follows is a selected album of some of the participants in the "great conversation" about the changed and changing evaluation of capital punishment. Most of them shared a general awareness that something was wrong with a society that relied upon this practice. They were early critics who likely would have agreed with contemporary sociologist Peter Berger in his assessment of the anomalous nature of capital punishment:

> The final fiction [is that] nobody did any killing at all. It was the law itself that killed. But the law, as we know, is incapable of killing. Only men kill. And a man is dead. There must, then, be something radically wrong with the whole argument.

> We would contend that the process is one of *bad faith* from beginning to end. It is a lie that prosecutor and judge have no option....It is a lie that the jury can dismiss from their minds the question of punishment....It is a lie that their positions dictate to the governor or the pardons board what course of action they must take. No matter what method of deceit is finally used in the execution itself, it is a lie that nobody is doing any killing. A man is dead and his killers are known. They are Mr. Smith, the DA; Mr. Brown, the judge;

Mr. Jones, the warden—and so on...to the executioner. This is the reality. The rest is fiction, mythology, alibi.[40]

A. England

1. WILLIAM BLACKSTONE (1723–1780)

Blackstone published his famous commentaries on English law in the five years immediately following the appearance of Beccaria's work. He had much to say about capital punishment as it was being practiced in the Britain of his day, when the need for legal reform was most urgent. He was not an abolitionist by any stretch, but that makes his testimony all the more telling. He was staunchly convinced that there was something terribly wrong with a nation that relied heavily on the death penalty:

> Punishments of unreasonable severity, especially when indiscriminately inflicted, have a less effect in preventing crimes....Sanguinary laws are a bad symptom of the distemper of any state, or at least of its weak constitution....A multitude of sanguinary laws...do likewise prove a manifest defect either in the wisdom of legislative or the strength of executive power. It is a kind of *quackery* in government, and argues a want of solid skill, to apply the universal remedy, the *ultimum supplicium,* to every case of difficulty.[41]

Blackstone was far ahead of his time in penetrating the fog of popular mythology with its inflated claims about the merits of the death penalty. He had no fear in letting the world know from his legal studies that this emperor had no clothes.

2. JEREMY BENTHAM (1745–1832)

"The origin of philosophical and critical opinion about criminal law may have originated with Beccaria, but effective agitation for criminal-law reform in England began with Jeremy Bentham. He provided the thrust and philosophical elements to English law-reform."[42] One pertinent observation Bentham made became the center of a discussion in France after Napoleon, when a new law code was being prepared. Bentham pointed out the relevance of class. The laws are the work of the upper class, which envisaged death as a great evil and a shameful death as the greatest of evils. But these lawmakers showed how little they were aware that, for the lower class to whom these laws were meant to apply, human life was cheap and harsh and brutal, so that they did not attach nearly the same value to it.

This was an early dent that Bentham put in the myth of deterrence by bringing it into contact with empirical reality, concluding that the death penalty was in fact not very "useful" and should thus be abolished for most crimes.[43] As practiced at the time, it was invariably used against the poor for the benefit of the rich. That was true in the twelfth century; it was true in Bentham's time. As he put it, "There is no regular justice for them at all, unless it be for hanging them, or something in that style...99 men out of a hundred" are outside the law's protection.[44]

Bentham addressed the subject of capital punishment in two different works separated by more than half a century. The first is the more detailed and novel for its time (1775), since it was written only twenty years after Beccaria's attack and twenty years before Kant's rebuttal of Beccaria. But it was an important contribution to the philosophical investigation that was gradually helping to dismantle the privileged position that capital punishment had enjoyed for so long. The most valuable analysis and assessment of Bentham's significance in this process has been that provided by Professor Hugo A. Bedau.[45]

To see the new elements in this conversation, one need only look at the objections to using death as a punishment from Bentham's utilitarian perspective. Penal laws, he was convinced, should have a dozen characteristics, and some of these militate against the very idea of executing the one being punished; it simply does not make any sense. There are simple and stark incompatibilities that make the very idea of death as a penalty a contradiction in terms. Two of the most telling of these properties Bentham described thus:

"An 8th property...might be styled...*disabling efficacy*." By this he meant that a good punishment ought to disable a man "from doing mischief, without, at the same time, disabling him, in a great measure, from doing good, either to himself or others." But, as is obvious, "the punishment of which the efficacy in this way is the greatest is evidently that of death. But...this punishment is in an eminent degree *unfrugal;* which forms one among the many objections there are against the use of it, in any but very extraordinary cases." Here is a form of the common-sense argument that death simply goes too far. It "disables" completely and is therefore unacceptable; it is not in any rational sense a punishment at all, but only *useless annihilation,* making proper punishment totally impossible.

> The 11th and last of all the properties that seem to be requisite in a lot of punishment, is that of *remissibility.* The general presumption is that when punishment is applied, punishment is needful; that it ought to be applied, and therefore cannot want to be remitted. But in very particular, and those always very deplorable cases, it may by accident happen otherwise.

The instance referred to, of course, is that of wrongful conviction, "where the sufferer is innocent of the offense" but appeared guilty at the time the sentence was passed. The worst of these instances of irremissibility occur where the punishment was "whipping, branding, mutilation, and capital punishment. The most perfectly irremissible of any is capital punishment."[46]

Of course, it is still easy enough to dismiss the occasional killing of innocent people as unfortunate but inevitable in a fallible human system. The degree to which one is disturbed by this is probably as good a barometer as any of what value one really puts on human life itself. Philosopher William Frankena found in his perceptive study of pro-life movements "three rather different kinds of respect for life."[47] These are helpful distinctions that can bring greater light to an often opaque conversation.

3. SAMUEL ROMILLY (1757–1818)

Romilly was the grandson of "a Huguenot refugee who left France, of his own volition, during a period of religious persecution, forfeiting his right to the family inheritance." As a young barrister traveling from town to town he saw firsthand "the results of the imbecile state of the law whereby over two hundred offenses were punishable by death."[48] He himself was not an abolitionist, but he dedicated the last ten years of his life to campaigning to get parliament to abrogate the penalty of death for the theft of five shillings and other such trivial offenses. When his bill was defeated the first time in the House of Lords, 31-11, Romilly was especially bitter about the fact that seven Anglican bishops had voted against it. In fact, "six times, in 1810, 1811, 1813, 1816, 1818, and 1820, the House of Commons passed Bills to abolish capital punishment for shop-lifting to the value of five shillings, and six times the House of Lords threw out the Bills."[49] But it is clear that in the longer run Romilly contributed greatly to the cause of changing national consciousness.

4. DANIEL O'CONNELL

Daniel O'Connell, the famed criminal defense lawyer who became the great champion of Irish freedom and Catholic civil rights, and who also called for the end of slavery and the acknowledgment of the rights of women, gave a speech in London in 1832 on the death penalty. In it he is reported to have said that experience had confirmed him in this opinion:

> "There should not be in man the power of extinguishing human life, because the result was irreparable; because the injury that might be done could not be compensated, if the beings were not infallible who inflicted the punishment...and because, while we thought we were vindicating the law of society, we might be committing the greatest outrage that could be perpetrated on our fellow-creatures."[50]

Statements such as this by a leading Catholic layman have not been given the attention they deserve. Because the theologians and canon lawyers were silent by force of circumstances did not mean that there was no Catholic participation in the campaign to recover perspective on capital punishment, as has often been claimed. A fuller study of the many Catholic laymen involved in law and the criminal justice system who were abolitionists of one kind or another remains to be done, but there are enough ready examples to warrant the task.

5. WILLIAM EWART (1840/1850)

The "spiritual heir" of Romilly, William Ewart introduced bills to eliminate death as the penalty for various kinds of theft.

But in March of 1840 he took the floor to make a "historic resolution to abolish capital punishment entirely."[51] Like Romilly, he kept at it year after year until 1850, when he ended his speech with the assurance that "the reform which we support is founded on sound principles of punishment, on the lasting interests of humanity, and on the genuine spirit of the Bible."[52]

Even though it would be another 115 years before his "historic resolution" would finally be implemented in England, its great significance should not be missed. The campaign for abolition had matured through articulating the multidimensional case against the death penalty, highlighting the fact that it was as much on religious as on humanitarian grounds that the struggle was being made. The fact that churchmen continued to support executions as legitimated by God only meant that the churches would continue to discredit themselves until the fuller appreciation of their own message about the value of human life could be retrieved by collaborators like Romilly and Ewart.

Part of the reason for the delay undoubtedly was the strange argument over public versus private executions that occurred at this time. The campaign to end public spectacles and do the killing quietly in the prison yard diverted attention from the abolitionist cause as such. Some thought that moving the scaffold inside would end any deterrent effect and thus end capital punishment. Others disagreed and thought that hiding the butchery would make it easier to increase the frequency of executions. Obviously no one knew exactly what would happen, but the bill passed and the last public execution in England took place in 1868.[53] Some thought that the end of the "circus executions" was motivated by fear on the part of the authorities that the crowds might get out of control, which they sometimes did. But it may well have been that "it was not fear but disgust which was the primary motivating factor. The crowd was not so much a terror to the upper classes as a reproach."[54]

6. JOHN JESSOP (1864)

Anglican priest John Jessop is mentioned here as a kind of personification of the changing situation. He had been a prison chaplain for ten years when he was called to testify before the Royal Commission on Capital Punishment, set up in 1864 largely due to the work of William Ewart. Unlike many of his colleagues who could not adjust to the idea of living without the death penalty, Jessop was a member of a small, interesting class—a cleric who had had firsthand experience of ministering to death-row prisoners and was personally transformed by it. He had accompanied at least four men to the gallows in the course of his ministry. His testimony to the Royal Commission was that this experience had led him to discard the traditional ecclesiastical ideology and come to a very different assessment of capital punishment, viz., that it was

> religiously, politically, and socially...*indefensible*. It was contrary to the tenets of the Bible, it depraved the most depraved of the population who were those who attended; it lowered the estimation of the sanctity of life; it demoralized and was no deterrent.[55]

This kind of collision of ideology with reality convinced him that Europe's commitment to the use of capital punishment on any religious grounds was untenable, despite the dogged resistance of the old guard in parliament.[56]

B. France

1. JOSEPH DE MAISTRE (1753–1821)

De Maistre is admittedly out of place here. He is included not only as a curiosity piece at the other end of the spectrum in the history of thought about capital punishment, but as a tragic illustration of what inclusion of capital punishment can do to religious thought, and vice versa.

De Maistre was the architect of the strangest version of a full-fledged mythology of the scaffold ever constructed within Catholicism. The French Revolution had left this prominent and talented layman "a ferocious critic of every form of constitutionalism and liberalism, an ultramontane legitimist, a believer in the divinity of authority and power....His world had been shattered by the satanic forces of atheistical reason; and could be rebuilt only by cutting off all the heads of the hydra of the revolution in all its multiple disguises."[57] John Courtney Murray, S.J., characteristically expressed his criticism in a kindlier manner by saying of de Maistre that "just as (the Revolution) reversed his Gallicanism to an ultra-montanism, so also did it lead to a critical contempt of every doctrine of the *philosophes*."[58]

The world view that de Maistre somehow arrived at as an expression of his Catholic faith had the executioner firmly installed as a fixture at its very heart:

> He (the executioner) is made like us externally. He is born like all of us. But he is an extraordinary being, and it needs a special decree to bring him into existence as a member of the human family—a fiat of the creative power. He is created by a law unto himself....All greatness, all power, all subordination rest on the executioner. He is the terror and the bond of human association. Remove this mysterious agent from the world, and in an instant order yields to chaos: thrones fall, society disappears. God, who has created sovereignty, has also made punishment.[59]

This ghastly vision was certainly not shared, and was in fact repudiated by most of his Catholic contemporaries, but it stands as an extraordinary example of the bizarre excesses to which glamorization of capital punishment could lead, denying even the possibility of a world from which it could ever be abolished.[60] The post-Napoleonic law code had restored a multitude of crimes to the capital category, and the atmosphere was such that the guillotine was getting plenty of use. The earliest year in which criminal statistics were kept in France was 1825. In that year there were 134 recorded executions, and in 1826 the number rose to 150.[61]

One of the most notorious of the laws was the so-called Law of Sacrilege, added by Charles X in 1825. He thought it would win him favor with the Catholic hierarchy if he made it a capital crime to profane church vessels that contained communion hosts (amputation of the right hand prior to being hanged was added for good measure). The law became the object of a solemn condemnation after the events of July 1830, but this kind of royal utilization of the capital code for political purposes helped to strengthen the growing suspicions that the real reasons behind the continued use of the death penalty were latent and crude.

2. ALPHONSE DE LAMARTINE (1790–1869)

Lamartine was renowned chiefly for his lyric poetry and was already a member of the French Academy when he was elected to the Chamber of Deputies in 1833. His first teacher had been a Jesuit priest who made a deep and lasting impression on him. One of his most admired poems was his *Hymn to Christ,* dedicated to Manzoni, whom he had met on a trip to Florence. His relations with the church were stormy, especially in mid-life when several of his works were placed on the Index, and his theological ideas went in a variety of odd directions. But his voice, lifted against capital punishment, which he saw as an aberration that should be removed from society, resisted and criticized the widespread and complacent acceptance of church-and-state-sanctioned bloodshed. He gave three memorable speeches advocating abolition in 1836, 1837, and 1838.

Lamartine's historical vision was influenced by that of Chateaubriand in seeing his day as

> one of those recurring epochs of social reconstruction... when the public conscience begins to question itself on one of the most terrible anxieties of its legislation, demanding if it be true that there is any social value in shedding blood, if it be true that the hangman is the carrier-out of a kind of priesthood of humanity, and if it be true that the scaffold is the last argument of justice.

De Maistre had been dead for fifteen years, but his gallows ideology still had to be confronted in the circles of some of his Catholic followers.

Lamartine had no doubt that all three of the above propositions were false, and he explained why and how he had reached this position:

> If at the beginning of its existence, society, in its dearth of means of repression, thought that the right to strike down the guilty was its supreme argument, its only means of self-preservation, it has been able to strike without crime because the striking was done in good conscience. But is it the same today? Today society is armed with powers of repression and punishment that do not require the shedding

of blood, and is enlightened with a light strong enough to substitute moral sanction, corrective sanction, for the sanction of murder. Can this society legitimately remain homicidal? Nature, reason, science—all reply, No!

His view was "unorthodox" in that he did not think society ever had or ever could have any right to kill. The law, in using capital punishment,

> seemed just while the conscience of man knew no better...but it was a carnal law....It made society the avenger of the individual, and the murderer of the murderer. Society has a holier mission—to preserve the individual from crime without setting him an example of murder, to respect and enforce the moral law without violating the natural law, to restore the work of God and proclaim against the voice of all men and against itself this great social divine principle, this dogma eternal, I mean the inviolability of human life.

Lamartine offered many quotable quotes, such as this, from his first speech:

> What is it that hinders society from washing its hands of this business of blood forever? Only one thing—an error, a prejudice, a lie—the belief that the death penalty is still necessary....Is the murder of man by society the proper method of making sacred before the eyes of men the inviolability of human life? No voice will answer us except the paradoxical voice of these glorifiers of the hangman, who attribute to God the thirst for blood, and preach war, this wholesale murder, as a work of providence....Religion replies to these men with the Gospel.

But perhaps the best of his brief remarks with lasting applicability is a terse sentence from his third speech: "It is not death that we must learn to fear; it is life that we must learn to respect."[62]

3. CHARLES LUCAS (1803–1889)

No one in French history is more closely identified with the cause of abolishing the death penalty than Charles Lucas. In 1827 he entered an essay contest and wrote on the topic of the

death penalty. His essay not only won major prizes but determined the direction of the rest of his life. In 1830 he was
appointed Inspector General of French Prisons, a post in which
he earned the reputation of being the founder of penitentiary
science, working diligently to improve French prisons until his
retirement in 1865. During all his years of service he tried to find
an efficient replacement for the death penalty. While he made a
strong philosophical case against it on principle, arguing for the
inviolability of human life, and a comparable theological case for
its being contrary to the spirit of Christ, he also boldly challenged its utility, sharing the view of Bentham that, of all penalties, it was the least effective.

The experience of France was a bit happier than that of England in the latter part of the nineteenth century. Imbert traces the
story through the various locales, citing statistics and monitoring
changes, but the most significant fact is that as of 1863, there
were no further executions of any kind, public or private. The
death penalty was kept on the books in the Penal Code of 1867,
but any time a criminal was condemned to death, clemency was
automatic. There were no executions down to 1918, and the one
that occurred then was an exception in a military context.[63]

It is interesting to put this record together with normal
Catholic teaching at the time. The grand theory was always
there, being taught in the seminaries and defended in the manuals. But that was the death penalty de jure; de facto abolition had
already occurred for most ordinary circumstances.[64] The penal
code had been cleaned up, the absurdity of having hundreds of
capital crimes on the books had been left aside, and the number
of actual executions was greatly reduced. There was no great
need for a well-lubricated guillotine. Its continued presence was
chiefly symbolic, a holdover from the past; it did not make much
actual difference.

4. VICTOR HUGO (1802–1885)

Hugo was assured a place in the front rank of abolitionists
due to three of his celebrated works: *The Last Day of a Condemned
Man* (1829), *Claude Gueux* (1834), and *Les Miserables* (1863). He
was greatly influenced by Voltaire and shared his profound revulsion for the death penalty. He joined vigorously in public

protests against state killings. The most famous were his campaigns to spare the lives of John Tapner in Guernsey in 1854 and of American John Brown in 1859, as well as his letter to Queen Victoria in 1883, asking her to grant clemency to the Irish militant O'Donnell. Hugo was convinced that "blood is washed away with tears, not with blood."[65]

Others labored long and hard against the death penalty, but few if any had the dogged determination of Victor Hugo.

> I do not know any aim more elevated, more holy, than that of seeking the abolition of capital punishment; with sincere devotion I join the wishes and efforts of those philanthropic men of all nations who have laboured, of late years, to throw down the patibulary tree,—the only tree which revolution fails to uproot! It is with pleasure that I take my turn to give my feeble stroke, after the all-powerful blow which, seventy years ago, Beccaria gave to the ancient gibbet, which had been standing during so many years of Christianity.

C. Belgium

1. JEAN-JOSEPH THONISSEN (1816–1891)

A highly respected Belgian Catholic jurist, statesman, and professor at Louvain University, Jean-Joseph Thonissen published a small volume in 1862 entitled *The Supposed Necessity of the Death Penalty*.[66] It raised a fierce controversy at the time but was in part responsible for the fact that no further executions were held in Belgium for years. Thonissen's influence did not stop there. He was well aware that most Catholic theologians took a very dim view of the abolitionist movement and saw dire consequences for the future if it were ever successful. So, three years after the publication of his book, he wrote a calm, reflective essay, entitled "The Problem of the Death Penalty from the Viewpoint of Catholic Dogma."[67]

Thonissen was by no means soliciting recruits for the abolitionist movement but only trying to reassure his conservative colleagues that there was no great need to worry about the declining use of the death penalty. He rehearsed the biblical material amply, concluding that the death penalty found full sanction there, but then began to make his basic case. Just because states like France and Belgium had abolished from their law codes certain statutes covering crimes that were presented as capital offenses in the Bible did not mean the legislators were thereby defying God.

> There is no need to hide behind a biblical text and insist that it is absolutely imperative that it be part of modern law. It is quite all right to accept the reality of some changed social circumstances. As Christians and as citizens of a free state, we have the obligation to study and resolve [penal] problems as we can.

He gives as one obvious example the replacing of execution with life imprisonment for some criminals.

His final appeal reveals how some of the work of the abolitionists had made its mark on his thinking. "If the necessity of the death penalty is not demonstrated, it may certainly be suspended on a trial basis....If less severe penalties suffice, they should be used." He noted that "between 1846 and 1856 alone, England and France saw ten people condemned to death whose innocence was later established juridically." His admiration for some of the abolitionist leaders, whom he described as among "the most eminent lawyers in France, England, and Germany" (Mittermaier was mentioned by name), led him to challenge his Catholic colleagues to see that "the honor of our flag, no less than the demands of Christian charity, require that we not allow this important question to be discussed without us and in spite of us." There was no "Catholic dogma" preventing Catholics from joining hands in the struggle for abolition. His conclusion was both accurate and welcome, but there were obstacles that would prevent such collaboration for most of another century.

D. Italy

1. GIUSEPPE COMPAGNONI (1754–1833)

Compagnoni's book *The Elements of Democratic Constitutional Law* was published in Venice in 1797 and publicly burned before the assembled faculty at the University of Ferrara, from which he was dismissed in 1799 because of his "ultra-liberal" views. However objectionable any of his ideas may have been, he is remembered today as the first and only man in Italy to maintain in 1792 the right of the Jews to juridical emancipation. On the subject of the death penalty, however, writing at precisely the same time as Kant, he argued on utilitarian grounds that society never for any reason whatsoever had any right to kill.

> Staying alive is the primary need of man and therefore his primary right. His life is the principal object he brings to the social contract. Losing that means losing everything. Since preservation of life and all its rights is the basic rationale of the contract, it is false to assert the contrary by stipulating conditions of losing it....Man does not sacrifice some portion of his rights on entering society, but rather assures and augments all of them.[68]

The final statement was an open disagreement with Beccaria, but Compagnoni felt very strongly about it. "Whatever else the state might do to punish a criminal, one thing was clear: It cannot kill him in cold blood!" This was seen as an outrageous position in its time, but there is an interesting parallel in this new secular context to what we saw earlier in the religious context. It was from the fringe, the "philosophical heretics," that the intuition of the inalienable nature of the right to life first received its clearest expression in secular terms, just as it was from the fringe, the "theological heretics," that the intuition of the sacredness/inviolability of life first began to be stressed in the process of Christian retrieval.

2. PIETRO ELLERO (1833–1933)

Ellero was born the year Compagnoni died. In a long and distinguished career devoted to the reform of the Italian legal code he founded in 1861 at Padua a unique magazine called *The Journal for the Abolition of the Death Penalty,* which was published until 1865. He had already set forth his basic ideas in a book entitled *On Capital Punishment* in 1858, when he was only 25 years old. Later he taught law at the University of Bologna and was a leader in the "revolt of the academics," protesting what were viewed as indefensible parts of Christian "tradition." He not only foresaw but confidently predicted nearly a century before the fact that "even the Catholic Church will some day reject capital punishment, just as it did slavery."[69] It was not easy to see how this could ever happen, given the alienation and fierce animosities of the time.

3. MSGR. GIUSEPPE C. ZANGHY (1829–1878)

It is surprising to learn that there was an Italian cleric who published a work against the death penalty in 1874. Monsignor Giuseppe Zanghy's book entitled *Catholicism and the Death Penalty* is hard to come by.[70] As summarized and criticized by Skoda, Zanghy seems to have held that, even for the gravest crimes, death as a penalty was "contrary to the spirit of the Catholic Church." The quotation attributed to him by Skoda is that "the Church has manifested its spirit as one of mildness, far removed from any kind of bloodshed, a spirit based on the Bible, the teachings of its Fathers and Doctors, its pontifical decrees, and its own history." Admittedly this sounds a bit on the triumphalistic side rather than a serious account of the history.

He is also cited, however, as dismissing any appeal to the capital laws of the Old Testament as irrelevant, contending that they could not be considered binding on Christians. They were only due to the "peculiar conditions of the time and the great inclination of the Jews of that day to delinquency." This too is not a very reassuring "scientific" remark. The only additional information given by Skoda is that Zanghy admitted that "the Doctors of the Church had justified capital punishment," but, he maintained, they did so only with the greatest reservation.

How was this assessment received by fellow Catholic scholars of the nineteenth century? Skoda admitted that there was no "systematic and doctrinal response" that refuted the arguments of the abolitionists, but that occasionally some of the controversial questions were touched on in periodicals, especially the Jesuit publication *La Civiltà Cattolica* and a few others. He lamented the fact that there was no single comprehensive work defending the Catholic "tradition." He seems to have hoped that he would find someone who had stepped forward and argued the full Catholic case in support of the death penalty in a more effective way. But the nineteenth century ended without the appearance of any such contribution.

E. Spain

1. MANUEL PÉREZ DE MOLINA (1854/1878)

Nineteenth-century Spain had its horror stories, as might be expected. One of the more notorious was the execution of a well-known professor named Ruzafa, who was condemned to death in 1826 for being a deist and refusing to remove his hat when viaticum was carried past him on the street. The case led Benjamin Wiffen to write a letter asking: "When will life be sacred in Spain?"

But there were more promising developments too, especially after the revolution of 1854, the year in which the first Spanish petition for abolition of capital punishment for political crimes was introduced. That was also the year in which the work of Manuel Pérez de Molina, a progressive lawyer opposed to the death penalty, appeared. *Society and the Scaffold: The Death Penalty Historically and Philosophically Considered* used Beccaria as its point of departure but went on to develop a double-thesis, philosophical and religious: (1) the death penalty is not truly a penalty but is immoral, useless, and incompatible with the principles of penal science; and (2) it was never justified by Jesus Christ and is not justified by belief in the immortality of the soul.[71] The work seems to have found an audience, since in 1878 a revised edition with a different subtitle (*Impugnación de la Pena de Muerte*) was published. It was to be exactly another century before abolition was finally achieved.

F. Germany

This "sampler of voices" criticizing the death penalty in nineteenth-century Europe is of necessity very incomplete. Its purpose is to point out some of the ways in which a faded Christian value had nonetheless survived and resurfaced as an option for the heirs of the tradition in which it had been obscured. Nowhere was this process more complex than in Germany. because it was there that so many divergent voices clashed in what may have been the broadest intellectual exchange over the dilemmas of capital punishment ever to take place anywhere. Our four selections for brief hearings are an influential Protestant theologian, a celebrated jurist, a historian with a broad sweep, and an unusual Catholic moral theologian.

1. FRIEDRICH SCHLEIERMACHER (1768–1834)

Schleiermacher's full position was not published till nearly a decade after his death. It is an interesting variation on Beccaria's appeal to the social contract. Everyone who agrees to live in the society thereby agrees to be punished for criminal behavior, but Christian rulers ought to know that they cannot impose a punishment other than what one has a right to invoke upon himself. But

> no one has the right or is ever allowed to kill himself. This means that the *death penalty has absolutely no place in a Christian state.* There has always been disagreement on this, but no argument can possibly refute this conclusion....True, the purpose of the penal code is to assure obedience to the law, but this is meaningless when we execute the criminal....Perhaps one might say that some crimes are so terrible that the criminal should never again enjoy life and that the death penalty is an act of mercy for him. But this is *totally unchristian,* for God's grace is far greater than any human act."[72]

Part of the complication here is the fact that Schleiermacher was struggling with the obvious reality of an increasingly secular state while assuming nonetheless that his mission was to promote the building of an increasingly Christian state. It was easy to fade from one to the other, confusing the reality that existed with the ideal he hoped for.

> The development of the state *requires*...the *abolition* of the death penalty....As states become more Christian, they also become aware that it is not only superfluous and useless but also simply immoral. If we do not see that, it only means that we are stupid....The guilt of using the death penalty rests on no single individual but on the whole society....All Christians must constantly work for the abolition of the death penalty.[73]

Keeping in mind that the chief alternative among Protestants at the time was the fierce retributivism of Kant and Hegel, the lines are drawn all the more sharply. Schleiermacher's Calvinism involved him in some problematic philosophical positions, especially concerning freedom of the will.[74] His determinist views on this question were unacceptable to both Lutherans and Catholics. Thus, just as in the case of Beccaria, the cause of abolishing the death penalty was closely associated with objectionable philosophical views, leading many to assume that the two "mistakes" were interconnected—and in many individual cases they may well have been. Schleiermacher himself felt that there was "undeniably something to be said for immortality, [but] he could not convince himself of it."[75]

2. KARL J. A. MITTERMAIER (1787–1867)

Born in Munich, Mittermaier first visited Heidelberg as a student in 1808 and returned to accept a chair of law in 1821, soon becoming a highly regarded teacher and scholar. He also served as speaker of the Lower House in Baden from 1833 to 1840 but withdrew from politics entirely after the turbulent events of 1848. During those years, however, he strove mightily to bring about the abolition of capital punishment. His most lasting contribution was his book, which was published in an English adaptation in 1865.

In the preface to this work a personal friend, Charles H. Schaible, provides a highly laudatory biographical sketch:

> Mittermaier's name will never perish, and posterity will remember him with thankful reverence for his disinterested exertions in the cause of humanity, and especially for his efforts to bring about the abolition of capital punishment— a remnant of barbarous times, which will soon be swept away by the spread of knowledge and of sound views of jurisprudence.[76]

The eighteen chapters of the English adaptation of his book show the broad approach of Mittermaier, who found fault with capital punishment from start to finish. His arguments included the full spectrum of objections that had been emerging for a

century: humanitarian, legal, pragmatic, sociopolitical, psychological, historical, and religious grounds, all of them accumulat-
ing to result in an overwhelming outweighing of any alleged
advantages to executing criminals. Many of the arguments were
formulated in as eloquent a manner as was to be found anywhere
in the intervening years. For instance:

> Man has only the authority to deprive his neighbour of his
> civil rights; he has no claim to interfere with the rights which
> belong to him in his capacity as a human being....No infer-
> ence justifies the legislator in killing the man. He might per-
> haps withdraw the right of citizenship...but the withdrawal of
> this protection by no means justifies Death Punishment.[77]

Mittermaier stayed abreast of developments in Europe and
America. He visited England and Scotland in 1850 but was never
able to fulfill his dream of coming to the United States to meet
the abolitionist leaders and see firsthand the results of the
promising ante-bellum movement. He made no claim to being a
prophet but was convinced that it was only a question of time till
the death penalty, like its twin-barbarity—slavery—would be erad-
icated from the civilized world.

> The science of jurisprudence, legislation, and experience
> combined tend to the abolition of Capital Punishment.
> When this result will be brought about we do not presume to
> say. But as soon as the persuasion has become general that
> Capital Punishment is neither necessary nor expedient, it
> will disappear just as withered leaves fall from the trees in
> autumn.[78]

3. ERNST WILHELM HERMANN HETZEL (1820–1906)

The broadest historical work on the death penalty in nineteenth-century Germany was Hetzel's 540-page tome on the cul-
tural-historical evolution of capital punishment. In the first part
he surveyed the practices in ancient "paganism," including
under this label the laws and customs of ancient Egypt, China,
Persia, and India, then Greece and Rome. By page 40 he was into
the second part, devoting only ten pages to Judaism. Then he
turned to the third part, devoting nearly four hundred pages to

the history of Christianity. This he divided into six periods. The first five were: (1) the New Testament; (2) Early Christian writers up to Constantine (325); (3) From Constantine to Charlemagne (771); (4) From Charlemagne to the Reformation (1517); and (5) From the Reformation to Beccaria (1764)—these five periods took up one hundred pages. So part 6 (From Beccaria to 1869) was clearly his major interest and concern, constituting the bulk of the book. He closed it out with forty pages of reflections on six aspects: juridical, political, philosophical, anthropological, theological, and historical. Then he lined up in fascinating fashion thirty-five pages of bibliography since Beccaria, breaking the works into two opposing columns, those written by opponents of the death penalty (Gegner) on the left, and those written by supporters (Anhänger) on the right.

Hetzel made it very clear where his own sentiments lay. In fact, in the appended list of books he put his own as the last and latest work in opposition to capital punishment. Just looking at his outline it is obvious where his chief interests were; for example, he dispatches the Middle Ages in fifteen pages (although it should be acknowledged that he included therein notice of a remarkably large sample of both the best and the worst moments of Christian conduct regarding bloodshed).

Hetzel stood with Schleiermacher against Kant, noting that, despite all the Old Testament legislation, "Christ and his apostles nowhere defended the death penalty." He had reviewed enough history to realize and acknowledge that for at least the last five hundred years "the Christian church through most of its leading representatives claimed that the death penalty was divinely mandated." It was only very recently that "Christians on all sides" had begun to change, appropriately extending the application of the principle of Christian love even to the realm of the death penalty. (He had not been able to find any Catholic representatives to include as yet.)

Hetzel waxed eloquent in elaborating on the fact of incompatibility, intertwining religious and secular arguments against executing people. For instance, he reminded the utilitarian that "it is unethical to punish someone more harshly simply for the aim of possibly deterring others from crime." As for the theological retributivist, he noted: "You think that the earthly legislator shares in the justice of God and that the authorities are fulfilling God's will. But weak human beings lack the most important means for doing such work, namely omniscience, true justice, and omnipotence." In concluding, he insisted that it should be evident that for "practical Christianity the death penalty is impossible; it is godless, i.e., against the express will of God in the ethical world-order. In a word, it is simply unethical."[79]

On his very last page, in giving hopeful examples of Christians turning away from capital punishment in increasing numbers, Hetzel saw fit to include mention of a recent case in which "the highest ecclesiastical court in Rome, with the approval of the pope, upon application by the excommunicated king of Italy, in March 1869, commuted the death sentences of Ajani and Luzzi to life imprisonment."[80] It could be taken as a harbinger, in very dark days, of better things to come from the Vatican a century later.

4. FR. FRANZ X. LINSENMANN (1878)

We close this chapter with an unexpected Catholic voice. Fr. Franz Linsenmann, professor at the University of Tübingen, differed from many of the Catholic moral theologians of his time in that he tried to grapple directly with a variety of problems raised by the Enlightenment rather than simply condemning and dismissing all "modernism." He probed such diverse questions as the ethical foundations of academic freedom, the teaching of Meister Eckhart, the morality of lotteries, and the purposes of punishment. Taking a critical look at the problem of the death penalty, he treated it at surprising length in his 1878 textbook.[81]

Linsenmann was without doubt a rather unique phenomenon. His pioneering position on capital punishment was not based on questionable quibbles about Bible interpretation. It was an approach of common-sense moderation, working within the general framework of the Catholic moral theology of the day. He had no hesitation acknowledging the potential legitimacy of capital punishment (the centerpiece since 1210 of the state's "right" to execute), but he had great difficulty taking seriously some of the arguments used by fellow moralists to justify its standard use. His was, in many ways, a voice of the future, even though that future was still nearly a century away and its contours not yet discernible.

Linsenmann began his treatment of capital punishment by acknowledging that the assumed right of the state to kill felons might possibly be supported by a "universal consensus of mankind" argument, so widespread was the practice historically. He noted that theoretical abolitionists were only a relatively recent and as yet small minority; that some states that had abolished the death penalty had also quickly restored it; and that even where it was not often used, it was kept on the books in case of emergencies under martial law and the law of the sea. But since all this in itself did not really prove either the legitimacy or the necessity of capital punishment, appeal to the Bible was usually turned to by Catholic moralists, at least by way of confirmation.

Part of Linsenmann's independence of spirit was manifest in the fact that he took empirical factors seriously and used the Bible thoughtfully. He left the Old Testament aside, simply noting as a point of common knowledge that death was a penalty often found in the law codes of ancient Israel. But he chose to begin his reflections by calling attention to a New Testament passage as at least implicitly reflecting the right of those in authority to impose the death penalty. In John 19:10f., when Pilate in frustration says to the silent Jesus, "Do you not know that I have power to release you and power to crucify you?" Jesus reminds him that he would have no such power if it were not given to him from above. Likewise in reviewing Romans 13:1ff., Paul's famous passage about the civil authority wielding the sword, Linsenmann remarks that this image "can hardly be understood as representing anything other than the authority's right over life and death....The New Testament presupposes the right of capital punishment as at least a given."[82]

Thus far he was still in step with his conservative predecessors and contemporaries in his conclusions, if not in precisely how he reached them. But then he began to carve out new territory, making his own original contribution:

> Scientific investigation has not just the theoretical task of justifying the use of the death penalty, but also the practical task of determining in what circumstances it is to be applied. In our time neither the *legitimacy* nor the *necessity* of the death penalty can be deduced from the nature and goals of

punishment; on the contrary, as far as penal theories go, all agree that the essential purposes of punishment can be met just as well or better by other kinds of penalties than by death. Indeed, there is further agreement that, far from appearing just or necessary, execution *contradicts* the standard purposes of punishment, since it does not undo an injustice but is simply an act of raw power intentionally destructive of human life.[83]

This was indeed the striking of a very different chord in a Catholic textbook, and it was not one that would begin to reverberate very widely for nearly another century. Linsenmann managed to get past the age-old stumbling-block by drawing the distinction between theory and practice. One did not have to contradict Innocent III in order to see the current incongruity of the modern secular state indulging in the regular practice of killing people as a standard part of its ordinary regimen. Nor did Linsenmann stop at the above statement. Aware that he was advocating a move to higher ethical ground than was customary, he elaborated on the significance of this new stance. It was not a departure from but a *return to* the best of Christian ethical principles:

> It is imperative to recognize that the death penalty can be justified only if it is *absolutely necessary* from the perspective of self-defense. Just as war is justifiable only as self-defense against an *external* threat to society, so the death penalty can be justified only as self-defense against an *internal* threat to society. Hence it follows that a situation of civil order and security can be reached in which individual dangerous elements can be controlled with lesser penalties than death, so that with declining use capital punishment eventually becomes *superfluous.* Indeed, the goal to be devoutly desired would be to restrict its use by law. Abolition of the death penalty is simply a political or cultural question; there are no legal or moral grounds preventing it.

It is difficult to appreciate today what an uncommon statement this was, coming from an established Catholic moral theologian of the time. Well into our own century it was not uncommon for manuals of moral theology prepared for use in seminaries to hold positions like the following: "No government can renounce the right of inflicting capital punishment." And some even went on to embrace the position held by a popular Irish manualist, Fr. Joseph Rickaby, S.J., that "the power to inflict (the death penalty) could never be dispensed with."[84]

Behind these disparate positions was the intense philosophical debate that agitated Germany throughout the nineteenth century. Linsenmann as a young man at Tübingen may well have heard Mittermaier speak on the subject. But the lack of significant Catholic participation was a cause of chagrin to him as an educator:

> The learned journals and the popular newspapers abound with this controversy; so moral theology simply has to take a position; what is at issue and in great need of being verified is the *basis* for the legitimacy and necessity of a punishment which runs counter to the Commandment "Thou shalt not kill."

Linsenmann devotes the rest of his treatment to this foundational question, reviewing the prevalent theories about the nature and purposes of punishment. As for the first—deterrence—he finds two real problems: (a) it is a secondary aim in the sense that it cannot justify a mode of punishment that is not already necessary and legitimate on other grounds; and (b) even as a subordinate purpose it is highly questionable whether the death penalty ever serves it at all. He was inclined to believe that capital punishment had "never actually hindered serious crimes." In support of this he told of a chaplain (cited in Holtzendorff's 1875 study of murder and the death penalty in Germany) who had accompanied 167 prisoners to the gallows and knew for a fact that at least 161 of them had at some time been personally present at earlier hangings. Against deterrence claims, he also agreed with Beccaria that "cruel and bloody punishments do not so much deter as deaden the sensibilities of people."[85] Here he alluded to the black humor that invariably surrounded the scaffold, noting that "a hanging was referred to as a wedding; the gallows was the bride, the convict was the groom, the hangman was the celebrant, who tied the knot with the rope, and the body swinging in the air at the end of the rope was doing the wedding-dance." He saw this as a psychological response to tragedy. The practice of executing was so horrific that some kind of comic relief had to be sought to disguise it as something other than what it really was.

Another troublesome position that a society's commitment to the death penalty led to was the assumption that human dignity, the *imago Dei,* the sacredness of the person, the unique value of the individual, all this was simply forfeited, handed over, lost, or destroyed by the evil action of the wrongdoer. Koch and Preus asserted outright that "the dignity of manhood is inviolable *only* as long as the individual respects it in himself."[86] No great effort ever seemed to be made to ground this common belief, presumably because it was felt to be implicit in the very act of executing someone. But the validity of such a claim of forfeiture that canceled the very right to life would at some point have to be dealt with. An answer to this challenge was crucial. Was there really any credible foundation for this notion? Is talk about the "image of God" or the "sanctity of life" anything more than rhetoric if it can be "forfeited" and go up in smoke upon a person's misconduct? No easy answer was forthcoming.

From Beccaria to Linsenmann was a long stretch, and we have hardly touched on the massive cultural changes that occurred in that period. But these two men can be taken symbolically as representing a "double enlightenment" process, one secular, the other religious, which inevitably intertwined and overlapped in the nineteenth century, accounting for some of the stop-and-go cycles of abolitionist movements.

CHAPTER 7

From Vatican I to Vatican II

I. LATE NINETEENTH-CENTURY EUROPE

In 1848 in the Frankfurt Parliament the founder of the Catholic social movement in Germany, Baron (later Bishop) Wilhelm Emmanuel von Ketteler, was among those who voted in favor of abolishing the death penalty. This serves as a good reminder of how radically the later events of 1848 altered things. Catholic would-be liberals were transformed into conservatives, and the course of progressive thought was effectively stunted for the following century. Hopes for the dawning of a more "enlightened" age were extinguished by the fears provoked by the chaotic revolutions.

The assassination of the papal prime minister, Pellegrino Rossi, could be taken as symbolic. The plans of the forward-thinking new pope, Pius IX, died with Rossi, and an era of resistance to all change set in. His 1864 *Syllabus of Errors* was a declaration of war on everything modern, and, with the loss of the papal states in 1870, despite having succeeded in pushing the dogma of papal infallibility through Vatican I, he chose to "retreat to the citadel and brood on the evils of democracy and modernity."[1]

Among the positive results of the loss of the temporal domain, however, was the fact that the popes were thereby freed from the burden of ever again being involved administratively in the grisly business of capital punishment. This existential liberation in itself was worth far more than anything lost, for it opened the way for rethinking the issue in the future and possibly coming up with a strategy to retrieve some long-faded values in and for future generations.

But in the meantime, the theory that had been developed in the post-Trent period had its own momentum for continuing, especially due to two factors, one political, the other pedagogical.

A. The Politics of Retention

As Richard Evans has observed, the death penalty was "an instrument of state politics" more than an aspect of penal policy because of the symbolism it bore. In both Protestant and Catholic circles, efforts were made to tie retention of the death penalty to religion's "traditional values" and to tie abolitionist movements to the breakdown of society and the emergence of atheism and agnosticism. So, even as the First Vatican Council convened in Rome (1870), the accents of religion could also be heard in the political maneuverings of the Reichstag, and the voice was that of none other than Otto von Bismarck.

> [In addressing an 1870 session] the Chancellor was struck by the "overestimation on the part of the opponents of the value which they attach to life in this world, and the importance which they ascribe to death...[which] is only a transition from one life to another....Death is of central importance as a punishment for those for whom it is the peace, the sleep which Hamlet longs for, dreamless."...He urged the deputies not to give way to the "morbid sentimentality of the times," nor to share in the "pathological tendency...to treat the criminal with more care and consideration and more inclination to protect him from injustice than his victims."[2]

As in countless political contexts before and since, the difference between being for or being against capital punishment was painted as an aspect of the difference of being on the angelic or being on the demonic side in the great cosmic struggle.

B. The Pedagogy of Retention

The pedagogical factor, in the case of Catholicism, was the provision of relatively uniform seminary manuals. These ahistorical works helped to maintain the impression that the positions they advanced were perennial, immutable "traditions" of the church maintained over the centuries. They were effective instruments for keeping things as they were, especially after Leo XIII's 1879 encyclical *Aeterni Patris,* promoting the adoption of Thomistic philosophy and theology. Coordinated manuals, based on the principle "gratia supponit naturam," reinforced one another on the proper content of seminary instruction. Since reason and revelation are in harmony, philosophical and theological arguments work in tandem, allowing the stronger case to be made invariably for "traditional" positions, such as routine support for capital punishment.

For example, Viktor Cathrein, a Swiss-born Jesuit who was a leading neo-Thomist, wrote a moral philosophy manual that first appeared in 1895 and subsequently went through many editions and was widely used. Its philosophical thesis #99 was the declaration that "the political power has the right of establishing the death penalty for certain more atrocious crimes."[3] In good Scholastic fashion he first presents the *status quaestionis* to alert the reader as to where this proposition came from and why it was being taught as part of the "preferred" philosophical outlook that would well serve Catholic clergymen of the day:

1. From the time of Beccaria many proponents of liberalism have condemned the death penalty as unjust and inhumane. As a result of their efforts the death penalty has in many places been either entirely abolished or fallen into disuse because the governing power commutes the sentences to life in prison. Those writing against the death penalty in recent times have been, e.g., Ahrens, Holtzendorff et al. 2. Against them we contend that the civil authority has the right to establish the death penalty at least for certain more serious crimes, such as homicide.

The proof of the proposition: The state has this power IF it is necessary to impede crime effectively. But it is necessary. Ergo...

Proof of the major: Killing someone is not intrinsically evil unless it is unjust. But God, the supreme Lord of life, can not only take away the life of anyone, but can also give that power to the civil authority. But if this is necessary to safeguard society, we conclude properly that such authority has been received from God. For it has received all the rights needed for proper governance of the republic.

Proof of the minor: The civil authority must, as far as possible, effectively see to the security of citizens and public order. It must especially impede the gravest crimes most effectively, such as homicide, which takes away not only all one's earthly goods but also the person, many times unprepared for the eternal judge. But often it is only the death penalty that is effective enough to deter. For, a) some men are so wicked that society cannot otherwise protect itself from new crimes except by cutting them off from society. Ergo, it is lawful to kill them....And, b) in a large crowd many are always to be found who can only be impeded from committing atrocious crimes by the fear of death alone. So the civil authority not only can but must threaten them with death because it has the responsibility to do all it can to provide public security.

One striking feature of this entire presentation, in view of the real history behind it, is the total absence of any reference to the formerly colossal problem of executing heretics. Once Protestants and Catholics, respectively, stopped burning one another at the stake, discussions of the death penalty could be conducted with a much loftier tone. Cathrein's placid syllogisms may all be perfectly valid in form, but his easy assumptions, for example, about the deterrent force of the death penalty, were wide open to empirical challenge, as eventually would have to be recognized and conceded.

His treatment of the death penalty goes on with the elaboration of two scholia and six objections with appropriate responses, all of which provide interesting reflections of the social context. In the first scholion, for instance, he cautiously avoids the argument that some others were using to defend capital punishment as the *only* proportionate response to murder. "We abstain from this argument because it presupposes a theory of expiation, which is too vague as a principle for human judgment." Perhaps it was because he was consciously "doing philosophy," that is, using reason alone rather than appealing to revelation, that he skirted this "religious" argument, which was so prominent elsewhere.

Throughout his treatment, however, he constantly appealed to the authority of Thomas Aquinas, even invoking those problematic quotes seen earlier, including the analogy of amputating a gangrenous member in order to save the whole body. The requisite question mark had not yet been attached to that metaphor, and its applicability had not yet been challenged. All in all, however, a case can certainly be made that this low-key, thoughtful approach by a leading supporter of capital punishment like Cathrein was already a major step in the right direction. The excess baggage that had so burdened earlier scholars had in a way been confiscated by the armies of the *Risorgimento,* making a more academic discussion of the whole issue possible. But before fuller recovery could happen, some very troubled times were destined to postpone the retrieval.

II. EARLY TWENTIETH-CENTURY EUROPE

If Pius IX's *Syllabus of Errors* had put many things on hold in 1864, the slowdown became a standstill with the double assault of Pius X repressing "Modernism" in 1907. *Lamentabili* and *Pascendi* reprobated so many ideas and propositions so harshly that one of the chief effects was a chill that lasted down to Vatican II. This atmosphere must be taken into account to understand some of the fruitless battles that raged early in this century. The following example is one that had a direct bearing on the capital-punishment debate.

A. George G. Coulton's Critique (1923)

Cambridge University historian G. G. Coulton (1858–1947) was involved in a series of altercations with Catholics over medieval history. Coulton invariably had better historical information than his opponents, and he was not above taunting them for their ignorance of Christian church history, especially some of its less flattering episodes. One of these battles shed light on the entanglement with capital punishment in prosecuting heretics.

The seventeenth-century syllogism seen earlier, concluding that all Protestants ought rightly to be executed immediately as violators of the Roman imperial law against the *crime of heresy,* was more than a merely logical exercise. It was incorporated into standard works defending Catholic practices. It was one of the "burdens of bloodshed," a liability that came with the "tradition" justifying the use of the death penalty. When in power, it was used; when out of power, it was suspended.

Coulton faulted two Catholic authors (Fr. Joseph Rickaby and Fr. Leslie Walker), who footnoted the text of Aquinas ("heretics are to be compelled to hold the faith") to claim that "the heretics whom medieval writers had in view were the heretics of their own time, that is, apostate Catholics. The Protestant of our day falls under St. Thomas' first class," that is, unbelievers, and therefore are not subject to the penalties of heresy. Coulton would have none of this and made fun of their effort to foist this historical inaccuracy on uninformed readers in such an off-handed way. He made his points effectively, and they may be summarized in somewhat condensed fashion as follows:

> 1) A heretic can confer valid baptism; therefore, any Protestant who has been sprinkled with water and intentionally baptized in the name of the Father, Son and Holy Ghost is truly baptized. 2) The infant thus baptized becomes at once *fidelis*. 3) No matter what, he can never lose this character. 4) Therefore, he became at baptism subject to the church and remains legally so till death. 5) The church as a "perfect society" has full rights of coercion and punishment over its subjects. 6) These include not only spiritual punishments, but also corporal, even the ultimate punishment of death. 7) Formal heresy is a capital crime. 8) It becomes formal when one refuses *pertinaciously* to accept a teaching of the church. 9) It is not for the individual, nor the state, nor society in general to decide pertinacity. 10) The sole judge of this is the Roman Catholic Church.[3a]

Coulton dug into the authors to show that this was indeed the teaching of all the great Catholic moralists from Aquinas to Bellarmine and Suárez, and more recently, right down to two well-known Jesuit scholars at the turn of the century (historian Theodor Granderath, who died in 1902, and canon law professor de Luca of the Gregorian University, whose 1901 work was prefaced with a long letter of praise by Pope Leo XIII).

When his critics objected, Coulton added fuel to the fire by noting that the position was still being defended by Alexis Lépicier, professor at the Propaganda Fide College (and later cardinal). In the 1910 edition of one of his books Lépicier asked: "How must we deal with heretics? Are they to be tolerated or altogether exterminated? Has the Church the right of punishing them with death?" In his reply he pulled no punches:

> I am aware that there are many who think that the Church has no right to sanction the death-penalty, whether for heresy or for any other crime. But their decision cannot be called probable, since it does not appear plainly how this negation is compatible with the constitution of the Church or with historical facts....Many heretics have been condemned to death by the just judgment of the Church, which has the right of executing pertinacious heretics...if she judge this advisable.[3b]

The loss of the papal states in 1870 was the social precondition for abandoning this kind of ecclesiological imperialism, but, as Coulton reminded everyone, it had not yet disappeared. Up until the settlement with Mussolini in 1929, there were still those whose "immutable" ecclesiology required that the church, as a "societas perfecta," have that crown jewel of state power, the right to kill, even if it chose not to use it.[4]

Even though it will take us out of strict chronology and on somewhat of a tangent, this would seem to be the best place to summarize briefly how complete the contemporary effort has been to renounce the remnants of this tenacious death-penalty strain that plagued church circles in so many ways.

B. The Vatican's Death-Penalty Statute (1929–1969)

In the 1929 Concordat Vatican City retained a statute that was cloned from the Italian legal code in force at the time, reserving death as the penalty for anyone who tried to assassinate a pope within Vatican City.[5] It was still on the books during the years of the Second Vatican Council. In light of all the rethinking of both the nature of the church and of capital punishment, it was an increasingly anachronistic embarrassment, so Pope Paul VI had it quietly removed in 1969 when other necessary adaptations were also being made in the "fundamental law" of Vatican City.

Although notice of the removal of the death-penalty statute appeared "buried" in the Vatican's Latin *Gazette* in August 1969, the fact did not come to general public attention for nearly a year and a half, and even then, almost accidentally. In January 1971 Pope Paul VI raised his voice in criticism of executions being planned in both Spain and the Soviet Union, calling on the respective leaders to grant clemency to political prisoners. A Rome newspaper taunted the Vatican for hypocrisy, saying that Vatican City itself still had a death-penalty statute on its books. The press corps thereupon descended on the Vatican, asking insistently whether this were true, and a Vatican spokesman calmly provided them with the reference to the 1969 *Gazette.*

The report of this episode the next day in the *New York Times* concluded ominously with the observation that "no one has tried to kill a Pope in the city-state in this century."[6] When the first such assassination attempt was made, ten years later, on the life of Pope John Paul II, his reaction was exactly the opposite of what the law would have provided. Instead of calling for "legal" bloodshed, he offered Christian forgiveness, demonstrating in action what was at the time already well on its way back to the center of Christian theory in regard to the death penalty. Revenge was finding itself less welcome than before.

If it had not been for the cataclysmic disruption of European societies in the Second World War, however, it might well have taken much longer for the full abolition of the death penalty to be achieved. The nineteenth-century events we have noted led to the rise of what has been called "closed Catholicism" as part of its survival tactics in an increasingly hostile society. John Whyte, in tracing this phenomenon, discerned four stages in its development:

1. The beginnings of closed Catholicism (c.1790–1870);
2. The development of closed Catholicism (c.1870–1920);
3. The peak period of closed Catholicism (c.1920–1960); and
4. The decay of closed Catholicism (since 1960).

Whyte goes on to say:

> Catholics in continental Europe found themselves responding to what they saw as liberal aggression, by making a pan-conservative alliance with other right-wing forces. This alliance proved electorally unprofitable, and closed Catholicism largely grew out of the efforts of Catholics to distance themselves from these unpopular allies.[7]

Some of the consequences of these developments for Catholic theology have been chronicled and analyzed by Gerald McCool, especially what happened in the seminary manuals of Roman theology. We have seen in the case of Viktor Cathrein's work an example of the philosophical manuals. Their counterpart in theology, according to McCool, had as their purpose

> the clear exposition of safe "received" Thomistic doctrine rather than the stimulation of original thought. The verbalism, caution, and excessive recourse to the authority of the Angelic Doctor which characterized these manuals upset even Catholic scholars like Pierre Duhem who were sympathetic to the Thomistic revival.

One of the best and brightest of the leaders in this period (Cardinal Louis Billot) "had no feel for history and showed little interest in it. Scripture, exegesis, and positive theology were played down in his teaching and writing." Among the "tragic consequences for Catholic theology" was the fact that this "prevented the Roman theologians...from solving, or even appreciating, the genuine questions with which modern historical science and modern philosophy confronted the Church at the time of the modernist crisis."[8] These factors help to account for the fact that, except for an occasional maverick like Linsenmann, the manualists guaranteed sanctuary for the age-old belief in the divinely authorized death penalty as a necessary part of the eternal plan for both church and state. The historical and biblical studies that could have challenged this reigning mythology had not yet taken root.

C. E. Thamiry's Standard Defense (1928)

One way of testing where things stood in early twentieth-century European Catholic thought is to consult the *DTC,* the prestigious, comprehensive multi-volume French *Dictionnaire de Théologie Catholique.*[9] It is a monumental record of much of the best Catholic scholarship of the day, and it carried in volume ten a lengthy entry on the death penalty written by Edouard Thamiry. In it he cited an 1867 article by a French author named Hello, who called attention to the total absence of Catholic theologians in the eighteenth- and nineteenth-century controversies over capital punishment. Thamiry, after acknowledging the accuracy of the remark, noted however a lone dissenter, an Abbé LeNoir, who in the very year of Hello's article (1867) went on record against the death penalty in Bergier's *Dictionnaire de Théologie.*

LeNoir, however, hardly advanced the cause in any serious way, since all he did was adopt a curious millenarianism modeled on the evolutionary scheme popularized by Auguste Comte, distinguishing three ages in the history of humanity. In the first age, as envisioned by LeNoir, there was no death penalty, since God had put a mark on Cain to protect him and others from such punishment. But in the second age—in which we still find ourselves— capital punishment was wrongly introduced in blatant violation of natural law, and God has merely tolerated it along with all the other evils of this time of darkness and tribulation. But when Christ returns in glory to bring in the third age, the reign of pure law and complete Christianity, the death penalty will disappear entirely. Meantime, until that millennium arrives, capital punishment must be seen for what it truly is: an illegitimate, barbaric, ungodly practice in open violation of God's own law.

Understandably, Thamiry was unimpressed with LeNoir's unorthodox fantasies and he especially found the attempted use of scripture in support of these novel notions both "too tendentious and too subtle" to be taken seriously, "even in a philosophical utopia, let alone before the reality to which Catholic doctrine refers." But it is obvious that his dismissal was not limited to the wilder parts of LeNoir's speculations. For Thamiry, the writings of the entire abolitionist school were packed with "illusions coming from two principal sources," the lamentable influence of utilitarianism, and the total neglect of natural-law doctrine. The latter mistake was especially due to the errors stemming from Rousseau's *Social Contract* theory. The only way to remove the confusion, as far as Thamiry was concerned, was to return to the basic principles of natural law, in light of which the legitimacy of the death penalty could once again be clearly seen as formulated in classical Catholic theology.

The article is a *tour de force,* neatly organized in neo-Scholastic fashion, combining appeals to natural law, both individual and social, and to divine positive law (as found in traditional readings of the scriptures), and following with the usual references to events in Christian history to show that "the right (of the state to impose the death penalty) has never been contested in the Church, although clerics have always been forbidden to take part in capital cases." The grand finale, in traditional style, comes with his systematic response to major objections:

First are his replies to objections from legal considerations:

a. Capital punishment is not a case of using a human person as a means instead of an end, because it only destroys the corporal life for the sake of justice and the safety of society.

b. Capital punishment is not a case of violating a person's natural right to life, because society also has a natural right and the criminal by his action has forfeited his right, allowing the state to exercise its right. (He cites Aquinas's example of the criminal being reduced by his crime to the level of a beast enslaved by evil instincts.)

c. Capital punishment is not automatically evil just because it is an act of killing a human being. The law of legitimate self-defense against a criminal, as in the case of defense against an unjust enemy in war, is an exception to the rule of not killing, and such are in reality acts of virtue.

d. Capital punishment is not illegitimate just because it happens to collide with Rousseau's hypothesis that the rights of civil authority are derived from the consent of its citizens. This erroneous notion ignores natural law based on the fact that all civil authority comes from God.

Then come Thamiry's answers to four more objections that arise from practical considerations:

a. Life imprisonment, contrary to Beccaria's contention, is not as effective a deterrent as execution, and it is an illusion to think otherwise.

b. To claim that condemning criminals to perpetual hard labor would be more useful to society is to put material utility ahead of moral utility. Experience demonstrates that being soft in repressing criminals is a kind of betrayal of the good citizens of the society.

c. The death penalty does not violate the medicinal purpose of punishment because there are two different recipients of
the medicine. It is true that one of them, the criminal, is not
healed by his execution, but the other one, society, is healed by
the criminal being removed from it. The first duty of the state is
the defense of the general good, and the death of the criminal is
the only means at its disposal to perform that defense.

d. The fact that capital punishment means no possibility of
reversing judicial errors does not militate against its legitimacy;
it only means that capital cases must be tried very carefully.
Judges should pronounce death sentences only when there is
complete certainty of the guilt of the convict.

Thamiry concludes by expressing his conviction that he has
satisfactorily demonstrated that capital punishment is a necessary instrument that the state simply must have in its hands if it is
to accomplish its essential mission and achieve its primary goal.

Thamiry had clearly exercised diligence in striving to inform
himself about the objections raised by opponents of the death
penalty. Each of the above theses is in answer to positions articulated since Beccaria, and some of them undoubtedly have merit.
But there is irony in his complacent repetition of the "tradition,"
protecting the legitimacy, even necessity, of the state's having the
right to execute at the very time when, next door in Germany, the
executioner's axe was about to be replaced with guillotines in
preparation for the Nazi bloodbath. In retrospect, at least, it is
regrettable that churchmen did not speak with greater reserve
about any political entity having an unqualified right to kill.
Hindsight suggests how much more appropriate would have been
greater concentration on the more basic human right, the right to
life, which was under unprecedented challenge.

D. Jacques Leclercq's Novel Challenge (1937)

Leclercq, teaching at Louvain University, was one of the earliest Catholic moralists to break ranks and call for a full reevalua-
tion of the traditional uncritical Catholic support for capital
punishment. He was exceptional in being able both to distance
himself enough from the tradition to level strong criticism from

within, and at the same time to let Beccaria belatedly have his due as the pioneer of a most desirable reversal. The outspoken canon alienated many in voicing his regrets about the past. Reviewing the history of the death penalty's use in Christendom, he noted how it always went hand in hand with war. He pointed out that it was due to negative reaction against the pacifism of heretics (Waldensians, Anabaptists, Quakers) that Catholic theologians found themselves in the awkward position of being concerned with practically nothing else but defending the state's right to kill, both in war and in capital punishment.

"Here as in many other matters, it was St. Augustine who fixed the tradition," he claimed, and for centuries the accent was put on defending the legitimacy of the general principle without any concern to determine its actual limits. The Catholic tradition had become "schizoid," mixing a Christian standard for clerics (no bloodshed) and a natural-law standard for laymen (sanctioned violence). But, as of the thirteenth century, church courts did not hesitate to hand heretics over to "the secular arm" for execution, thus eviscerating any impact of that distinction. In putting all their efforts into defending the legitimacy of the civil authority in doing this dirty work for the church, argued Leclercq, churchmen never got around to fixing the limits of that power:

> Unfortunately, Catholic moralists shared the mentality of their time and even the best of them accepted the horrible spectacles of state killings....It does not make one very proud to be Catholic when one notes that even the holiest of Catholic moralists, like St. Thomas Aquinas and St. Alphonsus Liguori, did not dream of doing anything but demonstrating the right of the state to kill, without touching on the question of its limits, and that the reaction against this ancient penal practice came only from the rationalist circles of the 18th century....The state has the mission of protecting life and helping to enhance it as much as possible. If a man commits a crime, the state ought to help him to reform; killing him goes against the very reason of society....In our days, in the Western world, the death penalty has ceased to be legitimate, since states have sufficient means without it for protecting the social order.[10]

This devastating critique, astonishingly outspoken for the time, went beyond speculation about any abstract right and framed the question in a disturbingly practical way. Capital punishment as employed in modern society is condemned, not by denying the state's right to kill (which is not the issue), but by denying the necessity—and therefore the morality—of such use of violence today. It is an application of the last-resort principle, as in just-war theory. Unless that condition is fulfilled, the use of such lethal force as the death penalty is simply unwarranted, a public act of immorality, a camouflage for vengeance. The venerable acknowledgment of the state's right to kill is irrelevant in this modern context. Withholding the church's rubber stamp from the unwarranted use of the death penalty becomes a moral imperative, a common goal to be pursued by all who would promote a more humane and just society.

In this assessment of the situation Leclercq admittedly overstates the case. As we have seen, it was not "only from the rationalist circles of the 18th century" that the criticism came. Minority Christian groups were lamenting the practice well before Beccaria. Nonetheless, his main point is well taken, and the attention he called to the problem alerted many to the work remaining to be done if clarification and renewal were to be achieved.

E. Johannes Ude's Change of Heart (1934)

A different kind of dissent came out of Austria not long after Leclercq's Belgian blast. Fr. Johannes Ude, a former Graz seminary professor, was so affected by the execution of a retarded youth when capital punishment was reintroduced into Austria in 1934 that he literally underwent a conversion to total pacifism. He repented of having taught seminarians for long years that Christians could legitimately shed blood in capital punishment and war and of having maintained this position in his *Ethics* textbook, first published in 1912. While under arrest by the Nazis, he composed a manuscript devoted to repudiating these abandoned positions. He had arrived at the conviction that the traditional teaching was a sellout by which the gospel had been betrayed and Christians had sided with the forces of death.[11]

These two Catholic "conscientious objectors" to the death penalty were pilgrims traveling on two quite different roads to arrive at much the same practical conclusion—the unacceptability of the death penalty in modern society. Both would find many followers along their respective paths before the passing of many more years.

III. POST-WORLD WAR II EUROPE

As is all too well known, there has never been an era of greater slaughter of human beings than the twentieth century. The technology of death has been so highly developed and so widely used that holocausts, genocides, ethnic cleansings, obliteration bombings, atomic incinerations, and other such modes of previously unimaginable mass slaughter have provided numerous regions of the globe with unparalleled killing fields layered with corpses. It is no wonder that people with any kind of belief system that puts high value on human life would stop and examine their heritage to see if it were in any way implicated in this carnage. Such questioning was especially called forth when the full impact of the massive destruction of human life in the Second World War began to be realized.

Religious justification of war is obviously an extremely problematic issue, and capital punishment, as so clearly seen in the *Roman Catechism,* has invariably been paired with it, since the tradition came to view them as the two great exceptions to the commandment "Thou Shalt Not Kill." When European Christians had to begin rebuilding from the rubble of war in 1945, revulsion over the prospect of even further intentional destruction of life by resumption of the death penalty was widespread. Space considerations require that our attention be directed chiefly to Roman Catholic developments, but some note must be taken of the unusually broad theological discussion of the ethics of capital punishment that took place in northern Europe shortly after (and directly because of) World War II.

Theological renewal movements were the postwar seedbeds in which historical-critical studies that provoked much rethinking were being fostered. The challenge concerning capital punishment was how to dislodge it from its well-protected niche so that it could be openly examined the way that other issues were. A new group of French- and German-speaking Catholic theologians had entered into fuller conversation with Protestant colleagues than was ever previously possible.[12] The polemics that marred so much work and caused such distortions on all sides in the aftermath of the Reformation were finally being left behind and the field of conversation was becoming more inclusive. This welcome development, however, had its down side in that different traditions had grown up and been shaped in very different ways. More than a little confusion was naturally the result in the early efforts to work within broader horizons, and this was clearly the case with the complex issue of capital punishment.

A. Germany

The capital-punishment issue had special poignancy in postwar Germany. The shame and guilt inevitably experienced by many German Christians after what Adolf Hitler did to the country and the world, especially his brutal and systematic extermination of some twelve million human beings (Jews, Christians, and others) in the concentration camps, understandably raised profound questions about any talk of the right of the state to kill. In 1934 he had had twenty supplementary guillotines constructed and recruited special executioners to operate them. By 1945 German executions by guillotine alone numbered more than 16,500, and Nazi records boasted of a single executioner in that period who had killed 2,948 victims.[13]

These vivid memories were in the background when on May 24, 1949, Article 102 of the Basic Law of the Federal Republic was adopted, declaring simply: "The death penalty is abolished."[14] This not only provoked an extensive discussion of the politics of capital punishment, but prompted serious debate among theologians as well. In agitating for its reintroduction, a delegation of Christian Democrats in September 1952 called for it to be put to a free vote. This led to "the last great parliamentary debate on the death penalty, on October 2, 1952," the highlight of which was a "powerful speech from the Justice Minister Thomas Dehler," who spoke of the death penalty as "a foreign body in our penal system," an act which invariably "put the state on the same level as the criminals it was condemning."[15] The vote was close but the effort to reintroduce failed, 151 to 146 with two abstentions, so Germany has now been without capital punishment for nearly a half-century.

There were Christian thinkers of all kinds involved in the German debate of those years; they represented many different approaches and positions that are virtually impossible to categorize. Nonetheless, one scholar, working from a Lutheran context, designated the major Christian positions in a novel way.

1. GERHARD GLOEGE'S FRAMEWORK (1966)

Gloege tried to classify the participants according to the methodologies used in approaching the death penalty: (1) The *theological* approach (Lutheran/Evangelical authors); (2) The *Christological* approach (Calvinist/Reformed authors); and (3) The *ecclesiological* approach (Roman Catholic authors). This tidy arrangement has not been taken over in subsequent studies, probably because of its "pre-ecumenical" feel. It seems to imply that each denomination has a particular view of the death penalty derived from some distinctive element in its history or doctrine. But it quickly becomes apparent that this is by no means the case. The debate seems simply to go around in circles without the circles intersecting or illuminating one another.

The theological position, for example, seems to be the one with more substance than the other two, and its Lutheran spokesmen all start from a common position that "the criminal law of the state is based on the order of God the Creator."[16] This, of course, is the heart of Luther's doctrine of the two kingdoms, and its most articulate proponents in the postwar debate were Paul Althaus[17] and Walter Künneth,[18] who "justify the necessity of the death penalty with the authority of the state as a God-given institution."[19] Their appeal is principally to Genesis 9:6 and Romans 13:4 as the authoritative texts providing this justification.

The designation "theological," however, is not very helpful in that it does not account for the fact that some within the same tradition oppose the death penalty, and some outside that tradition support it, citing the same scriptures. Gloege himself was aware at the start that the framework was unsatisfactory. He complained of the discussion of capital punishment being a "labyrinth of opinions and judgments...a problem not only without a solution but even without a proper formulation of the question."[20] At best, in light of the complications, it might better be said from the start that "attitudes to the death penalty are only *partial* indicators of membership of a theological school."[21]

Describing the Calvinist position as Christological and making the Catholic position ecclesiological are even more objectionable, if meant to be useful labels. They suggest something quite other than intended. The latter, for instance, is characterized as stemming from "the view of the church as a community which must protect itself against lawbreakers," as if that told us much (or anything) about the struggle of spirit over this issue by Augustine, Aquinas, Bellarmine, or even Cathrein.

Granted, it is easier to find fault with a paradigm than to improve on it. Yet there should be better candidates for explanatory labels. For instance, the Lutheran doctrine of the two kingdoms played an obviously central role for both Althaus and Künneth, providing at least three elements out of which their support for capital punishment was constructed: (1) the sanctity of the moral legal order willed by God; (2) the idea of the need for expiation of wrongs; and (3) the divinely bestowed authority of the state to protect and defend its people. Althaus and Künneth drew on these from Luther's vision of divine order.

2. WERNER ELERT'S REALISM (1949)

The most interesting development from within, however, was that of Werner Elert.[22] He continued to endorse all of the above points as important to the Lutheran heritage, but his emphasis fell on the great significance of historical change and its impact on Christian ethics. Elert agreed completely with Althaus that the state has the power to use capital punishment in the pursuit of its God-authorized goals. But this was only the first step; nothing at all had yet been established about the justice or the necessity of any actual killing done by the state. This turned the conversation in a very different direction.

Churchmen of all persuasions often have trouble distinguishing between the ideal and the real, especially regarding their own institutions. A group of humans may have the highest goals but will always fall short of reaching them in practice. The historical record matters. One need not be a cynic to realize that states always have and always will abuse the death penalty. Any reasonable person familiar with the facts of life is led to conclude that, on the whole, states cannot be trusted to administer capital punishment impartially and proportionately. Count the "reigns of terror" in any century! We have an overabundance of evidence and experience. In the name of simple justice under the laws of God and society, any responsible Christian will not voluntarily allow to the state the power to take human life or approve of such use if it does. Traditional arguments sound fine in theory, but they simply do not apply in the reality of the sinful world of experience.

To label Elert's approach theological is no help at all. What he is articulating is a more accurate, more realistic assessment of the state.[23] Over a century earlier Lutheran Richard Rothe had already perceived the penal code as the center of the legal system and the key to a society's quality of life.[24] Rothe agreed with Schleiermacher on many things but disagreed with him on the death penalty. He favored it because he saw it as an expression of the divine order underlying all justice and thus all states.

Elert came to the conviction that modern excesses and abuses have unquestionably provided more than ample grounds for following a different path and abolishing the death penalty from ordinary law codes. The horrendous Nazi use of death as policy made the adoption of Article 102 by the government of postwar Germany the wisest, most necessary, and ethical choice available. The difference between Elert and his predecessors in the same tradition was that he made *the penal system* rather than the individual criminal the chief focus of attention. Instead of asking whether public safety needs to be defended at all costs from criminal behavior, he asserted that it was even more important that public safety be defended against systemic injustice.

Before leaving the Lutheran contributions to the debate, one other work may be mentioned. Hans-Peter Alt chose the death penalty as the subject of his doctoral work in theology at the University of Erlangen because of more than an academic interest in the topic. His father, as a chaplain in Munich's Stadelheim prison, had had the gruesome task of ministering to throngs of Nazi "death candidates" as they were marched off to execution. This experience had brought him to an adamant conviction that all state executions were contrary to God's will, and it was his fervent hope that his son would one day be able to "work through the problem systematically" to demonstrate why capital punishment was intrinsically evil, no matter how much the Christian tradition might have defended it in the past. Taking up this partisan challenge, the younger Alt presented his results to the Erlangen Theology Faculty in 1957 and a few years later published them for broader circulation.[25]

Alt embraced the position that capital punishment can be justified only in the rarest limit cases of true and urgent necessity, when the very existence of the state is under immediate threat, but that in normal times it can have no role and, rather than being left on the books, definitely should be abolished from the regular law codes of modern Europe. But the whole question of how the law of God and the laws of the state were interrelated in this regard remained obscure. Alt objected to Karl Barth's image of "two concentric circles," the spiritual kingdom and the secular kingdom, with Christ at the center of both. This was for him an "illegitimate mingling of the two kingdoms." He insisted that the unity of the kingdoms exists "only through the unity of God," that the same God rules in the sacred and the secular, "in anger and in grace, in law and in gospel," and that this unity can only be believed in, not demonstrated rationally, so that all attempts at human understanding fall short.[26] Some of Alt's critics found his objections to traditional support for the death penalty convincing but were less impressed with his efforts to construct a credible case against it.[27]

Alt sensed that one's view of the morality of capital punishment was greatly dependent upon how one "divided or combined" the sacred and the secular spheres of life. His mentors at Erlangen were Paul Althaus and Walter Künneth, and to them he dedicated his volume. The penal law of the state, according to Luther's doctrine of the two kingdoms, was a legitimate expression of God's law, including the law of punishing sinners. Alt criticized the Barthian view as illegitimately intermingling these two separate realms, with "unhelpful" consequences, but he found it difficult to do much more within his framework.

In retrospect, Alt's work can be seen as an early struggle

with what Gloege also ran into. The increasing openness to dialogue in the Christian theological world was creating unanticipated complications: the new woes of theological pluralism. As long as one stayed within a single confessional tradition, questions arose and answers could be forged systematically within the framework of that particular heritage. But by stepping outside, or above, or over against that framework, one soon heard other questions beginning to be asked and begging to be answered.

What should take priority among the purposes of punishment: retribution or forgiveness? revenge or rehabilitation? paying for the past or healing for the future? punishing the crime or reforming the criminal? At one end of such a spectrum of questions the death penalty could be evaluated as absolutely *unthinkable,* since it proposed the direct, intentional destruction of a human life created by God and redeemed by Christ; the very idea was in blatant contradiction of God's goodness, love, and mercy. At the other end, the death penalty could be evaluated as *essential,* the necessary exercise of lawful authority as delegated by God, the designated way for properly restoring the moral order disrupted by radical disobedience.

Christian theologians for four centuries had not had to deal with such radically diverse options. One of the great comforts of having a heritage or of belonging to an exclusivist sect was that it freed one from having to struggle with such wrenching issues by giving an answer as *the* answer, the distillate of the wisdom of one's forebears in faith. Catholics and Calvinists had to admit that they had never before seen the death penalty as viewed through a Lutheran prism. Lutherans had to admit that it looked very different if one set aside the doctrine of the two kingdoms. There were grounds for feeling confused...and frustrated.

3. KARL BARTH'S AMBIVALENCE (1952)

Gloege had dubbed the Calvinist approach Christological, but that was not especially meant as a compliment. Karl Barth was the best-known exponent, and Gloege summarized the distinctive contention of his approach thus:

> The Death penalty has been abolished on earth by the execution of Jesus Christ on Golgotha. The atonement of the

Son of God has annihilated it completely; nothing speaks for
it, everything speaks against it.

The position is as simple in its clarity as it is simplistic in its
derivation. It led him to attack vehemently any use of "expiation"
as a theological category applicable to the death penalty. He saw
such a notion as contradicting the central Christian belief in the
expiatory death of Jesus. His impressive eloquence on the topic
was never in dispute:

> Now that Jesus Christ has been nailed to the cross for the
> sins of the world, how can we still use the thought of *expia-*
> *tion* to establish the death penalty?...Capital punishment will
> surely be the very last thing to enter our heads....From the
> point of view of the Gospel, there is nothing to be said for its
> institution, and everything to be said against it.[28]

Though the rhetoric is forceful, multiple questions come thundering out of the past. Is this not more the voice of Servetus
rather than that of Calvin? Does it not do away not only with capital punishment but any kind of punishment after the meritori-
ous death of Christ? Barth himself drew back from the logical
consequences of his sweeping statement. As he goes on to
explain, he was not entirely opposed to capital punishment. His
insistence was rather that there should be no *ordinary* use of the
death penalty. It can never be justified...except in extraordinary
circumstances when the very life of the society is under immediate threat.

> Capital punishment must always be rejected and opposed as
> the legally established institution of a stable and peaceful
> state....It can have no place in the *ordinary* life of the state....It
> cannot possibly be a regular institution.

This is a bit tamer than earlier. Article 102 was appropriate.
The death penalty ought to be abolished from the "regular penal
system" of any state concerned with ethical standards. But, he continued, "in an absolute emergency when not just the *bene esse* but
the very *esse* of the state and its members is at issue, when 'to be or
not to be' is the question," [capital punishment has its place on

the] "extreme margin...on the far edge. [This very limited place] can be contested only by an illegitimate ethical absolutism."

In response to Barth's own sense of humor, his tongue-in-cheek critics have sometimes summarized his position thus: The death penalty has absolutely nothing to be said for it, but pacifism which opposes it absolutely also has absolutely nothing to be said for it. And, needless to say, the position of Catholics or Lutherans who see the death penalty as expiation also has absolutely nothing to be said for it.

Barth went on to discuss the two "exceptions" or boundary cases where death could be morally justified as the penalty: (1) high treason, and (2) tyrannicide. Consideration of the latter led him to speak of the plight of his friend, Dietrich Bonhoeffer, who was involved in the 1944 plot to assassinate Hitler. In this emotional context Barth invoked Calvin, Beza, and John Knox as allowing for extreme public emergencies in which it might happen that "God would raise up an avenger and deliverer whose destructive work would not be murder but would be done in obedience to His command." He went on to acknowledge that "this strange form of capital punishment might be the command of God," but that this would obviously be an extreme exception, only to be justified by a rare and extraordinary danger threatening the very survival of the state.

There is undoubtedly irony as well as confusion and inconsistency in some of this. Barth speaks only of a world that is already fully redeemed by Christ and takes no account of anything else. The dialectic between "the already and the not-yet" of Christian faith seems to be entirely missing here. It is appealing to say that the death penalty should never even be thought of because Christ died for all, but such a contention needs to be argued and probed, not merely proclaimed. If the position seems oversimplified, that is probably because it is.

But this illustrates once again the importance of the postwar debate in Germany. It was the first serious encounter and exchange of a variety of theological perspectives on the death penalty in Western Christian history. There was no precedent for such open theological debate monitored by the world press as it progressed. Some church members were wary or confused by the unparalleled ecumenical nature of the conversation where no one could silence new voices raising new questions and attempting new, "untraditional" answers. The time was ripe for some creative Catholic participation as well.

4. GUSTAV ERMECKE'S SPADEWORK (1958)

In designating the Catholic approach to the death penalty ecclesiological, Gloege had in mind an important fact. It was in the experiential realm of the church as a historical human community that the issue invariably arose. Just as in the case of war, early Christian churchmen did not have the luxury of an academic seminar to decide whether or not a certain line of behavior was ideally acceptable from the perspective of the teachings of Jesus. There were unavoidable troubles, and decisions about recourse to counter-violence had to be made if the community was to survive and function.

Medieval, Renaissance, Reformation, and Enlightenment developments found the Catholic tradition compromised on the question of the death penalty, taking little part in critical conversations about it. Beccaria got the Western world talking about it, but only a few pioneering Catholic voices, like Linsenmann and Leclercq, had broken the grand silence, to the chagrin of the managers. But in 1958 another voice was heard.

At his October installation as rector of the Philosophical-Theological Academy of Paderborn, Fr. Gustav Ermecke chose to test the waters and belatedly enter the debate that had been dominated by Protestant voices for a decade. He focused his address on the question that continued to loom large despite (or perhaps because of) the exchanges of Althaus, Barth, Elert, Gloege, Künneth, Thielicke, and Wolf, to mention only seven. Ermecke undertook an exploration entitled *Toward the Ethical Foundation of the Death Penalty Today*.[29] When his contribution appeared in print the following year, it provoked with good reason an unusual amount of interest and controversy, much of the latter due to misunderstanding of exactly what he was trying to do. His intent was to probe, in academic fashion, what philosophical-ethical grounds might be discovered on which to build a rational argument for the liceity (not the necessity) of the state's use of the death penalty, leaving aside all biblical-theological considerations. Limiting discussion to philosophical arguments alone is not easily done.

Ermecke began by expressing his conviction that there were three particular mistakes that one should try to avoid in modern discussions of the ethics of capital punishment:

1. Sentimentality, which can distract in either direction when one is trying to formulate rational arguments about the death penalty;

2. Failure to recognize the distinction between the liceity of capital punishment *in principle,* and the advisability of its application *in practice;*

3. Naive unawareness of the enormous complications resulting from the modern lack of any *core-consensus* philosophy in Western societies. This third mistake was to him the most troublesome of all. The absence of a common world view in an ever more pluralistic culture made many discussions virtually fruitless. Conflicting presuppositions and starting points abounded: secularist versus religious; individualist versus collectivist; objectivist versus subjectivist; naturalist versus supernaturalist; and so on.

In this maze of opinions Ermecke undertook the daunting task of adjudicating many current outlooks before the bar of reason alone. For instance, he pointed out that executing someone in order to deter others is absolutely without moral defense. Accepting such flimsy grounds for killing people could easily open the way to other grave abuses of state power, as the Nazi experience had so horrendously demonstrated. Claiming as grounds for execution the state's right of self-defense is likewise unacceptable. At the point of execution, the threat to society is no longer imminent; in any rational use of language, the imprisoned, chained, pacified culprit about to be killed no longer constitutes a "present danger."

Ermecke was touching very close to a troublesome truth that moralists had not been giving due attention, but he was not yet finished. He turned to consider the traditionally invoked "principle of totality." Aquinas's comparison of the state having the right to amputate a putrid member just as a physician cuts off a gangrenous limb Ermecke described as "a misplaced analogy, unworthy of any further repetition."[30] Likewise, he suggested, appealing to the "common good" as grounds for executing criminals is no longer acceptable on a couple of scores. One would first have to prove that imposing death is absolutely the only means to preserve that good, and even then, it was still doubtful whether such killing could ever be licit in light of the value of the human person.

Turning to Kant for a moment, he noted that the retributive claim of the need for restoration of the order of justice, which had been injured by the crime, was also highly questionable as an ethical ground for the death penalty.

> The moral order of values is no more upset in itself by a criminal violation than the order of arithmetic is deranged when someone makes a mistake in calculating.

The mistake must be dealt with, true, but there is no disrupted order that needs to be reestablished. This is an instance of the fallacy of an abstraction being treated as if it were concrete, a logical "category mistake."

Criticizing all of these elements, which were standard features of Catholic ethical tradition, Ermecke found himself in a very odd position. If there was to be a rational argument for the legitimacy of the death penalty, it would have to be based on grounds other than the usual ones that had been endlessly repeated within Catholic circles for centuries. The surprise move he then made is still the most original (and controversial) part of his discourse. He called attention to a statement made by Pope Pius XII to a medical convention in 1952:

> Even in the case of one condemned to death, the state does not dispose of the individual's right to life. It is reserved to the public power to deprive the condemned of the good of life in expiation of his crime after he has already dispossessed himself of his right to life.[31]

Ermecke quickly insisted that he was introducing these words "not because they come from the Pope, but because they are the expression of sound reason." The state can impose capital punishment only when—and because—the individual has already forfeited his right to life.

> The criminal has, in a way, committed social suicide, renouncing by his crime the community and his right to be part of it. The state is only carrying out what the criminal has already done: his exclusion, his civil and juridical death. The criminal condemns himself, the state only draws the consequences.[32]

Needless to say, Ermecke's "new" reasoning provided an alternate basis for the ethics of the state's practice of the death penalty that was (and is) itself highly debatable. Unaddressed in his argument is the crucial question of whether, when, how, and what kind of human rights can be so "forfeited." These questions are far more often begged than answered, due to their unusual difficulty.[33] But the major point of relevance here is to note how broadly and critically whole areas of the traditional complex of Catholic reasoning about the death penalty were so severely questioned and criticized, even though the questioning was coming only from the philosophical perspective of an established Catholic moralist. Whether one finds merit in a particular argument or not is relatively unimportant. The most significant part of Ermecke's intervention was precisely his heavy criticism directed at the usual arguments in support of capital punishment. Such probing of a previously sacrosanct domain was a major development that helped prepare the way for dismantling and moving beyond earlier liabilities.

B. France

The theological conversation about capital punishment which occurred in postwar Germany had no real parallel elsewhere. In France the most interesting early development was a work by a popular literary figure.

1. ALBERT CAMUS (1947)
In 1947 Camus (1913–1960) published his essay *Neither Victims nor Executioners*,[33a] observing that the unparalleled carnage and destruction of human life in the recent war had "killed

something within us." The only hope for a viable future, he was convinced, depended on making a radical change from a world "where murder is legitimate, and where human life is considered trifling" to one in which people would commit themselves to renounce "any truth which might oblige me, directly or indirectly, to demand a man's life." He did not mean a "world in which murder no longer exists (we are not so crazy as that!) but rather one in which murder is not legitimate." To refuse to "sanction murder" would entail coming to "a provisional agreement between men who want to be *neither victims nor executioners.*" And in trying "to define the values by which this international community would live," one of the first objectives would be "the drawing up of an international code of justice [in which the] Number One Article would be the abolition of the death penalty."

Camus somehow embodied much of a new spirit in postwar Europe. He was put off by the dogmatic aspects of both Christianity and Marxism, and articulated the estrangement of the individual in an alien universe. The finality of death seen up close invalidated so much in earlier outlooks. The old argument used to justify the theoretical legitimacy of the state's right to execute continued to be repeated by defenders of capital punishment, but it would never sound the same after Hitler. Camus revealed that he had personally made a kind of secular vow, which he challenged others to consider doing also:

> I will never again be one of those...who compromise with murder....All I ask is that, in the midst of a murderous world, we agree to reflect on murder and make a choice.

It would take another thirty-five years before France dismantled the guillotine and abolished the death penalty (1981), but the spirit of Albert Camus was one of the influential factors that led the country to that belated conclusion.

2. PAUL SAVEY-CASARD (1961)

Savey-Casard, a law professor in Lyons, wrote an unusually illuminating survey article entitled "The Catholic Church and the Death Penalty." In it he examined the thought of the major moral theologians of the past century and grouped them into three categories according to his understanding of their basic philosophy of punishment.[34]

The first group was made up of those with a retributive view, who gave priority to the need for expiation. They tended to emphasize the importance of restoring the moral equilibrium disrupted by the crime, and, as a result, they usually supported retention of the death penalty and advocated its regular use as necessary to sustain the moral order as intended by God. The three nineteenth-century exemplars he cited were Mgr. d'Hulst, Th. Meyer, and R. P. Hébert.

The second group was more pragmatic in approach, inclined to give priority to the goal of achieving the security of the public order. They too usually supported capital punishment but were much more influenced by utilitarian concerns and thus tended to "desacralize" the scaffold and emphasize especially the deterrence claim. If it was not clearly necessary for the maintenance of order, there was little need for the state to execute, and under favorable circumstances one might even agree to its [conditional] abolition. Among those in this group he listed V. Cathrein, Edouard Thamiry, Edouard Génicot, Arthur Vermeersch, and Ferdinand Cavallera.

Those in the third group were the relative newcomers, Catholics who were finding capital punishment to be unnecessary in a modern state and therefore unjustified. These were the men beginning to call for the explicit rejection of the death penalty in our time. The three moralists he included here were Jacques Leclercq, Joseph Vernet, and Bernard Häring, although he noted that not all held exactly the same position. Häring, for example, had suggested that besides the much-discussed "right to execute," the state also had the less commonly acknowledged "right to pardon," and this could be conferred by anticipation in a law abolishing capital punishment, as long as there was agreement that it was unnecessary.[35]

Savey-Casard concluded from his survey that there were certain points on which one could say that there was a firm, Catholic position, and other points on which there was much flexibility, allowing for the growth of both doctrine and practice in different directions. On his list of fixed points were the following:

1. The Church affirms that the state does not sin when it uses the power of the sword.
2. The Church affirms that, to be legitimate, the state must use this power not only with justice but also with prudence.
3. The Church affirms further its perennial horror of bloodshed, not permitting it for her own benefit, and prohibiting her clergy from directly participating in any way in capital judgments.

After these "fixed points," as far as Savey-Casard was concerned, one entered a wide-open domain of controversy, and "the differences of opinion among theologians deserve to be followed closely by jurists and sociologists as well."[36] What was most noteworthy about this pre–Vatican II piece was its openness, taking history seriously and accepting the validity of pluralism.

3. JOSEPH VERNET, S.J. (1962)

The signs of coming change were multiplying. The "caretaker" pope, John XXIII, had called a council, and the very year it was set to open a powerful article against the death penalty appeared in a French Catholic journal. The author, Joseph Vernet, a Jesuit who knew the French prison system well, described capital punishment as "illusory in its effects and barbaric in its application."[37] He took the purported aims of punishment one by one and found none of them valid in the modern context. Without getting into the details of the old debate about the right of the state to kill, he simply noted that, even if such existed, society could choose not to exercise it and to renounce the death penalty as inappropriate, since all its goals can be achieved in other ways. In his conclusion he challenged those Christians who would not prefer to "humanize and spiritualize" society by abolishing the death penalty to ponder the incident in Luke 9:55, where Jesus is portrayed as telling his fire-breathing disciples: "You do not know of what spirit you are!"[38]

C. England

1. REPORT OF THE ROYAL COMMISSION (1953)

The Royal Commission on Capital Punishment, which began its work in 1949, has been described as "almost certainly the most exhaustive and comprehensive investigation into the subject ever made."[39] Its published report ran over five hundred pages, and for those who took the time to read it, the death penalty could never again be viewed as it had been previously in the English-speaking world. Basically a conservative document, its original mandate was to do no more than "consider whether liability under the criminal law in Great Britain to suffer capital punishment for murder should be limited or modified."

The members of the commission understood the politics of these words as precluding them "from considering whether the abolition of capital punishment would be desirable."[40] But their diligent research laid to rest longstanding myths that had shrouded the death penalty for years. They cautiously con-cluded, after soberly surveying the results of numerous empirical studies, that "it is important...not to base a penal policy in rela-tion to murder on exaggerated estimates of the uniquely deter-rent force of the death penalty."[41] The notoriously conservative House of Lords acted "as though the Royal Commission had never sat and never reported," but the report was to have signifi-cant effect nonetheless. It definitively undermined the popular mythology of the death penalty, but that, of course, was not enough to change anything quickly. Meantime, a few other notable events had their own impact.

2. ARTHUR KOESTLER (1956)

Koestler's *Reflections on Hanging* appeared on the British scene in a more dramatic way than the Royal Commission's report. Like Beccaria's essay nearly two centuries earlier, it came from a secular rather than religious source, but it was motivated by a higher ethic that embarrassed many in religious circles into discontinuing their support for the death penalty. Koestler was especially hard on "bloodthirsty shepherds," the Anglican bish-ops serving in the House of Lords, who invariably chose to sup-port the death penalty, no matter what.

Some of Koestler's quotes, couched in the language of pop-ular psychology, struck a chord and had an impact that abstract treatments seldom do. People who had not previously thought very much about their easy acceptance of state killings were pulled up short by his graphic imagery:

> Deep inside every civilized being there lurks a tiny Stone
> Age man, dangling a club to rob and rape, and screaming
> "an eye for an eye." But we would rather not have that little
> fur-clad figure dictate the law of the land.[42]

Even though there was little direct Catholic involvement in
the British debate, it was more and more evident that voices like
Koestler and Camus won a significant following across the board.
There was simply no reasonable reply to the reminders they gave
of how deeply Christian moral leadership had been compromised
by its longstanding endorsement of a collapsing penal tradition.
Koestler called attention to the record, including

> certain sanguine Lords of the Church, from Archdeacon
> Paley, who taught that criminals were unredeemable, to the
> Bishop of Truro, who in the Lords' debate of 1948 suggested
> that, instead of abolishing the death penalty, we should
> extend its range. This type of illustrious clergyman has
> always shown great deference to the wisdom of the secular
> Lords of the Law.[43]

The last sentence, ironically, reveals that Koestler realized that
the Christian tradition at its best would be much more in support of abolition than retention, much more pro-life than pro-
death, other things being equal. At the end of the book this
comes out clearly in his statement that "the deliberate taking of
life by the State is unjustifiable on religious or philosophic or scientific grounds."[44] The problem, as he saw it, was how to get
Christian leaders to recognize this and retrieve their own best
principles and values.[45]

D. Italy

1. FR. FRANCISCUS SKODA (1959)

Though challenges were being raised all over Europe by the
mid-1950s, this did not mean that there were no defenders holding the line on this issue. We have already had occasion to call
attention to the work of Fr. Franciscus Skoda. His doctoral dissertation at the Lateran University in Rome in 1956 made a wholesale effort to defend the past. He sketched the common Catholic

stance since the time of Beccaria and was especially anxious to rebut those who were contending that all use of the death penalty was unethical. He wanted to demonstrate that the legitimacy of capital punishment was "always the constant doctrine of the church," and that all the major moral theologians agreed that

> killing done by public authority...was always recognized as licit....The Church has its immutable principles on the doctrine of human life, which is only a means for obtaining eternal happiness and is not the supreme human good, as many adversaries contend. The Church has immutable principles on the divine origin of authority and society, and on the legitimate use of violence in defense against an unjust aggressor. The Church values ecclesiastical tradition and has infallibility in explaining the Sacred Scriptures. Opponents of the death penalty, on the other hand, have a different conception of life and the origin of society and authority: they argue against the death penalty relying more on sentiment than on reason.[46]

Capital punishment (in the abstract) has here taken on extraordinary symbolic significance, serving as a virtual touchstone of orthodoxy. Because it was in possession, it was nine-tenths of the law, so one could safely conclude that its standard use was in accord with divine revelation. The burden of proof for claiming otherwise was squarely on the shoulders of any who would be critics. Since serious questions about its morality had always come from "dissidents and dissenters" who invariably rejected other orthodox Christian beliefs and practices as well, opposition to the death penalty was to be evaluated and explained as just one more departure from orthodoxy accompanying all the other errors of the unorthodox "innovators."

Skoda's work stands as a classic period piece, illustrating all the problems associated with pre–Vatican II triumphalism. He attributed the critique of Beccaria and all the others after him entirely to the rampant modern errors of "individualism, rationalism, and sentimentalism." Abolitionism was the work of anti-God forces. And yet, after all this, he grudgingly conceded in the end that

in modern times use of the death penalty is not required as
frequently as in earlier days....But this does not mean, as
many would have it, that the death penalty ought simply to
be abolished. For it can be used not only to render offenders
harmless but also to deter possible and probable criminals
from similar offenses.[47]

This sudden shift to a utilitarian argument of deterrence, after
seeing that changed circumstances have left his earlier position
indefensible, is astonishing, not to say irresponsible. He more than
suggests that it would be perfectly justifiable to execute people on
the outside chance that this might occasionally deter someone else
somewhere from committing some crime. The life of the condemned person is left completely aside, ignored as irrelevant or
something anyone can simply destroy without qualms.[48]

Such ready support for the death penalty without reservation, however, was not to stand unquestioned for long. By the
time Skoda's work was published, a new pope had been elected
and soon announced plans for a Second Vatican Council to deal
precisely with updating admittedly outdated areas put on hold in
the conflicts of the previous century. It is fascinating in retrospect to realize that in the same period that Skoda was working
within this ahistorical ideology, John Courtney Murray, S.J., was
working out the specifics of an alternative approach that would
point the way to liberation from this kind of dogmatic bondage.[49]
But before that could happen, a few other developments may be
mentioned that also helped prepare the way to needed change.

IV. ENGINEERING THE CATHOLIC RENEWAL

Where was the engine of change going to come from that
would challenge the gallows? World War II had left much of the
old European order in shambles and a chance for new beginnings
was at hand. Other Christian groups that were burdened with less
baggage than the Roman Catholic heritage took their stand earlier in favor of abolishing capital punishment. But for Rome, a
more gradual change was needed. In retrospect, the following
may be counted as some of the stepping stones put in place.

A. Seeds of Change from Pius XII (1939–1958)

Two encyclicals, both promulgated in 1943, played a role in initiating a change of climate in Catholic theology: (a) *Divino Afflante Spiritu* cautiously endorsed the use of historical-critical methods in biblical studies, thus opening the way for Catholic scholarship to move beyond the liabilities of a fundamentalist approach. The simplistic, ahistorical use of the Old Testament death-penalty texts, as routinely invoked in the traditional defense, was soon set aside, thereby removing one monumental problem from the scene. A whole new era of professional biblical investigation and application was dawning, and few specialists were as yet trained to work in this new context, but at least a start was made. (b) *Mystici Corporis Christi* focused attention on the need for a renewed ecclesiology, raising questions about the basic nature and functions of the church. After four centuries of anti-Protestant polemics, a point was finally reached when dialogue could replace dispute, and benefits accrue to all. It was this issue that was destined to take center stage in Vatican II. The rethinking of church priorities eventually had to raise questions about the bewildering anomalies of religious support for any intentional destruction of human life.[50]

B. Pope John XXIII (1958–1963)

The Second Vatican Council had already been announced, prepared for, convened, and its first session completed when Pope John XXIII took a major step on his own. He officially enhanced the vision and expanded the framework for subsequent thinking about the human condition. His positive endorsement of the primacy of human solidarity in his 1963 encyclical, *Pacem in Terris,* provided a firm basis for the eventual dismantling of support for the death penalty. He insisted:

> Any human society...must lay down as a foundation this principle: every human being is a person....By virtue of this he has rights and duties of his own...which are *universal, inviolable, and inalienable.* If we look upon the dignity of the human person in the light of divinely revealed truth, we cannot help but esteem it far more highly.[51]

This perspective called for serious rethinking of support for capital punishment. It fostered grave doubts about the morality of
"amputating" human beings as putrid limbs to be discarded as
garbage. To do so is an action of total despair in human potential
and flies in the face of any Christian evaluation of human life.
Pope John XXIII's central commitment to this "first universal-
ity," that of the inherent dignity of every member of the human
race, clearly required major attitude adjustment in regard to the
death penalty.

Earlier papal teachings about social questions "were almost
exclusively framed in concepts and language of the natural-law
ethic of scholastic philosophy. One searches in vain through the
writings of the popes during the hundred years before the council
for careful consideration of the biblical, Christological, eschato-
logical, or ecclesiological basis of the church's social role."[52] There
were reasons why this had been so, and one of them was the
unspoken assumption that "this world shared a unified intellectual
heritage in which Christianity and culture had been harmoniously
synthesized." Such a reading of the historical context of the
church's role in the twentieth century is "no longer accurate....Dif-
ferences of class, race, economic status, and political tradition
have made the West a far from unified society with a harmoniously
integrated culture....The council clearly recognized this."

C. Vatican Council II (1962–1965)

The bearing of the Second Vatican Council on thinking
about the death penalty can be reduced to parts of the teaching
of three of its documents.

1. *Lumen Gentium* (the *Dogmatic Constitution on the Church*)
was the first of the "the twin pillars of the ecclesiology" of Vatican II.[53] All we need to cite here is its very first paragraph, which
bears an emphasis with far-reaching consequences: "The Church
is a sacrament or sign of intimate union with God, and of the
unity of all mankind. It is also an instrument for the achievement
of such union and unity."[54]

If such an understanding is to be taken in any serious way, it
obviously calls for a reassessment of the kinds of actions and

policies that are appropriate to such a body. A sacrament or sign must signify, or it has lost its reason for being. If it is supposed to signify the *unity of humanity,* and also be an instrument helping to forge that unity, it can never justifiably involve itself in, or approve of, actions that contradict that unity by destroying or condoning the destruction of any human life or society.

The consequences of such a teaching can already be sensed with the mere statement of the general principle, but gradually particular areas of questionable conduct, like capital punishment, must come under scrutiny. Whatever one may say about earlier times of social chaos, the modern state must be held to higher standards. The "signs of the times" make it clear what kind of ecclesial witness is called for. What needs to be retrieved is precisely what was lost in earlier struggles—ideals of cherishing, promoting, protecting, and valuing human life as divinely conferred. What needs to be abandoned and opposed is the anti-life policies embraced by a culture of death. The implications of this church-as-sign theology become even clearer in the next document.

2. *Gaudium et Spes* (*Pastoral Constitution on the Church in the Modern World*), in many ways, captured more of the true legacy of Pope John XXIII than any of the other documents. Ten days before he died, Pope John summed up succinctly his hope and vision and reason for convoking Vatican II:

> Today more than ever...we are called to serve mankind as such...to defend above all and everywhere the rights of the *human person.*...It is not that the Gospel has changed; it is that we have begun to understand it better.[55]

A better understanding of the gospel is especially attempted in this, the longest and most intriguing of the Council documents. Once the church is defined as *sacrament of unity, servant of humanity, witness to human dignity, and defender of the human person,* the casual acceptance and defense of the death penalty becomes so anomalous and incongruous as to be incredible. The following *catena* of quotations is merely a sample of this document's challenging calls for a different kind of Christian presence in the modern world, which inevitably entails opposition to such pro-death conduct as capital punishment:

> The Council wishes to speak to all humans in order to shed light on the mystery of mankind and to cooperate in finding solutions to the outstanding problems of our time (10)....Faith throws a new light on everything...and thus directs the mind to solutions which are fully human...

> What does the Church think of mankind? What needs to be recommended for the upbuilding of contemporary society?...People are waiting for an answer to these questions (11).

> There is a growing awareness of the exalted dignity proper to the human person, since he stands above all things and his rights and duties are universal and inviolable....Hence the social order...must always work to the benefit of the human person (26).

> This Council lays stress on reverence for humanity: everyone must consider his every neighbor without exception as another self....A special obligation binds us to make ourselves the neighbor of every person without exception, and of actively helping him when he comes across our path (27).

> It is necessary to distinguish between error, which always merits repudiation, and the person in error, who never loses the dignity of being a person (28).

> The Church...is at once a sign and a safeguard of the transcendent character of the human person....All those dedicated to the ministry of God's Word must use the ways and means proper to the Gospel which in a great many respects differ from the means proper to the earthly city (76).

Many of these statements cannot meaningfully coexist with ready approval of the death penalty, since the two symbolisms collide head-on. Executions symbolize a society's total repudiation of a convict's personhood and denial of his or her membership in the human family.[56] They send a message that flatly contradicts the "better understanding" of the gospel.

3. *Dignitatis Humanae* (*Declaration on Religious Freedom*) has deeper American roots than the others. As its very title indicates, *Dignitatis Humanae* is totally centered on the dignity of the human person in his or her historical reality. Approval of any kind of direct and intentional destruction of human life blatantly contradicts its central thesis, to say the least.[57] Its opening sentence sets the tone: "Contemporary man is becoming increasingly conscious of the dignity of the human person" (1). Later, the proper role of the state is stressed: "The protection and promotion of the inviolable rights of man is an essential duty of every civil authority" (6). "All men must be treated with justice and humanity" (7). "Christ...left vengeance to God until the day of judgment....He bore witness to the truth but refused to use force to impose it" (11).

One later passage is an open admission of the historical mistakes that were made, leading to departures from the gospel ideals that we have surveyed:

> Although in the life of the people of God in its pilgrimage through the vicissitudes of human history there has at times appeared a form of behavior which was hardly in keeping with the spirit of the Gospel and was even opposed to it, it has always remained the teaching of the Church that no one is to be coerced into believing (12).

Had this teaching always been followed in practice, the death penalty would never have been inflicted on heretics. Then, of course, there would not have been any need for churchmen to defend the state's right to kill and have nothing else to say except prayers over the corpses of the condemned.

D. Early Voices of the Future

Even as the Council was still in session, the transformation of Catholic consciousness of capital punishment was underway. We note an English, an Irish, and a French work among the early manifestations of change.

1. The first English-language Catholic work reflecting the new era seems to have been that of Tidmarsh, Halloran, and Connolly, which appeared in Great Britain in 1963. Dominican the-

ologian Mannes Tidmarsh presented the opening essay, "a theoretical framework"; J. D. Halloran followed with "facts and figures," and K. J. Connolly closed with "some psychological aspects
of capital punishment." The foreword stated very simply that "the
purpose of this book is limited: it argues that the death penalty
for murder in this country at present is unnecessary and therefore
unjust."

Tidmarsh tackled the delicate problem of purpose in penal
theory. The decision to impose punishment on a person and its
actual imposition are social actions, part of the response to a
breakdown of the normal relationship between a society and its
members.

> [Punishment] is not a personal or private reaction. The
> judge...attends not only to the deserts and needs of the
> offender, but to the needs of society also....A punishment
> which prejudices rather than promotes the good order of
> society is plainly not just, no matter how guilty the offender
> may be nor how well founded the authority.

Tidmarsh thereby set the scene for Halloran, because now it is an
empirical question that comes to the fore in need of verification.
Myths are dismantled by "facts and figures," and Halloran came
up with a firm conclusion:

> There is no evidence whatsoever that capital punishment
> has a unique deterrent effect...[so]...there is no case for
> holding that capital punishment is necessary for the protec-
> tion or the good of society. Why then do we kill four or five
> people every year? The *burden of proof* concerning the value,
> the usefulness and the justice of this practice is surely on
> those who wish to retain it.[58]

Connally in his turn closed the case in forthright fashion:

> If we abolish capital punishment, we shall have lost nothing;
> we shall not have endangered society; and we may do some
> practical good, because our energies may be diverted to solv-
> ing the problem by new techniques.[59]

A new era had clearly begun. Not only did this work illustrate that there were articulate Catholic spokesmen, including clerics, finally joining in the call for abolition, but also that they had clearly done their homework and were contributing in very positive fashion to the cause, despite their relatively late arrival to the campaign.

2. A comprehensive two-part article in the *Irish Theological Quarterly,* written by Michael B. Crowe,[60] was the best historical overview of the issue to be found in English. But instead of merely defending the state's right to kill, "should this be necessary," he proceeded to point out the often-overlooked consequence that "outside circumstances of clear necessity, the right should be held in abeyance."[61]

In the same language as Halloran, Crowe acknowledged that the burden of proof "appears now to have been shifted definitely from those who would wish to abolish capital punishment to those who want to retain it." In other words, if it is not necessary, it is not justifiable; if it is not justifiable, it is not ethical. If it is not ethical, it ought to be abolished from civilized societies.

Crowe summarized the results of historical studies in a progress report on the reexamination of the tradition that was taking place:

> There is no conclusive argument for or against the death penalty in the Scriptures....The Fathers saw no decisive argument against it, although many of them refused to countenance Christian participation in its execution....The arguments in justification of capital punishment used by St. Thomas and his followers were moral and social rather than theological....At the Reformation what one might call the specifically theological arguments for and against the death penalty were ventilated....From the 18th century onward, theological considerations, whether in the service of retaining or of abolishing the death penalty, receded into the background of the controversies.[62]

3. As seen earlier, the French Catholic Church had some special baggage to deal with, some of it going back to the time of the tragic conflicts with the Huguenots. Ever since Bishop Bossuet's influential church history (1688) had identified "change" as the

characteristic error of Protestantism and perpetual identity
throughout the ages as the sign of Catholic truth, the stage was
set for interpreting the least alteration or novelty within Catholicism as heretical.

> In Lord Acton's estimate Bossuet was "the most powerful
> adversary the theory of (doctrinal) development ever
> encountered."...Controversy compelled men to choose
> between the alternative of changelessness and variation. The
> real solution was in neither of the two extremes. It is neces-
> sary to distinguish between variation as a sign of error and
> corruption, and development as a sign of life and truth.[63]

The rigid attachment to what was believed to be tradition
contributed to the *intégriste* rejection of the idea that there could
ever have been anything lacking in earlier positions or policies of
the church. A talented French scholar addressed this dilemma in
the specific case of the history of the death penalty and published his impressive results shortly after the Council.

Jean Imbert, a professor on the Faculty of Law and Economic
Sciences in Paris, was motivated to undertake the task by his growing realization of how little most people knew about "the evolution of capital punishment." His research had provided him with a
wealth of new information, and in his preface he warned readers
that, while the highest standards of impartiality would be
observed, nonetheless:

> Impartiality does not require abstention; the historian is not
> a robot; he can and must sometimes express his own opin-
> ion about the problems of his time, at the risk of otherwise
> shirking his duty as a human being. That is why the conclu-
> sion will have a more personal note than the rest of this
> work, and we ask in advance for the indulgence of those who
> may be shocked by it.[64]

At the end of his investigations Imbert expressed the "shocking" conclusion to which his research had gradually led him, that
is, the conviction that

in peacetime...there is no longer any justification whatsoever, either theoretical or practical, for the scaffold in a
country like France....Further use of the guillotine to sever a
few heads a year no longer has any value either as an example or a deterrent. Could you find one Frenchman in a million who even knows their names or why they are being
executed? There will always be criminals, but modern society has other means of protecting itself from them than this
radical and inhumane mode of elimination which for millennia has not succeeded in suppressing crime.

In his final paragraph Imbert acknowledged how strongly
he felt about his conclusions. Those who argue for retention of
the death penalty in a modern state, he pointed out, invariably
appeal to utilitarian grounds, many of them claiming that in the
last analysis this is their essential argument against abolition.
But, he wanted to know, how is it "useful"?

Do they not see that the facts provide an irrefutable denial
of that claim, because criminality is no different in the countries that use the death penalty and those that do not? These
"death-worshipping" theoreticians invariably call to mind
the teaching of Muyart de Vouglans who, in 1780, insisted
on the "utility of judicial torture and the absolute impossi-
bility of replacing it with as reliable an alternative." And yet,
torture disappeared from the arsenal of the means-of-proof
and punishments used by our tribunals for over two centuries without the march of justice suffering harm without
it; on the contrary! Just as torture was once expelled from
our judicial institutions, so now must the death penalty likewise be abolished.[65]

Italy had abolished the death penalty in 1948, and West
Germany had followed suit in 1949, so the theological debate
about its retention or abolition, strangely enough, came after it
was abolished in those countries; for Germany the discussion
had lasted basically fifteen years. It was during those same fifteen years that the great debate raged in Britain, until abolition
was achieved there in 1965. That left France, at the time that
Imbert was writing, in the embarrassing position of still having
the guillotine at a time when progressive European political,

legal, and theological opinion had reached a virtual consensus that such killing was no longer an appropriate penal practice for a civilized state.[66]

So, throughout the decade of the 1970s, the French debate continued, coming to something of a climax in 1978 when the French bishops intervened with a highly unusual document. They had been engaging in a lively campaign against the death penalty, but did so in their own way.[67] We will return to take a closer look at their document later when its uniqueness will be more readily apparent. But meantime our plan is to double back and sketch briefly the American Catholic experience regarding the death penalty down to this same post-conciliar period and beyond.

CHAPTER 8

The American Context

I. Eighteenth-Nineteenth-Century American Abolitionists
   A. Dr. Benjamin Rush (1787)
   B. Edward Livingston (1825)
   C. Robert Rantoul, Jr. (1836)
   D. John Greenleaf Whittier (1843)
   E. Charles Spear (1844)
   F. Walt Whitman (1845)
   G. Horace Greeley (1850)
   H. Frederick Douglass (1858)
   I. Marvin H. Bovee (1869)
   J. Newton M. Curtis (1892)

II. The Early Twentieth-Century U.S. Catholic Context
   A. *The Catholic Encyclopedia* (1910)
   B. Finley Peter Dunne (1914)
   C. Raymond T. Bye (1919)
   D. Clarence Darrow (1924)
   E. The Execution of Sacco and Vanzetti (1927)
   F. The Execution of Bruno Richard Hauptmann (1936)

III. The Post-World War II Era
   A. The Rosenberg Case (1953)
   B. The Chessman Case (1955–60)
      1. Fr. Donald R. Campion, S.J.
      2. Donal E. J. MacNamara
      3. John Cogley
      4. Governor Pat Brown

IV. A Study of Clerical Contrasts
   A. Msgr. Thomas Riley (Massachusetts) (1958)
   B. Msgr. Salvatore Adamo (New Jersey) (1964)

Because our chief interest is to trace the remarkable change in attitude toward the death penalty among the contemporary leaders of the American Catholic Church, it would have been possible to decide on a number of different starting points. The story is chiefly about the twentieth-century developments, but it is important to note that Christian voices of opposition to capital punishment are nothing new. They have been heard on these shores in significant numbers ever since the nation began. The following samples are meant merely to provide some sense of the broader American context.

I. EIGHTEENTH-NINETEENTH-CENTURY AMERICAN ABOLITIONISTS

The English colonizers who started settling in North America in the seventeenth century brought the gallows with them and used them regularly. By the time of the Revolution "all the American colonies had severe criminal codes. All except Rhode Island threatened capital punishment for ten or more crimes."[1] Even though Pennsylvania started out with a more lenient code, due to the Quaker moderation of William Penn, there was no objection in principle to the death penalty. There were, in fact, Quaker judges in Pennsylvania imposing hanging as the punishment for convicted murderers.

> Curiously, we do not find explicit protest within the Society against Quaker magistrates wielding the sword of justice in this way; so long as it seemed right for Friends to participate in government, they were evidently willing to approve their coreligionists in office curbing evil doers by means of the executioner's sword.[2]

Catholics were a very small minority and of little political significance both in colonial America and in the early national period. As their numbers grew, they certainly heard voices of

301

opposition as they began to be raised against the death penalty by some of their neighbors. State killings, as we have seen, were commonplace but so too were the nagging objections of minority Christian groups not wedded to the objectionable policies of the dominant culture.

The occasional allegation among free-thinkers that it was religion that started such killings and secularism that stopped them is manifestly untrue. But, on the other hand, the dark side of religion played all too large a role, as we have seen, in entrenching the death penalty in Europe and thereby in its colonies in the New World. But what is often unacknowledged is that it was also religion that helped to energize much of the call for abolition, and this can be seen in U.S. history perhaps as clearly as anywhere. Since the First Amendment guaranteed that there would be no established church, there was no pressure for any particular church to support capital punishment, even though most did. But this freedom meant that many more voices could be and would be raised against it, given its moral ambiguities and repugnance. Since some of the witnesses to a better way raised their voices against the death penalty out of Christian motivation, the traditional church support for the practice did not go unchallenged, but neither was it so intense here as in "the old country."

American abolitionism is literally as old as the U.S. Constitution. Beccaria's work was first published in English in 1767 and was well known in British colonial circles. It had been in circulation only twenty years when the first public call for complete abolition of capital punishment in the newly formed United States occurred. It was in Philadelphia, in the home of Benjamin Franklin, that a prominent, erudite American physician spoke his piece and revealed in doing so that he had stronger, more numerous, and more diverse objections to the death penalty than Beccaria had articulated.

A. Dr. Benjamin Rush (1787)

A special reason for recalling Dr. Benjamin Rush here is to emphasize that while the humanitarian impulse of the Enlightenment was obviously at work, so were the religious sentiments imbedded in the culture. His arguments were a striking combination of both kinds, and he showed himself well ahead of his time in the way that he joined the use of the Bible with the light of reason:

> Laws which inflict death for murder are, in my opinion, as unchristian as those which tolerate or justify revenge; for the obligations of Christianity upon individuals, to promote repentance, to forgive injuries, and to discharge the duties of univeral benevolence, are equally binding upon states. The power over human life is the sole prerogative of Him who gave it. Human laws, therefore, rise in rebellion against this prerogative, when they transfer it to human hands.

> (It was) the ignorance and cruelty of man, which by the mis-application of this text of scripture [Genesis 9:6], has so long and so often stained the religion of Jesus Christ with folly and revenge....There is no opinion so absurd or impious that it may not be supported by solitary texts of scripture. To collect the sense of the Bible upon any subject we must be governed by its whole spirit and tenor.

In his own understanding of Western history, Dr. Rush was convinced that it was "the effects of the Christian religion" that ultimately accounted for Western progress, for the "extirpation of slavery," the elimination of torture, the "diminution of the number of capital punishments, and the mitigation of the horrors of war." In saying this, of course, he had to make important distinctions. Christian values are not always reflected in institutional practices, and lifestyles all too easily fall short of ideals.

His final remarks reveal his realism: "I despair of making such an impression on the present citizens of the United States, as shall abolish the absurd and unchristian practice (of capital punishment)." But with confidence that wiser generations would arise in the future, he looked ahead, saying, "To you, the unborn generations of the next century, I consecrate this humble tribute to justice."[3]

B. Edward Livingston (1825)

"Probably no American opponent of capital punishment has been so influential as Edward Livingston." In a political-legal career divided between New York and New Orleans, he formulated the arguments that would be used by "hundreds of active anti-gallows reformers" in ante-bellum America. His was a more predominantly secular approach than that of Rush, but the religious component was clearly there nonetheless. He was well aware of the way in which the Bible was used by many supporters of the death penalty, and he addressed them directly: "Indeed, if I were inclined to support my opinion by arguments drawn from religion, the whole New Testament should be my text, and I could easily deduce from it authority for a system of reform as opposed to one of extermination."

In urging adoption by Louisiana of the code he had prepared, which allowed absolutely no use of capital punishment, he devised a common-sense argument that cleverly challenged his opponents:

> Your favorite (method) of death...has been fully tried. By your own account, all nations, since the first institution of society, have practiced it, but you yourselves must acknowledge, without success. All we ask, then, is that you abandon an experiment which has for five or six thousand years been progressing under the variety of forms which cruel ingenuity could invent; and which in all ages, under all governments, has been found wanting....You have made your experiment; it was attended in its operation with an incalculable waste of human life, a deplorable degradation of human intellect; it was found often fatal to the innocent, and it frequently permitted the guilty to escape....Tortures were superadded, which nothing but the intelligence of a fiend could invent...yet there was no diminution of crime; and it never occurred to you, that mildness might accomplish that which could not be effected by severity.

It is astonishing to hear an American politician of more than a century and a half ago publicly saying almost exactly what dozens of American Catholic bishops have been insisting on in recent years:

> The right to inflict death exists, but...it must be in defense, either of individual or social existence; and it is limited to

the case where no other alternative remains to prevent the threatened destruction. Societies have existed without it....In those societies, therefore, it was not necessary. Is there anything in the state of ours that makes it so?[4]

His words take on an eerie overtone when one recalls that he was addressing the legislators of the state of Louisiana, a state which today has chosen to return with a vengeance to the wretched business of intentional killing.

C. Robert Rantoul, Jr. (1836)

Rantoul was "America's most active and renowned opponent of capital punishment in the late 1830s....Both his parents were profoundly opposed to capital punishment, and his father, while serving in the Massachusetts legislature, sought repeatedly to strike it from the laws." Rantoul had a life-changing experience in 1830 when he defended a client whom he was convinced was innocent and who nonetheless was convicted and executed. His religious heritage was Unitarian, which raises some interesting questions about possible connections with Socinianism as a source of the family's opposition to the death penalty. In any event, he represents a further development in U.S. abolitionism. As seen above, Livingston granted a state's theoretical right to execute but denied that the conditions for exercising it were any longer fulfilled. Rantoul went further and took great pains to deny that any state ever had such a right. The influence of Beccaria on him was certainly evident, but the Anabaptist negative assessment of the state also seems to have contributed to his world view.

The whole object of government, as Rantoul saw it, was

for the protection of property, life, and liberty. It is not for the destruction of any of them....Having performed these duties (of protection), its office is at an end....The right of self-defense furnishes no foundation whatever...upon which to establish the right to take away life.[5]

When it comes to religious arguments against capital punishment, however, there is nothing in Christian history quite comparable to the barrage developed in the 1840s. Nowhere were the twin evils of human slavery and capital punishment more forcefully denounced as comparable violations of divine and human justice. A few examples are seen in the following writers.

D. John Greenleaf Whittier (1843)

Whittier (1807–1892) shared a room with Rantoul when both of them served in the Massachusetts legislature in 1835, but his opposition to capital punishment had even deeper roots than Rantoul's influence. His Quaker heritage is reflected in his powerful poem "The Human Sacrifice" (1843), which makes it clear that for him the most offensive feature of the penal system was the union of "gallows and gospel." The involvement of the Christian clergy as "the hangman's ghostly ally" he found unconscionable.

> Blessing with solemn text and word
> The gallows-drop and strangling cord;
> Lending the sacred Gospel's awe
> And sanction to the crime of Law...
> Two busy fiends attending there:
> One with cold mocking rite and prayer,
> The other with impatient grasp,
> Tightening the death-ropes' strangling clasp.

The poem gives fascinating testimony to the way the European objections were transplanted to these shores by the heirs of religious minority groups. Calls for church reform since the Middle Ages succeeded in many other areas, but not in this one. From Whittier's Quaker perspective, the gallows constituted a great embarrassment, a vestige of earlier religious institutional corruption.

> Last relic of the good old time,
> When Power found license for its crime,
> And held a writhing world in check
> By that fell cord around its neck;
> Stifled Sedition's rising shout,
> Choked the young breath of Freedom out,
> And timely checked the words which sprung

From Heresy's forbidden tongue.
While in its noose of terror bound,
The Church its cherished union found,
Conforming on the Moslem plan,
The motley-colored mind of man,
Not by the Koran and the Sword,
But by the Bible and the Cord!

E. Charles Spear (1844)

Spear (1801–1863), a Universalist minister, wrote a popular book entitled *Essays on the Punishment of Death* in 1844; the book made him "the foremost proponent of the abolition of capital punishment in New England."[6] He also started a prison-reform newspaper that was the heart of the movement from 1845 to 1857. The running debate in which he presented the anti-death-penalty case—and opponents like George B. Cheever[7] presented the pro-death-penalty case—probably involved the selected use of the texts of the Bible more than at any other time in history. One overall characteristic of these proof-texting exchanges, sometimes observable in similar debates in our own day, was the prominence of Old Testament texts as the chief ammunition of the retentionists and of New Testament texts as the counterpart of the abolitionists. These literalistic Bible battles read like antique catalogues today, since so much has happened in biblical studies in the interim that makes the simplistic interpretations of both sides outmoded and unpersuasive.

F. Walt Whitman (1845)

The bitterness toward the pro-gallows clergy found in the poetry of Whittier was more than equaled by the acerbic words of Whitman (1819–1892). His essay *A Dialogue* appeared in 1845 and climaxes with an attack on those who founded "the whole breadth and length of the hanging system...on the Holy Scriptures."

When I read in the records of the past how Calvin burned Servetus at Geneva and found his defense in the Bible; when I peruse the reign of the English Henry VIII, that great champion of Protestantism, who, after the Reformation, tortured people to death for refusing to acknowledge his spiritual supremacy, and pointed to the Scriptures as his authority; when through the short reign of Edward VI, another Protestant sovereign, and of the Bloody Mary, a Catholic one, I find the most barbarous cruelties and martyrdoms afflicted in the name of God and his Sacred Word, I shudder and grow sick with pity. Still...I bethink me how good it is that the spirit of such horrors...the blasphemy which prostitutes God's law, and the darkness of superstition which applauded them...have all passed away. But in these days when clergymen call for sanguinary punishments in the name of the Gospel, when...they throw themselves on the supposed necessity of hanging in order to gratify and satisfy Heaven...when they demand that our laws shall be pervaded by vindictiveness and violence, my soul is filled with amazement, indignation and horror...."O Liberty," said Madame Roland, "what crimes have been committed in thy name!" "O Bible!" say I, "what follies and monstrous barbarities are defended in thy name!"[8]

G. Horace Greeley (1850)

"Tens of thousands of rural Americans first heard of the evils of capital punishment while attending Horace Greeley's lyceum lectures."[9] An extremely influential advocate of social reforms, Greeley (1812–1872) summarized concisely his major objections to the death penalty in an article in 1850, organized around four propositions:

1. It teaches and sanctions Revenge...
2. It tends to weaken and destroy the natural horror of bloodshed...
3. It facilitates and often insures the escape of the guilty from any punishment by human law...
4. It excites a pernicious sympathy for the convict...[10]

The most interesting feature of his position is that it is the teaching of Jesus against revenge that is still given pride of place, while the rest of his reasons are of the pragmatic type popular in the budding social sciences.

H. *Frederick Douglass (1858)*

Governor John King was heavily petitioned to commute the sentence of a young man named Ira Stout, who had been convicted of murder and was scheduled to be hanged in Rochester, New York, in October 1858. Stout had organized a letter-writing campaign, and among those who signed up to hold a meeting the night before his scheduled execution was Susan B. Anthony. Frederick Douglass (1817–1895) chaired the meeting and delivered an address entitled "Capital Punishment Is a Mockery of Justice." His words on that occasion are of special interest, since they show the great affinity between slavery and capital punishment, and the need to abolish both. The address is too long to reproduce in whole here, but parts of it offer exceptionally good examples of retrieved Christian morality that are as timely today as they were when formulated. Some of the arguments are classical, but the eloquence of Douglass gives them a powerful new relevance. Note the four following passages of distinctly religious orientation as responsible for his rejection of the death penalty:

1. In proportion as the tide of barbarism has receded, a higher regard has been manifested for the God-given right to life, its inviolability has been strengthened in proportion to the development of the intellect and moral sentiments....Conscience, reason, and revelation unite their testimony against the continuance of a custom, barbarous in its origin, antichristian in its continuance, vindictive in its character, and demoralizing in its tendencies.

2. Any settled custom, precept, example or law, the observance of which necessarily tends to cheapen human life, or in any measure serves to diminish and weaken man's respect for it, is a custom, precept, example or law utterly inconsistent with the law of eternal goodness written on the constitution of man by his Maker, and is diametrically opposed to the safety, welfare and happiness of mankind; ...however ancient and honorable such laws and customs may be in the eyes of prejudice, superstition and bigotry, they ought to be discountenanced, abolished, and supplanted by a higher civilization and a holier and more merciful Christianity.

3. When a criminal is firmly secured in the iron grasp of the government, and on that account can no longer endanger

the peace and safety of society;...when he is wasted and ema-
ciated by heavy chains and horrid thoughts, and long con-
finement in a gloomy cell—when, as it is often the case, he is
completely transformed, both in temper and in spirit—the
execution of the death penalty on such an one is an act of
cold blooded enormity, and is as cowardly as it is cruel...and
instead of repressing and preventing the horrid crime of
murder, it really serves, by shocking and blunting the finer
and better feelings of human nature, to undermine respect
for human life and leads directly to the perpetration of the
crime which it would extinguish.

4. That punishment (the death penalty) is a form of revenge,
wreaking upon the criminal the pain he has inflicted on
another, wrong in principle and pernicious in practice; (it)
arises out of the lowest propensities of human nature, and is
opposed to the highest civilization;...it has no sanction in
the spirit and teachings of Christ, which everywhere abound
in loving kindness and forgiveness.[11]

I. Marvin H. Bovee (1869)

The chief reason for including Bovee (1827–1888) is
because of his book of 1869, which is one of the few in English in
the nineteenth century to focus entirely on the impropriety of
capital punishment in Christian ethics. "*Christ and the Gallows*
was a diverse and sometimes haphazard collection of arguments
from other reformers and letters from friends of the cause."[12]
One of Bovee's strengths, however, was to see clearly the degree
to which death flunked the test of fitting the definition of punishment, a point regularly and strongly made in many contemporary church statements.

> It is said that the punishment of crime is threefold in its
> nature, contemplating in its application three specific
> objects, first of which is reformation of the criminal; sec-
> ondly, the protection of society; and thirdly, the restraint
> imposed on the criminally inclined. If these be the objects
> of punishment, then, indeed, has the death penalty fallen
> far short of accomplishing either one of the objects named;
> for capital punishment destroys without reforming the crim-
> inal, while all history proves that in securing protection to

society, or in deterring commission of crime, its failure has been most marked and conspicuous. Accomplishing but little good and vast injury, it is, indeed, strange that so abhorrent a punishment should still be upon the statute books of many States professing high Christian civilization. My theory of punishment would be summed up in these words: Penalties that do not contemplate the reformation of the criminal are not punishments, but cruelties.

J. Newton M. Curtis (1892)

Curtis (1835–1910) is another figure of special interest for the way in which he combined religious and secular arguments against the death penalty. The heading of an address Curtis (R., N.Y.) made before the U.S. House of Representatives in 1892 indicates this duality in its very title: "The Death Penalty Undesirable, and Not Sustained by Divine Authority." In calling for total abolition he rehearsed the traditional ethics of self-defense, noting that a state cannot "find judicious warrant for going beyond the disarming and confining of a disorderly person. A single step beyond the line of safety is one step in the direction of that condition of society where brute force, not reason, rules." Then he immediately pushed on to note that "in advocating this principle we are early warned not to legislate against the laws of God and the criminal codes of civilized states."

This led Curtis to discuss the dispute over the correct translation of Genesis 9:6, and then to lament the fact that some insist on going no further than the Old Testament:

> [They have] stuffed their ears with cobwebs of brutal prejudice, that the lessons taught by the Sermon on the Mount might not enter their hearts; have veiled their eyes with vengeance, that they might not see how He, in the extreme agony of His suffering for man, forgave His persecutors...and took to His home the repentant thief. They may search in vain through the chronicles of theocracy for the record of a single execution for murder under His administration of nearly thirty centuries....Age and universality have ever been the ready arguments of those who have stood in the way of progress.[13]

The fact that such arguments against the death penalty, inspired by and relying on the straightforward content of the gospel, were being set forth on the floor of the U.S. Congress over a century ago is a sobering reminder that the tradition of state killings has long been under severe suspicion of being something quite other than what most of its proponents made it out to be. It cannot be overlooked that from the twelfth-century Waldensians to these nineteenth-century Americans, the drumbeat of protest against capital punishment as contrary to Christian teaching and spirit has been constant, even though the opponents have usually been in the minority, at least until the late twentieth century.

II. THE EARLY TWENTIETH-CENTURY U.S. CATHOLIC CONTEXT

The turn of the century was "the end of the beginning" in the history of the U.S. Catholic Church.[14] The immigrant church was coming into its own. In 1903 James Cardinal Gibbons was the first American prelate to vote in a papal election, and five years later the American church was removed from missionary status on the Vatican's organizational chart. With more than sixteen million members by 1910, it was beginning to be a force to contend with. One sign of its maturing was the publication (between 1907 and 1912) of a fifteen-volume encyclopedia. Volume ten, which appeared in 1910, contained a treatment of capital punishment that is worth examining as a reflection of its time.[15]

A. The Catholic Encyclopedia (1910)

The encyclopedia was a source of justifiable pride at the time of its publication. Its articles represented some of the best international scholarship of the day, and its editors had as their explicit goal the publication of "full and authoritative information on the entire cycle of Catholic interests, action, and doctrine." When the volume containing a five-page entry on "punishment, capital" appeared, the article was attributed to John Willey Willis. It is worth reviewing for some of the things that can be derived from it about outlooks and attitudes of the time, a time when a vigorous U.S. penal reform movement succeeded in getting nine more states to abolish the death penalty.[16] Even though there was no official Catholic participation in the movement, there has not been enough study to determine how and how many Catholic laypeople may have been involved at the grassroots level.

Dr. Willis, a native Minnesotan, converted to Catholicism in 1884 at the age of 30. A distinguished teacher, lawyer, and judge, he twice ran for Congress unsuccessfully.[17] He was well read and asserted near the beginning of his article that "the idea of capital punishment is of great antiquity and formed a part of the primal concepts of the human race." He proceeded with the story of Cain-Abel, followed by some of the other Old Testament data, generally treating them in an even-handed way, although at one point he makes the remark that "no more cruel form of punishment for offences deemed capital existed in ancient times than that which prevailed among the Jews, i.e., stoning to death." When the full panoply of human ingenuity in inflicting pain is taken into account, there were certainly several other methods that could more than reasonably vie for that title.[18]

Turning to the ancient Greeks, Willis notes that they "punished homicide, committed by design, and many other offences with death." After a few further details he takes up ancient Rome, observing that "the Roman law was notably severe in regard to public offences," and gives some of the more graphic examples, ending up with a treatment of the types of crucifixion.

He then devotes all of three sentences to the Christian Middle Ages, saying that

> in spite of the zealous humanitarian efforts of the Church, cruel punishments were commonly employed, and the death penalty was very frequently inflicted. This severity was, in general, an inheritance from the Roman Empire, the jurisprudence of which, civil and criminal, pervaded Europe. One of the most horrible forms of punishment, derived from ancient Roman usages, was burning at the stake.

With that said, he suddenly leaps to the sixteenth century to tell of the "popular frenzy" over witchcraft, which "the Statute of

Elizabeth in 1562 made a crime of the first magnitude (and) the Act of James VI in 1603...provides the penalty of death....The number of victims in Scotland from first to last has been estimated as more than four thousand." He then reports that "the same overmastering dread (of witches) pervaded New England. Many persons were convicted of witchcraft and were tortured, imprisoned and burned. One of the leaders...was the Reverend Cotton Mather who...betrayed in the prosecution of witches absolute fanaticism and merciless cruelty."

The selectivity of material here borders on the bizarre. To understand (not excuse) how this could happen, it helps to keep in mind the depth of anti-Catholic feeling in much of the country at this time. Willis apparently saw no need to mention any of the darker episodes of Catholic history, such as the Spanish Inquisition.[19] He chose rather to cite only Protestant abuses, singling out statistics about Scotland without mention of comparable figures that could have been cited from numerous Catholic areas. One can only theorize that this was done because he thought that Catholic abuses were already far too frequently criticized and caricatured in the hostile public writings of the day, and he had an opportunity to balance the record somewhat for his Catholic audience. The climax of this partiality and defensiveness comes in the next paragraph:

> Canon law has always forbidden clerics to shed human blood and therefore capital punishment has always been the work of the officials of the State and not of the Church. Even in the case of heresy, of which so much is made by non-Catholic controversialists, the functions of ecclesiastics were restricted invariably to ascertaining the fact of heresy. The punishment, whether capital or other, was both prescribed and inflicted by civil government. The infliction of capital punishment is not contrary to the teaching of the Catholic Church, and the power of the State to visit upon culprits the penalty of death derives much authority from revelation and from the writings of theologians. The advisability of exercising that power is, of course, an affair to be determined upon other and various considerations.

This is a noble effort to put the best face on an embarrassing history. As long as such special pleading was the order of day, there was little prospect for achieving a more balanced picture or setting the record straight. The smoke of confessional battles was still hanging too heavily over the battlefields, causing blind spots that could only be remedied by the advent of a more ecumenical atmosphere when concern for the whole spectrum of truth could take its proper place above the tactics of partisan debate.

The rest of the article is actually quite good, with note taken of how Blackstone objected to the frequency of capital punishment, especially for petty crimes, while Boswell and friends took ghoulish pleasure in watching executions and the dismemberment of convicts. Willis granted that Beccaria "makes a most impressive argument in favour of penal servitude for life as a substitute for the judicial killing of criminals," and he also found it worth quoting Voltaire's remark that "a man after he is hanged is good for nothing...hanging is a benefit to nobody but the executioner." With no mention of its having been placed on the Roman Index of Forbidden Books, he favorably cited the entire passage in which Beccaria had contended that the death penalty "is pernicious to society, from the example of barbarity it affords," then he asked rhetorically, "Is it not absurd that the laws, which detect and punish homicide, should, in order to prevent murder, publicly commit murder themselves?"

Without expressing an opinion on the worth of these unorthodox ideas, Willis went on to note a few dissenting views, observing that "the battle is still raging between advocates and opponents of capital punishment, (but)...the policy at present pursued by the nations of the world generally favours capital punishment." He finished the article with a rundown of the nations and states where the death penalty had been abolished and those where it still continued to be practiced, with mention also of their particular methods of execution.

As a period piece it is an interesting essay that conveys much information about the long and complex history of capital punishment. At the same time, the noted deficiencies were probably caused by the author's awareness of the widespread U.S. anti-Catholicism of his day and the resultant Catholic "siege mentality" that would give no comfort to the "enemy" by taking the chance of publicly acknowledging known shortcomings on "his side."[20] He obviously manifested much more sympathy for some

of the Beccarian reforms than would have been likely had the
article been written by a cleric trained on the seminary manuals
of the day. But, like most Catholic scholars of the post-Enlighten-
ment period, he saw the abolitionist debate as something prefer-
ably to steer clear of, due to the antipathies and objectionable
philosophies with which it was suffused and surrounded. One
might watch with interest from a safe distance but choose not to
participate unless (or until) some changes occurred in both
church and society that would make greater participation more
feasible.[21]

B. Finley Peter Dunne (1914)

If official Catholic voices were silent, however, that did not
mean that there were no second thoughts about the system on
the popular level. One noteworthy account was by Finley Peter
Dunne, the popular Chicago Irish-American journalist who had
created the humorous figure of Martin Dooley. The account
appeared in the *American Magazine* and told of his assignment as
a cub reporter nearly thirty years earlier to cover the hanging of
three Italian laborers. It is not a protest piece as such, but the
sorry spectacle is viewed with gentle cynicism.

> As [the valet] placed the white hood on the first man and
> adjusted the rope, the priest stepped forward and in the level
> voice prescribed by the custom of the Church began to read
> the most awful of human supplications for divine mercy,
> "The Litany for the Dying." He read it in Latin. Italian men
> of the present day are not noted for their piety, but these
> unfortunates recalled vaguely, through a mist of sin and irre-
> ligion, words which they had heard in their childhood, and
> they interrupted the prayer with cries of "Ora pro nobis."
> They knew no more....The priest closed his book and
> stepped back. His fine face was white from pity and horror.

The description continues, telling of the botched execution of
one of the three. "The clumsy mechanics of the operation had
failed. For fully five minutes the base crowd watched the awful
spectacle with frank enjoyment." Dunne does not elaborate on
the details, but his sarcasm in closing is trenchant:

The Majesty of the Law had been vindicated. Justice was tri-
umphant. Right was made plain to the blindest and a splen-
did example of punishment put before the eyes of intending
sinners.

N.B. There were just as many capital crimes in the year following the infliction of this notably exemplary punishment
as in the year before.[22]

C. Raymond T. Bye (1919)

The twin evils of war and capital punishment have always had
multiple interrelationships, and in the cycles of U.S. history whenever war fever was high, abolitionist interest tended to be low. After
World War I the movement to do away with the use of the death
penalty reexerted itself, and solid works like that by Raymond T.
Bye were available for serious consideration. Bye was convinced
that his dissertation at the University of Pennsylvania in 1919

had established the thesis that capital punishment has no
proper place in the penal system of the United States....It is
but a question of time when this disgraceful barbarity will
be swept away in the better order that is gradually creeping
over the world.[23]

His optimism proved premature. But a few other incidents stand
out as influential in keeping the issue alive in all segments of
post–World War I America. The numbers of actual executions
would rise to record levels, but the arguments against it would
continue to find articulate proponents.

D. Clarence Darrow (1924)

Anyone living in the United States in the 1920s could hardly
have been insulated from the irreverent wit of the Great Mouth-
piece, Clarence Darrow. Darrow reveled in being a kind of American Voltaire, poking fun at institutional religiosity at its most
peculiar and recalling the worst failings of the past. In a memorable face-off with Judge Alfred Talley at New York's Metropolitan
Opera House on September 23, 1924, debating whether capital
punishment was a wise policy, he mockingly recalled

the good old days when you could kill people by the millions because they worshipped God in a different way from that which the State provided, or when you could kill old women for witchcraft!...Those were the glorious days of capital punishment. And there wasn't a judge or a preacher who didn't think that the life of the State depended upon their right to hang old women for witchcraft and to persecute others for worshipping God in the wrong way.[24]

The next year Darrow and a few other activists founded the American League to Abolish Capital Punishment. By his stinging wit he forced many people to rethink old prejudices. While he undoubtedly offended some, the ethical edge of his criticisms had to give one pause. The question had to be faced: Why did good-intentioned institutions like churches involve themselves in supporting such violent practices as capital punishment with all its ugly and unflattering features?

E. The Execution of Sacco and Vanzetti (1927)

The irregularities of this notorious case, riddled with seven years of "egregious violations in due process of law,"[25] had to strike close to home for an immigrant church that included many poor Italians. If the principle of capital punishment was not at issue, the manner of its use certainly was, and impartial observers could not fail to notice the way in which its victims were selected from the lower economic and social classes. This troubling fact had to temper Catholic support for capital punishment, even though the penny catechisms were still presenting it as a normal part of God's eternal plan.

This ideology of support was in fact an influential element in institutionalizing injustice. Herbert Ehrmann, a young lawyer in the Sacco-Vanzetti defense, was devastated by what he saw in that trial. The jury was ready to hang the "foreigners" before it even had time to read the evidence. Looking back on it twenty-five years later, he wrote from his own experience:

If the jury is composed of the dominant or "in-group" and the defendant and his witnesses belong to an "out-group"— as they frequently do—the defendant's evidence is often discounted to zero. The jury tends to believe that foreigners, Negroes, or members of any minority group will lie for one another and "stick together" under all circumstances.[26]

One positive consequence of the case was that it brought Ehrmann and his wife Sara into the ranks of active reformers with the formation of the Massachusetts Council for the Abolition of the Death Penalty, by which many seeds of reform were planted and a reliable core of opponents was ensured for the future.[27]

F. The Execution of Bruno Richard Hauptmann (1936)

The execution of Sacco and Vanzetti took place in the same year that Charles Lindbergh made his solo flight across the Atlantic. Nine years later the execution of Bruno Richard Hauptmann, accused of kidnapping and killing the Lindbergh baby, had the earmarks of another possible miscarriage of justice. The pressure to solve the case and apply the death penalty quickly swept aside the lingering doubts that would otherwise have led to further appeals and the possible dismissal of the case against Hauptmann. But the rise of Adolf Hitler and the beginning of World War II soon diverted attention and postponed the mounting of any strong campaign against abuses in administering capital punishment.

III. THE POST-WORLD WAR II ERA

A. The Rosenberg Case (1953)

In the heyday of McCarthyism the planned execution of Julius and Ethel Rosenberg as communist spies was the object of worldwide criticism. Its impact on Franco-American relations caused a major headache for the newly installed Eisenhower administration. The archbishop of Paris had joined with four former prime ministers and other French dignitaries as well as some eight thousand French citizens calling for clemency. Among the thousands of Americans besieging the White House with letters and telegrams of protest, some twenty-three hundred clergymen of all denominations, along with atomic scientists

Harold Urey and Albert Einstein, signed an appeal pleading with the president to prevent the execution.

Pope Pius XII was also besieged by appeals from Catholics the world over demanding to know why he had not made an attempt to intervene.

> Finally, the Vatican press responded by revealing the fact that the Pope had indeed transmitted an oral appeal, using the Apostolic Delegate, the archbishop of Laodicea, as intermediary. The Pope's message had asked for mercy for the Rosenbergs "out of motives of charity proper...without entering into the merits of the case." The appeal, however, had apparently been received by President Truman's Attorney General, J. Howard McGrath, who did not see fit to inform the President, much less the press, of the Pope's intercession.[28]

The timidity of the papal protest stands in contrast to the more recent direct interventions, but it must be viewed in historical context. It was at least a halting, tentative step on the road to recovering the pastoral practice of St. Augustine, disapproving all executions, especially those based on political motives. The burden of proof needed to be shifted to the advocates of death. In this case the moral outrage of millions of ordinary people was directed not against the death penalty as such but against its blatantly political use.

> Given his view of the overriding importance of a strong intelligence service and his visceral anticommunism, Eisenhower considered the existence of possibly mitigating factors, in the case of both the Rosenbergs or of Ethel in particular, to be of minimal importance. The primary consideration was that going through with the executions would send a message to the Communists that from now on American nationals recruited into Soviet espionage networks would be treated with the utmost severity.[29]

But it simultaneously sent other messages as well, especially about how little one really valued human life if one were ready to destroy it in order to make political points that could be made in far less costly ways.

In the *Catholic Worker* Dorothy Day shared her "Meditation on the Death of the Rosenbergs" with her readers. Her sadness, as always, was rooted in her Christian "fellow-feeling" (*com-pas-sio*): "My heart was heavy...knowing that Ethel Rosenberg must have been thinking with all the yearning of her heart of her own soon-to-be-orphaned children." Day struggled to leave aside the questions raised by those who thought the Rosenbergs were innocent. For her, the larger question was already there to be confronted even if they were guilty:

> Leaving all that out of account, accepting the verdict of the court that they were guilty, accepting the verdict of the millions of Americans who believed them guilty, accepting the verdict of President Eisenhower and Cardinal Spellman who thought them guilty—even so, what should be the attitude of the Christian but one of love...?

> If they were spies for Russia, they were only doing what we also do in other countries...but they indeed were serving a philosophy, a religion, and how mixed up religion can become. What a confusion we have gotten into when Christian prelates sprinkle holy water on scrap metal, to be used for obliteration bombing...or bless a man about to press a button which releases death on 50,000 human beings, including little babies, children, the sick, the aged, the innocent as well as the guilty.

After reading the details of the execution the next morning, she took comfort from the report that "at the last Ethel turned to one of the two police matrons who accompanied her and clasping her by the hand, pulled her toward her and kissed her warmly. Her last gesture was a gesture of love."[30]

C. The Chessman Case (1955–1960) [31]

The popular success of Caryl Chessman's *Cell 2455 Death Row* brought international attention and sympathy to his case, raising doubts and questions in the minds of many about justice in the penal system. There is no doubt that the Chessman debate focused attention in such a way that something new began to happen in American religious circles. The year 1956 stands out as the time when official church statements publicly opposing capital punishment began to enter the general news. The Methodist Church was apparently "the first of the major denominations in America to make the abolition of capital punishment its official position."[32] A few weeks later the United Church of Canada became "the second church to officially go on record as being opposed to capital punishment."[33] The Unitarians (1956) and Universalists (1957) also made early statements and, when they merged in 1961, issued a strong new resolution giving no fewer than five grounds for members to "exert all reasonable efforts toward the elimination of capital punishment."[34]

1. FR. DONALD R. CAMPION, S.J.

It was five months before Caryl Chessman was executed in California that Fr. Donald R. Campion wrote the cover story in *America* magazine asking "Should Men Hang?" Campion had studied and worked with noted criminologist Thorsten Sellin at the University of Pennsylvania and knew whereof he spoke.[35] He provided a context for understanding the case for abolition. He called attention especially to

> the growth of a critical attitude toward claims long made on behalf of the death penalty. Further research into the validity of these claims, particularly those concerning the alleged deterrent effect of this punishment, may well hasten the abandonment of the death penalty everywhere in civilized society. Then the gallows, the electric chair, the guillotine and the gas chamber can be relegated to our museums. There they will take their appointed places alongside the rack, the thumb-screw and other rightfully discarded instruments of earlier systems of justice.[36]

Few indeed were the American Catholic voices that as yet spoke with such a combination of confidence and clarity against the death penalty. But there were some.

2. DONAL E. J. MACNAMARA

The dean of the New York Institute of Criminology, Donal E. J. MacNamara, wrote a letter in reply to Campion. He contended that "Catholics have not been as silent" as the article intimated, noting that in early 1959 he (MacNamara) had been elected president of the American League to Abolish Capital Punishment; that Archbishop Bernard J. Sheil, auxiliary of the Chicago archdiocese, had "accepted the chairmanship of the Illinois Committee to Abolish Capital Punishment"; and that Fr. Charles Sheedy, C.S.C, dean at the University of Notre Dame, was "a member of our national board and presided over a large and enthusiastic assembly at Notre Dame earlier this year."[37]

MacNamara, among other noted accomplishments in a distinguished career, demonstrated how far ahead of most of his fellow lay Catholics he was in a powerful statement published in 1961. He admitted that he had not only been a supporter of the death penalty for over twenty years of his career in police and prison work, but that he had actually participated in a number of executions. He described, however, how total his "conversion" to abolitionism had been, and enumerated ten reasons that had led to his opposition:

1. Capital punishment is criminologically unsound...
2. Capital punishment is morally and ethically unacceptable...
3. Capital punishment has demonstrably failed to accomplish its stated objectives...
4. Capital punishment in the United States has been prejudicially and inconsistently applied...
5. The innocent have been executed...
6. There are effective alternative penalties...
7. Police and prison officers are safer in non-death-penalty states...
8. Paroled and pardoned murderers are no threat to the public...
9. The death penalty is more costly than its alternatives...
10. Capital punishment stands in the way of penal reform.

His conclusion left no doubt about the strength of his convictions:

> Capital punishment is brutal, sordid, and savage. It violates the law of God, and is contrary to the humane and liberal respect for human life characteristic of modern democratic states....It

makes the barbaric *lex talionis* the watchword....It encourages disrespect for our laws, our courts, our institutions.[38]

As is obvious, Donal MacNamara was a pioneer among U.S. Catholic lay men and women who grasped the importance of adopting a different outlook on this important ethical question well before most others did.

3. JOHN COGLEY

Two months before the execution of Chessman, John Cogley, editor of the lay Catholic journal *Commonweal,* also showed uncommon insight in confronting the problem:

> Though I am aware of the abstract arguments for the State's right to take a life, I remain uneasy about the morality of capital punishment....I am not convinced that the ultimate penalty is really necessary for the protection of society, and a cold-blooded killing that is not necessary, even if performed by a State executioner, strikes me as irrational. For that reason alone it is morally questionable....Society might now feel that Christianity requires the elimination of capital punishment, as it ultimately eliminated human slavery, even though slavery as an institution was, and still is, abstractly defended by conscientious theologians. Certainly the Chessman case has forced us to think about these things.[39]

This argument (that the death penalty is unnecessary and therefore immoral) had been articulated by Canon Leclercq more than two decades earlier in Europe, but was as yet by no means common, especially on these shores. It was neither the absolute, universal rejection of killing found in pacifism nor the blanket acceptance of killing found in many of the moral theology manuals, but a common-sense application of a standard ethical principle on the moral use of force. The comparison of the death penalty to the case of slavery (which many nineteenth-century American Christian theologians, both Catholic and Protestant, had defended) also struck a sensitive chord in a nation on the verge of launching a massive civil-rights movement. It was a time, not for defending or making excuses for past mistakes and injustices, but rather for finding ways to overcome the obstacles and implement the practice of greater justice for the future. Slavery and the death penalty, with their common history in American experience, had been accurately paired by Cogley as equally proper objects of abolition.

4. GOVERNOR PAT BROWN

One of the more ironic twists in the Chessman story was the role the Catholic governor of California, Pat Brown, played. On the one hand, he was responsible for enforcing the law, but on the other, he was personally opposed to the death penalty. He did all he could to delay the execution, giving Chessman more time and calling the California legislature into special session to consider once more the proposal to abolish capital punishment from the state. The address that he made on that occasion is quite unusual for its time. Brown, like MacNamara, had come to his position of total rejection of the death penalty more from his own experience than from any overt religious influence.

> As an act of public conscience from the experience of over a decade and a half in law enforcement work, I ask the legislature to abolish the death penalty in California. There are powerful and compelling reasons why this should be done....Although I believe the death penalty constitutes an affront to human dignity and brutalizes and degrades society, I do not merely for these reasons urge this course for our state....Society has both the right and the moral duty to protect itself against its enemies....But the naked, simple fact is that the death penalty has been a gross failure. Beyond its horror and incivility, it has neither protected the innocent nor deterred the wicked....[It] has cheapened human life...is invoked too randomly...and there can be no meaningful exemplary value in a punishment the incidence of which is but one [execution] in fifty [homicides]....No available data...gives support to the grand argument that [it] exerts any substantial effect on the incidence of homicide....The twelve Southern states, all zealously applying the death penalty, have the highest homicide rate....It is primarily inflicted on the weak, the poor, the ignorant, and against racial minorities....Only last year, 1959, out of 48 executed in the U.S., 27 were Negroes. I believe you will find these figures compelling evidence of the gross unfairness and social

injustice which has characterized the application of the death penalty....And there looms always the ugly chance that innocent men may be condemned....I issue this call...as a matter of conviction and conscience....The entire history of our civilization has been a struggle to bring about a greater measure of humanity, compassion, and dignity among us.[40]

IV. A STUDY IN CLERICAL CONTRASTS

The experiences of two American Catholic clergymen appointed to state commissions deliberating the future of capital punishment in their respective states turned out to be totally opposite. Separated by a half-dozen years, their accounts remain on the record as symbolic of the two different worlds that were colliding in this transitional period. There may well have been others who served in similar capacities around the nation, but these two stand as prototypes.

A. Msgr. Thomas J. Riley (1958)

Msgr. Riley served on the Massachusetts' Governor's Special Commission on Capital Punishment and ended up as one of a minority of two members who opposed abolishing the death penalty in that state, finding such a proposal to be "inopportune at this time." The text of the majority report was printed in *The Catholic Lawyer,* followed immediately by an account of the minority viewpoint written by Riley (who in the meantime had been appointed auxiliary bishop of Boston).[41] It is a straightforward account of the standard pre–Vatican II clerical position. It appealed to logic, psychology, sociology, and philosophy, in proper legal and abstract fashion, and from start to finish never found it necessary or appropriate to mention anything whatsoever about the teaching of Jesus. He does concede that

> no one can deny that there have been grave abuses connected with the exercise by the state of its right to inflict the death penalty. History records the regrettable facts that men have been put to death by state governments for trivial reasons, in brutal and abhorrent ways, and in satisfaction of

the basest of human passions. We should not, however, allow the abuses connected with the exercise of the right of capital punishment to obscure our understanding of the considerations which justify this right in principle. We should not argue that, because the death penalty has often been imposed for minor crimes, there can never be a crime of major proportions for which it would be a necessary means for the protection of society. We should not identify the death penalty itself with the gruesome methods which have been employed in particular situations or by individual executioners. We should not infer from the fact that motives of hatred or vengeance are often associated with the inflicting of capital punishment that such motives constitute the only reasons for which the death penalty could be demanded or justified.

Riley certainly demonstrated his awareness of many of the problems associated with the death penalty but desperately held to assumptions that were proving unstable. For instance, he acknowledged two conditions that, if unfulfilled, would render capital punishment unethical:

> The infliction of capital punishment can be justified only if it serves as a deterrent in relation to future possible crimes of the same order, and only if less drastic measures toward the same end will not be sufficiently effective.

His confidence that neither of these crucial conditions was in fact fulfilled was unshakable, no matter what the social scientists might say. Distrustful of any and all kinds of statistics, he held out with the firm conviction that "here too there may be hidden factors which may alter the significance of the data presented."

Yet there is something ominous in Riley's admission that sometime in the future circumstances might conceivably change. Unlike some of his earlier counterparts, he could envision the possibility of a world without capital punishment, a society in which abolition would be appropriate. But,

> we have not yet reached the stage of moral development at which it would be prudent to remove a safeguard judged to be necessary by many who are charged with the heavy

responsibility of protecting human life against criminal attack....If the death penalty is necessary, we must resort to it.

Most striking is Riley's unlimited faith in the effectiveness of the death penalty, no matter the evidence to the contrary. And yet, his final sentence, whether out of frustration or foresight, acknowledged that "once we can say, however, that it can be dispensed with, our arguments in favor of it lose all force." It was almost as if he had a premonition of what was coming.

B. Msgr. Salvatore J. Adamo (1964)

A few years after Riley's experience, Msgr. Salvatore Adamo served on the New Jersey Commission to Study Capital Punishment and found himself in exactly the opposite position. He too was one of a two-member minority, but this time the minority was in favor of abolition. The Second Vatican Council was well under way and Adamo was an early exponent of the kind of change resulting from its renewed ecclesiology. He outlined his position in a journal geared to his fellow clergy, knowing that his stance was not as yet likely to be acceptable to many of them. He observed that some who were otherwise inclined to oppose capital punishment were alienated from doing so by the more extreme statements made by some of the abolitionists. This was a version of the very problem that kept many from enthusiastically joining hands with earlier abolitionist advocates.[42]

Unlike Riley's abstract, professorial approach, Adamo's position was rooted in New Jersey realities. He examined the backgrounds, both ethnic and religious, of those convicted of capital crimes and how they had actually fared. Of seventy-six convicted in fifteen years in New Jersey, he noted that twenty-nine had had their sentences commuted to life (over 30 percent). Protestant convicts had a one-in-two chance of commutation, whereas Catholic convicts had a one-in-eight chance. All twenty-six Italian convicts were executed, as were fifteen out of seventeen Americans of Italian descent. The one Irish convict was executed, while all three Irish-Americans were given life. That the system was slanted and unfair to certain ethnic groups was bad enough in any kind of penal arrangement. But when the penalty is death, such lethal inequities are simply intolerable in any civilized nation.

Adamo's was the voice of the future, just as Riley's was the voice of the past on the capital-punishment issue. The shift of focus from abstract theory about the state's right to the concrete practice of killing unfairly selected people was dramatic. Capital punishment, said Adamo, "is basically an act of *vengeance*. It neither corrects the criminal nor helps the dead victim. It satisfies only the desire to avenge a murder or some other terrible crime." Such plain talk had lasting echoes.

It is noteworthy that the arbitrary aspect of the death penalty in twentieth-century America had become a major issue precisely as its use was in decline. The all-time high for U.S. executions was in 1935 when 199 convicts were executed. Thereafter, the numbers ran thus:

Year	Number Executed
1940	124
1945	117
1950	82
1955	76
1960	56
1965	7

Something was clearly happening, and many were predicting that the death penalty would soon vanish from American life the same way that slavery, judicial torture, and other inhumanities had.

The continuing decline in executions extended through the sessions of the Second Vatican Council. There were forty-seven U.S. executions in the year that the Council opened (1962); twenty-one in the year of the second session; fifteen in the year of the third session, and only seven the year the Council ended. In the next year, 1966, only one execution took place. The NAACP Legal Defense Fund had launched an effective assault on the death penalty, challenging its use under the Eighth and Fourteenth Amendments. The Fund had already helped sponsor (in 1965) a systematic study of some three thousand rape cases in the South to examine how race affected sentencing. This led to "class action lawsuits for the first time on behalf of death row prisoners in Florida and California where Governors Kirk and Reagan threatened to reinstate executions."[43] The de facto moratorium on executions that resulted—as of 1967—was aided by the fact that many Americans were souring on the Vietnam War and the troublesome questions it too was raising about the ethics of intentional killing.

V. DEVELOPMENTS IN THE LATE 1960s

A. *The New Catholic Encyclopedia (1967)*

In the aftermath of Vatican II, the project of an updated Catholic encyclopedia was completed under the auspices of the Catholic University of America. It was slightly more than a half-century since the first Catholic encyclopedia, and much had changed in the church, nation, and world.

Fr. Donald Campion, S.J., provided the entry on capital punishment. It is an interesting contrast to the Willis article of some six decades earlier. Only about half as long, it reflects awareness of all that had been going on in the social sciences with the dismantling of the traditional mythologies. Campion sets the tone early with the observation that primitive peoples used the death penalty "not only to retaliate for murder or treason, but also to appease spirits offended by sorcery, incest, or sacrilege." The religious roots of the practice of sacrificing victims in a society are never far away, even in the most secular of societies.

The article then proceeds in three parts: (1) "Ancient Practices"; (2) "Catholic Recognition of Capital Punishment"; and (3) "Modern Challenges to Capital Punishment."

In the first part the article discusses the practices found in the legal codes of the Middle East (Israelite, Babylonian, Assyrian, and Hittite), with a few words about Rome and Greece.

Under "Catholic Recognition of Capital Punishment" he takes note of the ambivalence within the tradition. "Two patterns of grave punishment emerged in Europe before the Middle Ages. The law of Germanic peoples...tended to see homicide and attacks on person or property as wrongs done to individuals. The proper penalty in such cases came to be a fine paid to the injured party or his heirs. Capital punishment was employed elsewhere, however," This is the first antithesis: how best to make the criminal "pay"—with his goods or with his life? The second antithesis is the fact that, on the one hand, the church's pronouncements contained "at least tacit recognition of the state's competence to execute criminals...with due regard for justice," but, on the other hand, "expressions of the Church's own horror of bloodshed" and its belief in the importance and reality of God's mercy ("As I live, says the Lord God, I swear I take no pleasure in the death of the wicked man, but rather in the wicked man's conversion, that he may live" [Ezek 33:11]).

Campion points to the recurrence of a form of this antithesis in the New Testament in Matthew 5:38, which "Christians have tended to hear...as an exhortation to be quick to waive lawful rights out of love even for an erring neighbor. Along with it, however, they have recalled St. Paul's defense of civil authority (Romans 13:4)." At this point he jumps ahead to 1955 where he finds much the same dialectic in an address of Pope Pius XII: the competence of the state to punish, but the priority of remediation over retribution as the higher goal of punishment. The latter point is straight from Aquinas, and Campion remarks about him that "while upholding capital punishment in principle on grounds of retribution, social defense, and deterrence, he sounded an interestingly modern note by the priority he gave to rehabilitation as a penal aim."

The final part of Campion's article discusses modern challenges to capital punishment. If Willis gave the impression in his work that, as a Catholic layman informed in the legal field, he admired some of the contributions of Beccaria, Campion left nothing to guesswork. He paid genuine tribute to Beccaria as the one who opened the modern debate:

> On the basis of his own theory of society, he rejected the state's right to take a citizen's life. Far more influential, however, was his critique of the death penalty as cruel, unreasonable, and ineffective....He merits the title of father of modern penal reform.

It is an admirable instance of historical-critical judgment, distinguishing the wheat from the chaff. You do not have to accept Beccaria's questionable political philosophy in order to give credit where credit is due.

Campion went on to review some of the reform movement's achievements, then openly acknowledged that

> relatively few Roman Catholics in the U.S. or elsewhere have been active in these debates. When Catholic theologians have dealt with the topic, they have tended to repeat affirmations of the state's competence to inflict death as a penalty....It should be noted, however, that Pius XII, in his extensive statements on crime and punishment, never explicitly defended or denied the state's right to impose the death sentence, even while he defended its right to have a retributive intention in its penal administration.
>
> Any further Catholic thought on the topic will undoubtedly reflect a new emphasis on the notion of the inalienable rights of the human person as set forth in recent authoritative documents such as John XXIII's *Pacem in Terris*. It may also reveal reliance on a dynamic conception of natural law and of the nature of man and society that has been manifested in the deliberations on the Church in the modern world by Vatican Council II. At that point, the state of the question may come to embrace not merely the relative effectiveness or social necessity of capital punishment, but also the basic right of the state to employ it as a matter of normal social policy.[44]

That is exactly what happened in the next quarter-century.

B. A National Moratorium on State Executions (1967)

In the 1960s the convictions of a growing number of defendants in capital cases were being appealed to the federal courts on challenges to the constitutionality of state capital laws. Lawyers from the Legal Defense and Educational Fund (LDF), founded by the NAACP, and from the ACLU assisted in these filings, and by 1967 several key cases had gone as far as the U.S. Supreme Court and were awaiting action. As a result, an unofficial moratorium began that year after two executions: that of Aaron Mitchell by California on April 12, 1967, and that of Luis José Monge by Colorado on June 2, 1967.[45] The appealed cases that were piling up for Supreme Court review were seeking to challenge the death penalty as a form of "cruel and unusual punishment" in violation of the eighth and fourteenth amendments to the Constitution, and played an important role in focusing national attention on that claim.

VI. THE NATIONAL COUNCIL OF CHURCHES OF CHRIST, U.S.A.'S REJECTION OF THE DEATH PENALTY(1968)

Vatican II had had as one of its major goals the improvement of relations with other Christian churches. American efforts were still at a very early stage when the largest ecumenical organization in the country unanimously adopted a statement calling for abolition of the death penalty. This inevitably drew greater attention to the question, promoting a livelier conversation about capital punishment than American Catholics had ever been involved in before. In the national debate provoked by the moratorium, a significant number of member churches had already spoken out on their own when the National Council adopted a joint statement by a vote of 103 church bodies in favor of the document and none opposed.

The statement gave ten reasons for opposing the death penalty, and standing at the head of the list was:

1. Belief in the worth of human life and the dignity of human personality as gifts of God.[46]

The language and emphasis could have come straight from Pope John XXIII's encyclical *Pacem in Terris* of five years earlier. There were more than adequate grounds for ecumenical harmony at this point, even though no formal Catholic statements about capital punishment were yet in circulation. The principles were there, begging to be applied. It was only a matter of time.

The rest of the statement, as with most such group documents, reflected the varied interests and emphases of different member churches, some simply compromises, some more persuasive than others.

  2. A preference for rehabilitation rather than retribution in
     the treatment of offenders.

The tension between these two classical purposes of punishment
is proverbial, and it is obvious that the death penalty serves only
the latter while making nonsense of the former. The fact that
Karl Menninger's *The Crime of Punishment,* calling for reform in
the basic psychology of our penal system, was receiving much
public attention at the time may have been a factor.[47]
  The remaining reasons for opposing capital punishment
were the following:

  3. Reluctance to assume the responsibility of arbitrarily ter-
     minating the life of a fellow-being solely because there
     has been a transgression of law;
  4. Serious question whether the death penalty serves as a
     deterrent to crime...;
  5. The conviction that institutionalized disregard for the
     sanctity of human life contributes to the brutalization of
     society;
  6. The possibility of errors in judgment and the irreversibil-
     ity of the penalty which make impossible any restitution
     to one who has been wrongfully executed;
  7. Evidence that economically poor defendants, particu-
     larly members of racial minorities, are more likely to be
     executed than others because they cannot afford exhaus-
     tive legal defenses;
  8. The belief that not only the severity of the penalty but also
     its increasing infrequency and the ordinarily long delay
     between sentence and execution subject the condemned
     person to cruel, unnecessary and unusual punishment;
  9. The belief that the protection of society is served as well
     by measures of restraint and rehabilitation, and that soci-
     ety may actually benefit from the contribution of the
     rehabilitated offender;
  10. Our Christian commitment to seek the redemption and
     reconciliation of the wrong-doer, which are frustrated by
     his execution.

The first, the seventh, and the last of the ten reasons are probably the most telling from a Christian or strictly religious perspective; the fifth and the eighth are parallel to concerns of Beccaria; the fourth, the sixth, and the ninth derive especially from modern social-science studies. Gathered together with no further commentary, they are something of a hodge-podge but certainly make a cumulative case that provides much food for thought. As a period piece the most striking feature of the statement, in contrast to nineteenth-century Protestant American utterances about capital punishment (whether pro or con), is the fact that the Bible as such is not invoked as the basis for the position taken. Some of the reasons for this are obvious, but it may also be a factor in explaining why the statement never did get very broad exposure.[48]

CHAPTER 9

The U.S. Bishops' Turnaround

337

Due to the national moratorium on executions, the question of the death penalty seemed less pressing as the decade of the 1970s started than it otherwise might have. No state killings were actually taking place, but death sentences were still being meted out in courtrooms, resulting in foreboding increases of populations on death row. It was the lull before the storm, and many were busy doing their homework. The way chosen to record what happened in the next twenty-five years is to proceed annually, selecting the more memorable events, incidents, and statements. This crucial quarter-century in which the great metamorphosis of Catholic leadership occurs will be detailed in the next three chapters covering the periods 1971–1983, 1984–1990, and 1991–1996.

I. GETTING STARTED (1971)

Thirteen U.S. religious organizations (Protestant, Jewish, and Catholic) filed an *amicus* brief with the Supreme Court, urging that the death penalty be ruled unconstitutional. Reflecting the post–Vatican II ecumenical atmosphere, two of the thirteen groups were Catholic: the National Catholic Conference for Interracial Justice, and the National Coalition of American Nuns.

The USCC's Department of Social Development, prompted also by the crises occurring in U.S. prison systems (Attica, the Presidio, San Quentin, the Tombs, and so on), prepared a seven-page brief for the bishops, incorporating the impressive results of the Washington Research Project's study *The Case Against Capital Punishment.* The conclusion of the brief was that "it would seem clear that capital punishment cannot be justified and so should be abolished as a matter of Federal law."[1] The scene was thus set. The death penalty—moratorium or not—was a problem that would not go away. It demanded attention while the outcome in the courts was awaited.

II. HISTORIC FIRSTS (1972)

A. *Indiana's Bishops Step Forward*

The first group of Catholic bishops to issue a clear, public call for abolition of the death penalty in its state seems to have been that of Indiana. The opening lines of their statement were to become the regular refrain for the future:

> Human life is sacred. Each human being is unique, never to be repeated. Human life is precious. It is the height of God's physical creation. All the "things" in the world do not equal in value one human life....There is no greater loss than that a human life be destroyed, wasted, or ruined.[2]

This was a very different tone from the past. In fact, the next paragraph sounds as if it could be openly quarreling with the 1566 *Roman Catechism*'s defense of the death penalty:

> God has told us quite clearly that it is sinful to kill. The force of this commandment, however, is blunted by all of these so-called legitimate exceptions. Society seems to say that this divine command...can be ignored for so many "valid," mitigating reasons.

The bishops make it clear, however, that they are not out to condemn the past but are simply trying to respond to "a growing realization of the sacredness of life," which requires "men of religious conviction and principle...to raise their voices continuously in defense of life. They must question every taking of life. They must see that life is not taken lightly or thought of as cheap. Any needless, purposeless taking of human life is an affront and threat to all of life."

B. *Furman v. Georgia*

In this historic case the U.S. Supreme Court ruled five to four that, as it was being administered by many states, the death penalty was unconstitutional, a "cruel and unusual" form of punishment violating the eighth and fourteenth amendments. For a time many thought that the nation might be on the verge of abolishing the death penalty, as so many other nations of the Western world had done or were doing. But, "the disarray in the opinions of the (Supreme Court) majority and the political opposition to the Court's ruling that quickly spread across the land sowed ample seeds of discontent."[3]

It has been said that "*Furman* will stand in American legal history as one of the most peculiar decisions for both what it did and what it refrained from doing. It did not resolve the basic problem of validity of capital punishment; the issue was, in 1972, too dubious and controversial. Instead, by answering a narrower question it banned the death penalty as applied in the cases at hand."[4] It was the first time the Supreme Court had ever heard arguments on the validity of the death penalty as such, and the result was that nine separate opinions were submitted, clustered in three categories: abolitionist (Marshall and Brennan); strict constructionist (Blackmun, Burger, Powell, and Rehnquist), and neutral (Douglas, Stewart, and White). Another point of interest about the decision which was widely commented upon was the breakdown of the 5-4 vote. Those in the majority all had served under chief justice Earl Warren; the dissenting minority was made up of the four Nixon appointees.[5]

Some hard decisions faced the bishops, especially some of the older and more conservative ones who had long been defending the death penalty automatically in the uncritical Tridentine fashion routinely taught in seminary manuals. Early statements of opposition were often timid, as past support was replaced by various degrees of objection based on a variety of new elements. Besides the new application of the old principle ("unnecessary therefore immoral"), other arguments now in circulation and new factors affecting the discussion caused confusion and uncertainty.

1. The new emphasis on the inalienable nature of human rights and respect for human dignity seemed to collide with the less humane record of the past.

2. It seemed increasingly inconsistent to oppose the deliberate destruction of human life in abortion and euthanasia while actually advocating the deliberate destruction of human life in capital punishment.

3. The growing number of empirical studies were finding little if any validity in traditional deterrence claims; did not these increasing doubts as to whether capital punishment actually did what was claimed for centuries mean that a doubtful conscience had been created, and that it should therefore (according to traditional principles) be resolved in favor of life, not death?

4. The undeniable arbitrariness and bias against the poor in the selection of U.S. victims had to trouble anyone with a conscience. In other ages one might have ignored this aspect, but how could that still be the case in a time when all were being newly reminded of the church's "option for the poor"?

5. The extreme difficulty in rationally justifying the deliberate killing of a human person as an action that served any of the legitimate purposes of punishment demanded attention. In this age of greater psychological sophistication could one be sure that the real but latent motive of capital punishment was not something else, such as revenge?

This surprising new complex of problems surrounding capital punishment had to be dealt with. Serious Christian "shepherds" had a responsibility to work out practical and realistic pastoral positions to advise conscientious believers how they might respond to such a growing challenge in a divided society.[6]

The five bishops of Florida issued an early statement expressing "our hope that the time is not far distant when capital punishment will be abolished altogether." But, sensing that this was not in the cards for the near future, they went on to call for:

> adequate workable safeguards...to forestall the injustices (of the past). The redemptive and rehabilitative aspects of punishment should more insistently be stressed rather than its retributive aspect. Life should be taken only in extreme necessity.[7]

The influence of Vatican II was evident. There was no sign of the old insistence on defending first and foremost the right of the state to kill. But there was still hesitancy to go further.

Bishop Joseph Green of Reno, in testimony before the Nevada legislature, urged that "alternatives" to capital punishment be considered: "We have only slowly and painfully come to see that the issue of life's value and dignity is on a moral continuum. We must not only oppose the killing of the innocent....Our belief that God alone gives and sustains life suggests that he alone properly takes it."[8] The message varied in strength but was increasing in frequency, repeated by more and more bishops as they appropriated the "new attitude" called for.

III. NEW CHALLENGERS (1973)

A. Bishop Joseph Durick

In February Bishop Durick of Nashville took the initiative to write an unusual pastoral letter on prison reform and pastoral priorities entitled "Humanity Demands It."[9] The second half was given over to the problem of capital punishment and spoke against it in more decisive terms than were as yet common among American bishops. Durick compiled supportive quotations from a broad group as he went along—Karl Menninger, Ramsey Clark, Clarence Darrow, the Catholic Bishops of Canada, Protestant theologian Charles Milligan, and Jewish theologian Israel Kazis. In this company he marched to the conclusion that "the argument that the death penalty deters crime is of strong question. The theological arguments in its behalf are weak. Let us treasure life, not gamble with it. I would earnestly ask that the death penalty not be renewed in Tennessee."

Two years later, when Durick resigned as bishop of Nashville to go into prison ministry full-time, he made it clear that his opposition to the death penalty was largely inspired by his unforgettable experience of Vatican II.

> The last thing that Paul VI said to the bishops of the world on the last day of the council was this: Go out into the world and make every effort possible in every way to restore the dignity of man and all that it implies! I stand foursquare with modern theologians who hold that...capital punishment does not fit into the greater contemporary theological awareness of the worth of each individual on earth.[10]

B. *Congressman Robert Drinan, S.J.*

The open acknowledgment that things were in considerable flux was soon illustrated on another level. On March 14, 1973, Fr. Robert F. Drinan, S.J., backed by twenty-six other congressmen, introduced federal legislation to abolish the U.S. death penalty outright. His speech on the House floor was a powerful call for abolition, giving a lengthy list of objections to capital punishment. He concluded by saying:

> in my view the taking of a human life is morally unacceptable; capital punishment does not serve as a corrective measure....It is not a deterrent to crimes....It is a violation of due process because there are no standards to guide judge or jury....It allows discrimination by race and class....It violates the mark of a civilized society because it contradicts the ideal of human dignity....It is cruel and excessive and irrevocable punishment.[11]

This overwhelming repudiation of the death penalty in principle and in practice was indeed relatively new in most Catholic circles. It was not what most had been raised on, and, for that very reason, many still had serious reservations about some of the arguments and deep uncertainty about so complete a tranformation of position. The special problem for many was not knowing what to do about the "tradition" question. Bossuet's old rhetoric about the immutability of orthodoxy and the suspicion of heresy attached to every change were still the norm for many.

C. *Canadian Catholics Step Softly*

Five "guidelines for discussion" of the question of capital punishment were issued in the debate in Canada, but the bishops "stopped just short of taking a clear anti-capital-punishment stance."[12] They knew there was continuing disarray in the ranks, so they called for further study. But in doing so, three elements in their guidelines clearly revealed how much things had changed already and what might be expected in the near future:

1. We consider it an illegitimate use of the Bible...to quote texts in order to argue, in our time, for the retention of the death penalty.
2. To a Christian, whose starting point is reverence for the sanctity of life, the death penalty can surely be only a desperate resort. A Christian must be utterly convinced of its social necessity before supporting it.
3. Our question is not whether the death penalty is an effective deterrent; our question is whether it is an absolutely necessary deterrent.[13]

A broad consensus was emerging on the impropriety of capital punishment and thus the advisability of its abolition, but that practical conclusion was being arrived at by people coming from different directions, basing their opposition on different grounds. There was confusion and disagreement enough that any kind of guidance and clarification would be seen as especially timely and appreciated.

IV. CONTROVERSY AT THE U.S. BISHOPS' MEETING (1974)

Such was the climate and setting when events led the U.S. bishops to confront the issue in 1974. Bishop James Rausch as General Secretary of the NCCB/USCC initiated the request for a preliminary document. He asked Msgr. Harrold A. Murray to have his department take on the project, and Murray in turn asked Mr. John Cosgrove to coordinate the effort. Cosgrove contacted the president of the Catholic Theological Society, Fr. Richard McBrien, and asked him to suggest three men in the Washington area whose guidance might be helpful. He received the names of Fr. J. Bryan Hehir, Fr. Richard McCormick, S.J., and Fr. Charles Curran.[14] The three clerics met with Cosgrove on May 8, and came up with the recommendation that lay philosopher-theologian Dr. Germain Grisez, who was already on record as opposed to capital punishment,[15] be asked to prepare a background study for the use of the bishops' subcommittee. Dr. Grisez, who was already committed to teach at the University of Saskatchewan that summer, accepted the task nonetheless.

THE DEATH PENALTY

A. *Bishop Unterkoefler's Subcommittee*

Bishop Ernest Unterkoefler of Charleston, South Carolina, as chairman of the subcommittee on Social Development and World Peace, was the one responsible for coming up with a proposed statement on capital punishment for the bishops to consider endorsing. In a mid-June exchange of letters he agreed with Grisez that the bishops "cannot come out flatly against a seeming tradition to condemn capital punishment."[16] He went on to suggest that, with Pius XII's 1955 allocution and John XXIII's *Pacem in Terris*, "I sense that foundations can be found for the development of Catholic teaching against the exercise of the right of the State to administer capital punishment."

Grisez completed and sent back from Canada a fifty-one-page paper on July 10 for the subcommittee's use, suggesting that Russell Shaw might be enlisted to draft a shorter version based on this longer one. Cosgrove, in a July 16 memo to Bishop Rausch, reported that Grisez's draft had been received and forwarded to Bishop Unterkoefler and his subcommittee, and that they would all be meeting in his office on July 23 to take action. That meeting of the subcommittee resulted in a seven-page document, which was forwarded to the Administrative Board.

At the Administrative Board meeting in September, Bishop John Dougherty summarized the background of the document and recommended that it be submitted to the bishops for adoption in November. Bishop Daley asked whether it was wise to make a statement on capital punishment when the teaching of the church on the matter was not clear and such a document might thus cause confusion in the minds of some Catholics. Bishop Dougherty responded by suggesting that, if seen in the broader context of the church's concern for life in every form and at every moment, such a document would be a significant help in the formation of Catholic consciences on the value of life.

Bishop Rausch observed that Catholic conferences in several states had already asked for guidance on the question when the matter came up in their respective legislatures. So he moved that the statement be distributed for *modi* from the bishops and be included on the agenda for consideration at the general meeting. He noted that, even if rejected, it would provide the opportunity for valuable discussion among the bishops. His motion carried and several *modi* were received in the following weeks, leading to some minor revisions. The statement, as revised, was then distributed to all the bishops.

At the November Adminstrative Board meeting right before the general meeting, Bishop Dougherty noted that several states had recently reintroduced capital punishment and others were considering doing the same, so it seemed an especially appropriate time for the bishops to discuss the issue. Cardinal Krol expressed concern over parts of the draft that he had found "contradictory and unclear." Bishop Dougherty's motion to put it before the general meeting for action, seconded by Bishop O'Keefe, carried nonetheless.

In moving the statement for adoption at the general meeting, Bishop Dougherty stressed that "the purpose of the statement is to enhance human dignity and to promote social justice." Bishop Unterkoefler seconded the motion and was asked to lead the discussion. He emphasized that it was appropriate for the bishops to give leadership on this issue, noting that the two foundations of the statement were the sacredness of human life and the quality of human dignity. He said the committee was recommending the policy of *non-use* of the death penalty at the present time, without getting into the question of the right of the state to impose the death penalty.

Bishop Joseph McDevitt rose to oppose the statement, pointing to several alleged inconsistencies in the text. He thought the bishops might weaken their influence by taking a stand on such a "moot question." In response to an inquiry from Archbishop Whealon, Unterkoefler pointed to a number of conditions present in contemporary American society that called for just such a statement: "a growing disrespect for life...a tendency to have retribution through violence," and the possibility of rehabilitation, even for murderers, as had been the case with the murderer of St. Maria Goretti.

Cardinal Carberry expressed concern over whether the acceptance of the document implied rejection of the teaching of the church regarding the limited right of the state to take life. He referred to a study published by Columbia University, which supposedly showed a sharp increase in the number of murders since the moratorium on capital punishment, and he questioned the statement's use of two quotations from *Gaudium et Spes*. Bishop Unterkoefler countered that the latter were not being used as proof-texts but as generally supportive; he also cited his personal, first-hand experiences of the inhumanity of executions, several of which he had attended when stationed in Virginia.

Bishop Walter Sullivan of Richmond then spoke in favor of the statement, recounting his experience on a Virginia study commission where most of those initially favoring the death penalty, after several days of evidence, ended up convinced that it should not be restored. He asked whether the motive of capital punishment was not in reality the desire for vengeance or retaliation, and if these can ever be consistent with the gospel. Bishops Roach, Evans, Durick, and Howze all spoke in favor, while Bishop Fearns expressed reservations about the way the scriptures were used in the draft and suggested that further study was called for. Bishop Grutka, who had headed the commission on prison reform the previous year, spoke in favor of the statement, observing that he had never met a prison chaplain or a professional corrections officer who thought capital punishment was an appropriate solution.

Cardinal Krol, while not saying explicitly if he was for or against the statement, asked whether its language could not be sharpened, whether its allegation of discriminatory application was sufficiently compelling, whether there was sufficient evidence to say that it was not being applied even-handedly, and whether it was sufficiently clear that the *right* of the state was not being denied but merely the *opportuneness* of using capital punishment today. Bishop Unterkoefler thereupon closed the discussion, saying that notes had been taken on the objections and a revision would be made to incorporate what they could from the suggestions presented.

Unterkoefler returned the next day with a revised version, but the criticisms continued. Bishop Weldon wanted more concern expressed for the victims and their families; Bishop McFarland did not find the draft's stated rationale "compelling"; Bishop Begin strongly opposed its adoption, saying that "the Church has guaranteed the right and obligation of the state to protect its people," and he doubted that the people would ever accept such a document from the bishops.

Bishop Dozier thereupon spoke strongly in support of the document, and Bishop Grutka said that the bishops "should have a position which is pro-life in every respect" and should thus advocate alternatives to capital punishment.

Cardinal Krol expressed an additional concern that the statement did not do justice to the legitimate vindictive aspect of punishment. Then, when he finally called for a vote on the document, it received "the distinction of being the only statement ever formally defeated by the assembly." It was rejected, 119 to 103 (with 3 abstentions).[17]

By way of substitution Bishop John May of Mobile, Alabama, put forward a brief resolution, saying simply:

> The United States Catholic Conference goes on record as opposed to capital punishment.

But Cardinal Carberry objected and moved to table the resolution. His motion carried. The next day, however, Bishop Dougherty requested Bishop May to repeat his motion, and Bishop Durick seconded it. A written vote was then called for and the outcome showed 108 in favor and 63 opposed. "At first Cardinal Krol ruled that a resolution also needed a two-thirds vote, but Bishop May said he offered a simple motion which needed only a majority vote."[18]

Because of all the squabbling and confusion, ending in a less than ringing endorsement of even a simple motion of opposition, the stage was not exactly set for an energetic national reeducation campaign anytime soon. In fact,

> because it was accepted by a simple (rather than a two-thirds) majority, some of the dissenting bishops later publicly disagreed about its standing. They felt it was not a binding opinion of the American church.[19]

It was clear that in late 1974, while a majority of the U.S. Catholic bishops were opposed to reinstating the death penalty (which at that time had not been used in the nation for seven years), there was still a vocal minority wedded to the Tridentine rather than the Vatican II outlook. On the other hand, because the majority had not reached consensus on the *reasons* for their opposition, those supporting capital punishment were able to take advantage of the disarray and contend that nothing had really changed. The old tradition of defending the death penalty was still in place. Further questions needed to be answered by those opposed before a real change could be made. Was capital punishment to be condemned as wrong in practice, wrong in principle, or both? The rejected draft had acknowledged the need for further serious study, and twice it quoted from *Gaudium et Spes* (27 and 50) to "indicate the spirit according to which we must weigh the issue."[20] There was still heavy work to be done, but there was also qualified help on hand.

V. THE "BICENTENNIAL BIFURCATION" (1976)

In February 1976 the religious leaders representing most of the major denominations in the state of Rhode Island spoke out against executions:

> It is no longer an adequate and justifiable way of dealing with the problem of serious crime in our midst....The belief that the person has an inalienable dignity demands our affirmation that the imposition of the death penalty is unwarranted within our present capabilities and in our present circumstances.[21]

Among the signers of the statement was Bishop Louis Gelineau of Providence.

Around the same time Bishop Bernard Flanagan of Worcester, Massachusetts, objected to the proposed legislation to make the death penalty mandatory for certain crimes. He called it

> a brutal—some would even describe it as barbaric—form of punishment which would be counterproductive to the church's crusade for the sanctity of life...and is completely out of accord with modern developments of the penal system with its emphasis on the reform and rehabilitation of the criminal.[22]

But then came the mid-year surprise.

A. *Gregg v. Georgia*

On July 2, 1976, two days before the celebration of the U.S. bicentennial, the Supreme Court upheld seven to two the constitutionality of capital-punishment statutes formulated along the lines of those of Georgia, Texas, and Florida. The votes of Justices Stevens, Stewart, and Powell "swung the Court in favor of guided discretion" by which they felt the arbitrariness issue that had been so central in *Furman* "had dissipated considerably."[23] Justices White, Burger, Rehnquist, and Blackmun concurred, leaving only Brennan and Marshall to dissent. The latter, besides challenging the majority's contention that executions served any legitimate governmental end, criticized them for relying on the 1975 study of Isaac Ehrlich, a highly controversial, not to say idiosyncratic, "econometric" calculation of deterrence, which Justice Marshall found to be "of little, if any, assistance in assessing the impact of the death penalty."[24] But for some unapparent reason Justice Stewart saw fit to rely on it in his lead opinion, and it was in fact the only empirical study he cited in support of his statement that, in regard to the deterrent effect of the death penalty, "the results simply have been inconclusive."

In the interim Ehrlich's results have been judged to be so flawed as to "deserve no place in the debate on capital punishment."[25] The striking difference between *Furman v. Georgia* in 1972 and *Gregg v. Georgia* in 1976 was the way in which the latter aligned with the public opinion polls. "We have been told that the justices of the Supreme Court, like the rest of us, read the headlines; but it is rare for the Court to trot them out so blatantly as it did here. I fail to see a single defensible principle of punishment or of constitutional interpretation underlying the *Gregg* plurality's use of the data it cited....Only a little imagination is required to guess what a comparably cautious, not to say timid, Court would have ruled twenty years earlier in *Brown v. Board of Education*."[26]

This decision, in retrospect, can be viewed as a major parting of the ways. From this time forward the majority of the U.S. Supreme Court justices and the majority of the U.S. Catholic bishops were at loggerheads. The reinstatement of the death penalty enjoyed wide approval in the public opinion polls, but it collided squarely with the enhanced, Vatican II-inspired vision of human dignity. The two bodies were functioning on very different levels. Whatever the Court's technical conclusion on the constitutionality of capital punishment, the bishops' firm judgment was that any further use of it would be morally indefensible in the penal system of a modern state on a variety of grounds. "The Court rejected the view that evolving standards of decency now condemn the death penalty."[27] But their rejection seemed to be more a case of not wanting to accept those standards, which were certainly perceived as there and being accepted by more and more nations as the required criteria for a modern civilized society. It was especially troublesome that the morality issue seemed to be left completely out of the picture because the focus was so narrowly on the legal.

The Catholic Bishops Conferences of Florida, Indiana, Nevada, and Tennessee lost no time in expressing their disapproval, issuing statements unequivocally opposing the reintroduction of the death penalty. Similar significant statements of opposition from individual bishops and other state conferences multiplied impressively as the painful process of "contested accommodation" went on in the conscientious attempt to resolve this crucial question.[28]

B. Canada Abolishes Capital Punishment

Ironically, two weeks after the Supreme Court cleared the way for the United States to resume executions, the Canadian Parliament moved in the opposite direction, the latest nation to accept the evolving standards by abolishing capital punishment. In analyzing why, there was no doubt that "the position of the Canadian bishops was a contributing factor....There was (also) a strong call for abolition from other religious communities in Canada." Two months before the vote, Bishop Emmett Carter, president of the Canadian Catholic Conference, had addressed a parliamentary panel on the subject in both English and French, asserting that abolition was "the better alternative." The Conference had already declared that capital punishment is acceptable only in a society which is not yet sufficiently well established to defend itself in any other way against those elements which would put in jeopardy the life of its citizens; this last is clearly not the case in Canada....The spirit of the Gospel directs us toward forgiveness, clemency, and reconciliation.[29]

A fascinating parallel to the Canadian Catholic experience was that of the Presbyterian Church. Mary Templer reviewed the process in her thesis, tracing the highlights thus: "In 1954 the Presbyterian Church in Canada stated that it was in favor of capital punishment. The church drew up a statement...which was adopted by the 80th General Assembly." This held sway until 1976, when developments led it to "a complete reversal of its position" as a result of three basic changes that gradually made their impact: (1) a new understanding of "how Scripture is to be used," (2) a new understanding of what the principle of justice demands, and (3) a concern about the collapse of the previously central deterrence theory which has been "disproved by every study that has been done."[30]

Templer found one negative result that was also paralleled in the United States Catholic experience:

There is indeed a problem with transferring information from the head office in Toronto to both ministers and lay people of local churches. This was indicated by the fact that only one in five ministers interviewed was familiar with the church's positions on capital punishment...and none of the lay people interviewed were familiar with them.

How to close the gap in Christian education was a monumental problem, since so many people seemed to assume that there was "nothing new" to be learned beyond what they had been told as children.

C. Portugal's Century of Abolition

Portugal had long given the lie to the claim that a state could not function without killing. In 1967 it celebrated the centennial of its abolition of the death penalty with an important worldwide conference. With the 1976 adoption of a new Constitution, the guarantee was written in and underlined in crystal-clear terms in two statements of Article 25: (1) "Human life is inviolable," and (2) "In no case will there be the penalty of death."[31]

D. A Pontifical Commission's Advice

After the 1974 controversy the U.S. bishops consulted the Pontifical Commission for Justice and Peace seeking advice for dealing with the impasse that had occurred over the document prepared by Bishop Unterkoefler's subcommittee. The Pontifical Response from Rome in 1976 helped to clarify the situation and solidify opposition to any continued use of the death penalty. This document probably swung the balance for many bishops who had hesitated over the question of the "orthodoxy" of the change.

One of the document's observations struck a chord (and used a word) that would soon be ringing at the center of the entire debate: "The U.S. bishops have spoken out and acted firmly in defense of life against abortion and euthanasia....There is an inner logic that would call Catholics, with their sense of the sacredness of life, to be *consistent* in this defense and extend it to the practice of capital punishment."[32] Those inclined to continue to support the death penalty were increasingly faced with the allegation of being inconsistent with respect to valuing human life.

The Pontifical Response also offered four points that well summarized the basic conclusions of the historical scholarship of the previous half-century:

1. "The Church has never directly addressed the question of the State's right to exercise the death penalty." This was in answer to extremists on the right who were contending that previous church support made retention of the death penalty a virtual Catholic dogma that could never be changed.

2. "The Church has never condemned its use by the State." This was in answer to an extreme position on the left, contending that the early church officially taught an absolute pacifist position. While there were some, perhaps many, individual early Christians who were pacifists, it is also clear that there were many who were not, and authoritative statements of

an institutional nature on the subject of the death penalty are lacking.

3. "The Church has condemned the denial of that right." This was obviously a reference to the profession of faith that Pope Innocent III required of Waldensians reconciled to the church in 1210. The fact that the statement had been included in Denzinger's handbook tended to provide it with an inflated significance. We have reviewed the host of uncertainties about it above. Without knowing for sure exactly what the Waldensian position was, one cannot read more into this brief statement than its prima facie meaning. The fairest way to treat it is to balance it with the first statement.

4. "Recent popes have stressed the rights of the person and the medicinal role of punishment." This could be viewed as the most important statement in the Response. It pointed to the undeniable developments, at least since *Pacem in Terris,* giving a priority to personalist thought that is ultimately incompatible with the outright endorsement of capital punishment in modern circumstances. Faithfulness to the gospel requires the elimination of past distortions once they are exposed as such. When these two factors—the rights of the human person and the proper role of human punishment—are placed at the center of the discussion, defense of the morality of the death penalty today becomes problematic in the extreme.

At the Bicentennial Call to Action Conference in Detroit in October 1976 abolition of the death penalty was explicitly advocated in two of the eight documents adopted.[33] Then, on December 27, Cardinal William Baum of Washington, D.C., took the occasion of the Christmas season to call attention to the Pontifical Response, with its accent on the value of human life, and to express his own conviction in the shadow of the national halls of power—the Supreme Court and the Congress—that "contemporary attempts to restore capital punishment represent a setback in the growing moral awareness of humanity concerning the God-given gift of life."[34] It was not a good year for those who prefer clergy to be held firmly in cultural captivity.

VI. THE UNITED STATES RESUMES EXECUTIONS (1977)

On January 17, 1977, a firing squad in Utah complied with convict Gary Gilmore's request to be killed, thus putting an end to the ten-year moratorium on executions and firing the shots that signaled the official return of the United States to the practice of capital punishment.

A. *Reactions to the Gilmore Execution*

Three different Catholic reactions appeared in the press, symbolic of the complex and shifting scene in post–Vatican II Catholicism: (1) the total rejection of capital punishment as immoral on principle; (2) the continued traditional defense of the state's right to use it, with no objection to the way it was being used, and (3) rejection of the exercise of that right on the grounds of new insights and changed conditions.

1. The week after Gilmore's execution *L'Osservatore Romano* carried an article by the Italian Franciscan theologian Gino Concetti with the headline: "Can the Death Penalty Still Be Considered Legitimate?" It was a strongly worded statement of a pacifist position not much heard in Rome in earlier days. Concetti made it clear that he was only speaking for himself, but his statement caught wide public attention, especially because of where it appeared. In the article Concetti asserted that

> in light of the word of God, and thus of faith, life—all human life—is sacred and untouchable. No matter how heinous the crimes...the criminal does not lose his fundamental right to life, for it is primordial, inviolable and inalienable, and thus comes under the power of no one whatsoever. If this right is so absolute, it is because of the image which, at creation, God impressed on human nature itself. No force, no violence, no passion can remove or destroy it. In virtue of this divine image, every human is a person with dignity and rights.[35]

2. An article by Francis J. Furey, archbishop of San Antonio, Texas, appeared in his diocesan newspaper, *Today's Catholic*. In it he expressed his approval of what the state of Utah had done. He insisted that to say that capital punishment did not deter crime

was "a lot of hogwash" and that the church had no position on this question anyway.

> It is a divisive issue....There are arguments on both sides. However, to say that the U.S. hierarchy, as such, is opposed to capital punishment is just a plain lie....The church has always supported the right of the state to impose the death penalty in order to protect itself and its citizens. The question is when and in what manner this right should be used. In the humble opinion of this writer, the when is NOW and the manner depends on circumstances. I am thoroughly convinced that people who commit heinous crimes, such as brutal murder, and other crimes against society, should be made to pay with their most precious possession, their life. Only in this way can the punishment be made to fit the crime.[36]

Furey's statement was, in a sense, the swan song of the "old school." Unaffected by Vatican II, it held tenaciously to the so-called traditional position and found Concetti's pacifism so utterly bewildering that there was virtually no room for dialogue. The two views clashed so totally that neither side seemed able to understand how the other could be taken seriously as an orthodox position of Catholic Christians. It seemed like a controversy between inhabitants of different planets.

Such polarization often renders debate impossible, since the opponents do not have enough in common to say anything constructive to one another. But in this instance, a third position was calling for expression, one that was neither pacifist nor traditionalist. It had found the support of the majority of the U.S. bishops in 1974.

3. Joseph Bernardin, archbishop of Cincinnati and president of the NCCB/USCC, issued a statement saying, in part, that

> a return to the use of capital punishment can only lead to further erosion of respect for life and to the increased brutalization of our society....I do not challenge society's right to punish the capital offender, but I would ask all to examine the question of whether there are other and better approaches to protecting our people from violent crimes than resorting to execution. The more pertinent question is:

what course of action best fosters *respect for life,* all human life, in a society such as ours in which such respect is sadly lacking? In my view, more destruction of human life is not what America needs in 1977.[37]

In a memo communicating with the Executive Committee of the NCCB/USCC before releasing this statement, Bernardin reported that "pressure has been put on me to say something... and, in particular, the Conference's position on the subject....My statement is based on the (1974) resolution....I hope you will be satisfied with my handling of this matter."

In the same week Bishop Ernest Unterkoefler appeared before the judiciary committee of the South Carolina legislature to testify against the proposed state legislation reinstating the death penalty. Initially scheduled to be held before Gilmore's execution, his appearance had been postponed and actually took place on January 26. In his testimony Unterkoefler noted that he had served for three years as a chaplain at the State Penitentiary in Virginia, and during that time "walked the last mile to the electric chair with six men, one of whom I know was innocent." This was but one of his many reasons for opposing the death penalty. Others included the fact that "taking the criminal's life does not bring back the victim's life....It is doubtful that it deters....It is inhumane....It involves the body politic in the same type of action as the criminal....It totally violates the imperative of the Judeo-Christian tradition of forgiveness, mercy, and charity to the repentant sinner."

The USCC Committee on Social Development and World Peace also spoke, putting out a statement called *Crime and Community.* A four-paragraph section on capital punishment recalled the bishops' 1974 resolution of opposition:

We continue to support this position, in the belief that a return to the use of the death penalty can only lead to the further erosion of respect for life in our society.

It went on to note that history shows that it has been used in a discriminatory way against the poor, that recent studies definitely continue to question its effectiveness as a deterrent, and that the legislative effort to introduce lethal injection as a supposedly humanitarian feature "merely seeks to conceal the reality of cruel and unusual punishment. We find this practice unacceptable."

Another practice was found unacceptable this same year by none other than the U.S. Supreme Court. As it allowed executions to be resumed, it excluded rape from the list of capital crimes in *Coker v. Georgia* (the only state in which it was still included). This removed one of the most emotional and symbolic issues from the debate. The court acknowledged that death was a "grossly disproportionate and excessive" punishment for rape.[38]

B. *Amnesty International Adopts the Stockholm Declaration*

Another essential part of the story of 1977 took place in Sweden. A flurry of worldwide activity occurred as it became clear that the United States was not bluffing. Utah was only the first to break the moratorium and open the "bloodgates," despite the contrary movement in the civilized world. Six preparatory regional meetings were held in preparation for an unprecedented international gathering in December in Stockholm, where over two hundred delegates to the Amnesty International Conference on the Abolition of the Death Penalty opened a new chapter in the struggle by endorsing a declaration that called for "total and unconditional opposition to the death penalty" throughout the world and asked everyone for "commitment to work for (its) universal abolition."[39] The work of Amnesty International from this time on would guarantee that a nation's continued killings could no longer be merely internal affairs with no notice taken elsewhere. They would henceforth receive international scrutiny and analysis and be regularly monitored and reported to the world at large by observers who challenged the alibis and excuses that executing states were invoking.[40]

VII. "EVOLVING STANDARDS OF HUMAN DECENCY" (1978)

A. *Spain Abolishes Capital Punishment*

In 1978 an extraordinary change was welcomed around the world. Spain, in the preamble to its 1938 capital-punishment law, introduced by Generalissimo Francisco Franco, had stated that the death penalty required neither explanation nor justification because "it is reality itself which imposes it and prescribes it." In 1978 Spain abolished that "reality." It was only three years after the international furor over Franco's having five terrorists shot despite the strong pleas of Pope Paul VI and others for clemency. (Franco himself died only two months after the incident.) Alberto Iniesta, auxiliary bishop of Madrid and more outspoken than most, had let it be known that he had six objections to the death penalty: It is useless, it is immoral, it is unnecessary, it is pessimistic, it is unjust, and it is anti-Christian.[41] But he also lamented the fact that "the [Spanish] episcopate as a whole has not made its views known either way, either for or against the death penalty." Iniesta himself had introduced a proposal at the December 1977 meeting of the Spanish bishops, asking that they petition the suppression of the death penalty, but it was not accepted. The Franco legacy was still too strong. But the "evolving standard of decency" was sufficiently alive among other segments of Spanish society to free the law code of the death penalty without the bishops' help.

B. Denmark Abolishes Capital Punishment

The Danish Parliament, by a vote of 100 to 46, removed all remaining applications of the death penalty from the law books in March 1978. There had not been an execution since the last one for war crimes in 1950.

VIII. PROTESTING U.S. EXECUTIONS (1979)

A. Archbishop John Quinn

In April Archbishop John Quinn of San Francisco, acting as president of the NCCB, sent a telegram to the governor of Alabama asking for a grant of clemency shortly before the scheduled execution of John Louis Evans. Quinn expressed his conviction that "effective and humane alternatives can be developed without resorting to capital punishment....A return to the death penalty is not the right answer."[42]

B. *Florida's Bishops and John Spenkelink*

On May 25 the state of Florida electrocuted John Spenkelink, the first involuntary victim executed in the United States since 1967, and it seemed clear that the floodgates were being opened. Bishop René Gracida of Pensacola-Tallahassee issued a challenging letter outlining all the objections to capital punishment and urging Floridians "to call upon the governor to refrain from signing any more death warrants." Governor Robert Graham had already signed two more by the following month, when all seven of Florida's bishops joined in a public expression of their deep dismay, noting that "it is our hope and prayer that (as a nation) we will turn away from capital punishment."[43] The "Bicentennial Bifurcation" was beginning to look more like the Great Divide.

C. *Political Responsibility: Choices for the 1980's*

In October Nevada became the third state to resume executions by killing Jesse Bishop, who, like Gilmore, went to his death willingly.[44] That same month the Administrative Board of the USCC issued a twelve-page statement called *Political Responsibility: Choices for the 1980's,* which included a paragraph on capital punishment, reaffirming that

> we believe that there are better approaches to protecting our people from violent crimes than resorting to executions....Our society should reject the death penalty and seek methods of dealing with violent crime which are more consistent with the Gospel vision of respect for life and Christ's message of healing love.

At the November 1979 bishops' meeting, Bishop René Gracida made a formal request that the Committee on Social Development and World Peace be asked to prepare a new statement that would "clearly state our belief in the inappropriateness of capital punishment as an instrument of public policy in our time, and which would call for the abolition of capital punishment in our nation."[45] The five years since the previous draft statement had been rejected had brought dramatic changes to the national scene. The response to Gracida's request was to hold center stage at the bishops' next annual meeting in Washington.

IX. A YEAR OF INITIATIVES
VS. CAPITAL PUNISHMENT (1980)

A. Bishop Gracida in Brooklyn

Bishop Gracida had been doing a special study of capital punishment when he was invited to give a Lenten lecture in a series in the Cathedral-Basilica of St. James in Brooklyn, New York. His chosen topic was "Capital Punishment and the Sacredness of Life." In the course of the lecture he acknowledged that "I am indebted...to Professor Germain Grisez for much of this research into the penal code of ancient Israel." He also incorporated the points made by the Pontifical Commission in its 1976 Response and noted that

> certain Catholic thinkers...have argued that the use of the death penalty is itself a morally unjustifiable attack upon human life. That is my own position. I deny to political society any special dominion over life, and I maintain that the good end of just punishment cannot justify the bad means of killing a person.

Toward the end of his presentation he added a supplementary argument of a practical nature: In light of all the evidence of the "inability of our penal system and our judicial system to mete out punishment fairly and equitably, it seems to me that, if the death penalty cannot be imposed and executed fairly, then it should be abolished." He closed with an allusion to his experience in World War II, which had made him

> acutely aware not only of the Nazi Holocaust but also of the frightful cost in human lives that the Allied victory required....If we have learned anything we must surely have learned by now that all human life is sacred and worthy of defense, even the life of a convicted criminal. To execute criminals is to brutalize society and to render more easy the taking of human life in other circumstances. May the risen

Christ...encourage us to weigh seriously the challenge posed to us by the use of capital punishment as an instrument of public policy in these United States. May we join together to achieve its abolition.[46]

B. Georgia's Bishops Protest Killings

In June the two Catholic bishops of Georgia (Thomas Donnellan of Atlanta and Raymond Lessard of Savannah) and Episcopal Bishop Bennett Simms of Atlanta issued a joint statement three days before the scheduled execution of Jack Potts, recalling that "four years ago the restoration of the death penalty by the Supreme Court prompted a joint statement of opposition by us. Now, in the face of its looming actual use...we protest it in practice." They gave four principal reasons for their opposition:

> First is the holiness of human life....Second, we hold that the Christian purpose of punishment is reformatory and retributive, not vindictive. Vengeance is morally inadmissible on Christian grounds....Third, the violent taking of one human life to serve notice on other lives is decidedly cruel....Finally...we have made our way slowly toward more just and compassionate treatment of one another in the human family....The abolition of the death penalty seemed to us such a forward move. Its restoration is a backward step. Its actual use in our state demeans us all.[47]

It still did not seem possible that the states actually were going to follow through and set up in late twentieth-century America the anachronistic machinery of death that popular frustration over increasing crime was calling for.

Meanwhile, the bishops' subcommittee preparing the requested statement on capital punishment this time had more advance notice and thus actually had the draft completed by June with the help of Georgetown theologian Fr. John Langan, S.J. It had been distributed to the bishops in time for several *modi* to be received before it was taken up at the annual meeting. In one of them Archbishop Philip Hannan of New Orleans asked that the statement not exclude terrorists from execution, and, in another, Cardinal Krol noted that some of the arguments presented were actually criticisms of shortcomings in the practical application, not of the principle of capital punishment itself.

C. Six Bishops on Death Row in Texas

It was also in the month of June that six U.S. bishops took part in an unusual experience to gain better firsthand understanding of the increasing reality of capital punishment in this country. Frank Butler, a USCC staff member, was part of the group and later wrote a moving account of what transpired.[48] They visited the state prison at Riverside, Texas, and there met with not only the warden but several inmates awaiting execution on death row. Their emotion-wrenching experience as they conversed with and joined in prayer with men marked for death, several of whom were from poor Catholic families, highlighted one feature that was often to be noted in the ensuing debate: those churchmen who had had some firsthand experience with the ugly reality of these prisons, filled with fellow human beings treated as animals being readied for slaughter, had a far more pastoral response, judging any kind of support for such inhumanity to be incompatible with Christian ethics. Churchmen whose experiences had been more in the academic or abstract administrative realm were more likely to be the ones who had problems updating their theology. Seminary manuals had been concerned with perpetuating the ideology worked out in the polemical contexts of earlier centuries. The two different world views reflected made men of good will, who shared much in most other respects, incapable of understanding one another on the issue of capital punishment.

D. The Historic NCCB Meeting

A significantly different atmosphere had developed and a quite different document from the 1974 one lay before the bishops at the November 1980 meeting. Bishop Edward Head of Buffalo, New York, gave the document's background as he introduced it. He pointed out that it was meant "to provide a substantive rationale" for their earlier resolution, which had simply put them on record as opposed to capital punishment. He described the draft as making a prudential, pastoral judgment about the application of the death penalty in the current American context....This judgment is based, first of all, on positive Christian values such as the dignity of all human life, faith in God as the Lord of life, and Christian forgiveness....This document clearly does not reject the traditional Catholic view that the state has the right to take the life of a person guilty of a very serious crime. Granting this principle, however, the document asserts that capital punishment should not be imposed under the conditions of contemporary American society.[49]

The final point that Bishop Head made before turning to the statement itself was about

the great need for education of Catholics and of all Americans on this subject. Much more than a printed statement is needed...if we are to help the average Catholic work toward effective and humane ways to deal with the evils of serious crime. Our committee will ask the Office of Social Development to produce and distribute educational materials in the form of study guides and other resources to be used in our Catholic parishes and dioceses. We hope this will help to stimulate an effective implementation of the policy statement by promoting a serious reflection on capital punishment in the light of Christian values.[50]

In retrospect it is interesting to note this expression of awareness of the magnitude of the educational challenge ahead. It was not a challenge that was to be met very effectively for more years than they could have guessed at the time. In presenting the text Bishop Head also guided the process of submitting eleven proposed modifications and twelve amendments to the bishops for voice vote. The only proposed change his committee had not accepted was that of Archbishop Hannan, who wanted in effect to make an exception from the start and support the retention of capital punishment for "terrorists striving for the establishment of a regime that would disregard human rights." That amendment was now moved and seconded for consideration on the floor by the entire body of bishops, and when the call was made, it was solidly defeated by voice vote.

Bishop Gracida then rose to thank the committee for "the excellent pastoral statement" formulated in response to his request of a year earlier. "Events in our nation, and particularly in the southern states, during this past year have served to increase rather than diminish the need for the Conference to give the reasons for our stated opposition to the use of the death penalty." He mentioned that his request had been not his only, but that all the "bishops of Region IV voted unanimously to urge that (request)."

In recommending that his fellow bishops vote in favor of adopting the statement, Bishop Gracida showed his awareness of the division alluded to earlier and emphasized that the document was

> clearly a pastoral statement. It is not a doctrinal statement. It does not address in a formal way the fundamental question: Does the state have the right to deliberately take human life in the name of justice? It is proper that this statement not seek to answer that question since the magisterium of the Church has not formally addressed that question and has not provided us with a clear teaching on the subject. Yet the statement prepared by the Committee clearly acknowledges that the tradition of the Church has implicitly recognized the existence of the right of the state in this matter.[51]

Bishop Kinney spoke in favor of the statement, saying that while serious crime is a problem, "killing those who commit it is no solution." Bishop Rausch also spoke in favor, noting that "if the statement reminded people of the dignity of those guilty of capital crime, it might also be a reminder of the dignity of those imprisoned for lesser crimes."

There were, however, some who felt it necessary to argue further in support of the "traditional" position. The most dramatic intervention was that of Bishop Joseph Madera of Fresno, who told of the horrors wrought by a serial killer, some of whose victims he had personally known. He pointed out that "Christ accepted the right of Pontius Pilate to condemn him to death, and St. Thomas Aquinas taught that the common good should be preferred to the individual good."

Bishop Joseph Daley then announced that he was "ambivalent because of the question of innocent victims of crime" and said that he planned to abstain from the vote. A written ballot was then taken. When the results were tallied, Bishop Thomas Kelly reported that 217 votes had been cast, 145 of them in favor of the statement, 31 of them opposed, and 41 abstaining. One could find both good news and bad news in this outcome. It was a definite improvement in that a number of additional bishops had come to oppose capital punishment in the intervening span of six years (in 1974, 103 bishops voted against the first draft, then 63 opposed the simple motion replacing it, whereas now only 31 voted against the 1980 statement). On the other hand, because it was the most controversial vote ever taken, it did not bode well, especially for launching any kind of effective national reeducation campaign. It gave room for those who were so inclined to ignore the document once more, and Catholics who did not understand or were less than enthusiastic about the position taken could point to a handful of prelates who were looking the other way.

The statement opposing capital punishment has three major parts. In Part One, an overall judgment is made that "in the conditions of contemporary American society, the legitimate purposes of punishment do not justify the imposition of the death penalty. Furthermore, we believe that there are serious considerations which should prompt Christians and all Americans to support abolition of capital punishment."

Part Two describes "four Christian values that would especially be promoted by abolition": First, it would "send a message that we can break the cycle of violence, we need not take life for life." Second, it would manifest "our belief in the unique worth and dignity of each person from the moment of conception, a creature made in the image and likeness of God." Third, it would testify to our conviction that "God is indeed the Lord of life...(thus) removing a certain ambiguity which might otherwise affect the witness that we wish to give to the sanctity of human life in all its stages." Fourth, it is "more consonant with the example of Jesus."

Part Three singles out six difficulties inherent in the current practice of capital punishment in the United States:

1. It "extinguishes possibilities of reform and rehabilitation for the person executed as well as the opportunity for the criminal

to make some creative compensation for the evil he or she has done. It also cuts off the possibility for a new beginning and of moral growth in a human life which has been seriously deformed."

2. It "involves the possibility of mistake....Because death terminates the possibilities of conversion and growth and support that we can share with each other, we regard mistaken infliction of the death penalty with a special horror."

3. It "involves long and unavoidable delays."

4. It "brings with it great and avoidable anguish for the criminal, for his family and loved ones, and for those who are called on to perform or to witness the execution."

5. "In the present situation of dispute over the justifiability of the death penalty and at a time when executions have been rare, executions attract enormous publicity, much of it unhealthy, and stir considerable acrimony in public discussion."

6. "There is a widespread belief that many convicted criminals are sentenced to death in an unfair and discriminatory manner....It is a reasonable judgment that racist attitudes and the social consequences of racism have some influence in determining who is sentenced to die in our society. This we do not regard as acceptable."

The Conclusion acknowledges a number of complicating factors and the need for reforming a variety of policies connected with current practice, among them the following examples:

1. We do not propose the abolition of capital punishment as a simple solution to the problems of crime and violence....There is a special need to offer sympathy and support for the victims of violent crime and their families.

2. Important changes are necessary in the correctional system in order to make it truly conducive to reform and rehabilitation of convicted criminals and their reintegration into society.

3. We also grant that special precautions should be taken to ensure the safety of those who guard convicts who are too dangerous to return to society.

Due to the complexity of the problem of crime today, some sincere people support the death penalty. But the bishops set out to "urge them to review the considerations we have offered which show both the evils associated with capital punishment and the harmony of abolition with the values of the Gospel."[52]

The die was cast. After the adoption of the statement more and more bishops raised their voices in public opposition to the death penalty as its use was reintroduced in state after state. Former defenders of capital punishment among the bishops were either converted or remained silent about the issue, while public protests from the state conferences of bishops became both stronger and more frequent as the pace of the killings escalated.

X. CATHOLIC ANTI–DEATH PENALTY ACTIVITIES PROLIFERATE (1981)

A. *Voices at Home and Abroad*

A new organization called Law Enforcement Against Death (LEAD) arose early in the year to work for abolition of the death penalty. Patrick Murphy, former commissioner of the New York City Police Department, was among its leaders. He was at this time the president of the Police Foundation. His no-nonsense approach combined the best of both ethical and empirical arguments:

> The state should protect life, not take it. Even in consensual cases, with the offender expressing a desire to be put to death, the state should not assume the role of executioner. Unfortunately, the public doesn't understand the issue in depth. People read about a horrible crime and say the death penalty is a valid way of responding to it, because they feel frustrated and want a simple solution. But the death penalty applies to only a fraction of cases, and it would not be an effective deterrent in reducing crime to any significant degree. You frequently hear elderly people speak out in favor of it. This is because their level of fear is extremely high and so they tend to grasp at anything in the way of apparent solution. They and others don't perceive the abuses accompanying the death penalty—such as the fact that most condemned inmates are poor and members of minority groups. People with more education tend to have a greater awareness of the inequities. They realize that the

mobster who's able to afford a first-rate, highly paid lawyer is much less likely to be sentenced to death than a poor black who's given a court-appointed attorney.[53]

As the state of Indiana prepared to execute Steven Judy in early March, the archbishop of Indianapolis, Edward O'Meara, expressed his opposition:

> This will be Indiana's first legal execution since 1961....The resumption of executions in our own state does not seem to me to say the right thing about our respect for human life in general. There is no convincing positive proof that the taking of Judy's life will diminish the likelihood of such a horror happening again in our midst. Actually, the opposite could well be the case, for one violence usually creates another violence.[54]

Judy was electrocuted on March 9, and that same month the results of a Gallup Poll were published, showing two-thirds of Americans in favor of capital punishment for murder, the highest percentage in twenty-eight years.[55]

Also during March the Italian Bishops Conference responded to the popular call for reintroducing the death penalty for terrorists, especially after the assassination of former prime minister Aldo Moro. The bishops denounced the "culture of death" that was thriving in Italy as elsewhere, but insisted that the proper Christian response was to focus more than ever on the conversion called for by the gospel.

> Today the Church is called with new urgency to defend life....Man is a creature made in God's image. Even when that image is obscured by grave sin, it remains sacred....Evil is not conquered by evil, death is not overcome by another death. Victory is won only by the power and intelligence of love.[56]

The first year of the Reagan administration found the death penalty much in the news. In April, New York's Governor Hugh Carey vetoed legislation that would have reinstated the death penalty in the Empire State. Supreme Court Associate Justice William Rehnquist publicly criticized his colleagues for tolerating multiple appeals and long delays in cases involving capital punishment. Bishop Ernest Unterkoefler was among those invited to Washington, D.C., to testify before the U.S. Senate Judiciary Committee, which was considering proposals to reintroduce federal executions for various crimes. After telling of his personal experience of accompanying six men to the electric chair during his time in Virginia, knowing for certain that at least one of them was innocent, he went on to summarize the contents of the 1980 statement against such conduct by the state, and ended by insisting to the lawmakers that "humane alternatives can be developed without resorting to such simplistic and atavistic practices as capital punishment."[57]

In May over forty-five thousand West Germans signed a petition calling for abolition of the U.S. death penalty and delivered it to the U.S. Embassy in Bonn.

B. France Abolishes Capital Punishment

In October, France passed law #81–901, the first article of which declares simply: "The death penalty is abolished." The two-centuries-old use of the guillotine was over. Unlike the case of Spain three years earlier, the Catholic bishops and other French religious groups had made their voices heard, calling strongly for abolition.

In December, Amnesty International released its annual report, judging the retention of the death penalty by the United States to be a basic, institutionalized violation of human rights.[58]

This was also the year of the attempted assassination of Pope John Paul II (May 13), which subsequently seemed to have a notable new existential bearing on his attitude and statements in connection with the death penalty, with forgiveness, and with the valuing of human life.

XI. THE ANTI–DEATH PENALTY CAMPAIGN CONTINUES (1982)

A. Holland Abolishes Capital Punishment

In April, the Parliament of the Netherlands by a large majority adopted a constitutional provision, article 114, stating that "the death penalty may not be imposed." The Dutch had not held an execution in thirty years, the last one being in 1952 for war crimes. The last execution for a peacetime offense had been in 1860.[59]

B. Disturbing Domestic Developments

1. In March the five-member board of the Massachusetts Catholic Conference, headed by Cardinal Humberto Madeiros, issued a statement opposing proposed legislation to reintroduce the death penalty in that state. Two weeks later Msgr. Francis Lally of the USCC appeared before a House subcommittee and testified that it is a reasonable judgment that "racist attitudes and the social consequences of racism have some influence in determining who is sentenced to die in our society. This we do not regard as acceptable."[60] The variety of injustices associated with the administration of capital punishment seemed uglier and uglier.

2. In August, New Jersey Governor Thomas Kean signed the bill that restored the death penalty in that state and specified lethal injection as the mode of state killings for the future.

3. Meanwhile, the fourth volunteer convict, Frank Coppola, was executed by the state of Virginia. Governor Charles Robb, in refusing to commute the sentence, pointed to Coppola's desire to die, and received a "sympathy" call from President Reagan, who reminisced about his own refusal to grant a stay of execution once when he was governor of California.[61] Meantime, the population of death rows nationally exceeded the one thousand mark, and speculation about a coming bloodbath seemed a realistic concern to many.

4. On December 7 Texas won the race to go into the history books as the first state in the union to use a more "humane" mode of extermination—lethal injection. The victim was Charlie Brooks, the first black man executed since the *Furman* decision. He was one of two drug addicts who had killed a salesman with a single shot. Each accused the other. Both were found guilty and sentenced to death. The other one, Woodie Loudres, got his conviction overturned on appeal, then in a plea bargain settled for a forty-year term. Charlie Brooks was not so lucky.

For six years he made appeals on this and other grounds, but one after another his appeals failed. In his last plea to the U.S. Supreme Court, he won support from an unusual quarter—Jack Strickland, the prosecutor who had convicted both him and Loudres. "Only one shot was fired," said Strickland, "and you don't know who fired it. One guy lives and one guy dies [and it] strikes the citizen as unfair."

That very day, ironically, the Fifth Circuit Court of Appeals ruled in another capital case that a prisoner could not be executed unless the jury found that he himself, and not a codefendant, had committed the murder.[62]

The controversy about the ethics of physicians taking part in adminstering lethal injection, in contradiction of the Hippocratic oath, rose to new intensity now that the invitation to such collaboration was a grim reality facing the entire medical community. Three different drugs in different syringes and different doses were administered to Brooks by two physicians, and the eye-witnesses found it was far from being a "humane" scene in many respects.[63]

XII. THE MOMENTUM PEAKS (1983)

A. *The Pope, the Bishops, and the Executed*

On January 15 Pope John Paul II made an address to the Vatican diplomatic corps in which he included mention of capital punishment. The Associated Press release of the next day asserted that

> Pope John Paul II condemned the death penalty today, the first time a Pope has spoken out against capital punishment....The Pope asked for clemency for prisoners condemned to death, especially those sentenced to die for political reasons. He criticized governments that "make a certain number of people disappear, without trial, leaving their families in a cruel state of uncertainty," in what Vatican observers said was an allusion to Argentina's junta.[64]

The first sentence of the release seems quite clearly to be a product of a journalist's overactive imagination, unless the pope had said something more than what followed in the release. Willam F. Buckley, Jr., had some fun with it a few weeks later:

> [The speech]...was being interpreted by the abolitionists as a major ethical event, whereas what the Pope called for was "clemency and mercy for those condemned to death"—but listen: "especially for those who have been condemned for political motives." The word "especially" seemed to give it away. That is to say, the Pope a) believes in clemency, an exhortation as old as Christianity. But b) tacitly acknowledges that clemency is more appropriate in some cases than in others—particularly it is appropriate for convicted men whose crimes were political. The Pope here postulates something the abolitionists are entirely unwilling to do: which is that there is a distinction between superior, and lesser, claims for clemency.[65]

It seemed safe to say that, if the pope said nothing more than what was in the release, the bulk of Buckley's remarks were on target (whoever his "abolitionists" were). It was simply one more case of a pastor interceding for clemency, à la St. Augustine. And, in fact, Pope John Paul II made the same kind of request again only two months later during his visit to Central America, pleading for the lives of six Guatemalan "terrorists." In a singular display of gaucherie, the Guatemalan honchos put an emphatic end to the discussion by shooting all six men three days before the pope arrived in their country.[66] Arbitrary capital punishment can dramatically terminate otherwise bothersome discussions.

In April the state of Oklahoma was scheduled to hold its first execution and was making arrangements to do so by lethal injection. Even though the execution was later stayed, it served as the occasion for the two bishops of Oklahoma (Archbishop Charles Salatka of Oklahoma City and Bishop Eusebius Beltran of Tulsa) to issue a statement opposing both the execution itself and the projected method. Stressing that violence only begets more violence, they noted that "society is not best served by adding the violence of execution to the violence of murder." After summarizing the other arguments against it, they went on to address lethal injection as "objectionable on two scores." First, it necessarily involves health-care professionals, whose occupation is to maintain human health and prevent death, so that using them to kill is "both repugnant and open to dangerous developments." And second, "the very ease with which death is accomplished by drugs...could lead to easier imposition of the death penalty." They go on to mention the regrettable involvement of the German medical profession in the Nazi massacre of millions as an horrendous example of what such a regrettable trend could lead to.[67] (Their words took on added gravity in 1992 when the U.S. Justice Department proposed lethal injection as the mode for federal executions with a mandated presence of at least one physician to pronounce death. Medical professionals protested loudly, and in 1993 the requirement was dropped, but physician participation was not prohibited.[68])

In September the state of Mississippi rejoined the purveyors of death, executing Jimmy Lee Gray and receiving criticism for doing so in an especially barbaric fashion.[69] It was only the latest of several botched cases in this year alone. Gray convulsed for eight minutes in the gas chamber and "his head kept striking a steel pole on the back of the chair." His moans echoed throughout this torture and were described as "blood chilling."[70]

The most memorable episode of the year 1983 involving the Catholic Church and the death penalty in the United States, however, was the prolonged and highly publicized case of Robert Austin Sullivan, who was finally killed by the state of Florida on November 30, after Pope John Paul II and many others, including the bishops' conferences of both Florida and Sullivan's home state of Massachusetts, had made appeals for clemency on his behalf.[71] The case took on added interest due to the rumor in circulation that a priest had heard the confession of a man who could have provided Sullivan with the perfect alibi. He "claimed to have been with Sullivan the night of the murder but would not come forward because he had accompanied Sullivan to a gay bar, and the priest would not violate the confidentiality of the confessional."[72]

The Sullivan case was in some ways reminiscent of that of Caryl Chessman a quarter of a century earlier. Sullivan had been on death row for more than ten years; he was middle-class, college-educated, wrote well, and was something of a charmer; he organized his own elaborate "legal defense fund" and stayed in touch with and received assistance from hundreds of volunteers whom he had befriended, including Bishop René Gracida, in whose diocese he was imprisoned and executed. On that day "there were protests at the governor's mansion, vigils at the prison, a candlelight prayer service at the Catholic church in Starke....Sullivan recited the 62nd Psalm. Then he was banished from human society via electricity."[73]

Two weeks after Sullivan's death there were executions on consecutive days, the first time such a thing had happened in decades: Robert Wayne Williams in Louisiana on December 14, and John Eldon Smith in Georgia on December 15. But this was only the beginning; 1983 was the last year in which the number of U.S. executions amounted to less than double-digits.[74]

B. Cardinal Bernardin's Call for Consistency

In hindsight another event in 1983 stands as a significant development in American Catholic thinking on the death-penalty issue. On December 6 Cardinal Joseph Bernardin delivered the Gannon Lecture at Fordham University in New York City, and its content both set the tone and the agenda for the coming years.[75] The more immediate focus was on the issue of war and peace, since this was the year in which the U.S. bishops' pastoral letter "The Challenge of Peace" made major headlines and provoked unparalleled public discussion of the just-war theory and the nuclear threat. But in presenting the framework for understanding that issue, Bernardin directed attention to the consistency perspective.

> The central idea in the letter is the sacredness of human life and the responsibility we have, personally and socially, to protect and preserve the sanctity of life. Precisely because life is sacred, the taking of even one human life is a momentous event.[76]

He spoke of the "perceptible shift of emphasis in the teaching and pastoral practice of the Church in the last 30 years. To summarize the shift succinctly, the *presumption against taking human life* has been strengthened and the exceptions made ever more restrictive." After this key statement, capital punishment was explicitly brought up as the illustration. While the right of the state to use it had long been acknowledged,

> the action of Catholic bishops and of Popes Paul VI and John Paul II has been directed against the exercise of that right by the state. The argument has been that more humane methods of defending the society exist and should be used. Such humanitarian concern lies behind the policy position of the NCCB against capital punishment, the opposition expressed by individual bishops in their home states against reinstating the death penalty, and the extraordinary interventions of Pope John Paul II and the Florida bishops seeking to prevent the execution in Florida last week.

In light of what has been seen about the shift (or drift) of churchmen away from the value or central concern for human life in earlier Christian history, the case can be made that Cardinal Bernardin had here put his finger on exactly what was needed, a retrieval of what had been lost, along with a mentality that could admit that history can help to liberate as well as it has sometimes enslaved. Aware of the importance of what he was venturing into, he continued:

> I wish to probe the *rationale* behind the shift and indicate what it teaches us about the need for a consistent ethic of life. Fundamental to the shift is a more acute perception of the multiple ways in which life is threatened today....What is new is the *context* in which these ancient questions arise, and the way in which a new context shapes the *content* of our ethic of life.

Eleven years later Bernardin agreed to share some personal recollections of the circumstances surrounding that memorable evening:

> I had always thought in those terms [i.e., the consistent ethic of life], but had not articulated it formally until my Fordham lecture in 1983. The immediate circumstance that led me to it was this. I had been invited by Archbishop Roach, who was president of the conference, to succeed Cardinal Cooke as chairman of the (at that time) "ad hoc committee on pro-life

activities," and I agreed to do so as long as it was understood
that I would have the authority, as it were, to link various life
issues, because there were many of our "middle-management
people" (priests, religious, lay people working in our parishes
and institutions) who were certainly anti-abortion but who
felt that we could be much more credible if we were "anti-any-
thing-that-diminished-human-life," not only abortion, and
were in favor of anything that would enhance life.

I made it very clear that by the consistent-ethic I was articulating I was not saying that all the problems or all the issues
were the same...but that they were all related in some way.
Some of the people who didn't like the consistent-ethic
accused me of down-playing abortion, just making it one
issue among many, but if you read the talks which I gave
(over a period of several years I gave ten major talks in
which I developed it), you will see that I made it very, very
clear that they are not all the same or equally important, but
they are all important and all related, and to be truly "pro-
life," you have to take all of those issues into account.[77]

When asked about his awareness of influences that sparked
his thought in this direction, he replied:

Certainly Bryan Hehir was a major consultant, and once I
even wrote to Cardinal Ratzinger (not officially but unoffi-
cially, as a theologian), asking him to give me his reaction to
what I had been articulating, and in due time I got a private
letter from him (not in his capacity as Prefect of the Congregation), indicating that he felt that basically I was on the
right track and he made a couple of suggestions to improve
it. That's not generally known.

When asked if he thought there was any sentiment that the
stated repudiation of the death penalty by the vast majority of
bishops was too strong for some, he replied:

I'm not aware of any internal episcopal efforts to back down
or weaken the 1980 statement. As a matter of fact, I've seen
statements on the part of individual bishops and provincial
conferences restating their opposition to the death penalty,

even in circumstances that were not popular. But I do think this: that we do not have a large percentage of our people with us, so it is going to require a great deal of work. There's a real challenge here and, if it really is the case that 75% to 80% of our people do not agree, well then, that means we really have a job ahead of us to explain to them why we take this position.

When asked if he felt that the U.S. Catholic bishops as a whole shared his own strong feelings on the importance of this issue, he answered:

It may well be that there is an individual bishop here or there who still does not agree with the change of stance, but certainly the vast majority has signed on....I do think that, as we become a more and more violent society, the acceptance or support of this position will be more eroded. You get a case like the Dahmer case up in Milwaukee, or even nights like last Tuesday here in Chicago when six people were killed in different acts of violence, not in accidents but intentionally, by weapons—knives and guns. The more that goes on, the more people will be inclined—out of frustration—to say "get rid of them" by capital punishment, but there is no real evidence to show that the death penalty is a deterrent....It's revenge, and that attitude will intensify on the part of many as the violence escalates. But as far as the Catholic educational effort is concerned, I see no evidence that it will do anything but increase its opposition. For example, I know that the Illinois Catholic Conference is working hard on it. I do not have a crystal ball, but I see no reason to think that our concern to enlighten people on this emotional issue will diminish.

The year 1983 thus marked a significant point in the struggle of American Catholic leadership to withdraw support from the death penalty and join in the drive for a consistent ethic of life. The reasons had been more than adequately worked out on paper, but the task of communicating them effectively to the Catholic laity and the broader public was proving to be more daunting than expected ten years earlier, when the majority of the bishops had endorsed the resolution opposing all capital punishment (1974).[78] The next ten years would provide more grounds for abolishing the death penalty than they could possibly have imagined, as several Southern states seemed to be in competition to see which could become the greatest international embarrassment.

CHAPTER 10

Consolidating Consistency
(1984–1990)

I. A Time of Tension (1984)
    A. Tennessee's Bishops Plead for a Better Way
    B. North Carolina Politics and a Woman's Death
    C. Florida's Christian Leaders Dissent

II. Questions and Executions (1985)
    A. Catholic Controversy in Illinois
    B. Australia Abolishes Capital Punishment
    C. Virginia—Killing the Mentally Retarded
    D. Texas—Killing Juvenile Offenders
    E. California's Bishops Give Unambiguous Witness

III. The Death March Continues (1986)
    A. South Carolina vs. the World
    B. *Lockhart v. McCree*—Death-Prone Juries

IV. The Beat Goes On (1987)
    A. Objections from Bishops' Conferences Grow
    B. Amnesty International Reports on the
       USA Death Penalty
    C. *McCleskey v. Kemp*—The Race Factor
    D. Mississippi and Filipino Bishops Choose Life
    E. The Cooper Case, the Pope, and a Journey of Hope

V. The Hyper-Politicized Death Penalty (1988)
    A. Florida Kills "Dean" Darden
    B. To the White House via Death Row

VI. The Sky Grows Darker (1989)
    A. Bishops' Reaction to Missouri's Death Machine
    B. The Experience of Two Catholic Governors
    C. The *Penry* Decision on Killing Juveniles
    D. Alabama Electrocutes Ronnie Dunkins
    E. Polar Opposites in Print

I. A TIME OF TENSION (1984)

It is worth pausing here to ponder briefly upon the magnitude and significance of the change that had occurred in only a few short years. U.S. Catholic Church leaders had long been accustomed to supporting most government policies as a matter of course, and as a simple matter of good citizenship. Such ready compliance had come under some stress in the late 1960s with the Vietnam War, and again with the abortion ruling *Roe v. Wade* in 1973. Then came the "Bicentennial Bifurcation" on the death penalty with *Gregg v. Georgia* in 1976. The discomfort of the growing split over life-and-death issues (war, abortion, capital punishment) climaxed in 1983 with the emergence and prominence of both the "Peace Pastoral" and the "consistent-ethic-of-life" argument. The bishops were now expressing their opposition to government policies more than ever before, and the fundamental issue in all of them was the dignity of the human person.

The material in the next two chapters, sketching developments in U.S. use of capital punishment from 1984 to 1996, is meant to illustrate the bifurcation in action. Just as the bishops' opposition to state executions was solidifying, the states ironically were not only returning to the use of the death penalty with increasing frequency, but were doing so with more passionate public support. How did the bishops respond to this unpleasant new situation of finding themselves in mounting opposition of their own state governments? It is safe to say that one general characteristic was well-tempered caution. As Cardinal Bernardin expressed all too clearly, they knew they were leading where only a minority of the laity were as yet ready and willing to follow.

Their dilemma was extremely delicate. They fully granted the horrendous nature of the crimes inflicted by vicious criminals on hapless victims and their families. The death penalty was admittedly a different kind of life issue than the others. Churchmen of earlier ages, especially when church and state were deeply intertwined, had allowed executions, blessed them

383

and used them liberally. Emotion and tradition now combined to ask agonizingly: Why not now? Are today's killers any more deserving of being spared than those of other eras?

It was a painful question, but too much had happened since Vatican II to allow such sentiments to prevail. Their turnaround was based too firmly on principle. The events of recent years had brought the bishops to see and to agree that execution as a penalty was henceforth totally precluded. Even the most despicable of criminals could not be executed once the "new understanding of the gospel" and the fuller appreciation of the nature of human rights were endorsed. By taking this stand, the bishops realized that they were not only disagreeing with the conclusions but also with the premises of the popular punitive outlook. The call to be consistent in supporting the value of life was increasingly urgent even as it was increasingly counter-cultural.

George Orwell had turned 1984 into such a social nightmare decades before it arrived that its actual advent was in many ways a relief, but hardly so with regard to the U.S death-penalty conundrum. The degree to which opposition to the death penalty was countercultural in American society in 1984 was dramatically revealed, especially in the Old South. The parallels between approving slavery and approving capital punishment have always been disturbingly close. Whereas many church people tried to justify the former as divinely authorized in the nineteenth century, many church people tried to justify the latter as divinely authorized in the twentieth century. In taking their stance for life late in the twentieth century regarding the death penalty, U.S. Catholic leaders were departing from the kind of passive acceptance of the status quo that marked many of their nineteenth-century counterparts on the question of slavery. The American Catholic Church was in a smaller, less prominent situation when the major battles over slavery were fought; that is not the case in this parallel conflict.

A. Tennessee's Bishops Plead for a Better Way

In May, as Tennessee faced the possibility of its first execution in twenty-four years, the two Catholic bishops (James Niedergeses of Nashville and J. Francis Stafford of Memphis) issued an unusual joint pastoral letter. Just as in the case of the 1972 Indiana Catholic

Conference statement seen earlier, it was a good example of the work of a broad-based, Vatican II–inspired Catholic Public Policy Commission that provided informed counsel and extensive lay and clerical experience for the bishops to draw upon. The commission provided ample evidence for concluding that violence was "the most serious social problem of the day." The pastoral letter started with somber empirical data: "In the years from 1980 through 1982, 1,389 persons were murdered in Tennessee. There were 5,086 reported rapes and 24,297 robberies." This resultant picture led the bishops to ask a troubling question: "Has ours become a society imprisoned within a climate of violence?...It is easy to be engulfed by feelings of vengeance and the urge to retaliate." But besides all the stories of people and their horrendous sufferings from violence, heard from many sources, the bishops realized that their prime responsibility was to remind all that "there is another story that makes claim upon us—the life of Jesus our Lord."

This unusually sensitive reflection on the relevance of Jesus as God's Word of reconciliation, following the Way of suffering love, gave the pastoral a distinctive theological tone. It engaged in a kind of discourse that led to

> a presumption in favor of life...a presumption which binds all Christians: we should do no harm to our neighbor; how we treat our enemy is the key test of whether we love our neighbor; and the possibility of taking even one human life is a prospect we should consider in fear and trembling. The cutting edge of this presumption against our doing violence, especially lethal violence, demands that we oppose the death penalty. We give a firm NO to legalized execution: It is a judgment that flows from the new commandment of Jesus. Hence, we would be negligent in our duty as bishops if we did not speak out! We are convinced that capital punishment does not cultivate an attitude of respect for the sanctity of human life in our society.

The exceptional eloquence of the letter did not end there. It went on to ask another pertinent, embarrassing question:

> [Because] we Christians must also remember that even the murderer does not forfeit the God-given right to be called

"neighbor"...(and since) Jesus' radical call to conversion
ever unsettles our neat categories: Can we in any honest way
say that we love the murderer and still pull the lever which
executes him or her? Regardless of the gravity of his crime,
would you be able to execute your blood brother? ...We must
learn to forgive even when no spirit of contrition is shown
us!...By taking another life through capital punishment, we
do not reverse the cycle of violence. We do not even diminish it; we accelerate it....Capital punishment is "the outward
sign of an inward mind-set that believes that the scales of justice can be balanced by violent means."

Seldom has the contemporary Christian case against the death
penalty found more felicitous expression. The centuries of
church support were acknowledged as an undeniable part of the
record, but then "the present climate of violence in our world"
was pointed to as prompting church members to turn around
and start anew,

> to reassess this moral issue and oppose legalized executions
> by the state. In the midst of the complexities of this moral
> issue, we charge all to examine closely the reasons for their
> judgment. With certainty we can say: A position founded in
> any way on revenge is at serious variance with the gospel call
> to suffering love! Revenge is a cancer which destroys us.

A closing paragraph admitted the pain involved in developing
"an entirely new attitude" toward violence, undoubtedly a tall
order, but "it can be done through the transforming grace of
Christ. We too pray that capital punishment will not happen
again in the state of Tennessee. It is unworthy of us."[1]

As at other times in history, the people of Tennessee were
reminded that they were standing at an ethical crossroads; the
cultural pro-death sentiments were strong, appealing dramatically to the worst instincts and prejudices. Neighboring states
were already vying for the lead in the number of legally termi-
nated lives. Many wanted Tennessee to join in the violence,
resuming the state ritual of sacrificing scapegoats, while articulate Christian leaders pointed in the other direction under the
influence of the gospel. A dozen years later the state of Tennessee

still had the commendable distinction of not having given in. Despite the allure of the culture of violence, Tennessee in 1995 was still "choosing life," having put no one to death. But the numbers of persons piling up in the warehouses were continuing to mount ominously.

B. North Carolina Politics and a Woman's Death

The execution that probably caught the most media attention in 1984 was that of the first (and only) woman so condemned in over twenty years. Velma Barfield, a 51-year-old North Carolina grandmother, never denied her guilt in fatally poisoning four people, including her mother and fiancé. Hers was a classic case for testing attitudes toward and beliefs about penal theories and religious conversions. In prison she underwent an extraordinary change and spent much of her six and a half years doing all she could to help other prisoners. She corresponded with Ruth Graham, wife of the Rev. Billy Graham, and Mrs. Graham advised her that her story needed to be told and contacted a publisher for her. With the help of a professional writer, Cecil Murphey, Barfield's story was put on record and published soon after her execution as *Woman on Death Row*.

Barfield was to an unfortunate degree a victim of the political calendar. If ever a case was to be made for clemency, it was hers. But Governor James B. Hunt, Jr., was locked in a bitter battle, to win the U.S. Senate seat away from incumbent Jesse Helms, who had recently smeared Hunt with allegations of effeminateness and worse. The outcome of the Barfield case may well have been different at another time, but in the foul atmosphere of the day a gubernatorial act of clemency—for which Hunt was pressured by many church people—would surely have been used as further evidence of Hunt's not being "macho."[2] Two days before the election was held, the state of North Carolina had Velma Barfield injected with lethal drugs as two different groups gathered outside Central Prison in Raleigh. When her death was announced to them, "one group broke into jeers and cheers. Minutes later they disbanded. The other—and larger—group of about two hundred people kept a vigil with lighted candles. Many of them had been in prayer for more than two hours before the execution."[3]

Governor Hunt lost the election anyway; Velma Barfield lost her life but not her dignity. She confessed her crime, asked forgiveness of all, and volunteered her usable organs for medical transplant. "She then said she did not fear death, because she had put her trust in the Lord....She put on her pink cotton pajamas and walked to the room where she was executed by lethal injection."[4] It was a moment of special shame.

In the days leading up to the execution, an unusual contrast emerged in the reactions of the two Catholic bishops of North Carolina. Bishop Joseph Gossman of Raleigh, in whose backyard the execution took place, clearly expressed his disapproval, saying that he was saddened but not surprised by Hunt's action. He added, "Forgiveness doesn't come easily in a world and in a society that seeks to get even." He pointed positively to the recent example of Pope John Paul II publicly forgiving the man who had tried to kill him in St. Peter's Square.

Bishop Michael Begley of Charlotte, on the other hand, reacted in the pre–Vatican II "old school" manner. He noted that Barfield had "caused some painful deaths. The state has a right to decide on the death penalty and this is one instance when they chose that right." He insisted on the necessity of the legal system being "truly and fairly applied," but expressed his conviction that it was being so applied in Barfield's case.[5] Despite the 1980 NCCB Statement, its basic teaching had still not persuaded all.

C. Florida's Christian Leaders Dissent

Less than a month after Barfield's execution in North Carolina, however, the leaders of twenty-six Christian communities in Florida, including all eight of its Roman Catholic bishops, joined forces in issuing a firm statement of opposition to their state's becoming the "capital-punishment capital" of the country. "Our responsibility is to bring to bear upon this problem of major consequence in Florida the moral teaching of the wider Christian community." They noted that there were more than two hundred persons on Florida's death row, more than any other state in the union, and that there had already been seven executions that year. "Between 1979 and October 1, 1984, the state has attempted to execute more than 60 other persons."

They called attention to a practical complication, lamenting the "acute poverty of practically all death-row inmates" who, as a result had to rely on volunteer attorneys who were greatly over-burdened due to the large number of cases and the complexity of the proceedings. "The inordinate demands upon the time and energy of attorneys [has] made qualified volunteers harder and harder to recruit."

In light of this critical situation, they continued, "We urge the Christian people of Florida and all other residents of Florida to reflect with us on the moral consequences of the present course of action in our state." Attention was then turned to the main task of presenting a Christian perspective on an intolerable situation:

> We hold that capital punishment is not necessary to any legitimate goal of the state and that its use threatens to undermine belief in the inherent worth of human life and the inalienable dignity of the human estate. Our belief in the value of human life stems from the worship we offer to the Creator of human life and from the teaching of Scripture that each human is created in the image of God....
>
> [Capital punishment] is inconsistent with our efforts to promote respect for human life, to stem the tide of violence in our society, and to embody the message of God's redemptive love. In times when life is cheapened and threatened on all fronts, the value and uniqueness of every human life merit profound respect, strong reaffirmation, and vigorous proclamation.

They added a thoughtful third part on the Bible, stressing that "Jesus offered his disciples an alternative to violence, a new way," and then, in an unusual fourth part, they sensitively expressed their concern for the victims of crime.

> The fundamental issue here is the restoration of peace: peace in the hearts of the broken, peace in the hearts of the violent, peace in the hearts of all members of the community. This peace rests in the confidence that God will judge fairly and mercifully. It removes from the hands of those

who govern the stain of what is at best a morally ambiguous
death policy. The use of capital punishment in Florida must
be discontinued....We seriously question that it does any
good, and we are deeply convinced that it does a great deal
of harm. Our principal objection to it lies in what we believe
to be its immorality.[6]

All in all, 1984 stands out as a year in which two exceptional
appeals for American Catholics to convert to a new attitude
toward the death penalty came from the religious leaders
addressing the problem of particular states bent upon killing:
Tennessee and Florida. The quality of discourse in the formulation of objections coming from Catholic leaders against the
death penalty had reached a truly impressive elevation in the ten
years since the first unelaborated statement.

II. QUESTIONS AND EXECUTIONS (1985)

A. Catholic Controversy in Illinois

In March Haven Bradford Gow published an article challenging the validity of Cardinal Bernardin's consistent-ethic-of-
life argument. His effort was to show that, whatever the case for
Catholic consistency, there certainly was no Catholic consensus.
Gow alleged that

> many Catholic lay persons and theologians persist in their
> view that it is not a contradiction for religious people to
> oppose abortion-on-demand and, at the same time, favor
> capital punishment for, say, someone who has raped and
> murdered a child. They reason that the unborn child is
> innocent of wrongdoing, while the rapist-murderer has
> taken the life of another human being.[7]

The most interesting thing about the article was the bevy of
witnesses whom Gow assembled to testify for his position and
the array of arguments with which they attempted to refute the
position embraced by Bernardin. The first witness was Rocco
Cordaro, described as "a 68-year-old YMCA staff member...a
faithful husband...father of three sons and a daughter...and a

devout Catholic who sharply dissents from the controversial stand" of the National Conference of Catholic Bishops. This "dedicated Catholic" considered the bishops "misguided" by having "concern for the criminals instead of the victims of crime and their families....Why should we feel more sympathy for the killers instead of for the families of the victims?"

Next came Fr. Richard Roach, S.J., described as "a Marquette University scholar," who argued that "it is not a contradiction for religious people to oppose abortion and, at the same time, support capital punishment....The deadly deed can be the right thing to do." It is only murder, the direct or intentional killing of the innocent, that is prohibited. With a mighty leap he reaches the conclusion that "trying to put abortion, capital punishment, and war in one package makes chaos of Catholic morals."

Next in line was "Catholic scholar Fr. James Reilly, M.S., (who) also supports capital punishment, pointing out that the official teaching of the Roman Catholic Church favors the death penalty." When anyone claims that capital punishment is a morally unjustifiable attack on the sanctity of human life, Fr. Reilly said he considers it his duty "as a Catholic priest and as a citizen to point out that that statement goes directly counter to the official teaching of the Roman Catholic church," and he cites the *Roman Catechism* of 1566 as his proof.[8]

The third Catholic cleric enlisted to testify for Gow's case against the cardinal was Fr. Pierre Lachance, O.P., of St. Anne Parish in Fall River, Massachusetts:

> Thomas Aquinas reflects the common and traditional teaching of the Church, allowing capital punishment for serious crimes, when the crime is proved and when the common good requires it....Traditional Catholic teaching maintains that capital punishment is morally justified and a much needed deterrent to criminals....(It) is the most effective deterrent to crime....Society must be protected against criminals. That is legitimate, so that capital punishment becomes legitimate and necessary if it is the only effective way to safeguard the common good. This means that the individual who poses a threat to the life of others loses his own right to live.

Gow then summoned three conservative Protestant clergymen who all insisted on the need for the literal application today
of the Old Testament law codes read as requiring death as the regular penalty for a host of crimes. One of the three, Rev. Reuben
Hahn of Mt. Prospect, Illinois, even maintained that "not to
inflict the death penalty is a flagrant disregard for God's law."

To climax the appeal to knowledgeable authorities, the final
testimony came from none other than J. Edgar Hoover, who
affirmed vigorously the crucial effectiveness of the death
penalty's deterrent power, no matter what the social scientists'
studies might show. Gow closed by drawing a parallel between
the legitimacy of war and of the death penalty: "If society has the
moral right and obligation to act in collective self-defense
against aggression emanating from *without*...then society likewise
has the moral right and obligation to defend itself against
aggression emanating from *within*."

The regularity with which this whole arsenal of last-ditch
arguments missed the point is intriguing, but what is most astonishing is the complete absence throughout of any reference at all
to the teaching of Jesus. The document stands in stark contrast,
for example, to the pastoral letter of the bishops of Tennessee,
seen above. Meantime, the abuses inseparable from the practice
of systematic destruction of life continued to multiply.

In May Cardinal Bernardin had a chance to respond,
addressing the Criminal Law Committee of Cook County. It was
the only one of his ten public addresses on the consistent ethic of
life in this period that focused entirely on the issue of the death
penalty. Fully aware of the ultra-conservative objections, he went
immediately to the key to transcending them: the ability to see,
appreciate, and adapt to changed circumstances. He described
the situation thus:

> Traditional Catholic teaching has allowed the taking of
> human life in particular situations by way of exception, as,
> for example, in self-defense and capital punishment. In
> recent decades, however, the presumptions against taking
> human life have been strengthened and the exceptions made
> ever more restrictive. Fundamental to this shift in emphasis is
> a more acute perception of the multiple ways in which life is

threatened today. Obviously such questions as war, aggression and capital punishment have been with us for centuries; they are not new. What IS new is the CONTEXT in which these ancient questions arise, and the way in which the new context shapes the CONTENT of our ethic of life.

Within the Catholic Church, the Second Vatican Council acknowledged that "a sense of the dignity of the human person has been impressing itself more and more deeply on the consciousness of contemporary man" (Declaration on Religious Freedom, #1). This growing awareness of human dignity has been a dominant factor within Western culture. Within the United States, the struggle to appreciate human worth more fully is found in the civil rights movement and in the public debate about our foreign policy toward totalitarian regimes of both the right and the left.

The world had changed, the United States had changed, the Catholic Church had changed, the status of the death penalty had changed. The paradox was that just as an enhanced awareness of the dignity of the human person was flourishing, so too there was

a growing recognition of the frailty of human life today.... Today, life is threatened on a scale previously unimaginable. This is why the U.S. Catholic bishops and others have been so visible and vocal in the public debate this past decade or two, asserting belief in the sacredness of human life and the responsibilities we have, personally and as a society, to protect and preserve the sanctity of life.

A consistent ethic of life is based on the need to ensure that the sacredness of human life...will be defended and fostered from womb to tomb, from the genetic laboratory to the cancer ward, from the ghetto to the prison.

It would be difficult to find a better brief summary of the new context that had led to the call for an entirely new attitude toward capital punishment, but then Bernardin immediately went on to do the same kind of concise presentation of the issue itself. In direct response to his critics, he put it on the line: "The question is not whether the State still has the *right* to inflict capital punishment, but whether it should *exercise* that right. In present circumstances, are there sufficient reasons to justify the infliction of the evil of death on another human person?"

Calling attention to the proliferating statements of different Catholic groups in opposition to capital punishment, Bernardin ventured to state that their reasoning "basically...followed two lines of thought. First, they review four traditional arguments justifying capital punishment: retribution, deterrence, reform and protection of the State. Based on their review, the religious leaders have argued that *these reasons no longer apply* to our age." Attention is called to the bishops' 1980 statement for further elaboration on these. But this is only part of the story. The second line of thought is the positive, the retrieved Christian value that ought to far outweigh any pain in giving up the past. "As religious leaders we argue that *there are gospel insights which bespeak the inappropriateness of capital punishment.*"

Bernardin spells out three of these insights:

1. The example of Jesus, offering forgiveness at the time of his own unfair death;

2. God's boundless love for every person, regardless of human merit or worthiness;

3. The biblical imperative of reconciliation wherever there is division between persons.

> I do not believe they are unique to the Christian vision. People of good will recognize that these values ennoble human experience and make it more complete. Commitment to these values changes one's perspective on the strengths and weaknesses of the human family....It is when we stand in the perspective of a higher court—that of God's judgment seat— and a more noble view of the *human person,* that we seriously question the appropriateness of capital punishment.

The final part of his address was taken up with some of the recent Gallup poll findings that were particularly troublesome, especially increasing U.S. support for executions. Why had 30 percent of the population turned to favoring capital punishment in the previous nineteen years (42 percent in 1966 to 72 percent in 1985)? Why did 51 percent say they would still favor the death penalty even if studies showed conclusively that it does not deter crime? Thirty percent admitted openly that their one and only reason was simple: *revenge.*

> We desperately need an attitude or atmosphere in society which will sustain a consistent defense and promotion of life....Attitude is the place to root an ethic of life. Change of attitude, in turn, can lead to change of policies and practices in our society. We must find ways to break the cycle of violence which threatens to strangle our land. We must find effective means of protecting and enhancing human life.[9]

Seldom have American Catholics had a more cogent call to adopt a higher ethic. But judging from the opinion polls, many were either not listening or not accepting.

B. Australia Abolishes Capital Punishment

The month of May was memorable on the world scene as well. Another of the developed, democratic nations embraced the new international ideal and rejected the death penalty. Australia's last state with capital punishment decided to abandon it. The process had been a long one, but de facto there had not been an execution for the previous eighteen years, and even that one had been strongly protested by church groups and others. The stages on the Australian road to full abolition were thus: Queensland, 1922; Tasmania, 1968; Victoria, 1975; South Australia, 1976; Western Australia, 1984; and New South Wales, 1985.[10] As a British penal colony in earlier times, Australia had seen more capital punishment than most places.[11] It was thus ironic to note that at the very time this progress was achieved, an even earlier British penal colony—the state of Georgia—was busy going in the opposite direction, returning to the business of executions.

C. Virginia–Killing the Mentally Retarded

In June the state of Virginia executed Morris Odell Mason, a mental retardee. The case sparked protests that would be frequently repeated as such executions multiplied nationwide.[12] The Supreme Court showed itself unlikely to provide relief. In

September, Justice Thurgood Marshall spoke to a group of U.S. Court of Appeals' judges and officials in Hershey, Pennsylvania, telling them that the rights of prisoners on death row to challenge their sentences were being denied by "fundamentally unfair" procedures and inadequate legal representation. He called on courts and state governments "to allow more time for deliberation in death-penalty appeals."[13] His was a lonely voice of protest against the pro-death-penalty tide in the punitive climate of the day, but his concern for the priority of justice was very much in line with what the Catholic bishops in state after state were publicly contending was required of them as Christian leaders who could no longer condone the deliberate destruction of human life if they were to take the retrieved values seriously.

D. Texas–Killing Juvenile Offenders

In September the state of Texas executed Charles Rumbaugh, whose crime had been committed when he was 17 years old (he had killed a jeweler in the course of a robbery). Amnesty International took the public stand that if Texas went through with the execution, it would be in violation of international agreements already made. But Texas was far from being the only offender in this regard. "In June 1988, 30 prisoners in 14 states were under sentence of death for crimes committed when they were under 18 years of age."[14]

E. California's Bishops Give Unambiguous Witness

That same month "the proximity of the first execution in our state after a moratorium of 18 years" led the twenty-six Catholic bishops of California to affirm unanimously their opposition to the death penalty, the morality of which, they noted, "may be too readily taken for granted, and its destructive consequences too easily overlooked." Aware that this had not always been pointed out in earlier years, they called attention to the fact that

for some years now Catholic leaders, including Pope Paul VI and Pope John Paul II, have questioned whether capital punishment can any longer be justified. As recently as November 28, 1983, John Paul II made a plea to the governor of Florida for a stay of execution "for humanitarian reasons." Several individual bishops of the United States and at least ten state conferences of bishops have issued statements opposing capital punishment.

Their tone revealed that, even though the position being advocated had been publicly endorsed by most Catholic leaders for over a decade, they were aware of and tried to be sensitive to the continuing resistance of many Catholics who did not yet understand the full reasons for the turn-around. After going over some of those reasons again, the California bishops acknowledged forthrightly that as yet

> not all Christians may come to this conclusion when they apply general principles and gospel values to the concrete historical situation. Nonetheless, our intention in this statement is to affirm our opposition to the use of the death penalty and challenge the people of California, particularly our own Catholic faithful, to examine the issue of capital punishment in the light of the fundamental moral and religious questions it involves. We dare to take this position and raise this challenge because of our commitment to a *consistent* ethic of life by which we wish to give unambiguous witness to the sacredness of every human life from conception through natural death, and to proclaim the good news that no person is beyond the redemptive mercy of God.[15]

In December, Archbishop Roger Mahony of Los Angeles, in a statement on Jewish-Catholic dialogue urging Californian Catholics and Jews to join together in considering many issues, included among them the question of capital punishment. He observed that this "emotionally charged issue (might)...engage us to the limit of our religious core, resting on our understanding of human dignity. This is a dangerous area, perhaps one which gives some indication of how deep our dialogue has rooted itself these past 20 years."[16]

III. THE DEATH MARCH CONTINUES (1986)

A. South Carolina vs. the World

Early in 1986 the news focused on preparations for the execution of another juvenile, this time in South Carolina. Mother Teresa and U.N. General Secretary Pérez de Cuellar were among those calling for mercy for Terry Roach, but the international protests only served to stiffen local resolve, and Roach died in the electric chair on schedule. Attorney David Bruck described the banality of the senseless killing:

> They take a living person, who took 25 years to create—and even Terry Roach, as damaged as he was, was unique, there never has been anyone like him and there never will be again, all of modern science cannot create his fingernail—and within just a few seconds they converted him into a piece of junk to be wrestled out on a stretcher and carted away. To me, the message was that human beings are junk and if you don't believe it—watch this....It is the easiest thing. Murderers can do it, anyone can do it. We can do it. Watch this! It was banal....It was dehumanizing. Not only to him. It was a ritual that denied the importance and uniqueness of any of us.[17]

B. Lockhart v. McCree—Death-Prone Juries

The U. S. Supreme Court reversed a circuit court's ruling in an Arkansas case concerning "death-prone" juries. The practice of excluding from jury service in capital cases anyone who was opposed to the death penalty in principle had been ruled unconstitutional. The Supreme Court found no grounds for objecting to the practice and reversed the decision. "The result is that defense counsel enters every capital trial knowing that the accused does not stand to be judged by a true cross-section of the general public, but rather by a carefully winnowed segment of the community from which every opponent of the death penalty has been excluded."[18] The basic American sense of fair play seemed to have been abandoned. Some drew the disturbing conclusion that "the present Court holds that maintaining the smooth functioning of our system of capital punishment is a higher priority than protecting the rights of capital defenders."[19]

Jury interviews conducted by researchers were revealing another unsettling element, even apart from the death-prone factor. In one North Carolina case, out of forty-nine jurors questioned, "only two were able to tell us properly what the legal requirements of mitigating testimony were. And in every instance where the jurors were mistaken, their mistake made a death sentence more likely. The misunderstandings are very deep."[20] The intentional exclusion of more balanced personalities increased the likelihood that juries would be unfair. Evidence developed by a recent study suggests that juries composed of "death-qualified jurors are more likely to be white, punitive, and authoritarian. Hence, they are more likely, on this evidence, to exhibit a tendency toward racially biased decisions."[21]

IV. THE BEAT GOES ON (1987)

Eighteen executions had taken place in both 1985 and 1986, but 1987 saw the number climb to twenty-five, one of whom "may have been innocent, another was mentally retarded, and a third was executed after a 4–4 vote of the Supreme Court denied him a stay of execution."[22]

A. Objections from Bishops' Conferences Grow

1. Pennsylvania: In January, the bishops of Pennsylvania reacted to the state legislature's reinstatement of the death penalty by a brief but pertinent message expressing their conviction that it would only further advance the already prevalent "destructive anti-life attitude. We believe that the question confronting us today is not whether the state *may* impose capital punishment, but whether it *should*." After reviewing the principles involved, their conclusion was clear: "We believe that in the context of our times it is in the best interests of the people of this commonwealth not to impose the death penalty. Accordingly, we oppose capital punishment as unnecessary and inappropriate."[23] The Catholic bishops of the Quaker State had come to share one

mind and heart with traditional Quakers, favoring the protection of human life over any kind of bloodshed rather than getting caught up in the popular mythology.

2. Ohio: In March, the bishops of Ohio decided that it was time to speak out again about the ominous situation facing that state. No one had been executed for twenty-four years, but since the 1981 reinstatement of capital punishment, seventy prisoners had piled up on death row. In one of the best researched statements of the day, the bishops laid out the history by which the problem of church support for the death penalty arose in the past, and the more recent developments due to which "the church had been challenged to think further about this difficult issue in the context of our complicated situations." The resulting turnaround occurred:

> As a result of prayerful reflection on our country's experience...and the state of our criminal justice system...and because respect for human life faces an unprecedented crisis today, reflection on the death penalty has taken on a new seriousness, depth, and urgency. The new situation has led to new emphases in the church's teaching. In this century state power has been misused in horrible ways by regimes which have unjustly used the death penalty on millions; an ethos of abortion and euthanasia has spread like a plague; starvation stalks millions; nuclear war is treated as one among many military options, even though it is capable of destroying all human life. It is no exaggeration to say that human life is threatened as seriously in our time as it has ever been threatened.
>
> In such a context it is important to remember that all persons have value that comes from God even when they might seem utterly lacking in any value. Therefore, persons convicted of crimes must not be treated as though they were not persons, but only objects of fear and vengeance. No human life, no matter how wretched or how miserable, no matter how sinful or how lacking in love, is without value. Precisely when persons appear worthless and expendable and when people are tempted to destroy them, the church must speak out in defense of their lives. We advocate working toward a consistent ethic of life....So much of life is broken and

wounded by violent crime. Its destructive effects extend to many people and last for many years. We all feel rage and hurt....The desire to strike back is strong. Yet Christians know that this response is contrary to the human vocation to love, show mercy, and forgive.[24]

B. *Amnesty International Reports on the USA Death Penalty*

In February, Amnesty International published an unprecedented exposé of what was happening in the United States. It came, however, at a time when President Reagan had led the United States to ignore any kind of international criticism, no matter what its ethical warrant.

Amnesty International's findings were summarized and documented in eighteen points, most of which either had already been or would soon be objects of concern expressed in the public statements of many of the U.S. Catholic bishops. The objections ranged from killing juveniles ("these executions put the USA out of line with most other countries"), to killing the mentally ill, to the wide regional disparities (63 percent killed in the old Confederacy, only 4 percent in the Northeast, and so on), to the total arbitrariness of those selected for execution, to the obvious role of race in that process ("53 of the 58 prisoners executed between January 1977 and May 1986 had been convicted of killing whites"), to the "systematic exclusion of opponents of the death penalty from juries" and "the use of peremptory challenges to exclude blacks from sitting on capital trial juries, especially if the defendant is black," to the assignment of inexperienced, often incompetent counsel to "many indigent offenders charged with capital crimes," to a whole array of "procedural bars to appealing on issues that should have been raised at the time of trial," to the increasing unwillingness of federal courts "to consider new constitutional questions in capital cases," to "the very narrow view of the role of clemency" taken by governors and pardons boards, due to the decline in civil discourse that had come to mark the politics of the day.

The overarching question was why the American people, with their heritage of generosity and fair play, had allowed such a heavily flawed system and situation to arise and flourish. The report could only speculate that popular support for the practice of such injustices in a modern democratic nation "may not be based on accurate information about the actual use of the death penalty and its effects on society." In other words, there may be a large ignorance factor at work. The polls showed that support for the death penalty by the American people was far from unqualified. "Were the public fully aware of the sound moral and practical reasons for not using the death penalty and of the alternative measures needed to protect society from violent crime, its support for the penalty would be likely to diminish."[25] It was precisely the filling of this vacuum with accurate information and understanding that many of the U.S. Catholic leaders saw as the greatest challenge confronting them. Ten specific cases had been singled out as especially objectionable and in need of attention in the name of human decency.[26]

C. McCleskey v. Kemp–The Race Factor

In April, in striking contrast to Amnesty International's sensitivity, the U.S. Supreme Court sounded a very different note in handing down its five-four decision in *McCleskey v. Kemp,* declaring that Georgia's capital-punishment system was constitutional despite the fact that killers of white people were four times more frequently sentenced to die than killers of black people. The decision was a kind of throwback to *Dred Scott,* turning a blind eye to the effects of racism in the legal system. This "profound retreat from its stance in *Furman*"[27] raised troubling questions about the fairness of the Court. The four dissenting justices (Brennan, Marshall, Blackmun, and Stevens) gave strongly worded opinions, arguing that the risk of racial discrimination in the application of the Georgia statute clearly made it unconstitutional. "We as a people ignore this man and what his case stands for at our peril," warned Justice Brennan.

> We remain imprisoned by the past as long as we deny its influence on the present. The destinies of the two races in this country are indissolubly linked together. The way in which we choose those who will die reveals the depth of moral commitment of the living.[28]

The majority, however, embraced the view that system-wide statistical evidence did not impeach the exercise of sentencing discretion by individual capital jurors. "This faith of the Court in capital jurors' exercise of discretion," long part of American mythology, found no support in either empirical data or contemporary studies.

One curiosity of the case was the role that the work of Professor David C. Baldus played.[29] On the one hand, the Court accepted the validity of his figures, which were based on a study of more than two thousand Georgia murders of previous decades. His conclusions were carefully argued, not claiming that race was always decisive, but showing that "the race of both victim and defendant helped determine whether the defendant would be condemned to death or receive a lighter sentence."[30] But then, the majority of the Court rejected McCleskey's appeal, which claimed exactly what Baldus had demonstrated was part of "the Georgia way." They did so, as far as dissenting Justice William Brennan could figure, out of fear that "recognition of McCleskey's claim would open the door to all aspects of criminal sentencing." But that, in turn, suggested that what they were really afraid of was "too much justice."[31]

The greatest irony, however, came a few years later when Justice Powell, who cast the swing vote for the majority, revealed that he had changed his mind, regretted this vote, and had come to believe "that capital punishment should be abolished."[32] This is one of the legal nightmares associated with the death penalty. The lives of human beings are caught in the wheels of a not only fallible legal system but one that continues to kill even when its badly divided membership manages a slim, momentary majority. Bureaucratic brutality is nothing new in penal systems, but it is scandalous to provide it with any kind of religious support.

Msgr. Daniel Hoye, USCC general secretary, issued this statement after the shock of McCleskey:

> The U.S. Catholic Conference is deeply disappointed....We disagree with the court's judgment in this matter. The fact that capital punishment is applied in a racially discriminatory way has been one of the reasons for our continued opposition on moral grounds to the application of the

death penalty. The evidence submitted in the McCleskey case strengthens our conviction that the death penalty is frequently applied in an irrational and discriminatory fashion.[33]

The decision also showed another troubling feature: protection of human life did not seem to take high priority for this Court. In both *Lockhart* and *McCleskey*

the Court rejected empirical arguments that were strongly endorsed by the scientific community in order to uphold the constitutionality of the administration of the death penalty. The parsimonious explanation for the failure of social science data to influence the Court in death penalty cases seems to be that the outcome of these cases is frequently a foregone conclusion.[34]

The ensuing controversy over built-in factors of discrimination, injustice, inhumanity, and corruption in the capital-punishment system focused in May on the Florida case of Shabaka Sundiata Waglimi. Waglimi had spent most of his adult life (from age twenty-three to age thirty-seven) on death row before the state of Florida, finally pressured into granting him a new trial, decided that it had no defensible case against him and abandoned prosecution.[35]

Such injustices had to raise increasingly troubling questions in the minds of decent Americans as the nationwide pace of executions accelerated. Defense lawyers in the Death Belt were being overwhelmed by excessive caseloads, with the result that more convicts were being left without adequate defense opportunities. In August an unprecedented three executions took place on the same day, one each in Alabama, Florida, and Utah.

D. Mississippi and Filipino Bishops Choose Life

Also in May, on the day that Edward Earl Johnson was executed, the three bishops of Mississippi (Brunini, Houck, and Howse) issued a statement expressing their disapproval, saying that abolition of the death penalty rather than its continued use would "send a message that we can break the cycle of violence....

We will never overcome the violence in our lives by the use of more violence."[36] Johnson's case brought broader protest because it was another instance where new evidence had been uncovered that raised strong doubts about his guilt, but Mississippi proceeded to kill him in the gas chamber before the doubts about his guilt could be resolved.

During this same period the new Constitution of the Philippines was ratified by an overwhelming majority of the voters, and it included in its Bill of Rights the abolition of the death penalty "unless the Congress hereafter provides for it." The battle obviously was not over, but there was at least a temporary advance, the first Asian nation in modern times to choose abolition. More than five hundred prisoners were on death row, most of them convicted by military tribunals during the Marcos martial law period (1972–1981), and President Corazon Aquino announced that she would commute all of these sentences. The Catholic bishops had taken a firm and courageous stand, voting 34-6 in favor of a statement against the restoration of the death penalty, but Vice-President Ramos swore to do all he could to achieve restoration.[37]

E. The Cooper Case, the Pope, and a Journey of Hope

September also brought unprecedented news: Pope John Paul II interceded not once but twice in the same month in two different U.S. death-penalty cases. First, he once again asked a Florida governor (this time Martinez) to spare the life of an inmate on death row, and once more he was flatly turned down. A week later he appealed to Indiana authorities for clemency for Paula Cooper, an 18-year-old who, at the age of 15, had stabbed her 78-year-old Bible teacher to death. Whether the pope's plea for clemency played a role or not, the Indiana Supreme Court eventually barred the execution of Cooper in July 1989, but not before a petition signed by over a million people was presented to the Secretary General of the United Nations in the effort to obtain a reprieve for Cooper.[38]

One of the most noteworthy outcomes of this case was a transformation experienced by the victim's grandson. Bill Peske was present when Paula Cooper was convicted of murdering his grandmother, but what most impressed him was Cooper's elderly grandfather being escorted from the courtroom in tears. The picture stayed with him, and four months later he envisioned his grandmother, the victim, also in tears. His interpretation was straightforward: "My grandmother believed in forgiveness, and I was convinced that she wanted someone in our family to have the same compassion that she would have had for Paula and her family. It seemed to fall on my shoulders." Peske was a founding board member of Murder Victims Families for Reconciliation (MVFR) and originated the idea for the Journey of Hope, inviting people from around the world to a two-week march in witness to the fact that "vengeance is not the answer."[39]

V. THE HYPER-POLITICIZED DEATH PENALTY (1988)

U.S. Supreme Court Chief Justice Rehnquist set the tone for the next several years by telling a national conference in Williamsburg, Virginia, that he was going to ask a committee of judges "to study the possibility of setting up rules to limit last-minute appeals by death-row inmates."[40] He followed through by naming former justice Lewis F. Powell, Jr., as chair, and the drive was thus under way to curtail capital appeals so as to get on more quickly with the killing.

A. Florida Kills "Dean" Darden

On the Ides of March the state of Florida saw fit to kill William Jasper Darden, the "Dean of Death Row," on the seventh death warrant issued in his fourteen years there. Supreme Court Justice Harry Blackmun expressed the opinion that "if ever a man received an unfair trial, Darden did." Rev. Joe Ingle stayed with him through the preparations and heard him utter as his last words, before dying calmly, that he bore neither guilt nor ill will toward any. "I am at peace with myself, with the world, with each of you; I say to my friends and supporters around the world: I love each and every one of you. Your love and support have been a great comfort to me in my struggle for justice and freedom."[41]

In June, Frank J. Monahan, director of the USCC Government Liaison Office, submitted identical testimony to both the Democratic and the Republican Party leadership, explaining that the bishops "join in the public debate not to impose some sectarian doctrine, but to speak for those who cannot speak for themselves...to share our experience in serving the poor and vulnerable, and to voice our hope that our nation might be an effective force for true justice and genuine peace." In general, he noted that "we are convinced that a consistent ethic of life should be the moral framework from which we address all issues in the political arena," while on the specific issue of capital punishment, he repeated that "we oppose the use of the death penalty....(Its use) can only lead to further erosion of respect for life....Our nation should seek means of dealing with violent crime which are more consistent with human dignity."[42] That same month the state of Louisiana had the distinction of staging the one-hundredth execution in the United States since *Gregg v. Georgia* allowed the reintroduction of state killings.

B. To the White House via Death Row

In September, Vice-President George Bush, on the presidential campaign trail in California, received "wild applause" from high-school students in Concord after expressing his strong support for the death penalty.[43] In October he introduced the case of Willie Horton into his battle with Massachusetts governor Michael Dukakis, and the level of the campaign's discourse declined significantly. Being avidly in favor of swift executions had somehow become symbolic of being qualified for public office. As veteran Washington, D.C., police officer Ronald Hampton summed it up later, "The driving force behind the death penalty in this country are politicians who use the issue in an attempt to appear 'tough on crime.' Our criminal justice system is breaking down for lack of direction and funds while some pour more money into the black hole of capital punishment. The death penalty does not prevent crime."[44] But it does, when properly manipulated, produce votes in modern America.

VI. THE SKY GROWS DARKER (1989)

A. Bishops' Reaction to Missouri's Death Machine

On January 6 the state of Missouri made history by being the first to use a new lethal-injection machine invented by the controversial "Holocaust revisionist" Fred Leuchter. No more shooting, hanging, gassing, or electrocuting. Modern technology could do better than that:

> It has the appearance of being more "scientific"....It is clinical. The equipment includes intravenous lines, prescription drugs, a hospital gurney, medical technicians, doctors, and an execution protocol in which the condemned person is sedated prior to being executed....The theory is that the inmate simply "goes to sleep."[45]

The first victim was a repentant, reformed, well-liked prisoner; the warden had come to trust and like him and had often called upon him for help when he had to deal with problems involving other inmates. George "Tiny" Mercer's execution, graphically described on British Television as the senseless destruction of human life, eerily reminiscent of Nazi nighmares, made many wonder what was happening to America. Leuchter himself was proud of the event, telling author Stephen Trombley that "it was an interesting first, not only for myself and the machine, but also for the state of Missouri, it being the first execution conducted there in many years, it being in Middle America, and it being in the middle of the Bible Belt."[46]

In April the eight Catholic bishops of Missouri, in trying to make a statement about these sad developments in their home state, chose Good Friday to express their dismay over the resumption of state killings. Tiny Mercer was dead, and next on the list was Heath Wilkins, who had been 16 years old at the time of his crime. The U.S. Supreme Court was scheduled to hear oral argument the next week, so the Missouri bishops spoke out: "In the shadow of this sad event we, the Roman Catholic bishops of the state, wish to call attention to the dire effects of this form of punishment." They reviewed once again the arguments in the 1980 statement against capital punishment, explaining carefully.

"What is reported in the media confirms the fear that the real reason for capital punishment is revenge....But to inflict pain and suffering on another because of his or her acts is not within the highest call of a Christian. This is vengeance, and vengeance does not belong to the Catholics and Christians of Missouri." They continued with a forceful reminder:

> While capital punishment bespeaks a desperate people, its abolition would be an unmistakable sign of hope....As a society, we must respond to crime. For Christians, that response must be in accord with our belief in the "Lord of life" who creates all people in his image and clothes them in human dignity. We see the likeness of God and the value of life in an innocent child. We must learn to see the same in a criminal even as we condemn the sin committed....Forgiveness is needed, but it alone is not enough. The road that leads to capital punishment is a long one. It begins with broken homes, poor education and the lack of a nurturing environment....Accordingly, capital punishment falls especially on the underprivileged of our society. The situation before us defies any simple solution. We must work to eradicate the social factors that foster crime....We must be sensitive and supportive to the needs of the victims of crime. We must be concerned about the common good, but we must realize that the imposed death of any convicted man or woman will never contribute to it. It is our hope that in due time capital punishment in the state of Missouri will be overturned and that the people of the state will establish respect for all human life as the cornerstone of all laws and social policy.[47]

The high quality of this episcopal response—in contrast to all that was going on and being said in so much of the media at the time—was truly striking. It may well be looked back upon as one of the finer moments in U.S. Catholic leadership, a time when Christian values were publicly brought to bear in timely fashion on a deteriorating social order.

B. The Experience of Two Catholic Governors

In the spring of 1989 Governor Mario Cuomo vetoed, for the seventh time in as many years, legislation that would have

restored the death penalty in New York State. This time, unlike
some of the earlier occasions, the Catholic bishop of Albany,
Howard J. Hubbard, joined Cuomo in denouncing the death
penalty. But the New York legislature was coming ever closer to
having the numbers to override the veto. (Donald J. Trump took
out full-page ads in four New York newspapers to express his
righteous indignation at increasing lawlessness in the city by calling for the great panacea: reinstatement of the death penalty.[48])

This was also the year when former California governor Pat
Brown published his afterthoughts about having sent thirty-six
prisoners to their deaths during his two terms in office over a
quarter-century earlier. The book gave readers an unusual look
into the mental anguish that the very presence of capital punishment in a state's legal system can cause for officeholders with any
kind of conscience. Brown gave his reflections, not only on the
thirty-six who were executed, but also on the twenty-three whose
sentences he commuted from death to life imprisonment, a far
higher percentage than usual, and he noted the heavy political
costs connected with doing so.[49]

C. The Penry Decision on Killing Juveniles

In June the U. S. Supreme Court ruled five-four in *Penry v.
Lynaugh* that execution of mentally retarded convicts and juveniles was not forbidden by the Constitution. The decision,
among other things,

> sent echoes of disbelief and dismay reverberating across the
> nation....John Paul Penry...a convicted Texas killer, [is] a
> mental child in a full-grown body. His I.Q. falls somewhere
> between 50 and 63....He suffers from organic brain damage
> which likely occurred during and after his breach birth.[50]

Tom Wicker characterized the decision as an especially "cruel
reading of the Constitution."[51] Others found it "morally repugnant," a "tragic injustice," and "downright horrifying."

> The question is not one of compassion or empathy for the
> murderer, but of a profound conviction that an advanced
> civilization should not require such an abominable punish-

ment for such vulnerable defendants....The use of the death penalty as retribution in any of its theories holds no validity for persons with mental retardation.[52]

D. Alabama Electrocutes Ronnie Dunkins

The next month Alabama executed Ronnie Dunkins, combining in one case all the concerns about racial discrimination, loaded juries, poverty, inexperienced counsel, and mental retardation. The details, including the botched execution, were described movingly by a pen-pal witness, Evangelical theologian Dale Aukerman, who was led by the experience to wonder what would happen if, in light of the "utterly compelling Christian case" against the death penalty,

> tens of thousands of pastors on every Sunday after (or maybe before) a week with one or more executions, would mention the killing and seek to dissociate followers of Jesus from it? Church bulletins and newsletters could do the same. A hotline would supply the information. What if, at the time of every execution, there would be protest vigils for life?[53]

Such questions were being raised with a new intensity in view of the increasing ugliness of the system. But there was also continued refusal to change.

E. Polar Opposites in Print

In September, Cardinal Bernardin appeared before the U.S. Senate Judiciary Committee, speaking for the U.S. bishops, whom he described as

> deeply committed to defending the sanctity of human life....We believe human life is so precious that the state should not take the life of any person, even one who has taken another life. Society must send a message that we can break the cycle of violence, that we need not take life for life.

Ironically, this was the same month that a journal connected with the University of Notre Dame published an article that flatly rejected what the bishops had been laboring to communicate over the previous decade and openly assured Catholics that nothing whatsoever had changed, that the church was still as avidly pro-capital-punishment as in the past. The author, Michael Pakaluk, a college teacher, constructed some very unusual arguments. For instance, he claimed that although all the studies show that "there is no evidence that the death penalty deters," this is a negative conclusion. Common sense dictates that "it will be some sort of deterrent... [and thus] we are justified in acting on this conviction, until there is conclusive evidence to the contrary." Among other things, he reversed the burden of proof that should favor life and gave preference rather to death.

Along the same line he continued, "It is prudent to err on the side of using capital punishment." Why? Because, if we use it and it is not a deterrent, guilty persons die; if we do not use it and it is a deterrent, "more innocent persons are murdered. Clearly, we ought to err in the first way, not the second." Such was presented as if it were a serious rebuttal of all the post–Vatican II church's hard-won positions in defense of human life and dignity.

The most audacious part of the article, however, was the author's consignment of abolitionists to the ranks of infidels by a rather circuitous route:

> There are some who argue that society might, in an extraordinary and supererogatory way, display its respect for human dignity by refraining from capital punishment. This is the approach, I believe, that is taken by the Pope. On this view, to administer the death penalty is good; to withhold it, knowing that one could administer it, is better. Note, however, that a society may adopt this high ethical ideal only after it has understood and accepted the traditional teaching of the Church. This is a proposal to show mercy, which is possible only if the fittingness of punishment is first acknowledged. Only after someone realizes that he can lawfully inflict the death penalty can his choice to withhold it be a free act of generosity. But our society is in a very different condition; few persons understand the Church's teaching, and few of those who press for the abolition of the death penalty accept it. For us, the abolition of the death penalty would be regress, not progress.[54]

What is most ironic about this formulation is its basic mis-understanding of what the pope, the bishops, and other aboli-tionists of our day have been insisting on. They are not "refraining" out of mercy from using the right to kill (while hold-ing it ominously in reserve). They are rather recognizing the pri-ority of the *right to life,* which is sacred and not to be intentionally destroyed. It is not a question of whether to be nice; it is a ques-tion of whether to be moral. The statements in *Evangelium Vitae* further clarify this for anyone who somehow missed it. The strangest implication is Pakaluk's insinuation that all the bishops "pressing for abolition" do not know or accept the "real" teach-ing of the church.

In October, Amnesty International's annual report told of thousands of documented killings by government agents in at least two dozen countries during 1988. "Most of the victims died because of their political or religious beliefs, their ethnic identi-fication, or simply because they associated with people consid-ered enemies of the authorities." Concern was expressed about the way the death penalty was being used legally in fifty-eight countries (nearly half of the 133 investigated), including the United States. It noted that while eleven prisoners had been exe-cuted in the United States during the year 1988, there were 2,182 other inmates under sentence of death, waiting on the death rows of thirty-four of the fifty states.[55]

VII. INCREASING U.S. DEVIANCE (1990)

A. Cardinal Bernardin and Consistency "after Webster"

1. In March, Cardinal Bernardin was invited to give a progress report at Georgetown University, speaking on the con-sistent ethic of life after *Webster;* he was to assess how things stood seven years after his Fordham address, thus framing the national debate about value-of-life issues. As indicated by the topic, his chief concern was to assess the impact of the Supreme Court's July 1989 *Webster* decision on the abortion issue. Not only discussing but also practicing consistency, he reviewed other life issues as well, including a brief look at capital punishment.

Noting that the consistent-ethic's opposition was "rooted in the conviction that an atmosphere of respect for life must pervade a society, and resort to capital punishment does not enhance this attitude," he obviously could find no good news to speak of. "The number of men and women condemned to die grows each year; the general public does not share the conviction of the consistent ethic on capital punishment; and we have recently had the spectacle of people running for public office on the basis of whom they are prepared to kill."

With this frank assessment of the bizarre atmosphere that had come to characterize the political scene, he was nonetheless not about to despair.

> Even though the Catholic tradition, in principle, allows states to resort to capital punishment, and in spite of the public consensus which presently exists, I am convinced that a consistent ethic cannot change on this question. But we must be prepared for a long, strenuous effort with no solid hope for early progress....But we should resist the sectarian tendency to retreat into a closed circle....To be both prophetic and public, a countersign to much of the culture, but also a light and leaven for all of it, is the delicate balance to which we are called.[56]

B. The Encyclopedia of World Crime

This standard publication came out around the same time and gave in its treatment of capital punishment a description of the American situation that suggested grounds for the sadness reflected in Bernardin's assessment. It observed:

> The United States is one of only a handful of nations which continue to regard the death penalty as a natural deterrent to crime. Forty-one countries...have now outlawed capital punishment on humanitarian grounds. Within the U.S. advocates of the death penalty argue that the checks and balances within the judicial system are exact and that the chances of the "wrong man" being put to death are remote. However, the history of capital punishment in the U.S. is full of incidents that contradict this assertion.[57]

The image of this country in the 1990s as being an anomalous backward society, perpetuating an anachronous and inhumane penal system for no rational purpose, was engraved on the record for posterity to ponder.

C. Justice William Brennan Retires

Another loss occurred in July when failing health forced 84-year-old Supreme Court Justice William Brennan to retire, leaving Thurgood Marshall in lonely isolation as the only other member of the Court opposed in principle to state killings. The two of them had been central in recognizing execution as cruel and unusual punishment in *Furman v. Georgia* in 1972 and had resisted all subsequent efforts to increase the bloodshed. There was no small irony in the fact that Brennan, whose relations with the U.S. Catholic hierarchy had been so stormy over the divisive issues of abortion and federal aid to parochial schools, was so much in harmony on the capital-punishment issue. As the only Catholic on the Court when he was appointed by President Eisenhower in 1956, he had practically been disowned because of his support for *Roe v. Wade*. "At least two Catholic publications called for his excommunication."[58] But he got little credit from those same quarters for his pro-life position on the death penalty. The case could certainly be made that neither he nor the most vocal of his critics had embraced a fully consistent ethic of life. Such was the ethical confusion that Cardinal Bernardin had been trying to address.

D. The Bishops of Florida Appeal Again

The bishops in the Death Belt were naturally the ones who were most frustrated by all the death-promoting developments in their states. Unwilling to back off from their commitment to the value of human life, the bishops of Florida spoke out again in September 1990, reiterating what they had said (1) in 1972 when the moratorium was still in force, (2) in 1979 when Florida killings began again with John Spenkelink's execution, and (3) in 1983 and 1984 when Florida led the nation in executions. The bishops had hoped that their state might by now have "arrived at the stage where it places primary value on the inviolable dignity of every individual and the sacredness of each human life." But such was obviously not the case.

So, they saw fit to attempt to instruct once more in the most basic manner, to spell out the reasons, to repeat in compact form ten objections or grounds on which their opposition to the death penalty was based, no matter what was the case in earlier years. Killing was simply no longer "an appropriate form of punishment for murder or other serious crimes": (1) It contributes to disrespect of human dignity and human life, and contributes to the atmosphere of violence; (2) it is not a deterrent; (3) it is applied in discriminatory fashion; (4) mistakes can be and have been made; (5) it precludes the possibility of reform or rehabilitation; (6) it necessarily involves long delays, which are themselves cruel and unusual punishment; (7) these cause anguish to the families of both victims and criminals; (8) the attendant publicity arouses animosity and escalates the level of violence; (9) there is no such thing as a "humane way for the state to kill" someone....All forms of execution are brutal and brutalizing; and (10) the ability of a judge to override a jury's recommendation of a life sentence is especially offensive.

> Abolition of the death penalty would help break the cycle of violence...manifest belief in the unique dignity of every individual... acknowledge God as Lord of life, and would be more consonant with the spirit of the Gospel.[59]

There were undoubtedly still Catholics who were in favor of Florida's life-destroying program, but at least it could not be said that it was because the countercultural case against the practice had not been made to them in powerful Christian terms by the Catholic leadership.

E. Virginia Executes Wilbert Evans

Another strange execution occurred in Virginia over the lone dissent of Supreme Court Justice Thurgood Marshall. Wilbert Evans had been convicted of a murder and sentenced to death in 1984 on one of the two grounds allowed in Virginia law, the single aggravating circumstance that he was judged to represent "a future danger to society." Without that finding he could not have been given a death sentence. When a prison riot occurred and he played a crucial role in quelling it and saving the lives of several hostages, preventing the rape of one of the nurses, and effectively pleading with his inmates not to hurt anybody, at least eight prison officials testified to his unusual behavior and the bloodshed he had prevented.

The appeal for a stay of execution on the grounds that his conduct belied the jury's earlier estimate of his "future dangerousness" was granted by a Richmond District court, then lifted by the Fourth Circuit Court of Appeals, which in turn was upheld a day later by the U.S. Supreme Court because of "late-arriving evidence which could unleash endless litigation." Once more, Justice Marshall berated his colleagues for their inverted, insensitive priorities:

> The state's interest in "finality" is no answer to this flaw in the capital-sentencing system. It may indeed be the case that a state cannot realistically accommodate post-sentencing evidence casting doubt on a jury's finding of future dangerousness; but it hardly follows from this that it is *Wilbert Evans* who should bear the burden of this procedural limitation....If it is impossible to construct a system capable of accommodating ALL evidence relevant to a man's entitlement to be spared death,—no matter when that evidence is disclosed—then it is the system, not the life of the man sentenced to death, that should be dispatched.
>
> The indifferent shrug of the shoulders with which the Court answers the failure of its procedures in this case reveals the utter bankruptcy of its notion that a system of capital punishment can coexist with the Eighth Amendment. A death sentence that is *dead wrong* is no less so simply because it is not uncovered until the eleventh hour. A system of capital punishment that would permit Wilbert Evans's execution, notwithstanding as-to-now unrefuted evidence showing that death is an improper sentence, is a system that cannot stand.[60]

There is little question what the history books will have to say about this one. Once again the death penalty proved itself an agent of corruption, depriving the society that condones it of basic human decency.

CHAPTER 11

New Setbacks and Advances
(1991–1996)

I. A Season of Sorrow (1991)
   A. Justice Thurgood Marshall Retires
   B. Georgia Kills Warren McCleskey
   C. Louisiana Kills Andrew Lee Jones

II. The Death Penalty *Redivivus* (1992)
   A. Texas Kills Johnny F. Garrett
   B. Arizona Religious Leaders Speak Out
   C. California Kills Robert A. Harris
   D. *Catholics Against Capital Punishment* Started
   E. The *Universal Catechism* Published
      1. Its Teaching on Capital Punishment
      2. The European Controversy

III. Grim Reminders (1993)
   A. A Northwest Hanging Party
   B. *Herrera v. Collins*
   C. Sister Helen Prejean's *Dead Man Walking*
   D. Walter McMillian's Alabama Nightmare

IV. Pleading for Sanity (1994)
   A. Bishops Speak Out
   B. Justice Blackmun's Reversal

V. Choosing Life (1995)
   A. Strong Words from North Dakota
   B. Pope John Paul II's *Evangelium Vitae*
   C. A Challenge from Charleston, South Carolina
   D. *The HarperCollins Encyclopedia of Catholicism*
   E. South Africa Abolishes the Death Penalty

VI. Twenty Years After *Gregg v. Georgia* (1996)
   A. A Worrisome Winter
   B. A Somber Summer

I. A SEASON OF SORROW (1991)

A. Justice Thurgood Marshall Retires

Chief Justice Rehnquist wrote the six-three ruling that overturned two earlier decisions which prevented prosecutors in a capital case from introducing evidence about the character of a murder victim and the effect of the crime on the murder victim's family. He described the earlier Court decisions as having "unfairly weighted the scales in favor of the defendants, who are allowed to present mitigating evidence." It was the last straw for Justice Thurgood Marshall, who, along with Stevens and Blackmun, was furious. Justice Stevens called it "a sad day for a great institution." Marshall, in the final words of his distinguished career of championing the legal rights of the disadvantaged, noted:

> Power, not reason, is the new currency of this Court's decision-making....Cast aside today are those condemned to face society's ultimate penalty. Tomorrow's victims may be minorities, women, or the indigent. Inevitably, this will squander the authority and the legitimacy of this Court as a protector of the powerless.

Marshall issued his angry dissent and two hours later announced his retirement, "as much out of disgust as ill health."[1] It was the end of an era and the passing of a major ethical voice from the Court.

For years Marshall had been the justice who stood closest to the Catholic bishops' retrieved position on capital punishment. He had been a major influence in getting the Court to rule in *Furman v. Georgia* that the death penalty was unconstitutional. As he put it repeatedly in his years on the Court, "the Eighth Amendment itself was adopted to prevent punishment from becoming synonymous with vengeance." He knew whereof he spoke, having grown up in an era "when lynching was commonplace in America. He had great difficulty viewing a state execution in Georgia, Mississippi, or any of the places where racism was virulent, as little more than a lynching." He gave two principal reasons for his total opposition to capital punishment:

> 1. the death penalty is excessive; and 2. the American people, fully informed as to the purposes of the death penalty and its liabilities, would in my view reject it as morally unacceptable.[2]

The first reason reflected the depth of his respect for the human person. Punishment, to be punishment, must stop short of killing the person. Execution flunks the definition; it is not punishment but extermination. The second reason reflected the depth of his faith in the power of education to change the way human beings live. To the objection that the country was using the death penalty regularly at the very time that the Constitution was being written, he calmly replied: "That's true. They also put people in jail for debt...and did a lot of other things that we don't do now."[3] Among the most obvious of these immoralities were human slavery and judicial torture. These former "essentials" have long since been abolished from law codes in which they used to be granted the secure status of "natural institutions."

Less than six months later, during the Senate Judiciary Committee's hearings prior to confirming him as Marshall's replacement, Clarence Thomas assured the examining senators that he would have "no problem upholding the death penalty in appropriate cases."[4] The legacy of Thurgood Marshall on the Supreme Court had been securely placed on indefinite hold.

B. Georgia Kills Warren McCleskey

In this same season the state of Georgia pressed ahead and executed Warren McCleskey, even though questions about his guilt had not been resolved. His case had come before the Supreme Court three times, raising recurring questions about "Southern justice" as found in "perfunctory death penalty trials where everybody knew before the trial started what the outcome would be, as a way around the bad press it was getting for lynching people. These kinds of 'legal lynchings' still take place in capital trials around the country today."[5] But by limiting the appeals process and hastening executions, the Court could also cut down on the amount of bad press provoked by some trials.

C. Louisiana Kills Andrew Lee Jones

One such unfair trial led to the execution of Andrew Lee Jones in Lousiana's electric chair in July, but not before it had had an unusual impact overseas. The *Andrew Lee Jones Fund* was created in Great Britain to help raise money to provide qualified legal assistance to the poor on U.S. death rows, who were often kept there because of incompetent and ineffective counsel.[6]

II. THE DEATH-PENALTY *REDIVIVUS* (1992)

A. Texas Kills Johnny F. Garrett

On January 3, Pope John Paul II and the Catholic bishops of Texas urged a stay of execution for Johnny Frank Garrett, who had killed a 76-year-old nun in 1981. On January 6, just one hour before his scheduled execution, Governor Ann Richards issued a thirty-day reprieve in response to these pleas, in order to allow time for the Texas Board of Pardons and Paroles to hold a clemency hearing. On January 22, Bishop Leroy Matthiesen of Amarillo, speaking for Archbishop Flores and the seventeen other bishops of Texas, released to the press a copy of a letter he had written to the Texas Board, testifying to his personal knowledge that Garrett had been raised in a "thoroughly dysfunctional family." On February 5, the Board voted 17-0 against commuting Garrett's death sentence, and on February 11, the state of Texas executed Johnny Frank Garrett despite all the pleas for clemency. The bishops of Texas let their collective disapproval of their state's action be known:

> We raise our voices in union with those of Pope John Paul II, of Archbishop Cacciavillan, papal pro-nuncio to the U.S., as well as with the voices of Amnesty International, the Franciscan Sisters of Mary Immaculate of Amarillo and with the voices of other religious communities as well as with other groups and individuals.[7]

B. Arizona Religious Leaders Speak Out

On the same day that the Texas bishops were opposing the planned killing of Garrett in their state, an ecumenical statement signed by nine Christian leaders in Arizona was released protesting the planned gassing of murderer Donald E. Harding. Noting that there were 102 persons on Arizona's death row at the time, these leaders voiced their unity in opposing capital punishment:

> We want to bear witness that the death penalty cannot be justified as a legitimate tool of society's justice system. The denominations we represent in Arizona have spoken nationally against the death penalty....Our opposition relies principally on our faith vision of human dignity and solidarity....We believe that punishment should be primarily redemptive, reformative, and restorative....Capital punishment does not lead us to these goals, either for the victim or for the criminal....The use of the death penalty is inconsistent with the Christian calling to honor the sanctity of all of human life....To succumb to the retaliatory violence of capital punishment is abdicating our responsibility as Christians and as human beings.[8]

C. California Kills Robert A. Harris

On April 21, Robert Alton Harris was executed in the gas chamber in California, the first such event in twenty-five years. A flood of international protest surrounded this incident as well. The London *Times* could not believe the barbarity of it and suggested that "in any other country...it would be universally condemned as a cruel violation of human rights." In France *Le Monde* described it on page one as "a sinister spectacle."[9] In Italy *L'Osservatore Romano* headlined it as a cruel and barbaric act done by "a treacherous justice."

Convicted of killing two teen-agers fourteen years earlier, Harris had received four separate stays of execution from the Ninth Circuit Court of Appeals, each one being overturned by the U.S. Supreme Court. He died more than six hours after schedule on his final day, and there were unforeseen glitches. The Roman newspaper listed numerous barbarities to which it objected: "the cyanide gas, the inhuman agony, the confusing swing of hopes, postponements and statements, all the while being tied to the chair in the gas chamber, watching with desperate eyes the small group of journalists and witnesses coldly gathered behind a thick, bulletproof window."[10]

What guaranteed worldwide attention for the Harris case was, first, the lawsuit initiated by San Francisco TV station KQED against the warden of San Quentin over whether the execution could be televised; and second, the "mesmerizing study about the spectatorship of murder" written by Wendy Lesser with the Harris case as its centerpiece.[11] As Lesser notes at the end, the court compromise was to have the execution videotaped for possible use in future cases involving the constitutionality of gas-chamber executions, but at the same time to prevent it from being released to the media or the public.

L'Osservatore Romano, in protesting both of these executions (California and Texas), included several remarks that caught attention. "The paper detected a primitive instinct of vendetta in developed and well-off societies." Cardinal Fiorenzo Angelini remarked on the anomaly of groups that oppose abortion but support the death penalty: "This is incoherent and an unacceptable contradiction." In former times, it was noted, Catholic theologians admitted the death penalty as legitimate, "but, today, it is no longer admissible."[12]

D. Catholics Against Capital Punishment

The formation of Catholics Against Capital Punishment was announced in January 1992. Its explicit goal is "disseminating more widely the teachings of the Roman Catholic Church...(in particular, the statements of the U.S. bishops)...which characterize capital punishment as inappropriate and unacceptable in today's world."[13] The CACP newsletter quickly established itself as a valuable resource, compiling information and monitoring developments, reprinting relevant statements, and telling of the solid work being done by many in the current struggle to abolish the "anachronous barbarism" of capital punishment from U.S. society.

The fourth issue of CACP (July 30) called attention to the death that month of Albert Pierrepoint at the age of 87. He had started his "fine art of hanging" in 1931 when his uncle Tom asked him to come along as an assistant at an execution in Dublin. He was Britain's chief executioner from 1946 till he retired in 1956, and in the course of his career had hanged 433 men and 17 women. He could be viewed as a kind of personification of the century: a man deeply involved in state killings for twenty-five years, who then turned against capital punishment. Pierrepoint became an outspoken critic in his latter days, doing all he could to get the death penalty abolished and to prevent its return when advocates were calling for it in the wake of the horrors of terrorism. In 1974, for instance, he countered the claim that executions deterred crime or did anything else positive by stating bluntly: "Capital punishment, in my view, has never achieved anything except revenge."[14]

In November of this same year *In Spite of Innocence* by Hugo A. Bedau, Michael Radelet, and Constance Putnam was published. It told of "the ordeal of 400 Americans wrongly convicted of crimes punishable by death," twenty-three of them persons who were erroneously executed in the United States during this century alone. Mario Cuomo, governor of New York, said of it that "the text documents how human mistakes, passions and prejudices have led to the unjust conviction and erroneous execution of too many Americans. This compelling evidence cannot be ignored."[15]

E. *The* Universal Catechism *Published*

A new Catholic catechism appeared in Europe in late 1992 in French, Spanish, and Italian, and was greeted with a variety of reactions. The English version was delayed for two years because of translation controversies and other complications. It was finally published as *The Catechism of the Catholic Church* in 1994. Archbishop William Levada of Portland, Oregon, gave an account of its background at a special symposium before the appearance of the English translation, mentioning that over three million copies were sold in Europe in its first year, even though "this new catechism was written in the first place for bishops."[16] The catechism included a treatment of the death penalty that soon became the target of criticism in Europe, and the controversy that arose is of interest especially in light of subsequent developments.[17]

1. ITS TEACHING ON CAPITAL PUNISHMENT

The core principle of the seventy-one-paragraph treatment of the fifth commandment is articulated in the lead paragraph:

> Human life is sacred because from its beginning it involves the creative action of God and it remains forever in a special relationship with the Creator, who is its sole end. God alone is the Lord of life from its beginning until its end; no one can under any circumstance claim for himself the right directly to destroy an innocent human being. (2258)

This is the crucial, central emphasis, the principle beyond compromise brought to bear on all actions touching human life. The consistency of this focus is what makes this treatment of the death penalty superior to its counterpart in the *Roman Catechism* of 1566.

The skeleton outline of the section is impressive, signaling that the treatment is very different from that of its Tridentine forerunners:

5th Commandment—"YOU SHALL NOT KILL"

I. RESPECT FOR HUMAN LIFE
    The Witness of Sacred History   (2259–62)
    Legitimate Defense   (2263–67)
    Intentional Homicide   (2268–69)
    Abortion   (2270–75)
    Euthanasia   (2276–79)
    Suicide   (2280–83)

II. RESPECT FOR THE DIGNITY OF PERSONS
    Respect for the Souls of Others:
        Scandal   (2284–87)
    Respect for Health   (2288–91)
    Respect for the Person and Scientific
        Research   (2292–96)
    Respect for Bodily Integrity   (2297–98)
    Respect for the Dead   (2299–2301)

III. SAFEGUARDING PEACE
    Peace   (2302–06)
    Avoiding War   (2307–17)

The first and most striking feature of this commentary on the meaning of the fifth commandment, communicated by the very outline, is the simple fact that *capital punishment,* as such, does not even appear as a separate topic! In the *Roman Catechism* it was right there at the start, holding an ominously prominent place; it was the first "Great Exception," which was carefully safeguarded before one started prohibiting all the other kinds of killing; its time-honored pedestal was lofty and guaranteed. Not so here. Rather, the overwhelming message conveyed even by the outline is the primacy of the total respect for life that cannot be morally dispensed with.

THE WITNESS OF SACRED HISTORY

2259—First, the story of Cain's murder of his brother Abel is reviewed as classically revealing "the presence of anger and envy in man....Man has become the enemy of his fellow man. God declares the wickedness of this fratricide." So, while it highlights Cain's sinful disrespect for human life and all the tragic evils this violent killing will bring upon humanity, it misses the opportunity to point out another important lesson in respect for human life: God's respect for Cain's life, not executing him or having someone else do so for his murder of Abel, but actually putting a mark on him to protect him from such a fate. This is one of the places where Pope John Paul II did some fine-tuning in his 1995 encyclical; and it will reportedly be improved in the Latin edition scheduled to appear in mid-1997.[18]

2260—"The covenant between God and mankind is interwoven with reminders of God's gift of human life and man's murderous violence." The quotation from Genesis 9:6 follows: "Whoever sheds the blood of man, by man shall his blood be shed; for God made man in his own image." But, surprisingly, this text is recalled not as a proof-text for the death penalty, as was the constant interpretation in the past, but as a proverb, a truism, a sad poetic comment on the results of human sin. It is not read as a call for blood but as a lament over its inevitability, given human weakness. This is a good example of the retrieval of a biblical text from an ideological morass in which it had been entangled for centuries. The recovered context requires that the text be read as part of the overall instruction in respect for the value of human life, which the commandment inculcates for everyone, not as a sanction for retaliatory killing, which is its complete antithesis.

2261—The text continues, in no way softening the horrendous evil of homicide: "The deliberate murder of an innocent person is gravely contrary to the dignity of the human being, to the golden rule, and to the holiness of the Creator. The law forbidding it is universally valid: it obliges each and everyone, always and everywhere." There is, as mentioned earlier, some ambivalence here with the restriction to respecting innocent life, but that may derive from the fact that the text just quoted (Ex 23:7: "Do not slay the innocent and the righteous") is so phrased. What to do, ideally, about the guilty and the unrighteous is simply not the subject under discussion at this point and thus is not directly addressed here.

2262—With the general principle restated in unambiguous terms, notice is then given to the explicitly expanded teaching of Jesus, which forbids not only the act of murder but also any and all acts of "anger, hatred and vengeance. Going further, Christ asks his disciples to turn the other cheek, to love their enemies. He did not defend himself and told Peter to leave his sword in its sheath." It would be difficult to find fault with this "witness to sacred history" insofar as priorities, principles, and perspective are concerned. The positive requirements of the commandment not to kill have been spelled out in challenging terms, appealing to the example of Cain as the one most to avoid, and the example of Jesus as the one most to obey and imitate.

LEGITIMATE DEFENSE

2263—This second heading under "Respect for Human Life" is the crucial portion where the problem of capital punishment must be dealt with. The 1566 *Roman Catechism* had told pastors that "it should first be taught what kinds of killing are not forbidden by this Commandment,"[19] and the traditional headings of the earlier catechism refer to these as "exceptions" to the commandment. But here the authors begin rather by insisting that "the legitimate defense of persons and societies is *not* an exception to the prohibition against the murder of the innocent that constitutes intentional killing." One senses that there were probably some heavy arguments over how to formulate this delicate area, and that the final redaction (#2263, 2264 and 2265) settled for some of the classical quotes of Aquinas, justifying the killing of an aggressor in self-defense on the principle of double effect, carefully including the caution that "if a man in self-defense uses more than necessary violence, it will be unlawful."

2266—It is at this point and in this context that Aquinas's "social security" argument for capital punishment is presented:

> Preserving the common good of society requires rendering the aggressor unable to inflict harm. For this reason the traditional teaching of the Church has acknowledged as well-founded the right and duty of legitimate public authority to punish malefactors by means of penalties commensurate with the gravity of the crime, not excluding, in cases of extreme gravity, the death penalty.

The text (still #2266) goes on to give a brief summary of Scholastic penal theory, contending that

> the primary effect of punishment is to redress the disorder caused by the offense. When his punishment is voluntarily accepted by the offender, it takes on the value of expiation. Moreover, punishment has the effect of preserving public order and the safety of persons. Finally punishment has a medicinal value; as far as possible it should contribute to the correction of the offender.

As it stands, this is a singularly inadequate presentation, added on the heels of an unargued defense of the tradition of killing malefactors, but not including a single word about the intense controversy to which the contents of these two paragraphs have been subjected over the past two centuries, and especially during the last thirty years. One gets the impression that an editorial committee must have disagreed and ended up in compromise, with the more traditionalist members writing these first two paragraphs, then those who were more aware of current developments being allowed to add the following paragraph as at least a measure of concession to modernity:

> 2267—If bloodless means are sufficient to defend human lives against an aggressor and to protect public order and the safety of persons, public authority should limit itself to such means, because they better correspond to the concrete conditions of the common good and are more in conformity to the dignity of the human person.

Here too Pope John Paul II apparently found the catechism wanting and sharpened the teaching in this section by his 1995 encyclical. It is also worth noting that at least the French, Canadian, United States, Irish, Italian, and Filipino Catholic Bishops' Conferences had all gone on record with statements that went considerably beyond the catechism's basic position on the issue of the death penalty well before the catechism was published. This undoubtedly explains some of the dismay with which it was greeted in some quarters.

But one also can be thankful for small favors. The above teaching, even if not incorporating as complete a repudiation of the death penalty as many desired, is nonetheless a significant modification of the tradition. It admits that historical changes have occurred, that "bloodless means" better corresponding to modern conditions do in fact exist, that there are alternatives to killing available in a modern state, that a nonviolent way should always take priority, and that such are "more in conformity to the dignity of the human person," as has been emphasized wherever the spirit of Pope John XXIII and Vatican II has been given a hearing. The death penalty is as outmoded and unjustified as chopping off hands, plucking out eyes, disembowelling bodies, and other such practices that were regularly blessed in the past.

Two other relevant passages come later, in the second part under the heading "Respect for the Dignity of Persons, the fourth section—Respect for Bodily Integrity." The issue is torture, an inherent part of capital punishment, making it by definition cruel and unusual punishment:

> 2297—Torture which uses physical or moral violence to extract confessions, punish the guilty, frighten opponents, or satisfy hatred is contrary to respect for the person and for human dignity.

In light of the invaluable work of Amnesty International in our day, it is gratifying to see this straightforward acknowledgment of the outright immorality of torture—the twin of capital punishment. But even more welcome is the next paragraph, which is the kind of confession that was simply impossible, for example, in the cultural context of Cardinal Bellarmine's time:

> 2298—In times past, cruel practices were commonly used by legitimate governments to maintain law and order, often without protest from the Pastors of the Church, who themselves adopted in their own tribunals the prescriptions of Roman Law concerning torture. Regrettable as these facts are, the Church always taught the duty of clemency and mercy. She forbade clerics to shed blood. In recent times it has become evident that these cruel practices were neither necessary for public order, nor in conformity with the legitimate rights of the human person. On the contrary, these practices led to ones even more degrading. It is necessary to work for their abolition. We must pray for the victims and their tormentors.

Once again, it is tempting to engage in a hermeneutic of suspicion and hypothesize about divided authorship. Could the above paragraph have been written by the same author as the previous paragraphs? If one accepts paragraphs 2297–2298 as accurate in evaluating the immorality of torture today, how could one avoid applying them equally to capital punishment? In the final analysis, paragraph 2298 may eventually be recognized as the crown jewel of this part of the catechism, the statement that articulates most richly the Catholic retrieval of what is required for a contemporary Christian assessment of the right to life, with which the death penalty is in diametrical opposition.

2. THE EUROPEAN CONTROVERSY

Passages like 2298 represent a greater step forward than others do in promoting sensitivity to the realm of human rights. But there are obviously different assessments of capital punishment in Catholic (just as in other) circles today. The catechism as published is a mix, a compromise document reflecting competing positions as the process of change continues. It is unquestionably an immense improvement over the *Roman Catechism* of 1566, but not nearly as good on capital punishment as some of the bishops' statements, for example, those of the Indiana and Tennessee bishops made years before the new catechism came out.

Why the early complaints about the catechism's treatment of capital punishment? One of the first to attempt a broader analysis was Fr. Denis O'Callaghan, an Irish moral theologian, who painted this picture:

> Behind the condemnation by all civilized societies of the gross abuse of capital punishment in some parts of the world, behind the emotional exchange on the relative merits of various methods, there is the radical query about the very substance of the death penalty as an ethically legitimate option in any circumstances....The expectation had certainly been, for the minority who had considered the issue, that as formal principle, the death penalty would no longer have a place in Catholic ethics.[20]

It was from this well-informed minority that the expressions of disappointment first came. The catechism had simply not gone far enough. They had hoped to see a clear, outright, general condemnation of any and all capital punishment as an abomination to be abolished with the same kind of total rejection as were the sins of human slavery and judicial torture. This the catechism did not do. It chose to stay with the safer self-defense and double-effect principles of Thomas Aquinas. But it used those principles not to support but to repudiate the use of capital punishment in modern society.[21]

One unfortunate factor introduced early into the dispute was an insinuation of political motivation—that the Vatican chose not to include a blanket condemnation of the death penalty so as not to embarrass the United States. Such an allegation found little credibility, especially given the consistency with which Pope John Paul II had issued "embarrassing" calls for clemency or commutation in individual U.S. cases. Fr. O'Callaghan, however, had a more intriguing conjecture. All one has to do is look at the teaching of the two catechisms (1566 and 1992) to realize that we are dealing with a monumental change or development. Given the problems connected with such changes in a tradition-minded institution like the Catholic Church, the real marvel is that so much change has been accomplished in so short a time. O'Callaghan pointed especially to a fascinating psychological factor:

> In contemporary debate the death penalty issue sees conservative and liberal exchanging what had come to be accepted as their standard ideological positions. As a consequence, both feel uncomfortable. The conservative finds himself supporting his side of the case (pro-death-penalty) on the principle of the end justifying the means through a utilitarian set of premises. The liberal finds himself supporting his side (anti-death-penalty) on the plea that here is something which no circumstances can justify, something which falls constructively within the purview of intrinsic evil. Like other issues where human life is at stake it is important that the death penalty continue to be seen as matter for serious debate.[22]

One possibility may be that the position adopted in the catechism and in many of the bishops' statements can best be viewed as a mediating stance, not an endpoint. Going back to Gilmore's execution in 1977, the liberal stance of Concetti and the conservative stance of Furey were so far apart as to make it virtually impossible for them to understand one another. The mediating position of Bernardin carried the day because it combined old and new, repudiating the practice of capital punishment in our day without repudiating the principles on which that practice had earlier been based. That was its advantage, but that did not mean it was the end of the line. Many felt that it was still necessary to drive the stake through the heart of the monster lest it rise again. Deeper changes were at work that would ultimately require rearticulation so that the message would find a form that said finally (to paraphrase Pope Paul VI at the UN on the parallel problem of war): "No more capital punishment; capital punishment never again!"[23]

The catechism in this perspective represents a significant advance. It emphasizes the ironic impropriety of the state continuing to kill murderers so as to show that murder is wrong. Fr. Compagnoni explicitly called attention to the parallel between the modern work of Amnesty International, monitoring the abuses and violations of human rights committed by any and all governments, and the prophetic witness of early Christians with their commitment to a lifestyle that illustrated their full obedience to God's command: "Thou shalt not kill."[24] By its very position, however, the catechism leaves the door open for further progress.

This may be what Cardinal Ratzinger meant in his widely-quoted comments when the catechism was introduced on the thirtieth aniversary of the opening of Vatican II (December 7, 1992). He assured his audience that the catechism "does not simply detach itself from 2,000 years of tradition...but develops a road, an evolution," restricting its use today to "extreme situations." For some European Catholics, however, this "progress" was perceived as too little too late. One poll reported that

> more than half the Italian clergy disagreed with the catechism's guidelines on the death penalty. It showed that 52% of Italy's priests opposed executions in principle and said they were unable to back the view outlined in the text.[25]

This example highlighted a difficulty inherent in the very idea of a "universal" catechism. On this issue the socio-politico-cultural conditions make extremely important differences. Those Europeans whose nations have already lived for a generation or more without the death penalty are in a better position to understand why it is past time to do away with the traditional mythology. The new catechism was already behind the times for many Europeans, and thus a distinct disappointment.

Some ten months after the catechism appeared, another public exchange with Cardinal Ratzinger took place. It was at the October 5, 1993, Vatican press conference introducing Pope John Paul II's new encyclical on moral theology, *Veritatis Splendor*. Ratzinger was asked once again how capital punishment could still be regarded as a legitimate response to crime. His preference this time was to hand the microphone to Albert Chapelle, a Belgian Jesuit. In his reply the latter noted that "many Western episcopates have judged that in a law-based state, in times of peace, the death penalty would no longer be legitimate....The catechism does not contradict this teaching in any way."[26]

What had brought the dispute back to the front page was an editorial three days earlier in *La Civiltà Cattolica*. The editorial said that the staff also had hoped for an outright condemnation of capital punishment in the catechism but realized the practical problem: the death penalty is still legal in many countries and enjoys the support of public opinion. The catechism, by putting strong limits on its use and advocating bloodless means as preferable, was trying to "change the Catholic segment of public opinion."[27] The practical policy goals coincided; the theoretical grounds diverged. The catechism, for the time being, represented the less progressive position, but the discussion was far from over.

III. GRIM REMINDERS (1993)

A. *A Northwest Hanging Party*

The New Year got off to a strange start as a media circus moved its heavy equipment into Walla Walla, Washington, to cover every detail of the gruesome hanging of Westley Allan Dodd. The state of Washington had not staged a legal hanging for thirty years, so more than a hundred reporters turned up for the occasion. Nostalgia for the days of simpler justice in the "Wild West" apparently drew the throngs, but this time there was an interesting difference. The local Catholic Church, St. Patrick's, with the full collaboration of its pastor, Fr. Kevin A. Codd, provided its parish hall to serve as headquarters for the groups of protesters, and Sister Susanne Jabro, C.S.J., of the Seattle Archdiocesan Detention Ministry Office, coordinated prayer vigils for the protesters. After the announcement, at 12:15 A.M. on January 5, that the execution was over and Dodd was dead, the producers of the media show went home, but Fr. Codd then tried to make some sense of what had happened. He found no pious grounds in biblical allusions to killing malefactors but offered his own down-to-earth analysis:

> A morbid sense of attraction to things gruesome...brought this circus to our town. The questions...almost always came back to the noose. [It was] an act of barbarism [that brought them], a show not intended to do justice but to give us our turn to say, "Hang the son-of-a-bitch!" It is our chance to see vicariously what our forebears actually saw: a man swinging from a tree by the neck...so that we might feel for ourselves the surge of satisfaction at having killed the beast....The truth, of course, is that the beast is not really dead.[28]

B. Herrera v. Collins

On January 25, the U.S. Supreme Court rendered another controversial decision, contending that under the Constitution a death-row inmate who presents newly discovered evidence, that— if proven—could establish his innocence, is not ordinarily entitled to a new hearing in federal court.

The appeals court had offered the opinion that "actual innocence" was irrelevant if it had not been determined in the original trial. Herrera's attorneys had appealed to the Supreme Court, and now five justices concurred with the lower court, refusing to block the execution, while the other four agreed to hear arguments related to the Eighth Amendment's application. Is it cruel and unusual punishment to execute a convicted capital murderer who may be innocent on the basis of evidence obtained after the conviction is final? The surprising decision was that such new evidence need not be considered.[29]

The decision was so shocking to Senators Howard Metzenbaum (D-Ohio) and Mark Hatfield (R-Oregon) that they introduced legislation which, if passed, would explicitly allow a prisoner to obtain judicial review of such evidence.

> If we fail to respond to the court's opinion in *Herrera,* I believe we will make a mockery of the 14th Amendment's guarantee that no state shall "deprive any person of life...without due process of law."...When a government lawyer can stand before the Supreme Court and argue that knowingly convicting an *innocent* person does not violate the

Constitution, then I think we have to ask whether our zeal for capital punishment has begun to blind our sense of justice.[30]

There was a final touch of irony in the fact that former Justice Thurgood Marshall died the night before the release of this decision, in which "the Supreme Court again spoke in the voice of indifference, again shaped the law untempered by justice....[Marshall] was the greatest lawman of the age...who knew that even a Constitution born in racism was redeemable if one used the values at its core to deal humanely with the life around us." He once noted that, while we have a great Constitution today, "it didn't start out that way." Only the humane interpretations of Justices like Brandeis, Warren, Brennan, and Marshall "replaced cramped formalism with decency."[31]

The state of Texas proceeded to kill Leonel Herrera in May, despite strong new evidence that he was not guilty of the murders for which he had already spent eleven years in jail.

C. Sister Helen Prejean's Dead Man Walking

With the appearance of *Dead Man Walking,* U.S. Catholic discussions of the death penalty entered a new phase. As Garry Wills remarked in his review:

> She tells her story with a quiet eloquence...yet we learn, by the narrative's cumulative force, how the killing process hardens, coarsens, corrupts and deadens those who serve it, from governors down to the anonymous executioners who do not even want to be identified with what they do.[32]

Sister Prejean's book is a powerful, experiential account of the inevitable heartbreak and challenge of maintaining a credible Christian ministry toward both convicted murderers and their victims' survivors.[33] But most of all, the book is a healthy illustration of the "entirely new attitude" required when gospel values are brought back to the evaluation of capital punishment. When *Dead Man Walking* later appeared as an Academy-Award-winning film (directed by Tim Robbins and starring Susan Sarandon and Sean Penn), Sister Helen's message suddenly had a far broader audience and an unparalleled impact, leading thousands to give more serious thought to this painful subject than ever before.

D. Walter McMillian's Alabama Nightmare

In March one of the horror stories of the century had a relatively happy ending when the state of Alabama finally had to release Walter McMillian, who had spent six years on death row waiting to be executed for a murder he had no part in and knew nothing about. His story reads like an incident out of the most racist days of the distant past, so much so that he was asked to tell it to the U.S. Senate Judiciary Committee the month after his release. Not only had his whole family and church community testified that he was with them and nowhere near the murder scene when it occurred, but he was not even a suspect seven months after the event, when a lynch gang of state police and others suddenly arrested him, telling him he was charged with sodomy. "I asked them what that meant....They never told me where, when or how I had committed this crime....The charge was later dismissed by the Court because there was no factual evidence."

But a prisoner then claimed that McMillian's truck (which the prisoner wrongly described) had been seen near the murder scene months before. McMillian was charged on the grounds of this "perjured hearsay" and was actually placed on death row immediately and kept there for a year before his case even came to trial. Then "fine, upstanding members of the black community" testified in his favor, but "they were no match for a white, convicted felon (who testified against him)....A self-proclaimed murderer had more credibility to my nearly all-white jury than the upstanding members of our community." McMillian knew that his release was a fluke. He had seen seven other Alabama prisoners executed during his time on death row. "From my cell you could smell the stench of burning flesh....My life will never be the same."[34]

And yet the killing continued. Brazilian lawyer Belisario Dos Santos, a member of the Justice and Peace Commission of the Archdiocese of São Paulo, acknowledged the terrible abuses of which his own government was blatantly guilty but then asked an obvious question about what the United States was doing:

Agents of the state kill without judicial proceedings inside the prisons, and the same agents of the state execute children, poor people and black people, extra-judicially....However, I don't know which is worse, the hypocrisy before the systematic immunity of the killers, or the perversion of a judicial system which, because of technicalities, allows executions with racist juries, inexperienced attorneys, and the conviction of innocent people in a game that is more political than judicial.[35]

Whichever one may consider worse, both are stark violations of the right to life expressive of the dignity of the human person.

IV. PLEADING FOR SANITY (1994)

A. Bishops Speak Out

In January the six bishops of Kansas called on all Kansans to join with them in fighting attempts to reinstate the death penalty. Thirty-eight states had already done so since the Supreme Court had struck it down in *Furman v. Georgia* in 1972. The bishops declared their firm belief that the death penalty "takes us down the wrong road," fueling vengeance, diverting energies from forgiveness, and greatly diminishing respect for all human life.

In May, eight days before mass-murderer John Wayne Gacy was executed, the Catholic Conference of Illinois released a statement of the bishops reaffirming their principled opposition to all capital punishment. They explained once more that this opposition is due to their belief that life is sacred and that "destroying it is in violation of our responsibility to protect and enhance it at all stages of its development."[36]

Also in May, the bishops of the state of Washington (retired Seattle archbishop, Raymond Hunthausen, his successor, Thomas Murphy, Spokane bishop, William Skylstad, and Yakima bishop, Francis George) described the planned execution of convicted murderer Charles Campbell in these terms:

[It is] inequitable, vengeful and ineffective in deterring crime....At a time when society cries out for an end to violence, the death penalty...involves us all in the business of killing...undermines God's love of law and forgiveness...perpetuates violence, fuels vengeance, and greatly diminishes respect for human life.[37]

In June the bishops of Louisiana felt compelled to "raise a voice of reasoned dissent" against the growing use of the death penalty in their state:

> We are convinced that there is a more responsible way to address the growing incidence of murders and other acts of violence in our midst. We are aware that since 1722, when the first legal execution in Louisiana was recorded, there have been about 1,000 executions in our state. Twenty-one have taken place in the last 10 years. Homicides have not decreased. We are convinced that violence begets violence; death begets death....Our problem is this: Capital punishment plunges us farther into the culture of death. We are convinced that we must choose consistently for life. This means forgoing a right to impose the death penalty in order to reverse the culture of violence and death. We favor a deliberate and courageous decision to break the cycle of violence. We must choose life.

B. Justice Blackmun's Reversal

It was also in 1994 that Justice Harry A. Blackmun changed his position after more than two decades on the U.S. Supreme Court—and found the death penalty no longer acceptable:

> From this day forward, I no longer shall tinker with the machinery of death. For more than 20 years I have endeavored...to develop procedural and substantive rules that would lend more than the mere appearance of fairness to the death penalty endeavor. Rather than continue to coddle the Court's delusion that the desired level of fairness has been achieved and the need for regulation eviscerated, I feel morally and intellectually obligated simply to concede that the death penalty experiment has failed....The death penalty remains fraught with arbitrariness, discrimination,

caprice, and mistake....I believe that the death penalty, as currently administered, is unconstitutional.[38]

Blackmun's change of heart had no practical impact, since it came as a dissent to a majority decision not to review the case of a Texas man who was sentenced to die. Less than two months [later], the eighty-five-year-old justice retired from the Court.[39]

V. CHOOSING LIFE (1995)

A. *Strong Words from North Dakota*

In January the North Dakota Catholic Conference issued a statement entitled "Crime and Punishment," invoking the teaching and language of the recently published catechism and insisting:

> If bloodless means are available...the state should reject use of the death penalty....Bloodless means are available in North Dakota....Although the prospect of imminent death may motivate the offender to undergo a conversion or change of heart, other means can accomplish the same end. In addition, since the death penalty deprives the criminal of life, it cannot lead to the type of rehabilitation that can allow the offender, even if incarcerated, to participate in the community of persons.[40]

The statement, however, was more than a mere rehash of the catechism. It set forth opposition to capital punishment in unusually strong and clear terms, pointing out its basic incompatibility with Christian faith today:

> The test of every public policy...is whether it enhances or threatens human life and dignity....We must not approach such a matter lightly or leave it to the winds of public opinion. It demands great scrutiny and a rightly formed conscience. Above all, we must root our approach to punishment, especially punishment by death, in respect for the sanctity of human life and the dignity of all persons, and the preservation and enhancement of the common good.

Another interesting point was the bishops' special educational effort to correct what they recognized as a long-standing misconception:

> It is important to distinguish between *retributive justice*—the redressing of the disorder caused by the offense—and the spirit of *vindictiveness*. All persons, even those most affected by the crime, ought to accompany acts of punishment with an attitude of forgiveness. Moreover, it is erroneous to believe that unless the death penalty is carried out, proper retribution cannot take place. In Catholic tradition, the state has the right, but not the duty, to exercise the death penalty. There is no obligation to use the death penalty; other means can restore the order of justice.

Another feature of this short but potent statement was its expression of concern for victims and their families:

> We acknowledge the shattering pain that comes with violent crime. We mourn as a community all who have lost loved ones to acts of violence. It is the particular responsibility of the faith community to provide support to the victims and foster healing. We also urge all people to participate in and support acts of reconciliation between victims of tragic crimes and criminal offenders so that we may share in the incomparable experience of forgiveness and underscore the meaning of "Love your neighbor as yourself."

One could hardly ask for a clearer example of what had happened in church teaching about capital punishment in the three decades since the close of Vatican II. A Catholic statement such as this would have been literally unimaginable in earlier days.

A practical illustration of the new spirit came in March, when Sister Joanne Marie Mascha, 58, was murdered on the grounds of Ursuline College in a suburb of Cleveland. A 21-year-old man was arrested as a suspect. The Ursuline Sisters immediately petitioned the prosecutors not to seek the death penalty. Sister Maureen McCarthy, the Ursuline superior general, told the press: "I am sure Joanne Marie would be the first to ask forgiveness....I cannot think we can possibly eliminate violence with more violence. I think if you are pro-life...you have to be consistent with all life."[41] Not only had the message been heard, but it was being lived and passed on.

B. *Pope John Paul II's* Evangelium Vitae

In that same month Pope John Paul II released his encyclical *Evangelium Vitae,*[42] in which he had more to say about capital punishment than had any previous pope in a comparably authoritative document. His spirited repudiation of death as a punishment was all but total, to the consternation of many. The treatment of the subject in the catechism was obviously on his mind, and at least three times he seemed anxious to clarify or fine-tune what had been written there.

Paragraph #9 further elaborates on the significance and applicability of the Cain-Abel narrative by noting that "God, who is always merciful even when he punishes, 'put a mark on Cain, lest any who came upon him should kill him' (Gen 4:15)." The striking lesson of contemporary relevance that the pope draws from this is that "not even a murderer loses his personal dignity, and God himself pledges to guarantee this." This intriguing remark is obviously meant as the beginning rather than the end of an extended conversation. It is a call for probing the biblical story on deeper levels, much as is encouraged in contemporary literary studies. As Ricardo Quinones points out:

> The very prevalence of the Cain-Abel story...would indicate an essential concern for matters of justice, and this cuts across the board, from regenerate Cain, to the dramas of envy, to Cain of future history. Utilization of Cain-Abel is in most instances *prima facie* evidence that one is addressing community ethics in the most serious sense, that one is addressing principles of validation for acts of innovative change.[43]

Paragraph #27 of the encyclical offers an interesting judgment on recent history. Despite the virtually universal acceptance of and reliance upon capital punishment in Catholic circles in so much of earlier history, the time for radical change has come, and there is no longer any reason for reluctance on the part of the Catholic community in embracing total abolition of the death penalty. The pope voices his personal conviction that "we should count among the signs of hope...the growing public opposition to the death penalty."

But it was paragraph #56 that was probably the most noticed statement in the entire encyclical, and certainly the most relevant regarding capital punishment. After quoting from the recent catechism, Pope John Paul sharpened its teaching more pointedly by insisting that criminal punishment "ought not go to the *extreme of executing* the offender except in cases of absolute necessity: in other words, when it would not be possible otherwise to defend society." Such cases, moreover, are at best "very rare, if not practically nonexistent."

Cardinal Ratzinger commented, when he was introducing the encyclical to the press, that the catechism would obviously have to be modified as a result. Fr. Richard McCormick remarked that this "papal position will make all supporters of capital punishment—including some anti-abortionists—squirm."[44]

The routine practice of capital punishment is here branded as devoid of ethical sanction because it does not meet the requirements of basic moral principles. Priority is thus restored to the presumption that "thou shalt not kill" (because human life is sacred), since that presumption can almost never be offset today. The two positions that collide here (absolutely no killing vs. absolutely no killing except in "practically nonexistent" cases) predictably gave rise to controversy over the encyclical, just as had been the case with the catechism.[45] Both the catechism and the encyclical stop short of absolute repudiation of all capital punishment, but the encyclical closes the gap to a sliver. Debate between adherents of these two anti-death-penalty positions can profitably continue, since both are far higher expressions of regard for the dignity of human life than any pro-death-penalty position.

Despite their difference, both of these positions lead to the same policy conclusion: the death penalty as part of an ordinary law code today is wrong and should not be retained as part of a modern state's penal system. It cannot be accepted as *ordinary* punishment, because by definition it is never absolutely necessary in ordinary circumstances. The debate concerns only whether there is a possible context in the rarest of instances and the most highly unusual (extraordinary) circumstances, when an occasional execution might possibly be justified. If this were the only question that ever had to be handled in practice, it would be no problem at all. Adherents of both positions would "practically always" be in agreement, while one side "only extremely rarely, if ever" allowed an execution.

But the real problem comes from the position at the opposite end of the spectrum, seeing nothing wrong with state killings as a routine practice. It is this position that must share the blame for the array of injustices, irregularities, and outright corruption that stem from having an "ordinary" capital-punishment statute in any jurisdiction, such as in the majority of the states.[46] When the mythology is stripped away, the central driving force behind the death penalty today is invariably the thirst for *revenge*. That is why the death penalty is

> unambiguously and courageously opposed by Catholic religious leadership. The use of the death penalty is not retributive justice, it does not appropriately protect society, it is not an effective deterrent....From both a moral and practical perspective, the death penalty should not be a part of public policy. Instead, actions in regard to social justice would better be based on an option for the sacredness and dignity of all human life.[47]

The greatest irony lies in the fact that authorizing capital punishment allows the state to treat human life in exactly the same objectionable manner as the murderer does—intentionally destroying it.[48]

C. A Challenge from Charleston, South Carolina

In May, Bishop David Thompson, who had succeeded Bishop Ernest Unterkoefler as bishop of Charleston, South Carolina, continued the latter's heritage and issued a statement that highlighted the teaching of the recent encyclical. He knew he was speaking to many who were still resisting the change, and thus decided to address them directly:

> I realize that capital punishment enjoys strong support in many states of our country, including South Carolina. My point in writing this statement is not necessarily to stir up compassion for the people who are on death row, but rather to identify a better course of action....People can and do feel the desire for retribution and vengeance. At the same time, however, I think our state has to challenge those feelings with strong convictions regarding the value of human life, even as it confronts our culture of violence, called by the Kerner Commission, "as American as apple pie."[49]

In the same straightforward fashion he expressed his personal position clearly:

> I oppose the death penalty, and I shall work with my brother bishops and others of good will to present to the citizens of our respective states our solid conviction that capital punishment as a penalty in the United States needs to be abolished. Then and only then shall we demonstrate that one can resist violence and confront a culture of violence without behaving violently. I am convinced that the hidden victim of public executions is the public conscience, along with the public's respect for the sacredness of life at all levels.

D. The HarperCollins Encyclopedia of Catholicism

The status of the capital punishment debate in 1995 was also reflected in two articles found in a new reference work, the *HarperCollins Encyclopedia of Catholicism.*

First, Fr. John Langan, S.J., who was involved in the formulation of the bishops' 1980 statement, was the author of a brief entry on capital punishment. He summed up the situation in a nutshell by noting:

> Catholic teaching has been reluctant to condemn capital punishment in principle; but most recent popes and bishops have favored abolition and have appealed for clemency in particular cases.

In explaining the problems that have brought about this practical repudiation of earlier outlooks, he listed five grounds for doing so:

    a. doubts about its necessity or usefulness as a means of
       preserving public order;
    b. the possibility of error in the judicial process;
    c. the repellent and inhumane character of the act;
    d. its incompatibility with the teaching of Jesus on
       forgiveness; and
    e. inconclusive evidence on its effectiveness as a deterrent.[50]

The case against death as punishment, expressed in such concise
and forthright language, has eroded the old position of support to
the point of collapse. By the time one unpacks each of these five
arguments, abolition emerges as a modern categorical imperative.

Langan himself had cogently shown the crucial importance
of the third of these five grounds as a result of the post–World
War II flowering of human-rights theory. Over a dozen years earlier he had traced in convincing fashion three stages in the
painful process by which Catholicism had gradually been able to
appropriate this understanding (symbolized roughly by the century of changes stretching from Pius IX and his *Syllabus of Errors*
in 1864, through advances by Leo XIII and Pius XII, to John
XXIII's *Pacem in Terris* in 1963). Initially,

> human rights theory in an explicit and politically dynamic
> form confronted Catholicism as an alien force, and it has
> taken Catholicism a long time to appropriate it.[51]

But it is safe to say that the third ground—contemporary human
rights theory—combined with the fourth ground—contemporary
understanding of the gospel—more than any other factors have
made further justification or toleration of capital punishment in
Catholic thinking unacceptable and unlikely for the future.

A second entry, by Fr. J. Bryan Hehir, whom Cardinal
Bernardin acknowledged as a major influence on his own thinking, is a brief treatment of the consistent ethic of life, which has
played an important role in helping many to see the need for
rejecting the death penalty. Defining this ethic as "a moral
framework to protect human life," Hehir identifies it as having

> two different sources. First, societal conditions...create a
> range of threats to human life. The issues of abortion, capi-

tal punishment, modern warfare, euthanasia, and socio-economic issues of justice all pose distinct challenges to protecting human life and promoting human dignity....The premise of the consistent ethic is that a relationship exists among these issues.

Second, in analyzing the nature of these threats to life, the consistent ethic proposal draws upon the structure and key concepts of Catholic moral theology....[It] is designed to test the Catholic moral vision in terms of two questions: which issues are defined as moral concerns, and how moral principles are used across a spectrum of issues. It is also designed to provide a means for the Catholic community to engage the broader civil society on these same issues.[52]

In virtually every episcopal or state conference's protest against capital punishment in recent years, these are the factors that have provided the central rationale: (1) a fuller understanding of human rights, especially the right to life; (2) a fuller understanding of the gospel, especially the teaching of Jesus on relating to one's fellow beings and renouncing revenge; and (3) a fuller understanding of the need for consistency. The resulting perspective leaves little room at all for further approval of any kind of deliberate destruction of human life by the state or any other agency.

E. South Africa Abolishes the Death Penalty

On June 6, 1995, a historical moment was marked when South Africa's highest court abolished the death penalty as unconstitutional and a form of cruel and inhumane punishment that "does not appear to deter crime and cheapens the value of human life in a society already plagued by violence."[53] The decision was 11-0 and was grounded on Article 9 of the new Constitution, which drew upon the United Nations' *Universal Declaration of Human Rights,* adopted in 1948. It states very simply that "every person shall have the right to life." The court explicitly asserts that these words are binding on everyone, including the government. The lives of the 440 prisoners on death row in South Africa in June 1995 were spared by this extraordinary achievement of

President Nelson Mandela and his government. "Inevitably everyone is wondering whether the decision...will prompt the United States to reconsider its policy, which has resulted in more than 3,000 persons on death row."[54]

Any such reconsideration, however, did not seem likely in the national mood of 1995. The United States ended up killing fifty-six men in that year alone, the highest number of executions in a single year since 1957. Texas led the way with nineteen, and there was no indication that 1996, another presidential election year, would be different.

VI. TWENTY YEARS AFTER *GREGG V. GEORGIA* (1996)

A. A Worrisome Winter

The New Year brought news from Illinois that Guinevere Garcia had stopped all appeals and declared she wanted to die. Her execution was scheduled for January 17. But Governor Jim Edgar, who had never granted clemency to anyone on death row, stepped in the day before and commuted Garcia's sentence. Unlike the case of Velma Barfield in North Carolina twelve years earlier (the only woman executed in twenty years), Garcia was not a political liability, so the decision was not nearly so costly.[55] In fact, due to the attention drawn by the powerful advocacy of human-rights activists on Garcia's behalf, especially Bianca Jagger, the governor's action ironically brought him some favorable press. It was not entirely clear what his motivation was, since he said his action was not based on the history of extraordinary physical abuse that Garcia had endured for years before she killed her abusive husband, but that her case "never should have been eligible for the death penalty."[56]

But, after this promising start, good news was scarce. In the same month the state of Delaware marched Billy Bailey to a fifteen-foot gallows, put a black hood over his head, tied his feet together, and dropped his body through a trapdoor, letting him twist for eleven minutes of strangulation before he was pronounced dead. The very next day the state of Utah deployed a firing squad of five men with deer rifles to shoot John Taylor, who was strapped to a black steel chair twenty-three feet away with a black hood over his head and a white target pinned on his heart.

As other nations around the world watched these bizarre events in bewilderment, the domestic climate seemed more and more accepting of such barbarous conduct. Cardinal Bernardin and the other bishops of Illinois selected February 18 as the Sunday on which to have a reaffirmation of opposition to the death penalty read in the 1,069 Catholic parishes of Illinois. The statement repeated the insistence on the sacredness of human life and the responsibility of the state to protect and enhance the lives of all at all stages of development, noting that executions were "an inappropriate response" on both moral and practical grounds. One interesting point was that part of the liturgical reading for the day was the eye-for-an-eye text from Leviticus, so attention was called to the erroneous but popular understanding in the hope of correcting it:

> [Leviticus 24:20] is not a prescription for revenge nor a goad to further bloodshed, but a guideline to keep people from going beyond the original offense and escalating violence....Justice cannot be achieved through vengeance...and vengeance is never a worthy human motive.[57]

The following week the UN Commission on Human Rights issued the results of a special investigation, documenting the fact that many death sentences in the United States "continue to be handed down after trials which fall short of international guarantees for a fair trial." The probe cited six recent instances where death was the sentence despite doubts about guilt. Twelve others were sentenced to death despite serious mental retardation, a violation of human rights the commission termed "particularly disturbing."

In March, Cardinal John O'Connor of New York caused a stir and illustrated in action how difficult and demanding the adoption of "an entirely new attitude" really is on this delicate question. He reiterated in summary form the "traditional teaching of the church" about the "right and duty of legitimate police authority to punish malefactors by means of penalties that are commensurate with the gravity of the crime—not excluding, in cases of extreme gravity, the death penalty." Then he went on to emphasize that he opposed its use in our day, just as the Holy Father and the catechism do.[58] The problem was that the connection between these two factors was not explained. This is the pedagogical challenge that will undoubtedly have to be grappled with for at least a generation.

B. A Somber Summer

The picketing of the Supreme Court by dozens of Catholic religious in May was no surprise. Members of the National Convocation of Jail and Prison Ministry used the occasion of their twenty-second annual meeting to do so. Then in June another group, the National Coalition to Abolish the Death Penalty, also held its meeting in Washington and included a peaceful protest march, with picketing, prayer, and fasting in front of the Supreme Court, to mark the occasion of the twentieth anniversary of *Gregg v. Georgia*.

That anniversary was also marked, in one way, by the U.S. Congress Anti-Terrorism bill, and, in another way, by the International Commission of Jurists' publication of its stinging critique of the nation's death-penalty record. The commission's 265-page report described the "grossly flawed" system, mentioning, among other shortcomings, the following:

> Prosecutors have unbridled discretion, victims' relatives have too much influence, juries are skewed, judges are unduly swayed because they are often elected, public defenders are scarce and inexperienced...and death sentences are inadequately reviewed by federal courts.[59]

After observing what had happened in the course of twenty-five years, two points could be quite safely made about the struggle of the U.S. Catholic bishops to provide solid Christian pastoral leadership on the emotional issue of capital punishment.

1. They had, for the most part, accomplished the extraordinary personal transformation to an "entirely new attitude" as required by the "fuller understanding" of the gospel after Vatican II. A quarter of a century is, after all, an extremely short period of time for such a massive adjustment to be made. The

challenge was all the greater because it coincided with an equally extraordinary period of escalating punitive attitudes on the part of the American public.

2. The collision of these two contrary "attitude adjustments" has resulted in making the bishops' reeducation programs for the Catholic people at large surprisingly ineffectual. The popular American addiction to the death penalty is constantly reinforced in and by the media, which often drown out the countercultural call for abolition.

There are, however, reasons for thinking that the situation will improve with fuller information and better educational opportunities for people with a basic sense of decency who have not been challenged previously to rethink their support for this anomalous practice on specifically religious grounds. As long as the debate remains solely on the pragmatic level, conducted only on the interpretation of social-scientific data, it is intractable. There will always be arguments on both sides on that level and from that perspective.

But the real issue, the central issue, the deciding issue, is the assessment of the human person. If the "mad dog" or the "putrid limb" analogies are acceptable, the debate is over and it is time to get on with the execution of such monsters. But if "made in the image of God" is taken as having any serious content, then the debate is also over, and it is time to get on with the work of finding higher ways of dealing with human failure than willful destruction of divine handiwork.

Instead of a Conclusion

I. A SUMMARY, OF SORTS

There is no easy way to narrate the magnitude of the transformation that has been taking place simultaneously in European and American Catholic circles over the past quarter-century. The revolutionary repudiation of capital punishment, generated since the Second Vatican Council, is extremely impressive, even though not yet total. There are few, if any, counterparts where such rapid change of mind and heart and policy statement concerning a literal matter-of-life-and-death has occurred. It has been nothing short of miraculous, when one recalls the typical resistance to change so charactcristic in much of institutional Catholicism in recent centuries.[1]

But capital punishment is clearly a unique exception in an embarrassing realm of ethics: a deliberate act of killing, traditionally approved and uncritically blessed by the church, at least since the early Middle Ages. One can only ask why and how this lonely, unlikely exception, the one and only case of allowing direct destruction of human life, was able to squeeze its way onto a sacred pedestal and gain its long-privileged support historically in moral theology. Some of the more unpleasant elements of the answer to that question have been traced. The details of the rapid reversal of recent years, however, resulting in the Catholic reappraisal of state killings, have not yet been fully chronicled. Many hard-working activists in one part of the world have been largely unaware of their counterparts laboring elsewhere, but there is every indication that a definitive corner has been turned in this generation, and the future will be far different from the past in its assessment of the lingering remnants of capital punishment.

As of March 1995, Pope John Paul II made it considerably more difficult for anyone inclined to continue to favor the death penalty to expect support from Rome. The word went forth that the contemporary understanding of the Christian gospel, combined with the general post–World War II awareness of the

457

nature of basic human rights, had found one another and
embraced, as Pope John XXIII had proposed they should do
over three decades earlier. Catholic approval of state-sponsored
executions was at an end.

A perspective brought by greater temporal distance from
these events will be needed, however, before it can be understood exactly how this total rejection of capital punishment can
be best explained. Professor Germain Grisez, who played an
early role in the story of the U.S. bishops' first statement of opposition in 1974, has more recently suggested a dynamic framework
in which to understand what has happened:

> In the past, capital punishment sometimes may have seemed
> justified as a defensive measure....Today, however, this
> defensive function plainly can be served in other ways. Thus,
> it is hardly possible to see how the use of the death penalty
> can be reconciled with Christian conceptions of human dig-
> nity and the sanctity of every human life....It seems that
> Catholic teaching on capital punishment can develop, just as
> Catholic teaching on coercion in matters of religion and on
> slavery have.[2]

This is certainly a helpful way to view the change, seeing it
in the same light as other dramatic turnarounds since the nineteenth century, required by fuller awareness of the dignity of the
human person, such as in thought about religious freedom and
human slavery. But those very parallels suggest that the "new
understanding" of the gospel may ultimately lead to a more comprehensive repudiation of capital punishment than, for example,
that still found in the 1992 catechism. The refinements already
made by the pope in 1995 point in that direction. In the meantime, it is important to point out that even the position of less-
than-total repudiation comes down to much the same practical
policy today. If such a thing as a morally justified execution is, in
the encyclical's language, "practically nonexistent," that means
in turn that "practically" every execution in the country today is
in violation of Christian conscience, and therefore is appropriately protested as a matter of course.

That message needs to be clarified and amplified in concrete terms: deliberate killing of human beings is not an acceptable option. The magnitude of a crime, its hideous, heinous, gruesome, grotesque circumstances and details, are not and cannot be the issue. Life is the issue, and deliberately destroying human life, all human life, any human life, is wrong, period. Punishment, yes. Death, no. People are not to be killed—not by any "right" of the state, not in God's name, not for revenge, not to deter another, not at all. That is the nature of the right to life, the dignity of the human person, the law of God, and the teaching of Jesus.[3]

Linsenmann and Leclercq were pioneers who sounded the alarm that something was amiss in the longstanding Catholic approval of the death penalty. But both of them were easily marginalized in their day as mavericks who did not have to be listened to; nonetheless, they planted important seeds of doubt in the minds of subsequent generations.

The September 1952 address of Pope Pius XII, to which Ermecke called attention, may be considered the beginning of the loosening-up process. Pius had said:

> Even in the case of the execution of one condemned to death, the state does not dispose of the right of the individual to life. It is thus reserved to the public power to deprive the condemned of the good of life, in expiation of his fault, after he by his crime has already been dispossessed of his right to life.

Ermecke realized that, while fully supportive of capital punishment, such an analysis voided any theory that would justify it on the basis of the state's having a "right to kill" as such. True, that was not the point the pope was making at the time, but it was a departure from the repeated past. Capital punishment so viewed was already in a very different position. It was still being justified, but only because the criminal himself was believed to have thrown away God's gift and forfeited his own right to life. The grounds of justification of execution were thus shifted dramatically: the state had no God-given right to kill its citizens, only the power to carry through with the formalities of the "social suicide" that the criminal himself had committed by his crime.

Admittedly this was a legal fiction, but at least it set the scene for dismantling the mythology of the death penalty based on the state somehow sharing in a vindictive God's power to slaughter evildoers. All that needed to be added was an equally radical questioning of the idea of "forfeiture" applied to the right to life, and suddenly the entire traditional Catholic assessment of capital punishment was not just up in the air but out in the cold.[4]

Even as Ermecke was probing the ideas of Pius XII in the mid-1950s, Fr. Franciscus Skoda manned the barricades, contending that it was "secular" abolitionists who were raising all these questions and that none of them should be taken seriously. Since the critics rejected so much else in the church's teaching, why react any differently when they turned their attack on the sacred death penalty? It was safe to assume that Pius XII could not possibly be saying anything other than what St. Thomas Aquinas and everyone else before and after him had always said about the state having the unquestionable right to kill.[5]

That was, in fact, the gist of an article written in *Civiltà Cattolica* in 1960 by Antonio Messineo, S.J., who contended:

> The Church, from the Fathers to St. Thomas Aquinas down to our own day, with unswerving unanimity, taught the legitimacy of capital punishment, and that therefore it could confidently be affirmed that the death penalty was in perfect accord with Christian thought.[6]

Such was the atmosphere in 1960, the very year that California executed Caryl Chessman and that Pope John XXIII set up preparatory commissions for convening a council to update Catholic thought. Ironically, twenty-one years later, after the Italian bishops conference along with so many others had unequivocally condemned the proposed restoration of capital punishment, that same journal carried an enlightened editorial setting forth the post-conciliar Catholic position, noting that death as a penalty flunks every conceivable test in penal theory, not to mention its blatant violation of belief in God as the Lord of life.[7]

But in those twenty-one years a sea change had occurred.

Catholic leaders who approved of the renewal fostered by Vatican II realized before long that the prevailing view of the death penalty in 1965 was an anachronous embarrassment. This did not mean that Catholic proponents of capital punishment had entirely disappeared, but the progress made was perhaps best indicated by the fact that the most vocal opponent of the new abolitionism chose not to reveal his identity. The angry but anonymous author was sure that an international Communist plot was behind the change.[8]

When the pressing need to change began to be felt on these shores, besides the activities of the U.S. Catholic Conference, the Canadian Catholic Conference (1973) put out a surprising public challenge, suggesting that it was time for Canadian Catholics to start thinking about the death penalty in an entirely different way: "The focus ought not to be on the convicted murderer....The focus should be on *us:* should Canadians as a community try to break the escalating spiral of violence by refraining from violence?"[9]

For most Americans, however, it was probably in 1977, when the Gilmore execution ended the ten-year moratorium and drew worldwide criticism, that the mixed voices of reaction in different Catholic quarters became most noticeable. There was, as seen earlier, the wholesale repudiation expressed by Fr. Gino Concetti, the moderate repudiation expressed by Cardinal Joseph Bernardin, and the continued approval voiced by Archbishop Francis Furey.

Meantime, outside the American context, there were other Catholic circles in which the death penalty had become more and more repugnant. Some of these were playing a significant role in the international debate over the value of life, the dignity of the human person, and the inviolability of human rights. The works discussed below, while not the only ones that could be chosen, have certainly helped illuminate and motivate many contemporaries who are working to eliminate capital punishment, not only from its formerly comfortable place in Catholic moral theology, but, more important, from its still lethal place in law codes that continue in use around the world.

II. BREAKING GROUND FOR A MORE
RADICAL REJECTION

A. *Jean-Marie Aubert, France (1978)*

The role of Aubert and his book *Christians and the Death Penalty* was unusual. It was, if not the earliest, certainly one of the most persuasive and influential presentations of the retrieved Catholic position at the very time when the debate over abolition was at its height in France. It surely helped people of faith to join in the struggle to dismantle and retire the guillotine, which was finally successful in 1981.[10]

Aubert's work was occasioned by a highly emotional letter written to him by a person who was deeply upset by the document issued by the Social Commission of the French Catholic bishops in January 1978 entitled "Must the Death Penalty Be Retained in France?: Elements for Reflection." The letter writer expressed his "stupefaction" upon reading this "shameful" text, which he knew Aubert (along with Père Yves Congar, O.P.) had a large part in composing. In his book Aubert reprinted both the commission's document and the critic's letter, which went on to accuse the French bishops of being blind and naive in their repudiation of capital punishment and actually causing scandal by being duped into accepting a "secular tradition, while rejecting what the Church has always taught about the liceity and propriety of the death penalty." Aubert's 144-page work was a running commentary on the original document, trying to convey to his upset critic how things had changed and why the post–Vatican II church could no longer function as the staunch defender of the direct destruction of human life as it had in the days of Joseph de Maistre.[11]

Some awareness of the peculiar history of France may help one to appreciate the extreme bitterness of Aubert's critic. In the aftermath of the French Revolution, far-right groups, sometimes called *intégristes,* deplored the Revolution and (like de Maistre), adopted "a rigid view of their faith, emphasizing the virtues of order and hierarchy in the political and the spiritual realms. Their pet bugaboos are the 'laic state'...religious experimentation, and progressivism." Their inclinations were, on principle, to see "only a fully Catholic state as completely acceptable," and to "consider their own opinions as orthodoxy and the opinions of others as heterodoxy....Any possibility of real understanding between the left and right tendencies of French Catholicism seems out of the question."[12]

Nonetheless, Aubert was determined to try, knowing that the *intégristes* were a relatively small, though very vocal, minority, and that in any event his efforts would certainly be appreciated by the masses of ordinary Frenchmen who had their own questions about the unusual document that had been put forth by the national bishops' commission. That document had four parts (and correspondingly Aubert's book has four chapters). It started out with the simple admission that "France is one of the rare nations of Western Europe, along with Ireland and Spain, which have retained the death penalty."[13] More and more voices were clamoring for its abolition, but the split between partisans and adversaries did not fall along political or religious lines. In former times the church admitted the arguments of those who thought it necessary for security, but was that definitive? "Have not social and cultural contexts evolved?" The bishops had asked the commission to put together some elements for reflection, first of all for Catholics, to throw light on this difficult problem from the perspective of renewed Christian faith after Vatican II.

It was clearly an unusual kind of document, not at all in the dogmatic mode, implying that the church did not claim to have all the answers to current questions in its tradition. New, serious problems had arisen, and had to be faced seriously. The first part therefore proceeded to examine the "motives and arguments in the debate about the death penalty" at the most basic level. When a murder occurs, our first reaction is outrage; the public identifies with the victim; it feels compelled to answer violence with violence, death with death. But is it not irrational to allow this raw instinct to prevail? Does society claim to protect the lives of some by destroying the lives of others? Does not the state, which is supposed to provide order in the society, demonstrate instead the supreme violence by choosing to punish by means of a premeditated homicide? This does not fit any of the conditions of valid self-defense or the standard aims of punishment as ordinarily set forth in Catholic thought. It is simply and obviously an act of vengeance and ought to be acknowledged as such, no matter what the usual excuses for it have been historically.

Aubert's second chapter was a meditation on European Christian history and the great cultural changes that had taken place within it—and the wrenching readjustments called for as a result. "The death penalty is one of the last vestiges of a bygone age...a shameful anachronism no longer supported by the culture," and that is part of why the scaffolds were first moved inside the prison yards and curtains were drawn over what used to be festive public spectacles.[14] A certain humility has to be observed when one realizes that one's own generation has engaged in the unparalleled obscenities of the Nazi Holocaust. But it is also essential to realize that certain late medieval "Christian" developments pertaining to the death penalty could be seen as contributing to that disaster as well. The historical failure of Christian churchmen to teach and preach the high ideal of nonviolence, of no bloodshed and no revenge, was an area calling for humble repentance, and even more important, for total repudiation for the future.

Reinforcing the propriety of these sentiments were modern works such as those recalling poet François Villon. Villon was twice condemned to die and spent harrowing time on death row in fifteenth-century France. While he was not a very admirable person, the picture he left of the so-called Christian France of his day was horrendous. Every petty potentate had his gallows at the crossroads. The archbishop, the abbot, the duke, the governor, and so forth could and did exterminate their respective undesirables—and boasted that they were authorized by God in doing so. The spires of the great Cathedral of Notre Dame shared the Parisian skyline with the great Gibbet of Montfaucon, a huge structure of impressive engineering skill. It could accommodate up to sixty simultaneous hangings, leaving the corpses of its victims swinging in the breeze until the birds picked clean the bones.[15] This lavish destruction of human life had the authorization of the church, which routinely contended that it was the divinely ordained mode of organizing and protecting society. Whatever one does with this history, its assumptions simply cannot be carried forward into the present. Rather than defending such a tradition, Aubert suggested, one might better search for the source of the errors that brought it into being and replace them with "an entirely new attitude" that takes greater account of faded Christian ideals.

The third chapter, "Myth and the Reality of the Death Penalty," is too rich to summarize here. It is enough to note Aubert's assessment of some of the most bizarre notions attached to blood and its "purity," to sacrifice and expiation, and to all the other misused biblical concepts employed in earlier European history to justify scaffold brutalities:

> We ought to admit that the real reason behind the death penalty is that old barbaric reflex, the *lex talionis,* simple straightforward revenge, officially perpetuated violence.[16]

To refuse to see this is to choose to keep this life-destroying mythology alive and deliberately align oneself with the dark forces of death. There is no viable Christian defense of the death penalty as practiced in a modern state.

Chapter four, "The Call to Non-violence," presents Aubert's most pressing challenge. It is here that one gets some sense of the difference between what the French bishops were trying to do in their document compared with what the American bishops attempted in their formulation at much the same time. The United States had just opted, after *Gregg v. Georgia* (1976), to go back into the business of wholesale killing after a ten-year moratorium. France, on the other hand, was still for the most part in a de facto moratorium and was being asked to go further, to join the movement in the international community and make it de jure by officially abolishing the death penalty. Much of the most vocal resistance was due to the escalating problem of terrorism. The French colonial past, especially in Algeria, complicated the scene, but there was nothing quite comparable in France to the violent, corrosive legacy of black slavery and its subsequent lynching escapades, which had blighted decades of U.S. experience. This legacy gave the American use of the death penalty its ugliest characteristic. There was less political will in the United States for the message of the U.S. Catholic bishops to resonate. Theirs was a countercultural voice in the (political) wilderness, leading to the Bicentennial Bifurcation.

The condemnation of the death penalty called for by church leaders in France, however, at least outside *intégriste* circles, was grounded much more radically. It delved into a fuller appreciation of the dignity of the human person as reflecting the God of life. Aubert was able to speak eloquently and with greater confidence than the American bishops:

> Vatican II...completely altered the context in which the death penalty must now be viewed....At this level of historical analysis, we can only conclude that it is definitively anachronous, but we cannot stop there....It is an evil, barbaric institution, unworthy of any and every society. Its rejection is not only motivated by reasons of history, but especially on more profound grounds of an existential order...reasons rooted in the depths of human reality as expressed in the idea of the human person. It is necessary to go that far, to the very source of our problem, in order to stir the will sufficiently to reestablish nonviolent relations among people and eliminate capital punishment.

This is only the first part of his final meditation, the next sentence of which launches into the question: "What is the human person?" The reply goes on for several pages, insisting on the "untouchable" nature of the person, which capital execution totally and irresponsibly violates.[17]

What the French bishops' commission obviously (and intentionally) ignored as virtually insignificant, given the context, was any discussion whatsoever of "the state's right to kill," the very notion the old school had found so central. Theologians who had embraced that "right" in earlier centuries were themselves virtually blind to its objectionable, unchristian, intolerable aspects, which had come into view with the changed circumstances. The unfortunate situation of the church openly approving the direct, intentional destruction of human life needed to be not only abandoned but repented of. Aubert and his colleagues called for a "radical" conversion, an altered perspective on the part of modern Christians, uprooting an evil that had lost its disguise.

One other difference in the two approaches was the way the French bishops appealed to the laity, inviting them to raise their awareness and their ethical standards and to take up the cause of human dignity "in an entirely new way" by speaking out in total opposition to the guillotine. How successful they were in actually changing minds or mentalities is another question, but the fact remains that France did indeed repudiate the death penalty within three years. It had in fact already seen its last use the year before the document came out.[18]

B. Niceto Blázquez, O.P., Spain (1989)

We have met the work of the Spanish Dominican theologian Niceto Blázquez before, both his pioneering study of St. Augustine and his advances in the critique of St. Thomas Aquinas on the death penalty. He has probably done more extensive historical research and reflection on the subject than any other contemporary Catholic scholar. His 1989 book, which he dedicated to the Chinese students slaughtered by state-authorized killers that year in Tiananmen Square, is entitled *Estado de Derecho y Pena de Muerte*. It consists of six chapters, starting with an overview of (1) the legal situation of the death penalty in the contemporary world; then looking back to (2) Christians and the death penalty up to the twelfth century; then focusing more closely on (3) its justification in the twelfth century; then reviewing his own earlier study of (4) its place in St. Thomas; then taking a look at certain changes in (5) its place in Francisco de Vitoria; and finally looking ahead (6) toward a new mentality. We can only try to excerpt a few of the rich contributions from this fascinating plate of multiple offerings, from which we have already borrowed more than once.

Blázquez had watched and pondered the scene in both the United States and Europe for over a decade after Aubert's work. One recurring phenomenon especially disturbed him. Even though country after country had abolished the death penalty, every time there was a heinous crime, a popular outcry for restoring capital punishment would invariably arise and be given great attention in the media. The reigning assumption continued to be, without any discussion of it anywhere, that the state had this unquestioned universal right to decree death as a penalty, even if it had (temporarily) abolished the practice.

This was the legacy that had to be addressed. Blázquez was convinced that

> NOBODY, neither the Church nor the State nor anyone
> else, has the right to kill "legally" by setting up some juridi-
> cal ritual. The death penalty, no matter who accepts it as
> "legal," objectively is always and everywhere an immorality,
> no matter what subjective motives are invoked to justify it.
> My basic proposition with this study is to discuss and deny to
> the State this presumed right, based on the very essence of
> Christian ethics and human rationality, leaving aside the
> emotions and visceral passions fed by historical fanaticisms
> and scholastic interests. I would be most satisfied if with
> these pages I could contribute to making people think more
> and better about a problem that is so serious and has been
> so poorly treated throughout history.[19]

Blázquez looks more closely at the public statements of recent popes, starting with Pius XII, and notes the 1952 state-ment to which Ermecke had called attention. There was no way to read his words other than as reflecting acceptance of the Thomistic theory of the civil authority having the right to punish grave offenders with death. But Blázquez goes on to examine Pius's talks on aspects of penal thought in 1953, 1954, 1955, and 1957, which often touch on the purposes of punishment but never again mention the death penalty. Pius's 1957 remarks on the "vindictive" aim of punishment are formulated in such a way that they actually seem to rule out death as qualifying, since part of the goal of vindictive punishment is "to induce the person's conversion," which is obviously excluded by execution.

Blázquez is perfectly aware that an argument from silence proves nothing, but nonetheless finds it intriguing that in the very quarter-century when most of the nations of the Western world were rethinking from all angles the rationale of capital punish-ment, the writings of the popes observed a "systematic silence" in which the very words *death penalty* (or equivalents) were not even to be found—not in Pius XII's many addresses (after 1952), not in any of Pope John XXIII's or Pope Paul VI's speeches or writings. Meantime, beginning with the timid gesture of Pius XII in 1953 (in the Rosenberg case), personal intervention for clemency or commutation in certain cases began to be common. Paul VI, even before he became pope, had intervened on behalf of a condemned man, and in an incident during his visit to the Philippines as pope, he pardoned on the spot the one who attacked him personally, just as John Paul II did after the 1981 assassination attempt in St. Peter's Square. A clearer message was being sent in the personal conduct of the popes than in any articulated theory.

What Blázquez was driving at was this: if the state had some special right to execute, a claim which the manualists had made so much of for centuries, it surely was not something of any obvious significance that was being taught by any of the modern popes. In fact, their systematic silence might better be interpreted as their hope to avoid providing the very idea of the death penalty with any further support. If one wants to speak of "the mind of the church" on this, the best place to look, Blázquez contends, is paragraphs 27–28 of *Gaudium et Spes* (Vatican II's *Constitution on the Church in the Modern World*):

> Everyone should look upon his neighbor (without any exception) as another self, bearing in mind above all his life and the means necessary for him to live it in a dignified way....Today there is an inescapable duty to make ourselves the neighbor of every man(27)....
>
> The teaching of Christ even demands that we forgive injury, and the precept of love, which is the commandment of the New Law, includes all our enemies(28).

After this powerful text Blázquez merely remarks:

> Here is the universal norm. No mention of the death penalty; explicit condemnation of every kind of killing; solemn proclamation of the Gospel principle of forgiving enemies. All this convinces us that the presumed ethical liceity of the death penalty as a legal punishment is not to be found anywhere in any text or any context of the Council.[20]

In the course of reviewing all the published statements by church groups over the past thirty years, he includes a brief look at the 1980 statement of the U.S. bishops and finds both its content and its methodology to be "much poorer than that of the French (1978 Reflections), but not thereby lacking in pastoral value."[21] What this whole section reveals is that a significant behind-the-scenes effort was going on at this time to try to get some kind of official statement from Rome. A 1978 conference held in Madrid had lodged a complaint alleging that the Holy See had not provided any guidance on this extremely important issue. Of course, that was the famous "year of three popes," when many other pressing problems necessarily absorbed Rome's attention.

The closest thing to a formal response to the complaint came at the Twelfth Conference of European Ministers of Justice, which was held in Luxembourg in 1980, the same year as the U.S. Catholic bishops' statement against capital punishment. The apostolic nuncio of Brussels, Igino Cardinale, addressed the conference on the subject.[22] He pointed to the fact that Vatican City had abolished the capital punishment statute in 1969, and that it had not been invoked for many long years before that. He remarked that the *Code of Canon Law,* by its complete lack of treatment of the death penalty, showed the basic stance of the church. He also went on to express the hope that modern conditions would continue to show the death penalty to be essentially useless and thus permit its eventual abolition by all nations, a situation that the church would be most pleased to see develop. Then he added:

> Up to the present the common teaching of the Church has not condemned the principle of the death penalty...but current theological investigations have been undertaken pointing toward a *revision* of this position. Already at the level of certain episcopal conferences this has been done. The fact that a similar condemnation in principle has *not yet* taken place for the Church ought not to lessen the urgency of working in this direction. The Church must do its part, but is persuaded that public authorities have a corresponding responsibility to diagnose the conditions that will finally allow for the full suppression of the death penalty.

What these "current theological investigations" were or where they were taking place was still not clear to Blázquez at the time of writing, eight or nine years later. But there had already been one voice out of Rome that he found compelling in its frontal attack on capital punishment, that of Franciscan moralist Gino Concetti in his two articles of 1977 and 1978, which graced the front pages of *L'Osservatore Romano*. The first article, as we have seen, protested the resumption of U.S. executions with the shooting of Gary Gilmore in Utah, and the second one protested the planned poisoning (lethal injection) of a woman on death row in Texas (which did not occur). That any modern state had a "right" to engage in such immoralities was simply beyond belief, being incompatible with everything Christianity stood for. It was thus nothing but a display of pure power used unethically in direct violation of the "inviolable right to life," which cannot be denied to any human being because of errors or crimes.

> The human being always retains this right, no matter what his behavior. Killing a person does not correct, expiate, or heal anything. To destroy the untouchable gift of life is to commit homicide, pure and simple. Over and above any and all excuses or theories, it must be recognized that the death penalty is *incompatible* with the respect and dignity due to the human person, according to the Gospel.[23]

Blázquez found himself in complete agreement with Concetti, and having come to the end of his survey, expressed an overall conclusion:

> Modern episcopal abolitionism is valid at the strictly pastoral level, but at the level of doctrine and principles, it falls far too short. To help it to overcome the defective arguments of the past which were used in support of capital punishment, I propose the use of an alternative argument based on the perspective of *human rights*.

Here he summarizes the line of thought which he had worked out in the first three chapters of his 1980 book *Human Rights,* inspired by the thought of St. Thomas Aquinas.[24] It is a solid challenge and invitation to a gospel-based position that is pro-life in more than name or slogan. If life is the fundamental natural right, life protected from all violence, the death penalty is an assault upon the very foundation from which all other rights flow. If we cannot come to share the conviction that we must respect the lives of all, sooner or later we are all liable to become victims of the injustices of naked power.

Blázquez's final conviction is expressed thus:

> Neither Christian theology nor human reason offer enough moral basis to attribute to the State the power to decide judicially on the eventual death of criminals as a just punishment....The death penalty, as a juridical punishment, is equivalent theologically to a rash usurpation of the radical power of God over human life, and is an institutionalized violation of the Christian command to forgive enemies. Rationally speaking, it is equivalent to a violation of the natural law by its radical negation of the foundation for all other human rights, life itself....The death penalty constitutes an immorality in itself, and is the gravest possible act of *state-injustice*.[25]

C. Gino Concetti, O.F.M., Italy (1993)

We have already encountered the Italian Franciscan theologian Gino Concetti a number of times.[26] A professor of moral and political theology at the Antonianum in Rome, he has in the past two decades published books about morality and political parties, euthanasia, organ transplants, AIDS, sexuality, and war. His ethical writings have received wide attention, not only because of his location in Rome, but also because his strong and clear opinions on current issues have often been surprisingly fresh, persuasive, and nontraditional.

Despite his early interest and participation in the controversy over capital punishment and the two articles noted above by Blázquez, it was another fifteen years before his monograph on the subject appeared. Called simply *The Death Penalty*, it was well positioned to attract significant attention because of Concetti's familiarity with the full range of recent developments. In a historical section he traced the modern Catholic change in stance as stemming directly from Pope John XXIII's *aggiornamento*, which fostered opening new paths and the stripping away of outmoded elements in church tradition. As he saw it, these things were changed because from the start they were "the fruits of deviation from, or of incomplete comprehension of, Revelation."

Reflection on the death penalty, even though the topic was not directly addressed in the Council, was stimulated by the renewal; within a few years of Vatican II it had become clear to many that a "radically different solution than in the past" was called for. Concetti cited six post–Vatican II European Catholic moralists (excluding himself for the moment) who had publicly sought to take into account the cultural evolution that had occurred and to work out accordingly a more or less new solution to the death-penalty conundrum. All of these authors had departed to some degree from the standard position of the past, recognizing that more had to be said than the mere repetition of the past defense of the state's right to kill.[27] It was imperative that justice be done by taking full account of two modern phenomena:

1. the contemporary growth in awareness of human dignity, which is a major "sign of our time"; and

2. the renewed realization that the spirit of the gospel requires merciful treatment even of those who have gravely sinned against God and society.

One cannot simply argue the question of morality in terms of natural law and claim to be doing Christian ethics. The gospel must be allowed to have its say, or one is only engaging in secondary speculation.

The six moralists Concetti referred to had all published relatively recent textbooks that included some treatment of the death penalty, so he took them in the order in which their books appeared (at least in their Italian editions):

1. ANSELM GÜNTHÖR

Günthör published his work in 1977, which illustrates that the conversation about the ethics of capital punishment has being going on quite energetically in Rome for the last two decades, much as it has in the United States. Günthör, in fact, sounded very much like some of the American bishops of that time. He insisted that the new circumstances had to be taken into account, but he was not yet prepared to say exactly how or how far. He noted the need for openness, but then ventured to go only as far as to say that "the death penalty could not be considered immoral in all instances." The major change thereby reflected would seem to be the shift in the burden of proof. The presumption now should always be in favor of life, not death. No use of death is licit except in the very rarest of circumstances. There may be a stronger case to be made against capital punishment, but it will take time for it to be formulated, and it is probably to be sought by further probing of the renewed consciousness of the dignity of the human person.[28]

2. BERNARD HÄRING, C.SS.R.

Häring is by far the best known of the six moralists, at least in the English-speaking world. He has touched on and dealt with the death penalty numerous times during his long and distinguished career at the Alphonsianum in Rome and elsewhere, but it is his statement in his 1981 work, *Free and Faithful in Christ,* that Concetti focuses on. Häring states his position in terms of classical probabilism:

> I would say that at the present time there are two probable opinions within Christianity and within the Catholic church. There are those who think that the death penalty can and should be inflicted on dangerous criminals, in order to protect innocent people. This opinion finds favor especially in view of those skilled terrorists who, time and again, escape and cause new slaughter.

> Personally, I incline to the opinion that *abolition* of the death penalty is the *better course*...[because] it corresponds more closely to Jesus' non-violent message and to his own gentle spirit, as well as to the witness of his disciples. Surely dangerous criminals must be kept where they cannot continue to harm others; but our main task is to heal those who have fallen into the mind-set of violence.

> One of my main arguments in favor of abolition of the death penalty is the fact that in the past most states have participated in mass murder through war or violent oppression of those who were claiming justice. And military and civil tribunals have all too often and too lightly condemned people to death without sufficient proof of the crime and/or with no proportion to the fault committed.

> It is my conviction that a state has *no right* to uphold the death penalty unless it has done all in its power to give better education and to care for a more just and humane environment.[29]

The most striking aspect is Häring's openness in taking history seriously. His last statement is especially interesting, in light of all the quarreling over the "right" of the state to kill. He has taken to heart the objections raised by Abbé Jacques Leclercq some fifty years earlier and seems to be suggesting to those who claim that the murderer "forfeits" his own right to life by taking the life of another that perhaps the state "forfeits" *its* right to execute by its own engagement in legal injustices and abuses.

In any event, Häring by no means stopped with his 1981 position; his impressive 1986 work, *The Healing Power of Peace and Nonviolence,* shows him moving relentlessly toward ever greater incorporation of gospel teaching into Christian ethical responses to violence.[30]

3. SANDRO SPINSANTI

Spinsanti, while agreeing that the two positions described by Häring may be considered probable in the abstract, thinks that one must take into account the concrete fact that practically all the countries of Europe have abolished the death penalty both de jure and de facto. He then invokes a principle endorsed in *Verbum Dei* (*Constitution on Revelation*) that affirms that "tradition progresses in the Church...in various ways, including the sense of spiritual realities coming from believers' own experience" (par. 8). The new awareness of many today is the way of nonviolence. It has seldom been tried before, and it is working. Earlier moralists could not even conceive of a society without the death penalty as its cornerstone, because they had never experienced anything else. The doctrinal renewal, stemming from the Council and experiencing the practical success of living in a nonviolent manner, should raise Christian awareness to a new level, and this will have to find articulation in a new way. The new formulations may sound very much like the experiential terms of some earlier groups, such as the "peaceful" strain that prevailed among some of the early Anabaptists.

By giving such prominence to the experiential, Spinsanti has pointedly raised the doctrinal development issue. While the two opinions may have both been probable in earlier days, it would seem that the more the nonviolent option works, the more the "right" of having recourse to the violent option erodes. This is simply another way of saying that the death penalty is unethical today because it has been shown to be unnecessary (as well as contrary to the spirit of Christ).[31]

4. LINO CICCONE

In Concetti's assessment, Lino Ciccone takes an even more courageous step by openly concluding that the death penalty is simply illicit today. He reaches this conclusion in reviewing four points:

> a. for centuries there existed a position that held that the state had a right to kill certain grave malefactors;

> b. this position was justified in moral theology right down to our own times;

> c. the magisterium supported this position, however, only indirectly and incidentally, and never gave it direct or full attention;

> d. in our time, especially since Vatican II, theologians and the magisterium of entire episcopal conferences have been delineating new positions, repudiating the death penalty almost unanimously, and, in many cases, denying outright that the state has the right to kill.[32]

Concetti knew that the fourth point is the sore spot of the whole debate. Denying that the state has such a right "is the greatest and the most significant novelty in this last position," and it is also Concetti's own position. It was this which had called so much attention to his front-page article about Gilmore's execution in *L'Osservatore Romano* in 1977.

5. K. H. PESCHKE

Peschke holds a position described by Concetti as "suspended between biblical tradition and innovation." He concedes that the state has a right to *punish,* but is not at all sure that extends to a right to *kill.* "It cannot be proved that the state unconditionally has the right to inflict death, but neither can it be proved that it is purely and simply obliged to abolish the death penalty." Concetti finds this non-position a bit too "academic" and probably due to the lingering influence of the old school. But Peschke too has contributed to the erosion of the old arguments. Instead of finding two probable opinions, all Peschke could find was two *possible* opinions about the morality of using the death penalty.[33]

6. MARCIANO VIDAL

Vidal is a professed disciple of the outspoken Spanish bishop Alberto Iniesta, whose forceful opposition to all capital punishment was already well articulated in the 1970s. Vidal simply builds on Iniesta's original barrage. The death penalty is unethical six times over: because it is "inutile...immorale...non-necessaria...pessimista...ingiusta...antichristiana." Concetti agrees wholeheartedly, but thinks it would be better not to use the term *abolition.* What we really ought to be talking about is *prohibition* of the death penalty. It is not enough just to get it abolished from the law codes; it must be absolutely forbidden as sinful and immoral, a kind of conduct that is no more worthy of consideration than murder itself, of which it is a subspecies.[34] It is improper to give the impression that it is ever an ethically acceptable option.

After this survey of contemporary opponents of capital punishment, Concetti goes on to review the teaching of the magisterium, including the statements of the French, American, and Italian bishops' conferences, and the paragraphs from the new catechism, noting the mounting Catholic rejection of the death penalty. He then spends a chapter on the major contributions of lay thinkers, five of them in this century: Aldo Casalinuovo (1939), Ernesto Eula (1963), Norberto Bobbio (1982), Ezzat A. Fattah (1983), and Sergio Cotta (1988). Their cumulative assault on capital punishment has resulted in the contemporary international repudiation that finds increasingly strong expression in the documents adopted and propagated by the United Nations. These documents are then reviewed in their essentials in the following chapter, including the climactic 1977 Stockholm Declaration, calling upon all governments in the world "to bring about the immediate and total abolition of the death penalty," and upon the United Nations to declare unambiguously that "the death penalty is contrary to international law."

Concetti sees this international movement functioning as "the critical conscience of humanity for the protection of the dignity of the human person and of human rights." It has taken centuries for this clarity about the inviolability of human life to evolve. Christians have a great responsibility to try to understand this extraordinary situation. If they have in the past been part of the problem, contributing to the corruption created for societies by the very presence of capital statutes in their law codes, the modern campaign against the culture of death is an unparalleled opportunity for the Christian church not only to reverse the mistakes of the past but to witness to the gospel for the future, promoting the higher ethic of the sanctity of human life.

> The death penalty, besides being an act of barbarism, is a theological and juridical *absurdity*. Considered strictly in its objective reality, it is the violent destruction of the life of a human being, a human person....It is a deliberate act of homicide...a double infraction of standards, one committed against humanity, the other committed against God.

It is for this reason that Catholic theologians everywhere, Concetti concludes, are especially called upon today to work for its elimination. As for what to do about correcting or reversing history, his basic call is for simple honesty. There are hosts of reasons to be taken into account in explaining why things happened the way they did, but the inescapable conclusion is that

> in the area of human rights (e.g., religious freedom, democracy, etc.), Catholic culture has been *sluggish* in plumbing the depths and poorly disposed to facing up to the instances uncovered by other forces, showing the submerged patrimony of Christian values....The basic fact that can no longer be ignored is that the death penalty is *irreconcilable* with the message of the Beatitudes, and thus is in open conflict with the principles and the spirit of Jesus. Any conception of the State as absolutized or sacralized to the point of having a

"legal right" of using violence and bloody repression against human persons rather than being bound to guarantee and protect their inviolable and inalienable right to life is contradicted by the Gospel.[35]

This is why Concetti feels so strongly about the need for the radical repudiation of the death penalty; he denies that the state has any right to commit "legal homicide." He makes a special plea to Msgr. Guzzetti, "one of the best-known postconciliar theologians opposed to the death penalty," but whose rejection has been less than total. "By the fact that the principle of the absolute inviolability and untouchability of human life is limited by making a distinction [between innocent and non-innocent life], an unacceptable dichotomy is introduced between theory and practice."

There is much more to be said about and learned from Concetti's work. It is interesting to note that his book was published in Rome during the days after the release of the new catechism (1992) and before the release of the encyclical *Evangelium Vitae* (1995), with its sharper repudiation of the death penalty. Thus it would not be rash to suspect that Concetti's work may well have played a role in the way that Pope John Paul II stiffened his opposition to capital punishment precisely in that period.

D. William Schabas, Canada (1993–1996)

The recent writings of Professor Schabas of the University of Quebec Law Faculty are also powerful reinforcements of this particular line of thought. Pope John Paul II in his 1995 encyclical dubbed the worldwide trend toward abolition of capital punishment a providential "sign of the times," in other words, an instance of the manifestation of positive human progress in outgrowing and overcoming institutionalized evil. It marches hand in hand with the appeals of Vatican II for greater social justice and world peace, stressing that abolition of the death penalty is not optional or secondary for the modern world, and the struggle to extend it can be part of a modern Christian sense of mission.

During the decade from 1948 to 1957, six countries put an
end to the death penalty. During the decade from 1958 to
1967, the figure climbed to eight. From 1968 to 1977, the
total was fifteen. From 1978 to 1987, nineteen countries
abolished capital punishment. Ten countries abolished the
death penalty between 1988 and 1991....If the trend continues uninterrupted, sometime prior to the year 2000, a
majority of the world's states will have abolished the death
penalty.[36]

This dimension of our overall story has received all too little attention, due to the provincialism that so often limits local
news media. While great credit must undoubtedly be given to
Vatican II for opening up conditions in the church that have promoted broad new theological work, this did not happen in a vacuum. The achievements of the United Nations and its many
associated agencies in moving the world forward in the struggle
for greater humanity and justice are manifold. From any perspective interested in the civilizing process, the advances in international law in the past half-century are uncontestably
extraordinary, and the promise for a better and more just human
future is very much tied up with continued progress in this
regard.

The first limitation on the death penalty in international
law appeared in the 1929 Geneva Convention, dealing with prisoners of war. But it was in December 1948 that the historic *Universal Declaration of Human Rights* was adopted, with Article 3
clearly affirming that "everyone has the right to life, liberty and
security of person." From that seed a mighty tree has grown and
is flourishing in many parts of the world.

When the U.S. Constitution stated that no person "shall be
deprived of life...without due process of law," it legitimized
the death penalty, subject to certain controls. But the *Universal Declaration*...and the *American Declaration*...let the right to
life stand alone, unblemished by its fatal exceptions....Their
drafters contemplated abolition of the death penalty, but
were unwilling to proclaim it openly. Yet the general recognition of the right to life, without exception, has proven far-
sighted, for it has allowed the two *Declarations* to retain their

relevance and to grow as part of an abolitionist future that their authors only faintly discerned.[37]

The language is technical but the instruments are real. Since 1948 treaties have been signed and protocols agreed to which progressively defend the right to life more effectively and make the abolition of the death penalty "a common standard for mankind." This may be the last, best hope for weaning the United States away from its morbid attraction to capital punishment. For instance, the International Covenant on Civil and Political Rights, which the United States has been a party to since 1992, states in Article 6 that in those countries that have not yet achieved the ideal of abolishing the death penalty, at least it "shall not be imposed for crimes committed by persons below eighteen years of age." But several States have ignored this restriction, causing the United States to be cited for basic human-rights violations. Condemning and executing juvenile offenders is an old American custom. More than 340 youngsters were hanged or electrocuted in this century before the 1967 moratorium, and at least a half-dozen have been killed in the past few years, with more to come. Something has to give if the United States expects to maintain membership in the international community of law-abiding nations.[38]

III. *ON THE THRESHOLD OF THE THIRD MILLENNIUM*

In closing, one other work that appeared in 1993 needs to be noted briefly, if only because of its symbolic importance. *The Death Penalty on the Threshold of the Third Millennium* contains fourteen papers that were prepared for an international colloquium, held in the south of France, honoring Professor Antonio Beristain, director of the Basque Institute of Criminology in San Sebastián, Spain.[39] Beristain had been one of the first to envision and articulate what the high ideal of a truly Catholic position after Vatican II would have to be if the Council Fathers were to be taken seriously. His challenging vision was already clearly articulated in the 1970s:

> The message of Jesus Christ...is a yeast that can and should
> ferment the institutions of law, purifying its structural injus-
> tices throughout....The Gospel demands that punishment—
> avoiding revenge, cruelty and expiation—be useful,
> dignified, and necessary to the common good and well-
> being of the citizens directly affected by it, that it also
> respect the personal dignity of the offender and that it con-
> tribute to his social reinsertion. In the light of Catholic the-
> ology, the death penalty cannot be accepted because it lacks
> all the fundamental principles demanded of any legal sanc-
> tion by the Gospel.[40]

In the recent Festschrift a grand tour of the modern world
scene is provided, highlighting the work of Amnesty International, celebrating Professor Beristain for his work for human
rights in Spain during and after the Franco dictatorship, and otherwise describing the good news of progress elsewhere. But
when it comes to reporting on the United States, law professor
Leonard L. Cavise of DePaul University of Chicago had the
somber chore of recounting the status of state killing in the worst
current offender-nation in the West.

A. Leonard Cavise

Cavise narrated without embroidery what had been happening; the result was a grim picture of both present and future.
"The current make-up of the Supreme Court offers nothing positive for abolitionists." The retirement of Justices Brennan and
Marshall, replaced by Souter and Thomas, left an extremely conservative court committed to the ruling mythology of capital
punishment, and the prospect of any "judicial relief," such as in
1972, was off in the far distance, to say the least. Prospects for
any "legislative changes" at the state level were likewise dismal;
even "laws prohibiting the execution of offenders under 18 years
of age only passed in six of the state legislatures." The number of
capital crimes in many was increased, the use of the right to
appeal was decreased, and the same trends on the state level prevailed at the federal level under President Bush. Looking ahead a
few months to the fall 1992 elections, Cavise's crystal ball was
clear enough to avoid false hopes:

Even though a change of administration would affect the political composition of the judiciary, it is doubtful that it would have any impact on the desire of legislators to authorize, and of juries to impose, the penalty of death.[41]

Aside from this dark cloud, however, there were reports of significant sunlight elsewhere in the world.

B. Jean Pinatel

Pinatel, the honorary president of the International Society of Criminology, reported in Cario's book on the 1988 international conference on the death penalty that had been held in Syracuse, Sicily, bringing together members of the four major international associations representing penal law and criminology. What most impressed Pinatel was the fact that at that time three of the four associations, and the president of the fourth, speaking for himself personally, were all on record as totally opposed to capital punishment. He himself was convinced that in fact the criminological data establish scientifically that the death penalty has no useful role to play. But he also realized that "this scientific position collides with the sentiments of public opinion concerned about safety."

This poses a strange problem, and Pinatel uses a medical analogy to sketch it. Suppose a biological discovery, based on demonstrated scientific evidence, collides with a popular public opinion, based on ignorance, which denies the medical claims but has no concern to come up with any kind of refuting evidence. Granted, "criminology is not medicine," but its widely agreed-upon results ought to count for something. It is thus highly desirable that colloquia like this one take account of and recognize the gravity of this paradoxical situation. "The morbid attachment to the death penalty which can be observed among many of our contemporaries...throws a disquieting light on human nature." Stanley Milgram's experiments at Yale gave us some idea of its complexity, showing people easily disposed to engage in a surprising degree of unwarranted cruelty to others.

> The readiness to act as executioners is much more common among people than we would like to believe, and this enables

us to see in a new light how deep are the roots of support for the death penalty.[42]

C. Pierre Marbot

Marbot reported for Amnesty International, documenting again the worldwide trend toward abolition but lamenting the fact that one of the great democratic nations from which the world usually expects far better has been accelerating its rush in the opposite direction:

> A judicial review of capital affairs, done by Amnesty International, showed that between 1972 and 1987 more than forty innocent people had been condemned to death in the U.S. and 23 innocent persons had actually been executed since the beginning of this century.[43]

Several of the other chapters had to do with issues raised by efforts to restore the death penalty in countries where it had been successfully abolished. But there were two other substantial offerings that developed precisely the contemporary coalescence that we have noted several times and that is the most fascinating and productive phenomenon of our time. The death penalty is in the latter stages of full retreat and total repudiation in Europe because of two movements. Insofar as those two movements have also emerged in the United States, the same wave of full repudiation has occurred (and is occurring) here, wherever the interaction of the two has been most productive. Fittingly, the spokesman in this volume for the first of these movements is the honoree himself, Professor Antonio Beristain, addressing "Philosophical and Religious Aspects of the Death Penalty"; the spokesman for the second is Peter Csonka, executive administrator of the Council of Europe, in a chapter entitled "The Death Penalty: The Viewpoint of Human Rights."[44]

D. Antonio Beristain

We have earlier seen many of the points made by Beristain, as far as Christian theology is concerned. His grasp of European history assures that he always offers interesting new insights. After looking at various fictions under which capital punishment disguised itself, Beristain warns that while some things have changed, others have not.

> Across the centuries capital punishment has been a religious penalty inflicted in the name of society considered as a sacred body....The myth sometimes enveloped the reality: upon the sword of the executioner in Fribourg, Switzerland, were written the words: "Lord Jesus, You are the Judge!" The executioner found himself invested with a sacred function: he was a man who destroyed the body so as to liberate the soul by divine sentence....Yesterday it was the myth of the sacrality of power. Today, the desacralization of the world has further eliminated all ideological justification of the right to kill....In reality, the only foundation for the death penalty resides in fanatical, religious, expiationist, vindictive arguments, exactly as was the case for torture. If we allow the death penalty, we must also allow torture....But we reject all of these excuses.[45]

It is this unmasking of what was formerly thought of as "religion" that characterizes Beristain's vision. This recognition of the respective roles of sacralization and desacralization is precisely what modern biblical studies have helped to clarify. Walter Harrelson made the point very explicitly in his rethinking of the commandment "Thou shalt not kill":

> Human life cannot be taken—not even by means of capital punishment administered by the most just and thoroughgoing system of justice conceivable—unless it is done on behalf of God. But that rules out capital punishment entirely, in a day when no society would wish, presumably, to act directly on God's behalf....The commandment stakes out the claim of God over all life and serves notice to all human beings— but especially to those who claim the biblical heritage as binding on them—that God's claim upon life is to be given priority in the decisions taken by a community or its individual members.[46]

E. Peter Csonka

Csonka's contribution covers in necessarily brief fashion much of the same ground that was seen in the work of William

Schabas. The use of the death penalty is being kept under scrutiny worldwide today in a way never previously possible. Even when outlaw nations continue to disregard the ever more specifically defined ethical standards of world conduct, it is no longer as it was in the past. One administration or ten administrations may manage to ignore world opinion and sustain barbaric codes, but their misdeeds can and will now be publicized and criticized until a change of heart occurs or the pressure of world opinion makes it commercially desirable to stop the killing.

Csonka traces the "spectacular emergence" of human-rights theory in international law since World War II, noting the controversy that went on over the initial affirmation of the right to life in the preparatory sessions when the *Universal Declaration of Human Rights* was being formulated in 1948. A minority wanted to affirm outright at that time that the death penalty violates the right to life, but they did not have the votes to get it into the original text. It is fascinating to note some of the timing of developments here, for it was in 1966 (the year after Vatican II closed) that the International Covenant on Civil and Political Rights was adopted. It was in 1978 (the year Pope John Paul II was elected) that the American Convention on Human Rights went into effect.

Since those days, when for a brief ten-year period America, too, due to a handful of dedicated civil-rights lawyers, stopped the killings and was among the de facto abolitionist countries, the retrogression has been appalling, raising profound questions about American society. But the cases brought so far against the United States, especially over executing juveniles, may be only the beginning of a long line of such challenges.[47] These challenges could be exactly what is necessary to start the upward trend of a new cycle.

> Trying to be neither cynical nor too optimistic, one can legitimately say that the international community has made considerable progress in the past 40–45 years toward the abolition of the death penalty from this planet.[48]

There is every reason to think that that advance will continue.

IV. TO LIVE IS TO HOPE

Whatever happens on the American political scene, however, there is no doubt about the goal of the vast majority of American Catholic leaders and moral theologians. Nor is there doubt about the direction of the international human-rights community. All will be attempting to further the lessons that have been learned since mid-century and to clarify their foundation: every human being is a person. Every person has universal, inviolable, inalienable rights. Basic to all other rights is the right to life. This right cannot be forfeited by misconduct. Thus everyone has a right not to be killed. Therefore the state has no right to kill.

Further work certainly is required in the challenging task of more fully elaborating solid intellectual foundations for the protection of human life and dignity, especially in a time when a culture of death seems to be preferred in many quarters. The best of Catholic tradition ought to be able to make a positive contribution here, if the tendency to defend the detours of the past can be minimized.[49]

The above survey of some of the more progressive Catholic thinking in Europe about the unacceptability of capital punishment should not leave the impression that there is not comparable work being done in this country. As suggested earlier, it may well be that the most important contribution in the long run will be from those who help today's Catholic faithful to deal with the process and reality of change. On this issue there has been ample American insight, starting with John Courtney Murray and Bernard Lonergan.

Avery Dulles has written lucidly on the dialectic that is required to avoid the extremes at both ends of the spectrum. "The conservative aspect of tradition would be misunderstood unless one took into account another aspect, which we might call innovative, or at least *renovative.*" The contemporary repudiation of capital punishment is a departure from misguided policies adopted for special reasons in particular periods of the past. But those policies were the original departure, the departure from a higher ethical ideal. That is the sense of retrieval, return, renewal, renovation, due to the achievement of greater insight.

> The relationship between tradition and innovation in religion is thus a dialectical one of mutual priority and dependence. If tradition is a matter of dwelling in the already given, innovation may be seen as a process of breaking out. Paradoxically, it is by dwelling in the tradition that we get the force and insight to break out and, so to speak, see for ourselves....Tradition is not an incessant repetition of the already given. It demands, and in a sense includes, its own opposite, innovation.[50]

Perhaps the greatest contribution that could be made to the entire movement to change minds and hearts about the death penalty would be to find ways to get people to focus more thoughtfully and prayerfully on the meaning of human life. As long as one is immersed in the sensory overload of TV and movies that present endlessly unrelieved violence and killing as the unquestioned norm, human life is likely to be seen not only as cheap but worthless. Capital punishment fits right in as one more way of inflicting senseless death.

But if the churches dare to undertake serious reeducation, sharing more articulately the vision of human life that best illuminates the tragedy of capital punishment, they can make a difference. If priority is given to establishing the basis for human dignity, if the uniqueness of the human person is highlighted, if not only the inalienable right to life but also the belief that life is literally divine gift and mystery become an important part of the discussion, there will be no need nor reason nor inclination to go back and try to defend the "shortcomings" of an earlier age. Rather, we can start the conversation on a very different level, with appropriately eloquent terms such as these:

> Capital punishment denies the givenness and totality of human life....It implies that men know more about life than they do....It is a denial of the human mystery....It is therefore always morally wrong, no matter what the justifications....It destroys the very purpose for which human life exists, a never-ending search for human meaning. No one has the right to frustrate this human dimension by imposing death....Capital punishment is a capitulation to human despair, the antithesis of morality and ethics....It is worse

than either abortion or euthanasia, because, unlike the latter, it is justified in terms of a volitional act by the subject of the killing. Hence, capital punishment is a more direct attack on the totality of human life because it attacks the spiritual subject for what in fact he has done.[51]

In the end, as in the beginning, the case for respecting human life prevails: from a Christian perspective, the death penalty has nothing to be said for it, and everything to be said against it. The goal set by Amnesty International to abolish it from the entire human community is in full accord with the requirements of the love of God, the love of neighbor, and of basic human decency. Whatever "right to kill" may have accrued to states in circumstances of the past, it has been fully superceded by the "right to life" of the human person in the circumstances of the present.

NOTES

Introduction

[1]*National Catholic Reporter* (April 7, 1995), 3.

[2]David E. Anderson, *National Catholic Reporter* (May 12, 1995), 3.

[3]René Girard, *Violence and the Sacred* (Baltimore, Md.: Johns Hopkins University Press, 1977). Cf. Michael E. Hardin, "Violence: René Girard and the Recovery of Early Christian Perspectives," *Brethren Life and Thought* 37 (1992), 117: "Christians who participate in social roles which demand some form of retaliation or punishment might need to be challenged to ask whether they have bought into the mechanism of sacred violence."

1. The Death Penalty and Early Christianity

[1]Cf. Jean Marie Aubert, *Chrétiens et Peine de Mort* (Paris: Relais Desclée, 1978), 15f., where he laments the "naive biblicism" that distorts the texts about the death penalty by "absolutizing the letter" and ignoring the fact that they must be interpreted very carefully in light of "the progress made in modern biblical exegesis."

[2]David E. Medley, *The Relevance of the Image of God to Capital Punishment in the Old Testament* (Ph.D. dissertation, Southwestern Baptist Theological Seminary, Fort Worth, Tex., 1979), labels the problem "the great paradox" of the Bible—the presence of a general command to all humans not to kill, accompanied by specific commands to kill for certain offenses. After struggling with the issue, he ends up favoring guarded retention of the death penalty in modern society: "Although the criminal law of the Old Testament should not be applied in every detail to modern society, an understanding of these laws is basic to answering the questions raised by capital punishment today. They emphasize the dignity of man and the sovereignty of God" (157).

[3]Students of the approach of René Girard have especially been preoccupied with this work. See, for example, Raymund Schwaiger, *Must There Be Scapegoats?* (Harper & Row, 1987), and James G. Williams, *The Bible, Violence and the Sacred: Liberation from the Myth of Sanctioned Violence* (Harper, 1991).

[4]S. Mendelsohn, *The Criminal Jurisprudence of the Ancient Hebrews* (original ed. 1890; 2d ed., New York: Hermon Press, 1968), 44–52. For a somewhat broader kind of summary, see Edwin M. Good, "Capital Punishment and Its Alternatives in Ancient Near Eastern Law," *Stanford Law*

Review 19 (1967), 947–77, where he organizes the entire Near Eastern legal data on capital cases into five categories:

1. Offenses against *Persons*: Murder; Kidnapping; Assault; Negligence; Sorcery and Curse, and Sexual Offenses: Rape; Adultery; Fornication; Prostitution and Procurement; Incest; Homosexuality; Bestiality; and Polyandry (very rare; only in one Sumerian allusion). Self-Induced Abortion; Death under Distraint; Offenses Regarding Slaves.

2. Offenses involving *Property*: Theft; Breaking and Entering; Breach of Contract; and False Exchange.

3. Defiance of *Authority*: General Disregard; Treason and Sedition; Neglect of Duty and Malfeasance; Perjury.

4. *Religious* Offenses: Wrong Observance; Neglect of Observance; Unpermitted Observance; and the BAN (Hebrew = HEREM).

5. *Procedural* Requirements: Royal Trial; Cases of Ordeal; Requirements of Evidence; and Substitution in Cases of Capital Punishment.

⁵Cf. Gerald J. Blidstein, "Capital Punishment—The Classical Jewish Discussion," *Judaism* 14 (1965), 164: "Jewish law abolished capital punishment in fact not by denying its conceptual moral validity but rather by allowing it *ONLY* this conceptual validity."

⁶Talmud, Makkot I,10, quoted by Edna Erez, "Thou Shalt Not Execute: Hebrew Law Perspective on Capital Punishment," *Criminology* 19:1 (May 1981), 37.

⁷Ibid., 38.

⁸Cf. Thorsten Sellin, *The Penalty of Death* (Beverly Hills/London: Sage Publications, 1980), 15: "This aversion to the use of capital punishment was not a new phenomenon in Israel....This is evident from legal doctrine and practice as early, at least, as two centuries before the fall of Jerusalem....That this aversion would persist in later centuries was only natural, considering the recurrent brutal persecutions the Jewish people would suffer for their faith." On the other hand, there is no question about the severe, literal interpretation of the capital laws by Philo of Alexandria. See esp. Book III, xv–xvii of his *On the Special Laws*, trans. F. H. Colson (Cambridge, Mass.: Harvard University Press, 1937; Loeb Classical Library, volume 7 of 12), 527ff.

⁹John McMaster, *The Divine Purpose of Capital Punishment* (London: Kegan Paul, Trench, Trübner, & Co., 1892), xv.

¹⁰See Gary Scott Smith, ed., *God and Politics: Four Views on the Reformation of Civil Government* (Philipsburg, N.J.: Presbyterian and Reformed Publishing Co., 1989), "Part One: Theonomy."

¹¹Rousas J. Rushdoony, *The Institutes of Biblical Law* (The Craig Press, 1973), 231. Some of the recent internal disputes are described by

H. Wayne House and Thomas Ice, *Dominion Theology: Blessing or Curse?* (1988), with the conclusion that "the Reconstructionists are firm about most positions....These include...application of the death penalty for virtually all of the capital crimes listed in the Old Testament law, including adultery, homosexuality, fornication, apostasy, incorrigibility in children, blasphemy, and perhaps sabbath-breaking, along with murder and kidnaping"(40).

[12]Carl F. H. Henry, "Does Genesis 9 Justify Capital Punishment? Yes," in *The Genesis Debate*, ed. Ronald F. Youngblood (Grand Rapids, Mich.: Baker Book House, 1990), 241.

[13]Ibid., 244. Henry is here summarizing, and presumably agreeing with, the view expressed by Gordon H. Clark, "Capital Punishment," in *Baker's Dictionary of Christian Ethics*, ed. Carl F. H. Henry (Grand Rapids, Mich.: Baker Book House, 1973), 81.

[14]Malcolm A. Reed, "Does Genesis 9 Justify Capital Punishment? No," *The Genesis Debate*, 231.

[15]Cf. E. E. Hobbs and W. C. Hobbs, "Contemporary Capital Punishment: Biblical Difficulties with the Biblically Permissible," *Christian Scholar's Review* 11 (1982), 250–62.

[16]See Paul Heinisch, *Theology of the Old Testament* (Collegeville, Minn.: Liturgical Press, 1950), 172. The arbitrariness of this kind of "dispensational" argument was itself more than problematic.

[17]Christian Reformed Church in North America, Statement on Capital Punishment (1981), in *The Churches Speak on: Capital Punishment*, ed. J. Gordon Melton (Detroit, Mich.: Gale Research, 1989), 72. This thoughtful statement is the work of a committee chaired by Reformed theologian Henry Stob, with Clarence Vos as the principal author of the section on the Old Testament.

[18]Ibid., 73.

[19]Terence E. Fretheim, "The Book of Genesis," *The New Interpreter's Bible* (Nashville, Tenn.: Abingdon Press, 1994), I:399.

[20]Karl Bruno Leder, *Todesstrafe: Ursprung, Geschichte, Opfer* (Wien-München: Meyster, 1980), chapter 2, summarizes the extensive studies of S. R. Steinmetz, *Ethnologische Studien zur ersten Entwicklung der Strafe* (Groningen, 1928).

[21]Christian Reformed Church, in *The Churches Speak on: Capital Punishment*, 94. (The New Testament consultant on the committee that formulated the document was Professor Louis Vos of Calvin College.)

[22]See Paul W. Meyer, "Romans," *Harper's Bible Commentary*, ed. James L. Mays (San Francisco, Calif.: Harper & Row, 1988), 1163.

[23]C. E. B. Cranfield, *Romans: A Shorter Commentary* (Grand Rapids, Mich.: Wm. B. Eerdmans, 1985), 323f.

[24]John Barton, "Reading and Interpreting the Bible," *Harper's Bible Commentary*, 8.

[25]Aubert, 21.

[26]See Ernest Barker, ed., *From Alexander to Constantine: Passages and Documents Illustrating the History of Social and Political Ideas 336 B.C.–A.D. 337* (Oxford, 1956), esp. Part V ("Ideas of the Christian Church down to Constantine").

[27]See Bernhard Schöpf, *Das Tötungsrecht bei den frühchristlichen Schriftstellern bis zur Zeit Konstantins* (Regensburg: F. Pustet, 1958).

[28]Athenagoras, *A Plea for the Christians*, chapter xxxv, in *The Ante-Nicene Fathers*, vol. 2, *Fathers of the Second Century*, ed. A. Roberts and J. Donaldson (Grand Rapids, Mich.: Wm. B. Eerdmans, 1967), 147.

[29]Minucius Felix, *Octavius* xxx, 6, trans. G. H. Rendall, Loeb Classical Library, vol. 250 (Cambridge, Mass.: Harvard University Press, 1931), 409.

[30]See Lisa Sowle Cahill, *Love Your Enemies: Discipleship, Pacifism, and Just War Theory* (Minneapolis, Minn.: Fortress Press, 1994), 48. After reviewing current studies of Tertullian, she concludes by describing him as "a pacifist but not a separatist."

[31]Schöpf, 153. He is referring to a remark of Tertullian in his work *On the Resurrection of the Flesh*, 16, where he says he would not drink from a "cup infected with the breath of an executioner." For the sordid story of three centuries of British hangmen, see Brian Bailey, *Hangmen of England: The History of Execution from Jack Ketch to Albert Pierrepont* (New York: Barnes & Noble, 1992).

[32]Clement of Alexandria, *The Stromata, or Miscellanies* Book I, chapter xxvii, in *The Ante-Nicene Fathers*, II: 339.

[33]Schöpf, 158.

[34]Origen, *Against Celsus*, 7:26. See Cahill, 53.

[35]Ibid., 8:73. "We in this way are much more helpful to the kings than those who go into the field to fight for them. And we do take our part in public affairs, when along with righteous prayers we join self-denying exercises....And none fight better for the king than we do. We do not indeed fight under him, although he require it; but we fight on his behalf, forming a special army—an army of piety—by offering our prayers to God" (*The Ante-Nicene Fathers*, IV: 668).

[36]Robert Markus, *The End of Ancient Christianity* (New York: Cambridge University Press, 1990), 101.

[37]See Johannes Quasten, *Patrology*, vol. 2, *The Ante-Nicene Literature After Irenaeus* (Utrecht: Spectrum Publishers, 1953), 82: "Origen is the first to declare the Church to be the city of God here on earth...existing for the time being side by side with the secular state....It is at present a

state within a state, but the power of the Logos working in her will result in overcoming the secular state." There are obviously some very serious questions still in need of resolution.

[38]For more recent discussion of some of the "inconsistencies and even outright contradictions" (p. 293) in some of the ways Origen explicates New Testament images of the Church, see Verlyn D. Verbrugge, "Origen's Ecclesiology and the Biblical Metaphor of the Church as the Body of Christ," in *Origen of Alexandria: His World and His Legacy*, ed. Charles Kannengiesser and William L. Petersen (Notre Dame, Ind.: University of Notre Dame Press, 1988), 277–94.

[39]*The Ante-Nicene Fathers*, 5: 277.

[40]Ibid., 351.

[41]Michael Grant, *The Climax of Rome* (Boston, Mass.: Little, Brown, 1968), 234, estimates that "perhaps the total number of those who died in all parts of the empire was about three thousand."

[42]J.-P. Migne, PL 6: 708A (liber VI, caput 20), 15–17: "Ita neque militare justo licebit, cujus militia est ipsa justitia; neque vero accusare quemquam crimine capitali; quia nihil distat utrumne ferro an verbo potius occidas; quoniam occisio ipsa prohibetur. Itaque in hoc Dei praecepto nullam exceptionem fieri opportet, quia occidere hominem sit semper nefas..." (English translations are in *The Ante-Nicene Fathers* VII: 187; and Louis J. Swift, *The Early Fathers on War and Military Service* [Wilmington, Del.: M. Glazier, 1983], 62f.).

[43]David G. Hunter, "The Christian Church and the Roman Army in the First Three Centuries," in *The Church's Peace Witness*, ed. Marlin E. Miller and Barbara N. Gingerich (Grand Rapids, Mich.: Wm. B. Eerdmans, 1994), 179.

[44]J. Helgeland, R. J. Daly, and J. P. Burns, *Christians and the Military: The Early Experience* (Philadelphia, Pa.: Fortress Press, 1985), 36.

[45]See Ramsay MacMullen, *Christianizing the Roman Empire A.D. 100–400* (Yale University Press, 1984), 88f.: "The use of armed force...belongs peculiarly to the closing decades of the fourth century....Without that, pagan intransigence simply could not be overcome." Robin Lane Fox, *Pagans and Christians* (New York: Harper & Row, 1986), 23, has reservations about the narrow time frame in MacMullen's thesis, but not about the essential point: "The rise of Christianity induced a much sharper rise in religious intolerance and the open coercion of religious belief. Christians were quick to mobilize force against the pagan cults and against their own unorthodox Christian brethren, a reaction which was not the late creation of Constantine and his reign."

[46]Jean Imbert, *La Peine de Mort: Histoire–Actualité* (Paris: Armand Colin, 1967), 40.

[47]Adolf von Harnack, *History of Dogma,* (trans. Neil Buchanan from the 3d German ed. (1897) (New York: Russell & Russell, 1958), 5:331, claimed that "in one respect the Church had a softening and beneficial effect. It restricted to an extraordinary extent the capital punishment closely connected with outlawry....Even in the Roman period the Church in Gaul exerted itself to soften the Roman administration of justice where the latter admitted capital punishment. It continued its efforts with success in the Merovingian age, so that arrangements were more and more frequently made in substitution for the death penalty. The chief argument urged by the Church was doubtless that God did not will the death of the sinner, and that Christ died an atoning and sacrificial death for all. Thus Christ's death obtained an extraordinary importance. It became the grand achievement, whose value even softened the earthly right of punishment."

[48]Aubert reflects on the ambivalence and irony of the so-called Constantinian conversion: "If the Empire adopted Christianity, Christianity in return adopted the institutions and law of the Empire, in particular the Roman conception of the death penalty, without questioning it or influencing the legislation" (14). He goes on to suggest some reasons for this, but the anomaly remains to be explained more fully.

[49]Michael Grant, *The Fall of the Roman Empire* (New York: Collier, 1990), 160. He also notes the single exception—Valentinian's short-lived policy of universal toleration launched in A.D. 371 and standing out "as a beacon during a millennium and a half in which, for the most part, rulers of the leading nations continued to think and act otherwise."

[50]Clarence A. Forbes, "Firmicus Maternus," *New Catholic Encyclopedia* (New York: McGraw-Hill, 1967), 5: 935f.

[51]Clarence A. Forbes, *Firmicus Maternus: The Error of the Pagan Religions, #37* in *Ancient Christian Writers: The Works of the Fathers in Translation* (New York: Newman Press, 1970), 15.

[52]Ibid., 68 (chap. 12:5).

[53]Ibid., 115f. (chap. 29:1–4). Joseph Lecler, S.J., *Toleration and the Reformation* (London: Longmans, 1960) I: 42, says of the above passage of Maternus: "This is the first time, we believe, that Christians appealed to the Old Law to justify violent procedures against error. Unfortunately, the example would not be forgotten."

[54]Grant, *The Fall of the Roman Empire,* 156. See also Nicolas Cheetam, *Keepers of the Keys* (New York: Chas. Scribner's Sons, 1983), 22. It was also during the pontificate of Damasus I that Emperor Theodosius I (379–395) began his vigorous campaign to "Christianize" the entire Empire by Roman law.

[55]Emperor Julian the Apostate (361–363) claimed that under his

predecessor Constantius many Christian heretics were put to death. If true, then the execution of Priscillian and his companions would obviously not be the first such. But there is no corroboration of Julian's claim from any other source, and it is generally not regarded as reliable. See Leonard W. Levy, *Treason Against God: A History of the Offense of Blasphemy* (New York: Schocken Books, 1981), 367.

[56]See P. R. Coleman-Norton, *Roman State and Christian Church: A Collection of Legal Documents to A.D. 535* (London: SPCK, 1966), II:#203—Rescript of Maximus to Pope Siricius on Support of Orthodoxy (after Siricius had protested the Priscillianist executions). The Rescript has nothing explicit to say about the death penalty but is of interest for the imperial use of power for church purposes that it reflects. Maximus, newly baptized, referred to the heresies as "diseases difficult to heal that would harden if they were not completely destroyed."

[57]See Henry Chadwick, *Priscillian of Avila* (Oxford: Clarendon Press, 1976), esp. chapter 3, "Priscillian's End and Its Consequences." It seems that St. Optatus of Milevis in Africa, Priscilian's contemporary, in his treatise *De Schismate Donatistarum* 3.6, was the first bishop to champion the State's infliction of capital punishment on heretics and schismatics. A liberal exegesis of the Pauline precept in 1 Corinthians 5:5 was enough to establish the doctrine of the delivery of such persons "for the destruction of the flesh, that the spirit may be saved." See also Samuel N. C. Lieu, *Manichaeism in the Later Roman Empire and Medieval China* (Manchester University Press, 1985), 116: "Priscillianism...thus became one of the first main victims of the anti-Manichaean legislation even though neither side in the controversy could demonstrate any real knowledge of Manichaeism, and what Priscillian knew he anathematized."

[58]S. L. Greenslade, *Church and State from Constantine to Theodosius* (London: SCM Press, 1954), 54.

[59]Epistula XV (J.-P. Migne, *PL* 54:679–80). Michael Grant calls attention to the year 394, "when the Christians first achieved a decided majority in the Senate. The age of ambivalence, of possible latitude of thought, was gone from the ancient Roman world for ever" (*The Climax of Rome,* 256).

[60]N. Q. King, *The Emperor Theodosius and the Establishment of Christianity* (London: SCM Press, 1961), 50–59, details the "juggernaut" of legislation by Theodosius I (379–395) "against all the heretics": Encratites, Saccofori, and Hydroparastatae were to suffer the death penalty; a variety of penalties was proposed for Manichaeans, Arians, Pneumatomachoi, Eunomians, Apollinarians, and others. King remarks (51) that "half-way through this law [of A.D. 382] the legislator seems to have lost his head. This is the first time the death penalty was laid down

for wrong belief. The hateful principle of inquisitor and informer was now also introduced." He goes on to suggest that it may well have been a factor in the execution of Priscillian a couple of years later, since "in a letter Maximus equated Priscillianism with Manichaeism and this may be a direct reference to the law we are studying."

[61]Neil B. McLynn, *Ambrose of Milan: Church and Court in a Christian Capital* (Berkeley, Calif.: University of California Press, 1994), 315.

[62]Ibid., 323.

[63]Ibid., 330.

[64]It is the history of this strange subterfuge of having "recourse to the secular arm" that was the focus of international seminars held in Spain and in Italy in recent years. See the works of Niceto Blázquez.

[65]English translations of Ambrose's "Two Books Concerning Repentance" are found in the *Select Library of Nicene and Post-Nicene Fathers,* 2d series (Grand Rapids, Mich.: Wm. B. Eerdmans, 1969 reprint), vol. 10: 327–59.

[66]Ambrose, *Duties of the Clergy,* III: 4. English translation in *Nicene and Post-Nicene Fathers,* vol. 10, 71f.

[67]C. 5, canon 13 (Migne, *PL* 13:1181ff.).

[68]*Epistula* VI, c.3, n.7, cited by F. Compagnoni, "Capital Punishment and Torture in the Tradition of the Roman Catholic Church," *Concilium* 120 (*The Death Penalty and Torture*) (October 1978), 41. See also E. Demougeot, "A propos des Interventions du Pape Innocent I dans la Politique Séculière," *Revue Historique,* 212 (1954), 25.

[69]Compagnoni, 41.

[70]Migne, *PL* 24: 843: "non est effusio sanguinis, sed legum ministerium."

[71]Migne, *PL* 25:85. Ezekiel 9:1b reads thus in the Vulgate: "appropinquaverunt visitationes urbis, et unusquisque vas interfectionis *habet* in manu sua." Jerome comments: "Non dixit *habebat,* ut Septuaginta transtulerunt. Neque narrat praeterita, sed praesentia futuraque demonstrat. Qui igitur malos percutit in eo quod mali sunt, et habet vasa interfectionis, ut occidat pessimos, *minister est Domini.*"

[72]John Chrysostom, *Homily 46 on Matthew 13:24–30,* in *Nicene and Post-Nicene Fathers of the Christian Church,* ed. Philip Schaff (Grand Rapids, Mich.: Wm. B. Eerdmans, 1975 reprint), 10:288f.

[73]Augustine, *Letter 34,* 1. See Herbert A. Deane, *The Political and Social Ideas of St. Augustine* (New York: Columbia University Press, 1963), 178f.: "In spite of all the efforts of the Empire to restrain the violence of the Donatists,...the movement was stronger in 391, when Augustine became a priest, than it had ever been before....In 395 Augustine became

a bishop and began an extensive campaign against the Donatists in Hippo and throughout Africa."

[74]*Letter 93, 5:17.* See Peter Brown, "St. Augustine's Attitude to Religious Coercion," *The Journal of Roman Studies,* 54 (1964): 107–16. Brown traces the evolution of Augustine's thought and his gradual loss of patience in the Donatist crisis, concluding that "his charity seems to vary greatly with the degree to which he was personally involved in the suppression of a powerful rival. He is a sensitive and conscientious pastor up to his victory over the Donatists; but, in 420, he can appear, for an instant, as a harsh and cold victor."

[75]H. Hetzel, *Die Todesstrafe in ihrer kulturgeschichtlichen Entwicklung: Eine Studie* (Berlin: W. Moeser, 1870), 84, quotes a passage of the Donatist bishop Petilianus: "Do you really think you are serving God by murdering us with your own hand? You are wrong if you think so, for God has no priestly hangmen. Christ, in his death for humanity, gave Christians the example of dying, not of killing. But you allow the rulers of this world, who would be Christians, not to act as Christians, since you lead them to use the weapons prepared for the enemies of the state against Christians." For the original Latin, see Paul Monceaux, *Histoire Littéraire de L'Afrique Chrétienne,* tome cinquième: *Saint Optat et les premiers Ecrivains Donatistes* (Paris: 1920; reprint Bruxelles 1963), Appendice 1, "Pamphlet de Petilianus contre l'Eglise Catholique," 319–28. Augustine refuted the allegations of Petilianus, pointing out that it was the Donatists who were doing most of the killing until the imperial forces intervened. The intensity of the rhetoric illustrates how deep the mutual alienation was by this time.

[76]See Cahill, 78: "Nowhere is the incongruity between the religious identity of the church and its pragmatic compromise with violence more evident or more jarring than in Augustine's supposition that physical force may be used to encourage Christian faith." See also William C. Placher, *A History of Christian Theology* (Philadelphia, Pa.: Westminster, 1983), 115: "(Augustine's) decision has often been cited as the beginning of a thousand years of all the horrors of the Inquisition, and that goes too far, but calling in the army to enforce a theological decision did set a precedent that would haunt Christendom."

[77]Greater care in the use of the term *the Inquisition* is obviously required in light of modern studies. As J. B. Russell notes (*Dissent and Order in the Middle Ages* [New York: Twayne Publishers, 1992], 54f.): "There was never such an entity as 'THE Inquisition.' Two common misperceptions must be obliterated. The first is that a centralized institution in the Middle Ages called 'The Inquisition'...ever existed; in fact, such an institution is pure fantasy. Prosecutions of heretics did exist, conducted

by a variety of authorities, especially bishops and princes....But 'there was never a permanently constituted congregation and tribunal against heresy until the 16th century.' And second, Inquisitions were by no means restricted to, or even focused on, investigation or prosecution of dissent."

[78]N. Blázquez Fernández, *La Pena de Muerte según S. Agustín* (Madrid, 1975), traced the history of the controversy over proper interpretation of Augustine on the death penalty, then did his own careful analysis of the Augustinian texts.

[79]Hurtado de Mendoza, *Scholasticae et Morales Disputationes de tribus virtutibus,* 1631. Sect. I, Disputatio 86: "Whether heretics can or cannot be condemned to death." As cited by Blázquez, Hurtado concludes (755): "Itaque sensit Augustinus licuisse Imperatoribus nece haereticos coercere."

[80]Blázquez, 11: "El ilustre teólogo (Hurtado) llega a la conclusión breve y precisa de que, según Agustín, el exterminio de los herejes por parte de las autoridades civiles no sólo sería legítimo, sino también piadoso y laudable."

[81]Otto Schilling, *Die Staats und Soziallehre des hl. Augustinus* (Freiburg im Breisgau, 1910), 178–80.

[82]Cited by Gustave Combes, *La Doctrine Politique de Saint Augustin* (Paris: Librairie Plon, 1927), 188–92 (au sujet de la peine de mort). Combes agrees that Augustine acknowledged the legality of the death penalty but concludes that he struggled all his days with the troubling question whether it was a just law. "Does the right of life and death belong to anyone other than God? And if it belongs only to God, should men not renounce arrogating it to themselves?" Not being able to suppress the law, he did what he could to suspend its effects. "Augustine is hostile toward the death penalty because it respects neither the rights of God nor the dignity of man."

[83]N. Noguer, "La doctrina politico-social de San Agustín, esp. sobre el castigo de los herejes," *Razón y Fe* 35 (1913), 349–65.

[84]N. Merlín, "Doctrina auténtica de san Agustín sobre el castigo de los herejes," *Espana y América* II (1913), 104–17.

[85]Geoffrey Keating, *The Moral Problems of Fraternal, Paternal and Judicial Correction According to St. Augustine* (Roma: Pontifical University Gregoriana, 1958), 113–23.

[86]Blázquez, 207–10.

[87]As Blázquez puts it, "He would always defend and presume the good faith of the executors on the subjective level, but would say nothing about the objective morality of the executions themselves" (208).

[88]St. Augustine, *The City of God,* Book I, chapter 21 (Garden City, New York: Doubleday Image Books, 1958), 57.

[89]Blázquez, 209: "JAMÁS hasta la pena de muerte o a esas torturas que en la práctica suelen resultar más bien una expresión perfecta de la venganza...que la justicia." Deane (see n. 73), comes close to expressing the position of Blázquez: "It is clear that Augustine is firmly opposed to the use of capital punishment against the Donatists, no matter what crimes they may have committed, and that he believes that in all criminal cases the death sentence should be used only when it is absolutely necessary" (329).

[90]Blázquez, 210.

[91]Brown, 337.

[92]See William R. Stevenson, Jr., *Christian Love and Just War: Moral Paradox and Political Life in St. Augustine and His Modern Interpreters* (Macon, Ga.: Mercer University Press, 1987), 150: "Although we may be led to Augustine...it is far from obvious what we should do with him when we get there. What part or parts of him should we bring back to our own time and condition?...The whole of Augustine, in other words, is much more than his parts." That very fact makes grappling with his positions all the more worthwhile and potentially fruitful.

[93]Clyde Pharr, trans., *The Theodosian Code and Novels and the Sirmondian Constitutions* (Princeton, N.J.: Princeton University Press, 1952), 236 (Book 9, Title 14—*On the Cornelian Law on Cutthroats,* 2: given on the kalends of July in the year of the consulship of Tatianus and Symmachus).

[94]St. Augustine, *Letters,* vol. 3 (#131–64), trans. Sr. W. Parsons (New York: FOTC, 1953), 10f.

[95]Augustine, in *Select Library of Nicene and Post-Nicene Fathers,* 1st series, vol. 1, trans. J. G. Cunningham, 470f. A special irony is added to the story by the fact that these two brothers whom Augustine so eloquently urged to forgo torture and execution in punishing the Donatist terrorists were themselves both decapitated the following year when they fell afoul of the system and were implicated by Marinus, Count of Africa, in the revolt of Heraclian. Augustine visited Marcellinus in prison and testified to his upright character. Cardinal Baronius centuries later added his name to the Roman Martyrology (see P. Roche, "Marcellinus, Flavius," *New Catholic Encyclopedia* 9:189).

[96]See, e.g., Robert Markus, *The End of Ancient Christianity* (New York: Cambridge University Press, 1990), 134: "Augustine's theology had carefully kept a space for an intermediate realm of the 'secular' between the 'sacred' and the 'profane'; his own inclinations...were to defend this area from encroachment by the 'sacred,' from clerical interference and

ecclesiastical domination. But his differentiated and complex vision faded from the world of his successors."

[97]Besides Pharr, see the examples in Edward Peters, ed., *Heresy and Authority in Medieval Europe: Documents in Translation* (Philadelphia, Pa: University of Pennsylvania Press., 1980), 44–47. For the tangled story of Theodosius' involvement in the extraordinary strife that occurred between the "Robber Council" of Ephesus (449) and the Council of Chalcedon (451), see Colm Luibheíd, "Theodosius II and Heresy," *Journal of Ecclesiastical History*, 16 (1965), 13–38.

[98]See Michel Rouche, "The Early Middle Ages in the West," in *A History of Private Life*, ed. Paul Veyne (Cambridge, Mass.: Belknap Press of Harvard University, 1987): "The wise elders who framed the Salic Law rehearsed a whole litany of violent acts culminating in murder, punishable by the so-called wergeld, 'man-gold'....Only gold could stem the flow of blood." But he also goes on to note "the curious Frankish custom of putting thieves to death but fining murderers."

[99]Katherine Fischer Drew, *The Laws of the Salian Franks* (University of Pennsylvania Press, 1991), 50. The three capital cases are all in capitulary VI: 1) incest; 2) rape; and 3) homicide "without cause."

[100]Paul Savey-Casard, *La Peine de Mort: Esquisses Historique et Juridique* (Genève: Librairie Droz, 1968), 24.

[101]Ibid.

[102]Imbert, after listing these, emphasizes that this unusually bloody capitulary is the exception rather than the rule, and "is to be explained—not justified—by the frequent relapses of Saxons into idolatry and revolt" (51). But there was also a vengeance factor involved; see Aland, *A History of Christianity*, I: 257f.

[103]For a good sample of decrees, see P. R. Coleman-Norton, *Roman State and Christian Church: A Collection of Legal Documents to A.D. 535* (London: SPCK, 1966), vol. 1—A.D. 1 to 177; vol. 2—A.D. 178 to 486; vol. 3—A.D. 487 to 652. The one quoted above was issued in 419 by Emperors Honorius and Theodosius to Monaxius, and eventually incorporated into Justinian's *Code* (IX, 47, 25): "We decree that those who instruct barbarians how to build ships, when the latter were previously ignorant of the art, shall be put to death."

[104]Liber IV, epistula 47, *PL* 77: 721: "quia Deum timeo, in mortem cujuslibet hominis me miscere formido." English translation in *Select Library of Nicene and Post-Nicene Fathers*, 2d series, vol. 12, 161.

[105]*Epistula* 97, cap. 25, quoted by Compagnoni, 47f.

[106]Glanville Downey, *Constantinople in the Age of Justinian* (University of Oklahoma Press, 1960; New York: Dorset Press reprint, 1991), 141.

[107]*The Secret History of Procopius,* trans. Richard Atwater (New York: Dorset Press, 1992), a scandal-mongering account by one of Justinian's courtiers, reflects the duality of the emperor's accomplishments. Chapter 18, for example, is entitled "How Justinian Killed a Trillion People" and chapter 29 "Other Incidents Revealing Him a Liar and a Hypocrite." As far as Procopius was concerned, Justinian was responsible for all wars, plagues, earthquakes, and other disasters that happened in his time: "the whole earth ran red with the blood of nearly all the Romans and the barbarians....His persecution of the Samaritans and the so-called heretics filled the Roman realm with blood," and he did all this by "some hidden power and diabolic force" (92–94).

[108]See K. Engisch, "Strafrecht," *RGG,* Band 6, col. 402. Also see William S. Thurman, "How Justinian I Sought to Handle the Problem of Religious Dissent," *The Greek Orthodox Theological Review* 13 (1968), 15–40.

[109]For an English translation, see S. P. Scott, *The Civil Law* (Cincinnati, Ohio: Central Trust Co., 1932; New York: AMS reprint, 1973), vol. 15. Averil Cameron, *Procopius and the Sixth Century* (Berkeley, Calif.: University of California Press, 1985), chapter 7–"Procopius and Christianity," offers helpful insight into this tangled story. He suggests that "Procopius's hatred for the official policy of persecution probably had personal roots" (120).

[110]Steven Runciman, *The Medieval Manichee* (Cambridge, 1947; reprinted 1960), 31–39 passim.

[111]Besides the Justinian *Code,* the law code known as the Eclogue was issued by co-emperors Leo III the Isaurian and his son Constantine V in 726. Nicolas Oikonomides, "Eclogue," *Dictionary of the Middle Ages,* vol. 5, 382, notes one curious development reflected in this document: "In a deliberate effort to infuse an element of humanity into the law...capital punishment is often replaced by mutilation, which does not endanger the salvation of the criminal's soul....Being the work of iconoclasts, the Eclogue was denounced in the 9th century as a 'perversion of the law' and formally abrogated."

[112]J. B. Russell, 10.

2. Movement in the Medieval Church

[1]Frederick H. Russell, *The Just War in the Middle Ages* (Cambridge: Cambridge University Press, 1975), 18. Russell is here commenting on Augustine's *Contra Faustum,* 22:70.

[2]See Thomas F. X. Noble, *The Republic of St. Peter: The Birth of the*

Papal State, 680–825 (Philadelphia, Pa.: University of Pennsylvania Press, 1984).

[3]J. B. Russell, 11.

[4]See Geoffrey Barraclough, *The Medieval Papacy* (Harcourt, Brace & World, 1968), 63: "Few popes in the century following Pope John VIII (872–882) died peacefully in their beds....John VIII himself was murdered; Stephen VI (896–97) strangled in prison; Benedict VI (973–74) smothered; John XIV (983–84) done to death in the Castel Sant'Angelo."

[5]Louis Duchesne, *The Beginnings of the Temporal Sovereignty of the Popes A.D. 754–1073* (New York: Burt Franklin, 1972 reprint of 1908 edition), 271. H. Hetzel, *Die Todesstrafe in ihrer kulturgeschichtlichen Entwicklung* (Berlin: W. Moeser, 1870), 97, makes the statement that good King Wenceslaus (928–936) was the first and only Christian prince in the first millennium and a half of Christian history to abolish the death penalty for Christian reasons, although the English kings Alfred the Great (871–901) and William the Conqueror (1066–1087) reduced its use to the single case of treason.

[6]Bernard Hamilton, *The Medieval Inquisition* (New York: Holmes & Meier, 1981), 22f.

[7]W. L. Wakefield and A. P. Evans, eds., *Heresies of the High Middle Ages* (New York: Columbia University Press, 1969), 72. See also Martin Erbstösser, *Heretics in the Middle Ages,* trans. Janet Fraser (Edition Leipzig, 1984), 62: "Heresy entered western Europe almost unnoticed, and indeed, the earliest recorded account of an individual heretic (Leuthard) seemed almost to be a description of an isolated episode."

[8]Wakefield and Evans, 81. See also Bernard Cullen, "Western European Heresies," *Dictionary of the Middle Ages* V (1985), 194.

[9]Jeffrey B. Russell, *Witchcraft in the Middle Ages* (Ithaca, N.Y.: Cornell University Press, 1972), 86f. "The heretics themselves ended in the flames, and the charge may have been invented by the orthodox to justify this mode of execution, unusual for the time. Or the reverse may be true: the punishment may have been designed to suit the actual crime."

[10]Russell, *Dissent and Order in the Middle Ages,* 28. Peter Brown, "Society and the Supernatural: A Medieval Change," *Daedalus* 104 (1975), 133, refines the point thus: "We find a sharpening and a redistribution of roles in society dramatically pinpointed in the sudden emergence of a new relationship between clergy and laity in the time of the Investiture Contest...a process as widespread and ineluctable as a change in the tide of Western society." For a review of the manifold often conflicting trends stirring in twentieth-century historiography of

this period, see John van Engen, "The Christian Middle Ages as an Historiographical Problem," *American Historical Review* 91 (1986), 519ff.

[11]Hamilton, 25.

[12]Wakefield and Evans, 89–93. The "presumed author" of this unique record was Anselm, a canon and later dean of the cathedral at Liège.

[13]M. D. Chenu, O.P., *Nature, Man, and Society in the Twelfth Century* (University of Chicago Press, 1968; Midway Reprint, 1983), chapters 6 and 7.

[14]Though there is still uncertainty over the degree to which Bogomilism, with its Manichaean style of dualism, may account for the rise of at least some of these heresies, its role as an important factor is a plausible thesis (see Adriaan H. Bredero, *Christendom and Christianity in the Middle Ages* [Grand Rapids, Mich.: Wm. B. Eerdmans, 1994], 199: "Divergent understandings of salvation imported into the Western church from Bulgaria during the eleventh century also played an important role. There the dualistic sect of the Bogomiles had arisen in the tenth century....Bogomilism spread along the trade routes to the West, where the church was hardly prepared to deal with this new phenomenon").

[15]Russell, *Dissent and Order in the Middle Ages,* 29: "Eucharistic heresy is one of the most common themes in medieval dissent. In some instances, the accounts are simply garbled and false; in others...the heretics misunderstood orthodox doctrine...; in yet others the heretics deliberately attacked the Eucharist in order to attack the authority of the clergy."

[16]Stanislaus Woywod, O.F.M., *A Practical Commentary on the Code of Canon Law,* rev. Callistus Smith, O.F.M. (New York: Joseph F. Wagner, 1952), 598. Canon 984 included among those who were ineligible for Orders "a judge who has pronounced a death sentence." Woywod provided an accurate and pertinent explanation: "The spirit of the sacred ministry is a spirit of mercy and forgiveness, wherefore the Church declares it improper to raise to the sacred ministry a person who has concurred in procuring the execution of a man, no matter how legitimate and guiltless such action may have been. From the earliest times of the Church men who had shed human blood, even apart from any guilt, were refused admission to the sacred ministry." Even though this restriction has sometimes been interpreted as merely a ritualistic taboo modeled on the ancient Israelite fear of "blood pollution," a more benign interpretation is also justifiable, seeing the prohibition as a kind of residual respect for life and abhorrence for any kind of deliberate bloodshed.

[17]See Henry Kamen, "Clerical Violence in a Catholic Society: The Hispanic World 1450–1720," in *The Church and War*, ed. W. J. Sheils (Oxford: Basil Blackwell, 1983), 201–16. The most bizarre example recorded is that of Antonio de Acuna, bishop of Zamora, Spain, "who in 1520 at the age of 60 set out to fight for the Comuneros at the head of 300 of his diocesan clergy, all armed to the teeth at his specific orders."

[18]Imbert, 55f. "Some late 12th century ecclesiastics, working in concert with civil authorities, themselves condemned heretics; such was the case of Guillaume aux-Blanches-Mains. Hardly a case of *Ecclesia abhorret a sanguine!* This confusion of powers did not last long. Soon the church pressured the lay power to do the executing....Sovereigns and judges could hardly avoid their cruel mission!" Imbert goes on to note that the unfortunate disappearance of most of the records of this period has allowed historians to differ wildly in estimating the number of actual executions that took place.

[19]Philip Dixon, *Barbarian Europe* (Oxford: Elsevier-Phaidon, 1976), 100.

[20]Peter Llewellyn, *Rome in the Dark Ages* (London: Faber & Faber, 1971), 280. A gifted man in a turbulent age, John VIII "failed in the tangle of local feuds and ambitions and through the defects of his own hasty, devious temperament....His pontificate marked the last attempt to revive a united Empire against common enemies" (281).

[21]J. N. D. Kelly, *The Oxford Dictionary of Popes* (New York: Oxford University Press, 1986), 110.

[22]The irony can hardly be missed in noting that John VIII, the first warrior-pope, was, as far as we know, also the first pope ever murdered. For an account of some of the intrigues in his ten years as pope, see Fred E. Engreen, "Pope John VIII and the Arabs," *Speculum* 20 (1945), 318–30.

[23]Uta-Renate Blumenthal, *The Investiture Controversy: Church and Monarchy from the Ninth to the Twelfth Century* (Philadelphia, Pa.: University of Pennsylvania Press, 1988), 64.

[24]E. Caspar, the editor of Gregory VII's letters, describes him as "the great innovator, who stands quite alone" (cited by R. F. Bennett in his introduction to his translation of Gerd Tellenbach, *Church, State and Christian Society at the Time of the Investiture Contest* [Oxford: Basil Blackwell, 1959], ix).

[25]See., e.g., 1 Thes 5:8, where faith and love are to be put on as a "breastplate" and the hope of salvation as a "helmet." 2 Corinthians 10:3f. makes it very clear that this imagery is not to be taken literally: "Though we live in the world, we do not wage war as the world does. The weapons we fight with are not the weapons of the world."

[26]H. E. J. Cowdrey, *Popes, Monks, and Crusaders* (London: Hambledon Press, 1984), xiii–20.

[27]See Colin Morris, *The Papal Monarchy: The Western Church from 1050 to 1250* (Oxford: Clarendon Press, 1989), 337: "The profound opposition to men of violence, which treated the knights as the medieval equivalent of gangsters, continued for a long time: the revealing pun *militia-malitia* is found in many twelfth-century writers. But the pope and bishops needed the knights....Before the end of the eleventh century there had been three distinct attempts to enlist the knights in God's service."

[28]Quoted by Frances Gies, *The Knight in History* (New York: Harper & Row, 1984), 20. Gies goes on to call attention to "an implication with enormous potential consequence: the knight was justified in exercising his profession of war only if he did it against the enemies of Christ." Hans-Werner Goetz, *Life in the Middle Ages* (Notre Dame, Ind.: University of Notre Dame Press, 1993), 179, notes the "three different concepts of knighthood": a) the noble warrior-knight; b) the graduate knight (assigned to perform a religious function); and c) the "romantic type of knight" we encounter in literature.

[29]Karen Armstrong, *Holy War: The Crusades and Their Impact on Today's World* (New York: Doubleday, 1991), 63.

[30]See Blumenthal, 117: "The terms *obedience* and *disobedience* are by far the most frequently encountered twin concepts in the more than 400 extant letters of Gregory VII."

[31]See R. I. Moore, *The Formation of a Persecuting Society: Power and Deviance in Western Europe 950–1250* (Oxford: Basil Blackwell, 1987), 70. Moore has some interesting suggestions which "diminish the extent to which the ecclesiastical perception of heresy as a monster ravaging outside the gate can be taken at face value."

[32]Charles Journet, *The Church of the Word Incarnate: An Essay in Speculative Theology,* trans. A. H. C. Downes (New York: Sheed & Ward, 1955), I: 280–94: "The Death Penalty and the Medieval Repression of Heresy," made as sympathetic a pre-Vatican II case as was possible without a great deal of whitewash. Journet took into account the unique cultural conditions that are sometimes overlooked by polemicists, such as the fact that "it was not the Church that introduced the death penalty for heresy. It had a popular origin....In the given cultural epoch the death penalty (was) universally accepted as just....It was not the Church but the secular arm itself...that extended the death penalty to the crime of heresy." All of this is true, but it is also true that these were nonetheless steps away from the tradition of Chrysostom and Augustine and

others who were more influenced by the gospel in this than by the deviations mentioned.

[33]Cahill, 125: "The Crusades represent a change from tradition in that they place violence (and especially killing) at the heart, not the periphery, of faithful discipleship." See also Chadwick F. Alger, panel discussion, in *The Holy War,* ed. T. P. Murphy (Columbus, Ohio: Ohio State University Press, 1976), 184f.: "Should the holy wars of Christianity be looked upon as a significant turning point for the religious institutions of Western society? Up to that point, there seems to have been a possibility that the Church could become a vital force in the implementation of its doctrines of nonviolence and brotherhood as behavioral norms for Western civilizations, but the Church undermined this potential when it became immersed in large-scale violence itself. This left a heritage of military symbolism that could be exploited by rising interests, and the potential the Church might have had for moral leadership against violence was undermined when the Church itself took up the sword....Thus it would seem that forever afterward, Western civilization was deprived of what could have been the key institutional base for restraining the use of violence."

[34]Cheetam, 102f. Also, Anton Weiler, "Christianity and the Rest: The Medieval Theory of a Holy and Just War," *Concilium* 200 (December 1988), 113: "In 1095 Pope Urban II preached a crusade....The Holy War made its effective entry into the Christian world. Christendom, ruled by pope and emperor, identified itself with the kingdom of God, and maintained its own existence and rights in the name of God with the sword—and extirpated the unbelievers."

[35]Henry Treece, *The Crusades* (New York: Barnes & Noble, 1962; 1994 reprint), 84f.

[36]Cowdrey, xiii–17f.

[37]James A. Brundage, "Holy War and the Medieval Lawyers," in Murphy, 103, notes "a suggestive parallel between Christian holy war and the Muslim jihad. No one to date has been able to demonstrate a direct influence of the one upon the other. There is, in fact, a good argument to be made that what they really have in common with each other is a common root in more ancient ideas." The most plausible common root, of course, is the biblical narrative of ancient Israel and its holy wars.

[38]G. R. Evans, *The Mind of St. Bernard of Clairvaux* (Oxford: Clarendon Press, 1983), 24.

[39]Bernard of Clairvaux, Letter 78, 11–12.

[40]Russell, *The Just War in the Middle Ages,* 37.

[41]See Jonathan Riley-Smith, *The First Crusade and the Idea of Crusading* (Philadelphia, Pa.: University of Pennsylvania Press, 1986), 8.

⁴²See Martin Erbstösser, *The Crusades* (New York: Universe Books, 1978), 86f.: "The departure of the individual contingents was associated with the first pogroms of the Jews in medieval Europe. Almost all the Jewish communities of the Rhineland cities in particular experienced trials and tribulations of a horrifying nature....Extortion, plundering and mass-murder were the loathesome results. The Jewish colonies in Metz, Speyer, Worms, Mainz, Cologne, Neuss, Xanthen and Trier were exposed to this terror in one form or another."

⁴³See the monumental work of Shlomo Simonsohn, *The Apostolic See and the Jews: History* (Studies and Texts #109) (Toronto: Pontifical Institute of Mediaeval Studies, 1991). After publishing six volumes reviewing all the surviving papal documents dealing with the Jews, from 492 (Pope Gelasius I) to 1555 (Pope Julius III), Simonsohn summarized his findings in this volume, telling the story of the centuries-old policy of papal protection of the Jews from misguided Christian zealots. The unfortunate erosion of this praiseworthy protective policy, however, especially in the fourteenth and fifteenth centuries, was due in part to the very changes we have been tracing concerning the death penalty.

⁴⁴Riley Smith 54f. See also L. A. T. Gryting, *The Oldest Version of the 12th Century Poem, La Venjance Nostre Seigneur,* Contributions to Modern Philology, no. 19 (Ann Arbor: University of Michigan Press, 1952).

⁴⁵Robert Payne, *The Dream and the Tomb: a History of the Crusades* (New York: Stein & Day, 1984), 36.

⁴⁶See Leona C. Gabel, *Benefit of Clergy in England in the Later Middle Ages* (New York: Octagon Books, 1969), which is a reprint of the 1929 original; also see George W. Dalzell, *Benefit of Clergy in America and Related Matters* (Winston-Salem, N.C.: John F. Blair, 1955).

⁴⁷Dalzell, 270. In English law the "neck verse" was the opening verse of Psalm 51 (King James Version): "Have mercy upon me, O God, according to thy lovingkindness: according unto the multitude of thy tender mercies blot out my transgressions." Dalzell observes that even if the convict could not memorize these twenty-two words, "he could mutter something. Thereupon the clerk of the court inquired of the ordinary, 'Legit vel non?' Here for a tense moment the life of the prisoner, who had perhaps filched half a crown, hung upon the conscience or caprice of the ordinary" (24ff.). In effect, this practice meant that only the uneducated poor went to the gallows.

⁴⁸Lawrence M. Friedman, *Crime and Punishment in American History* (New York: BasicBooks, 1993), 43, notes that "this strange device neatly illustrates one of the quaintest habits of the common law: its skill at changing a rule while pretending not to."

[49]Atto Vercellensis Episcopus, *De Pressuris Ecclesiasticis Libellus,* par I (Migne, *PL* 134: 61.)

[50]Peter Damian, Epistula 4, 9 (Migne, *PL* 144: 316).

[51]Guibert of Nogent, *Gesta Dei per Francos* (RHC Occ. 4. 124.). Also, Marcus Bull, *Knightly Piety and the Lay Response to the First Crusade: The Limousin and Gascony, c. 970–c.1130* (Oxford: Clarendon Press, 1993), 3f., provides additional exponents of the new ideology marked by "the symbiosis they believed existed between crusading and professed religion."

[52]Morris, 364.

[53]Peter Abailard [Abelard], *Sic et Non: A Critical Edition*, ed. Blanche B. Boyer and Richard McKeon (Chicago: University of Chicago Press, 1977), 523.

[54]Ibid., 524.

[55]See Hans Erich Feine, *Kirchliche Rechtsgeschichte:* Band I: *Die Katholische Kirche,* 3te Aufl. (Weimar: H. Böhlaus Nachfolger, 1955), 385ff.

[56]Benjamin Arnold, *German Knighthood, 1050–1300* (Oxford: Clarendon Press, 1985), 246.

[57]See Walter Ullmann, *The Growth of Papal Government in the Middle Ages* (London: Methuen, 1955/1970), 441.

[58]Forty-four thieves were hanged on a single day in Leicestershire, England, in 1124, just a few years before Hugh wrote his remarks (Harry Potter, *Hanging in Judgment* (New York: Continuum, 1993), 2.

[59]This particular collision of rights—the owner's right to private property versus the thief's right to life—has a curious history that cannot be detailed here. See Shaun J. Sullivan, O.F.M., *Killing in Defense of Private Property: The Development of a Roman Catholic Moral Teaching, 13th to 18th Centuries,* AAR Dissertation Series #15 (Missoula, Montana: Scholars Press, 1976).

[60]F. H. Russell, *The Just War in the Middle Ages* 202.

[61]Michael G. Mitchell, *Heretici Comburantur: An Inquiry into the Reasons for Burning Heretics in France and in the Empire in the 11th and 12th Centuries,* Yale University Ph.D. dissertation, 1990 (Ann Arbor, Mich.: UMI Dissertation Services, 1994), 213, concludes: "Canon law was generally opposed to capital punishment....Before Gratian the Church did not advocate harsh measures. Gratian...permits, though does not advocate, that convicted heretics be put to death. After Gratian we find mixed signals, but neither synodical canons nor papal decrees went to the extreme and ordered that heretics be executed. Nowhere in canon law is burning mentioned. However...certain passages of the Old Testa-

ment could have been on the judges' mind when they gave sentences of death by burning. Secular law was harsher."

[62]M. D. Chenu, O.P., *Toward Understanding St. Thomas* (Chicago, Ill.: Henry Regnery Co., 1964), 265: "From the last third of the 12th century, certain masters...were aleady using it (Lombard's *Sentences*) as a textbook, and the plan of its treatises, even when their speculative or practical lacunae were recognized, was rather generally adopted." Of course, the approval it received from the Lateran Council in 1215 assured its widespread usage.

[63]Mark A. Zier, "Peter Lombard," *Dictionary of the Middle Ages,* ed. Joseph A. Strayer (New York: Chas. Scribner's Sons, 1987), 9: 516f.

[64]Petrus Lombardus, *Libri IV Sententiarum* studio et cura PP. Collegii S. Bonaventurae in lucem editi, secunda editio (Ad Claras Aquas: ex typographia Collegii. S. Bonaventurae, 1916), liber III, dist. 37, cap.3, Tomus II: 718: "secundum litteram actus homicidii prohibetur, secundum spiritum vero etiam voluntas occidendi. Unde huic mandato secundum litteram fit superadditio in Evangelio, quia littera Evangelii exprimitur, quod Legis littera non exprimebatur."

[65]Philip S. Moore, C.S.C., *The Works of Peter of Poitiers, Master in Theology and Chancellor of Paris (1193–1205)* (Notre Dame, Ind.: University of Notre Dame Press, 1936), 43.

[66]Petrus Pictaviensis, *Sententiarum Libri Quinque* (Migne, *PL* 211:1150. For further data on Peter, see Philip S. Moore, chapter one, as well as Moore's article "Peter of Poitiers," *New Catholic Encyclopedia,* 11:227. For commentary on this section of his *Sentences,* see N. Blázquez, *Estado de Derecho y Pena de Muerte* (Madrid: Noticias S.A., 1989), 93.

[67]Petrus Pictaviensis, *Sententiarum Libri Quinque,* 1151: "Dicimus etiam sine praejudicio quia quod dictum est in Evangelio et in Apostolo, ad tempus dictum est; Spiritus enim divinus omnia medullitus considerans praevidit quod in tempore primitivae Ecclesiae, dum parvula erat, utile erat sustinere patienter. Sed modo auctus est numerus fidelium, et licet quod tunc non licebat."

[68]See John W. Baldwin, *Masters, Princes and Merchants: The Social Views of Peter the Chanter and His Circle.* (Princeton, N.J.: Princeton University Press, 1970). Pages 318–23 deal with Peter on capital punishment.

[69]The hanging and burning of Arnold of Brescia in 1155 was a disturbing anticipation of this policy. See G. W. Greenaway, *Arnold of Brescia* (Cambridge, 1931), 159: "Upon whose head lies the guilt of Arnold's blood?...The ultimate responsibility lies upon the Emperor (Frederick

Barbarossa), the Pope (Adrian IV) and the Senate alike, and...the two latter must divide between them the major portion of the blame."

[70]Edward Peters, *Inquisition* (Berkeley, Calif.: University of California Press, 1988), 47.

[71]See details in Baldwin, who also authored the article on Peter
the Chanter in the *Dictionary of the Middle Ages,* vol. 9, ed. Joseph R.
Strayer (New York: Chas. Scribner's Sons, 1987), 521f. There he sums
up by saying that Peter "felt that the application of capital punishment
to petty thievery, poaching deer in royal forests, and heresy had no
scriptural justification." Latin text in Baldwin, II:213: "In veteri testa-
mento nusquam legimus quod suspendendi sunt fures pro quan-
tocumque furto nec in lege iustiniana...nusquam legibus divinis vel
humanis sanctum est ut fur suspendatur nisi forte incorrigibilis sit.
Unde ergo tanta presumptio quod pro capa interficitur fur, et adulter
etiam non verberatur vel in aliquo mutilantur."

[72]Baldwin, *Masters, Princes and Merchants,* 322.

[73]See Malise Ruthven, *Torture: The Grand Conspiracy* (London:
Weidenfeld & Nicolson, 1978), 46.

[74]Walter L. Wakefield, *Heresy, Crusade and Inquisition in Southern
France 1100–1250* (Berkeley, Calif.: University of California Press, 1974),
86: "In 1198 a new and energetic pope began one of the most momen-
tous pontificates of the Middle Ages and set in motion events fateful to
the Albigensian heretics, to Languedoc, and to the church itself."

[75]Carl Erdmann, *The Origin of the Idea of Crusade* (Princeton, N.J.:
Princeton University Press, 1977), 246f. His general observation:
Anselm's "main work is a canonical collection...which opened a new
era in the history of canon law" (243).

[76]Paolo Golinelli, *Indiscreta Sanctitas: Studi sui Rapporti tra Culti,
Poteri e Societa nel Pieno Medioevo* (Roma: nelle Sede dell' Istituto Storico
Italiano per il Medio Evo, 1988), c. IV: Sant' Anselmo di Lucca, 117–55.
Anselm is described as "il nuovo santo vescovo guerriero."

[77]R. Kay, "Bonizo of Sutri," *New Catholic Encyclopedia,* 2:674f.

[78]Erdmann, 251.

[79]Ibid., 248–50.

[80]Constant Van De Wied, *History of Canon Law* (Louvain: Peeters
Press, 1991), 96f. See also Lynn K. Barker, *History, Reform and Law in
the Work of Ivo of Chartres,* diss., University of North Carolina, 1988, 27f.:
"Ivo's *Decretum* is a very large work, containing some 3760 texts....It contains nearly all the texts of Burchard of Worms' *Decretum* (about 1600 of
his 1784)." Barker shows persuasively that Ivo did "not subscribe to the
'Gregorian' view of history....In place of the so-called Gregorian image
of disparate eras in history (i.e., perfection-decline-reform), Ivo posits

history as a continuum in which reform is ongoing. He has replaced the Gregorians' historical rationale for sometimes radical change with his own historical basis for moderation" (180f.).

[81]Migne, *PL* 161: 689–746.

[82]Ibid., 966f.

[83]See Blázquez, *Estado de Derecho y Pena de Muerte,* 90.

[84]Kenneth Pennington, "Medieval Law," chapter 10 in *Medieval Studies: An Introduction,* 2d ed., ed. James M. Powell (Syracuse, New York: Syracuse University Press, 1992), 344.

[85]J. A. Clarence Smith, *Medieval Law Teachers and Writers, Civilian and Canonist* (Ottawa: University of Ottawa Press, 1975), 19: "As early as 1140 AD...(there was) a new compilation at Bologna of the sources...by a Camaldolese monk called Gratian...hardly anything else is known of him. He is last mentioned in 1143, and must have died then or very soon after." More recently John T. Noonan has convincingly challenged the centuries-old claim that Gratian was a Camaldolese monk. Cf. Noonan, "Gratian Slept Here: the Changing Identity of the Father of the Systematic Study of Canon Law," *Traditio* 35 (1979), 145–172.

[86]R. W. Southern, *Medieval Humanism* (New York: Harper & Row, 1970), 56, n.1.

[87]Sally Anne Scully, *Killing* ex officio: *The Teachings of Twelfth and Thirteenth Century Canon Lawyers on the Right to Kill,* Ph.D. diss., Harvard University, 1975, quote from text of opening unpaginated overview. Scully goes on to describe her work as "an analysis of the changes and contrasts over a century in lawyers' commentaries on Gratian's teaching. It documents the growing acceptance of war and killing as an acceptable aspect of the law of nature rather than an unfortunate if necessary derogation from the law of Scripture, particularly the pacifism of the New Testament."

[88]For the text, see J.-P. Migne, ed., *Decretum Gratiani* (Paris, 1855), Pars II, Causa XXIII, quaestio V (cols. 1213–38). Also available is a modern reprint of the 1879 edition by Emil Friedberg, *Corpus Iuris Canonici,* vol. 1, *Decretum Magistri Gratiani* (Graz: Akademische Druck und Verlagsanstalt, 1959), columns 889–965 (Causa XXIII).

[89]See Russell, 60: "Gratian's wholesale acceptance of Augustine's doctrine so convinced succeeding canonists and theologians that on this issue they were stimulated not to vigorous debate but to endless, unoriginal and tedious repetition of the assertion that love and patience did not prohibit warfare and killing." Also, see Stanley Chodorow, *Christian Political Theory and Church Politics in the Mid-Twelfth Century: The Ecclesiology of Gratian's Decretum* (Berkeley, Calif.: University of California Press, 1972), 229f., who provides a close read-

ing of this section of Causa 23, noting that for Gratian the New Testament passages "do not hinder the use of force because they refer to the attitudes of men, not to their actions."

[90]Scully, 23. Scully notes that "the first three questions are concerned with the abstract task of establishing legitimacy of any form of force, whether individual punishments or total war. Once the theory of the correct use of violence is spelled out, the questions, of which only numbers 4, 5 and 8 are consequential, deal with its concrete application."

[91]Ibid., 28–30.

[92]Ibid., 31.

[93]Ibid., 309.

[94]See Wolfgang P. Müller, *Huguccio: The Life, Works, and Thought of a Twelfth-Century Jurist* (Washington, DC: The Catholic University of America Press, 1994).

[95]Scully, 144ff. She notes that no critical edition of Huguccio's work had yet appeared, but she had access to two different manuscript versions. The citation reads: "clericis in nulla casu licet militare et ideo eis semper est peccatum militare" (C.20. q.3 c.3).

[96]Ibid., 153f.

[97]Ibid., 309.

[98]See Stephan Kuttner, "Johannes Teutonicus, das vierte Laterankonzil und die Compilatio Quarta," *Miscellanea Giovanni Mercati* (Vatican City, 1946).

[99]For a good contemporary treatment of this hard saying, which clears away some common distortions and misunderstandings, see Walter Wink, "Neither Passivity nor Violence: Jesus' Third Way," *Forum* 7:1–2 (March–June 1991), 5–28, and a later exchange between Wink and Richard Horsley in Willard M. Swartley, ed., *The Love of Enemy and Non-retaliation in the New Testament* (Louisville, Ky.: Westminster/John Knox Press, 1992), 126–36.

[100]B. W. Hancock and P. M. Sharp, "The Death Penalty and Christianity: A Conceptual Paradox," *Perspectives on Science and Christian Faith* 46:1 (March 1994), 61.

[101]Scully, 306–10, passim.

[102]Ibid., 35.

3. The Waldensian No and the Thomistic Yes

[1]See Susan K. Treesh, "The Waldensian Recourse to Violence," *Church History* 55 (1986), 294–306.

²See Jean Gonnet and Amedeo Molnár, *Les Vaudois au Moyen Age* (Torino: Claudiana, 1974).

³See Giovanni Gonnet, ed., *Enchiridion Fontium Valdensium (Recueil critique des sources concernant les Vaudois au moyen age) du IIIe Concile de Latran au Synode de Chanforan (1179–1532)* (Roma: Libreria Editrice Claudiana—Torre Pellice, 1958).

⁴See Wakefield and Evans, 203.

⁵Ibid., 205.

⁶Marie-Thérèse d'Alverny, *Alain de Lille: Textes Inédits, avec une introduction sur sa vie et ses oeuvres* (Paris: Librairie Philosophique J. Vrin, 1965), 161: "Les Vaudois sont alors plutot des perturbateurs que des hérétiques, 'objecteurs de conscience,' prédicateurs désordonnés sans mandat légitime..."

⁷Gonnet and Molnár describe the movement as "a center" characterized by its early basic beliefs that splintered into a "right wing" and a "left wing"—the right wing, presumably those who returned to the church, and the left wing, presumably those more radical than Waldès himself. These latter increasingly adopted additional heretical positions (104f.).

⁸Wakefield and Evans, 220.

⁹Ibid., 221. For another account, see Erbstösser, 96–105.

¹⁰Henricus Denzinger et...Adolfus Schönmetz, S.J., *Enchiridion Symbolorum Definitionum et Declarationum de Rebus Fidei et Morum,* ed. 36 emended (Romae: Herder, 1976), 257. The Latin text, showing the insert in parentheses, reads thus: "Non condemnamus iuramentum, imo credimus puro corde, quod cum veritate et iudicio et iustitia licitum sit iurare [Additum a. 1210: De potestate saeculari asserimus, quod sine peccato mortali potest iudicium sanguinis exercere, dummodo ad inferendam vindictam non odio, sed iudicio, non incaute, sed consulte procedat]."

¹¹Journet, I:282.

¹²Imbert is careful to use language attributing the position to "the disciples of Waldès," "the Waldensian sect," etc., rather than to Waldès himself (57).

¹³See Peters, *Heresy and Authority in Medieval Europe,* 139–43. Stephen of Bourbon, one of the inquisitors who dealt with the Waldensians, reported that they "say that all judges commit a sin in pronouncing the death penalty and they regard as murderers...those who preach war against the Saracens and Albigenses" (see Elizabeth Siberry, *Criticism of Crusading 1095–1274* [Oxford: Clarendon Press, 1985], 215).

¹⁴See Peter Biller, "Medieval Waldensian Abhorrence of Killing pre-c.1400," in *The Church and War,* ed. W. J. Sheils (Oxford: Basil Blackwell, 1983), 129.

¹⁵Alanus de Insulis, *De Fide Catholica contra Haereticos,* caput xxii (Migne, *PL* 210: 396D) probably written in the 1190s, according to Wakefield and Evans, 214). See also John M. Trout, *The Voyage of Prudence: The World View of Alan of Lille* (Lanham, Md.: University Press of America, 1979), 16f.

¹⁶Henry Charles Lea, *A History of the Inquisition in the Middle Ages* (New York: Russell & Russell, 1955 reprint of 1887 original), I:225: "The Church made every dignitary feel that his was an office in a universal theocracy wherein all interests were subordinate to the great duty of maintaining the purity of the faith."

¹⁷Imbert, 58f.

¹⁸The document containing the catalogue with the four statements in the sequence given is part of #53 in the collection of Wakefield and Evans, 359.

¹⁹See Potter, *Hanging in Judgment;* traces these developments in England.

²⁰See Edward Peters, *Torture* (London: Basil Blackwell, 1985), 53.

²¹Baldwin, *Masters, Princes and Merchants,* 323.

²²See Brenda Bolton, "Tradition and Temerity: Papal Attitudes to Deviants, 1159–1216," in *Schism, Heresy and Religious Protest,* ed. Derek Baker (New York: Cambridge University Press, 1972), 91, notes that "in 1215, after almost sixty years' experience in the formulation of different approaches to heretics, the Church had to decide on one particular policy and one particular path. Which direction would it take? It took the most traditional way and reversed those policies which seemed to create a dangerous precedent. Innocent III's temerity was not tolerated by the hierarchy which had continually expressed resentment against repentant heretics. The bishops saw their teaching and preaching authority under attack and knew that it was only possible for the Church to survive by keeping to the rules. Tradition triumphed. After 1215, the structure of the Church became too rigid to contain the contemporary phenomena of new religious groups and such spontaneous movements were...placed almost inevitably outside the communion of the Church."

²³It cannot be forgotten that an inseparable complication was their preaching of the Crusades. For example, Cathar Peter Garcias of Toulouse, who was executed for heresy in 1247, told his relative William Garcias, a Franciscan, that "he did not damn the Franciscans along with other ecclesiastical bodies, but he stated that the Order was worthless because it preached the crusade" (Siberry, 213f.).

²⁴George Duby, *France in the Middle Ages 987–1460* (Oxford: Basil Blackwell, 1991), 241: "The Pope had no doubt that Count Raymond was behind this murder....His solution was radical: nothing less than

the extermination of heretics by fire and the sword, and the repopulation of the devastated land (forfeited as booty) by true believers."

[25]Edward Burman, *The Inquisition: Hammer of Heresy* (New York: Dorset Press, 1984), 28.

[26]John Tedeschi, *The Prosecution of Heresy: Collected Studies on the Inquisition in Early Modern Italy, vol. 78* (Binghamton, New York: Medieval and Renaissance Texts and Studies, 1991), 7, wisely cautions against perpetuating confusion by making "sweeping generalizations, as Lea did," that ignore the fact that the Inquisition "far from being a monolithic structure, was an institution which experienced development and change...throughout its long history. The two stages, medieval and modern, must not be understood as a single phenomenon."

[27]Peters, *Inquisition,* 44ff., traces this trend from persuasion to coercion, noting that the earlier phase is often overlooked by historians. "As late as the pontificate of Innocent III it *(persuasio)* marked the initial response of the highest ecclesiastical levels to the problem of dissent, heresy, and challenge to ecclesiastical authority. Moreover, it obviously had substantial results. Although it is impossible to calculate the number that it brought back to orthodox belief and behavior by virtue of patience, tolerance, and instruction, the number is clearly substantial."

[28]Ibid., 33.

[29]See Zoé Oldenburg, *Massacre at Montségur: A History of the Albigensian Crusade* (New York: Dorset Press, 1961).

[30]Ibid., 40.

[31]Ibid., 41.

[32]Henry C. Lea, *The History of the Inquisition in the Middle Ages* vol. 2 (New York: Macmillan, 1908), 214.

[33]Peters, *Torture,* 65.

[34]See R. I. Moore, *The Formation of a Persecuting Society* (Oxford: Basil Blackwell, 1987).

[35]Walter Ullmann, *A Short History of the Papacy in the Middle Ages* (London: Methuen & Co., 1972), 257.

[36]James A. Weisheipl, O.P., *Friar Thomas d'Aquino: His Life, Thought, and Works* (Washington, DC: The Catholic University of America Press, 1983), 7.

[37]It is sobering to note the continuing bloodshed in the Catharist-Catholic conflict during Thomas's adult life and the involvement of many of his confreres in it as inquisitors. In 1239 the Dominican house at Orvieto was sacked. In 1242 the Cathari murdered several inquisitors at Avignonet; in the ensuing battle two hundred of them, including the Catharist hierarchy, were captured, questioned by inquisitors, and burned. The list of names of others derived by torture in this case

served for years in subsequent tracking down and "elimination." In a single day in 1249 eighty Cathari were burned at Agen, and in 1278, just three years after Thomas died, 178 Cathari "Perfecti" were burned at Verona, the last major step in "exterminating the gangrene." In 1279 the Dominican house in Parma was sacked (see Fredric L. Cheyette, "Cathars," in the *Dictionary of the Middle Ages* 3:181–91).

[38]See George Q. Friel, O.P., *Punishment in the Philosophy of St. Thomas Aquinas and Among Some Primitive Peoples* (Washington, DC: The Catholic University of America Press, 1939). Also, Etienne Gilson, *Moral Values and the Moral Life: The Ethical Theory of St. Thomas Aquinas* (Hamden, Conn.: Shoestring Press, 1961).

[39]II Sent., d.36, q.1, art.3, ad tertium (Parma ed.). For the chronology and context of his works, see Chenu, *Toward Understanding St. Thomas.*

[40]II Sent., d.42, q.1, art. 2.

[41]IV Sent., d.20, q.1, art.2, solutio 3.

[42]III *Contra Gentiles,* c.144.

[43]*Summa Theologiae* I–II, q. 87, art.1.

[44]See Huntington Cairns, *Legal Philosophy from Plato to Hegel* (Baltimore, Md.: Johns Hopkins Press, 1949).

[45]See W. C. de Pauley, *Punishment Human and Divine* (London: SPCK, 1925), 107.

[46]*Summa Theologiae* II–II, q. 68, art. 1. Taken in isolation this may sound like pure utilitarianism, but, as other passages make clear, Aquinas is not denying a retributive function in human punishment but simply contrasting it with divine punishment (Cf. Chana K. Poupko, "The Religious Basis of the Retributive Approach to Punishment," *The Thomist* 39 [1975], 528–41).

[47]*Summa Theologiae* II–II, art. 4 and art. 3, ad 2um.

[48]III *Contra Gentiles,* c. 146 (trans. Vernon J. Bourke, Notre Dame, Ind.: University of Notre Dame Press, 1975), 219–22.

[49]See R. I. Moore, "Heresy as Disease," in *The Concept of Heresy in the Middle Ages,* proceedings of the International Conference, Louvain, May 1973, ed. W. Lourdaux and D. Verhelst (Leuven University Press, 1976), 1–11.

[50]II–II, q. 11, art. 3, ad tertium.

[51]The phrase is used by M. B. Crowe, "Theology and Capital Punishment," *Irish Theological Quarterly* 31 (1964), noting that it "turns upon the state's function of preserving order and upon the relationship between individual and society"(41).

[52]II–II, q. 64, art. 2.

[53]Ibid., ad 3um: "A man who sins deviates from the rational order,

and so loses his human dignity insofar as a man is naturally free and an end unto himself. To that extent, then, he lapses into the subjection of the beasts....To kill a man who retains his natural dignity is intrinsically evil, but to kill a sinner can be good, just as it is to kill a beast, for, as Aristotle points out, an evil man is worse than a beast, and more harmful." A footnote appended to this rather embarrassing passage in the Blackfriars bilingual edition (*Summa Theologiae*, volume 38, by Marcus Lefébure, O.P., 1975) tries to tone down "this rather stark and apparently brutal article" by recalling a few earlier texts by which it is "filled out more acceptably."

[54]Crowe, 39. Crowe concludes that "St. Thomas' specific handling of the death penalty lacks many of the reservations and qualifications that one would like to see" and notes that even one of his most avid modern defenders (A. F. Utz, O.P.) conceded that "St. Thomas may have been over-ready to accept the concrete manifestations of capital punishment in his time, a fate that has overtaken more than one thinker since"(42).

[55]X. Basler, "Thomas von Aquin und die Begründung der Todesstrafe," *Divus Thomas* 9 (1931), 69–90, 173–202, on the eve of the Nazi takeover, found himself hard-pressed to defend Thomas against having these texts interpreted as supporting a totalitarian notion of the state. "According to the teaching of Aquinas, the state's right to punish does not flow simply from the security requirement of the common good, but from the fact that the state has been delegated as God's representative and avenger for the security of the moral order, because the state's penal practice is a service assigned to it within that moral order" (193).

[56]The section of the Blackfriars Latin-English edition of the *Summa*, v. 32 (trans. Thomas Gilby, O.P.), has footnotes that regularly put the reader on alert, noting that "contemporary with the writings of St. Thomas are the 7th and 8th Crusades....The spirit of fighting for Christendom was active until the 16th century (62)....This paragraph is more the blunt expression of the medieval social conscience than of a moral theology wary of heavy dragooning (63)....This article (11:3 on not tolerating heretics) can be appreciated only when its historical period is kept in mind" (89).

[57]Franciscus Skoda, *Doctrina Moralis Catholica de Poena Mortis a C. Beccaria usque ad nostros dies,* 1956 (Pesaro, 1959). Skoda quotes from more than a dozen moral theology manuals in his effort to show that "Doctrina theologorum catholicorum est concors et unanimis."

[58]Niceto Blázquez, "La Pena de Muerte—Lectura Critica del Pensamiento de Santo Tomás," *Studia Moralia* 23 (1985), 107–28.

[59]II–II, q. 64, art. 4 and 7.

[60]Blázquez, "La Pena de Muerte—Lectura Critica del Pensamiento de Santo Tomás," 125. He refers earlier (110) to "some Episcopal Conferences after Vatican II that undertook a pastoral campaign with an abolistionist mentality in the style of the early centuries of the church, inviting experts to engage in an open study to clarify the actual human and historical motives which gave rise to the theory of the 'secular arm.'" This article was apparently his contribution in response to that invitation.

[61]Ibid., 119. "El Aquinate se expresa con grand frialdad racionalista y se echa menos aquella profusión de consideraciones inspiradas en la misericordia y en el perdón cristiano, que tanto abunda en San Agustín."

[62]Ibid., 123.

[63]Brian Calvert, "Aquinas and the Death Penalty," *The American Journal of Jurisprudence* 37 (1992), 259–81.

[64]See Antonio Beristain, "Capital Punishment and Catholicism," *International Journal of Criminology and Penology*, vol. 5 (1977), 331: "In the light of Catholic theology, the death penalty cannot be accepted because it lacks all the fundamental principles demanded of any legal sanction by the Gospel. Many arguments support the opinion of those who in our cultural world blot it out as...unnecessary. Certainly it cannot be proved that this penalty is...necessary. Such serious sanction demands clear justification. Lacking it, the death penalty is unjust. The positive social development of the abolitionist nations invalidates the main theoretical reasons to the contrary."

[65]It is not out of place to mention the potential relevance of the Anglo-Saxon Penitentials for further study of this question. Whatever shortcomings they may have, they show how grave crimes in a Christian society that was not already addicted to sanguinary revenge and saddled with the savage penal policies of the Theodosian Code could settle for punishments other than death (cf. the texts in *Medieval Handbooks of Penance*, trans. John T. McNeill and Helena M. Gamer [New York: Columbia University Press, 1938/1990] (i.e., 1990]).

[66]Harold J. Berman, *Law and Revolution: The Formation of the Western Legal Tradition* (Cambridge, Mass.: Harvard University Press, 1983), 476ff.

[67]See, e.g., Karl Bruno Leder, *Todesstrafe: Ursprung, Geschichte, Opfer* (München: Meyster, 1980).

[68]Joannes Duns Scotus, *In quartum Sententiarum*, d.15, q.III, *Opera Omnia* (Paris, 1894), 18: 357–90. The passage about suicide is on page 379. See also the remarks of Blázquez, *Estado de Derecho y Pena de Muerte*, 134f.

[69]See Erbstösser, 149–54.

[70]Kurt Aland, *A History of Christianity,* Volume 1: *From the Beginnings to the Threshold of the Reformation* (Philadelphia, Pa.: Fortress Press, 1985), 348.

[71]Stephen Howarth, *The Knights Templar* (New York: Barnes & Noble, 1982), 284.

[72]See the account in John J. Robinson, *Dungeon, Fire and Sword: The Knights Templar in the Crusades* (New York: M. Evans & Co., 1991), 460ff.

[73]Yves Renouard, *The Avignon Papacy: The Popes in Exile 1305–1403* (New York: Barnes & Noble, 1994), 134.

[74]Miroslav Hroch and Anna Skybová, *Ecclesia Militans: The Inquisition,* trans. Janet Fraser (German original 1988; New York: Dorset Press, 1990), 44.

[75]G. G. Coulton, ed. and trans., *Life in the Middle Ages,* Volume 4: *Monks, Friars and Nuns* #105 (New York: Cambridge University Press, 1967 reprint of 1911 edition).

[76]Erbstösser, 201f.

[77]A. R. Myers, ed., *English Historical Documents 1327–1485* (New York: Oxford University Press, 1969), 850f.

[78]See J. B. Russell, *Dissent and Order in the Middle Ages,* 88.

[79]See Jarold K. Zeman, *The Hussite Movement and the Reformation in Bohemia, Moravia and Slovakia (1350–1650): A Bibliographical Study Guide* (Ann Arbor, Mich.: Michigan Slavic Publications, 1977).

[80]Aland, 371.

[81]James Westfall Thompson, *The Middle Ages, 300–1500,* 2d ed. (New York: Cooper Square Publishers, 1972), 2: 968.

[82]Peters, *Inquisition,* 69.

[83]Lawrence S. Cunningham, *The Catholic Heritage* (New York: Crossroad, 1983), 77f.

4. Renaissance and Reformation Dilemmas

[1]John Addington Symonds, *The Age of the Despots,* vol. 1: 291f. Symonds goes on to observe that the "history of Italy has at all times been closely bound up with that of the Papacy; but at no period has this been more the case than during these eighty years of Papal worldliness, ambition, nepotism, and profligacy, which are also marked by the irruption of the European nations into Italy and by the secession of the Teutonic races from the Latin church."

THE DEATH PENALTY

²Gabriel Maugain, *Moeurs Italiennes de la Renaissance: La Vengeance* (Paris: Les Belles Lettres, 1935), 7.

³Ludwig Pastor, *The History of the Popes,* ed. R. F. Kerr (St. Louis, Mo.: B. Herder, 1952), 2:307: "The account, which says that grief for this event killed Nicholas V, may be an exaggeration, yet there can be no doubt that the agitation and anxieties, which were its inevitable consequence, must have had a most injurious effect."

⁴See Kelly, 245. Pastor writes: "Pope Nicholas showed no further mercy. He regretted the fate of the gifted man, but decided to let justice take its course....He (Porcaro) was hanged on January 9 on the battlements of St. Angelo....His last words were: 'O my people, your deliverer dies today'"(3:228ff.). His associates were executed at the Capitol.

⁵Pastor, 3:325f.

⁶Ibid., 251f. Cf. the book detailing the marvelous exhibit of 1993— Anthony Grafton, ed., *Rome Reborn: The Vatican Library and Renaissance Culture* (Washington, DC: Library of Congress, 1993).

⁷Pastor, 4:311.

⁸For fuller contemporary accounts of this episode and similar violent events of the day, see "The Food of Conspiracy," a chapter in S. Bertelli, F. Cardini, and E. G. Zorzi, *The Courts of the Italian Renaissance* (New York: Facts on File Publications, 1985), 244ff., with Leonardo da Vinci's "dispassionate" sketch of the hanging of one of the conspirators, Bernardo di Bandino Baroncelli.

⁹See the account and summary of theories in Will Durant, *The Renaissance* (New York: Simon & Schuster, 1953), 424. Durant's final remark on Alexander's devious political schemes is that by adopting "the ways of the world, (the church)...gained a state and lost a third of Christendom."

¹⁰John C. Dwyer, *Church History: Twenty Centuries of Catholic Christianity* (New York: Paulist Press, 1985), 219.

¹¹See Max Salvadori, "The End of the Renaissance in Italy," in *The Renaissance Reconsidered: A Symposium* (Northampton, Mass.: Smith College Studies in History, 44 [1964]), 64: "Like Joan of Arc two generations earlier, Savonarola had been condemned as a heretic, (which neither of them was, as proved by later rehabilitation in one case and current efforts at rehabilitation in the other); even more than Joan, he was executed for political deeds. Political reasons induced Alexander VI to authorize his trial; for political reasons the Florentine Medici crowd rejoiced at his death, which was lamented by the republican minority. Neither the Pope nor the Medicis cared about Savonarola's theological position." The quotation of Savonarola against the death

penalty is cited in Catherine B. Avery, ed., *The New Century Italian Renaissance Encyclopedia* (New York: Meredith Corp., 1972), 847.

[12]Cheetam, 191f.

[13]Kelly, 257.

[14]See Pastor, 7:171ff., for details. Two accomplices of Petrucci, Battista da Vercelli and Marc Antonio Nino, "were hanged, drawn, and quartered...[after being] severely tortured on the way" to the Ponte St. Angelo. At which point Pastor says: "This barbarity was generally condemned" (184). The case of Baglioni was made all the more sordid by Leo's treachery. He had given a promise of safe-conduct. In defending himself, Leo is supposed to have said that "the safe-conduct he had given Gianpaolo was to come to Rome and said nothing about leaving Rome" (see Orville Prescott, *Princes of the Renaissance* [New York: Random House, 1969], 319).

[15]John Anthony Scott, Introduction to Sir Thomas More, *Utopia*, trans. Peter K. Marshall (New York: Washington Square Press, 1965), ix.

[16]Ibid., 91. See also Hugh Trevor-Roper, "Sir Thomas More and Utopia," *Renaissance Essays* (Chicago, Ill.: University of Chicago Press, 1985), 24–58.

[17]Some of the old Protestant-Catholic animosities continue to haunt the story of Sir Thomas. The portrayal of him as a bloodthirsty heresy-hunter in Foxe's *Book of Martyrs* was supplanted for a time by the admirable *Man for All Seasons* image, but then the former portrayal was "vehemently resurrected" by Richard Marius's biography *Thomas More* (New York: Knopf, 1984), which in turn has been challenged by Louis L. Martz's *Thomas More: The Search for the Inner Man* (New Haven: Yale University Press, 1990), whose plea to the modern reader is "Let us lay aside, then, this ancient and unfounded charge against More" (6).

[18]"Haereticos comburi est contra voluntatem Spiritus." See H. Roos, "Die Quellen der Bulle *Exsurge Domine*, " in *Theologie in Geschichte und Gegenwart,* herausgegeben von J. Auer and H. Volk (München: Festschrift M. Schmaus, 1957), 909–26.

[19]The statements in Latin and German with introductory background can be found in H. Denzinger, *Enchiridion symbolorum definitionum et declarationum de rebus fidei et morum,* ed. Petrus Hünermann, editio 37 (Freiburg im Breisgau: Herder, 1991), 354 and 487–92.

[20]Cf., e.g., Paul Althaus, *Die Todesstrafe als Problem der christlichen Ethik* (München: Verlag der Bayerischen Akademie der Wissenschaften, 1955).

[21]Translation from Ewald M. Plass, ed., *What Luther Says: An Anthology* (St. Louis, Mo.: Concordia Publishing House, 1959), II: 595.

[22]Ibid., II:1156. See also Luther's *Large Catechism* where his treat-

ment of the Fifth Commandment explains that "God has delegated his authority of punishing evil-doers to civil magistrates in place of parents; in early times, as we read in Moses (Dt 21:18–20) parents had to bring their own children to judgment. Therefore, what is forbidden here applies to private individuals, not to governments." (English version found in *The Book of Concord: the Confessions of the Evangelical Lutheran Church,* Theodore G. Tappert et al., ed. and trans. [Philadelphia: Fortress Press, 1959], 180f.)

[23]See Bernice M. Hamilton, *Political Thought in Sixteenth-Century Spain* (Oxford: Clarendon Press, 1963). Hamilton also authored the article on Vitoria in the *Encyclopedia Britannica* (1975), 19:493f.

[24]Niceto Blázquez, *Estado de Derecho y Pena de Muerte* (Madrid: Noticias, 1989), capitulo V: "La Pena de Muerte según Francisco de Vitoria," 158.

[25]Christopher Hollis, ed., *The Papacy: An Illustrated History from St. Peter to Paul VI* (London: Weidenfeld & Nicolson, 1965). "The Triumph of the Counter-Reformation: Marcellus II to Leo XI (1555–1605)," 149, organizes the period thus:

A. The suspension of the Council and the personal efforts at reform by Paul IV (1555–1559);
B. The third and final convocation of the Council by Pius IV (1559–1565);
C. The practical application of the Council by Pius V, Gregory XIII, and Sixtus V (1566–1590).

[26]Text and history of the CCC *(Constitutio Criminalis Carolina)* in Josef Kohler und Willy Scheel, *Die Carolina und ihre Vorgängerinnen,* 4 Bände (Scientia Verlag Aalen, 1968).

[27]Pastor, 12:506f.

[28]Pastor, 13:47, 219 and 451.

[29]Joseph Lecler, S.J., *Toleration and the Reformation* (London: Longmans, 1960), I:328ff., quotes Servetus himself, who admitted in a letter to Calvin that serious heresy, coupled with obstinacy, deserves capital punishment "both before God and man." Calvin wrote to Farel the day of the condemnation, giving indication of its unanimity: "The people of Basle are convinced. Those of Zurich are even more vehement than the others...and those of Schaffhausen approve. The pastors of Bern hold the same opinion." But Basle was not all that enthused, and Calvin knew there was disapproval of his action, so he wrote his *Declaratio Orthodoxae Fidei,* which Lecler calls "one of the most frightening treatises ever written to justify the persecution of heretics" (I: 333).

[30]Luther was dead by this time, but he may well have agreed with

the verdict. His objection had been to burning heretics; by denying the Trinity, Servetus fell under the charge of blasphemy.

[31]Lecler, I:342.

[32]Note the importance of defining *heresy* at this point. Was Servetus a heretic? Melanchthon was careful to refer to him as a "blasphemer" whose denial of the Trinity apparently put him in a non-Christian category like the Jews and Saracens, so Luther's restriction would still be preserved.

[33]Kelly, 264. See also William V. Hudon, *Marcello Cervini and Ecclesiastical Government in Tridentine Italy* (DeKalb, Ill.: Northern Illinois University Press, 1992).

[34]Pastor, 14:80: "The pope lived, as far as political and military matters were concerned, in a world of phantasy, which was in glaring contrast to the actual state of affairs."

[35]Ibid., 262f. "Nothing lay so dear to the heart of Paul IV as his Inquisition." The outbreak of popular violence at his death was a cultural given, part of the ritual of the vacant See (see Laurie Nussdorfer, *Civic Politics in the Rome of Urban VIII* (Princeton University Press, 1992), chapter 14, "The Vacant See," 229: "The first item on the agenda was revenge. Romans in the early modern period saved all kinds of grievances for the interregnum....Murders, beatings, and break-ins were common fare as people hurried to settle old scores while papal justice was in abeyance."

[36]Ibid., 272. As Cheetham sums it up: "Paul was a medieval absolutist...incapable of moderation...a harsh bigot (with a) pathological tendency to distrust and persecute....Cardinal Seripando condemned his use of the Inquisition as inhuman" (208ff.).

[37]Pastor, 14: 261.

[38]F. C. Church, *The Italian Reformers, 1534–1564* (New York: Columbia University Press, 1932; 1974 Octagon reprint), 221f. Pomponio and several others, including "a Waldensian in 1558" and a trio in 1559, are mentioned by Pastor (14:261) with references to other sources. He goes on to note that sixty or seventy prisoners were in the dungeons of the Inquisition at the time of Paul's death, and that "it can also be proved, not for Rome but for Bologna, that witches were burned there by order of Paul IV."

[39]Cf. Jean Plaidy, *The Growth of the Spanish Inquisition* (1960; Barnes & Noble reprint 1994), 116ff.

[40]Pastor, 16:341.

[41]See E. Iserloh, J. Glazik, H. Jedin, *Reformation and Counter Reformation* Vol. 5 of *History of the Church,* ed. H. Jedin and J. Dolan (New York: Crossroad, 1986), 489.

[42]Pastor, 16:387.

[43]Ibid.

[44]For example, Pastor, 16:179ff., tells of the bitter battle with the Huguenots in France. In the fall of 1561 all sixty churches and convents of Montpellier were sacked and 150 priests and monks were put to the sword.

[45]Pastor, 17:101. Subsequent examples are also from this volume, 302–12 and 93–100 passim.

[46]See Massimo Firpo, "Il Processo Inquisitoriale contro Pietro Carnesecchi (1566–67): Una Proposta di Interpretazione," chapter 6 of *Inquisizione Romana e Controriforma* (Bologna: Il Mulino, 1992), 359–82.

[47]G. K. Brown, *Italy and the Reformation to 1550* (New York: Russell & Russell, 1931, reprinted 1971), 207–14, sketches the controversial career of Paleario, noting that it was "on Pius V's request that he was sent to Rome....On July 2, 1570, he was hanged and then burnt on Ponte St. Angelo."

[48]Paul Lacroix, *History of Prostitution* (New York: Covici-Friede Publishers, 1931), II:1156.

[49]Pastor, 17:71. This was a dramatic break with a tradition dating at least from the time of Theodosius I (392). It lasted a bit longer in England, but there "in 1624, a one sentence statute ended at least eleven centuries of sanctuary privilege in England" (see Ignatius Bau, *This Ground Is Holy* [New York: Paulist Press, 1985]), 131, 157.

[50]Pastor, 17:93f. It was already mentioned in a report of September 13, 1567, that such a bull was widely expected. In June, 1570, the governor of Rome finally and with great difficulty dissuaded the pope "from inflicting the death penalty for adultery," and agreeing to the less rigorous policy that "adulterers should be punished by whipping, imprisonment, or banishment."

[51]H. Outram Evennett, *The Spirit of the Counter-Reformation* (Notre Dame, Ind.: University of Notre Dame Press, 1970; reprint of 1951 Cambridge lectures), 113: "The years 1534–88 are thus the crucial ones in this moral and institutional transformation of the cardinals and their work in the Church....The impetus which the Council gave...to moral reform...completed the process....A supply of active and eager men of a new generation was to hand for the staffing of the congregations of cardinals and for that of the tribunals and offices of the curia, men in whose lives the new spirituality of the Counter-Reformation was a living force....It would be...absurd to fail to recognize the enormous change since 1527. The inspired work of saints and the laborious efforts of Popes had completed what the shock of the sack of 1527 had begun."

[52]Kelly, 270. "When news of the St. Bartholomew's Day massacre

of Huguenots in France reached Rome, he celebrated it with *Te Deums* and thanksgiving services as a victory for the church over infidelity as well as the defeat of political treachery." In doing so, however, Jedin contends that he was "misled" and, in any event, "played no part in the preparation and execution of the crime." Jedin and Dolan, Volume. 5: 514.

[53]Cheetham, 212. Gregory's support for the Jesuits' educational mission is reflected in the naming of the Gregorian University in Rome.

[54]Robert M. Kingdon, *Myths About the St. Bartholomew's Day Massacres, 1572–1576* (Cambridge, Mass.: Harvard University Press, 1988), 217: "The memory of Coligny...assumed more and more obviously the character of a myth, especially within the Protestant community....[It] did not distort by falsification....Rather the myth distorted, to a degree at least, by selection."

[55]Pastor, 19:401, 457f.: "They generally suffered the death appointed for traitors, that is, they were hanged, disembowelled while still alive, their heart and bowels torn out, and their dead bodies quartered."

[56]Ibid., 301.

[57]Ibid., 307.

[58]Ibid., 302. Cf. also Hroch and Skybová, 94.

[59]Pastor, 19: 306.

[60]Ibid., 307.

[61]Ibid., 303–5.

[62]Pastor, 20:538. Gregory's success in recovering through legal procedures was partly to blame for the problem, since it left many "dispossessed and disgruntled nobles" who contributed to the "serious disorder and lawlessness" that marked the papal states at the time of his death (Kelly, 271).

[63]The title of the biography by Baron Joseph A. de Hübner, *Der Eiserne Papst* (Berlin: 1932). See also Joseph A de Hübner, *The Life and Times of Sixtus the Fifth* (London: Longmans, Green & Co., 1872), 2 vols. Some of the executions are described in 1:278ff. "Count Attilio Baschi of Bologna was executed as a parricide....Capt. Fossombrone, accomplice in a murder, was hanged....Nicolino Azzolino, captain of the pontifical guards, was executed for having wounded an ensign....Count Giovanni Pepoli...was condemned to death and strangled in prison, and his property...was confiscated....A Franciscan, guilty of several crimes, was hanged on the bridge of St. Angelo...Don Annibal Capello...was cruelly executed on the bridge of St. Angelo....A mother who had sold her daughter's honour was hanged on the bridge of St. Angelo, and the girl was forced to witness the execution....Rome looked

on in silence at these executions." One of the key bandit chiefs, Lamberto Malatesta, was arrested and beheaded, despite his connections to prominent Roman families.

[64]Pastor, 21:77. See also Cheetam, 214.

[65]*Bullarium Romanum,* vol. 8, part 2 (Roma, 1857), 585–91.

[66]Pastor, 21:83. Sixtus had a medal struck to mark the occasion with "Securitas Perfecta" engraved on it; he said he was ready to execute twenty thousand if that was what it took to stop the brigandage.

[67]Hubert Jedin, in Jedin and Dolan, 505, merely says without details or elaboration that Sixtus, "persuaded that the papacy's worldwide activity presupposed order in the Papal State,...ruthlessly suppressed the brigand disorder that had flourished in the time of Gregory XIII." The reader is left with the task of finding out from other sources the magnitude and details of this suppression.

[68]Hroch and Skybová, 95.

[69]Luigi Firpo, "Esecuzioni Capitali in Roma (1567–1671)," in *Eresia e Riforma nell'Italia del Cinquecento,* ed. Albano Biondi, et al. (DeKalb, Ill.: Northern Illinois University Press, 1974), 321.

[70]J. R. Nash, *Encyclopedia of World Crime* (Wilmette, Ill.: Crime-Books, 1990), IV:3286f.

[71]Firpo, 311.

[72]See Achille Pognisi, *Giordano Bruno e l'Archivio di S. Giovanni Decollato* (Torino; 1891), 63.

[73]Kelly, 276.

[74]Giovanni Aquilecchia, "Bruno, Giordano," *Encyclopedia Britannica (1975), Macropedia* 3:347.

[75]Philippe Ariès, *The Hour of Our Death* (New York: Oxford University Press, 1981), 308. For more of Bellarmine, see his *De Laicis sive Saecularibus or The Treatise on Civil Government,* trans. K. E. Murphy (New York: Fordham University Press, 1928), chapter 13.

[76]Vincenzo Paglia, *La Morte Confortata* (Roma: Ed. di Storia e Letteratura, 1982), sketches the many confraternities that arose, especially in sixteenth and seventeenth-century Italy, to care for the condemned.

[77]Heinrich A. Rommen, *The State in Catholic Thought: A Treatise in Political Philosophy* (B. Herder, 1945; reprint by Greenwood Press, 1969), 78.

[78]Potter, 206. He observes that "judicial killing was sanctioned by bishops, and its execution presided over by chaplains. Had the Church (of England) denounced it earlier, it would have withered and died, as indeed it did quickly and without hope of resuscitation in the 1960s.... Only in the 1950s, long after all other progressive religious and secular opinion had ranged itself against Capital Punishment did the Church

(of England) take a firm stand in favor of abolition. Of the other arguments that sustained it—deterrence and retribution—neither could prevail when the religious imprimatur had gone." As is evident, much of this Anglican experience was soon paralleled in many Roman Catholic circles as well.

⁷⁹Daniel Sueiro, *La Pena de Muerte y los Derechos Humanos* (Madrid: Alianza Ed., 1987), 252.

⁸⁰See Maurice Simon, *Un Catéchisme Universel pour l'Église Catholique: du Concile de Trente a nos Jours* (Leuven: University Press, 1992), 2–5.

⁸¹Petrus Canisius, *Catechismi Latini et Germanici,* ed. a patribus S.J. (Roma: University Gregoriana, 1933), 2 vol. The quotes that follow are from Volume I (Latin), 14, 17, 57 (Ante-Tridentine), and 99, 103, 164 (Post-Tridentine). The *Catechismus minor* has the fifth commandment (247) and an abbreviation of the answer concerning its external and internal requirements (248), but no elaboration beyond the mere naming of homicide as the first of the sins that cry to heaven (256).

⁸²See the special issue of *Concilium* 204 (August 1989), especially the historical sketch by Berard Marthaler, "The Catechism Genre, Past and Present," 41–49. Also see Simon, *Première Partie: Le Catéchisme au Concile de Trente* 1–62). He gives (54) the text of the decree passed on the last day of the Council directing the pope to guide four publication projects to completion: the revised Index of Forbidden Books, the Catechism, the Missal, and the Breviary. These four tasks were faithfully completed by Pius IV and Pius V in that order, one appearing every two years: 1564 (Index), 1566 (Catechism), 1568 (Missal), and 1570 (Breviary).

⁸³Pastor, 16:29. But Pastor goes on to note that the secular-priest-humanist-scholar Giulio Pogiani (or Poggianus) spent the last four months of 1564 polishing its Latin version, so that it is "due to him that (the catechism) may be described, even as to its style, as a classical work."

⁸⁴Ibid., 16:407: "This son of the celebrated Venetian printer, Aldus, was living in a state of great poverty at Padua, when the pope summoned him...and assigned to him an annual salary of 720 gold scudi." This, of course, was in part provoked by the appearance of the Protestant histories, the *Magdeburg Centuries.* The first volume came off the press in Basel in 1559 and "created great consternation among Catholics" because of its effective use of historical materials to back up theological positions, a relative novelty that opened an entire new era of Christian historiography.

The "war of the printing presses" was already in full swing with the Protestant-Catholic scurrilous-pamphlet conflict, but it was over a quarter of a century before a competent Catholic response on the level of the *Centuriators* appeared. The first volume of the *Annales* of Cardinal Baronius was published in 1588. See Cyril K. Pullapilly, *Caesar Baronius: Counter-Reformation Historian* (Notre Dame, Ind.: University of Notre Dame Press, 1975), 47.

[85]*Catechism of the Council of Trent for Parish Priests,* issued by order of Pope Pius V, translated into English with notes by John A. McHugh, O.P., and Charles J. Callan, O.P. (New York: Joseph F. Wagner, 1934), 420.

[86]Gerard S. Sloyan, "Catechism," *New Catholic Encyclopedia* 3:229, notes that the work is "quite unmarked by a polemical tone once it has mentioned 'pernicious errors' in the introduction." For examples of the kind of "snake-pit" theology that so often abounded in the late sixteenth century, see J. Megivern, "The Catholic Rejoinder," *Discord, Dialogue and Concord,* ed. Lewis Spitz (Philadelphia, Pa.: Fortress Press, 1978), final chapter.

[87]See E. P. Evans, *The Criminal Prosecution and Capital Punishment of Animals: The Lost History of Europe's Animal Trials* (London: Faber & Faber, 1987; reprint of 1906 edition with Foreword by Nicholas Humphrey), xxxi: "Both animal and witch trials seem to have become increasingly common in Switzerland and the adjoining French and Italian areas during the 15th century, and the coincidence is all the more striking because of the almost total absence of any earlier tradition of secular animal trials in Switzerland" (Humphrey, quoting from Elizabeth Cohen's article, "Law, Folklore and Animal Lore," *Past and Present* 110 [1986], 8–37).

[88]See Hugo Adam Bedau, *Death Is Different* (Boston: Northeastern University Press, 1987), especially the first two chapters.

[89]According to this application, one would have to see someone like Benedict Carpzow (1595–1666) as the ideal to be emulated by all Christian authorities. In his forty-five years as a magistrate, chiefly in Leipzig, he signed more than twenty thousand death-warrants, a rate of some 450 a year (see Imbert, 96). Full biographical data is given in Eberhard Schmidt, *Einführung in die Geschichte der deutschen Strafrechtspflege,* 2te Aufl. (Göttingen: Vandenhoek & Ruprecht, 1951), 144ff.

[90]A. Cohen, *The Psalms* (London: Soncino Press, 1945), 326f., notes that in former times this psalm was called "the Mirror for Magistrates" and recalls the admonition in Jeremiah 21:12: "O house of David, this is what the LORD says: 'Administer justice every morning; rescue from the hand of his oppressor the one who has been robbed.'" To think that such rescue requires use of the death penalty stands the whole biblical value system on its head.

[91]Sloyan, 229.

5. Post-Tridentine Troubles and Tribulations

[1]Richard S. Dunn, *The Age of Religious Wars, 1559–1715,* 2d ed. (New York; W. W. Norton, 1979), 1.

[2]For the bitter horrors that devastated France, see R. J. Knecht, *The French Wars of Religion 1559–1598* (London: Longman, 1989); a generation later the Thirty Years War (1618–1648) was "fought with unbelievable brutality on German soil. It decimated the population, depressed the peasants, and ruined the towns" (Geoffrey Barraclough, *The Origins of Modern Germany* [New York: Capricorn Books, 1963], 373).

[3]Jean Delumeau, *Catholicism Between Luther and Voltaire: A New View of the Counter-Reformation* (Philadelphia, Pa.: Westminster Press, 1977; French original, 1971), 126, discusses Jansenists and "how they resembled Protestants." Delumeau goes on to agree with folklore studies in contending that "the average European of the early 17th century was largely imbued with an animist mentality. It was impossible for his religion not to suffer from the effects" (163).

[4]Ibid., 173. Delumeau claims that in the eighteenth century "the new interest in the external world (science) would not have drawn people away from God if the Church too had appropriated this different mentality. The more fervent Christians seemed to many of their contemporaries 'like men of austere and insensitive temperament.' 'Boring' and 'pious' were taken as synonyms. To generations of increasing curiosity, religion frequently offered no more than 'a melancholy and mortifying practice.'....The two Reformations had struggled to restore its sacredness to Christianity; as a consequence they dehumanized it by forgetting to christianize the profane....They forced people who lived 'in the world' to choose between God and the world" (227f.).

[5]Richard J. Evans, *Rituals of Retribution: Capital Punishment in Germany 1600–1987* (New York: Oxford University Press, 1996), 39.

[6]R. Bellarmino, *De Controversiis Christianae Fidei,* III, c. 21–22 (Lugduni, 1596), 1312–20. An Italian translation is provided by Alberto Bondolfi, *Pena e Pena di Morte* (Bologna: EDB, 1985), 235–53.

[7]Johannes Gerhard, *Loci Theologici* (Berolini: G. Schlawitz, 1868), Tomus VI, locus xxiv, sectio v, membrum ii, articulus iii—De Suppliciis, 425–78.

[8]On page 445 he refers to the numbers of victims in several places. On page 447 he begins a treatment of the meaning of *zizania* in the parable and elaborates on it off and on for the next four pages.

[9]Richard J.Evans, *Rituals of Retribution,* 40f.

[10]The Libraries of Harvard University and UC-Berkeley have copies of this work. The title page says: *Juris Publici Quaestio Capitalis:*

Sintne Protestantes Jure Caesareo Haeretici, et Ultimo Supplicio Afficiendi, etc. Contra Sanguinarium Gaspar Schoppii Classicum, tractata a JUSTO MEIERO, 3.

[11]Also spelled Kaspar Schoppe (1576–1649), he was a philologist converted to Catholicism in 1598. He moved to Rome, where he won favor for his fierce anti-Protestant writings in the Thirty Years War. His hatred, however, also targeted the Jesuits, against whom he wrote seventeen polemical works. He died in lonely anger against the world (See J. Mercier, *Dictionnaire de Théologie Catholique* [hereafter DTC], ed. A. Vacant, E. Mangenot, and E. Amann [Paris: Letouzey et Ané, 1923–1950], 14.2:1571–74).

[12]Peters, *Inquisition,* 83.

[13]Ibid., 84f.

[14]Ibid., 87.

[15]Henry Kamen, "Spain," chapter 12 in *The Reformation in National Context,* ed. Bob Scribner, Roy Porter, Mikulás Teich (New York: Cambridge University Press, 1994), 210.

[16]Ibid., 205.

[17]Richard Greenleaf, *The Mexican Inquisition of the Sixteenth Century* (Albuquerque: University of New Mexico Press, 1969), 26 and 209.

[18]The 1641 "Capitall Lawes of New England" ordered execution for all offenses found in the Bible, specifically (with biblical chapter and verse given in the law itself): idolatry, witchcraft, blasphemy, murder, bestiality, homosexuality, adultery, fornication, rape, kidnapping, perjury, and sedition. (Cf. the texts given in Richard C. Donnelly, Joseph Goldstein, and Richard D. Schwartz, *Criminal Law* [New York: Free Press of Glencoe, 1962], 310).

[19]Karl Rahner, "What Is Heresy?" chapter 19 in *Theological Investigations,* v. 5 *Later Writings* (Baltimore, Md.: Helicon Press, 1966), 476.

[20]See Reijo Wilenius, *The Social and Political Theory of Francisco Suárez* (Helsinki, 1963).

[21]Francisco Suárez, S.J., *Opera Omnia,* editio nova, a Carolo Berton (Parisiis: apud Ludovicum Vivès, 1858), vol. 12. Disputatio #23 runs from page 577 to page 586.

[22]See Nachman Ben-Yehuda, "Witchcraft and the Occult as Boundary Maintenance Devices," in *Religion, Science and Magic,* ed. J. Neusner, E.S. Frerichs and P. V. M. Flesher (New York: Oxford University Press, 1989), 233. See also, Jeffrey B. Russell, *A History of Witchcraft.* (London: Thames & Hudson, 1980), especially chapter 4: "The Witch-craze on the Continent of Europe."

[23]Norman Cohn, *Europe's Inner Demons: An Enquiry Inspired by the Great Witch-Hunt* (New York: Basic Books, 1975), 126–46.

[24]Christina Larner, "Crimen Exceptum? The Crime of Witchcraft in Europe," chapter 2 (49–75) in *Crime and the Law: The Social History of Crime in Western Europe Since 1500*, ed. V. A. C. Gatrell, Bruce Lenman, and Geoffrey Parker (London: Europa Publications Ltd., 1980), 55f.

[25]John Howard Yoder, "Against the Death Penalty," in *The Death Penalty Debate* (Dallas, Tex.: Word Publishing Co., 1991), 178.

[26]Anthony Kenny, *Wyclif* (New York: Oxford University Press, 1985), 97f.

[27]Peter Brock, *Studies in Peace History* (York: William Sessions Ltd., 1991), 2. Brock's studies have been invaluable in illuminating some of the "edges" of earlier Christian history.

[28]Anne Hudson, *The Premature Reformation: Wycliffite Texts and Lollard History* (Oxford: Clarendon Press 1988), 37.

[29]Howard Kaminsky, *A History of the Hussite Revolution* (Berkeley, Calif.: University of California Press, 1967), 393f., notes that "Chělcický's treatise *On Spiritual Warfare*...is clearly addressed to the Taborites; it reveals that the latter had attempted to justify their military action by the classic text of Romans 13:1–7. These passages had done duty for centuries of Christian compromise, and they had been richly exploited in the Prague literature *de bello* in the previous winter; the Taborites perhaps thought that they could make use of them without further ado. If so, Chělcický's treatise's definitive refutation must have given them second thoughts, for he had only to remark that Paul was writing not of Christian power but of pagan, Roman power, and that this very sword had put Paul to death."

[30]Matthew Spinka, "Peter Chělcický, the Spiritual Father of the *Unitas Fratrum*," *Church History* 12 (1943), 282. Brock, notes that although Peter was in general a great admirer of Wyclif, he strongly disagreed with Wyclif's qualified approval of war (6).

[31]Donald F. Durnbaugh and Charles W. Brockwell, Jr., "The Historic Peace Churches: From Sectarian Origins to Ecumenical Witness" in Miller and Gingerich, 183.

[32]Quotations from Spinka, 289.

[33]Ibid., 291.

[34]Tomas G. Masaryk, *The Meaning of Czech History*, ed. René Wellek (Chapel Hill, N.C.: University of North Carolina Press, 1974), 6: "In the course of these battles the voice of Chělcický was raised against the use of the sword, then the Bohemian Brethren came into being. After Chělcický, the mild Brethren found their spokesman in Komensky, but within a relatively short time, the Hussite movement underwent inner decay. The Brethren suffered persecution, not only from Rome but by rival Hussite factions as well. In the end the elite of the

Bohemian Brethren had to leave the country, with thousands of families taking part in the exodus."

[35]Durnbaugh and Brockwell, 184. Also see Franklin H. Littell, *The Anabaptist View of the Church: A Study in the Origins of Sectarian Protestantism,* 2d ed. (Boston, Mass.: Starr King Press, 1958), 43ff., who discusses "the problem of classification" and explains his preference for "Left Wing" because "it counts all the varicolored individuals and groupings associated with the movement at the first and later hanging on its periphery."

[36]C. J. Dyck, "Anabaptist Tradition and Vision," *Dictionary of Christianity in America,* ed. Daniel G. Reid (Downers Grove, Ill.: Intervarsity Press, 1990), 58f.

[37]See Pope John Paul II's words in Prague in May 1995. In canonizing Jan Sarkander, a Jesuit who had been tortured by Protestant authorities and died in prison in 1620, the pope averred that "the tragic events of past centuries must help to establish a new attitude and new relations...far from reopening painful wounds.... In the name of all Catholics I...ask forgiveness for the wrongs inflicted on non-Catholics during the turbulent history of these peoples. At the same time, I pledge the Catholic Church's forgiveness for whatever harm her sons and daughters suffered" (*The Tablet,* [May 27, 1995], 684).

[38]Conrad Grebel, Letter to Thomas Müntzer (Zürich, September 5, 1524), in *Spiritual and Anabaptist Writers,* volume 25 of the Library of Christian Classics, ed. George H. Williams (Philadelphia, Pa.: Westminster Press, 1957), 80.

[39]Harold Bender, *Conrad Grebel* (Scottdale, Pa.: Herald Press, 1950), 179, notes that Grebel based his position "upon the thought of the suffering church. Much has been said and written about 'a Sermon on the Mount ethic' among the Anabaptists...but there is no evidence that Conrad Grebel either here or...anywhere else derived his ethical principles exclusively or even primarily from the Sermon on the Mount. Not one citation from it is to be found in the entire scope of his writings, including his letters."

[40]Littell, 33, has the text of the condemnation ordering Sattler to be executed in the marketplace of Rottenburg am Neckar by having "his tongue cut off, his body torn six times with glowing tongs and still living thrust into a fire and burnt to powder."

[41]Ibid., 186. See also John H. Yoder, ed., *The Legacy of Michael Sattler* (Scottsdale, Pa.: Herald Press, 1973).

[42]D. B. Eller, "Hutterites," *Dictionary of Christianity in America,* 563f.

[43]Durnbaugh and Brockwell, 187.

⁴⁴Both quotations are found in *The Church, the State and the Offender,* Church and Society Series #3 (Newton, Kans.: Faith and Life Press, 1963), for the Board of Christian Service of the General Conference of the Mennonite Church (prepared for a conference held in Chicago in November 1961 by members of the Peace and Social Concerns Committee, chaired by Esko Loewen), 13.

⁴⁵Willem Balke, *Calvin and the Anabaptist Radicals* (Grand Rapids, Mich.: Wm B. Eerdmans, 1981), 289. The quotations of Calvin begin on 282.

⁴⁶Balke, 283.

⁴⁷Brock, 15.

⁴⁸Ibid. 18.

⁴⁹Magda Martini, *Fausto Socino et la Pensée Socinienne* (Paris: Librairie C. Klincksieck, 1966), 35f. Brock describes Socino as the one "who eased the transition from nonresistance and sociopolitical radicalism to sociopolitical conformity and the acceptance of war and self-defense....Under his guidance Antitrinitarian Anabaptism slowly evolved into Socinianism and thus became the progenitor of modern Unitarianism" (14).

⁵⁰All quotations are from Brock, 23–29 passim.

⁵¹Auguste Jorns, *The Quakers as Pioneers in Social Work* (Port Washington, N.Y.: Kennikat Press, 1969), 166. This is a reprint of the 1931 translation of the 1911 German original.

⁵²Margaret H. Bacon, *The Quiet Rebels: The Story of the Quakers in America* (New York: Basic Books, 1969), 132.

⁵³Jorns, 167.

⁵⁴See H. Larry Ingle, *First Among Friends: George Fox and the Creation of Quakerism* (New York: Oxford University Press, 1994), 121: "Fox was not a pacifist in the modern sense that he utterly rejected participating in all wars and violent conflicts. He could not imagine himself bearing the sword...but he also recognized that someone must wield the sword against evildoers."

⁵⁵Durnbaugh and Brockwell, 188.

⁵⁶Quoted by Margaret E. Hirst, *The Quakers in Peace and War* (London: Allen & Unwin, 1923), 57.

⁵⁷Jonathan Fryar, ed., *George Fox and the Children of the Light* (London: K. Cathie, 1991), 38.

⁵⁸Hirst, 138f. This "possibility of reformation" argument is characteristically Quaker. See, for example, Howard H. Brinton, *Friends for 300 Years: The History and Beliefs of the Society of Friends Since George Fox Started the Quaker Movement* (New York: Harper & Bros., 1952; reprinted by Pendle Hill Publications in 1965), 153: "By those who believe that the object

of punishment is reformation, capital punishment is obviously con-demned. That a human being should suddenly be deprived of the possi-bility of reformation or of making amends for his misdeeds is not only futile but morally wrong. If the taking of life is a crime for an individual, it is also a crime for the state."

[59]Elfrida Vipont, *The Story of Quakerism Through Three Centuries* (Richmond, Ind.: Friends United Press, 1977; reprint of 1954 original), 133f. Bellers's ideas for improving social conditions "were so far in advance of his time that their value has only been recognized in com-paratively recent years." Vipont goes on to list several of them.

[60]Jorns, 169f. The statement may well be true, understood as refer-ring to abolition as a project of a legal reform program. As far as desiring its complete elimination from the system, however, the disappearance of the gallows had long been the dream of several Christian groups, as we have seen: Waldenses, Wycliffites, Hussites, and a variety of Anabaptists.

6. Enlightenment: Religious and Secular

[1]Peter Gay, *The Enlightenment: An Interpretation–The Rise of Modern Paganism* (New York: Vintage Books, 1966).

[2]Daniel Sueiro, *La Pena de Muerte y los Derechos Humanos* (Madrid: Alianza Editorial, 1987), 248f.

[3]Maurice Andrieux, *Daily Life in Papal Rome in the 18th Century* (New York: Macmillan, 1969), 103f. See also Michel Foucault, *Discipline and Punish: The Birth of the Prison,* trans. Alan Sheridan (New York: Vin-tage Books, 1979), 61: "In these executions...there was a whole aspect of the carnival, in which the rules were inverted, authority mocked, and criminals transformed into heroes. The shame was turned around."

[4]Richard J. Evans, *Rituals of Retribution,* 901.

[5]This point was often made in apologetical writings. See, e.g., Fr. J. D. Conway in his column in *The Catholic Mind* (May 1959), 122: "The Church is naturally inclined, by history, doctrine, spirit, and example, to *favor abolition* of the death penalty in our modern society, but...she is prevented from taking that position firmly because of the false philoso-phies proposed by leading abolitionists. They contradict her doctrines, and she must refute their errors *before siding with them in their practical conclusions.*"

[6]Paul Hazard, *The European Mind (1680–1715)* (Cleveland and New York: The World Publishing Co., 1963), 446. The French original appeared in 1935.

⁷Bettina Strub, *Der Einfluss der Aufklärung auf die Todesstrafe* (Zürich: Juris Druck, 1973).

⁸Cesare Beccaria, *Dei delitti e delle pene.* Quotations here are from the English translation published in London by F. Newberry in 1775, edited and introduced by Adolph Caso, *An Essay on Crimes and Punishments,* 4th ed. (Boston, Masss.: Brandon Publishing Co., 1983; 2d ed. 1992).

⁹Piers Beirne, *Inventing Criminology: Essays on the Rise of "Homo Criminalis"* (Albany: SUNY Press, 1993), 29ff.

¹⁰Ibid., 16–19. Beirne contends that "nearly every page...is marked by Hutcheson's towering influence on Beccaria's thinking" (28). He points out that the manuscript form of Scotsman Francis Hutcheson's *System of Moral Philosophy* (1755) had been circulating on the continent as early as 1738. Montesquieu's *Esprit des lois* (1748) is far more "radical" than Beccaria's in some of its analyses of what was wrong with the law, e.g.: "The mischief arises from a notion which some people have entertained of *revenging the cause of the Deity.* But we must honor the Deity and leave him to avenge his own cause." Cf. Frank E. Manuel, ed., *The Enlightenment* (Englewood Cliffs, N. J.: Prentice-Hall, 1965), 113.

¹¹There were exceptions. A Spanish Benedictine, Martín Sarmiento (1695–1772), published a work two years earlier than Beccaria's, maintaining for the first time "in the modern style" that the death penalty should be abolished because the criminal is "more useful to society alive than dead" and serves longer and better as an example to deter others as a prisoner than as a corpse. Cf. "Muerte, Pena de," *Enciclopedia Universal Ilustrada Europeo-Americana* (Barcelona: Hijos de J. Espasa, 1907), 37:89.

¹²Crowe, 47.

¹³Henry Paolucci, in the introduction to his translation of Cesare Beccaria, *On Crimes and Punishments* (Indianapolis, Ind.: Bobbs-Merrill, 1963), xvii. Cf. also the chronology of editions presented by Ornella Vocca, *Evoluzione del Pensiero Criminologico sulla Pena di Morte* (Napoli: Casa E. Jovene, 1984), 9, noting that the original anonymous edition (Livorno) had no divisions into either chapters or paragraphs; the second edition (Monaco) was divided into forty numbered paragraphs; the third (Lausanne, 1765) edition had forty-five paragraphs; and two other editions (Harlem) had forty-seven paragraphs.

¹⁴As a result of the revisions, the numbering differs in different editions. In Paolucci, e.g., the torture paragraph is #12 and the death penalty paragraph #16, based on the 1958 Italian edition of Sergio Romagnoli; whereas in the 1983 International Pocket Library edition (which is a reprint of the 1775 London translation of F. Newberry, 4th

ed.,with an introduction by Adolph Caso [Boston, Mass.: Branden Publishing Co.; 2d ed., 1992]), the torture paragraph is #16 and the death-penalty paragraph is #28.

[15]John Paul II, *Evangelium Vitae,* para. 56. English translation in *Origins* 24:42 (April 6, 1995), 709: "The nature and extent of the punishment...ought not go to the extreme of executing the offender except in cases of absolute necessity....Such cases are very rare if not practically nonexistent."

[16]Robert and Beatrice Kastenbaum, *Encyclopedia of Death* (New York: Avon Books, 1989), 86: "The victims most put to suffering (in 16th century England) were priests who refused to recant and convert to the Church of England. The priest might be dragged through the cobblestone streets, then placed on the gallows. The executioner was expected to half-hang the condemned man to produce shock and agony just short of death. The next step would be to plunge a knife into his body, tear out the entrails and show them to the still living victim. The offender might then be drawn and quartered while, possibly, still alive."

[17]Voltaire, "Commentaire sur le livre *Des Delits et des Peines,*" in *Oeuvres Completes de Voltaire: Mélanges IV* (Paris: Garnier Frères, 1879; reprinted Nendeln / Liechtenstein: Kraus, 1967), 554.

[18]Quoted in Edward Peters, *Inquisition*...181. His fascinating treatment of "Voltaire and the 'Tyrants of the Mind'" runs from 177 to 184.

[19]See Strub, 152f.

[20]Commentary on Beccaria, attributed to Voltaire (c. 1770), quoted by Basil Montagu, ed., *The Opinions of Different Authors Upon the Punishment of Death,* 2d ed. (London: Longman, Hurst, Rees, Orme, & Brown, 1816), 178. His final comment about Machaut was: "Nature never intended such men for magistrates, but for executioners."

[21]Voltaire, 556.

[22]Cited by Skoda, 18, as *Commento filologico critico sopra i delitti e le pene secondo il gius divino* (Livorno, 1786), in chapter 30 of which he wrote: "Se si vuol dare la morte ai rei perché cosi commanda la vecchia legge, bisogna osservarlo intieramente e rinunziare alla nuova."

[23]Pastoret, *Des Lois Pénales,* published in 1790, first discussed the opinions of the "three staunchest defenders—Montesquieu, Rousseau, and Mably," refuting them one by one, then gave a full and favorable account of the opinions of the abolitionists, describing deterrence as a myth, and making an array of suggestions for penal reform (See Imbert, 120).

[24]Citations from George Rudé, ed., *Robespierre, Great Lives Observed* series (Englewood Cliffs, N.J.: Prentice-Hall, 1967). J. M. Thompson, *Robespierre* (New York: Howard Fertig, 1968), I: 139, observes in compar-

ing the two addresses that "there is no conduct so incalculable as that of a fanatic."

[25]Marcel Normand, *La Peine de Mort* (Paris: Presse Universitaire, 1980), 22, estimates that the total number of executions during the revolution was about forty thousand. According to Donald Greer, *The Incidence of the Terror During the French Revolution* (Gloucester, Mass.: P. Smith, 1966 [c. 1935]), 113, the record month was January 1794, a year after Louis's death, when 3,517 were beheaded.

[26]See Michel Vovelle, *The Revolution Against the Church: From Reason to the Supreme Being* (Columbus, Ohio: Ohio State University Press, 1991), for relevant observations on this anomaly.

[27]Immanuel Kant, *Metaphysik der Sitten, in Kant's Werke,* Band VI (Berlin: Prussian Academy edition, 1907), 334f. Cf. English translation of John Ladd, *The Metaphysical Elements of Justice: Part One of the Metaphysics of Morals* (New York: Bobbs-Merrill, 1965), 105: "aus theilnehmender Empfindelei einer affectirten Humanität."

[28]Edmund L. Pincoffs, *The Rationale of Legal Punishment* (New York: Humanities Press, 1966), 29: "The positions are, on the face of it, contraries. Both cannot be true, though both could be false."

[29]The most influential of these was Richard Rothe, *Theologische Ethik,* 5 volumes, 2d. ed. (1867–71). Prominent English-speaking Protestant clergy of the Kantian school were John N. McLeod, *The Capital Punishment of the Murderer, an Unrepealed Ordinance of God* (New York: R. Carter, 1842), and George B. Cheever, *Punishment by Death: Its Authority and Expediency* (New York: J. Wiley, 1843).

[30]Don Scheid, "Kant's Retributivism," *Ethics* 93 (1983), 262–82. Scheid contends that Kant is "not so unreasonable as many have made him out to be," and is "best interpreted as a partial retributivist."

[31]See David Ross, *Kant's Ethical Theory* (New York: Oxford University Press, 1954), 53ff. for treatment of the three forms of Kant's categorical imperative.

[32]Steven S. Schwarzschild, "Kantianism on the Death Penalty (and Related Social Problems)," *Archives for Philosophy of Law and Social Philosophy* 71 (1985), 343–372. Cohen taught philosophy at Marburg for 36 years before resigning in political protest in 1912.

[33]See M. Margaret Falls, *A Retributivist Condemnation of Capital Punishment,* diss., Vanderbilt University, 1986. Falls presented a condensed form of her argument in "Against the Death Penalty: A Christian Stance in a Secular World," *The Christian Century* 103 (1986), 1118f.

[34]Schwarzschild, 348.

[35]See Eugene B. Block, *When Men Play God: The Fallacy of Capital Punishment* (San Francisco, Calif.: Cragmont Publishing, 1983).

[36]Mario A. Cattaneo, "Cristianesimo e Pensiero Giuridico Liberale," in *Cristianesimo, Secolarizzazione e Diritto Moderno,* ed. Luigi L. Vallauri and G. Dilcher (Milano: Giuffrè, 1981), 1212f: "The principle of the human person as end, not means...has a crucial juridical relevance...as is evidenced by the way in which some have recognized it as the true and proper foundation for an entire philosophy of law."

[37]Michael Endres, *The Morality of Capital Punishment: Equal Justice Under the Law?* (Mystic, Conn.: Twenty-Third Publications, 1985), 25–30.

[38]Raphael Gallagher, C.Ss.R., and Brendan McConvery, C.Ss.R., *History and Conscience: Studies in Honour of Fr. Sean O'Riordan, C.Ss.R.* (Dublin: Gill & Macmillan, 1989), 3.

[39]Translated from the Italian by Rev. John T. Mullock (Dublin: James Duffy, 1847), 2 volumes. The tone and agenda are set in the opening statement of the author's preface: "My object in writing this work is to prove that the Roman Catholic Church is the only true one among so many other Churches, and to show how carefully the Almighty guarded her, and brought her victoriously through all the persecution of her enemies."

[40]Peter Berger, *The Precarious Vision: A Sociologist Looks at Social Fictions and Christian Faith* (New York: Doubleday, 1962), 87f.

[41]Sir William Blackstone, *Commentaries on the Laws of England,* Book IV, chap. 1, sec. 3.

[42]David D. Cooper, *The Lesson of the Scaffold: The Public Execution Controversy in Victorian England* (Athens, Ohio: Ohio University Press, 1974), 30.

[43]Imbert, 136.

[44]Quoted by Ross Harrison, *Bentham* (London: Routledge & Kegan Paul, 1983), 200f.

[45]Hugo Adam Bedau, "A Utilitarian Critique of the Death Penalty," in Bedau, 64–91.

[46]Jeremy Bentham, *An Introduction to the Principles of Morals and Legislation,* ed. J. H. Burns and H. L. A. Hart (London and NY: Methuen, 1970; reprinted in 1982), 181–84.

[47]See O. Temkin, W. K. Frankena, S. H. Kadish, *Respect for Life in Medicine, Philosophy, and the Law* (Baltimore, Md.: Johns Hopkins University Press, 1976).

[48]C. G. Oakes, *Sir Samuel Romilly: "The Friend of the Oppressed"* (London: Allen & Unwin, 1935), xii.

[49]Cooper, 33.

[50]Quoted by René A. Wormser, *The Law: The Story of Lawmakers, and the Law We Have Lived by From the Earliest Times to the Present Day* (New York: Simon & Schuster, 1949), 225.

[51]Ibid., 45.

[52]Potter, 76.

[53]Cooper, 153: "Lord de Ros had heard that during the Peninsular War there was an extraordinary contrast between the effects of public and private executions. Public executions, he insisted, resulted in better discipline in the British Army, while frequent private executions in the French Army did not discourage the rampant desertions there. Although the Duke of Wellington executed only 13 of his soldiers, he made a greater display of them than did the French who had executed 250."

[54]Potter, 87.

[55]Ibid., 91.

[56]Viscount Templewood, *The Shadow of the Gallows* (London: Victor Gollancz, 1951), 37, summarized the frustrating maneuverings thus: "The result, therefore, of a century of debate has been to leave the death penalty much as it was in 1862." This led him to ask if "the British public have been for so many generations habituated to the idea of hanging criminals that the possibility of abolishing death sentences is almost inconceivable?"

[57]Isaiah Berlin, "Joseph de Maistre and the Origins of Fascism" (1960 essay reprinted in his collection *The Crooked Timber of Humanity* (New York: Vintage Books, 1992), 105f.

[58]John Courtney Murray, S.J., "The Political Thought of Joseph de Maistre," *The Review of Politics* 11 (1949), 73. Murray faulted de Maistre for a lack of insight: "He failed to realize that the ascendant bourgeois class had attained sufficient strength to endure no longer the presence of the favored class of nobility."

[59]Joseph de Maistre, *Les Soirées de Saint-Pétersbourg, in Oeuvres complètes de J. de Maistre,* IV, 32f., cited by Berlin, 116ff. The lurid account goes on in even worse detail, describing how the executioner stretches the prisoner on the wheel. Cf. the translation in Alister Kershaw, *A History of the Guillotine* (New York: Barnes & Noble, 1993), 90: "Nothing can be heard but the sound of the bones breaking beneath the bar, the yells of the victim...the shattered members entwine in the spokes; the head hangs down, the hair is on end, the mouth, gaping like a furnace, no longer emits anything but bloody, intermittent words pleading for death. He (the executioner) has finished; his heart beats, but it is with joy; he applauds himself, he says in his heart: no one uses the wheel better than I...he holds out his bloodstained hand, and from a distance, Justice throws a few pieces of gold into it."

[60]Cf. J. Hébert, O.P., "La Justice Criminelle et la Peine de Mort," *Revue Thomiste* 2 (1894), 309–32 and 614–37, a classic statement of the polemics of a century ago. Hébert says ironically: "We have not camouflaged our opinion. We believe—without condemning abolitionist

nations—that the maintaining (of the death penalty) is a duty, if one wishes to defend the social order efficaciously and to safeguard the full rights of justice by the grand law of expiation" (631).

[61]Imbert, 139.

[62]E. S. Buchanan, trans. and ed., *Lamartine Impugns Capital Punishment* (Three Speeches in Favour of its Abolition Delivered in Paris in 1836–1838) (New York: Chas. A. Swift, Inc., 1930), 2–5.

[63]Imbert, 164.

[64]This is not unlike contemporary America, where people insist on having the death penalty on the books more than carrying out actual executions. Bedau, analyzing some of the polls, observes that it seems that "the public does not want actual executions so much as it wants the possibility thereof" (148).

[65]See Imbert, 170. Also, Victor Hugo, *The Last Day of a Condemned Man, and Other Prison Writings,* trans. with intro. and notes by Geoff Woollen (New York: Oxford Paperbacks [the Worlds Classics], Oxford University Press, 1992).

[66]V. C. Terlinden, "Thonissen, J. J.," in *Biographie Nationale publiée par L'Académie Royale des sciences, des lettres et des beaux-arts de Belgique* (Bruxelles: Emile Bruylant, 1932), XXV:114. Among articles on the death penalty written by Thonissen were several special studies including one on the death penalty in the Talmud and another on a thirteenth-century controversy over the legitimacy of the death penalty (See Hetzel, 488f.).

[67]J. J. Thonissen, "Le Problème de la Peine de Mort au point de vue du Dogme Catholique," *Revue Générale* 1 (1865), 76–87.

[68]Italo Mereu, *Giuseppe Compagnoni primo constituzionalista d'Europa* (Ferrara: De Savia, 1968), contended that Compagnoni's works as pioneering philosopher, historian, linguist, and jurist have not yet received due study and appreciation. He summarizes Compagnoni's criticism of Beccaria in *La Morte Come Pena,* (Milano: Espresso Strumenti, 1982), 105–113.

[69]Italo Mereu, *La Morte Come Pena*, 135. Also, Skoda, 26. Ellero made this prediction in his 1881 work *Tratti Criminalistici,* when Pius IX had imprisoned himself in the Vatican against the modern world. In 1887 Giuseppe Brini published *Le Opere Sociali di Pietro Ellero* in appreciation of his long and productive career.

[70]Skoda, 19, gives the reference thus: Mons. Giuseppe Coco Zanghy, *Il Cattolicismo e la pena di morte* (Catania: 1874). It was apparently the expansion of a paper he delivered in Venice earlier that year. The 1993 index volume of the Italian publication *Synaxis,* 33f. (kindly provided to me by the research department of *L'Osservatore Romano*) offers some

sketchy biographical notes on Zanghy from the eulogy given at his funeral. He apparently had an unusual gift for languages as well as very broad academic interests, and taught in virtually every area of the curriculum of the diocesan seminary in his native Catania. The cardinal-archbishop of Catania, G. B. Dusmer, chose him as his accompanying theologian at Vatican Council I. Zanghy's position becomes all the more fascinating in light of the timing. Mereu details the fierce political struggle surrounding the "Abolitionist Project of 1868" when an entire legislative committee unanimously called for the elimination of capital punishment but was outmaneuvered by the "law and order" forces by 1874 (146ff.).

[71]All this material is drawn from Alberto Gil Novales (professor, University of Barcelona), "Peine de Mort et Valeur de la Vie: Espagne (1820–1921)," *Actes du Colloque sur la Peine de Mort dans la Pensée Philosophique et Litteraire* (Université de Paris-Sorbonne, 1980), 53–59.

[72]Friedrich Schleiermacher, *Die christliche Sitte nach den Grundsätzen der evangelische Kirche,* ed. L. Jonas (Berlin: G. Reimer, 1843), 248.

[73]Ibid., 249f.

[74]See Richard B. Brandt, *The Philosophy of Schleiermacher* (New York: Greenwood Press, 1968), 29–35, on his "ethical determinism."

[75]Ibid., 34.

[76]John MacRae Moir, ed., *Capital Punishment, Based on Professor Mittermaier's Todesstrafe* (London: Smith, Elder & Co., 1865), xxviii.

[77]Ibid., 188.

[78]Ibid., 218.

[79]Hetzel, 474–81 passim.

[80]Ibid., 484. This would have been Pius IX and King Victor Emmanuel II just eighteen months before the armies of the latter took possession of Rome and Pius "shut himself up in the Vatican and moved no more in the city" (E. E. Y. Hales, *The Catholic Church in the Modern World* [New York: Doubleday, 1958], 143).

[81]F. X. Linsenmann, *Lehrbuch der Moraltheologie* (Freiburg im Breisgau: Herder, 1878), 471–82. Besides moral theology, Linsenmann also taught pastoral theology and patristics at Tübingen as of 1867; he served as academic rector in 1887 and was named bishop of his home diocese of Rottenburg in 1898, but his sudden death from a stroke turned the day set for his installation into the day of his funeral. See Alfons Auer, "Franz Xaver Linsenmann (1835–1898)," *Katholische Theologen Deutschlands im 19. Jahrhundert,* herausgegeben von Heinrich Fries und Georg Schwaiger (München: Kösel-Verlag, 1975), Band III: 215–40.

[82]Linsenmann, 472. He goes on to note that the symbol was derived in the first instance from the military sword, used against exter-

nal enemies, but that since it naturally came to serve also as the instrument for punishing society's internal enemies—criminals—the sword
passed into popular consciousness as the symbol of judicial power as
well as of military power.

[83]Ibid., 473.

[84]Quoted with something less than full endorsement by Anton
Koch and Arthur Preuss, *A Handbook of Moral Theology* (St. Louis, Mo.:
B. Herder, 1924), 155.

[85]Linsenmann, 475.

[86]Koch and Preus, 160.

7. From Vatican I to Vatican II

[1]Dwyer, 326.

[2]Richard J. Evans, *Rituals of Retribution*, 338f. See also Dwyer, 326:
"At the very moment at which democratic movements were far
advanced in some European countries and were beginning to stir in all
the others, the Catholic church turned against the tide, and created a
kind of papal absolutism which, paradoxically, rested on a broad consensus of the worldwide church."

[3]Victor Cathrein, S.J., *Philosophia Moralis in Usum Scholarum,* editio quinta (Freiburg: Herder, 1905), 467.

[3a]G. G. Coulton, "The Death Penalty for Heresy from 1184 to
1921 A.D.," *Medieval Studies* 18 (London: Simpkin, Marshall, Hamilton,
Kent and Co., 1924), 42.

[3b]Coulton, 62f.

[4]For a history of this eighteenth-century construct ("societas perfecta") as applied to the church, see Roland Minnerath, *Le Droit de L'Église
à la Liberté du Syllabus à Vatican II,* #39 in series *Le Point Théologique,* ed.
Charles Kannengiesser (Paris: Éditions Beauchesne, 1982), 31ff.

[5]See Skoda, 61 (*Legge Vaticana,* 7 giugno 1929, n. II, a. 4). The article parallels the November 25, 1926, Italian law, n. 2008, art. 1.: "Chi-
unque commette un fatto diretto contro la vita, l'integrità e la libertà
personale del Re o del Regente, *e punito con la morte.*" Skoda ironically
cited the statute (ten years before its suppression) as part of his "proof"
that the church had nothing against the death penalty.

[6]*New York Times,* January 16, 1971, 33:2. Mussolini, in his new
Penal Code of 1930, like fellow fascists Hitler in Germany and Franco
in Spain, increased the number of capital crimes considerably. But
these and most others were removed and the death penalty basically
abolished in Italian Law #224, August 10, 1944. It was retained for

wartime, and eighty-eight Nazifascisti collaborators were executed between April 1945 and March 1947, the last formal Italian executions (see Amnesty International, *When the State Kills* [New York: AIUSA, 1989], 155).

[7]John H. Whyte, *Catholics in Western Democracies: A Study in Political Behaviour* (New York: St. Martin's Press, 1981), 118.

[8]Gerald A. McCool, *Catholic Theology in the Nineteenth Century: The Quest for a Unitary Method* (New York: Seabury, 1977), 238–40 passim.

[9]*DTC,* Tome X, col. 2501.

[10]Jacques Leclercq, *Lecons de Droit Naturel,* IV: Première Partie: *Vie, Disposition de soi* (1937; rev. ed. 1946), 89–97. For some of the controversy surrounding Leclercq in the 1950s, see James M. Connolly, *Voices of France* (New York: Macmillan, 1961), 155f.

[11]Johannes Ude, *Du sollst nicht töten* (Dornbirn, 1948). Skoda attributes Fr. Ude's change of heart (and mind) to the sufferings he endured in prison from the Nazis (21).

[12]Scc T. Mark Schoof, O.P., *A Survey of Catholic Theology 1800–1970* (New York: Paulist Press, 1970). Among the foremost were Chenu, Congar, deLubac, Häring, Moeller, Rahner, and Schillebeeckx.

[13]Alfred Naud, *Tu ne tueras pas* (Mayenne: Floch, 1963), 9. Other ghoulish information provided by Naud is that in 1944 alone a single German executioner killed 1,399 prisoners, on average four a day. In ten months of 1944–1945, the special executioners severed 10,071 heads. At Plötzensee there were seventy executions in one night. The guillotines mobilized on the occasion of this massacre operated nonstop for eleven hours.

[14]Ibid., 211f.

[15]Richard J. Evans, *Rituals of Retribution,* 794f.

[16]Gerhard Gloege, ed., *Die Todesstrafe als theologisches Problem* (Köln: Westdeutscher Verlag, 1966), 82.

[17]Paul Althaus, *Die Todesstrafe als Problem der christlichen Ethik* (München: Verlag der Bayerischen Akademie der Wissenschaften, 1955).

[18]Walter Künneth, *Politik zwischen Dämon und Gott: eine christliche Ethik des Politischen* (1954).

[19]Gloege. See also Martin Honecker, "Capital Punishment in German Protestant Theology," *Concilium* 120 (October 1978), 54–63.

[20]Gloege, 10.

[21]Honecker, 60.

[22]Werner Elert, *Das christliche Ethos.* (Tübingen, 1949), para. #17, 4 (155–57).

[23]See Hans Dombois, ed., *Die weltliche Strafe in der evangelischen Theologie* (Witten: Luther-Verlag, 1959).

[24]Richard Rothe (1799–1867), *Theologische Ethik,* 5 volumes, (Wittenberg: Zimmermann, 1867–71).

[25]Hans-Peter Alt, *Das Problem der Todesstrafe* (München, 1960).

[26]The understanding of the two kingdoms has been much disputed. See F. Edward Cranz, *An Essay on the Development of Luther's Thought on Justice, Law, and Society* (Cambridge, Mass.: Harvard University Press, 1964), 177: "Luther develops a theology of the world only for Christians in a Christian society; he affirms a Christian secularization and not a secularization without qualification....Only Christianity teaches us not to 'mix' the two realms, which the natural man cannot even distinguish....Hence we must recognize how wide a gap separates Luther from later forms of secularism and that from the standpoint of these later forms we can ask questions which for Luther are irrelevant."

[27]A. Janssen, "Autour du problème de la peine de mort," *Ephemerides Theologicae Lovanienses* 37 (1961): 86–97, did an extensive review of the major German contributions. He had criticisms of particular points, but his chief goal was to give the arguments a wider hearing in a debate that he considered far from over. His impression was that these authors, including Alt, showed that it is easier to demonstrate the shortcomings of the arguments of others than to propose a fully convincing argument of one's own.

[28]Karl Barth, *Church Dogmatics* III/4 (New York: Chas. Scribner, 1951), 443 (1961 English translation). Subsequent quotations are passim through page 449.

[29]Gustav Ermecke, *Zur ethischen Begründung der Todesstrafe heute* (Paderborn: F. Schöningh, 2te. erweiterte Aufl., 1963).

[30]Ibid., 31: "In the future this analogy must be repudiated....The principle of totality applies to physical organisms only, but is not applicable to moral organisms. Today the death penalty must be grounded in a different way than was done by Thomas. In his day he could not have had an inkling of the extremes to which such an organic conception of the state could lead."

[31]Pius XII, Allocution to Congress of Histopathologists, *Acta Apostolicae Sedis,* 44 (1952), 787. English translation in *The Catholic Mind* (1953), 305–13. The part quoted is on page 311. Summaries and sources for the ensuing controversy are given in Ermecke, 36ff.

[32]Janssen, 89f., in reviewing Ermecke's work, states his chief contribution "is to have called attention to this argument little used previously."

[33]See Bedau, chapter 2: "The Right to Life and the Right to Kill."

[33a]Albert Camus, *Neither Victims Nor Executioners,* trans. Dwight Macdonald (New York: Continuum, 1980–).

^{33b}Ibid., 59. In 1957 Camus wrote another moving autobiographical essay called "Reflections on the Guillotine," reinforcing and appearing with Arthur Koestler's "Reflections on Hanging." He described his position thus: "Today I share absolutely Koestler's conviction: the death penalty besmirches our society, and its upholders cannot reasonably defend it." (Essay is included in Albert Camus, *Resistance, Rebellion, and Death,* trans. Justin O'Brien [New York: Alfred A. Knopf, 1961] 175–234. Quote is on page 179.)

[34]Paul Savey-Casard, "L'Eglise catholique et la peine de mort," *Revue de science criminelle et droit pénal comparé* (1961), 773–85. He later published his fuller historical-juridical study, *La Peine de Mort: Esquisse Historique et Juridique.*

[35]This rather progressive position was that of Häring before Vatican II. He went beyond it in subsequent years, as will be noted.

[36]Savey-Casard, "L'Eglise Catholique et la peine de mort," 785.

[37]Joseph Vernet, S.J., "Peine Capitale, Peine Perdue" *Etudes* (1962), 193–209.

[38]This saying is not in all translations because it is only in a few of the early Greek manuscripts. But Vernet's point holds nonetheless. See Joseph Fitzmyer, S.J., *The Gospel according to Luke I–IX* (Garden City, N.Y.: Doubleday, 1981), 830.

[39]Sydney Silverman, in the Afterword to Arthur Koestler, *Reflections on Hanging,* (New York: Macmillan, 1957), 210.

[40]*Royal Commission on Capital Punishment 1949–1953 Report* (Westport, Conn.: Greenwood Press, 1980 reprint of 1953 original), 3.

[41]Ibid., 274.

[42]Koestler, 100. On page 168 he comes back to the image and says: "The point is not to deny the existence of the fur-clad little man in us, but to accept him as part of the human condition, and to keep him under control."

[43]Ibid., 41.

[44]Ibid., 169.

[45]Brian Bailey, *Hangmen of England: The History of Execution from Jack Ketch to Albert Pierrepont* (New York: Barnes & Noble, 1992), 194: "Although I have been against the death penalty ever since I was old enough to think about it seriously, I feel a sense of shame in belonging to a society which, calling itself civilised, failed for so long to realise that civilisation and capital punishment are mutually exclusive."

[46]Skoda, 1–4 passim.

[47]Ibid., 132.

[48]Honecker put his finger on this key point: "The change in attitude to capital punishment during the Enlightenment came about

because the duty of the authorities to punish was no longer accepted as the only argument; the person of the offender was brought into the discussion. Capital punishment began to be held to be incompatible with the respect due to the humanity, first of the person punished, and later of those carrying out the punishment"(55). This is the most frequently missed point in the modern controversy.

[49]Cf. J. Leon Hooper, S.J., in his introduction to the writings of John Courtney Murray, S.J., *Religious Liberty: Catholic Struggles with Pluralism* (Louisville, Ky.: Westminster/John Knox Press, 1993), 43: "The Roman Catholic debate on truth and freedom appears to revolve around what is normally called a cognitional theory, that is, a way of visualizing the truths that make us free. When those truths are conceived in what Murray called a classicist manner, they are thought to be permanent, complete, immutable, and immediately present to the privileged knower. The truth of what the rest of us hold is measured by the relationship, the correspondence, between what we claim and the privileged knower knows."

[50]The movement toward greater "ecclesial consciousness," promoted by Pius XII, intensified through the next two decades, with the result that "the first purpose assigned the Council by John XXIII was to examine more deeply the nature of the Church" (see Joseph Gremillion, ed., *The Church and Culture Since Vatican II* [Notre Dame, Ind.: University of Notre Dame Press, 1985], 320.)

[51]John XXIII, *Pacem in Terris*, 9–10. See Peter Riga, *Peace on Earth: A Commentary on Pope John's Encyclical* (New York: Herder & Herder, 1964), 74: "Such a forceful elucidation of the infinite worth of the human person and of his sacred rights cannot be found in any previous papal document."

[52]David Hollenbach, *Justice, Peace, and Human Rights: American Catholic Social Ethics in a Pluralistic World* (New York: Crossroad, 1988), 5. The following quotations are from the same.

[53]Richard P. McBrien, "The Church," chapter 8C of *Modern Catholicism: Vatican II and After*, ed. Adrian Hastings (New York: Oxford University Press, 1991), 84.

[54]Ibid., 89. As McBrien observes: "This is clearly one of the most significant emphases in the entire constitution, and indeed in the whole Council itself....[It] has extremely important practical consequences; specifically, it means that the Church must signify what it is."

[55]See Peter Hebblethwaite, *John XXIII: Pope of the Council* (London: G. Chapman, 1984), 498.

[56]See Barry Nakel and Kenneth A. Hardy, *The Arbitrariness of the Death Penalty* (Philadelphia, Pa.: Temple University Press, 1987).

[57]See Pietro Pavan, in *Commentary on the Documents of Vatican II,* ed. H. Vorgrimler (New York: Crossroad, 1989), 4: 53, commenting on the opening statement that gives the work its very title *(Dignitatis Humanae).*

[58]M. Tidmarsh, O.P., J. D. Halloran, K. J. Connolly, *Capital Punishment: A Case for Abolition.* (London and New York: Sheed and Ward, 1963), 101.

[59]Ibid., 167.

[60]Crowe, 24–61, 99–131.

[61]Ibid., 130.

[62]Ibid., 128.

[63]W. J. S. Simpson, *A Study of Bossuet* (London: SPCK, 1937), 200f.

[64]Imbert, 7.

[65]Ibid., 219.

[66]Between 1966 and 1977, nine convicts were executed in France by guillotine, the last one on September 10, 1977. When the death penalty was abolished in 1981, there were seven people on death row (see Amnesty International, *When the State Kills,* 134f.).

[67]Paul-Ernest Dieterich, *Vergleichende Studie der Französischen und Deutschen Moralisten angesichts der Todesstrafe* (Paris: Institut Catholique, 1980), studied the contrasts between the French and German Catholic experience in opposing the death penalty. His thesis director was Henri de Lavalette, S.J., who was a prominent participant in the French debate. Dieterich isolated a series of differences, most of them stemming from historical and cultural circumstances. For example in Germany the debate preceded Vatican II and was thus largely confined to Protestant theologians (except for Ermecke), whereas in France it was post–Vatican II and largely Catholic. Neither was there the high degree of intra-Catholic public disagreement and conflict in Germany that there was in France. In this regard, the U.S. Catholic experience paralleled the French more than the German, but has not as yet enjoyed comparable success.

8. The American Context

[1]Philip E. Mackey, *Voices Against Death: American Opposition to Capital Punishment 1787–1975* (New York: Burt Franklin & Co., 1976), xiif. The material in this section is largely drawn from Mackey's valuable book.

[2]Peter Brock, *The Quaker Peace Testimony 1660–1914* (York, England: Sessions Book Trust, 1990), 94.

[3]Mackey, 3–13 passim.

[4]Ibid., 23f.

[5]Ibid., 36, 45. Cf. David Brion Davis, "The Movement to Abolish Capital Punishment in America, 1787–1861," *American Historical Review* 63 (1957), 35: "In contrast to pacifists like (Rev. Henry Clarke) Wright and romantic poets like (John Greenleaf) Whittier, Rantoul represented the spirit of the Enlightenment. He attacked capital punishment for the secular reason that it violated natural law as interpreted by reason. Yet even Rantoul was aware that in America rational theory had to be supplemented with appeals to Scripture."

[6]Louis P. Masur, *Rites of Execution: Capital Punishment and the Transformation of American Culture, 1776–1865* (New York: Oxford University Press, 1989), 124.

[7]Cheever, *Punishment by Death.*

[8]Mackey, 108f.

[9]Ibid., 111.

[10]Ibid., 116–18.

[11]*The Frederick Douglass Papers,* ed. John W. Blassingame (New Haven, Conn.: Yale University Press, 1979), vol. 3 (1855–63), 242–48 passim.

[12]Mackey, 123 and 127.

[13]Ibid., 143f.

[14]James Hennesey, S.J., *American Catholics: A History of the Roman Catholic Community in the United States* (New York: Oxford University Press, 1981), 204–20.

[15]The title page of *The Catholic Encyclopedia* names five editors: C. G. Herbermann, E. A. Pace, C. B. Pallen, T. J. Shahan, J. J. Wynne, S.J., "assisted by numerous collaborators" (New York: The Gilmary Society).

[16]See Mackey, xxxiv: Between 1907 and 1917, "while nine states ended capital punishment, six more and one territory won abolition votes in at least one house of their legislatures....Hundreds of magazine and newspaper articles were devoted to the reform."

[17]*The Catholic Encyclopedia and Its Makers* (New York: The Encyclopedia Press, 1917), 187.

[18]Geoffrey Abbott, *The Book of Executions: An Encyclopedia of Methods of Judicial Execution* (London: Headline, 1994), describes seventy such methods.

[19]The article on the *Inquisition* (in volume eight) was written by a Swiss Jesuit, Joseph Blötzer, and is a much longer (pp. 26–38), far more ideological piece than that of Willis.

[20]Cf. Jay P. Dolan, *The American Catholic Experience* (Garden City, N.Y.: Doubleday & Co., 1985), 201–3, "Anti-Catholicism was a leftover

from the Protestant Reformation....Although support for the anti-Catholic crusade had diminished considerably since the 1850s, it remained a threat well into the 20th century," tending to "harden the lines of the Catholic cultural ghetto, thus expanding the gap between Catholics and Protestants."

[21]As Dolan expressed it in his earlier work, *The Immigrant Church: New York's Irish and German Catholics, 1815–1865* (Baltimore, Md.: Johns Hopkins University Press, 1975), 168f. "In withdrawing from an unfriendly society and concentrating on its own internal development, the church had few models to follow except those of the old country. In looking to the past for their response to current needs Catholics inevitably adopted a conservative social program....As an immigrant institution, the church's task was to conserve the old order and to strengthen the self-identity of Catholics in a predominantly Protestant culture. In this situation religion could not function as a catalyst for social change: it was forced to serve as a link with the past."

[22]Mackey, 164–66.

[23]Raymond T. Bye, *Capital Punishment in the United States* (Philadelphia, Pa.: Committee on Philanthropic Labor, 1919), 98 and 101.

[24]Mackey, 171.

[25]M. L. Radelet, H. A. Bedau, C. E. Putnam, *In Spite of Innocence* (Boston, Mass.: Northeastern University Press, 1992), 97.

[26]Herbert Ehrmann, in Mackey, 215f.

[27]Mackey, xl.

[28]Ronald Radosh and Joyce Milton, *The Rosenberg File: A Search for the Truth* (New York: Holt, Rinehart & Winston, 1983), 376f.

[29]Ibid., 380.

[30]Thomas C. Cornell and James H. Forest, eds., *A Penny a Copy: Readings from the Catholic Worker* (New York: Macmillan Co., 1968), 160–62.

[31]For a comprehensive review of the case, see William M. Kunstler, *Beyond a Reasonable Doubt? The Original Trial of Caryl Chessman* (New York: William Morrow & Co., 1961).

[32]J. Gordon Melton, *The Churches Speak on: Capital Punishment: Official Statements from Religious Bodies and Ecumenical Organizations* (Detroit, Mich.: Gale Research, 1989), 135. The brief statement says: "We stand for the application of the redemptive principle to the treatment of offenders against the law, to reform of penal and correctional methods, and to criminal court procedures. We deplore the use of capital punishment."

[33]Ibid., 129. The Canadian statement has three parts: (a) "We affirm our belief that capital punishment is contrary to the spirit and

teaching of Christ; (b) we urge the government to develop alternative methods and abolish capital punishment as soon as possible; and (c) we urge the Board of Evangelism and Social Service to initiate and direct a study through the church of how we may best fulfil this responsibility."

[34]Ibid., 157. The grounds are: "respect for the value of every human life must be incorporated into our laws;...modern justice should concern itself with rehabilitation, not retribution;...it has not been proved...a deterrent to crime; human judgments are not infallible, and no penalty should be used which cannot be revoked in case of error;...it has not always been used impartially among all economic and racial groups in America."

[35]Sellin and Campion collaborated (and testified before a Joint Committee of the Canadian Parliament in 1955) on an aspect of the deterrence question: "Does the Death Penalty Protect State Police?" Their empirical study of twenty-seven different police forces led them to conclude that it did not. The data and their reflections were reprinted by Hugo A. Bedau, ed., *The Death Penalty in America* (New York: Doubleday, 1964; rev. ed., 1967). Campion concluded: "The data available...do not lend empirical support to the claim that the existence of the death penalty in the statutes of a state provides a greater protection to the police than exists in states where that penalty has been abolished"(314).

[36]Donald R. Campion, S.J., *America* 102 (December 5, 1959), 321.

[37]Donal E. J. MacNamara, *America* 102 (January 16, 1960), 462.

[38]Donal E. J. MacNamara, "The Case against Capital Punishment," *Social Action* (April 1961), 4–15. This statement was also reprinted by Bedau, *The Death Penalty in America,* 182–94.

[39]John Cogley, "Capital Punishment and Caryl Chessman," *Commonweal* 71 (March 18, 1960), 671.

[40]Edmund (Pat) Brown with Dick Adler, *A Governor's Education on Death Row: Public Justice, Private Mercy* (New York: Knightsbridge Publishing Co., 1989), 42–46. An ironic aspect of this story is that Governor Brown, a staunch opponent of the death penalty, imposed it thirty-six times, while Governor Ronald Reagan, a staunch proponent of the death penalty, imposed it only once. The explanation, of course, is that most of Reagan's time as governor fell during the ten-year moratorium on killing, so he had little opportunity to impose it.

[41]Thomas J. Riley, "The Right of the State to Inflict Capital Punishment," *The Catholic Lawyer* 6 (1960), 279–85. The majority report is entitled "Capital Punishment: The Issues and the Evidence," 269–78 and 300. Riley taught moral theology at St. John's Seminary in Brighton, Massachusetts for twenty-five years. He was appointed auxil-

iary bishop of Boston and served in that capacity from 1959 till his retirement at 75 in 1976. He died in August 1977.

[42]S. J. Adamo, "Capital Punishment: Yes or No?," *Homiletic and Pastoral Review* 65 (1965), 300ff.

[43]William J. Bowers, *Legal Homicide: Death as Punishment in America, 1864–1982* (Boston, Mass.: Northeastern Univerrsity Press, 1984), 17.

[44]Donald R. Campion, S.J., "Capital Punishment," *New Catholic Encyclopedia,* 3:79–81.

[45]These final executions had their own bizarre aspects. Governor Ronald Reagan of California avoided any part in the hearing and let his clemency secretary, Edwin Meese, accelerate the process of getting Mitchell (who was raving "I am the Second Coming of Jesus Christ!") to the gas chamber as quickly as possible. Monge, like Gilmore ten years later, gave up all appeals and wanted to die, thus using the state as his assisted-suicide agency.

[46]See Melton, p. 120. Adopted by the General Board on September 13, 1968, by a 103–0 vote the statement concludes by urging the member churches to "actively promote the necessary legislation to secure (abolition), particularly in the 37 states which have not yet eliminated capital punishment."

1956 stands out as "the start of something new." As already noted, the Methodists, the United Church of Canada, the Unitarians and the Universalists had all gone public with formal statements of opposition.

In 1959 Reform Judaism took a forthright position. The statement of the Union of American Hebrew Congregations opposing capital punishment was the most fully developed formal objection of any that had been issued by an American religious body up to that time.

[47]Karl Menninger, *The Crime of Punishment* (New York: Penguin Books, 1968).

[48]Timing was another factor. Issued within months of the assassinations of Dr. Martin Luther King, Jr., and Sen. Robert Kennedy, and as the national controversy over Vietnam escalated, these other particular death-related concerns understandably received greater attention than the perennial capital-punishment issue.

9. The U.S. Bishops' Turnaround

[1]Attachment to a March 25, 1974, USCC communication to the bishops.

[2]"Capital Punishment: Grave Doubts," *Origins: NC Documentary Service* 1:32 (January 27, 1972), 529 and 531.

[3]Bedau, *Death Is Different*, 92.

[4]Jan Gorecki, *Capital Punishment: Criminal Law and Social Evolution* (New York: Columbia University Press, 1983), 10.

[5]Michael Meltsner, "On Death Row, the Wait Continues," in *The Burger Years: Rights and Wrongs in the Supreme Court 1969–1986*, ed. Herman Schwartz (New York: Viking, 1987), 170.

[6]Something of the drama involved in working toward a solution is captured by Thomas J. Reese, S.J., *A Flock of Shepherds: The NCCB* (Kansas City, Mo.: Sheed & Ward, 1992). Abolitionism could not be dismissed as one more conflict between "liberals" and "conservatives," since moral theologians from across the spectrum could now be found among its advocates.

[7]*Statements of the Catholic Bishops of Florida 1972–1983* (Florida Catholic Conference), 3.

[8]*Origins* 2:37 (March 8, 1973), 583f.

[9]*Origins* 2:41 (April 5, 1973), 650 and 659f.

[10]*Origins* 6:25 (Dec. 9, 1976), 395. Reprinted from a Dallas newspaper.

[11]Robert F. Drinan, S.J., *God and Caesar on the Potomac: A Pilgrimage of Conscience. Writings and Addresses on Justice and Peace* (Wilmington, De.: M. Glazier, 1985), 140f.

[12]Melton, 3.

[13]*Origins* carried all of the texts cited; they are also reprinted in Melton.

[14]Frs. McCormick and Curran had already made their own positions clear in writing that same year. The former had published his in *Theological Studies,* explaining that "Human life should be taken only when doing so is the lesser of two evils, all things considered....This is the *substance* of the Christian tradition if our best casuistry in other areas is carefully weighed and sifted; for the permissible exceptions with regard to life-taking (self-defense, just war, capital punishment, indirect killing) are all formulations and concretizations of what is viewed in the situation as the lesser human evil" (reprinted in McCormick, *Notes on Moral Theology 1965–1980* (Lanham, Md.: University Press of America, 1981), 515.

Fr. Curran had clearly articulated his position in more detail well before most others: "Traditionally, Catholic theology in the light of the state's obligation to protect the common good has accepted the right of the state to resort to capital punishment in cases of proportionately grave crimes. Today many theologians would disagree with the older teaching. Prudentially and historically it does not seem that capital punishment can be justified. One would have to justify capital punishment on the basis of the reasons for which punishment exists...1)...It does nothing to rehabilitate; 2)...It has not served as a salutary deterrent...3)...It is not the only way of vindicating justice. Why should another life be taken if this is not necessary? The original victim is not brought back to life by the death of the assailant. Often such a concept of vindictive justice seems closer to revenge than a just form of punishment. Since human life is so important a value, I do not think that the state should take human life when it cannot be shown to be absolutely necessary. But the arguments as proposed in favor of capital punishment do not in my judgment prove the need for [it]." (Charles E. Curran, "Human Life," *Chicago Studies* 13 (1974), 284.) This assessment accurately anticipated the general conclusion and the specific arguments that would be widely adopted in Catholic leadership circles over the following quarter-century.

[15]See, e.g., Germain G. Grisez, "Toward a Consistent Natural Law Ethics of Killing," *The American Journal of Jurisprudence* 15 (1970), 91: "Since I do not accept the justifiability of intentional killing, I do not see how capital punishment can be justified."

[16]Bishop Unterkoefler died in 1991. I express my gratitude to his former vicar general, Msgr. Charles H. Rowland, who, despite his busy schedule as pastor of St. Joseph's Church in Columbia, South Carolina, graciously researched and made copies for me of some of the bishop's file of material on capital punishment.

[17]Thomas Reese, S.J., ed., *Episcopal Conferences: Historical, Canonical & Theological Studies* (Georgetown University Press, 1989), 114; also in his *A Flock of Shepherds,* 149.

[18]Hugh J. Nolan, ed., *Pastoral Letters of the U.S. Catholic Bishops, vol. 3: 1962-1974* (Washington, D.C.: NCCB/USCC, 1983), 464.

[19]Melton, 3f.

[20]Page 3 of the typed draft (provided to the author by a USCC archivist).

[21]*Origins* 5:40 (March 25, 1976), 629.

[22]*Origins* 5:35 (February 19, 1976), 550.

[23]Lee Epstein and Joseph F. Kobylka, *The Supreme Court and Legal Change: Abortion and the Death Penalty* (Chapel Hill, N.C.: University of North Carolina Press, 1992), 113.

[24]Ibid.

[25]Richard O. Lempert, "Desert and Deterrence: An Evaluation of the Moral Bases for Capital Punishment," *The Penalty of Death: Final Report of the Annual Chief Justice Earl Warren Conference on Advocacy in the United States* (Washington, D.C.: The Roscoe Pound American Trial Lawyers Foundation, 1980), 87.

[26]Bedau, *Death Is Different,* 170.

[27]Epstein and Kobylka, 115f.

[28]See J. Seidler and K. Meyer, *Conflict and Change in the Catholic Church* (Rutgers University Press, 1989), 24f.

[29]All quotations are from Thomas G. Dailey, "The Church's Position on the Death Penalty in Canada and the United States," *Concilium* 120 (October 1978), 122.

[30]Mary Templer, *The Right to Life and Death: What Do Presbyterians Say?* M.A. thesis, University of Windsor, 1992. Quotations are from pages 11, 44, and 133.

[31]See Amnesty International, *When the State Kills,* 193.

[32]*Origins* 6 (December 9, 1976), 391.

[33]Ibid., 392–95.

[34]Ibid., 473f.

[35]The author went on to challenge all who would defend the state as having the right to destroy human life, then dismissed appeals to deterrence and security as irrelevant and superficial, and finally concluded: "Death is not the best solution; on the contrary, it seems to us it is the worst solution....In the light of faith, all spilling of human blood is an offense to God and to the life which he created. Christ died for all so that the crimes of Cain would no longer be multiplied."

[36]*Origins* 6:35 (February 17, 1977), 563.

[37]Ibid, 564. Bernardin continues: "I hope our leaders will seek methods of dealing with crime that are more consistent with the vision of respect for life and the gospel message of God's healing love." The final quotation is from USCC archival material.

[38]The studies of Marvin Wolfgang and others by this time had shown how heavily discriminatory the use of the death penalty against black men had been historically. Bowers summarizes the statistics on racial discrimination in state-imposed executions in U.S. history (67–102).

[39]*The Death Penalty: Amnesty International Report* (London: AI Publications, 1979), 199.

[40]*United States of America: The Death Penalty* (London: AI Publications, 1987) is an unusually comprehensive report with grim statistics, overall information, and gruesome details of the twentieth-century U.S. practice of the death penalty up to 1985. It recommends abolition on grounds of human decency (189).

[41]Alberto Iniesta, "The Death Penalty: Legislation and Practice in Spain," *Concilium* 120 (October 1978), 24f.

[42]*Origins* 8:44 (April 19, 1979), 693. A temporary stay of execution was granted the next day, but time ran out for Evans in 1983, when he died a horribly botched death in the electric chair. One of his lawyers,

Russell F. Canan, tells the gruesome story in "Burning at the Wire, the Execution of John Evans," in *Facing the Death Penalty: Essays on a Cruel and Unusual Punishment,* ed. Michael L. Radelet (Philadelphia, Pa.: Temple University Press, 1989), 60–80.

[43]*Origins* 9:6 (June 28, 1979), 81–84.

[44]During this period "the only men being executed in America were those who gave up on their appeals and demanded death. On October 22, 1979, in Nevada, Jesse Bishop went willingly to the executioner. No one was executed in 1980. In Indiana, Steven Judy was voluntarily executed on March 9, 1981. Then there was another hiatus of seventeen months before the next volunteer came along—Frank Brooks in Virginia....Across the country, state and federal courts were finding that their new laws...were in fact riddled with glitches. The death-row population...was greater than it had ever been, bumping up toward a thousand" (David von Drehle, *Among the Lowest of the Dead: The Culture of Death Row* [New York: Random House, 1995], 195).

[45]*Minutes of the 26th General Meeting of the USCC* (November 10–13, 1980), 18.

[46]René H. Gracida, "Capital Punishment and the Sacredness of Life," in *Shepherds Speak: American Bishops Confront the Social and Moral Issues that Challenge Christians Today,* ed. D. M. Corrado and J. F. Hinchey (New York: Crossroad, 1986), 108–25.

[47]*Origins* 10:7 (July 3, 1980), 101.

[48]Frank Butler, "A Terrible Farewell," *Our Sunday Visitor* (November 9, 1980), 9f. The six were Bishop Ernest Unterkoefler of Charleston, S.C.; Bishop René Gracida of Pensacola-Tallahassee, Fla.; Bishop Andrew Grutka of Gary, Ind.; Bishop John Morkovsky of Galveston-Houston and his auxiliary, Bishop John McCarthy; and Bishop Thomas Kelly, O.P., USCC general secretary.

[49]*Minutes,* 20f.

[50]Ibid., 22.

[51]Ibid., 24f.

[52]*Origins* 10:24 (November 27, 1980), 373–77.

[53]Quoted by George M. Anderson, S.J., "The Death Penalty in the United States: The Present Situation," *America* 147 (November 20, 1982), 307.

[54]*Origins* 10:40 (March 19, 1981), 626.

[55]*New York Times* (June 14, 1981), 28:1.

[56]Text included in Bondolfi, 275f. The high level of public frustration and anger over the brazen acts of organized crime was eloquently expressed by Giorgio Almirante, *Pena di Morte?* (Roma: Ciarrapico Editore, 1981). What was most unusual about his plea was the fact that he

knew and respected and accepted most of the renewed post–Vatican II thinking but desperately tried to make the case for terrorists being the one exception to the rule.

[57]*Origins* 11:1 (May 21, 1981), 15.

[58]One Catholic clergyman unimpressed by the bishops' opposition to the death penalty was Msgr. Alphonse Fiedorczyk. He had his moment of national attention while presiding at the funeral of a policeman killed by burglars in Darien, Connecticut. In the course of the burial service he publicly urged the two thousand officers and firemen in attendance to work for greater use of the death penalty to fight the growing crime rate. The most interesting thing was that this old-time Catholic position was considered rare enough to be reported as news (*New York Times,* June 4, 1981), II, 2:5.

[59]Amnesty International, *When the State Kills,* 183.

[60]*Origins* 11:41 (March 25, 1982), 646.

[61]*New York Times* (August 11, 1982), 1:1, and (August 12, 1982), 21:1.

[62]Frederick Drimmer, *Until You Are Dead: The Book of Executions in America* (New York: Citadel Press, 1990), 71f.

[63]Cf. "Execution by Injection: Doctors Say No," *Science Digest* (March 1984), 36: "Ward Cascells, a cardiologist at Massachusetts General Hospital and co-author of two articles in the *New England Journal of Medicine* on the subject, says that 'there are many potential complications that could result in a slow and painful death for the convict.'" This is a tertiary argument, after the principal ones: 1) No matter what the mode, it is improper for physicians, guardians of life, to function as its terminators, and 2) it is specious to designate any method "humane" that willfully destroys human life. Cf. Dow, "Physicians Ponder Role as the Agent of Death," *American Medical News* (September 4, 1987), 9.

[64]*New York Times* (January 16, 1983), I, 5:2

[65]*National Review* 35 (February 18, 1983), 207.

[66]See the editorial in *America* 149 (December 17 1983), 382. It concludes with the observation that "although their recent record for stopping executions is discouraging, as moral leaders the Pope and the bishops have no alternative but to continue their efforts to end this brutal and brutalizing form of criminal justice."

[67]*Origins* 13 (June 3, 1983), 74f.

[68]See *Breach of Trust: Physician Participation in Executions in the United States,* published jointly in 1994 by the American College of Physicians (Philadelphia, Pa.), Human Rights Watch (New York, Washington, Los Angeles, and London), National Coalition to Abolish the

Death Penalty (Washington, D.C.), and Physicians for Human Rights (Boston, Mass.).

[69]*New York Times* (September 2 1983), I. 10:1.

[70]CF. Arthur S. Miller and Jeffrey H. Bowman, *Death by Installments* (New York: Greenwood Press, 1990), 145.

[71]*Origins* 14:5 (June 14, 1984), 68, marginal note says "the bishops filed a friend-of-the-court brief on Sullivan's behalf in the Florida Supreme Court." Although it was denied, a federal appeals court judge granted a temporary stay. "During the two-day stay, Archbishop Edward McCarthy of Miami transmitted to Florida Gov. Bob Graham a message from Pope John Paul II, asking mercy for Sullivan. However, Graham did not accede to the pope's request and Sullivan was executed as scheduled, Nov. 30, in the electric chair."

[72]*The Christian Century* 100 (December 21–28, 1983), 1175.

[73]von Drehle, 219. The author goes on to note that "by the end of 1983, every state in the Death Belt had weighed in....The wheels appeared to be turning at last: Within a year, six executions had been carried out and none of them had been volunteers."

[74]According to the *Statistical Abstract of the United States 1994,* 114th ed., 218, the totals were: 1984—21; 1985—18; 1986—18; 1987—25; 1988—11; 1989—16; 1990—23; 1991—14; 1992—31.

[75]Joseph Bernardin, "A Consistent Ethic of Life: An American-Catholic Dialogue." The text of the lecture can be found in several places. It is the first in a series of ten talks published in *Consistent Ethic of Life* (Chicago, Ill.: Sheed & Ward, 1988), 1–19. This collection also contains four critiques and a response to each, presented by eight scholars at a symposium on the consistent-ethic held at Loyola of Chicago on November 7, 1987. It closes with a response from Bernardin, "The Consistent Ethic of Life: Stage Two" (245–56).

[76]Ibid., 5. The following quotation is on page 7.

[77]From a phone conversation with the author, recorded on December 29, 1994.

[78]An example of someone who apparently could not see the least reason for change was Raphael T. Waters, "The Moral Justification of Capital Punishment," *Social Justice Review* 73 (1982), 99–106. The essay is as grand an act of faith in the death penalty as can be found short of Joseph de Maistre. Unlike John Paul II's assessment of the abolitionist trend as a providential sign of our times, Waters maintained that one of the great disasters of our day "playing a major role in the destruction of society is the almost universal ban on capital punishment." Like other abstract romanticizations of state killings, this exercise in pre–Vatican II neo-Scholasticism has no reference anywhere to either the teaching

or spirit of Christ. Exterminating criminals is seen as part of the order of "nature...in an exercise of the noblest of civic virtues—political prudence exercised in matters of social justice." The reality of directly and intentionally killing a human person with full premeditation by officials of the state is carefully camouflaged in the most abstract language possible.

10. Consolidating Consistency (1984–1990)

[1] *Origins* 14:5 (June 14, 1984), 65–72.

[2] Cf. the editorial "Vengeance Is Wrong," *Christianity and Crisis* 44 (October 29, 1984), 388f: "In early July a Chapel Hill newspaper that supports Helms came out with an unsubstantiated, later retracted, front-page story under the headline 'Jim Hunt is Sissy, Prissy, Girlish and Effeminate.'...The goal of defeating Jesse Helms, however laudable an end, does not justify this execution as a means....The governor claims that his decision had nothing to do with politics. If that is the case, Mr. Hunt, why not leave vengeance to the Lord?"

[3] From the Epilogue in Velma Barfield, *Woman on Death Row* (Nashville, Tenn.: Oliver Nelson Books, a division of Thomas Nelson Publishers, 1985), 162.

[4] William H. Willimon, "Death in North Carolina," *The Christian Century* 101: 37 (November 28, 1984), 1116.

[5] *Origins* 14:20 (November 1, 1984), 306.

[6] *Origins* 14:28 (December 27, 1984), 471f.

[7] Haven Bradford Gow, "Should Religious Support Capital Punishment?" *Human Events* (March 2, 1985), reprinted as "Religious Views Support the Death Penalty," in *The Death Penalty: Opposing Viewpoints,* ed. D. L. Bender and B. Leone (St. Paul, Minn.: Greenhaven Press, 1986), 79–85. Gow is identified as "a Wilbur Foundation Literary Fellow in Arlington Heights, Illinois."

[8] The O'Reilly quotations were from his article "Why the Death Sentence Is Needed," *Homiletic and Pastoral Review* 84:8 (May 1984), 54–57, where he concluded with this prediction: "The present appalling number of murders being committed daily...will continue and possibly even increase until our legislators and courts (and our liberal theologians and at least some of our bishops) are finally forced to acknowledge what our average citizens knew all along, viz., that capital punishment...is the only effective barrier which can and will effectively stem and eventually reverse the crime wave now virtually sweeping our Country."

[9]Bernardin, 59–65.

[10]See Amnesty International, *When the State Kills*, 102f.

[11]Robert Hughes, *The Fatal Shore* (NY: Vintage Press, 1986).

[12]"A June 1987 report by the Clearinghouse on Georgia Jails and Prisons estimated that 20% of the prisoners under sentence of death in the state may have below-average intelligence or be severely mentally handicapped" (cited by Amnesty International, *When the State Kills*, 229).

[13]*New York Times* (September 7, 1985), I, 24:1. Cf. Mark Tushnet, *The Death Penalty* (Constitutional Issues v. 2) (New York: Facts on File, 1994), 131: "The Supreme Court's concern about delay exacerbates the problem of inadequate counsel....When defendants have inadequate lawyers and are rushed from sentencing to execution, the chance of a gross miscarriage of justice increases."

[14]Amnesty International, *When the State Kills*, 227.

[15]*Origins* 15:18 (October 17, 1985), 301–3.

[16]*Origins* 15:30 (January 9, 1986), 502.

[17]David Bruck, in *A Punishment in Search of a Crime: Americans Speak Out Against the Death Penalty*, ed. Ian Gray and Moira Stanley for Amnesty International U.S.A. (New York: Avon Books, 1989), 85.

[18]Bedau, *Death Is Different*, 147.

[19]Welsh S. White, *The Death Penalty in the Nineties: An Examination of the Modern System of Capital Punishment* (Ann Arbor, Mich.: University of Michigan Press, 1991), 207.

[20]Margaret Vandiver, "Capital Juror Interviews," in *The Machinery of Death*, ed. Enid Harlow, David Matos, and Jane Rocamora (New York: AIUSA, 1995), 75.

[21]Gregory D. Russell, *The Death Penalty and Racial Bias: Overturning Supreme Court Assumptions* (Westport, Conn.: Greenwood Press, 1994), 128.

[22]AIUSA: *The Death Penalty: Developments in 1987* (January 1988), summary.

[23]*Origins* 16:32 (January 22, 1987), 580.

[24]*Origins* 16:41 (March 26, 1987), 726–28.

[25]*USA: The Death Penalty* (London: Amnesty International Publications, 1987), 182–87.

[26]Juvenile Offender: Terry Roach; Mentally Ill: Alvin Ford, Arthur Goode, Odell Mason, Gary Alvord, David Funchess; Appeals Problems: Charlie Brooks, James Autry, Alvin Stephens, and Roosevelt Green.

[27]William J. Bowers, "Popular Support for the Death Penalty: Mistaken Beliefs," in Harlow, Matos, and Rocamora, 71f.

[28]Quoted by Louis D. Mitchell, "The Death Penalty under

Review Again," *The Month* 20 (October 1987), 381. Mitchell concludes that "if sentencing disparities are an inherent part of the jury
system, as Justice Powell offered in his majority position, it can logically be concluded that no government can fairly administer the
death penalty."

[29]David C. Baldus, George Woodworth, and Charles A. Pulaski,
Jr., *Equal Justice and the Death Penalty: A Legal and Empirical Analysis*
(Boston, Mass.: Northeastern University Press, 1990).

[30]Michael Kronenwetter, *Capital Punishment: A Reference Handbook*
(Santa Barbara, Calif.: ABC-CLIO, 1993), 38.

[31]Ibid., 39. For background on this case, see Phillip J. Cooper, *Battles on the Bench: Conflict Inside the Supreme Court* (Lawrence, Kan.: University Press of Kansas, 1995), 84ff.

[32]John C. Jeffries, Jr., *Justice Lewis F. Powell, Jr.* (New York: Chas.
Scribner's Sons, 1994), 451.

[33]*Origins* 16:47 (May 7, 1987), 818.

[34]Phoebe C. Ellsworth, "Unpleasant Facts: The Supreme Court's
Response to Empirical Research on Capital Punishment," in *Challenging Capital Punishment: Legal and Social Science Approaches,* K. C. Haas
and J. A. Inciardi (Newbury Park, Calif.: Sage Publications, 1988), 208.

[35]Waklimi tells his tragic story of legal injustice and describes the
bewildering humiliations to which he was subjected by the state of
Florida in Gray and Stanley, 210–15.

[36]*Origins* 17:4 (June 11, 1987).

[37]*London Tablet,* 246 (August 29, 1994), 1082. Congress reinstated
the death penalty seven years later (January 1994), not only for murder
but for a dozen other crimes as well, including rape. The United States
was obviously in no position to criticize.

[38]*New York Times* (March 5, 1989), I, 8:5.

[39]Bill Peske, "The Seeds of Compassion," in Harlow, Matos, and
Rocamora, 64–68. Marie Deans of Virginia founded MVFR.

[40]*New York Times* (January 28, 1988), I, 10:1.

[41]Quotations are in Gray and Stanley, 188 and 199.

[42]*Origins* 18:5 (June 16 1988), 76f.

[43]*New York Times* (September 20, 1988), II, 6:6.

[44]Ronald Hampton, "The Death Penalty: Racial Bias, Cost, and
the Risk of Executing the Innocent," in Harlow, Matos, and Rocamora,
101–4. Hampton is executive director of the National Black Police
Association, a specialist in developing community relations.

[45]Stephen Trombley, *The Execution Protocol: Inside America's Capital
Punishment Industry* (New York: Crown Publishers, 1992), 71f. He
recounts that the "manual" method, which Texas had already used on

over forty prisoners by the time he was writing, had been "plagued with glitches and botched executions...and about 80% had had one problem or another." Then he has Leuchter himself explain and describe his easy-death machine and how it came to be.

⁴⁶Ibid., 263.

⁴⁷*Origins* 18:46 (April 27, 1989), 789.

⁴⁸*New York Times* (May 1 1989), II, 6:6.

⁴⁹Edmund (Pat) Brown with Dick Adler, *A Governor's Education on Death Row: Public Justice, Private Mercy* (New York: Knightsbridge Publishing Co., 1989).

⁵⁰Emily F. Reed, *The Penry Penalty: Capital Punishment and Offenders with Mental Retardation* (Lanham, Md.: University Press of America, 1993), 1. Further, "his mother was only 18 when he was born and almost died from loss of blood during his difficult birth. She suffered a nervous breakdown...and was committed to a mental hospital for the first ten months of his life. When she returned home she began a decade long campaign of abuse and torture....Penry was burned with cigarette butts all over his body." At age 22 he raped and stabbed to death a woman who was the sister of a Dallas football star.

⁵¹*New York Times*, op-ed column (June 27, 1989), I, 2.

⁵²Emily Reed, 7.

⁵³Dale Aukerman, "The Execution of Ronnie Dunkins," *Christian Century* 106 (August 30, 1989), 785.

⁵⁴Michael Pakaluk, "Till Death Do Us Part: Does the Death Penalty Satisfy Christian Standards of Justice and Compassion?" *Crisis* 7 (1989), 23–28.

⁵⁵"Amnesty International's Report on Human Rights," in *Historic Documents of 1989* (Washington, D.C.: Congressional Quarterly, 1989), 597.

⁵⁶Text in *Commonweal* (April 20, 1990), 242–48.

⁵⁷Jay Robert Nash, "Capital Punishment," *Encyclopedia of World Crime*, IV: 3284.

⁵⁸Samuel A. Mills, "Parochiaid and the Abortion Decisions: Supreme Court Justice William J. Brennan, Jr., versus the U.S. Catholic Hierarchy," *Journal of Church and State* 34 (1992), 766.

⁵⁹*Origins* 20:16 (September 27, 1990), 263f.

⁶⁰Thurgood Marshall, "Dispatch the System, Not the Man" (dissenting opinion), reprinted in *Harper's Magazine* (January 1991), 28ff.

11. New Setbacks and Advances (1991–1996)

[1]Timothy M. Phelps and Helen Winternitz, *Capitol Games* (New York: Hyperion, 1992), 162.

[2]Carl T. Rowan, *Dream Makers, Dream Breakers: The World of Justice Thurgood Marshall* (Boston, Mass.: Little, Brown & Co., 1993), 381.

[3]Ibid., 386.

[4]*New York Times* (September 17 1991), A, 14:3.

[5]Stephen B. Bright, "Race, Poverty and Disadvantage in the Infliction of the Death Penalty in the Death Belt," in Amnesty International, *The Machinery of Death*, 124. See also W. Witzhigh Brundage, *Lynchings in the New South* (Urbana, Ill.: University of Illinois Press, 1993).

[6]The Andrew Lee Jones Fund was set up to help able law students with intern awards and scholarships. Its administrative office is at 199 Strand, London, WC2R 1DR.

[7]*Origins* 21:32 (January 16 1992), 517.

[8]Ibid. In addition to Catholic Bishop Thomas O'Brien of Phoenix, the signers included Episcopal, Lutheran, Presbyterian, Quaker, UCC, Christian (Disciples), and Unitarian-Universalist leaders.

[9]Quoted in the Catholics Against Capital Punishment newsletter (hereafter CACP) (June 17, 1992), I:3, 2.

[10]*Origins* 21:47 (April 30, 1992).

[11]Wendy Lesser, *Pictures at an Execution: An Inquiry into the Subject of Murder* (Cambridge, Mass.: Harvard University Press, 1993).

[12]*London Tablet* 246 (May 2, 1992).

[13]Based in Arlington, Virginia, the national coordinator, Frank McNeirney, organized this group with the hope that it could "encourage Catholic members of Congress to push harder for an end to capital punishment."

[14]CACP 1:4 (July 30, 1992), 4. For details of Pierrepoint's career, see Brian Bailey, *Hangmen of England* (New York: Barnes & Noble, 1992), 157–83.

[15]Mario Cuomo, quoted on the dust jacket of the book published by Northeastern University Press.

[16]*Origins* 23:42 (April 2, 1994), 736. A "first reading" during this curious period of unexplained delay of the English version had been offered by Lawrence S. Cunningham, "The New Catechism," *Commonweal* 120:5 (March 12, 1993), 8–12, including the observation that "there is no evidence that contemporary biblical criticism has made any impact on the catechism's formulation" (10).

[17]The *London Tablet* monitored reactions throughout the early

months and devoted its May 28, 1994, issue to various perspectives, including those of Bernard Häring and Hans Küng.

[18]CACP 5:2 (June 10, 1996), 1: "The official Latin text of the *Catechism of the Catholic Church*...may include a more definitive and stronger denunciation of the death penalty than the initial modern-language editions, it was indicated recently by Catholic News Service." The information was attributed to Archbishop Crescenzio Sepe. In first introducing the catechism, Bishop Allessandro Maggiolini, a member of the commission that drafted it, had acknowledged that in searching for a justified execution nowadays it was "hard to find an example that is morally clear" (quoted in a report by Kenneth Woodward, et al., "New Rules for an Old Faith," *Newsweek* [November 30, 1992], 71).

[19]McHugh and Callan, 421.

[20]Dennis O'Callaghan, "Debating the Death Penalty," *The Furrow* 43 (1992), 610–16.

[21]Cf. Paolo Ferrari da Passano, S.J., "La Pena di Morte nel Catechismo della Chiesa Cattolica," *La Civiltà Cattolica* (1993 IV), 14–26, and Charles DeCelles, "The American Bishops and Capital Punishment," *Social Justice Review* 84 (September-October 1993), 152: "To replace capital punishment with something less brutal when possible is to act more in tune with the message of Jesus. It is to attain a higher level of ethical sensitivity. To rise to a higher level of ethics is what the American bishops are challenging us to do."

[22]O'Callaghan, 616.

[23]Pierre Moreau, "Autour de la peine de mort," *Lumière et Vie* #216 (Février 1994) 43:71–83, defends the catechism's position by making a distinction between morality and law, contending that the death penalty should be kept on the books, "si minime soit-elle," for symbolic purposes. He finds "Never again!" appropriate words for an exorcist but not for "a politician or legislator who must be ever ready to adapt to new situations." He seems to overlook the superior symbolism of abolition.

[24]Francesco Compagnoni, "La Pena di Morte nel 'Catechismo della Chiesa Cattolica,'" *Rivista di Teologia Morale* 25 (1993), 266.

[25]CACP 2:1 (January 29, 1993), 2.

[26]Albert Chapelle, quoted by Cindy Wooden, Catholic News Service, *North Carolina Catholic* (October 24, 1993), 1.

[27]Ibid., 8.

[28]Rev. Kevin A. Codd, "The Hanging of Westley Allan Dodd," *America* (January 30, 1993), 5f.

[29]Cf. J. W. Marquart, S. Ekland-Olson, J. R. Sorensen, *The Rope, the Chair, and the Needle: Capital Punishment in Texas, 1923–1990* (Austin, Tex.: University of Texas, 1994), 195f.

[30]Quoted in CACP 2:3 (April 28, 1993), 1f.

[31]Michael Meltsner, "The Late Justice," *The Nation* (February 15, 1993), 198.

[32]Garry Wills, "Living Others' Deaths," *The New York Review of Books* (September 23, 1993), 3.

[33]Helen Prejean, *Dead Man Walking: An Eyewitness Account of the Death Penalty in the United States* (New York: Random House, 1993).

[34]Walter McMillian, "Statement to the U.S. Senate Judiciary Committee, April 1, 1993," in Harlow, Matos, and Rocamora, 156–62. In 1996 the court ruled that McMillian could sue for damages.

[35]Belisario Dos Santos, Jr., "The Human Rights Context," in Harlow, Matos, and Rocamora, 188f.

[36]*Origins* 24:1 (May 19, 1994), 2.

[37]*Origins* 24:3 (June 2, 1994), 2.

[38]*Historic Documents of 1994:* "Blackmun Renunciation of the Death Penalty, February 22, 1994," 161–171 (Washington, D.C.: Congressional Quarterly, 1994).

[39]Ibid. Blackmun's public statement about his change of heart did have a significant impact in that it inspired the Minnesota Advocates for Human Rights to create the Justice Harry A. Blackmun Education Project "to show the public what Justice Blackmun saw...to bring to the public debate the facts about capital punishment in the United States."

[40]*Origins* 24:38 (March 9, 1995), 627.

[41]*Origins* 24:45 (April 27, 1995), 766.

[42]English translation in *Origins* 24:42 (April 6, 1995).

[43]Ricardo J. Quinones, *The Changes of Cain: Violence and the Lost Brother in Cain and Abel Literature* (Princeton, N.J.: Princeton University Press, 1991), 245.

[44]Richard A. McCormick, S.J., "The Gospel of Life," *America* 172:15 (April 29, 1995), 12.

[45]Lino Ciccone, *Non Uccidere: Questioni di Morale della Vita Fisica* (Milano: Edizioni Ares, 1984), 82, notes the two positions and the fact that "some episcopal statements, e.g., the U.S. and the Canadian, explicitly affirm that the state has such a right, whereas others, like the French, leave themselves open to the opposite thesis, even while not explicitly saying so. It is, however, an extremely significant fact that not one—neither an episcopal conference nor an individual bishop—has taken a public stand in favor of continued use of the death penalty today."

[46]Bruno Schüller, S.J., "Todesstrafe," *Lexikon für Theologie und Kirche* (Freiburg: Herder Verlag, 1965) X: 230, found at least three different tendencies in the ways in which earlier moralists dealt with the so-called "right of the state to kill" question. He elaborated somewhat on

two of them later in *Die Begründung sittlicher Urteile: Typen ethischer Argumentation in der Moraltheologie* (Düsseldorf: Patmos Verlag, 1980), 245ff.

[47]James Joyce, S.J., "Capital Punishment: A Hard Saying," *Church* 3:3 (1987), 28.

[48]John Howard Yoder, "A Christian Perspective," *The Death Penalty in America*, ed. H. A. Bedau, 3d ed. (New York: Oxford University Press, 1982), 374, makes the crucial point that "Christians, especially Christians who at other times and places have testified to their high respect for the sacredness of human life, are letting their silence speak for them. Their indifference testifies that as far as they are concerned this matter is one about which the Lord they profess to represent has no opinion. Is this silent testimony of conformity the one we want to give? If we confess his lordship, we must believe....If we believe it we must proclaim that killing criminals is not God's will, even for a sub-Christian society."

[49]*Origins* 25:5 (June 15, 1995), 86.

[50]John Langan, S.J., "Capital Punishment," in *The HarperCollins Encyclopedia of Catholicism*, ed. Richard P. McBrien (San Francisco, Calif.: HarperSanFrancisco, 1995), 224f.

[51]John Langan, S.J., "Human Rights in Catholicism," *Human Rights in Religious Traditions*, ed. Arlene Swidler (New York: Pilgrim Press, 1982), 32.

[52]J. Bryan Hehir, "Consistent Ethic of Life," *The HarperCollins Encyclopedia of Catholicism*, 358f.

[53]Lynne Duke, "South Africa Abolishes Death Penalty," *The Washington Post* (June 7, 1995), A25.

[54]Robert F. Drinan, S.J., "Even South Africa Drops Death Penalty," *National Catholic Reporter* (July 28, 1995), 20.

[55]*New York Times* (January 21, 1996), iv, 2:1.

[56]Quoted in CACP 5:1 (April 26, 1996), 5.

[57]Ibid., 4.

[58]Ibid., 1. There was plenty of media coverage, usually praising or blaming the cardinal rather than analyzing his statement.

[59]Dateline Geneva, AP wire, July 16, 1996.

12. Instead of a Conclusion

[1]Cf., however, Thomas M. Gannon, S.J., ed., *World Catholicism in Transition* (New York: Macmillan, 1988), especially the opening chapter by David Martin, "Catholicism in Transition," 3–35; and chapter six by Aurelio Orensanz, "Spanish Catholicism in Transition," which ends

with these words: "The church played a significant role in bringing Franco into power and in eroding that power, in bringing about social-ism and in criticizing it. Few churches in Western Europe keep a similar check against the megalomania and mythology of the state. The frag-mentation of the Spanish church into various tendencies, movements, theological schools and sensitivities will always be a safeguard against its own errors and the errors of Spanish society at large"(145).

[2]Germain Grisez, *The Way of the Lord Jesus,* vol. 2, *Living a Christ-ian Life* (Quincy, Ill.: Franciscan Press, 1993), 893f.

[3]Roderich Martis, *Die Funktionen der Todesstrafe: eine kritische Analyse zur Realität der Todesstrafe in der Gegenwart* (Bonn: Forum Verlag Godes-berg, 1991), 281. The different functions of the death penalty can be iden-tified empirically, no matter what the "party line" might claim. There are usually combinations of them, some acknowledged, some not. The scape-goat function is usually there; at the level of the political decision-maker the symbolic function of the no-nonsense statesman is important; but above all is the function of instrument of repression, which makes for great campaign rhetoric in power-politics ("tough on crime") but invari-ably results also in allowing all the abuses of power that go with it.

[4]Msgr. Giovanni B. Guzzetti, "Pena di Morte e Morale Cattolica," *La Rivista del Clero Italiano* (Milano: Vita e Pensiero, 1981), 750–63. The flurry of activities and writings about the death penalty in the early 1980s was largely the result of calls for its reintroduction as a response to terrorism. Msgr. Guzzetti, a widely known moral theologian on the Theological Faculty of Milan, wrote this impressive piece to show how "the Christian world took no part, neither its theologians nor its hierar-chy," in the early nineteenth-century abolitionist movement, but rather supported executions uncritically. But he notes a change in the second half of that century, as a group of more enlightened manualists began to highlight the distinction between the "question of right" (principle) and the "question of fact" (application). He counts M. Liberatore and T. Meyer in the first group, forerunners of change, and D. Prümmer and A. Vermeersch in the latter, guardians of the tradition.

[5]There were others who went farther than Skoda in this regard. Cf., e.g., Bertrand de Margerie, "Prohibe o desaconseja la revelación de Cristo la pena de muerte?" *Tierra Nueva* 45 (1963), 12–20. N. Blázquez, O.P., *Estado de Derecho y Pena de Muerte* (Madrid: Noticias, 1989) gives an analysis and blistering review of this and a later article by the same author in *Revue Thomiste* 3 (1983), 349–417, describing them as "unfortunate, distorted, and shocking" in their rabid defense of capital punishment.

[6]A. Messineo, S.J., "Il diritto alla vita," *Civiltà Cattolica* (1960/II), 449–62.

[7]"Riflessioni sulla pena di morte," *Civiltà Cattolica* (1981/I), 417–28. The author took note of the growing number of Catholic abolitionists and accounted for this as due "above all to a more profound comprehension of the spirit of the gospel and of the functions of the church in the modern world." Of course, there had been a few articles in the interim that had already heralded the change, one in 1976 and another in 1979. The former, by G. Perico ("Ritorno alla Pena di Morte?"), said that due to the changes in historical conditions, a penal system that retained the death penalty in our day "appeared to be more and more anachronistic and inopportune." The latter, by Giovanni Caprile, S.J., ("Recenti Orientamenti Episcopali sul Problema della Pena Capitale," 148–63), covered approvingly the worldwide movement of Catholic bishops conferences, including the U.S. bishops, to speak out against the death penalty.

[8]"Catholicus," *Pena di Morte e Chiesa Cattolica: Annotazioni Critiche* (Roma: Giovanni Volpe, 1981), 30: In the preface he speaks of "priests, pastors and professors of religion here and there who ceaselessly make pronouncements expressing only their personal, questionable, opinions. But what would have to be said if one deferred to the doctrine universally taught up to yesterday, faithful to the unanimous tradition of Catholic thought?" In answer he devotes 100 pages to covering much the same ground as Skoda had a quarter-century earlier. The major concern was to defend as sacred the right of the state to kill. That was denied "only by some Protestants, like the Anabaptists and Waldensians, and later by philosophers and jurists of the Enlightenment...but in the Church the theological literature has always unanimously recognized the civil authority's right to inflict the death penalty."

He recounts that his manuscript had already been handed over to the publisher when the *Civiltà Cattolica* editorial appeared, causing the author to dash off a twenty-five-page rebuttal as an appendix. He was agitated by developments since Vatican II, especially "the absurd opposition of many presumed Catholics who, deceived by the hypocritical propaganda of leftist parties...raise scandalous voices against one of the most elementary rights-duties of human society, defended as legitimate by the Church of all times" (49). He was convinced that only pacifist infiltration of the church could account for this putting aside of the right of the state which "all the 'manuals' of moral theology and philosophy indicate as 'certain,' "una dottrina solidissima universalmente insegnata, accettata, praticata." Then comes the long list of consenting manualists: Scavini, Gury, Ballerini, Tummolo, Iorio, Telch, Bonacina, Merkelbach, Aertnys,

Damen, Arregui, Sebastiani, Ferreres, and Tanquerey "the very prince of manualists, known by all Italian priests" (122).

[9]Melton, 2. Cf. also Philip S. Keane, S.S., *Christian Ethics and Imagination* (New York: Paulist Press, 1984), 133: "What happens imaginatively or symbolically when we deliberately put someone to death?...Capital punishment always raises the question: Can we afford to say about ourselves what capital punishment says about us?"

[10]Jean-Marie Aubert, *Chrétiens et Peine de Mort* (Paris: Relais Desclée, 1978).

[11]Brigitte Andre, "Un événement considérable," *Informations Catholiques Internationales* #523 (Février 1978), reviewed the emotional reactions from left to right found in the French press, summing them up thus: "[The bishops' statement] came too soon, it came too late; it was the right time, it was the wrong time....Has there ever been the proper 'moment' for preaching the Gospel?"(14).

[12]William Bosworth, *Catholicism and Crisis in Modern France: French Catholic Groups at the Threshold of the Fifth Republic* (Princeton, N.J.: Princeton University Press, 1962), 183. The second quotation is from 319f. The situation he describes is not unlike what happened in some U.S. Catholic circles after Vatican II.

[13]Spain abolished capital punishment that same year (1978), and Ireland did likewise in 1990.

[14]Aubert, 44f.

[15]For a graphic English translation of Villon's stark poems, see Robert H. Anacker, *François Villon* (New York: Twayne Publishers, 1968), 95f. ("Facing Execution"). For a sketch of the skyline with Notre Dame and the great gibbet, see Robert Laffont, ed., *Histoire de Paris et des Parisiens* (Paris: Pont Royal, 1958), 54.

[16]Aubert, 67.

[17]Ibid., 90f.

[18]See Amnesty International, *When the State Kills,* 134. "Between 1966 and 1977 nine people...were executed by guillotine [in France]. The last execution was carried out on 10 September, 1977....Seven people were under sentence of death when the death penalty was abolished [1981]."

[19]Blázquez, *Estado de Derecho y Pena de Muerte,* 43.

[20]Ibid., 169f.

[21]Ibid., 185.

[22]Msgr. Igino Cardinale, "Declaration," *La Documentation Catholique* #1790 (1980), 701.

[23]Concetti, quoted in Blázquez, *Estado,* 195.

[24]Ibid., 197, and Blázquez, *Los Derechos del Hombre* (Madrid, 1980).

²⁵Ibid., 199.

²⁶Gino Concetti, O.F.M., "Può ancora ritenersi legittima la pena di morte?" *L'Osservatore Romano* (January 23, 1977), 1.

²⁷Gino Concetti, O.F.M. *"Pena di Morte* (Roma: Piemme, 1993). His summary of the six authors mentioned takes up pages 26–35.

²⁸Anselm Günthör, *Chiamata e risposta* (Roma: Edizioni Paoline, 1977), III, 557f.

²⁹Häring, C.SS.R. *Free and Faithful in Christ,* vol. 3: *Light to the World* (New York: Crossroad, 1981), 37f. The English and Italian versions both appeared in 1981, but the German was out already in 1978.

³⁰Bernard Häring, C.SS.R., *The Healing Power of Peace and Nonviolence* (New York: Paulist Press, 1986).

³¹S. Spinsanti, *Vita fisica,* in T. Goffi and G. Piana, eds., *Corso di Morale, vol. 2: Diakonia* (Brescia: Queriniana, 1983), 254–56.

³²Ciccone, 92.

³³K. H. Peschke, *Etica Christiana* II (Roma: Pontificia Università Urbaniana, 1985), 366–69.

³⁴M. Vidal, *L'Etica Christiana* (Roma: Borla, 1992), 226f.

³⁵Concetti, *Pena di Morte,* 84–89.

³⁶William A. Schabas, *The Abolition of the Death Penalty in International Law* (Cambridge, England: Grotius Publications, 1993), 285f.

³⁷Ibid.

³⁸See Schabas's summary of the international situation in Harlow, Matos, and Rocamora, 22ff.

³⁹Robert Cario, ed., *La Peine de Mort au Seuil de Troisième Millénaire: Hommage au Professeur Antonio Beristain* (Toulouse: Editions Erès, 1993).

⁴⁰Antonio Beristain, "Capital Punishment and Catholicism," *International Journal of Criminology and Penology* 5 (1977), 321–35. Beristain explained that he wrote this article in the summer of 1975 in Freiburg, Germany, when Franco was still in charge in Spain. In that context he said: "We shall disregard almost entirely the opinions of the ecclesiastical hierarchy. For many centuries the official representatives of the church have so identified themselves with the holders of power, so neglected the defense of the weak and the oppressed, that they have even posed the problem of the death penalty in a manner contrary to that required by the Gospel."

⁴¹Leonard L. Cavise, "La Peine de Mort aux Etats-Unis," in Cario, chap. 4, 35–53.

⁴²Jean Pinatel, "La Peine de Mort," in Cario, chap. 1, 13f. The four organizations are: The International Association of Penal Law, headed by H. Jescheck (neutral as an organization); The International Society

of Social Defense, described as strongly abolitionist by leader S. Rozès; The International Penal and Penitentiary Foundation, led by Norwegian H. Röstad, who noted that the majority of its member-states were totally abolitionist; and The International Society of Criminology, for which G. Canepa reported "two essential conclusions: (1) that research old and new has found no grounds for believing the death penalty deters; and (2) that from a criminological viewpoint the death penalty violates the goals of both resocialization and prevention."

[43]Pierre Marbot, "La Peine de Mort dans le Monde d'aujourd'hui," in Cario, chap. 2, 16f.

[44]Beristain's essay is chapter 5 (55–71); Csonka's is chapter 8 (105–21).

[45]Beristain, in Cario, 60f. The rest of the essay turns to other reflections that are not yet common: the philosophical and theological implications of purposely destroying and of approving the destruction of human beings. Such nihilism is incompatible with religious faith. A philosophical counterpart of this discussion revolved around Leonardo Sciascia's *Porte Aperte* (Milano: Adelphi, 1987). Cf. Francesco D'Agostino, "*Porte Aperte:* La Pena di Morte come Problema," *Rivista Internazionale di Filosofia del Diritto* 69 (1992), 393–403.

[46]Walter Harrelson, *The Ten Commandments and Human Rights* (Philadelphia, Pa.: Fortress Press, 1980), 119f.

[47]See Christina M. Cerna, "U.S. Death Penalty Before the Inter-American Commission on Human Rights," *Netherlands Quarterly of Human Rights* 10 (1992), 155–65.

[48]Csonka, 121.

[49]For a recent example of the problems created by resistance to change, see John M. Haas, "*The Gospel of Life* and the Death Penalty," *Crisis* 13 (July-August 1995), 20–23. He comes to the conclusion that "Catholics who have opposed abortion but supported capital punishment...are not holding contradictory positions but are being consistent." Such use of language complicates the educational task to say the least.

[50]Avery Dulles, S.J., *The Reshaping of Catholicism* (San Francisco: Harper & Row, 1988), 44f.

[51]Peter J. Riga, "Capital Punishment and the Right to Life: Some Reflections on the Human Right as Absolute," *University of Puget Sound Law Review* 5 (1981), 35ff.

BIBLIOGRAPHY

Abailard, Peter. *Sic et Non: A Critical Edition.* Translated by Blanche B. Boyer and Richard McKeon. Chicago: University of Chicago Press, 1977.

Abbott, Geoffrey. *The Book of Executions: An Encyclopedia of Methods of Judicial Execution.* London: Headline, 1994.

Adamo, Salvatore J. "Capital Punishment: Yes or No?" *Homiletic and Pastoral Review* 65 (1965): 300ff.

Aland, Kurt. *A History of Christianity: From the Beginnings to the Threshold of the Reformation.* Volume 1. Translated by James L. Schaaf. Philadelphia, Pa.: Fortress Press, 1985.

——. *A History of Christianity: From the Reformation to the Present.* Volume 2. Translated by James L. Schaaf. Philadelphia, Pa.: Fortress Press, 1986.

Althaus, Paul. *Die Todesstrafe als Problem der christlichen Ethik.* München: Verlag der Bayerischen Akademie der Wissenschaften, 1955.

Anacker, Robert H. *François Villon.* New York: Twayne Publishers, 1968.

Anderson, George M., S.J. "The Death Penalty in the United States: The Present Situation." *America* 147 (November 20, 1982), 307ff.

Andrieux, Maurice. *Daily Life in Papal Rome in the 18th Century.* New York: Macmillan, 1969.

——. *Rome.* Translated by Charles Lam Markmann. New York: Funk & Wagnalls, 1968.

Ariès, Philippe. *The Hour of Our Death.* Translated by Helen Weaver. New York: Oxford University Press, 1981.

Armstrong, Karen. *Holy War: The Crusades and Their Impact on Today's World.* New York: Doubleday, 1991.

Arnold, Benjamin. *German Knighthood 1050–1300.* Oxford: Clarendon Press, 1985.

Atwater, Richard, ed. *The Secret History of Procopius.* New York: Dorset Press, 1992.

Aubert, Jean-Marie. *Chrétiens et Peine de Mort.* Paris: Desclée, 1978.

Aukerman, Dale. "The Execution of Ronnie Dunkins." *Christian Century* 106 (August 30, 1989), 785ff.

Bacon, Margaret H. *The Quiet Rebels: The Story of the Quakers in America.* New York: Basic Books, 1969.

Bailey, Brian. *Hangmen of England: The History of Execution from Jack Ketch to Albert Pierrepont.* New York: Barnes & Noble, 1992.

Baker, Derek, ed. *Schism, Heresy and Religious Protest.* Papers of the Ecclesiastical History Society. Cambridge University Press, 1972.

Baldus, David C., George Wordsworth, Charles A. Pulaski, Jr. *Equal Justice and the Death Penalty: A Legal and Empirical Analysis.* Boston, Mass.: Northeastern University Press, 1990.

Baldwin, John W. *Masters, Princes, and Merchants: The Social Views of Peter the Chanter and His Circle.* I—Text; II—Notes. Princeton, N.J.: Princeton University Press, 1970.

Balke, Willem. *Calvin and the Anabaptist Radicals.* Grand Rapids, Mich.: Eerdmans, 1981.

Barfield, Velma. *Woman on Death Row.* Nashville, Tenn.: Oliver Nelson Books, 1985.

Barker, Ernest, ed. *From Alexander to Constantine: Passages and Documents.* Oxford: Clarendon Press, 1956.

Barker, Lynn K. *History, Reform and Law in the Work of Ivo of Chartres.* Ph.D. dissertation (microfiche). University of North Carolina, 1988.

Barraclough, Geoffrey. *The Medieval Papacy.* New York: Harcourt Brace, 1968.

——, ed. *The Christian World: A Social and Cultural History.* New York: Harry N. Abrams, 1981.

Barstow, Anne Llewellyn. *Witchcraze: A New History of the European Witch Hunts.* San Francisco, Calif.: Pandora/Harper, 1994.

Basler, H. "Thomas von Aquin und die Begründung der Todesstrafe." *Divus Thomas* 9 (1931): 70–202.

Beccaria, Cesare. *On Crimes and Punishment.* Translated by H. Paolucci. Indianapolis, Ind.: Anonymous, 1963.

Bedau, Hugo Adam. *The Courts, the Constitution and Capital Punishment.* Lexington, Mass., and Toronto, 1977: Lexington Books and D. C. Heath & Co., 1977.

——. *The Death Penalty in America.* New York: Oxford University Press, 1964 and 1982.

——. *Death Is Different.* Boston, Mass.: Northeastern University Press, 1987.

——, ed. *The Death Penalty in America.* New York: Oxford University Press, 1982.

Beirne, Piers. *Inventing Criminology: Essays on the Rise of "Homo Criminalis."* Albany: SUNY Press, 1993.

Bellamy, John. *Crime and Public Order in England in the Later Middle Ages.* London: Routledge & Kegan Paul, 1973.

Bellarmine, Robert. *De Laicis sive Saecularibus: The Treatise on Civil Government.* Edited and translated by Katherine E. Murphy. New York: Fordham University Press, 1928.

Ben-Jehuda, Nachman. "Witchcraft and the Occult as Boundary Maintenance Devices." *Religion, Science and Magic.* Edited by J. Neusner, E. S. Frerichs, and P. V. M. Flesher. New York: Oxford University Press, 1989.

Bender, Harold. *Conrad Grebel.* Scottsdale, Pa.: Herald Press, 1950.

Benestad, J. Brian. *The Pursuit of a Just Social Order: Policy Statements of the U.S. Catholic Bishops, 1966–80.* Washington, D.C.: Ethics and Public Policy Center, 1982.

Berger, Peter. *The Precarious Vision.* New York: Doubleday, 1962.

Beristain, Antonio. "Capital Punishment and Catholicism." *International Journal of Criminology and Penology* 5 (1977): 321–35.

Berlin, Isaiah. *The Crooked Timber of Humanity: Chapters in the History of Ideas.* New York: Alfred A. Knopf, 1991.

Berman, Harold J. *Law and Revolution: The Formation of the Western Legal Tradition.* Cambridge, Mass.: Harvard University Press, 1983.

Bernardin, Joseph Cardinal. *Consistent Ethic of Life.* Chicago: Sheed & Ward, 1988.

Bertelli, Sergio, Franco Cardini, and Elvira Garbero Zorzi. *The Courts of the Italian Renaissance.* New York: Facts on File Publications, 1985.

Blassingame, John W., ed. *The Frederick Douglass Papers.* Volume 3 (1855–1863). New Haven, Conn.: Yale University Press, 1979.

Blázquez, Niceto Fernández, O.P. *Estado de Derecho y Pena de Muerte.* Madrid: Noticias, 1989.

——. "La pena de muerte: Lectura crítica del pensamiento de Santo Tomás." *Studia Moralia* 23 (1985): 107–28.

——. *La pena de muerte según san Agustín.* Madrid: Ediciones Augustinus Revista, 1975.

——. *Los Derechos del Hombre.* Madrid, 1980.

Blidstein, Gerald J. "Capital Punishment—The Classical Jewish Discussion." *Judaism* 14 (1965), 164.

Block, Eugene B. *When Men Play God: The Fallacy of Capital Punishment.* San Francisco, Calif.: Cragmont Publishing Co., 1983.

Blumenthal, Uta-Renate. *The Investiture Controversy: Church and Monarchy from the 9th to 12th Century.* Philadelphia, Pa.: University of Pennsylvania Press, 1988.

Bolton, Brenda. "Tradition and Temerity: Papal Attitudes to Deviants,

1159–1216." In *Schism, Heresy and Religious Protest.* Edited by Derick Baker. New York: Cambridge University Press, 1972.

Bondolfi, Alberto. *Pena e Pena di Morte. Temi etici nella storia.* Edited by Luigi Lorinzetti. Bologna: Edizioni Dehoniani, 1985.

Bosworth, William. *Catholicism and Crisis in Modern France: French Catholic Groups at the Threshold of the Fifth Republic.* Princeton, N.J.: Princeton University Press, 1962.

Bowers, William J. *Legal Homicide: Death as Punishment in America, 1864–1982.* Boston, Mass.: Northeastern University Press, 1984.

———. "Popular Support for the Death Penalty: Mistaken Beliefs." In *The Machinery of Death.* New York: Amnesty International USA, 1995.

Braithwaite, William C. *The Beginnings of Quakerism.* Second edition. Revised by Henry J. Cadbury. Cambridge University Press, 1961. First edition 1912.

Brandt, Richard B. *The Philosophy of Schleiermacher: The Development of His Theory of Scientific and Religious Knowledge.* New York: Greenwood Press, 1968.

Bredero, Adriaan H. *Christendom and Christianity in the Middle Ages: The Relations Between Religion, Church, and Society.* Translated by Reinder Bruinsma. Grand Rapids, Mich.: Eerdmans, 1994. Dutch original 1986.

Brinton, Howard H. *Friends for 300 Years: The History and Beliefs of the Society of Friends Since George Fox Started the Quaker Movement.* Reprint by Pendle Hill Publications in 1965 of 1952 edition. New York: Harper & Row, 1952.

Brock, Peter de Beauvoir. *The Political and Social Doctrines of the Unity of Czech Brethren in the 15th and early 16th Centuries.* Volume 11. Slavistic Printings and Reprintings. Edited by C. H. van Schooneveld. Leiden University's-gravenhage: Mouton & Co., 1957.

———. *The Quaker Peace Testimony 1660–1914.* York, England: Sessions, 1990.

———. *Studies in Peace History.* York, England: Sessions, 1991.

Brown, Edmund (Pat), with Dick Adler. *A Governor's Education on Death Row: Public Justice, Private Mercy*. New York: Knightsbridge Publishing Co., 1989.

Brown, Peter. *Augustine of Hippo: a Biography*. New York: Dorset Press, 1967.

——. "St. Augustine's Attitude to Religious Coercion." *Journal of Roman Studies* 54 (1964): 107–16.

Brundage, James A. "Holy War and the Medieval Lawyers." In *The Holy War*. Edited by Thomas Patrick Murphy. Columbus, Ohio: Ohio State University Press, 1976.

——. *Medieval Canon Law and the Crusader*. Madison, Wis.: University of Wisconsin Press, 1969.

Brundage, W. Witzhigh. *Lynchings in the New South*. Urbana, Ill.: University of Illinois Press, 1993.

Buchanan, E. S., ed. *Lamartine Impugns Capital Punishment (3 speeches 1836–1838)*. New York: Charles A. Swift, 1930.

Buchanan, William J. *Execution Eve*. Far Hills, N.J.: New Horizons Press, 1993.

Bull, Marcus. *Knightly Piety and the Lay Response to the First Crusade: The Limousin and Gascony, c. 970–c.1130*. Oxford: Clarendon Press, 1993.

Burman, Edward. *The Inquisition: Hammer of Heresy*. New York: Dorset Press, 1984.

Butler, Frank. "A Terrible Farewell." *Our Sunday Visitor* (November 9, 1980), 9f.

Bye, Raymond T. *Capital Punishment in the United States*. Philadelphia, Pa.: Committee on Philanthropic Labor, 1919.

Byrnes, Timothy A. *Catholic Bishops in American Politics*. Princeton, N.J.: Princeton University Press, 1991.

Cahill, Lisa Sowle. *Love Your Enemies: Discipleship, Pacifism, and Just War Theory*. Minneapolis, Minn.: Fortress Press, 1994.

Calvert, Brian. "Aquinas and the Death Penalty." *The American Journal of Jurisprudence* 37 (1992): 259–81.

Cameron, Avril. *Procopius and the Sixth Century.* Berkeley, Calif.: University of California Press, 1985.

Campion, Donald R. "Capital Punishment." In *New Catholic Encyclopedia.* New York: McGraw-Hill, 1967. 3:81.

——. "Should Men Hang?" *America* (December 5, 1959), 321.

Cantor, Norman F. *Inventing the Middle Ages.* New York: Quill: William Morrow, 1991.

Cario, Robert, ed. *La Peine de Mort au Seuil de Troisième Millénaire: Hommage au Professeur Antonio Beristain.* Toulouse: Edition Erès, 1993.

Catholicus. *Pena di Morte e Chiesa Cattolica.* Roma: Giovanni Volpe Editore, 1981.

Cathrein, Victor, S.J. *Philosophia Moralis in Usum Scholarum.* Quinta ed. Freiburg im Breisgau: Herder, 1905.

Cavise, Leonard L. "La Peine de Mort aux Etats-Unis." In *La Peine de Mort au Seuil de Troisième Millénaire: Hommage au Professeur Antonio Beristain.* Edited by Robert Cario. Toulouse: Editions Erès, 1993.

Chadwick, Henry. *Priscillian of Avila.* Oxford: Clarendon Press, 1976.

Cheetham, Nicholas. *Keeper of the Keys.* New York: Chas. Scribner's Sons, 1982.

Cheever, George B. *Punishment by Death: Its Authority and Expediency.* New York: J. Wiley, 1843.

Chenu, M. D., O.P. *Nature, Man and Society in the Twelfth Century.* Chicago: University of Chicago Press, 1968. Midway reprint 1983.

——. *Toward Understanding St. Thomas.* Chicago: Henry Regnery Co., 1964.

Chodorow, Stanley. *Christian Political Theory and Church Politics in the*

Mid-Twelfth Century: The Ecclesiology of Gratian's Decretum. Berkeley, Calif.: University of California Press, 1972.

Christoph, James B. *Capital Punishment and British Politics: The British Movement to Abolish the Death Penalty 1945–57.* Chicago and London: University of Chicago Press and Allen & Unwin, 1962.

Ciccone, Lino. *Non Uccidere: Questioni di morale della vita fisica.* Ragione e Fede #2. Milano: Edizioni Ares, 1984.

Codd, Kevin A. "The Hanging of Westley Allan Dodd." *America* (January 30, 1993), 5f.

Cogley, John. "Capital Punishment and Caryl Chessman." *Commonweal* 71 (March 18, 1960), 671.

Cohn, Norman. *Europe's Inner Demons: An Enquiry Inspired by the Great Witch Hunt.* New York: Basic Books, 1975.

Coleman, John A., S.J. *An American Strategic Theology.* New York: Paulist Press, 1982.

Coleman-Norton, Paul R., ed. *Roman State and Christian Church: A Collection of Legal Documents to A.D. 535.* Volume 2. London: SPCK, 1966.

Combes, Gustave. *La Doctrine Politique de Saint Augustin.* Paris: Librairie Plon, 1927.

Compagnoni, Francesco. "Capital Punishment and Torture in the Tradition of the Catholic Church." *Concilium* 120 (1978): 39–53.

——. "La Pena di Morte nel 'Catechismo della Chiesa Cattolica.'" *Rivista di Teologia Morale* 25 (1993): 263–67.

Concetti, Gino, O.F.M. *Pena di Morte.* Casale Monferrato: Edizioni Piemme, 1993.

Cooper, David D. *Lessons of the Scaffold: The Public Execution Controversy in Victorian England.* Athens, Ohio: Ohio University Press, 1974.

Cornell, Thomas C., and James H. Forest, ed. *A Penny a Copy: Readings from The Catholic Worker.* New York: Macmillan, 1968.

Coulton, G. G. "The Death Penalty for Heresy from 1184 to 1921 A.D." *Medieval Studies* 18 (London: Simpkin, Marshall, Hamilton, Kent and Co., 1924).

———. *Life in the Middle Ages.* Volume 4. *Monks, Friars, and Nuns.* Cambridge University Press, 1911. Reprint 1967.

Cowdrey, H. E. J. *Popes, Monks, and Crusaders.* London: Hambledon Press, 1984.

Cranz, F. Edward. *An Essay on the Development of Luther's Thought on Justice, Law and Society.* Cambridge, Mass.: Harvard University Press, 1964.

Crowe, M. B., O.P. "Theology and Capital Punishment." *Irish Theological Quarterly* 31 (1964): 24–61 and 99–131.

Cunningham, Lawrence. *The Catholic Heritage.* New York: Crossroad, 1983.

———. "The New Catechism." *Commonweal* 120 (March 12, 1993), 8–12.

Curran, Charles E., *American Catholic Social Ethics: 20th-Century Approaches.* Notre Dame, Ind.: University of Notre Dame Press, 1982.

———. "Human Life." *Chicago Studies* 13 (1974), 284ff.

D'Agostino, Francesco. "'Porte Aperte': la pena di morte come problema." *Rivista Internazionale di Filosofia del Diritto* 69 (1992): 393–403.

Dailey, Thomas G. "The Church's Position on the Death Penalty in Canada and the United States." *Concilium* 120 (1978): 121–25.

d'Alverny, Marie-Thérèse. *Alain de Lille: Textes Inédits, avec une introduction sur sa vie et ses oeuvres.* Paris: Librairie Philosophique J. Vrin, 1965.

Dalzell, George W. *Benefit of Clergy in America and Related Matters.* Winston-Salem, N.C.: John F. Blair, 1955.

da Passano, Paolo Ferrari, S.J. "La Pena di Morte nel Catechismo della Chiesa Cattolica." *La Civiltà Cattolica* (IV 1993): 14–26.

Davis, David Brion. "The Movement to Abolish Capital Punishment in America, 1787–1861." *American Historical Review* 63 (1957): 35ff.

Deane, Herbert A. *The Political and Social Ideas of St. Augustine.* New York: Columbia University Press, 1963.

DeCelles, Charles. "The American Bishops and Capital Punishment." *Social Justice Review* 84 (1993): 152ff.

Defourneaux, Marcelin. *Daily Life in Spain in the Golden Age.* Translated by Newton Branch. Stanford, Calif.: Stanford University Press, 1970.

Delumeau, Jean. *Catholicism Between Luther and Voltaire: A New View of the Counter-Reformation.* Philadelphia, Pa.: Westminster Press, 1977.

Demougeot, E. "A propos des Interventions du Pape Innocent I dans la Politique Séculière." *Revue Historique* 212 (1954): 25.

Denzinger, Henricus, ed. *Enchiridion symbolorum definitionum et declarationum de rebus fidei et morum* (quod emendavit, auxit, in linguam germanicam transtulit et adjuvante Helmuto Hoping edidit Petrus Hünermann). 37th edition. Freiburg im Breisgau: Herder, 1991.

Devine, Philip E. *The Ethics of Homicide.* Ithaca, N.Y.: Cornell University Press, 1978.

Dieterich, Paul-Ernest. *Vergleichende Studie der Französischen und Deutschen Moralisten angesichts der Todesstrafe.* Doctoral dissertation, Institut Catholique de Paris, 1980.

Dixon, Philip. *Barbarian Europe.* Oxford: Elsevier-Phaidon, 1976.

Dolan, Jay P. *The American Catholic Experience.* Garden City, New York: Doubleday, 1985.

——. *The Immigrant Church: New York's Irish and German Catholics, 1818–1865.* Baltimore, Md.: Johns Hopkins University Press, 1975.

Dombois, Hans. *Die weltliche Strafe in der evangelischen Theologie.* Witten, 1959.

Dombrowski, Daniel A. *Christian Pacifism.* Philadelphia, Pa.: Temple University Press, 1991.

Downey, Glanville. *Constantinople in the Age of Justinian.* New York: Dorset Press, 1960. Reprint 1991.

Drew, Katherine Fischer. *The Laws of the Salian Franks.* Philadelphia, Pa.: University of Pennsylvania Press, 1991.

Drimmer, Frederick. *Until You Are Dead: The Book of Executions in America.* New York: Citadel Press, 1990.

Drinan, Robert F., S.J. "Even South Africa Drops the Death Penalty." *National Catholic Reporter* (July 28, 1995), 20.

——. *God and Caesar on the Potomac: A Pilgrimage of Conscience. Writings and Addresses on Justice and Peace.* Wilmington, Del.: Michael Glazier, 1985.

Duby, Georges. *France in the Middle Ages 987–1460.* Oxford: Blackwell, 1991.

Duchesne, Louis. *The Beginnings of the Temporal Sovereignty of the Popes, AD 754–1073.* Translated by Arnold Harris Mathew. International Catholic Library. Volume 11. New York: Burt Franklin, 1908. Reprint 1972.

Dunn, Richard S. *The Age of Religious Wars, 1559–1715.* Second ed. The Norton History of Modern Europe. Edited by Felix Gilbert. New York: W. W. Norton & Co., 1979.

Durnbaugh, Donald F., and Charles W. Brockwell, Jr. "The Historic Peace Churches: From Sectarian Origins to Ecumenical Witness." In *The Church's Peace Witness.* Edited by M. E. Miller and B. N. Gingerich. Grand Rapids, Mich.: Eerdmans, 1994.

Dyck, C. J. "Anabaptist Tradition and Vision." In *Dictionary of Christianity in America.* Edited by Daniel G. Reid. Downers Grove, Ill.: Intervarsity Press, 1990.

Eisler, Kim Isaac. *A Justice for All: William J. Brennan, Jr., and the Decisions that Transformed America.* New York: Simon & Schuster, 1993.

Elert, Werner. *Das christliche Ethos.* Tübingen, 1949.

Ellsworth, Phoebe C. "Unpleasant Facts: The Supreme Court's Response to Empirical Research on Capital Punishment." In *Challenging Capital Punishment: Legal and Social Science Approaches.* Edited by K. C. Haas and J. A. Inciardi. Newbury Park, Calif.: Sage Publications, 1988.

Endres, Michael. *The Morality of Capital Punishment: Equal Justice Under the Law?* Mystic, Conn.: Twenty-Third Publications, 1985.

Engreen, Fred E. "Pope John VIII and the Arabs." *Speculum* 20 (1945): 318–30.

Enright, D. J., ed. *The Oxford Book of Death.* Oxford: Oxford University Press, 1983.

Epstein, Lee, and Joseph F. Kobylka. *The Supreme Court and Legal Change: Abortion and the Death Penalty.* Chapel Hill, N.C.: University of North Carolina Press, 1992.

Erbstösser, Martin. *The Crusades.* New York: Universe Books, 1978.

———. *Heretics in the Middle Ages.* Translated by Janet Fraser. Erfurt: Edition Leipzig, 1984.

Erdmann, Carl. *The Origin of the Idea of Crusade.* Translated by Marshall W. Baldwin and Walter Goffart. Princeton, N.J.: Princeton University Press, 1977.

Ermecke, Gustav. *Zur ethischen Begründung der Todesstrafe heute.* 2te. erweiterte ed. Paderborn: Ferdinand Schöningh, 1963.

Escamilla-Colin, Michèle. *Crimes et Chatiment dans L'Espagne Inquisitoriale.* Doctoral dissertation. Paris-Sorbonne, 1992.

Evans, Gillian R. *The Mind of St. Bernard of Clairvaux.* Oxford: Clarendon Press, 1983.

Evans, Richard J. *Rituals of Retribution: Capital Punishment in Germany 1600–1987.* New York: Oxford University Press, 1996.

Evennett, H. Outram. *The Spirit of the Counter-Reformation.* Notre Dame, Ind.: University of Notre Dame Press, 1970.

Ezorsky, Gertrude, ed. *Philosophical Perspectives on Punishment.* Albany, New York: State University of New York Press, 1972.

Falls, M. Margaret. "Against the Death Penalty: A Christian Stance in a Secular World." *The Christian Century* 103 (1986), 1118ff.

Feine, Hans Erich. *Kirchliche Rechtsgeschichte.* 3te ed., Band I: *Die Katholische Kirche.* Weimar: H. Böhlaus Nachfolger, 1955.

Finucane, Ronald C. *Soldiers of Faith: Crusaders and Moslems at War.* New York: St. Martin's Press, 1983.

Fleckenstein, Martin. *Die Todesstrafe im Werk Carl Joseph Anton Mittermaiers (1787–1867).* Rechtshistorische Reihe, Band 103. Frankfurt am Main: Peter Lang, 1992.

Forbes, Clarence A., ed. *Firmicus Maternus: The Error of the Pagan Religions.* Ancient Christian Writers #37. New York: Newman Press, 1970.

Fox, Robin Lane. *Pagans and Christians.* New York: Harper & Row, 1986.

Frankena, William. "The Ethics of Respect for Life." In *Respect for Life in Medicine, Philosophy and the Law.* Edited by O. Temkim, W. K. Frankena S. H. Kadish. Baltimore, Md.: Johns Hopkins University Press, 1976.

Fretheim, Terence E. "The Book of Genesis." *The New Interpreter's Bible.* 1994: 1:399.

Friedman, Lawrence M. *Crime and Punishment in American History.* New York: Basic Books, 1993.

Friel, George Q., O.P. *Punishment in the Philosophy of St. Thomas Aquinas and Among Some Primitive Peoples.* Ph.D. dissertation. Catholic University of America, 1939.

Fryar, Jonathan, ed. *George Fox and the Children of Light.* London: K. Cathie, 1991.

THE DEATH PENALTY

Gabel, Leona C. *Benefit of Clergy in England in the Later Middle Ages.* New York: Octagon Books, 1969.

Gallagher, John, C.S.B. *The Basis for Christian Ethics.* New York: Paulist Press, 1985.

Gallagher, John A. *Time Past, Time Future: An Historical Study of Catholic Moral Theology.* New York: Paulist Press, 1990.

Gannon, Thomas M., S.J., ed. *World Catholicism in Transition.* New York: Macmillan, 1988.

Gatrell, V. A. C. *The Hanging Tree: Execution and the English People 1770–1868.* New York: Oxford University Press, 1994.

Gay, Peter. *The Enlightenment: An Interpretation. The Rise of Modern Paganism.* New York: Vintage Books (Random House), 1966.

Gerhard, Johannes. *Loci Theologici.* Volume 6, locus 24. Berlin: G. Schlawitz, 1868.

Gies, Frances. *The Knight in History.* New York: Harper & Row, 1984.

Gillespie, L. Kay. *The Unforgiven: Utah's Executed Men.* Salt Lake City, Utah: Signature Books, 1991.

Gilson, Etienne. *Moral Values and the Moral Life: The Ethical Theory of St. Thomas Aquinas.* Hamden, Conn.: Shoestring Press, 1961.

Girard, René. *Violence and the Sacred.* Baltimore, Md.: Johns Hopkins University Press, 1977.

Given, James Buchanan. *Society and Homicide in Thirteenth-Century England.* Stanford, Calif.: Stanford University Press, 1977.

Gloege, Gerhard. *Die Todesstrafe als theologisches Problem.* Köln: Westdeutscher Verlag, 1966.

Goetz, Hans-Werner. *Life in the Middle Ages, from the 7th to the 13th Century.* Translated by Albert Wimmer. Notre Dame, Ind.: University of Notre Dame Press, 1993.

Goldhammer, Gary E. *Dead End.* Brunswick, Maine: Biddle Publishing Co., 1994.

Golinelli, Paolo. *Indiscreta Sanctitas: Studi sui Rapporti tra Culti, Poteri e Società nel Pieno Medioevo.* Roma: nelle Sede dell' Istituto Storico Italiano per il Medio Evo, 1988.

Gonnet, Giovanni. *Enchiridion Fontium Valdensium (Recueil critique des sources concernant les Vaudois au moyen age) Du IIIe Concile de Latran au Synode de Chanforan (1179–1532).* Volume 1 (1179–1218). Collana della Facoltà Valdese di Teologia-Roma, Torre Pellice: Libreria Editrice Claudiana, 1958.

Gonnet, Jean, and Amadeo Molnár. *Les Vaudois au Moyen Age.* Torino: Claudiana, 1974.

Good, Edwin M. "Capital Punishment and its Alternatives in Ancient Near Eastern Law." *Stanford Law Review* 19 (1967): 947–977.

Gorecki, Jan. *Capital Punishment: Criminal Law and Social Evolution.* New York: Columbia University Press, 1983.

Gow, Haven Bradford. "Religious Views Support Death Penalty." In *The Death Penalty: Opposing Viewpoints.* Edited by D. L. Bender and B. Leone. St. Paul, Minn.: Greenhaven Press, 1986.

Gracida, René H. "Capital Punishment and the Sacredness of Life." In *Shepherds Speak: American Bishops Confront the Social and Moral Issues that Challenge Christians Today.* Edited by D. M. Corrado and J. F. Hinchey. New York: Crossroad, 1986.

Grant, Michael. *The Climax of Rome.* Boston, Mass.: Little, Brown, 1968.

———. *The Fall of the Roman Empire: A Reappraisal.* Radnor, Pa.: Annenberg School Press, 1976.

Gray, Ian, and Moira Stanley. *A Punishment in Search of a Crime: Americans Speak Out Against the Death Penalty.* New York: Avon Books (for Amnesty International), 1989.

Greenaway, G. W. *Arnold of Brescia.* Cambridge, 1931.

Greenleaf, Richard. *The Mexican Inquisition of the 16th Century.* Albuquerque, N.Mex.: University of New Mexico Press, 1969.

Greenslade, S. L. *Church and State from Constantine to Theodosius.* London: SCM, 1954.

Greer, Donald. *The Incidence of the Terror During the French Revolution.* Gloucester, Mass.: P. Smith, 1935. Reprint 1966.

Gremillion, Joseph, ed. *The Church and Culture Since Vatican II.* Notre Dame, Ind.: University of Notre Dame Press, 1985.

Grendler, Paul F. *The Roman Inquisition and the Venetian Press, 1540–1605.* Princeton, N.J.: Princeton University Press, 1977.

Grisez, Germain G. "Toward a Consistent Natural Law Ethics of Killing." *The American Journal of Jurisprudence* 15 (1970): 91ff.

——. *The Way of the Lord Jesus. Living a Christian Life,* 2. Quincy, Ill.: Franciscan Press, 1993.

Gryting, Loyal A. T., ed. *The Oldest Version of the Twelfth-Century Poem, La Venjance Nostre Seigneur.* Contributions to Modern Philology #19. University of Michigan Press, 1952.

Guernsey, JoAnn Bren. *Should We Have Capital Punishment?* Minneapolis, Minn.: Lerner Publications Co., 1993.

Guroian, Vigen. *Ethics After Christendom: Toward an Ecclesial Christian Ethic.* Grand Rapids, Mich.: Eerdmans, 1994.

Guzzetti, Giovanni B. "Pena di Morte e Morale Cattolica." *La Rivista del Clero Italiano* (1981), 750–63.

Haas, John M. "The Gospel of Life and the Death Penalty." *Crisis* 13 (July-August 1995), 20–23.

Haliczer, Stephen, ed. *Inquisition and Society in Early Modern Europe.* Totowa, N.J.: Barnes & Noble, 1987.

Hallam, Elizabeth, ed. *Chronicles of the Crusades: Nine Crusades and 200 Years of Bitter Conflict for the Holy Land Brought to Life Through the Words of Those Who Were Actually There*. New York: Weidenfeld & Nicolson, 1989.

Hamilton, Bernard. *The Medieval Inquisition*. New York: Holmes & Meier Publishers, 1981.

Hancock, Barry W., and Paul M. Sharp. "The Death Penalty and Christianity: A Conceptual Paradox." *Perspectives on Science and Christian Faith* 46, no. 1 (March 1994): 61–65.

Happel, Stephen, and David Tracy. *A Catholic Vision*. Philadelphia, Pa.: Fortress Press, 1984.

Hardison, Ross. *Bentham*. London: Routledge & Kegan Paul, 1983.

Harlow, Enid, David Matas, Jane Rocamora, ed. *The Machinery of Death: A Shocking Indictment of Capital Punishment in the United States*. New York: Amnesty International USA, 1995.

Häring, Bernard. *Free and Faithful in Christ*. Volume 3 of *Light to the World*. New York: Crossroad, 1981.

———. *The Healing Power of Peace and Nonviolence*. New York: Paulist Press, 1986.

Hastings, Adrian, ed. *Modern Catholicism: Vatican II and After*. London: SPCK, 1991.

Hebblethwaite, Peter. *John XXIII: Pope of the Council*. London: G. Chapman, 1984.

Hébert, J., O.P. "La Justice Criminelle et la Peine de Mort." *Revue Thomiste* 2 (1894): 309–32 and 614–37.

Hehir, J. Bryan. "Consistent Ethic of Life." In *The HarperCollins Encyclopedia of Catholicism*. Edited by Richard P. McBrien. San Francisco, Calif.: HarperSanFrancisco, 1995. 358f.

Heinisch, Paul. *Theology of the Old Testament*. Collegeville, Minn.: Liturgical Press, 1950.

Hetzel, H. *Die Todesstrafe in ihrer kulturgeschichtlichen Entwicklung: eine Studie*. Berlin: W. Moeser, 1870.

Heyer, Friedrich. *The Catholic Church from 1648 to 1870*. Translated by D. W. D. Shaw. London: Adam & Charles Black, 1969.

Hirst, Margaret E. *The Quakers in Peace and War*. London: Allen & Unwin, 1923.

Hobbs, E. E. and W. C. "Contemporary Capital Punishment: Biblical Difficulties with the Biblically Permissible." *Christian Scholar's Review* 11 (1982): 250–62.

Hollenbach, David. *Justice, Peace and Human Rights: American Catholic Social Ethics in a Pluralistic World*. New York: Crossroad, 1988.

Hollis, Christopher, ed. *The Papacy: An Illustrated History from St. Peter to Paul VI*. London: Geo. Weidenfeld & Nicolson Ltd., 1964.

Holmes, Arthur F., ed. *War and Christian Ethics*. Grand Rapids, Mich.: Baker Book House, 1975.

Honecker, Martin. "Capital Punishment in German Protestant Theology." *Concilium* 120 (1978): 54–63.

Hooper, J. Leon, S.J. *Religious Liberty: Catholic Struggles with Pluralism*. Louisville, Ky.: Westminster/John Knox Press, 1993.

Hopkin, Charles Edward. *The Share of Thomas Aquinas in the Growth of the Witchcraft Delusion*. Ph.D. dissertation. University of Pennsylvania, 1940.

Hornus, Jean-Michel. *"It is not Lawful for me to Fight": Early Christian Attitudes Toward War, Violence, and the State*. Revision of *Evangile et Labarum* (1960). Translated by Alan Kreider and Oliver Coburn. Scottsdale, Pa.: Herald Press, 1980.

House, H. Wayne, and John Howard Yoder. *The Death Penalty Debate: Two Opposing Views of Capital Punishment. Issues of Christian Conscience*. Edited by Vernon Grounds. Dallas, Tex.: Word Publishing, 1991.

Howarth, Stephen. *The Knights Templar.* New York: Barnes & Noble, 1982.

Hroch, Miroslav, and Anna Skybová. *Ecclesia Militans: The Inquisition.* Translated by Janet Fraser. New York: Dorset Press, 1990. German original 1988.

Hudson, Anne. *The Premature Reformation: Wycliffite Texts and Lollard History.* Oxford: Clarendon Press, 1988.

Hughes, Emmet John. *The Church and the Liberal Society.* Princeton, N.J.: Princeton University Press, 1944.

Hughes, Robert. *The Fatal Shore.* New York: Vintage, 1986.

Imbert, Jean. *La Peine de Mort: Histoire-Actualité.* Paris: Armand Colin, 1967.

Ingle, H. Larry. *First Among Friends: George Fox and the Creation of Quakerism.* New York: Oxford University Press, 1994.

Iserloh, E., J. Glazik, and H. Jedin. *Reformation and Counter Reformation.* Volume 5 of *History of the Church.* Edited by H. Jedin and J. Dolan. New York: Crossroad, 1980.

Jackson, Owen R., O.S.A. *Dignity and Solidarity: An Introduction to Peace and Justice Education.* Chicago, Ill.: Loyola University Press, 1985.

Janssen, A. "Autour du problème de la peine de mort." *Ephemerides Theologicae Lovanienses* 37 (1961): 86–97.

John XXIII, Pope. *Peace on Earth.* New York: Herder & Herder, 1964.

Jorns, Auguste. *The Quakers as Pioneers in Social Work.* Port Washington, N.Y.: Kennikat Press, 1969. Reprint of the 1931 translation of the 1911 German original.

Journet, Charles. *The Church of the Word Incarnate: An Essay in Speculative Theology.* Volume 1: The Apostolic Hierarchy. Translated by A. H. C. Downes. London: Sheed & Ward, 1955.

Joyce, James, S.J. "Capital Punishment: A Hard Saying." *Church* 3 (1987): 28ff.

Kamen, Henry. "Clerical Violence in a Catholic Society: The Hispanic World 1450–1720." In *The Church and War.* Edited by W. J. Sheils. Oxford: Blackwell, 1983.

———. "Spain." In *The Reformation in National Context.* Edited by Roy Porter, Bob Scribner, and Mikulás Teich. New York: Cambridge University Press, 1994. Chapter 12.

Kaminsky, Howard. *A History of the Hussite Revolution.* Berkeley, Calif.: University of California Press, 1967.

Kastenbaum, Robert and Beatrice. *Encyclopedia of Death.* New York: Avon Books, 1989.

Kaufman, Natalie Hevener. *Human Rights Treaties and the Senate: A History of Opposition.* Chapel Hill, N.C., and London: The University of North Carolina Press, 1990.

Keane, Philip, S.S. *Christian Ethics and Imagination.* New York: Paulist Press, 1984.

Keating, Geoffrey. *The Moral Problems of Fraternal, Paternal and Judicial Correction According to St. Augustine.* Doctoral dissertation. Gregoriana (Rome), 1958.

Kelly, J. N. D. *The Oxford Dictionary of Popes.* Oxford: Oxford University Press, 1986.

Kern, Fritz. *Kingship and Law in the Middle Ages.* Translated and introduced by S. B. Chrimes. Studies in Medieval History #4. Oxford: Blackwell, 1956.

Kershaw, Alister. *A History of the Guillotine.* New York: Barnes & Noble, 1993.

King, N. Q. *The Emperor Theodosius and the Establishment of Christianity.* London: SCM, 1961.

Knecht, R. J. *The French Wars of Religion 1559–1598*. London: Longmans, 1989.

Koestler, Arthur. *Reflections on Hanging*. New York: Macmillan, 1957.

Kritzeck, James. *Peter the Venerable and Islam*. Princeton Oriental Studies #23. Princeton, N.J.: Princeton University Press, 1964.

Kronenwetter, Michael. *Capital Punishment: A Reference Handbook*. Santa Barbara, Calif.: ABC-CLIO, 1993.

Künneth, Walter. *Politik zwischen Dämon und Gott*. Berlin: Lutherisches Verlaghaus, 1954.

Kunstler, William M. *Beyond a Reasonable Doubt? The Original Trial of Caryl Chessman*. New York: William Morrow, 1961.

Kuttner, Stephan. "Johannes Teutonicus, das vierte Laterankonzil und die Compilatio Quarta." In *Miscellanea Giovanni Mercati*. Vatican City, 1946.

Lambert, Malcolm. *Medieval Heresy: Popular Movements from the Gregorian Reform to the Reformation*. Oxford: Blackwell, 1992.

Langan, John, S.J. "Capital Punishment." In *The HarperCollins Encyclopedia of Catholicism*. Edited by Richard P. McBrien. San Francisco, Calif.: Harper-SanFrancisco, 1995.

———. "Human Rights in Catholicism." In *Human Rights in Religious Traditions*. Edited by Arlene Swidler. New York: Pilgrim Press, 1982. 32ff.

Langbein, John H. *Torture and the Law of Proof: Europe and England in the Ancien Regime*. Chicago: University of Chicago Press, 1977.

Langer, Herbert. *The Thirty Years' War*. Translation of *Hortus Bellicus, der dreissigjährige Krieg* (1960). Translated by C. S. V. Salt. Poole Dorset, UK: Blandford Press, 1980.

Larner, Christine. "Crimen Exceptum? The Crime of Witchcraft in Europe." In *Crime and the Law: The Social History of Crime in Western Europe Since 1500*. Eds. Bruce Lenman, V. A. C. Gatrell, and Geoffrey Parker. London: Europa Publications, 1980.

Lasserre, Jean. *War and the Gospel.* Translated by Oliver Coburn. Scottsdale, Pa.: Herald Press, 1962.

Lea, Henry Charles. *A History of the Inquisition in the Middle Ages.* New York: Russell & Russell, 1877. Reprint 1955.

Lecler, Joseph, S.J. *Toleration and the Reformation.* London: Longmans, 1960.

Leclercq, Jacques. *Lecons de Droit Naturel.* Nouvelle, revue et corrigée (original 1937) ed. Volume 4—Les Droits et Devoirs Individuels: premiere partie: *Vie, Disposition de soi. Etudes morales, sociales et juridique.* Louvain: Société d'études morales, 1946.

Leder, Karl Bruno. *Todesstrafe: Ursprung, Geschichte, Opfer.* Wien-Münster: Meyster, 1980.

Lerner, Robert E. *The Heresy of the Free Spirit in the Later Middle Ages.* Berkeley, Calif.: University of California Press, 1972.

Lesser, Wendy. *Pictures at an Execution: An Inquiry into the Subject of Murder.* Cambridge, Mass.: Harvard University Press, 1993.

Levy, Leonard. *Treason Against God: A History of the Offense of Blasphemy.* New York: Schocken Books, 1981.

Lieu, Samuel N. C. *Manichaeism in the Later Roman Empire.* Manchester; Dover, N.H.: Manchester University Press, 1985.

Littell, Franklin H. *The Anabaptist View of the Church: A Study in the Origins of Sectarian Protestantism.* Second edition. Boston, Mass.: Starr King Press, 1958.

Llewellyn, Peter. *Rome in the Dark Ages.* London: Faber & Faber, 1971.

Loyn, H. R., ed. *The Middle Ages: A Concise Encyclopaedia.* London: Thames & Hudson, 1989.

Lynch, John. *Spain 1516–1598: From Nation State to World Empire.* Volume 10 of *A History of Spain.* Edited by John Lynch. Oxford: Blackwell, 1991.

MacBride, Sean, ed. *Crime and Punishment*. Dublin: Ward River Press, in association with Amnesty International—Irish Section, Association of Irish Jurists, and Prisoners Rights Organization, 1982.

Mackey, Philip E. *Voices Against Death: American Opposition to Capital Punishment, 1787–1975*. New York: Burt Franklin & Co., 1976.

MacMullen, Ramsay. *Christianizing the Roman Empire A.D. 100–400*. New Haven, Conn.: Yale University Press, 1984.

MacNamara, Donal E.J. "The Case against Capital Punishment." *Social Action* (April 1961): 4–15.

———. "Letter to America." *America* 102 (December 5, 1959), 321.

———. "Letter to America." *America* 102 (January 16, 1960), 462.

Maestro, Marcello. *Cesare Beccaria and the Origins of Penal Reform*. Philadelphia, Pa.: Temple University Press, 1973.

———. *Voltaire and Beccaria as Reformers of Criminal Law*. New York: Columbia University Press, 1942.

Magnuson, Torgil. *Rome in the Age of Bernini*. Volume 1: *From the Election of Sixtus V to the Death of Urban VIII*. Stockholm: Almquist & Wiksell International, 1986.

———. *Rome in the Age of Bernini*. Volume 2: *From the Election of Innocent X to the Death of Innocent XI*. Stockholm: Almquist & Wiksell International, 1986.

Mahoney, John. *The Making of Moral Theology: A Study of the Roman Catholic Tradition*. Oxford: Clarendon Press, 1987.

Markus, Robert. *The End of Ancient Christianity*. New York: Cambridge University Press, 1990.

Marquart, J. W., S. Ekland-Olson and J. R. Sorensen. *The Rope, the Chair, and the Needle: Capital Punishment in Texas 1923–1990*. Austin, Tex.: University of Texas Press, 1994.

Marshall, Thurgood. "Dispatch the System, Not the Man." *Harper's Magazine* (January 1991), 28ff.

Martin, Robert Paul. *The Death Penalty: God's Will or Man's Folly?* Avinger, Tex.: Simpson Publishing Co., 1992.

Martini, Magda. *Fausto Socino et la Pensée Socinienne.* Paris: Librairie C. Klincksieck, 1966.

Masaryk, Tomas G. *The Meaning of Czech History.* Ed. René Wellek. Chapel Hill, N.C.: University of North Carolina Press, 1974.

Masur, Louis P. *Rites of Execution: Capital Punishment and the Transformation of American Culture, 1776–1865.* New York: Oxford University Press, 1989.

Maugain, Gabriel. *Moeurs Italiennes de la Renaissance: La Vengeance.* Paris: Les Belles Lettres, 1935.

McBrien, Richard P. "The Church." In *Modern Catholicism: Vatican II and After.* Edited by Adrian Hastings. New York: Oxford University Press, 1991. 84–95.

———, ed. *The HarperCollins Encyclopedia of Catholicism.* San Francisco, Calif.: HarperSanFrancisco, 1995.

McCool, Gerald A. *Catholic Theology in the 19th Century: The Quest for a Unitary Method.* New York: Seabury Press, 1977.

McCormick, Richard A., S.J. *The Critical Calling: Reflections on Moral Dilemma Since Vatican II.* Washington, D.C.: Georgetown University Press, 1989.

———. "The Gospel of Life." *America* 172 (April 29, 1995): 12f.

———. *Notes on Moral Theology 1965–1980.* Lanham, Md.: University Press of America, 1981.

———, and Paul Ramsey, eds. *Doing Evil to Achieve Good: Moral Choices in Conflict Situations.* Chicago, Ill.: Loyola University Press, 1978.

McCune, Patricia Helen. *The Ideology of Mercy in English Literature and*

Law, 1200–1600. Ph.D. dissertation (history). University of Michigan, 1989.

McHugh, John A., O.P., and Charles J. Callan, O.P., eds. *Catechism of the Council of Trent for Parish Priests.* New York: J. F. Wagner, 1934.

McKenna, Andrew J. *Violence and Difference: Girard, Derrida, and Deconstruction.* Urbana and Chicago: University of Illinois Press, 1992.

McLeod, John N. *The Capital Punishment of the Murderer, an Unrepealed Ordinance of God.* New York: R. Carter, 1842.

McLynn, Frank. *Crime and Punishment in 18th-century England.* New York: Oxford University Press, 1991.

McLynn, Neil B. *Ambrose of Milan: Church and Court in a Christian Capital.* Volume 12: *The Transformation of the Classical Heritage.* Edited by Peter Brown. Berkeley, Calif.: University of California Press, 1994.

McMaster, John. *The Divine Purpose of Capital Punishment.* London: Kegan Paul, Trench, Trübner & Co., 1892.

McNeill, John T., and Helena M. Gamer, eds. *Medieval Handbooks of Penance.* New York: Columbia University Press, 1938/1990.

Medley, David E. *The Relevance of the Image of God to Capital Punishment in the Old Testament.* Ph.D. dissertation. Southwest Baptist Theological Seminary (Fort Worth, Tex.), 1979.

Melton, J. Gordon, ed. *The Churches Speak on: Capital Punishment.* Detroit, Mich.: Gale Research, 1989.

Meltsner, Michael. "On Death Row, the Wait Continues." In *The Burger Years: Rights and Wrongs in the Supreme Court 1969–1986.* Edited by Herman Schwartz. New York: Viking Press, 1987.

———. "The Late Justice." *The Nation* (February 15, 1993): 198f.

Mendelsohn, S. *The Criminal Jurisprudence of the Ancient Hebrews.* Second edition. New York: Hermon Press, 1968. Reprint of 1890 original.

Menninger, Karl. *The Crime of Punishment.* New York: Penguin Books, 1968.

Mereu, Italo. *La Morte come Pena.* Milano: Espresso Strumenti, 1982.

——. *Storia dell'Intoleranza in Europa: Sospettare e Punire. Il Sospetto e l'Inquisizione Romana nel'epoca di Galilei.* Milano: Arnoldo Mondadori Editore, 1979.

Messineo, A., S.J. "Il Diritto alla Vita." *La Civiltà Cattolica* 2 (1960): 449–62.

Miller, Arthur S., and Jeffrey H. Bowman. *Death by Installments.* New York: Greenwood Press, 1990.

Mills, Samuel A. "Parochiaid and the Abortion Decisions: Supreme Court Justice William J. Brennan, Jr., versus the U.S. Catholic Hierarchy." *Journal of Church and State* 34 (1992): 766ff.

Minnerath, Roland. *Le Droit de L'Eglise à la Liberté du Syllabus à Vatican II.* Volume 39. *Le Point Théologique.* Edited by Charles Kannengiesser. Paris: Beauchesne, 1982.

Mitchell, Michael George. *Heretici Comburantur: An Inquiry into the Reasons for Burning Heretics in France and the Empire in the 11th and 12th Centuries.* Ph.D. dissertation. Yale University, 1990.

Montagu, Basil, ed. *The Opinions of Different Authors upon the Punishment of Death.* Second edition. London: Longman, Hurst, Rees, Orme & Brown, 1816.

Moore, Philip S., C.S.C. *The Works of Peter of Poitiers, Master in Theology and Chancellor of the University of Paris (1193–1205).* Notre Dame, Ind.: University of Notre Dame Press, 1936.

Moore, R. I. *The Formation of a Persecuting Society: Power and Deviance in Western Europe 950–1250.* Oxford: Blackwell, 1987.

Moreau, Pierre. "Autour de la Peine de Mort." *Lumière et Vie* 43:1 (#216), Février, 1994, 71–83.

Morris, Colin. *The Papal Monarchy: The Western Church from 1050 to 1250.* Oxford: Clarendon Press, 1989.

Muldoon, James. *Popes, Lawyers, and Infidels: The Church and the Non-Christian World 1250–1550.* Liverpool: Liverpool University Press, 1979.

Müller, Ingo. *Hitler's Justice: The Courts of the Third Reich.* Translated by Deborah Lucas Schneider. Cambridge, Mass.: Harvard University Press, 1991.

Müller, Wolfgang P. *Huguccio: The Life, Works and Thought of a 12th Century Jurist.* Washington, D.C.: Catholic University of America Press, 1994.

Murphy, Thomas Patrick, ed. *The Holy War.* Columbus, Ohio: Ohio State University Press, 1976.

Murray, John Courtney, S.J. "The Political Thought of Joseph de Maistre." *The Review of Politics* 11 (1949): 73ff.

Myers, A. R. *English Historical Documents 1327–1485.* New York: Oxford University Press, 1969.

Nakel, Barry, and Kenneth A. Hardy. *The Arbitrariness of the Death Penalty.* Philadelphia, Pa.: Temple University Press, 1987.

Naud, Albert. *Tu ne tueras pas.* Mayenne: Floch, 1963.

Nielsen, Eduard. *The Ten Commandments in New Perspective: A Traditio-Historical Approach.* Translated by David J. Bourke. Studies in Biblical Theology: second series. Naperville, Ill.: Alec R. Allenson, 1968.

Nigg, Walter. *The Heretics: Heresy Through the Ages.* Translated by Richard and Clara Winston. New York: Dorset Press, 1962/1990.

Noble, Thomas F. X. *The Republic of St. Peter: The Birth of the Papal State, 680–825.* Philadelphia, Pa.: University of Pennsylvania Press, 1984.

Nolan, Hugh J., ed. *Pastoral Letters of the U.S. Catholic Bishops.* Volume 3 (1962–1974). Washington, D.C.: NCCB/USCC, 1983.

O'Reilly, James, M.S. "Why the Death Sentence Is Needed." *Homiletic and Pastoral Review* 84 (May 1984): 54–57.

Noonan, John T. "Gratian Slept Here: The Changing Identity of the Father of the Systematic Study of Canon Law." *Traditio* 35 (1979): 145–72.

———. *The Scholastic Analysis of Usury.* Cambridge, Mass.: Harvard University Press, 1957.

Novales, Alberto Gil. "Peine de Mort et Valeur de la Vie: Espagne (1820–1921)." In *Actes du Colloque sur la Peine de Mort dans la Pensée Philosophique et Litteraire.* Université de Paris-Sorbonne, 1980: 53–59.

Oakes, C. G. *Sir Samuel Romilly: "The Friend of the Oppressed."* London: Allen & Unwin, 1935.

Oakley, Francis. *The Western Church in the Later Middle Ages.* Ithaca, N.Y.: Cornell University Press, 1979.

Oberman, Heiko A. *The Dawn of the Reformation: Essays in Late Medieval and Early Reformation Thought.* Edinburgh: T. & T. Clark / Grand Rapids, Mich.: Eerdmans, 1986. Reprint 1992.

O'Brien, William J., ed. *Riding Time Like a River: The Catholic Moral Tradition Since Vatican II.* Washington, D.C.: Georgetown University Press, 1993.

O'Callaghan, Denis. "Debating the Death Penalty." *The Furrow* 43 (1992): 610–16.

O'Connell, Marvin R. *The Counter Reformation: 1559–1610.* New York: Harper & Row (Harper Torch books), 1974.

O'Connell, Timothy E., ed. *Vatican II and Its Documents: An American Reappraisal.* Theology and Life Series, #15. Collegeville, Minn.: The Liturgical Press, 1991.

Oikonomides, Nicolas. "Eclogue." In *Dictionary of the Middle Ages.* Edited by Joseph R. Strayer. New York: Scribner's, 1987: 382–85.

Oldenburg, Zoé. *Massacre at Montségur: A History of the Albigensian Crusade.* New York: Dorset Press, 1961.

Overberg, Kenneth R. *An Inconsistent Ethic? Teachings of the American Catholic Bishops.* Lanham, Md.: University Press of America, 1980.

Packard, Jerrold M. *Peter's Kingdom: Inside the Papal City.* New York: Chas. Scribner's Sons, 1985.

Paglia, Vincenzo. *La Morte Confortata, Riti della Paura e Mentalità Religiosa a Roma nell'Età Moderna.* Biblioteca di Storia Sociale #13. Roma: Edizioni di Storia e Letteratura, 1982.

Panico, Guido. *Il Carnefice e la Piazza: Crudeltà di Stato e violenze popolare a Napoli in età moderna.* Salerno: Edizioni Scientifiche Italiane, 1985.

Partner, Peter. *The Lands of St. Peter: The Papal State in the Middle Ages and the Renaissance.* Berkeley, Calif.: University of California Press, 1972.

———. *Renaissance Rome 1500–1559: A Portrait of a Society.* Berkeley, Calif.: University of California Press, 1976.

Pastor, Ludwig. *The History of the Popes.* Edited by R. F. Kerr. St. Louis, Mo.: B. Herder, 1952.

Pavan, Pietro. *Commentary on the Documents of Vatican II.* Edited by H. Vorgrimler. New York: Crossroad, 1989.

Pennington, Kenneth. "Medieval Law." In *Medieval Studies: An Introduction.* Edited by James M. Powell. Second edition. Syracuse, N.Y.: Syracuse University Press, 1992.

Perico, Giacomo. "Ripristinare la Pena di Morte?" *Aggiornamenti Sociali* 134 (1993): 23–37.

Peters, Edward. *Inquisition.* Berkeley, Calif.: University of California Press, 1988.

———. *The Magician, the Witch and the Law.* Philadelphia, Pa.: University of Pennsylvania Press, 1978.

——, ed. *Heresy and Authority in Medieval Europe: Documents in Translation.* Philadelphia, Pa.: University of Pennsylvania Press, 1980.

Pharr, Clyde, ed. *The Theodosian Code and Novels and the Sirmondian Constitutions.* Princeton, N.J.: Princeton University Press, 1952.

Phelps, Timothy M., and Helen Winternitz. *Capitol Games.* New York: Hyperion, 1992.

Pilarczyk, Archibishop Daniel. *Twelve Tough Issues.* Cincinnati: St. Anthony Messenger Press, 1988.

Pincoffs, Edmund L. *The Rationale of Legal Punishment.* New York: Humanities Press, 1966.

Placher, William C. *A History of Christian Theology.* Philadelphia, Pa.: Westminster Press, 1983.

Plaidy, Jean. *The Spanish Inquisition: Its Rise, Growth, and End.* Three works combined: The Rise (1959), Growth (1960), and End (1961). New York: Barnes & Noble, 1994.

Potter, Harry. *Hanging in Judgment.* New York: Continuum, 1993.

Powell, James M., ed. *Innocent III: Vicar of Christ or Lord of the World?* Second, expanded edition. Washington, D.C.: Catholic University of America Press, 1963/1994.

Prejean, Helen. *Dead Man Walking: An Eyewitness Account of the Death Penalty in the United States.* New York: Random House, 1993.

Prinz, Friedrich. *Klerus und Krieg im früheren Mittelalter: Untersuchungen zur Rolle der Kirche beim Aufbau der Königsherrschaft.* Monographien zur Geschichte des Mittelalters. Edited by Karl Bosl. Stuttgart: Anton Hiersemann, 1971.

Pritchard, John Laurence. *A History of Capital Punishment with Special Reference to Capital Punishment in Great Britain.* Port Washington, N.Y.: Kennikat Press, 1932/1971.

Pullapilly, Cyriac K. *Caesar Baronius, CounterReformation Historian.* Notre Dame, Ind.: University of Notre Dame Press, 1975.

Quasten, Johannes. *Patrology*. Volume 2: *The Ante-Nicene Literature After Irenaeus*. Utrecht: Spectrum Publishers, 1953.

Quinones, Ricardo J. *The Changes of Cain: Violence and the Lost Brother in Cain-Abel Literature*. Princeton, N.J.: Princeton University Press, 1991.

Rad, Gerhard von. *Holy War in Ancient Israel*. Translated by Marva J. Dawn. Grand Rapids, Mich.: Eerdmans, 1991.

Radding, Charles M. *The Origins of Medieval Jurisprudence: Pavia and Bologna 850–1150*. New Haven, Conn.: Yale University Press, 1988.

Radelet, Michael L., ed. *Facing the Death Penalty: Essays on a Cruel and Unusual Punishment*. Philadelphia, Pa.: Temple University Press, 1989.

———, Hugo Adam Bedau, and Constance E. Putnam. *In Spite of Innocence*. Boston, Mass.: Northeastern University Press, 1992.

Radosh, Ronald, and Joyce Milton. *The Rosenberg File: A Search for the Truth*. New York: Holt, Rinehart & Winston, 1983.

Rahner, Karl. *Theological Investigations*. Volume 5: *Later Writings*. Baltimore, Md.: Helicon Press, 1966.

Reed, Emily F. *The Penry Penalty: Capital Punishment and Offenders with Mental Retardation*. Lanham, Md.: University Press of America, 1993.

Reese, Thomas. *Episcopal Conferences: Historical, Canonical and Theological Studies*. Washington, D.C.: Georgetown University Press, 1989.

———, *A Flock of Shepherds: The NCCB*. Kansas City, Mo.: Sheed & Ward, 1992.

Regan, Augustine, C.SS.R. "Thou Shalt Not Kill" *Theology Today* #38. Edited by Edward Yarnold. Butler, Wis.: Clergy Book Service, 1979.

Renouard, Yves. *The Avignon Papacy: The Popes in Exile 1305–1403*. New York: Barnes & Noble, 1994.

Reynolds, E. E. *Campion and Parsons: The Jesuit Mission of 1580–81*. London: Sheed & Ward, 1980.

Riga, Peter J. "Capital Punishment and the Right to Life." *University of Puget Sound Law Review* 5 (1981).

Riley, Thomas J. "The Right of the State to Inflict Capital Punishment." *The Catholic Lawyer* 6 (1960): 279–85.

Riley-Smith, Jonathan. *The First Crusade and the Idea of Crusading.* Philadelphia, Pa.: University of Pennsylvania Press, 1986.

Romeo, Giovanni. *Aspettando il Boia: Condannati a morte, confortatori e inquisitori nella Napoli della Controriforma.* Firenze: Sansoni Editore, 1993.

———. *Inquisitori, esorcisti e streghe nell'Italia della Controriforma.* Firenze: Sansoni Editore, 1990.

Ross, David. *Kant's Ethical Theory.* New York: Oxford University Press, 1954.

Rouche, Michel. "The Early Middle Ages in the West." In *A History of Private Life.* Edited by Paul Veyne. Cambridge, Mass.: Belknap Press of Harvard University, 1987.

Rowan, Carl T. *Dream Makers, Dream Breakers: The World of Justice Thurgood Marshall.* Boston: Little, Brown & Co., 1993.

Rudé, George, ed. *Robespierre. Great Lives Observed.* Englewood Cliffs, N.J.: Prentice-Hall, 1967.

Rushdoony, Rousas J. *Institutes of Biblical Law.* Nutley, N.J.: Craig, 1973.

Russell, Frederick H. *The Just War in the Middle Ages.* Cambridge: Cambridge University Press, 1975.

Russell, Gregory D. *The Death Penalty and Racial Bias: Overturning Supreme Court Assumptions.* Westport, Conn.: Greenwood Press, 1994.

Russell, Jeffrey B. *Dissent and Order in the Middle Ages: The Search for Legitimate Authority.* New York: Twayne Publishers, 1992.

———. *A History of Witchcraft.* London: Thames & Hudson, 1980.

Ruthven, Malise. *Torture: The Grand Conspiracy.* London: Weidenfeld & Nicolson, 1978.

Sandys, Marla Rita. *Toward a Greater Understanding of Death Penalty Attitudes: An Examination of the Functions They Serve and an Exploration of Their Susceptibility to Change.* Ph.D. dissertation. University of Kentucky, 1990.

Savey-Casard, Paul. *La Peine de Mort: esquisse historique et juridique.* Geneve: Librairie Droz, 1968.

Schabas, William A. *The Abolition of the Death Penalty in International Law.* Cambridge, England: Grotius Publications, 1993.

——, *The Death Penalty as Cruel Treatment and Torture: Capital Punishment Challenged in the World's Courts.* Boston, Mass.: Northeastern University Press, 1996.

Scheid, Don. "Kant's Retributivism." *Ethics 93* (1983): 262–82.

Schilling, Otto. *Die Staats-und Soziallehre des hl. Augustinus.* Freiburg im Breisgau: Herder, 1910.

Schleiermacher, Friedrich, ed. *Die christliche Sitte nach den Grundsätzen der evangelische Kirche.* Berlin: G. Reimer, 1843.

Schmidt, Eberhard. *Einführung in die Geschichte der deutschen Strafrechtspflege.* 2te, vermehrte ed. Göttingen: Vandenhoeck & Ruprecht, 1951.

Schmidt, Gerhard. *Christentum und Todesstrafe.* Weimar: Verlag Deutsche Christen, 1938.

Schoof, T. Mark. *A Survey of Catholic Theology, 1800–1970.* Glen Rock, N.J.: Paulist Newman Press, 1970.

Schöpf, Bernhard. *Das Tötungsrecht bei den frühchristlichen Schriftstellern bis zur Zeit Konstantins.* Regensburg: Verlag F. Pustet, 1958.

Schüller, Bruno, S.J. *Die Begründung sittlicher Urteile: Typen ethischer Argumentation in der Moraltheologie.* Düsseldorf: Patmos Verlag, 1980.

———. "Todesstrafe." *In Lexikon für Theologie und Kirche.* Freiburg im Breisgau: Herder Verlag, 1965. 10: 230f.

Schwaiger, Raymund. *Must There Be Scapegoats?* New York: Harper & Row, 1987.

Schwarzschild, Steven S. "Kantianism on the Death Penalty (and Related Social Problems)." *Archives for Philosophy of Law and Social Philosophy* 71 (1985): 343–72.

Schwed, Roger E. *Abolition and Capital Punishment: The U.S. Judicial, Political, and Moral Barometer.* AMS Studies in Modern Society: Political and Social Issues, #16. New York: AMS Press, 1983.

Scott, George Ryley. *The History of Capital Punishment.* London: Torchstream Books, 1950.

Scott, S. P., ed. *The Civil Law.* Volume 15. Cincinnati, Ohio: Central Trust Co., 1932. Reprinted New York: AMS, 1973.

Scully, Sally Anne. *Killing ex officio: The Teachings of 12th and 13th Century Canon Lawyers on the Right to Kill.* Ph.D dissertation (history). Harvard University, 1975.

Seidler, J., and K. Meyer. *Conflict and Change in the Catholic Church.* New Brunswick: Rutgers University Press, 1989.

Seldes, George. *The Vatican–Yesterday Today Tomorrow.* New York: Harper & Bros., 1934.

Sellin, Thorsten. *The Penalty of Death.* Beverly Hills, Calif.: Sage Publications, 1980.

Shute, Stephen, and Susan Hurley, ed. *On Human Rights: The Oxford Amnesty Lectures.* New York: Basic Books, 1993.

Siberry, Elizabeth. *Criticism of Crusading, 1095–1274.* Oxford: Clarendon Press, 1985.

Simon, James F. *The Center Holds: The Power Struggle Inside the Rehnquist Court.* New York: Simon & Schuster, 1995.

Simonsohn, Shlomo. *The Apostolic See and the Jews: History.* Studies and Texts, #109. Toronto: Pontifical Institute of Medieval Studies, 1991.

Simpson, W. J. S. *A Study of Bossuet.* London: SPCK, 1937.

Skoda, Franciscus. *Doctrina Moralis Catholica de Poena Mortis a C. Beccaria usque ad nostros dies (1956).* Pesaro, 1959.

Smith, Gary Scott, ed. *God and Politics: Four Views on the Reformation of Civil Government.* Philipsburg, N.J.: Presbyterian and Reformed Publishing Co., 1989.

Smith, J. A. Clarence. *Medieval Law Teachers and Writers, Civilian and Canonist.* Ottawa: University of Ottawa Press, 1975.

Southern, R. W. *Medieval Humanism.* New York: Harper & Row, 1970.

Spinka, Matthew. "Peter Chĕlcický, the Spiritual Father of the Unitas Fratrum." *Church History* 12 (1943): 282ff.

Stahl, Paul Henri. *Histoire de la Décapitation.* Paris: Presses Universitaire de France, 1986.

Stevenson, William R., Jr. *Christian Love and Just War: Moral Paradox and Political Life in St. Augustine and His Modern Interpreters.* Macon, Ga.: Mercer University Press, 1987.

St. John-Stevas, Norman. *The Right to Life.* New York: Holt, Rinehart & Winston, 1964.

Strub, Bettina. *Der Einfluss der Aufklärung auf die Todesstrafe.* Zürich: Juris Verlag, 1973.

Sueiro, Daniel. La Pena de Muerte y los Derechos Humanos. Madrid: Alianza Editorial, 1987.

Sullivan, Shaun J. *Killing in Defense of Private Property.* Ph.D. dissertation. Graduate Theological Union, 1976.

Summers, Montague, ed. *The Malleus Maleficarum of Heinrich Kramer and James Springer.* New York: Dover Publications, 1971. Reprint of 1928 original published by John Rotker (London).

Swidler, Leonard, ed. *Human Rights: Christians, Marxists, and Others in Dialogue*. New York: Paragon House, 1991.

Symonds, John Addington. *The Age of the Despots: The Renaissance in Italy*. New York: G. P. Putnam's Sons, 1875. Reprint 1960.

Tedeschi, John. *The Prosecution of Heresy: Collected Studies on the Inquisition in Early Modern Italy*. Medieval and Renaissance Texts and Studies, #78. Binghamton, N.Y., 1991.

Teeters, Negley K., and Jack H. Hedblom. *"Hang by the Neck": The Legal Use of Scaffold and Noose, Gibbet, Stake, and Firing Squad from Colonial Times to the Present*. Springfield, Ill.: Charles C. Thomas, 1967.

Tellenbach, Gerd. *Church, State and Christian Society at the Time of the Investiture Contest*. Translation of *Libertas: Kirche und Weltordnung im Zeitalter des Investiturstreites* (Leipzig: W. Kohlhammer, 1936). Translated by R. F. Bennett. Studies in Medieval History. Edited by Geoffrey Barraclough. Oxford: Blackwell, 1959.

Templer, Mary. *The Right to Life and Death: What Do Presbyterians Say?* M.A. thesis. Department of Religious Studies, University of Windsor, Ontario, Canada, 1992.

Templewood, Viscount. *The Shadow of the Gallows*. London: Victor Gollancz, 1951.

Thamiry, E. In *Dictionnaire de Theologie Catholique*. See entry on the death penalty. Tome x, col. 2501.

Thompson, J. M. *Robespierre*. New York: Howard Fertig, 1968.

Thompson, James Westfall. *The Middle Ages, 300–1500*. Second edition. New York: Cooper Square Publishers, 1972.

Thomson, John A. F. *Popes and Princes, 1417–1517: Politics and Polity in the Late Medieval Church*. London: Allen & Unwin, 1980.

Thonissen, J. J. "Le Problème de la Peine de Mort au point de vue du Dogme Catholique." *Revue Générale* 1 (1865): 76–87.

Thurman, William S. "How Justinian I Sought to Handle the Problem of Religious Dissent." *The Greek Orthodox Theological Review* 13 (1968): 15–40.

Tidmarsh, M. *Capital Punishment: A Case for Abolition.* New York: Sheed & Ward, 1963.

Tierney, Brian. *The Crisis of Church and State 1050–1300.* Englewood Cliffs, N.J.: Prentice-Hall, 1964. Medieval Academy Reprints for Teaching, #21. Toronto: University of Toronto Press, 1988.

Treece, Henry. *The Crusades.* New York: Barnes & Noble, 1962/1994.

Treesh, Susan K. "The Waldensian Recourse to Violence." *Church History* 55 (1986): 294–306.

Trombley, Stephen. *The Execution Protocol: Inside America's Capital Punishment Industry.* New York: Crown Publishers, 1992.

Trout, John M. *The Voyage of Prudence: The World View of Alan of Lille.* Lanham, Md.: University Press of America, 1979.

Tushnet, Mark. *The Death Penalty: Constitutional Issues.* "A Harold Steinberg Book." New York: Facts on File, 1994.

Ude, Johannes. *Du sollst nicht töten.* Dornbirn, 1948.

Ullmann, Walter. *The Growth of Papal Government in the Middle Ages.* Second edition. London: Methuen & Co., 1962.

———. *A Short History of the Papacy in the Middle Ages.* London: Methuen & Co., 1972.

Vallauri, Luigi Lombardi, and Gerhard Dilcher. *Cristianesimo, Secolarizzazione, e Diritto Moderno.* Milano: Giuffrè Editore, 1981.

Van der Maat, Bruno A. *Los Cristianos ante la Pena de Muerte: Una Opcion.* Documento de Trabajo. Arequipa, Peru: CECYCAP, 1986.

Van de Wied, Constant. *History of Canon Law.* Louvain: Peeters Press, 1991.

Van Engen, John. "The Christian Middle Ages as an Historiographical Problem." *American Historical Review* 91 (1986): 519ff.

Vernet, Joseph, S.J. "Peine capitale, peine perdue." *Etudes* (1962): 193–209.

Vidal, M. *L'Etica Christiana.* Roma: Borla, 1992.

Vipont, Elfrida. *The Story of Quakerism Through Three Centuries.* Richmond, Ind.: Friends United Press, 1954. Reprint 1977.

Vocca, Ornella. *Evoluzione del Pensiero Criminologico sulla Pena di Morte.* Napoli: E. Jovene, 1984.

von Drehle, David. *Among the Lowest of the Dead: The Culture of Death Row.* New York: Random House, 1995.

Vovelle, Michel. *Mourir Autrefois: Attitudes collectives devant la mort aux XVIIe et XVIIIe siecles.* Mesnil-sur-l'Estrée: Firmin-Didot, 1974.

——. *The Revolution Against the Church: From Reason to the Supreme Being.* Columbus, Ohio: Ohio State University Press, 1991.

Wakefield, Walter L. *Heresy, Crusade and Inquisition in Southern France 1100–1250.* Berkeley, Calif.: University of California Press, 1974.

Wakefield, Walter L. and Austin P. Evans, eds. *Heresies of the High Middle Ages: Selected Sources Translated and Annotated.* Records of Civilization: Sources and Studies, #81. Edited by W. T. H. Jackson. New York: Columbia University Press, 1969.

Waters, Raphael T. "The Moral Justification of Capital Punishment." *Social Justice Review* 73 (1982): 99–106.

Weiler, Anton. "Christianity and the Rest: The Medieval Theory of a Holy and Just War." *Concilium* 200 (December, 1988), 113ff.

Weis, Eberhard. *Cesare Beccaria (1738–1794), Mailänder Aufklärer und Anreger der Strafrechtsreform in Europa.* München: Verlag der Bayerischen Akademie der Wissenschaften, 1992.

Weisheipl, James A., O.P. *Friar Thomas d'Aquino: His Life, Thought, and Works.* Washington, D.C.: Catholic University of America Press, 1983.

White, Welsh S. *The Death Penalty in the Nineties: An Examination of the Modern System of Capital Punishment.* Ann Arbor, Mich.: University of Michigan Press, 1991.

Whitelock, Dorothy, ed. *English Historical Documents c. 500–1042.* New York: Oxford University Press, 1955.

Whyte, John H. *Catholics in Western Democracies: A Study in Political Behaviour.* New York: St. Martin's Press, 1981.

Wilenius, Reijo. *The Social and Political Theory of Francisco Suárez.* Helsinki: SKK, 1963.

Williams, Alexander Jr. "Christian Ethics and Capital Punishment." *The Journal of Religious Thought* (1992): 49ff.

Williams, George H., ed. *Spiritual and Anabaptist Writers.* Library of Christian Classics #25. Philadelphia, Pa.: Westminster Press, 1957.

Williams, James G. *The Bible, Violence and the Sacred: Liberation from the Myth of Sanctioned Violence.* New York: Harper, 1991.

Wills, Antoinette. *Crime and Punishment in Revolutionary Paris.* Westport, Conn.: Greenwood Press, 1981.

Wills, Garry. "Living Others' Deaths." *New York Review of Books* (September 23, 1993): 3f.

Wormser, René A. *The Law: The Story of Lawmakers and the Law We Have Lived by from the Earliest Times to the Present Day.* New York: Simon & Schuster, 1949.

Woywod, Stanislaus, O.F.M. *A Practical Commentary on the Code of Canon Law.* Revised by Callistus Smith. New York: Joseph F. Wagner, 1957.

Yoder, John Howard. "A Christian Perspective." In *The Death Penalty in America.* Edited by Hugo Adam Bedau. Third edition. New York: Oxford University Press, 1982. 374ff.

———. ed. *The Legacy of Michael Sattler.* Scottsdale, Pa.: Herald Press, 1973.

Youngblood, Ronald F., ed. *The Genesis Debate.* Grand Rapids, Mich.: Baker Book House, 1990.

Younger, Kenneth. *The Hanging Question.* Edited by Louis Blom-Cooper. London: Duckworth, 1969.

Zeeden, Ernst Walter. *Das Zeitalter der Gegenreformation.* Herder-Bücherei Band 281. Freiburg im Breisgau: Herder, 1967.

Zeman, Jarold K. *The Hussite Movement and the Reformation in Bohemia, Moravia and Slovakia (1350–1650).* New York: Barnes & Noble, 1977.

Robert the Pious, King, 56
Robespierre, Maximilien, 222, 538n
Romilly, Samuel, 231–32
Rommen, Heinrich A., 161
Rosenberg, Julius and Esther: executed, 319–21, 468
Rossi, Pellegrino, papal prime minister: assassinated, 255
Rothe, Richard, Lutheran theologian, 273, 539n, 546n
Rousseau, Jean-Jacques, and social contract theory, 264
Rowland, Msgr. Charles H., viii, 555n
Rudolphus Glaber, chronicler, 55
Rufo, Richard, viii
Rumbaugh, Charles: killed by Texas, 396
Rush, Dr. Benjamin, pioneer abolitionist, 302–3
Rushdoony, Rousas J., theonomist, 13
Russell, Frederick, historian, 66
Ruzafa, Professor: executed for deism, 243

Sacco, Nicola, executed, 318
Salatka, Charles, Bishop of Oklahoma City, 374
Salviati, Francesco, Archbishop of Pisa, 137
Sarkander, Jan, S.J., 534n
Sarmiento, Martin, O.S.B., 537n
Sattler, Michael: executed, 199, 534n
Savey-Casard, Paul, 46, 282; classifies three types of Catholic moralists, 283–84
Savonarola, Girolamo, O.P.: executed, 138, 522n
Sawtrey, William, Lollard: executed, 126
Schabas, William, law professor, human rights specialist, 479, 486
Schaible, Charles H., 245
Scheid, Don, philosopher: on Kant's retributivism, 226
Schilling, Otto, 37–38

Schleiermacher, Friedrich, 244–45, 247
Schöpf, Bernhard, historian, 20–26,
Schoppius, Gaspar, 183, 532n
Schüller, Bruno, S.J., moral theologian, 566–67n
Schultz, Robert C., Lutheran theologian, ix
Schwarzschild, Henry, viii
Schwarzschild, Steven, 226
Scully, Sally Anne, historian of major canonists, 91–94, 513n
Sebastian, Saint, 63
Segarelli, Gerard, executed, 123
Sellin, Thorsten, Professor, 322, 492n, 552n
Seripando, Cardinal, 525n
Servetus, Michael: executed by Calvin, 147, 276, 307, 524n
Shaw, Russell, 346
Sheedy, Charles, C.S.C., Dean, Notre Dame University, 323
Sheil, Bernard J., auxiliary Bishop of Chicago, 323
Simmons, Carolyn, dean, viii
Simms, Bennett, Episcopal Bishop of Atlanta, 363
Simon, Maurice, historian of catechisms, 529n
Simons, Menno (Mennonites), 200–02
Simonsohn, Shlomo, historian: on the popes and the Jews, 509n
Siricius, Pope, 59
Sixtus IV, Pope (Francesco della Rovere), 136, 185
Sixtus V, Pope (Felice Peretti), 154, 157, 527–28n
Skilly, John, 194
Skoda, Franciscus, 242, 286–88, 460, 519n, 545n, 569n
Skylstad, William, Bishop of Spokane, WA, 440
Sloyan, Gerard: on Roman Catechism, 174, 530n
Smalcius, Valentinus, 204

GENERAL INDEX

Abolition and abolitionism, 142, 207,
213, 222, 227, 232, 237, 239, 242,
245, 250, 256, 262, 264, 282, 283,
285, 287, 297, 302, 305, 307, 322,
323, 325, 333, 339, 359, 362–63,
367, 371, 395, 432, 445, 448, 453,
463, 465, 474, 480
Abortion, 20, 21, 341, 354, 378, 390,
391, 400, 413, 415, 425, 448, 489
Abuse of death penalty, 273, 369
Act of Toleration (1689), 206
Acts, chapter, 5, 87, 144, 180
Ad Abolendam, 82
Ad Extirpanda (1252), "most terrible
of bulls," 110
Adultery, 81, 151, 526n
Aeterni Patris (1879), 256
Against Heretics (Alan of Lille), 103–5
Aggiornamento, 472
Agonized participation, 53
Ahistorical ideology, 288
Alabama, 360, 404, 411, 439
Albany, NY, 410
Albigensian Crusade, 109, 125
Algeria, 465
Alphonsianum (Rome), 474
Amarillo, TX, 423
Ambivalence in tradition, 330
America (Jesuit weekly), 322
American Civil Liberties Union
(ACLU), 332
American Convention on Human
Rights, 486
American League to Abolish Capital
Punishment, 318, 323
American Magazine, 316
Amnesty International, 359, 396,
423, 432, 482, 484, 489; 1977
Stockholm Declaration of "total
and unconditional opposition",
359; 1981 report notes U.S. viola-
tions, 371; 1986 warning to Texas

about killing juveniles, 396; 1987
unprecedented exposé of U.S.
abuses, 401–2, 556n; 1989 report
lamenting 2,182 persons on U.S.
death rows, 413
Amputation analogy. *See* Diseased
member analogy
Anabaptists, 197–205, 305, 475
Anagni, 151
Ancona, 136
Andrew Lee Jones Fund (British),
423
Angelic vs. demonic sides in cosmic
battle, 256
Anglican bishops, 232
Anglican priest, 233
Anglo–Saxon Penitentials and penal
policy, 520n
Anti–Catholicism in U.S. history,
314, 315, 550–51n
Anti–Communism, 320
Anti–sacerdotal heresy, 56, 61, 106
Anti–terrorism bill , U.S. Congress
(1996), 452
Antonianum (Rome), 472
Apostolici, The, 123
Appeal to laity by French bishops,
466
Arbitrariness of executions, 401
Archconfraternity of St. John the
Beheaded, 156, 157, 163
Arguments for the death penalty: the
celestial–security argument, 160;
the social–security argument, 117,
162
Arizona, 424
Arkansas, 398
Art of Dying Well (Bellarmine), 160
Article 102, West Germany abolishes
death penalty (1948), 270, 273,
276
Associated Press, The, 373